Organized Crime

The International Library of Criminology, Criminal Justice and Penology
Series Editors: Gerald Mars and David Nelken

Titles in the Series:

Organized Crime

Edited by
Nikos Passas

Department of Criminal Justice
Temple University, Philadelphia

Dartmouth

Aldershot • Brookfield USA • Singapore • Sydney

Published by
Dartmouth Publishing Company Limited
Gower House
Croft Road
Aldershot
Hants GU11 3HR
England

Dartmouth Publishing Company
Old Post Road
Brookfield
Vermont 05036
USA

British Library Cataloguing in Publication Data
Organized Crime. – (International Library
of Criminology & Criminal Justice)
 I. Passas, Nikos   II. Series
 364.1

Library of Congress Cataloging-in-Publication Data
Organized Crime / edited by Nikos Passas.
        p.   cm.
   Includes bibliographical references and index.
   ISBN 1-85521-437-7 : $129.95 (est.)
   1. Organized crime.   2. Organized crime–Prevention.   I. Passas,
Nikos.
   HV6441.0738   1993
   364.1'06–dc20

                                                                    93-25986
                                                                    CIP

ISBN 1 85521 437 7

Printed in Great Britain by Galliard (Printers) Ltd, Great Yarmouth

Contents

PART IV   ORGANIZED CRIME AND ECONOMIC STRUCTURES

PART V   REGULATION AND CONTROL OF ORGANIZED CRIME

Acknowledgements

The editor and publishers wish to thank the following for permission to use copyright material.

The American Academy of Political and Social Science for the essays: Donald R. Cressey (1967), 'Methodological Problems in the Study of Organized Crime as a Social Problem', *Annals of the American Academy of Political and Social Science*, **374**, pp. 101–12; Peter Reuter (1984), 'Police Regulation of Illegal Gambling: Frustrations of Symbolic Enforcement', *Annals of the American Academy of Political and Social Science*, **474**, pp. 36–47.

American Society of Criminology for the essays: Peter A. Lupsha (1981), 'Individual Choice, Material Culture, and Organized Crime', *Criminology*, **19**, pp. 3–24; Mark H. Haller (1990), 'Illegal Enterprise: A Theoretical and Historical Interpretation', *Criminology*, **28**, pp. 207–35; William J. Chambliss (1989), 'State-Organized Crime – The American Society of Criminology, 1988 Presidential Address', *Criminology*, **27**, pp. 183–208; Andrew Szasz (1986), 'Corporations, Organized Crime, and the Disposal of Hazardous Waste: An Examination of the Making of a Criminogenic Regulatory Structure', *Criminology*, **24**, pp. 1–27.

American Sociological Association for the essay: Ivan Light (1977), 'Numbers Gambling Among Blacks: A Financial Institution', *American Sociological Review*, **42**, pp. 892–904.

Archives Européennes de Sociologie for the essay: Diego Gambetta (1988), 'Fragments of an Economic Theory of the Mafia', *Archives Européennes de Sociologie*, **29**, pp. 127–45.

Daniel Bell (1953), 'Crime as an American Way of Life', *The Antioch Review*, **13**, pp. 131–54. Copyright © Daniel Bell.

Greenwood Publishing Group Inc. for the essay: Nikos Passas (1994), 'I Cheat, Therefore I Exist? The BCCI Scandal in Context' in W. Michael Hoffman, Judith Brown Kamm, Robert E. Frederick and Edward S. Petry Jr (eds), *Emerging Global Business Ethics* (from the Ninth Conference on Business Ethics. Sponsored by the Center for Business Ethics at Bentley College, Quorum Books, an imprint of Greenwood Publishing Group Inc., Westport, CT), pp. 69–78. Copyright © 1994 by the Center for Business Ethics, Bentley College. Reprinted with permission of Greenwood Publishing Group Inc. All rights reserved.

Kluwer Academic Publishers for the essays: Rensselaer W. Lee III (1991), 'Colombia's Cocaine Syndicates', *Crime, Law and Social Change*, **16**, pp. 3–39; Robert J. Kelly, Ko-Lin Chin and Jeffrey A. Fagan (1993), 'The Dragon Breathes Fire: Chinese Organized Crime in New York City', *Crime, Law and Social Change*, **19**, pp. 245–69; Bruce Bullington and

Series Preface

The International Library of Criminology, Criminal Justice and Penology, represents an important publishing initiative designed to bring together the most significant journal essays in contemporary criminology, criminal justice and penology. The series makes available to researchers, teachers and students an extensive range of essays which are indispensable for obtaining an overview of the latest theories and findings in this fast changing subject.

This series consists of volumes dealing with criminological schools and theories as well as with approaches to particular areas of crime, criminal justice and penology. Each volume is edited by a recognised authority who has selected twenty or so of the best journal articles in the field of their special competence and provided an informative introduction giving a summary of the field and the relevance of the articles chosen. The original pagination is retained for ease of reference.

The difficulties of keeping on top of the steadily growing literature in criminology are complicated by the many disciplines from which its theories and findings are drawn (sociology, law, sociology of law, psychology, psychiatry, philosophy and economics are the most obvious). The development of new specialisms with their own journals (policing, victimology, mediation) as well as the debates between rival schools of thought (feminist criminology, left realism, critical criminology, abolitionism etc.) contribute overviews offering syntheses of the state of the art. These problems are addressed by the INTERNATIONAL LIBRARY in making available for research and teaching the key essays from specialist journals.

GERALD MARS
Visiting Professor of Risk Management, Cranfield University

DAVID NELKEN
Visiting Professor of Law (Criminology), University College London

Introduction

Organized crime has been generating a mixture of public fascination and serious concern for decades, although its forms and modi operandi keep changing as they reflect diverse socio-economic and political conditions (Booth, 1990; Hess, 1973; Hobsbawm, 1959, 1969; Kaplan and Dubro, 1986; Kerner, 1973; McCoy, 1972, 1980; McIntosh, 1975). The latest worries stem from evidence suggesting that organized crime is becoming increasingly transnational and occasionally posing global security threats (Andelman, 1994; Arlacchi, 1992; Labrousse and Wallon, 1993; Pearce and Woodiwiss, 1992; van Duyne, 1993; Williams, 1994). This trend is also noted in analyses of the anomic consequences of the dismantling of the former Soviet Union (Handelman, 1994; Hersh, 1994; Serio, 1992). In the context of new technologies and geopolitical changes, the 1990s have already witnessed special concern regarding the illicit traffic in drugs and human beings, cross-border car theft and the smuggling of radioactive nuclear material. In 1994, Justice and Interior ministers from 22 European countries agreed on the 'Berlin Declaration', aiming at closer collaboration and mutual assistance with respect to these crimes. This initiative, modest as it was, highlighted the widespread recognition of the need for effective multinational cooperation in the fight against organized crime (Bossard, 1990; Lodl and Longguan, 1992; Nadelmann, 1993; Passas, 1991; Savona, 1993; Smith, 1989; Woodward, 1993).

Yet, despite a plethora of studies on organized crime, controversies regarding its definition, structure, functions, and how best to control it continue to this day (Abadinsky, 1994; Bynum, 1987; Kelly, 1986a; Potter, 1994; Ruggiero, 1993; Sieber and Bögel, 1993). Sensationalism, myths and misinformation have made it 'a topic much abused in the literature, both popular and academic' (Lupsha, 1986: 32). The only certainty seems to be that organized crime constitutes a serious social problem that survives aggressive efforts of regulatory and law enforcement agencies. The chapters of this book address these issues, while also focusing on various forms of organized criminal activity that have gained attention at different periods of time.

Defining and Studying 'Organized Crime'

Televised Congressional hearings and Presidential Task Forces in the US largely shaped the public understanding of organized crime from the 1950s into the 1970s, defining it as a predominantly Italian-American phenomenon (Kefauver, 1968; President's Commission on Law Enforcement and Administration of Justice, 1967). This official view was articulated in Cressey's (1969) influential work based on his privileged access to data collected by federal agencies. Cressey came under strong criticism for over-reliance on official data and, thereby, misrepresentation of the nature and structure of criminal groups. Although his theory of organized crime is still widely (and rightly) disputed, his methodological cautions have not lost their relevance. As Kelly (1992: 18) has pointed out, Cressey's work 'is more important for its methodology than for the thesis it advances'.

In Chapter 1, Cressey outlines a series of problems that any student of organized crime can expect to face. The most obvious hurdle is the secrecy of groups under study. It is hard to observe group members as they interact with each other and with outsiders. Reliable informants for the researcher are unavailable. In addition, the more violent or better organized a criminal group, the more dangerous it will be to investigate. Associations with influential people and organizations, legitimate transactions and the philanthropic activities of many criminal enterprises furnish more protective shields. Although participant observation has led to invaluable insights (Chambliss, 1988; Ianni and Reuss-Ianni, 1972 and Chapter 8 of this volume; Mieczkowski, 1986), this method carries significant risks and cannot be employed too often.

Journalistic sources of information may be helpful, but commercial interests and a tendency to simplify and then exaggerate often get in the way of contextualized and accurate reporting. Sometimes, press reports are not independent but merely summarize official reports and press releases or contain selective leaks from government bodies. Sensational and distorted accounts that keep appearing in the media serve as a warning against the use of such sources without independent confirmation of facts or checking with the reporters' original sources (Block, 1978; Nelli, 1976; Passas, in press; Schatzberg, 1993).

Autobiographies of former 'mobsters' suffer from these shortcomings too. Moreover, the reliability of these accounts has been challenged on the basis of frequent contradictions, a tendency at self-glorification, attempts to exculpate themselves, and manipulation by government bodies with which they may choose to cooperate in order to get immunity (Potter, 1994; Salerno and Tompkins, 1969).

The analysis of reports, court files and data collected by government bodies is an alternative solution. Yet there is no guarantee that official agencies concentrate on the most serious organized crime problems nor that they are bias-free (Albini, 1971; see also Chapters 3 and 4 of this volume). Further, access to this information is not always granted and official agencies may not cooperate fully with researchers. Due to the confidential nature of much information, it cannot always be shared with scholars. In other cases, corrupt officials may prevent the disclosure of compromising information. Other problems arise, however, when access is granted. Evidence is usually screened by controllers, informants and observers, and is influenced by their own interpretations. In some instances, agencies may be selective in what they release to the public, thus misrepresenting certain events or aspects of a phenomenon (Calder, 1992).

Moreover, law enforcement data are gathered, not with the view to assist social theorists, but in order to prosecute offenders successfully. This reinforces a propensity (also found among social scientists) to regard crime issues in terms of individuals rather than of structural or organizational problems. Thus, crime investigators may neglect or disregard information about the structure of illicit enterprises and interrelations with legitimate actors and mainstream society.

Cressey recommends the borrowing of methods from intelligence analysts, geographers and anthropologists who seek to make a lot out of little, to know the past from the present. He challenges a common belief that control bodies collect evidence on what are widely regarded as major social problems. In contrast he argues that, by focusing on a phenomenon or the activities of a particular group of people, controllers actually contribute to the perception or construction of a social problem. He thus warns about the myth-creation risk facing researchers who use these data and collaborate with people whose job it is to have their version of organized crime regarded as a social problem.

Writing in 1967, Cressey speculates that, despite its costs and significance, organized crime need not be constructed as a social problem. In support of this hypothesis, he notes the large demand for the illegal goods and services offered by criminals, a widespread feeling that the suppliers are not very criminal, and the inability of the law to regulate illegal organizations. Yet, public perceptions have changed since that time, especially regarding specific types of commodities such as illegal drugs. Cressey's last concern was addressed by subsequent laws that sought to define and control 'organized crime', including the Racketeer Influenced and Corrupt Organizations (RICO) statutes in the US (Ryan and Kelly, 1989). According to the Omnibus Crime Control and Safe Streets Act of 1968, 'Organized crime means the unlawful activities of members of a highly organized, disciplined association engaged in supplying illegal goods and services, including but not limited to gambling, prostitution, loan sharking, narcotics, labour racketeering, and other unlawful activities of members of such associations'.

This vague definition illustrates the frequent confusion of *acts* with *actors*, a problem also found in the white-collar crime literature (Shapiro, 1990). Sutherland's distinction of white-collar criminals effectively allowed gangsters to become 'the sole and indisputable occupants of organized crime' (Smith, 1991: 144). One of the earlier and best attempts to bring some conceptual clarity into the field is Maltz's contribution in Chapter 2. He addresses the problem of *ad hominem* definitions and offers a typology of organized crime. His definition-cum-typology refers to associations for the purpose of committing crimes and takes into account the means, objectives and manifestations of these associations.

Concentrating on criminal acts rather than offender characteristics is not only more consistent, but it also helps avoid mystification and stereotyping (Smith, 1990). Indeed, if our concern is with the gravity of offences committed rather than the identity of offenders, organized crime would take over much of the field now studied under the rubric of white-collar crime (Calavita and Pontell, 1993; Passas and Nelken, 1993). Nevertheless, neither this chapter nor subsequent efforts by Maltz (1985, 1990) and other scholars (Hagan, 1983) have settled the definitional debate. Partly, this is because it is difficult to define the phenomenon in a consistent and accurate way without unduly restricting the scope of academic inquiry. The diversity and complexity of phenomena studied under the label 'organized crime' suggest that a clear and precise definition may be neither possible nor desirable (Kelly, 1986b).

In Chapter 3, Smith criticizes conventional definitions of organized crime, challenges the view that 'if one understands Cosa Nostra he understands organized crime in the United States' (Cressey, 1969: 21), and offers a set of questions that can better guide research. He suggests that if one understands Italian-American crime families, one understands only part of the problem – and not necessarily the most serious part. Introducing his study on how a 'Mafia mystique' was created, he points out: 'The back of organized crime has been broken, the headlines scream, by indictment and conviction of groups of largely middle-aged or elderly Mafia leaders. We could almost sleep well, except for the two concurrent crime stories that command our attention: our national failure to control a drug trade in which the major trafficers [*sic*] are not Italian; and the rise in exorbitant white-collar crimes, either proven or still under investigation on Wall Street and in the defense industry. Put them next to "Mafia" and ask yourself: What is organized crime – *really*?' (Smith, 1990: xvi).

The relevance of Smith's cautions has not diminished with the passage of time. Although *cherchez les Italiens* is no longer the principal theme of organized crime control, the search for those 'different from us', the ethnic or the foreign, still informs anti-crime efforts, be they in terms of drug wars, illegal immigration, smuggling or banking offences (Potter, 1994: 10; Passas, in press). The first question Smith proposes concerns the role of illicit enterprises in the larger society. By substituting 'organized crime' with the more inclusive term 'illicit enterprises', he intends to avoid stereotypes and to underline analytical similarities with common business practices. This question is designed to facilitate inquiries into structural factors underlying such enterprises, to alert readers to historical parallels, and to promote cross-cultural comparative studies.

Next, drawing on organizational theory, Smith recommends research into the nature of the elements of an organization's environment that may affect the setting and attainment of its goals. The study of an illicit enterprise's clients, suppliers or competitors may result in more sophisticated and effective control strategies.

A third line of inquiry relates to the function and effects of violence. Smith's hypothesis is that violence may serve to maintain internal discipline, enforce market conditions and control competitors. Changes in the incidence of violence can thus reveal the relative stability of illegal markets, internal management problems, the degree of competition and conflict among different enterprises, etc.

Finally, Smith urges us to compare the function of corruption in illicit and licit enterprises. Such a comparison not only highlights further parallels between organized crime and legitimate business, but also challenges a common assumption that organized crime seeks to nullify government and the political process. Yet entrepreneurs – legal and illegal – may prefer to *use* the government to stabilize their market and fight competitors, rather than operate in an environment with a weak or inoperative government.

In Chapter 4, Reuter and Rubinstein expose a series of errors in official beliefs about organized crime. False beliefs, they argue, are generated by agencies which collect valuable information but analyse it inadequately. Such beliefs are dysfunctional from a public policy perspective, but may be perpetuated because they serve bureaucratic and political interests. Reuter and Rubinstein's study demonstrates the need to go beyond 'statistical reports and conversations with law enforcement officials' in order to transcend the veil of myth and disinformation. They do so by analysing primary data, such as wiretap transcripts and other information collected by police authorities that had not previously been examined in a systematic fashion. Their focus is on the structure and organization of illegal bookmaking and numbers games, but their findings may be generalized to other illicit enterprises (see Reuter, 1983).

The authors find that bookmakers are not terrifying mobsters; rather, they operate in a fragmented market characterized by low levels of violence and only episodic corruption. The evidence shows that bookmaking enterprises are often ephemeral and not part of a nation-wide coercive network. Violence, corruption and control of the market are more prominent features in the numbers business, but they should not be exaggerated. Profits in numbers are higher than in bookmaking, but not near official accounts. It appears that gambling is not the major source of finance for other criminal enterprises.

Policy makers will also note Reuter and Rubinstein's point that less aggressive enforcement in New York led to a decrease in police corruption, even lower concentration of the illegal market, and better prices to clients. The Mafia, on the other hand, is only one part of the underworld. An important function of the Mafia is to serve as a network of contacts that facilitate inter-city transactions. It also offers arbitration services when disputes arise in illegal markets (see also Chapter 9). In this light, effective law enforcement against the Mafia may ironically bring about an increase in the rate of violence.

Theoretical Frameworks and Interpretations

Inevitably, the questions we use to guide our studies and to systematize the available data emanate from distinct theoretical orientations and assumptions. For a long time, the theory of an alien conspiracy dominated by the Sicilian Mafia (Cressey, 1969; Kefauver, 1968; President's Commission, 1967) shaped research and law enforcement agendas. The obsession with the Mafia has led to the application of this Italian term to criminal groups in as historically and culturally diverse countries as Colombia, Japan and Russia. Effectively, this theory diverted attention from other criminal organizations and externalized the causes of organized crime. This section includes the most notable attempts to rectify this tendency.

In Chapter 5, Bell shows that organized crime cannot be understood in isolation from the American economy and political framework. He puts forward his classic theory that organized crime is not imported from overseas, but represents a 'queer ladder' of success. He observes that a variety of ethnic and religious groups, such as Irish, Germans and Jews, have participated in such crime (see also Haller, 1985). The problem is not limited to suspected Sicilian conspirators. Organized crime does not always have a predatory relationship with mainstream society; there are often mutual benefits, too.

Following the logic of Merton's theory of anomie (1968), Bell argues that newly-arrived immigrants resorted to organized crime as a means of attaining the American dream. In the context of discrimination, marginalization and blocked legitimate opportunity, organized crime provided an alternative ladder of social mobility. As different groups (e.g., Irish, Jews) were gradually assimilated and integrated into the legitimate economic and political structures, they moved out of crime to be replaced by new waves of immigrants (e.g., Italians). This argument is at the core of the 'ethnic succession' thesis which was adopted and elaborated by other scholars (Amir, 1986; Ianni and Reuss-Ianni, 1972; Ianni, 1974; O'Kane, 1992; Tyler, 1971).

In Chapter 6, Lupsha offers a critique of the ethnic succession theory. He does not regard organized crime as an adaptation of frustrated immigrants striving for social status and upward mobility, pointing out that many immigrants who participated in criminal enterprises did have access to legitimate opportunities. His remark that Italian-Americans play a dominant role in the orchestration of criminal enterprises in America is by now out of date. However, he makes the valid point that members of this ethnic group remained in illicit business despite growing integration.

Lupsha rejects the central role of economic factors and instead locates the source of the problem in American culture, rendering his analysis less easily applicable to other societies. He argues that people turn to crime by choice, in line with 'a perverse aspect' of American values which suggests that 'only "suckers" work, and that in our society one is at liberty to take "suckers" and seek easy money'. This theory is consistent with Merton's (1968) analysis of 'robber barons' and the anomie-inducing rewards of monetary success in American society, even if deviantly achieved. Lupsha also argues that people opt for criminal careers simply because they have the skills for the job and access to this type of opportunity. Thus, they often do not even consider what legal opportunities may be open to them. In this respect, Lupsha's analysis is congruent with Cloward and Ohlin's (1960) theory of illegitimate opportunity structures. This work therefore makes a contribution to the more general 'anomie tradition' of theorizing (Passas, 1994).

In Chapter 7, Smith pursues his suggestions made in Chapter 3 and outlines an 'enterprise perspective'. Through the concept of 'illicit enterprises', he shifts attention to the business-like character of organized crime and its analytical similarity to legitimate organizations and white-collar crime. He quarrels with the sharp positivist distinction between criminals and law-abiding citizens, and proposes a continuum or a spectrum that includes both legal and criminal business. In his own words, the enterprise perspective can be used to 'look at business at the edge of legitimacy where the pariah entrepreneur operates. This approach shows the importance of "standing" and "reputation" in our definition of social legitimacy, and their role in enabling (or preventing) movement of a pariah entrepreneur into the legitimate marketplace' (Smith, 1990: xix).

This model has the advantage of divorcing public policy considerations from fixations on particular people or groups. It requires less specific organizational structures and places illegal activities in the context of market and societal forces. An important policy implication of Smith's concept of illicit enterprises is that the government should do exactly the opposite of what it is doing with respect to legitimate organizations. The State promotes legitimate enterprises, increases their competitiveness or stabilizes the markets where they operate. Law enforcement should try to create the opposite conditions in the drug trade, arms trafficking or any other illicit business (Williams, 1993). Smith's approach has proved influential and has been employed in studies of crime outside the US (e.g., Arlacchi, 1986, who examines the 'entrepreneurial mafia' in the context of Calabria and Sicily and also the value shift from honour to wealth and power in the post-World War II era).

Structure and Networks of Criminal Enterprises

As we have seen, the paradigm of a well-structured confederation of criminals operating hierarchically under strict rules and centralized control has been discredited. The evidence points to a lack of rigid organization, locally controlled enterprises that operate on business principles (Anderson, 1979; Haller and Alviti, 1977; Reuter, 1983), and loosely structured patron-client relationships (Albini, 1971). This section highlights the diversity of existing illegal structures and networks through a series of case studies.

In Chapter 8, Ianni illustrates the advantages of field methods used by anthropologists in studying the social organization of the Lupollo 'family'. He describes the complementary relationship of the Lupollo's legal and illegal enterprises in an historical perspective. He attributes the Lupollo's movement from illegal to legal enterprises not only to the need to launder the proceeds of crime, but more importantly to a process of acculturation and upward social mobility. His analysis lends support to the queer ladder of success and ethnic succession theses since the Lupollo family, like other Italian-Americans in New York, pass their gambling rackets on to black, Puerto Rican and Cuban groups (see also Ianni, 1974; Ianni and Reuss-Ianni, 1972). Ianni does not find that this family fits the rational, enterprise model of organized crime. Indeed, he points to certain limits of structural analyses that do not capture the fact that Italian-American families are not 'consciously constructed formal organizations. Rather, they are traditional social systems, products of culture, and responsive to cultural change.'

In Chapter 9, Gambetta lays the groundwork for an economic theory of the Italian Mafia and argues that the commodity it provides is private protection. He postulates that the Mafia's aim is to produce, advertise and sell protection against interference from state authorities or outside competitors. As he describes the market (need) for protection and trust in an otherwise unpredictable environment, he observes that the Mafia does not necessarily generate demand by muscle and extortion. To the extent that there is extortion, he says, it is analytically similar to questionable but often legal practices of legitimate enterprises seeking to increase demand for the commodities they supply. Gambetta observes that there are benefits to recipients of Mafia protection in that they avoid competition from new entrants to the market. Of course, those attempting to enter the market will perceive the protection cost as extortionist.

According to Gambetta, violence may be used to mete out punishment and provide effective protection. The Mafia also needs to appear tough in order to show that it can protect and deter or remove competition. Thus in some instances, violence may occur in order to reinforce that perception. Finally, violence is a means of self-protection against the state. Gambetta's analysis suggests that the Cosa Nostra's function as an arbitrator of disputes arising in illegal markets in America (Reuter, 1983) may not be unique.

In Chapter 10, Light inquires into the role of numbers games in African-American communities. He argues that the institutional and cultural factors that must be considered in analysing poverty also explain the early prominence of blacks in numbers gambling. He shows that black heritage and religion alone cannot provide a complete explanation. After all, the game was later dominated by non-blacks; moreover, most black gamblers were Protestant fundamentalists whose emphasis on the work ethic was generally incompatible with gambling. In addition, participation rates have not been stable, but rose during recessions and declined with prosperity.

Anomie theory does not appear to fit the evidence of this study which suggests that betters do not expect a change in life-style if they win. Rather, they regard the game as a rational economic activity and refer to their bets as 'investments'. Paradoxically, betting is viewed as a means of personal savings. From the gambler's point of view, the game is convenient, appeals to race pride and the community spirit of the ghetto public, and may help convert change into lump sums. Light points to altruistic motives behind betting as well. After the federal government, the numbers industry used to be the biggest employer in slum areas. Also, numbers collectors would regularly seek contributions from their clients for 'hard-luck' cases. In this way, numbers games provided a mutual assistance network in times of need.

Numbers runners were often loan sharks as well and functioned as a source of consumer credit for their customers. Contrary to the common perception that such activities are parasitic and predatory on the needy, Light finds that numbers runners were leading philanthropists as well as the 'largest investors in black-owned business or ghetto real estate and the chief source of business capital in the ghetto'. The services offered by them were not provided by mainstream institutions which avoided such risky clients in red-lined areas. This problem was compounded by a lack of mutual sympathy between bankers and the poor, especially blacks. Light concludes that, in the context of this high turn-down rate, of real and perceived discrimination in lending which continues into the 1990s (Shlay et al., 1992; see also Chapter 18), of clashes of cultural standards and institutional barriers, numbers gambling has functioned as an alternative, if irregular, financial institution.

Chapter 11 is Gardiner's study of corruption in a Pennsylvania city in the 1950s and 1960s – a classic illustration on how case studies should be conducted and presented. He concentrates on vice and corruption, making clear that these can be understood only in their proper historical context. He outlines the functions and effects of illegal gambling and corruption, the ways in which protective shields prevent detection and disclosure of misconduct, and the conditions that give rise to the market catered for by illegal entrepreneurs and three types of corrupt public officials. He also indicates directions for possible reform.

Gardiner highlights the symbiotic, rather than antithetical, relationships between participants in illegal markets and those who operate in mainstream society. These findings are consistent with results of subsequent studies in other American cities (e.g. by Chambliss, 1988; Goldstock et al., 1990; Heinz et al., 1983; Potter, 1994; see also Chapter 12). Properly updated, this account may thus be used as a point of reference for comparative studies of corruption in different countries and different illegal markets (e.g., Clarke, 1983; *Economist*, 1992; Etzioni-Halevy, 1990; Grabosky, 1989; Lo, 1993; Lupsha, 1991; Pepinsky, 1992; Yayama, 1990).

In Chapter 12, Haller delves into the conditions that have affected cooperative relationships among illegal entrepreneurs in American cities. He adopts the enterprise perspective and defines illegal enterprises as 'the sale of illegal goods and services to customers who know that these goods and services are illegal'. Haller points out that systematic pay-offs to politicians and police have played a crucial role in the regulation of such markets as illegal gambling and red-light districts. This mutually beneficial relationship has contributed to a containment of damaging scandals as well as of competition from other criminal groups. Haller then discusses the role of business partnerships which allow for risk-sharing and the pooling of resources. He illustrates his partnership model by the examples of the Colonial Inn, an illegal casino in Florida, and the Cicero Enterprises in Illinois. Finally, he concentrates on two internal economic features of illegal enterprises that shape the way they cooperate with each other. One is the need to collaborate because each group handles different parts of the production and delivery process (i.e., manufacturers, importers, distributors, etc.). The other is specific to gambling operations and relates to the need of risk minimization against lucky streaks by betters.

Haller concludes by distinguishing La Cosa Nostra groups from the independent businesses of its members. The former, he argues, perform a role similar to a Chamber of Commerce or Rotary Club, facilitating legal and illegal business deals among their members. La Cosa Nostra also provides a degree of predictability in illicit business by eliciting normative standards and by functioning as a dispute resolution body.

This type of arrangement may be historically specific to certain types of crime in American cities. As Ruggiero (1993: 138) has noted, many illegal enterprises 'today transcend circumscribed territories' and 'make family-type structures obsolete...'. A feature of some major international criminal organizations is a 'growing interconnectivity with other transnational, nonstate actors' (Godson and Olson, 1993: 10). However, it would be misleading not to mention evidence on close links between *state* actors and elements of regional and international criminal enterprises (Block, 1991; Chambliss, 1988; Kwitny, 1987; Marshall, 1991; McCoy, 1972; Passas, 1993; Walsh, 1993; Weston, 1987; see also Chapter 25).

In Chapter 13, Chambliss makes precisely this point by investigating 'acts defined by law as criminal and committed by state officials in the pursuit of their job as representatives of the state'; these he refers to as state-organized crimes. He provides typical examples involving piracy, drug trafficking, arms smuggling, assassinations and civil rights violations. Chambliss challenges a unitarian view of the state by analysing conflicts among various government agencies. He regards such conflicts and the unavailability of legitimate methods for pursuing certain government policies as a key to explaining state-organized crime.

In Chapter 14, Lee focuses on Colombian cocaine syndicates. His description of competition and conflicts between the Cali and Medellín groups highlights once more the non-monopolistic nature of much organized crime, even in relatively small countries. This chapter was written before the death of Pablo Escobar and the subsequent weakening of the Medellín groups – developments precipitated by the actions of Cali groups which have now consolidated their position (Labrousse, 1994).

Lee also examines the relationship between drug traffickers with the political institutions in Colombia. He finds evidence supporting both the 'participation model' (i.e., ties to political structure) and the 'insurgency model' (i.e., conflict with legitimate power structures and cooperation with guerrilla groups). He draws attention to violence against many political figures, complex but essentially hostile relations with guerrillas, as well as the cartels' significant participation in the political and legitimate economic life of the country. Lee stresses that the traffickers' chief problem is with the government's anti-drug policy, not with the political system per se. Also, not unlike other powerful criminal enterprises, the Colombian cartels perform government-like functions in regions where the state is weak.

Lee then turns to the policy implications of his analysis. He notes certain contradictions in US anti-drug policy in South America and demonstrates that the attainment of all objectives at the same time is impossible (see also Chapter 25). He concludes that the main goal of reducing the drug trade can best be pursued by negotiation rather than by confrontation and military action.

In Chapter 15, Kelly, Chin and Fagan employ survey methods and interviews to explore the victimization of Chinese businesses by Asian crime groups in the city of New York. Four types of crime are examined here: (1) protection (insurance against harassment by themselves or rival gangs), (2) extortion (demand for money without the provision of any service in exchange), (3) overcharging business owners for goods the gangs sell them, and (4) enjoying the services of business owners without paying or at heavily discounted prices. These crimes cause a great deal of nuisance, but the total monetary costs are not too high.

Extortion is an important form of crime through which recruitment of new members and territorial control are facilitated. Victims are not likely to report these crimes due to fear of reprisal and a distrust of the criminal justice system. For this reason, lack of reliable data leaves many questions on the structure and organization of Chinese gangs unanswered.

The social context within which gangs operate is the fragmented and relatively disorganized Chinese immigrant community kept in a continuous state of transition by a constant flow of 'FOBs' (Fresh off the Boat). The authors provide some background information on the role of Triads and tongs, draw parallels with Italian-American and Sicilian organizations, but also stress important differences between them. Tongs, whose members are mostly law-abiding citizens, are viewed as cultural entrepreneurs, as 'middlemen' between the English-speaking community and the Chinese.

The authors argue that the breakdown of school and family controls, lack of legitimate opportunities, community isolation and disorganization all underlie the movement of detached immigrant youths into delinquency. They add, however, that a necessary intervening factor before youths join gangs is the internalization of Triad norms and values which have been transmitted to street gangs by the tongs (i.e., associations formed by Chinese workers in the 19th century). These processes legitimize youth gangs, facilitate social and economic relations with other groups, and provide a protective shield against social controls. The gangs are integrated in the community's social and economic life, operate in communities that are financially robust, and have ties with South Eastern societies. Finally, street gangs are associated with the unofficial 'government' of Chinatown and 'may perform useful police functions and control as much crime and violence as they produce'.

Organized Crime and Economic Structures

It is clear by now that criminal entrepreneurs often engage in legitimate business. They may do so in order to launder their proceeds, to diversify their sources of income, to increase their influence and power, and to gain respectability. Their relationship with control agencies and political organizations is often harmonious and mutually beneficial. In some cases criminal groups attach parasitically to legal enterprises. This section includes studies that illustrate how legitimate economic institutions may also benefit, often inadvertently, from the activities of criminal organizations.

In Chapter 16, Block and Chambliss's historical study offers insights into the social relations underlying the institutionalization of racketeering in American labour unions. Their focus is on miners, tailors and the Teamsters unions. They challenge conservative implications of functionalist arguments that account for causes of social phenomena by reference to their positive consequences. Against conventional wisdom, they argue that there is a functional, symbiotic relationship between racketeering activities and businesses. Ultimately, racket-ridden unions serve the interests of labour leaders and employers. This conspiratorial coalition, often initiated by employers, is conducive to the control of union workers, labour stability and higher profits. However, corrupt labour practices are detrimental to workers, their organizations and the institution of collective bargaining.

In Chapter 17, Passas offers one of the first attempts to place the scandal surrounding the Bank of Credit and Commerce International (BCCI) in a proper criminological context. After BCCI was closed down in 1991, it was described by government officials in the US and Britain as a 'criminal enterprise', a bank with a 'criminal culture' that perpetrated the largest bank fraud in history. Such statements were echoed in press accounts around the world that frequently mixed fact with fiction (Passas, in press). The case of BCCI is instructive as it highlights the vital role of financial institutions in organized crime. BCCI's clients included not only legitimate businesses and central banks of Third World countries, but also tax evaders, dictators, drug traffickers, arms smugglers and terrorists. The media feeding frenzy has led to an individualization of the problems highlighted by this scandal. As a result, structural factors underlying the demand for the illegal services provided at BCCI have largely been overlooked (Passas, 1993). Of course, BCCI itself committed a huge 'Ponzi' scheme (pyramid scheme), money laundering, deceitful accounting and other crimes.

Passas argues that, nevertheless, BCCI is more accurately described as a mirror of global evils rather than a source of global evils. BCCI may have perpetrated most of these crimes and may have extended illegal services or turned a blind eye to them when its survival was at stake. To the extent that this is true, transactions with illegal enterprises may have kept afloat a financial institution that also provided some desperately needed services to the Third World. Lord Bingham has remarked that 'The vices which brought BCCI down should not obscure the virtues which it showed in some places and which, perhaps, inspired its creation' (Bingham Report, 1992: §2.102). More importantly, BCCI has exposed a demand for illegal banking services that has not disappeared with its closure. This suggests the possibility that legitimate banks may also resolve financial difficulties by turning a blind eye to 'dirty money' and the shady business of some clients.

In Chapter 18, Brady shows how arson-for-profit schemes can be properly understood in the context of economic decisions that link racketeering syndicates with the banking, insurance and property industries. The scenario outlined by Brady is that banks illegally discriminate against (redline) low-income areas in which houses are abandoned and lose their value. Unpaid mortgages lead to foreclosures but, because of the general decline of such neighbourhoods, banks are left with a losing investment. Racketeers then offer to buy the problem buildings at a price higher than the market value, as long as the bank finances the new mortgage for the full price together with the costs of 'renovation'. Since the mortgage is backed by a major bank, insurance cover can be obtained for the full amount. Professional 'torches' may set some relatively minor fires, damages for which result in a series of insurance payments. In the meantime, renovations may never take place; corrupt contractors or building inspectors may write false reports about 'repairs'. Then, a big fire occurs that destroys the building. By state law, the insurance has to pay the mortgage holder first, which means that the bank is paid back the full mortgage.

Criminal operators make gains out of this scheme through bribes and phantom repairs at the expense of insurance companies. According to Brady, insurance companies are not very likely to complain for several reasons. They may be practising redlining themselves; they do not wish to appear too tough to their clients nor to lose costly civil counter-suits; they may fear that public attention will result in stricter regulation of their industry. They may also pass the losses on to consumers. However, the most important beneficiaries of such illegal schemes are the banks, even without explicitly joining in the conspiracy. Indeed, 'fire prone' speculators are among the best risks. The new and higher mortgage is paid, the banks no longer have the bad property on their books, and they break no law by contracting with someone who has a prior 'fire record' (unless, of course, they consciously join the conspiracy).

In Chapter 19, Szasz looks into the relationship between industries that generate hazardous waste and criminal groups that remove and dispose of this waste improperly. He outlines the conditions that facilitated the entry of organized criminals into the waste management market that was created by the passage of the Resource Conservation and Recovery Act of 1976. He argues that, in addition to flaws of implementation and enforcement, the most crucial factor was the very law that sought to address the public health problem of hazardous waste dumping. Through lobbying, the (legitimate) generators of toxic waste succeeded in shaping the new law in two important ways. Firstly, the government would not regulate their production processes, which could possibly have reduced the quantity of waste generated as a by-product. Secondly, the (legitimate) industries would not be responsible for the final disposal of their waste. This would be borne by state-licensed haulers and disposers. The large corporations also argued before the US Congress that an immediate enforcement of new standards could force them to close down because of a lack of proper facilities to treat such waste.

Criminal entrepreneurs found few difficulties in obtaining state licences, in contracting with corporations to dispose of their toxic waste, and dumping most of it illegally. Szasz points out that there is no evidence that generators of this waste intended the creation of an illegal market. Nonetheless, they derived several benefits from this situation: less government regulation, lower costs in the disposal of toxic waste, and protection against legal liability. In this way, legitimate corporations 'externalized' both the legal responsibility for their wastes and any stigma for the criminal acts that benefited their industry.

Regulation and Control of Organized Crime

Preceding chapters referred to policy issues and many concluded with policy implications. This theme becomes central in this section, with chapters addressing more directly the regulation and control of organized criminal activities.

Law enforcement practices can shape the environment and methods of criminal entrepreneurs in several ways. Corruption in social control agencies, which has been so frequently discovered and reported, is an important one. In Chapter 20, Sherman puts forward three models of such corruption as instances of organizational deviance. 'Cooptation' occurs when those subject to regulation pose a threat to regulators. Controllers may then absorb those subject to regulation into their policy-making process. This may result in a displacement of the official regulatory goals or 'licensing' of criminal activities (protection against arrest) in designated areas. The more an agency depends on its subjects to attain its goals, the more of this type of corruption can be expected. Sherman notes, for example, the dependence of elected officials on campaign funds and argues that this 'leads them to co-opt the gangsters who then make corruption an operative organizational goal of the police department'.

In his 'capture' model, an agency is exploited by those (e.g., politicians) who control its resources and can thus influence or constrain its activities. This power is treated as a commodity that may be sold to the highest bidder. Examples of this type of corrupt exploitation are frequently found where officials have direct control over an agency's personnel (e.g., in Watergate).

Finally, members of a control agency may take advantage of their position of power within the organization for personal benefit. Sherman points out that this kind of corruption is more likely in agencies that are relatively autonomous, independent or sheltered from outside controls. Police departments provide the most common examples of corrupt domination by powerful insiders.

In Chapter 21, Reuter focuses on police regulation of illegal gambling in the period 1933 to 1970. His analysis illustrates many of the problems that arise when the law prohibits activities which are in high demand and about which the public feels ambivalent. Under such circumstances, law enforcement can become largely symbolic, empty and formal. More importantly, such situations provide an environment ripe for corruption. Indeed, Reuter shows that vulnerability to law enforcement harassment generated incentives for making payments to local police and alliances with political figures. This brought about a domination of gambling operations by organized criminals, which was reduced only when federal anti-gambling efforts undermined the ability of local police to provide protection. This federal effort, the state's own entry into the gambling market, and shifting public attitudes on law enforcement priorities contributed to the decline in local police responsibility for gambling enforcement.

Decreases in corruption, violence and involvement of organized criminals are expected by many who argue for (at least) partial legalization and regulation of certain activities. In Chapter 22, Lowman outlines a Canadian experience in the control of street prostitution and recommends that the criminal justice approach be abandoned. His analysis is consistent with earlier findings in America that regulation may be a better alternative to prohibition (Best, 1987). Lowman argues that punitive strategies merely lead to displacement of the outlawed activities and do not protect prostitutes from often deadly street violence. He is critical of the suggestion that decriminalization simply creates a sexual free-for-all for men (see Matthews, 1986).

Matthews (Chapter 23) responds to Lowman's arguments for designating specific areas where prostitutes can offer their services. Instead, Matthews recommends a *negative* zoning policy designed to move street prostitution and kerb-crawling away from vulnerable neighbourhoods and areas where such activities have the most detrimental effects. He points to the low success of *positive* zoning in America and argues that decriminalization would bring about more commercialization and a rise in the supply of sexual services. The arguments made by these two authors typify current policy disagreements regarding other illegal commodities provided by criminal groups.

In Chapter 24, Albanese draws attention to the effect of public hearings and disclosures on law making and criminal justice policy. He illustrates how ideological beliefs influenced US Congressional investigations and shaped landmark legislation by examining the testimonies of Joseph Valachi, a Cosa Nostra member, and Carl Kotchian, president of Lockheed. Following Valachi's testimony, Congress allowed wider use of wiretaps and special grand juries under Title III of the Omnibus Crime Control and Safe Streets Act of 1968 and the Organized Crime Control Act of 1970. In the aftermath of the Lockheed scandal and Kotchian's detailed description of the reasons for, and methods of, secret payments to foreign governments to secure the sale of aeroplanes, Congress passed the Foreign Corrupt Practices Act of 1977. Albanese recommends the adoption of Smith's spectrum theory of enterprise (see Chapter 7) to enhance the ability of those in authority to predict illegal organizational behaviour and improve policy construction.

The last two chapters represent two very different perspectives on the control of drug trafficking and reflect the diversity of approaches under which anti-drug policies may be studied. In Chapter 25, Bullington and Block claim that American wars on drugs have been seriously compromised by foreign policy considerations, particularly those related to the

Cold War. This claim has also been made in a number of other studies (Chambliss, 1988; Labrousse and Wallon, 1993; Lee, 1989; Levine, 1993; McCoy, 1972; Scott and Marshall, 1991; US Senate, 1989). Bullington and Block argue that the emphasis on the fight against communist forces transformed US agencies (such as the Federal Bureau of Narcotics) into counter-intelligence bodies; drug traders were effectively divided into 'good' and 'bad' on the basis of their usefulness for these purposes. In the post-Cold War era, this study is still relevant as it underscores conflicts between foreign policy and law enforcement objectives that continue to provide a crime-facilitative context on an international level (Passas, 1993; Passas and Groskin, in press; on problems of controlling money laundering activities, see Levi, 1991).

In the last chapter, Reuter and Kleiman offer an economic analysis of drug enforcement. They point out that the intensification of US federal enforcement in the 1980s did not significantly affect the availability, retail price and consumption of marijuana and cocaine. Reuter and Kleiman argue that this may be explained by the structural features of these markets rather than by conflicts and lack of coordination among different agencies. They find that federal control efforts aimed at imports and high-level distribution increase costs and risks in those parts of the production-distribution process that do not significantly affect the retail price. Local law enforcement cannot be much more successful due to the huge scale of these markets and the significant number of middle-class users of these drugs (i.e., fewer transactions take place in the streets). The heroin market, on the other hand, is smaller and has a different consumer base, which makes it more vulnerable to tighter control efforts.

Each chapter of this book addresses different issues, markets, structures and relationships. The common thread linking them all is the idea that criminal groups and organizations can neither be understood nor controlled without a proper analysis of the social, economic, cultural and political contexts in which they operate. It is hoped that this book will prove helpful to students, researchers and policy makers alike.

References

Abadinsky, H. (1994), *Organized Crime*, 4th ed., Chicago: Nelson Hall.

Albini, J.L. (1971), *The American Mafia: Genesis of a Legend*, New York: Appleton-Century-Crofts.

Amir, K. (1986), 'Organized Crime and Organized Criminality Among Georgian Jews in Israel' in R.J. Kelly (ed.), *Organized Crime: A Global Perspective*, Totowa, NJ: Rowman & Littlefield, 172–91.

Andelman, D.A. (1994), 'The Drug Money Maze', *Foreign Affairs*, **73** (4), 94–108.

Anderson, A. (1979), *The Business of Organized Crime*, Stanford, CA: Hoover Institution Press.

Arlacchi, P. (1986), *Mafia Business: The Mafia Ethic and the Spirit of Capitalism*, London: Verso.

Arlacchi, P. (1992), 'Large Scale Crime and World Illegal Markets' in *Organized Crime: International Strategies*, Albuquerque: The University of New Mexico Latin American Institute, 47–61.

Best, J. (1987), 'Business is Business: Regulating Brothel Prostitution Through Arrests', *Research in Social Policy*, **1**, 1–20.

Bingham Report (1992), *Inquiry into the Supervision of the Bank of Credit and Commerce International*, London: HMSO.

Block, A.A. (1978), 'History and the Study of Organized Crime', *Urban Life*, **6**, 455–74.

Block, A.A. (1991), *Masters of Paradise: Organized Crime and the Internal Revenue Service in the Bahamas*, New Brunswick, NJ: Transaction.

Booth, M. (1990), *The Triads: The Growing Global Threat from the Chinese Criminal Societies*, New York: St Martin's Press.

Bossard, A. (1990), *Transnational Crime and Criminal Law*, Chicago: Office of International Criminal Justice.

Bynum, T.S. (ed.) (1987), *Organized Crime in America: Concepts and Controversies*, Monsey, NY: Criminal Justice Press.

Calavita, K. and Pontell, H.N. (1993), 'Savings and Loan Fraud as Organized Crime: Toward a Conceptual Typology of Corporate Illegality', *Criminology*, **31** (4), 519–48.

Calder, J.D. (1992), 'Al Capone and the Internal Revenue Service: State-Sanctioned Criminology of Organized Crime', *Crime, Law and Social Change*, **17**, 1–23.

Chambliss, W.J. (1988), *On the Take: From Petty Crooks to Presidents*, Bloomington: Indiana University Press.

Clarke, M. (ed.) (1983), *Corruption*, New York: St Martin's Press.

Cloward, R. and Ohlin, L. (1960), *Delinquency and Opportunity*, New York: The Free Press.

Cressey, D.R. (1969), *Theft of a Nation*, New York: Harper & Row.

Economist (1992), 'Money, Gangsters and Politics: An Everyday Story of Japan', 26 September, 31–2.

Etzioni-Halevy, E. (1990), 'Comparing Semi-Corruption Among Parliamentarians in Britain and Australia', in E. Oyen (ed.), *Comparative Methodology*, London: Sage, 113–33.

Godson, R. and Olson, W.J. (1993), *International Organized Crime: Emerging Threat to US Security*, Washington, DC: National Strategy Information Center.

Goldstock, R., Marcus, M., Thacher, T.D. and Jacobs, J.B. (1990), *Corruption and Racketeering in the New York City Construction Industry*, New York: New York University Press.

Grabosky, P.N. (1989), *Wayward Governance: Illegality and its Control in the Public Sector*, Canberra: Australian Institute of Criminology.

Hagan, F. (1983), 'The Organized Crime Continuum: A Further Specification of a New Conceptual Model', *Criminal Justice Review*, **8**, Spring, 52–7.

Haller, M.H. (1985), 'Bootleggers as Businessmen: From City Slums to City Builders' in D.E. Kyvig (ed.), *Law, Alcohol, and Order: Perspectives on National Prohibition*, New York: Greenwood, 139–57.

Haller, M. and Alviti, J. (1977), 'Loansharking in American Cities: Historical Analysis of a Marginal Enterprise', *American Journal of Legal History*, **21**, 125–56.

Handelman, S. (1994), 'The Russian "Mafiya"', *Foreign Affairs*, **73** (2), 83–96.

Heinz, A., Jacob, H. and Lineberry, R.L. (eds) (1983), *Crime in City Politics*, New York: Longman.

Hersh, S.M. (1994), 'The Wild East', *The Atlantic Monthly*, June, 61–86.

Hess, H. (1973), *Mafia and Mafiosi: The Structure of Power*, Fawnborough: Saxon House.

Hobsbawm, E.J. (1959), *Primitive Rebels*, Manchester: Manchester University Press.

Hobsbawm, E.J. (1969), *Bandits*, New York: Dell.

Ianni, F.A.J. (1974), 'New Mafia Black, Hispanic and Italian Styles', *Society*, **2**, 23–38.

Ianni, F.A.J. and Reuss-Ianni, E. (1972), *A Family Business*, New York: Russell Sage.

Kaplan, D.E. and Dubro, A. (1986), *Yakuza: The Explosive Account of Japan's Criminal Underworld*, Reading, MA: Addison-Wesley.

Kefauver, E. (1968), *Crime in America*, New York: Greenwood.

Kelly, R.J. (ed.) (1986a), *Organized Crime: A Global Perspective*, Totowa, NJ: Rowman & Littlefield.

Kelly, R.J. (1986b), 'Criminal Underworlds: Looking Down on Society from Below' in R. J. Kelly (ed.), *Organized Crime: A Global Perspective*, Totowa, NJ: Rowman & Littlefield, 10–31.

Kelly, R.J. (1992), 'Trapped in the Folds of Discourse: Theorizing About the Underworld', *Journal of Contemporary Criminal Justice*, **8** (1), 11–35.

Kerner, H.J. (1973), *Professionelles und Organisiertes Verbrechen*, Wiesbaden: Bundeskriminalamt (BKS).

Kwitny, J. (1987), *The Crimes of Patriots: The True Tale of Dope. Dirty Money, and the CIA*, New York: W.W. Norton & Co.

Labrousse, A. (1994), 'Géopolitique de la Drogue: Les Contradictions des Politiques de "Guerre à la Drogue"', *Futuribles* (185), 9–22.

Labrousse, A. and Wallon, A. (eds) (1993), *La Planète des Drogues*, Paris: Seuil.

Lee. R.W. (1989), *The White Labyrinth: Cocaine and Political Power*, New Brunswick, NJ: Transaction.

Levi, M. (1991), 'Regulating Money Laundering' in *British Journal of Criminology*, **31** (2), 109–25.

Levine, M. (1993), *The Big White Lie*, New York: Thunder's Mouth Press.

Lo, T.W. (1993), *Corruption and Politics in Hong Kong and China*, Milton Keynes: Open University Press.

Lodl, A. and Longguan, Z. (eds) (1992), *Enterprise Crime: Asian and Global Perspectives*, Chicago: Office of International Criminal Justice.

Lupsha, P.A. (1986), 'Organized Crime in the United States' in R.J. Kelly (ed.), *Organized Crime: A Global Perspective*, Totowa, NJ: Rowman & Littlefield, 32–57.

Lupsha, P.A. (1991), 'Drug Lords and Narco-Corruption: The Players Change but the Game Continues', *Crime, Law and Social Change*, **16** (1), 41–58.

Maltz, M.D. (1985), 'Toward Defining Organized Crime' in H.E. Alexander and G.E. Caiden (eds), *The Politics and Economics of Organized Crime*, Lexington: Lexington Books, 21–35.

Maltz, M.D. (1990), *Measuring the Effectiveness of Organized Crime Control Efforts*, Chicago: Office of International Criminal Justice.

Marshall, J. (1991), 'CIA Assets and the Rise of the Guadalajara Connection', *Crime, Law and Social Change*, **16** (1), 85–96.

Matthews, R. (1986), 'Beyond Wolfenden? Prostitution, Politics and the Law', in R. Matthews and J. Young (eds), *Confronting Crime*, London: Sage, 188–210.

McCoy, A. (1972), *The Politics of Heroin in Southeast Asia*, New York: Harper & Row.

McCoy, A.W. (1980), *Narcotics and Organized Crime in Australia*, Artarmon, NSW: Harper & Row.

McIntosh, M. (1975), *The Organisation of Crime*, London and Basingstoke: Macmillan.

Merton, R.K. (1968), *Social Theory and Social Structure*, New York: The Free Press.

Mieczkowski, T. (1986), 'Geeking and Throwing Down: Heroin Street Life in Detroit', *Criminology*, **24**, 645–66.

Nadelmann, E.A. (1993), *Cops Across Borders: The Internationalization of U.S. Criminal Law Enforcement*, University Park: Pennsylvania State University Press.

Nelli, H.S. (1976), *The Business of Crime*, New York: Oxford University Press.

O'Kane, J.M. (1992), *The Crooked Ladder: Gangsters, Ethnicity, and the American Dream*, New Brunswick, NJ: Transaction.

Passas, N. (1991), *Frauds Affecting the Budget of the European Community*, Report to the Commission of the European Communities, Brussels: EC Anti-Fraud Unit (UCLAF).

Passas, N. (1993), 'Structural Sources of International Crime: Policy Lessons from the BCCI Affair', *Crime, Law and Social Change*, **20** (4), 293–305.

Passas, N. (1994), 'Continuities in the Anomie Tradition', *Advances in Criminological Theory*, **6**, 91–112.

Passas, N. (in press), 'The Mirror of Global Evils: A Review Essay on the BCCI Affair', *Justice Quarterly*, January 1995.

Passas, N. and Groskin, R.B. (in press), 'International Undercover Operations' in G. Marx and C. Fijnaut (eds), *Undercover: Police Surveillance in Comparative Perspective*, Amsterdam: Kluwer.

Passas, N. and Nelken, D. (1993), 'The Thin Line Between Legitimate and Criminal Enterprises: Subsidy Frauds in the European Community', *Crime, Law and Social Change*, **19** (3), 223–43.

Pearce, F. and Woodiwiss, M. (eds) (1992), *Global Crime Connections: Dynamics and Control*, London: Macmillan.

Pepinsky, H.E. (1992), 'Corruption, Bribery and Patriarchy in Tanzania', *Crime, Law and Social Change*, **17**, 25–51.

Potter, G.W. (1994), *Criminal Organizations: Vice, Racketeering, and Politics in an American City*, Prospect Heights, Ill.: Waveland.

President's Commission on Law Enforcement and Administration of Justice (1967), *Task Force Report: Organized Crime*, Washington, DC: Government Printing Office.

Ruggiero, V. (1993), 'Organized Crime in Italy: Testing Alternative Definitions', *Social and Legal Studies*, **2** (2), 131–48.

Ryan, P. and Kelly, R.J. (1989), 'An Analysis of RICO and OCCA: Federal and State Legislative Instruments Against Crime', *Violence, Aggression and Terrorism*, **3**, 49–100.

Salerno, R. and Tompkins, J.S. (1969), *The Crime Confederation*, Garden City, NY: Doubleday.

Savona, E.U. (ed.) (1993), *Mafia Issues*, Milan: UN Crime Prevention and Criminal Justice Programme/ISPAC.

Schatzberg, R. (1993), *Black Organized Crime in Harlem: 1920–1930*, New York and London: Garland.

Scott, P.D. and Marshall, J. (1991), *Cocaine Politics: Drugs, Armies, and the CIA in Central America*, Berkeley and Los Angeles: University of California Press.

Serio, J. (1992), 'The Soviet Union: Disorganization and Organized Crime' in A. Lodl and Z. Longuan (eds), *Enterprise Crime: Asian and Global Perspectives*, Chicago: Office of International Criminal Justice, 155–70.

Shapiro, S.P. (1990), 'Collaring the Crime, not the Criminal: Reconsidering the Concept of White-Collar Crime', *American Sociological Review*, **55** (3), 346–65.

Shlay, A.B., Goldstein, I.J. and Bartelt, D. (1992), 'Racial Barriers to Credit: Comment on Hula', *Journal of Urban Affairs*, **28**, 126–40.

Sieber, U. and Bögel, M. (1993), *Logistik der Organisierten Kriminalität*, Weisbaden: Bundeskriminalamt.

Smith, D.C. (1990), *The Mafia Mystique*, Lanham, New York: University Press of America.

Smith, D. (1991), 'Wickersham to Sutherland to Katzenbach: Evolving an "Official" Definition of Organized Crime', *Crime, Law and Social Change*, **16** (2), 135–54.

Smith, H.E. (ed.) (1989), *Transnational Crime: Investigative Responses*, Chicago: Office of International Criminal Justice.

Tyler, G. (1971), 'Sociodynamics of Organized Crime', *Journal of Public Law*, **20** (3), 487–98.

US Senate (1989), *Drugs, Law Enforcement and Foreign Policy*, Committee on Foreign Relations, Report of the Sub-committee on Terrorism, Narcotics and International Operations, Washington, DC: US Government Printing Office.

van Duyne, P. (1993), 'Implications of Cross-Border Crime Risks in an Open Europe', *Crime, Law and Social Change*, **20**, 99–111.

Walsh, L.E. (1993), *Final Report of the Independent Counsel for Iran/Contra Matters*, Washington, DC: US Court of Appeals for the District of Columbia Circuit.

Weston, B.H. (1987), 'The Reagan Administration Versus International Law', *Case Western Reserve Journal of International Law*, 295–302.

Williams, P. (1993), 'International Drug Trafficking: An Industry Analysis', *Low Intensity Conflict and Law Enforcement*, **2** (3), 397–420.

Williams, P. (1994), 'Transnational Criminal Organisations and International Security', *Survival*, **36** (1), 96–113.

Woodward, R. (1993), 'Establishing Europol', *European Journal on Criminal Policy and Research*, **1** (4), 7–33.

Yayama, T. (1990), 'The Recruit Scandal: Learning from the Causes of Corruption', *Journal of Japanese Studies*, **16**, 93–114.

Part I
Defining and Studying
'Organized Crime'

[1]

Methodological Problems in the Study of Organized Crime as a Social Problem

By Donald R. Cressey

ABSTRACT: The secrecy of participants, the confidentiality of materials collected by investigative agencies, and the filters or screens on the perceptive apparatus of informants and investigators pose serious methodological problems for the social scientist who would change the state of knowledge about organized crime. There is overwhelming evidence that an organization variously called "the Mafia," "La Cosa Nostra," and "the syndicate" operates in the United States, but its activities are perceived as a "social problem" by "insiders" who have access to confidential information, not by most of the public. The social scientist has a duty to tell the members of his society when he believes they are in trouble. This is not necessarily unscientific because, once established as a social problem, a phenomenon can be studied scientifically with the help of funds appropriated for its eradication. Even if not established as a social problem, organized crime can be studied from the perspective of organizational theory. In this kind of study, social scientists will have to borrow methodological techniques from archaeologists and geologists, who manufacture data by reasoning that knowledge about inaccessible affairs can be obtained from considering affairs that are accessible to study. This kind of process can be used to create, from study of the structure of organized crime, information about criminals' norms and interaction processes.

Donald R. Cressey, Ph.D., is Professor of Sociology, University of California, Santa Barbara. He has been Professor of Sociology and Chairman, Department of Anthropology and Sociology, University of California, Los Angeles; Visiting Fellow in the Institute of Criminology, Cambridge University; and Visiting Professor of Law, University of Oslo. He is currently Chairman, Criminology Section, American Sociological Association, and has been President, Pacific Sociological Association, and member of the Council, American Sociological Association. Among his publications are Other People's Money (1953), Principles of Criminology (with E. H. Sutherland; 7th ed., 1966), The Prison (1961), and Delinquency, Crime, and Differential Association (1964).

THE report on organized crime prepared while I was a consultant
on organized crime for the President's
Commission on Law Enforcement and
Administration of Justice (hereinafter
referred to as the National Crime Commission) was written under conditions
which can best be described as "desperate." [1] Time pressures were such
that perplexing role problems and methodological questions could not even
be clearly formulated, let alone discussed. The secrecy of the participants,
the confidentiality of the materials collected by law-enforcement and investigative agencies, and the various filters
or screens on the perceptive apparatus
of both informants and investigators
pose serious methodological problems
for the social scientist who would change
the state of knowledge about organized
crime. Perhaps it is for this reason that
social scientists have tended to write
about organized crime only in descriptive terms, taking their clues from
the reports on Congressional hearings,
rather than in analytical terms. [2]

The basic methodological problems
stem from the fact that the society of
organized criminals, if it is a society,
is a secret society. The ongoing activities of organized criminals simply are
not accessible to observation by the
ordinary citizen or the ordinary social
scientist. Even to gain access to the
observations made by law-enforcement
and investigative bodies, one must have
"connections," such as appointment as

a consultant to the President's Commission. Because direct observations can
be made only with great difficulty, one
has a choice between four alternative
conclusions: (1) An organization of
"organized criminals" does not exist.
(2) An organization of "organized criminals" exists, but it is so secret that we
cannot learn anything about it that law-
enforcement personnel do not already
know. [3] (3) Any organization of "organized criminals" that exists must not
be much of a social problem or we
would know more about it. (4) An
organization of "organized criminals"
exists, but it must be studied by methods not ordinarily utilized by social
scientists.

Upon being invited to work for the
Commission, I discovered that I, probably like most social scientists, had unwittingly committed myself to the second (and perhaps the first) alternative.
After preliminary study, I drew eight
conclusions, described below, which
made it necessary to shift to the fourth
alternative. It should be noted that
each of the alternatives has its attendant risks. If one chooses the first
alternative, one must be prepared to
"explain away" the observations and
conclusions made by knowledgeable insiders such as police chiefs, directors of
police intelligence divisions, the Director
of the Federal Bureau of Investigation,
the members of Congressional investigating committees, and the President
of the United States. [4] If one selects

---

[1] Donald R. Cressey, "The Functions and
Structure of Criminal Syndicates," *Task Force
Report: Organized Crime*, U.S. President's
Commission on Law Enforcement and Ad-
ministration of Justice (Washington, D.C.:
U.S. Government Printing Office, 1967), Ap-
pendix A, pp. 25–60.

[2] Two noteworthy exceptions are Daniel
Bell, "Crime as an American Way of Life,"
Antioch Review, 13 (1953), pp. 131–154;
and Robert T. Anderson, "From Mafia to Cosa
Nostra," *American Journal of Sociology*, 61
(1965), pp. 302–310.

[3] This is a common assumption among law-
enforcement personnel. When I approached
one official with a plea for aid in obtaining
organized-crime data from his agency, his
first reaction was one of bewilderment. He
recalled the publications of the McClellan
Committee and the work of the participants
in Senator (then Attorney General) Kennedy's "organized crime drive," then asked:
"What can you do? What can you possibly
say that hasn't been said?"

[4] Mr. Charles H. Rogovin, Director of the
Organized Crime Task Force, sent a question-

the second alternative, one grants to law-enforcement bodies an infallibility which they do not deserve. If one chooses the third alternative, one's problem is similar to that of the person selecting the first alternative: one is likely to be accused of having one's head in the sand. If one selects the fourth alternative, one risks being categorized as a nonscientist whose reasoning is comparable to that of a "flying saucer nut" or a "Communist conspiracy nut" who knows that they are out there working against him even if he cannot see them. Selecting the fourth alternative also makes it essential that one quickly acknowledge that any conclusions one draws are probably erroneous and that the evidence which one uses has been screened by the perceptions of both informants and observers. What an informant or informer says is true is not necessarily what an observer says is true. And what a law-enforcement officer says he heard on a wire-tap or a "bug" is not necessarily what the speaker intended to convey in the conversation which was overheard.

It is difficult to account for my shift from the second alternative to the fourth. It is an oversimplification to say that "I was overwhelmed by the evidence." But I am certain that no

---

naire on organized crime to police departments in 71 cities. In some instances, federal-agency intelligence reports indicated the presence of organized crime where questionnaire respondents denied it, and six of nine cities not responding to the questionnaire are known by federal agencies to have extensive organized crime activities. See *Task Force Report: Organized Crime, op cit.*, p. 5. The Kefauver Committee described some local authorities who denied the existence of organized crime in their jurisdictions as "pathetically in error." —U.S., Congress, Senate, Special Committee to Investigate Organized Crime in Interstate Commerce, *Second Interim Report*, Senate Report No. 141, 82nd Cong. (Washington, D.C.: U.S. Government Printing Office, 1959), p. 7.

rational man could read "the evidence" that I read and still come to the conclusion that an organization variously called "Mafia," "La Cosa Nostra," or "the syndicate" does not exist. Such certainty, however, does not eradicate the fact that "the evidence" was somewhat staged. Mr. Henry S. Ruth, Jr., Deputy Director of the Commission, had invited law-enforcement and investigating agencies to submit reports on organized crime to the Commission. When the reports began to come in, it became apparent to the staff that provision had to be made for an analysis or, at least, a discussion of them. I was invited to do the job, but I accepted with reservations because, as indicated, I was not at all sure that a "Mafia," "La Cosa Nostra," or any other nationwide organization of criminals existed. Discussions with my friends and colleagues indicated, and continue to indicate, that this skepticism is widely shared by social scientists. I agreed to make some scouting trips to Washington in order to look at the reports with a view to trying to answer the question, neutrally phrased: "What is organized about organized crime?" My hunch was that the answer would be "Nothing." However, a few days spent reading the materials submitted to the Commission, a few days spent reading other, more confidential, materials, and a few days spent interviewing knowledgeable policemen and investigators convinced me that the following eight points are facts.

(1) A nationwide alliance of at least twenty-four tightly knit "families" of criminals exists in the United States.[5]

(2) The members of these "families" are all Italians and Sicilians, or of Italian and Sicilian descent, and those

---

[5] Because the "families" are fictive, in the sense that the members are not all relatives, it is necessary to refer to them in quotation marks. See Cressey, *op. cit.*, p. 39.

on the Eastern Seaboard, at least, call the entire system "La Cosa Nostra." Each participant thinks of himself as a "member" of a specific "family" and of "La Cosa Nostra" (or some equivalent term).

(3) The structure of each "family" —a structure consisting of positions for "Boss," "Underboss," Lieutenants, and Counselor, and for low-ranking members called "Soldiers" or "Button Men" —is well known to law-enforcement officials having access to informants. Other positions, such as "Buffer," "Money Mover," "Enforcer," and "Executioner" also are well known, but except in the case of "Enforcer," the terminology varies from place to place.

(4) The "families" are linked together by understandings, agreements, "treaties," and obedience to a nine-member "Commission" made up of the leaders of the most powerful of the "families."

(5) The "Boss" of each "family" directs the activities, especially the illegal activities, of the members of his "family."

(6) The names, criminal records, and the principal criminal activities of at least two thousand of the participants have been assembled.

(7) The members of this organization control all but a tiny part of the illegal gambling in the United States. They are the principal loan "sharks." They are the principal importers and wholesalers of narcotics. They have infiltrated labor unions, where they extort money from employers and, at the same time, cheat the members of the union. They own a large proportion of Las Vegas. They own state and federal congressmen and other officials in the legislative, executive, and judicial branches of government at the local, state, and federal levels. Some government officials are considered, and consider themselves, "members." The

members control some legitimate enterprises, such as vending machines, and they own a wide variety of retail firms, restaurants and bars, hotels, trucking companies, food companies, linen-supply houses, garbage-collection routes, and factories.

(8) The information about the Commission, the "families," and the activities of members is based on detailed reports from a wide variety of informants, wire-taps, and "bugs," not merely on the case histories of the participants in the Apalachin meeting or on Mr. Valachi's testimony before the McClellan Committee.[6]

In view of the fact that the significant "discoveries" during this preliminary period of study were revelations of facts well known to a large number of government personnel, and others, we speculated about the basis of my original skepticism and, therefore, about what I believe is the prevailing skepticism of many citizens. There seem to be three interrelated factors involved.

First, information on organized crime has, by and large, been presented to the public in a sensational manner. Policemen, well aware of the sensationalism present in televised Congressional hearings involving unsavory characters; in newspaper accounts of the activities of "muscle men," "gorillas," and "meat hooks"; and in popular books about "The Mafia Menace," say that the public is misled because the mass media insist on playing "cops and robbers" and "gang busters." Newspapermen find it virtually impossible to depict the participants as anything but gangsters who prey principally on each other. For example, there are few newspaper

6 See the testimony of Mr. Joseph Valachi in U.S., Congress, Senate, *Organized Crime and Illicit Traffic in Narcotics: Hearings Before the Permanent Subcommittee on Investigations of the Committee on Governmental Operations,* Parts 1 and 3, 88th Cong. (Washington, D.C.: U.S. Government Printing office, 1963).

accounts in which Mr. Lucchese is called "Mr. Lucchese" or Mr. Ricca is called "Mr. Ricca." The writer always displays his "inside knowledge" about how things *really* are by using the first name, parenthesis, corny "alias," parenthesis, last name. "Mr. Lucchese," when he was alive, could possibly have been someone who was corrupting my labor union, but "Three Finger Brown" could only have been a somewhat fictitious character in a "cops and robbers" story. Similarly, usury is almost always called "the juice racket," and this terminology lets the reader believe that the activity has nothing to do with him or the safety of his community. The criminals' terminology is similarly used when the word "scam" is used to describe bankruptcy fraud. Most of us can understand the seriousness of usury, bankruptcy fraud, and bribery, but we have a hard time realizing that our friends and neighbors are, in the long run, the victims of "the juice racket," "the scam racket," or "the fix." Probably of even more relevance to any prevailing skepticism is the fact that the murder of a La Cosa Nostra member by men acting under orders from the victim's "family Boss" is invariably described by the mass media as a "hit" or a "gangland slaying." In fact, a high proportion of such murders are executions of members who have secretly left the criminals' camp to join the forces of law, order, and decency. Calling the murder a "hit" makes it all but impossible for the reader to realize that control of a community's economic and political affairs by an alliance of criminals is serious business, certainly as serious as would be control of these affairs by Communists. The probability is high that any La Cosa Nostra member executed by his superiors has, for any of a number of reasons, been serving as an American spy, in much the same way that citizens of enemy nations sometimes work as American spies.

Second, there is a proclivity in our society, even among social scientists, to view criminality as an individual matter rather than as an organizational matter. The criminal's behavior is usually viewed, both popularly and scientifically, as a problem of individual maladjustment, not as a consequence of his participation in social systems.[7] Consistently, the law-enforcement process is, by and large, designed for the control of individuals, not for the control of organizations. Only in exceptional cases, such as those involving price-fixing or other monopolistic practices, are organizations put on trial. Accordingly, law-enforcement and investigating agencies necessarily must be more concerned with collecting evidence that will lead to trials of individuals than with evidence about the relationships between criminals or about the structure and operations of illicit organizations. Since the "organized crime files" of such agencies tend to be arranged with a view to prosecuting individuals, these agencies find it difficult to convince the public in general, and social scientists in particular, that "the problem of organized crime" is, in fact, different from "the problem of juvenile automobile theft."

Third, the confidential nature of much information plagues any law-enforcement agency that would "educate the public" or supply data for social scientists. One element in good intelligence work is silence. Further, when a case is before a grand jury or in the process of trial, disclosure of information by the government could well result in dismissal. Libel and

[7] For statements about some of the consequences of this perspective, see Edwin H. Sutherland and Donald R. Cressey, *Principles of Criminology* (7th ed.; Philadelphia: Lippincott, 1966), pp. 378–380, 548–550, and 675–680.

slander suits, and even political reprisals, are likely to threaten any policeman or investigator who tells what he
knows about organized criminals. There
is a great difference between knowing
something and proving it in a court of
law. When discussing the infiltration
of La Cosa Nostra members into legitimate business, one federal official said:
"As sure as I'm sitting here, two banks
in New York City are controlled by
hoodlums." But when he was asked
why the government does not throw
them out he responded: "It's one thing
to know it, it's quite another to prove
in court a violation of law." [8] Part of
what is known about organized crime
has been learned by means of wiretaps and "bugs," and disclosure of information obtained in this way is against
the law.

SOCIAL SCIENCE AND SOCIAL PROBLEMS

In most areas of study, it is no
longer permissible for the social scientist to use for scientific purposes data
that were gathered for nonscientific purposes. In the past, social scientists
happily and blithely analyzed materials
collected for administrative purposes,
perhaps generalizing from these "facts."
Now they know that the datum for
study is the process of assembling such
materials, not the assembly itself.[9]
For example, in the "social problems"
area of sociology, especially, it is only
a slight exaggeration to say that "a
social problem was created because certain data were assembled," rather than
"data on a social problem were assembled."· From this perspective, one im-

portant goal of the Commission's Task
Force on Organized Crime was the creation of a social problem. Even a cursory
examination of the Task Force Report
will indicate that we joined the ranks
of men who are paid to recognize organized crime as a social problem.
These men, mostly police officers and
prosecutors, know that the activities of
organized criminals are threatening the
foundations of American economic, political, and legal order, and they wish
that "the public" could be made aware
of its own plight. When they plead for
"education of the public," they are asking that a major social problem be
created.

A social scientist who is given access
to information ordinarily inaccessible
must be prepared to shift his role from
that of scientist to "social problem per-
ceiver" and then to "social problem
creator." For example, as he becomes
convinced that organized crime threatens a social order which he holds dear,
the temptation to join those who would
"educate the public" is great. But, of
course, such a move shifts his allegiance
away from the community of scientists
and scholars. We succumbed to this
temptation and spent as much time and
energy trying to convince "the public"
that they had a problem as we spent
analyzing organized crime as a social
system. We are convinced, however,
that the scientist has a duty, as an
"informed citizen," to tell the members
of his society when he believes they are
in trouble, even if they do not realize it.

Such rather propagandistic conduct
has long-range effects on social science
research. It has methodological implications because it crystallizes the notion
that organized crime should be studied
as a social problem rather than as, perhaps, a problem in basic economics,
anthropology, sociology, or political science. The underlying assumption seems
to be that as society becomes aware of

[8] Quoted in a column by E. Cony, *Wall
Street Journal*, November 18, 1963, p. 1.
[9] See Donald R. Cressey, "The State of
Criminal Statistics," *National Probation and
Parole Association Journal*, 3 (1957), pp.
230–241.

a danger, it will fund research studies of the danger, with a view to eradicating it. Perhaps social phenomena are extensively perceived as social problems only when some proposal for eradication (or, at least, change) is well publicized and well financed. Thus, "mental health" seems to have become a major social problem in the United States only after the National Institute of Mental Health was established to improve the nation's mental health. Somewhat as a consequence of the fact that mental health was established as a social problem in this way, social scientists discovered that they are experts on mental health problems. By the same token, creation of the new cabinet post, Secretary of Transportation, probably means that "transportation" soon will become a major social problem and that increasing numbers of social scientists will discover that they are experts on transportation problems. Using the same reasoning, "justice" has not been much of a social problem in the United States because the administration of justice has been hidden behind concepts such as "law enforcement," "prosecution," "trial," "prison," "attorney general," and "judge." The National Crime Commission did much to create a social problem in this area, and grants to social scientists for basic research are already becoming available.

It will not be easy to establish organized crime as a social problem, despite the fact that organized criminals already are exacting tributes from most Americans, and despite the fact that, by means of political corruption, organized criminals have already deprived many Americans of their right to cast an effective vote, to experience a fair trial, or, generally, to be honestly dealt with in political and economic relationships. There are three reasons for believing that this problem will not in the near future become a social problem, one of them a legal reason.

First, the American confederation of criminals thrives because a large minority of citizens demand the illicit goods and services that it has for sale. As Walter Lippmann observed at the end of the Prohibition era, the basic distinction between ordinary criminals and organized criminals turns on the fact that the ordinary criminal is wholly predatory, while the man participating in crime on a rational, systematic basis offers a return to the respectable members of society.[10] If all burglars were miraculously abolished, they would be missed by only a few persons to whose income or employment they contribute directly—burglary-insurance companies, manufacturers of locks and security devices, police, prison personnel, and a few others. But if La Cosa Nostra were suddenly abolished, it would be sorely missed because it performs services for which there is a great public demand. The organized criminal, by definition, occupies a position in a social system, an "organization," which has been rationally designed to maximize profits by performing illegal services and providing legally forbidden products demanded by members of the broader society in which he lives. Just as society has made a place for La Cosa Nostra by demanding illicit gambling, alcohol, and narcotics; usurious loans; and a cheap supply of labor, La Cosa Nostra has made places, in an integrated set of positions, for the use of the skills of a wide variety of specialists who furnish these goods and services. Organized crime cannot become a social problem until a much broader segment of society perceives that the cost of the services provided is too high.

[10] Walter Lippmann, "Underworld: Our Secret Servant," *Forum*, 85 (1931), pp. 1–4, 65–69.

Second, a large proportion of the persons demanding illicit goods and services believe that they are being supplied by criminals who are unorganized and who, for that matter, are not very criminal. A nice old man who accepts a few bets from the patrons of his restaurant does not seem very dangerous and, if treated in isolation, such persons cannot be perceived as much of a threat to the social order. Accordingly, they tend to be protected in various ways by their society. The policeman is likely to overlook bookmakers' offenses or merely to insist that they do not occur in his precinct; the judge is likely to invoke the mildest punishment the legislature has established; and the jailer is likely to differentiate such offenders from "real criminals." "Gambling" cannot become a social problem until it is widely known that bookmakers are not gamblers. The nature of their business is such that they must join hands with others in the same business.[11] Other illicit businesses have the same character. By joining hands, the suppliers of illicit goods and services (1) cut costs, improve their markets, and pool capital; (2) gain monopolies on certain of the illicit services or on all of the illicit services provided in a specific geographic area;[12] (3) centralize the procedures for stimulating the agencies of law enforcement and administration of justice to overlook the illegal operations; and (4) accumulate vast wealth which can be used to attain even wider monopolies on illicit activities and on legal businesses as well. Organized crime cannot become a social

problem until a much broader segment of society perceives that "organization," not gambling, is the phenomenon to worry about.

Third, "organized crime" is not against the law. What is against the law is smuggling and selling narcotics, bookmaking, usury, murder, extortion, conspiracy, and the like. Except when conspiracy statutes are violated, it is not against the law for an individual or group of individuals rationally to plan, establish, and develop a division of labor for the perpetration of crime, whether it be bookmaking or murder. Neither is it against the law for an individual to participate in such a division of labor.[13] None of the laws enacted for the regulation of legitimate organizations can be used to regulate La Cosa Nostra, and none of the laws enacted for regulation of membership in either legitimate (labor unions) or illegitimate (Communist party) organizations apply. For this reason, data cannot be routinely compiled on organized crime in the way that they are routinely compiled on, say, burglary and automobile theft. But the issue involves more than questions of assembling data. The legal lacunae permit directors of illicit businesses to remain immune from arrest, prosecution, and imprisonment unless they themselves violate specific criminal laws such as those prohibiting individuals from selling narcotics. Moreover, they permit law-enforcement agencies to ignore organized crime if they wish to do so, because any change in policy is not reflected in a set of statistics. Most

---

[11] See Cressey, "The Functions and Structure of Criminal Syndicates," *Task Force Report: Organized Crime, op. cit.,* pp. 34–36.

[12] See Thomas C. Schelling, "Economic Analysis and Organized Crime," *Task Force Report: Organized Crime, op. cit.,* Appendix D, pp. 114–126.

[13] On June 24, 1965, Senator John L. McClellan and Senator Frank J. Lausche introduced a bill which, despite its title, would have outlawed membership in specified types of criminal organizations: *Senate Bill 2187: A Bill to Outlaw the Mafia and Other Organized Crime Syndicates.* The bill apparently fell of its own weight, for constitutional reasons.

important, it makes it difficult for a wide segment of society to perceive "organized crime" as a social problem.[14]

FROM THE KNOWN TO THE UNKNOWN

Since it is doubtful that organized crime will be extensively perceived as a social problem in the near future, perhaps it can be studied as a problem in "pure" social science. In the last decade alone, social scientists have conducted thousands of studies of legitimate organizations. Variations in the effectiveness and efficiency of different kinds of divisions of labor, and in the conditions under which these arise, persist, and change have been observed in many settings, ranging from broad administrative systems to specific factories, firms, hospitals, and prisons.[15] The theory, techniques, and research results from these studies of formal and in-

[14] The severe restrictions on wire-tapping and "bugging" by the police, now being proposed, threaten to hamper this perception even more. The perception of existing "social problem perceivers," mostly government officials, in this area has been shaped, to a great extent, by sounds coming from telephone taps and "bugs." If these sounds are silenced, within ten years some of the current perceivers will probably be unable to perceive even the existence of organized crime, as was the case with some of them before they had the assistance of electronic devices. La Cosa Nostra members know that the law of evidence is old-fashioned, having been designed for criminals less rational and less ruthless than they are. Basically, the law requires material objects, papers, or a witness as evidence. The organized criminal systematically destroys all of these. The "bug," prudently used in cases where witnesses typically refuse to come forward, is a modern substitute for a witness. See G. Robert Blakey, "Aspects of the Evidence-Gathering Process in Organized Crime Cases: A Preliminary Analysis," *Task Force Report: Organized Crime, op. cit.*, Appendix C, pp. 80–113.

[15] For summaries of these studies, see James G. March, (ed.), *Handbook of Organizations* (Chicago: Rand McNally, 1965).

formal divisions of labor are directly applicable to illicit enterprises, and, moreover, it is quite possible that study of the arrangements in secret illicit enterprises will produce findings making it necessary to modify the organizational theory derived from studies of legitimate systems.

The principal handicap here stems from the fact that there are no "hard data" on organized crime. The information in the files of law-enforcement and investigating agencies, even those whose principal function is the assembling of intelligence information, is by no means oriented to providing assistance to social science theorists. As indicated above, law-enforcement agencies are necessarily concerned with apprehending and convicting individual criminals, and questions that social scientists would have them ask simply do not occur. Further, informants are not available for interview, and there is no known way to observe the everyday interactions of organized criminals with each other, with other criminals, or with noncriminals. These facts of life pose serious methodological problems for the social scientist who would learn something about the norms, values, and rules of organized criminal society, because such phenomena are social-psychological in nature and, therefore, are readily observable only in the context of interaction.

These problems were confronted as we tried to determine, while preparing the report, the essentials of "the code" of organized criminals. No "code" had been published, either by criminals or by observers, and since informants were not available for interview or observation, even an anthropologically oriented legal analysis of "primitive law" was impossible. We "solved" the problem by assuming similarities between groups whose consent to be governed is given only grudgingly, and for a price. Specifically, we argued that the relationship of prisoners to their governors, and the relationship of the populations of occupied nations to their governors, resemble the relationship of organized criminals to the governmental officials of their domain. On the basis of this argument, or assumption, we used "the code" of prisoners as an aid in the formulation of "the code" of norms governing the gross conduct of organized criminals.

We also traveled a rocky road from observations of social structure to generalizations about norms, but the methodological assumptions involved are not described in the report. We took a clue from archaeology, and it is quite possible that further study of the "logic of archaeology" (and of history and geology) will reveal solutions to methodological problems arising from the fact that, in the study of organized crime, the traditional social science techniques for data-gathering and data-analysis, and even the "logic of sociology," are inadequate. When the sociologist is unable to test the reliability and validity of observations, he is likely to conclude that no observation has in fact been made. But, over the years, archaeologists have created information and manufactured data by reasoning that knowledge about inaccessible affairs can be obtained from consideration of affairs accessible to study.[16] From bones, pots, tools, and other artifacts dug up by archaeologists, and from analysis of the relationships of these objects to each other, conclusions are drawn about the religious, political, and economic affairs of extinct cultures.[17]

If this kind of inferential process is applied to the problem at hand, we can use knowledge about the structure of organized crime to create information and manufacture data about both norms and interaction processes. It is true, of course, that our knowledge of structure is as yet quite fragmentary and restricted. Nevertheless, observations of structure can be made without conducting interviews or observing day-to-day affairs. The assumption is that, as such observations become well authenticated, we will be able to create increasingly good information about values and norms. As a preliminary step, it can be observed that analysis of only one position in the structure, "Enforcer," enables one to create information about complex governmental processes and a set of "laws." The Enforcer position was selected because all observers of organized crime agree that it exists and, moreover, because analysis of only one "gangland slaying" would establish that it exists, even if observers insisted that it did not.

Although little is known about the Enforcer position, a description of it makes it obvious that this position is one of a subset of positions existing within a broader division of labor designed to maximize organizational integration by means of just infliction of punishments on wrongdoers. Any person occupying the position of Enforcer makes arrangements for the injuring or killing of members.[18] The person oc-

---

[16] Intelligence agencies, of course, use the same kind of reasoning. "Strategic intelligence" consists, in part, of making a lot out of a little.

[17] See the discussion, and criticism, of this technique in A. R. Radcliffe-Brown, *Method*

in Social Anthropology (Chicago: University of Chicago Press, 1958).

[18] He also makes arrangements for injuring or killing persons who are not members of La Cosa Nostra, and this fact stimulates questions about the organizational boundaries of the criminal cartel and confederation. If the Enforcer has authority over persons who are not members of La Cosa Nostra, then it probably is proper to conclude that the boundaries of La Cosa Nostra are not the boundaries of "the organization" of organized

cupying the Enforcer position does not order the action, and he does not injure or kill anyone. He performs functions analogous to those performed by a prison warden or the prison official who makes the arrangements for imposing the death penalty. This means that the position must necessarily be integrated with a number of others, including a position for the person actually doing the killing or maiming and a position for the person giving orders to, and participating in "understandings" with, the person occupying the Enforcer position. Moreover, since these positions, like the Enforcer's functions, are political, they must necessarily be co-ordinated with other political functions of a legislative, adjudicative, or law-enforcement character. The presence of an Enforcer position in a division of labor can, in other words, be taken as evidence of the presence of comple-

criminals. We are confident that, from the perspectives of the Italian-Sicilian participants, "the organization" does not extend outside the "family," but we are not at all confident that street-level workers, who are outside the "family" and who might or might not be Italian or Sicilian, consider themselves outside the organization. This boundary problem is especially acute in areas like Chicago, where the term "La Cosa Nostra" is not extensively used, but where the organization is referred to as "the syndicate," "the outfit," or, simply, "the organization." It is significant that there is no plural form for any of these terms. "Outfit" and "organization" seems to refer to the local apparatus, which includes both Italian-Sicilians and non-Italian-Sicilians, while "syndicate" seems to refer to the amalgamation of all the "outfits" in the country. In the Report, we argue that the division of labor necessarily includes at least one position for a "corruptee," who usually is not a conscious member of La Cosa Nostra. The same arguments could be used to place within "the organization" all street-level workers occupying positions linked to the position of Enforcer and, through that link, to the entire apparatus. It is quite possible, of course, that "organized crime" is a series of organizations, perhaps overlapping, which interact with each other and with legitimate organizations.

mentary governmental positions, leading to the conclusion that La Cosa Nostra is a government as well as a business. The rationality evident in the creation of specialized occupations among working groups of criminals such as pickpocket troupes and check-passing rings has, in La Cosa Nostra, been extended to the creation of a cartel arrangement designed to minimize competition. It also has been extended to the creation of a governmental division of labor designed to maximize organizational integration.

The presence of an Enforcer position in a division of labor also can be taken as evidence that members of the organization must have created some functional equivalent of the criminal law, from which all government officials derive their authority and power. Whatever the content of this set of "laws," the presence of the Enforcer position signals the fact that it has been designed to minimize the degree of conflict and to maximize the degree of conformity among members. But a set of "laws" designed for this purpose must necessarily stress loyalty, honesty, rationality, respect for leaders, and patriotism; and we may therefore assume that such norms are stressed in the society of organized criminals.

The presence of an Enforcer position in a division of labor also signals the fact that punishments are to be imposed "justly," in a disinterested manner. Since punishments are imposed in this manner in order to maintain the consent of the governed, we may assume that the relationships between organized criminals are, to a great extent, determined by rules and expectations which insure that the consent of the governed is not lost. When justice prevails, the norms that govern the resort to adjudication serve to reduce conflict because they establish regularized expectations about the way in which disagreements will be settled.[19] Stated in reverse, the principle is that regularized expectations concerning the way in which disagreements will be settled are also the norms used in the adjudicative process. The presence of an Enforcer position, then, enables us to conclude that the day-to-day interactions of organized criminals are directed by norms which are also used in adjudication process. An adjudication process, in turn, signals the existence of a legislative process.

Although the above sketch is a gross oversimplification of the complex inferences which can be made about La Cosa Nostra norms from observation of one structural position, it does show that the

[19] See David Easton, *A Systems Analysis of Political Life* (New York: John Wiley & Sons, 1965), p. 264.

social scientist can create data on organized crime by reasoning from the known to the inaccessible, just as the archaeologist creates data, and just as the geologist proceeds as if the present were the key to the past. The social scientist who is an "organized crime expert" has an advantage over these other two types of scientists because he works with contemporary materials and therefore can comfortably make the assumption that "in the long run" the action scene which he has created by inference can be directly observed. This does not mean, of course, that eventually there will be no screens or filters on his perceptions. It means only that his perceptions will be strained through different screens and filters, those pertaining to "empirical observation."

[2]

CRIME & DELINQUENCY   July 1976

On Defining "Organized Crime"

The Development of a Definition and a Typology*

MICHAEL D. MALTZ

Associate Professor, Department of Criminal Justice,
University of Illinois at Chicago Circle

"Organized crime" means different things to different people; as a result, views of its seriousness vary. This paper discusses some of the problems in defining "organized crime." It offers a general rather than a single specific definition and develops a typology of different forms of organized crimes, permitting one to distinguish among the many disparate activities now lumped together and to eliminate the vagueness and contradictions surrounding use of the term "organized crime."

ORGANIZED CRIME plays a paradoxical role in American society. On the one hand, it has been described as a sinister criminal organization,[1] bent on squeezing exorbitant profits from the victims of its criminal enterprises. On the other hand, it has been called "one of the queer ladders of social mobility,"[2] a shortcut to success, American style, for groups without access to the legitimate means of power.

There is a similar divergence of views about white-collar crime, generally considered to be committed by those who have access to power but abuse it. While some decry the favored treatment given the white-collar criminal,[3] others maintain that white-collar crime greases the economy's wheels, that "foul is useful and fair is not. Avarice and usury and precaution must be our gods for a little longer still."[4]

The inconsistencies in the observations expressed above stem in part from the way the terms "organized crime" and "white-collar crime" are defined. There is very little agreement on what they constitute, in

---

*This paper is a revised and expanded version of the first section of "Policy Issues in Organized Crime and White-Collar Crime," in J. A. Gardiner and M. Mulkey, ed., *Crime and Criminal Justice: Issues in Public Policy Analysis* (Lexington, Mass.: D. C. Heath, 1975).

1. In a report of the Kefauver Committee (Special Committee to Investigate Organized Crime in Interstate Commerce). It is found in G. Tyler, ed., *Organized Crime in America* (Ann Arbor: University of Michigan Press, 1962), p. 11.

2. D. Bell, "Crime as an American Way of Life," in M. E. Wolfgang, L. Savitz, and N. Johnson, eds., *The Sociology of Crime and Delinquency*, 2nd ed. (New York: John Wiley, 1970), p. 166.

3. R. W. Ogren, "The Ineffectiveness of the Criminal Sanction in Fraud and Corruption Cases: Losing the Battle against White-Collar Crime," *American Criminal Law Review*, September 1973, p. 959.

4. John Maynard Keynes wrote this in 1930. Quoted in E. F. Schumacher, *Small Is Beautiful: Economics as if People Mattered* (New York: Harper & Row, 1974), p. 22.

comparison, say, with the specific crimes of "robbery" and "burglary." This paper discusses the problem in defining organized crime and white-collar crime. It develops a definition of organized crime and a typology of organized crimes (including some, but not all, types of white-collar crime), based on this discussion and on some of the previously propounded definitions. The aim of this alternative structure for defining the concept is to reduce the inconsistencies associated with organized crime and to provide new insights into its multifaceted nature.

Act or Group?

Central to the lack of consistent definitions is a semantic problem. The word "crime" is usually taken to mean the aggregate of specific "crimes"; i.e., *a crime* is a specific behavior or act and *crime* is the set of behaviors encompassing all crimes. In like manner we can call *an organized crime* a specific behavior or act. Yet when we talk of *organized crime* in the *generic* sense we usually refer not to a *set of behaviors* but to an *entity*, a group of (unspecified) people, a disease, a bogeyman: e.g., "Organized crime controls the scavenger industry in Westchester,"[5] "The Penetration of Legitimate Business by Organized Crime,"[6] "Why Organized Crime Thrives,"[7] and other anthropo-

morphisms. This confusion over the term leads to circular reasoning, as in "organized crime runs the narcotics distribution in New York City": the distribution of narcotics *is* an organized crime, and whoever runs it is *ipso facto* "in organized crime."

It has also been suggested that "organized crime as we know it in the United States requires an underclass of minority class ethnics in order to be operative."[8] But this presupposes a single form of organized crime—i.e., that which is committed by minority class ethnics.[9] The numbers operator may fit this description, but not the bookie who takes thousand-dollar bets; the narcotics pusher, perhaps, but not the marijuana importer; the truck hijacker, perhaps, but not the ones who fence the cargo. This again points out the confusion between the offender and the offense in defining organized crime.

White-Collar Crime Definitions

A similar situation exists with respect to the two formal definitions which have been attempted of white-collar crime. In 1949 Sutherland defined it as "a crime committed by a person of respectability and high social status in the course of his occupation."[10] In 1970 Edelhertz defined it as "an illegal act or series of illegal acts committed

5. R. Blumenthal, "Westchester Grip Tightened by Mob," *New York Times*, Oct. 13, 1974, p. 1.

6. M. K. Bers, *The Penetration of Legitimate Business by Organized Crime*, (Washington, D. C.: National Institute of Law Enforcement and Criminal Justice, Law Enforcement Assistance Administration, U. S. Department of Justice, 1970).

7. H. S. Ruth, Jr., "Why Organized Crime Thrives," *Annals*, October 1967.

8. F. A. J. Ianni's *Black Mafia: Ethnic Succession in Organized Crime* (New York: Simon & Schuster, 1974), p. 175.

9. We can assume that Ianni's "minority class ethnics" refers to a group identifiable by a common heritage and lacking access to political or economic power. Otherwise, even the WASP "power élite" can be considered a minority group.

10. E. II. Sutherland, *White Collar Crime* (New York: Dryden Press, 1949), p. 9.

by non-physical means and by con-
cealment or guile, to obtain money
or property, to avoid the payment
or loss of money or property, or to
obtain business or personal advantage."[11] Sutherland's definition is
an *ad hominem* definition of occupational crime,[12] based as it is on
an attribute of the *offender*.
Edelhertz' definition is based on
two attributes of the *offense*, the
means of execution and the objective.

The relationship between white-
collar crime and organized crime is
well established. Many observers
have noted the movement (or perhaps, maturing) of groups usually
associated with criminal activities
into legitimate business activities.
But the semantic problem arises
here, too. One study of organized
crime noted that "Organized crime
in business is usually referred to as
white collar crime, except when
committed by racketeers who enter
into business, in which case it is
called organized crime, even though
the criminal acts may be identical."[13]

Organized Crime Definitions

Criminolgists' greater interest in
organized crime has led to a number
of definitions. But the only attempt
to define "organized crime" in a
federal statute is found in the
Omnibus Crime Control and Safe
Streets Act of 1968: "Organized
crime means the unlawful activities of the members of a highly
organized, disciplined association
engaged in supplying illegal goods
and services, including but not
limited to gambling, prostitution,
loan sharking, narcotics, labor racketeering, and other unlawful activities of members of such organizations."[14] This definition is used by
the Law Enforcement Assistance
Administration for developing action programs to counter organized
crime, but it is too vague to be used
in a criminal code.[15] Other definitions are listed in the Appendix
(pp. 344-46).

Some common characteristics of
the listed definitions include (1) the
commission of crimes, in some cases
limited to certain types; (2) the
type of organization, in some cases
rigid, hierarchical, and disciplined;
(3) violence or the threat of violence, such as muscle, fear, and intimidation, or the need for an enforcer; and (4) corruption. Yet the
term "organized crime" can be
applied with validity (i.e., without
doing harm to the English language)
to only the first two characteristics
(and to the second only without
presuming organizational rigidity).
The last two elements may be
necessary for certain types of organized crime but not for all
"crimes that are organized."

---

11. H. Edelhertz, *The Nature, Impact and Prosecution of White-Collar Crime* (Washington, D. C.: U. S. Govt. Printing Office, 1970), p. 3.

12. R. Quinney, "The Study of White Collar Crime: Toward a Reorientation in Theory and Research," in R. D. Knudten, ed., *Crime, Criminology, and Contemporary Society* (Homewood, Ill.: Dorsey, 1970), p. 72, argues for reorienting Sutherland's concept of white-collar crime to a study of occupational crime.

13. IIT Research Institute and Chicago Crime Commission, *A Study of Organized Crime in Illinois* (Chicago: IITRI, 1971), p. 295.

14. Public Law 90-351, passed June 19, 1968. It is interesting to note that the Organized Crime Control Act of 1970 (Public Law 91-452, passed Oct. 15, 1970) does not define organized crime.

15. According to the *New York Times* of Jan. 24, 1975 (p. 33), the New York State Supreme Court ruled that the law creating the state's Organized Crime Task Force was unconstitutional because it did not define "organized crime."

For example, violence is not a necessary concomitant of organized crime. Rather, it can be viewed as a substitute for economic and political power for those who lack access to these subtler means of coercion.[16] As the criminal enterprise matures, it usually gains access to and begins to use these more sophisticated, covert, and powerful forms of persuasion. For those who start their criminal careers with such access we normally reserve the term "white-collar criminals."[17]

A Tentative Definition/Typology

When we analyze the different definitions of organized crime and white-collar crime, it is tempting to search for unifying concepts. This is made more attractive by the views of some that the only difference between the two types of crime is the type of person who commits the crime.

Rather than attempt a single definition to encompass all forms, it may be more fruitful to formulate a definition combined with a typology. As Clinard and Quinney point out,[18] the construction of a typology should be determined by the purpose at hand. Most existing typologies are related to the *offender* or to the social system in which he

is imbedded.[19] Typologies of *crimes* are normally based on legal definitions, although it is well known that the variation *within* a legal category is frequently as great as the variation *between* categories.[20]

When most people think of "organized crime," they conjure up visions of 1934 Duesenbergs racing across city streets and spitting machine-gun bullets from side windows. This type of activity still goes on, but not to the extent that it did forty years ago. Yet, if we are to take preconceptions into account, it does point out that whether or not violence is employed as a means of achieving the criminal objectives should be clear in our typology.

A typology based only on the *means* of committing crimes is inadequate. Take violence as an example: a store can be bombed by professional robbers, by an extortion gang, by a political extremist group, or by a building owner who wants to collect on the building's

---

16. This statement should not be construed as meaning violence-based organized crime is unimportant or that the writer condones violence. Violent crime, whether organized or unorganized, is abhorrent. But the term "organized crime" should not be taken to refer to this single type of organized crime when so many other types exist but are hidden from sight because all attention focuses on this one type.

17. G. Geis, *White-Collar Criminal* (New York: Atherton, 1968).

18. M. B. Clinard and R. Quinney, *Criminal Behavior Systems: A Typology*, 2nd ed. (New York: Holt, Rinehart and Winston, 1973).

19. Aside from the typology developed by Clinard and Quinney, *op. cit. supra* note 18, are those developed by J. B. Roebuck, *Criminal Typology: The Legalistic, Physical-Constitutional-Hereditary, Psychological-Psychiatric and Sociological Approaches* (Springfield, Ill.: Charles Thomas, 1967), and D. C. Gibbons, *Society, Crime, and Criminal Careers* (Englewood Cliffs, N. J.: Prentice Hall, 1968).

20. The lines between purse-snatching and robbery (J. E. Hoover, *Uniform Crime Reporting Handbook* [Washington, D. C.: Federal Bureau of Investigation, U. S. Dept. of Justice, 1966]) and between larceny under $50 and over (D. Seidman and M. Couzens, "Getting the Crime Rate Down: Political Pressure and Crime Reporting," *Law and Society,* Spring 1974, p. 457) are so fine as to be ambiguous, while the crime of robbery is too broad for research purposes (A. Normandeau, *Trends and Patterns in Crimes of Robbery [with special reference to Philadelphia, Pennsylvania, 1960 to 1966]*, unpub. Ph.D. dissertation, University of Pennsylvania, 1968, p. 4).

MICHAEL D. MALTZ

insurance. The *objective* of the organized crime, and the manifestation this objective takes, should also be factors in the typology.

Our tentative definition and typology, then, consists of the following elements:

A crime consists of a transaction[21] *proscribed by the criminal law between offender(s) and victim(s). It is not necessary for the victim to be a complainant or to consider himself victimized for a crime to be committed.*[22] *An organized crime is a crime committed by two or more offenders who are or intend to remain associated for the purpose of committing crimes.*

The means *of execution of the crimes include violence, theft, corruption, economic power, deception, and victim collusion or participation, which are not mutually exclusive categories; any organized crime may employ a number of these means.*

The objective *of most organized crimes is power, either political or economic.*[23] *These objectives, too,* *are not mutually exclusive and may co-exist in any organized crime.*

The objectives may take a number of different manifestations. *When the objective is political power, it may be of two types: overthrow of the existing order or illegal use of the political process. When the objective is economic power, it may manifest itself in three ways: through common crime* (mala in se), *through illegal business* (mala prohibita), *or through legitimate business* (white-collar crime).

The table (p. 343) shows a typology of organized crime based on this definition. Other characteristics might have been included. There are major differences in *organization,*[24] the nature of the *victim* may also be of interest, and the type of *law enforcement response* has a major effect as well.[25] However, including these or other characteristics would tend to confuse the issues on which this paper focuses: that organized crime consists of acts, not groups; that violence is but one of the means of executing the crimes; and that the crimes are committed for political as well as economic reasons.

---

21. See A. Kuhn, *The Logic of Social Systems* (San Francisco: Jossey-Bass, 1974), for a definition of "transaction" from the standpoint of social systems.

22. A narcotics user normally does not complain to the police about the dealer from whom he obtains his drugs, because he does not see himself as the victim of the dealer. But similarly the patient of a swindler advertising a fake cancer cure is not normally a complainant; in fact, he may even come to the defense of the swindler in a court proceeding.

23. Some of those convicted in the Watergate cases tried to justify their actions by stating that they had derived no financial gain from their actions. But money is not the only currency in use; political power is a more commonly used medium of exchange in Washington.

The distinction between political and economic power is, to some degree, academic. The

---

concentration of a great deal of economic power in one organization *becomes* political power— Exxon and General Motors may exert more (political) control over more lives than does a legislative body. On the other hand, political power always implies economic power—witness Mayor Richard Daley's award of Chicago's insurance business to his son's firm and the inordinate growth of the fortunes of Presidents Lyndon Johnson and Richard Nixon while they were in office.

24. Ianni, *op. cit. supra* note 8; D.R. Cressey, *Criminal Organization* (New York: Harper & Row, 1972).

25. Clinard and Quinney, *op. cit. supra* note 18.

TYPOLOGY OF ORGANIZED CRIME

MEANS	MANIFESTATION				
	ECONOMIC OBJECTIVE			POLITICAL OBJECTIVE	
	Through common crime *(mala in se)*	Through illegal business *(mala prohibita)*	Through legitimate business (white-collar crime)	Through the existing order	Against the existing order [a]
Violence	Predatory juvenile gang. Hijacking ring.	Gang wars for control of narcotics, etc. Extortion racket. Loan-shark enforcement.	Strike-busting. Enforcing strike on non-strikers by force.	Threatening (or killing) election opponents. Roughing up opposing voters.	Revolution. Kidnaping government officials.
Theft	Burglary ring. Stolen car ring.	Theft of rival organizations' goods (e.g., alcohol during Prohibition).	Burglary for insurance purposes. Stealing trade secrets; industrial espionage.	Watergate burglary. FBI "surreptitious entries" into political organizations' offices.	Theft of files from the Media, Pa., FBI office.
Corruption	—	Gambling and narcotics payoffs to police, judges, etc.	Paying kickbacks to purchasing agents, union officials, politicians.	Pardoning a convicted felon in return for political support.	CIA actions in Chile.
Economic Coercion	—	Betting heavily on a fixed sports event to bankrupt a bookie.	Price-fixing. Restraint of trade. Closing down a factory with an illegal strike.	Obtaining political support by selective enforcement of the antitrust law.	U.S. embargo of Cuba. Arab oil embargo.
Deception	—	Fixing a sports event.	Planned bankruptcy. Siphoning off corporate funds through a dummy corporation. Falsifying auto emission data to comply with EPA.	Watergate coverup.	Espionage.
Victim Participation	—	Prostitution. Narcotics. Gambling.	Home improvement schemes. Polluting a town dependent on the polluter for its livelihood.	—	

a. Note that these are crimes only within the existing political framework; if a revolution succeeds, the crimes are legitimated.

Rationale for the Definition/Typology

At first glance this definition and the typology in the table seem to complicate rather than simplify the problem. A single type of illegal activity—for example, a numbers racket—can encompass many types of organized crime. In its simplest form a numbers racket is an illegal business based on victim participation. If payoffs are made to law enforcement personnel, it is also corruption-based. If violence is used to prevent competition from moving in, it is also violence-based.

Yet these distinctions are very important. In recent years LEAA has granted a great deal of money to state and local law enforcement agencies to fight organized crime. Without a clear-cut definition of organized crime it is no wonder that the fight is being questioned.[26] When the police launch "an all-out attack on organized crime" by going after a numbers racket, is the object of their attack a relatively benign "ma-and-pa" numbers operation (i.e., a victim-participation-based illegal business), is it also corruption-based, or does it contain elements of violence as well? Distinctions of this type are necessary if the evaluation of organized crime programs, as required by LEAA, is to be worthwhile. Otherwise there is no way of knowing how effectively our law enforcement resources are being allocated.

Although this typology of organized crime is not exact, it permits one to distinguish among the many disparate activities now lumped together and to eliminate the vagueness and contradictions surrounding the use of the term "organized crime."

26. *Supra* note 15.

Appendix

SOME DEFINITIONS OF ORGANIZED CRIME

1. "While this criminal group is not by any means completely organized, it has many of the characteristics of a system. It has its own language; it has its own laws; its own history; its tradition and customs; its own method and techniques; its highly specialized machinery for attacks upon persons and property; its own highly specialized modes of defense. These professionals have interurban, interstate, and sometimes international connections."

Report of the Chicago City Council Committee on Crime, 1915, quoted in Tyler, *supra* note 1, p. 5.

2. "Organized crime is the product of a self-perpetuating criminal conspiracy to wring exorbitant profits from our society by any means—fair and foul, legal and illegal. Despite personnel changes, the conspiratorial entity continues. It is a malignant parasite which fattens on human weakness. It survives on fear and corruption. By one or another means, it obtains a high degree of immunity from the law. It is totalitarian in its organization. A way of life, it imposes rigid discipline on underlings who do the dirty work while the top men of organized crime are generally insulated from the criminal act and the consequent danger of prosecution."

Oyster Bay Conference on Combating Crime, 1965, quoted in R. Salerno and J. S. Tompkins, *The Crime Confederation: Cosa Nostra and Allied Operations in Organized Crime* (New York: Doubleday, 1969), p. 303.

3. "In the broad sense, the phrase 'organized crime' may include criminal organizations in a wide variety of sizes and types of unlawful enterprises. At its lowest levels, it includes youth gangs which have as their principal purpose the systematic commission of crime, or other small loosely knit groups which engage in single or multiple crimes, such as shoplifting, burglary, and confidence games. At its highest level, of course, it includes

DEFINING "ORGANIZED CRIME" 345

the large, well-run groups which engage in such hard-core activities as professional gambling, the importation and distribution of narcotics, loan sharking, or labor racketeering. Indeed, 'organized crime' is often identified solely with these hard-core activities. This, however, is a mistake. Like the similar phrase 'white-collar crime,' organized crime properly refers not so much to the activity as to the status of the people who engage in it."

G. R. Blakey, "Organized Crime and Corruption Practices," in S. A. Yefsky, ed., *Law Enforcement Science and Technology: Proceedings of the First National Conference on Law Enforcement Science and Technology* (Chicago: IITRI, 1967), p. 15.

4. "Organized crime is a cancerous growth on American society with ill effects that reach everybody in one degree or another. Though far less flamboyant than it was in the days of Al Capone and John Dillinger, it is vastly more powerful and dangerous than ever before, and the urgency of fresh, concerted action to stem and reverse the rising tide of criminality commands the highest priority."

N. A. Rockefeller, quoted in P. D. Andreoli, "Organized Crime Enterprises—Legal," in Yefsky, *op. cit. supra*, p. 21.

5. "Organized crime·is a combination of two factors: (1) lucrative income producing criminal activities, which because of their nature minimize risks of successful prosecution; (2) a criminal organization variously known as the Mafia, Outfit, Cosa Nostra or Crime Syndicate, which exercises monopolistic control of these activities through acts of violence, bribery, and other forms of corruption."

W. J. Duffy, "Organized Crime—Illegal Activities," in Yefsky, *op. cit. supra*, p. 29.

6. "Organized crime is a society that seeks to operate outside the control of the American people and their governments. It involves thousands of criminals, working within structures as complex as those of any large corporation, subject to laws more rigidly enforced than those of legitimate governments. Its actions are not impulsive but rather the result of intricate conspiracies, carried on over many years and aimed at gaining control over whole fields of activity in order to amass huge profits."

President's Commission on Law Enforcement and Administration of Justice, *Task Force Report: Organized Crime* (Washington, D. C.: U.S. Govt. Printing Office, 1967), p. 1.

7. "The Department of Justice, in its operations, considers organized crime to be twofold: first, a criminal syndicate consisting of families operating as criminal cartels in large cities across the Nation, banded together in an organization with what corresponds to a board of directors at the top to settle problems, such as jurisdictional disputes, and to enforce discipline; and second, any large continuous criminal conspiracy which has significant impact upon a community, a region, or an area of our country."

U. S. House of Representatives, Government Operations Committee, *The Federal Effort against Organized Crime: Report of Agency Operations* (Washington, D.C.: U.S. Govt. Printing Office, 1968), p. 4.

8. "An organized crime is any crime committed by a person occupying, in an established division of labor, a position designed for the commission of crime, providing that such division of labor also includes at least one position for a corrupter, one position for a corruptee, and one position for an enforcer."

D. R. Cressey, *Theft of the Nation: The Structure and Operations of Organized Crime in America* (New York: Harper & Row, 1969), p. 319.

9. "[W]e can define organized crime as any criminal activity involving two or more individuals, specialized or nonspecialized, encompassing some form of social structure, with some form of leadership, utilizing certain modes of operation, in which the ultimate purpose of the organization is found in the enterprises of the particular group . . . . [A] continuum of different types of organized crime . . . in-

346   MICHAEL D. MALTZ

cludes *political-social, mercenary, in-group*
and *syndicated* organized crime."

J. L. Albini, *The American Mafia: Genesis of a
Legend* (New York: Appleton-Century-Crofts,
1971), pp. 37, 48.

10. "Organized crime consists of the
participation of persons and groups of
persons (organized either formally or informally) in transactions characterized by:
(1) an intent to commit, or the actual
commission of, substantive crimes; (2)
a conspiracy to execute these crimes; (3)
a persistence of this conspiracy through
time (at least one year) or the intent that
this conspiracy should persist through
time; (4) the acquisition of substantial
power or money, and the seeking of a
high degree of political or economic
security, as primary motivations; (5)
an operational framework that seeks the
preservation of politics, government and
society in their present form."

IITRI, *supra* note 13, p. 264.

[3]

University of Florida Law Review

VOLUME XXIV FALL 1971 NUMBER 1

SOME THINGS THAT MAY BE MORE IMPORTANT TO UNDERSTAND ABOUT ORGANIZED CRIME THAN COSA NOSTRA

DWIGHT C. SMITH, JR.*

This article analyzes the problems in developing a real definition of organized crime within the context of its use as a starting point for cost-effectiveness analysis. The limitation of conventional definitions are reviewed, with particular attention being given to the significance of understanding Cosa Nostra as a key to understanding organized crime. As an alternative to that approach, some questions are posed that may lead to more useful conclusions about organized crime than the conventional assumptions concerning Cosa Nostra.

THE COST OF ORGANIZED CRIME

Why should anyone be concerned about the notion of organized crime? Various contemporary observers have attempted to answer this question, but the only clear consensus that emerges is that reasons can be advanced to satisfy any reader's predispositions toward anxiety.[1] If one wished to catalogue the "threats" that have been identified, the resulting list would range from economic and social concerns, through political apprehensions, to moral and philosophical dread. The common thread to be observed in all the answers, aside from a concentrated focus on the "bad guys" epitomized by the Crime Commission's references to Italians,[2] is a high proportion of pejorative exhortation in relation to the amount of objective analysis and factual proof provided to support the conclusions set forth.

There is one concern about orgainzed crime that has not been explored to any great extent: the concern of the taxpayer who looks for assurance that his involuntary contributions to the support of organized crime control have been well spent. The plight of the taxpayer is generally linked to the argument that organized criminals amass illicit fortunes on which no taxes

---

*Director of Institutional Research, State University of New York at Albany; Visiting Associate Professor of Police Science, John Jay College of Criminal Justice.

1. See THE PRESIDENT'S COMMISSION ON LAW ENFORCEMENT AND ADMINISTRATION OF JUSTICE, TASK FORCE REPORT: ORGANIZED CRIME (1967) [hereinafter cited as CRIME COMMISSION] which lists five separate "dangers" or "threats" of organized crime. See also D. CRESSEY, THEFT OF THE NATION (1969) [hereinafter cited as D. CRESSEY] which lists six.

2. "Today the core of organized crime in the United States consists of 24 groups operating as criminal cartels in large cities across the Nation. Their membership is exclusively men of Italian descent . . . ." CRIME COMMISSION, supra note 1, at 6.

are paid, thus increasing the relative burden on the less affluent, honest citizen. This argument, however, is unsupported by even a theoretical model of the economy of an illicit enterprise that would show its relationship to the licit economy. Without such a model we remain at the mercy of "guess-timates" as to the disproportionate share of government support shouldered by the honest taxpayer. Similarly, no effort has been made to compare the potential (or theoretical) loss of revenue through the tax evasion of organized criminals with the loss of revenue resulting from the tax avoidance of legitimate businesses. Some important questions remain to be explored here. For example: Is my disproportionate share of the tax burden made heavier because the men who operate the numbers rackets in New York City are not reporting income and thus avoiding taxes, or because oil companies have depletion allowances written into their tax returns? Of equal importance should be our concern for a return on the taxes we *do* pay for organized crime control.

The problem of organized crime control has not been posed in this fashion before. In the past, attention has been focused on developing a sufficiently persuasive rationale to justify both legislative authorization of certain tactical weapons[3] and sufficient funding of programs that will eliminate organized crime. The rationale has been presented largely in military terms: organized crime is an "enemy" and it is to be dealt with through a "war."[4]

This approach has its limits, not the least of them being that conventional military thinking is not attuned to the conceptual approach of cost-effectiveness analysis. An enemy seldom has a price tag. The commanding general is motivated by the objective of inflicting more punishment on the enemy than can be reciprocated, rather than by whether the cost of inflicting the punishment is greater than the ultimate benefit to his side.[5]

---

3. *E.g.*, wiretapping, revised court rules, limitations on activities of members of organized crime.

4. For one of the earliest treatments of this approach, see R. KENNEDY, THE ENEMY WITHIN (1960). A more recent Washington comment referred to the Omnibus Crime Control Act of 1970 as giving the federal government the means "to launch a total war against organized crime, and we will end this war." *See* N.Y. Times, Oct. 16, 1970, at 18, col. 1.

5. A cost-effectiveness analysis would have to investigate both positive and negative values associated with organized crime and its control. This is a difficult undertaking for law enforcement personnel raised on the philosophy that "the good guys wear white hats." To illustrate that difficulty: In the past two years I have asked my seminar students to prepare, on successive weeks, informal essays discussing "The Threats of Organized Crime" and "The Benefits of Organized Crime." The first essay appeared to be relatively easy to prepare, without any need for qualification; but even the thought of the second essay has provoked severe intellectual problems for some students. In 1969 over half the class could not discuss "benefits" without an accompanying disclaimer statement, exhorting the reader to remember that the dangers of organized crime were far worse than any paltry, theoretical benefits. The problem was most noticeable among students who were senior police officers and who had previously been assigned to special vice control squads. The difficulty was apparent even though the "benefits" assignment accompanied assigned reading of Gardiner, *Wincanton: The Politics of Corruption*, in CRIME COMMISSION, *supra* note 1, at 61-79.

Nonetheless, it may be that cost-effectiveness analysis is inappropriate in organized crime control. Many of the concerns associated with that area of enforcement are intangible and objectives of a control program may be impossible to associate with numerical values. Furthermore, although the *process* of criminal justice may be inherently sequential and continuous, it becomes operative through a *system* of criminal justice, which is ordinarily dysfunctional, often bewildering and discordant, and sometimes even irrational.[6] The law enforcement agency may effectively investigate organized crime and may allocate its resources well for that task; but its efforts may be thwarted by subsequent action based on conflicting objectives of another administrative unit within the criminal justice system. Despite these limitations, the process of undertaking a cost-effectiveness analysis might well be profitable, even if the concept is not adopted as a permanent evaluation tool. The attempt to apply it would require a more concrete specification of the nature of the problem, and of the objectives to be sought in relation to it, than has yet taken place. Clarification of public policy is desirable in any event; in this case, it would undoubtedly improve the law enforcement community's ability to tackle its share of the problem.

If a consensus *were* reached on the desirability of exploring a cost-effectiveness approach to organized crime control, the first task would be to define the problem of organized crime. To the casual reader of popular literature on the subject, this would not seem to be a difficult task. He might well conclude that with so many studies of "the problem" available, including one by a Presidential commission, the nature of organized crime and the directions in which its remedies lie must surely be clear by now.[7] Unfortunately, this is not the case. Because organized crime has not been well defined, remedies have been proposed that entail considerable law enforcement activity but little hope of resolving the problem. If one looks closely at what has been written about the nature of organized crime, the reasons for the definitional deficiency become clear. In simple terms, the characteristics that have been cited as keys to "understanding" organized crime are not the right keys at all. They open doors that lead down dimly lit paths to cul-de-sacs, while the reality of organized crime continues down the main line, unimpeded. "Understanding" is needed; but of the real phenomena, accurately defined.

THE PROBLEM OF DEFINITION

Assuming that there is a valid category of persons and events that can be called organized crime, it is apparent that there are three ways of approach-

---

6. For a more detailed discussion of the distinction between "process" and "system," see *The Information Requirements of Criminal Justice Administration*, in NEW YORK STATE IDENTIFICATION AND INTELLIGENCE SYSTEM, A NEW CONCEPT IN INFORMATION-SHARING 13-20 (1967).

7. The CRIME COMMISSION, *supra* note 1, devoted nearly ten pages (1-10) describing the nature of organized crime, and an almost equal amount of space (at 16-24) to suggesting remedies.

ing it: as a social phenomenon, to be analyzed and understood; as an illegally defined act, or state of being, for which a person can be prosecuted; and as a popular concept, to be communicated to the public.

These approaches are interrelated and cannot be considered apart from each other. Nevertheless, an adequate social definition must precede a legal definition if the latter is to have any enforcement value, and similarly, both the social and legal definitions must support the popular concept.[8]

This is not what has happened. Popular notions have been adopted as the basis for attempts at legal definitions. The popular notions are so burdened with stereotypes that it has been virtually impossible to undertake the necessary objective analysis that would produce an adequate social definition.

What are those stereotypes? As a sample, consider the results of an exercise that introduces the seminar on "Organized Crime in America" at the John Jay College of Criminal Justice. Without prior conditioning, students were asked to list the first ten responses evoked by the phrase "organized crime." The composite response of the ten terms most frequently mentioned in the last two years, in the order in which they occurred, was as follows:[9] Mafia, money, Italian, Cosa Nostra, gambling, narcotics, prostitution, organization, corruption, murder.

When forced to go beyond their immediate reactions, the students suggested other aspects of organized crime. Nonstereotype images such as interlocking businesses, control of industry, profit, affluence, supply, demand, and cross-country travel were mentioned. The trouble with these images, of course, is that they could be used just as well to describe a decent, law-abiding, upperworld, white, Anglo-Saxon member of the legitimate business community. This bothers many who have accepted the popular stereotypes that identify a group of social outcasts who do things for their own benefit to an innocent and unsuspecting public.

A colloquy in New Jersey a year ago demonstrated the unhappiness that emerges in the absence of expected stereotypes. It occurred as the state supreme court heard arguments from lawyers questioning the power of the fledgling State Investigation Commission to compel testimony about organized crime by conferring immunity from prosecution upon witnesses. During the arguments Chief Justice Joseph Weintraub pressed one of the lawyers for an explanation of the Cosa Nostra:[10]

---

8. The interrelationship of social and legal definitions is explored in some detail by D. CRESSEY, *supra* note 1, at 299-305. Unfortunately, he deals separately with the problem of the popular definition and thus misses the interrelationship of all three. *Id.* at 54-71.

9. I obtained 632 responses from the 65 students who participated in this exercise (some found the 9th and 10th responses difficult to articulate). Of this total, 209 were words or concepts expressed only once; the remaining responses were comprised of multiple listings of 80 words or phrases. The 10 listed here were mentioned 212 times, or one-third of the total responses. The order shown was derived by giving a value of 10 to the 1st word listed by each respondent and 1 to the 10th word listed, and by averaging the resulting score by the total listings of the word. By this calculation, "Mafia" (mentioned 37 times) had an average value of 8.8; "murder" (mentioned 11 times) had an average value of 4.6.

10. N.Y. Times, Dec. 16, 1969, at 50, col. 2.

The lawyer denied he had any personal knowledge of organized crime.

But based on "what [he had] heard and studied," he gave this description: "The Cosa Nostra is supposed to be a group of people banded together for selfish purposes to make money any way they can, with the emphasis on illegal means."

"That sounded like General Motors up until the last part," Justice Weintraub replied, drawing laughter from a packed courtroom.

What is organized crime — *really*? The stereotypes that form the concept amount to what Walter Lippman described years ago as "the pictures inside people's heads [of] the world outside."[11] If the pictures do not reflect reality, the definitions constructed to categorize them will be misleading.

Are the popular images of Mafia, Italian, and Cosa Nostra the reality of organized crime, or are they, in the imagery of Plato's famous allegory, simply shadows cast on the back wall of a cave by puppets held between our backs and the firelight at the entrance to the cave? Is the reality of organized crime a group of persons working together? Is it the activities they engage in — gambling, narcotics, extortion, murder, prostitution, usury? Is it a corporate-like structure built for illegal activities, but with significant and distinctive characteristics? Is it a series of basically independent social problems in which a particular group of entrepreneurs can be observed? Or is it a social phenomenon, generated by the demands of our society, and extending well beyond the cast of characters and the list of activities normally associated with it? Strikingly different definitions can be written for organized crime, depending on what is considered to be real about it.

Beyond the problem of stereotypes, a second barrier to understanding organized crime is a preoccupation with the criminality of it. Too much emphasis is placed on "crime" and not enough on "organized." While Professors Cressey and Schelling have both attempted to penetrate this barrier, with Schelling's effort being the more successful,[12] the barrier is still there. It encourages an assumption that the law stands in the middle of a large gulf separating legitimate and illegitimate activities. Consequently, no matter what point of departure is chosen, the generally perceived reality of organized crime distinguishes between criminals and law-abiding persons as being somehow inherently different; or between criminal activities as being of a different order from legitimate activities; or between criminal organizations as being different in both structure and operations from legitimate organizations.

Another barrier to a satisfactory definition is the focus on one side of the matter — the persons who commit organized crime. To be sure, there is recognition of the concept of the willing victim and of the distinction between predatory and service crimes. Despite those concepts, mental images are maintained of organized crime that have no relationship to its environ-

---

11. W. Lippman, Public Opinion 31 (1922).

12. Perhaps his advantage lies in being an economist rather than a criminologist. *See* D. Cressey, *supra* note 1; Schelling, *Economic Analysis and Organized Crime*, in Crime Commission, *supra* note 1, at 114.

ment; it appears as a force with its own motive power and an independently contrived *raison d'etre*.

The result of this approach has been the development of a "Mafia mystique," which came forcefully to the surface with the Crime Commission's comments about Italians, but reached its peak with Cressey's statement that "if one understands Cosa Nostra he understands organized crime in the United States."[13] Coincidentally, Puzo's bestseller,[14] *The Godfather*, provided the basis for a popular notion of Italian dominated syndicate crime that reinforced the official position of the Crime Commission. The cumulative effect on such declarations and fantasies prompted an unprecedented spurt of news articles that reinforced the mystique by reporting on "The Mafia" in relation to law enforcement activities against organized crime.[15] The popular, public inquiry of the press was in high gear until the Attorney General prohibited the use of the terms Mafia and Cosa Nostra by the Justice Department.[16] While his order temporarily affected the frequency of public references to these ethnically-identifiable labels, there is nothing to indicate that official beliefs have changed noticeably. "*Cherchez les Italiens*" still appears to be the principal theme of organized crime control.[17]

At the heart of that policy lies Cressey's detailed, though admittedly speculative, elaboration of the structure and functions of syndicated crime in the United States. His opponents, notably Morris and Hawkins, have con-

---

13. D. CRESSEY, *supra* note 1, at 21.

14. M. PUZO, THE GODFATHER (1969).

15. The *New York Times Index* listings under the heading "Mafia" show the name enjoyed some notoriety during the Kefauver hearings (13 listings in 1951) and again at the time of the McClellan hearings and the Appalachin meeting (16 and 13 entries, respectively, in 1958 and 1959). In intervening years, and after 1959, interest in "Mafia" almost disappeared from the newspaper. Since the Valachi revelations, "Mafia" has been a standard reference, with occasional cross-listings to "Cosa Nostra" and "Crime Syndicate." The following table indicates that the number of index listings was increasing arithmetically until the appearance of the Crime Commission report in 1967.

Year	Index Listings Under "Mafia"	Year	Index Listings Under "Mafia"
1963	18	1967	104
1964	17	1968	127
1965	40	1969	285
1966	60	1970, Jan.-June	185
		July-Dec.	85
		1971, Jan.-June	117

16. N.Y. Times, July 24, 1970, at 28, col. 4.

17. "[E]xcept when speaking for quotations, Federal investigators and state law enforcement officers continue to use the terms "Mafia" and "Cosa Nostra." The Federal agents, including those in the F.B.I., believe their position reflects the view of Mr. Hoover . . . ." Crutzner, *Dispute over "Mafia,"* N.Y. Times, Sept. 5, 1970, at 24, col. 2. This view may not be held by all law enforcement personnel, however. "Alfred J. Scotti, chief assistant district attorney of Manhattan, took issue with [Bronx District Attorney Burton B. Roberts'] use of the word Mafia, saying that in his 23 years in the district attorney's office 'I've never come across any evidence that would indicate that these groups [or] families operate as members of the Mafia.'" *See* N.Y. Times, Sept. 14, 1970, at 15, col. 1.

tended that his analysis is an over elaboration based more on myth than on justifiable speculation; they conclude that whatever lies behind the events normally categorized as organized crime can be eliminated if we "remove the criminal laws which both stimulate and protect it."[18]

While both sides of this argument may be partially correct, neither is a satisfactory approach to the problem of organized crime control. Their primary concern is with establishing, or challenging, Cosa Nostra as the key to understanding organized crime, when in reality it is an intellectual impasse. It is doomed at the outset because its origins are in contemporary stereotypes, a preoccupation with criminality, and a focus on perpetrators alone.

This concern for an accurate definition of organized crime is more than an abstract search for "Truth." A definition of a particular category of behavior will specify what is different about that category, what significant factors are common to a class of actions, and what factors separate the behavior covered by the category from other forms of behavior. If the category being defined is a criminal one, there will be a presumption that the differences have negative connotations. This is the case with organized crime: it is distinguished from other activities by unpopular behavior. But more importantly the activities categorized as organized crime are alleged to be the cause of a moral decay that is of considerable danger to American life.

Three serious problems of analysis appear at this point. First: Is Cosa Nostra so synonymous with organized crime that its elimination would signal the end of the phenomenon? Second: Are the activities identified as organized crime the totality of the causes of the decay in American life so that its elimination would eliminate this decay? Third: Are the activities that should properly be grouped as organized crime the *cause* of the threats identified with it, or merely its *symptoms*? The campaign against organized crime entails significant compromises with the balance between group security and individual privacy that existed even a decade ago; for the risks that organized crime control asks us to take, the underlying categorization and explanation of the phenomena under examination must be unequivocally sound. An inadequate definition process will not assure that soundness.

If this is the case, how should the problem of defining organized crime be approached? Very simply: by not looking for organized crime itself. As a contrived concept, at least in contemporary usage,[19] it does not possess its own logic, but requires interpretation from a variety of viewpoints. The question is not: "What is organized crime?" Rather, the question is: "What insights may be obtained from history, economics, sociology, psychology — even philosophy and theology — that would facilitate efforts to understand

18. N. MORRIS & G. HAWKINS, THE HONEST POLITICIAN'S GUIDE TO CRIME CONTROL 235 (1970).

19. There is a considerable difference between contemporary references to organized crime and the conceptual approach intended by John Landesco in his original use of the phrase. *See* J. Landesco, *Organized Crime in Chicago*, in ILLINOIS CRIME SURVEY, pt. 3, at 221 (1929). (Part 3 was reissued in 1968, with a *Foreword* by Mark Haller).

why the phenomena we categorize as organized crime occur, and what forces trigger their occurrence?"

The "Cosa Nostra Syndrome"

It is important to note that the alternative approach just described has been suggested previously, but has not yet been tried. Cressey drew attention to it in the concluding paragraph of his paper for the Crime Commission by saying: "New questions, different from those traditionally raised by police and prosecutors must be asked, and new evidence relating to the answers to those questions must be assembled."[20] While *Theft of The Nation*, an outgrowth of his paper, was an attempt to do just that, it has fallen short of the mark. Two noticeable changes in conceptual approach may account for this.

First, the suggestion that "New questions . . . must be asked" was linked to a plea that police intelligence files be opened to social science researchers from outside the law enforcement community. In turn, these suggestions were related to an earlier conclusion that: "What is needed is detailed and precise specification, by social scientists, law enforcement personnel, and legislators working together, of the formal and informal structures of illicit governments and businesses."[21] Contrast that conclusion with the manner in which it was restated in the book that followed:[22]

> We propose that social scientists, systems engineers, law-enforcement personnel, and legislators work together, probably in a new agency within the United States Department of Justice, to specify in detail the formal and informal structures of the illicit governments and businesses traditionally lumped together as "organized crime."

The proposal that "New questions . . . be asked" was not restated nor was the idea that intelligence files be made available to researchers. Rather, the explanatory comments immediately following the suggestion of a new agency within the Justice Department appears to have reversed the original intent:[23]

> Implicit in this proposal is the suggestion that a cadre of policemen be broadly trained for organized-crime work . . . . It is high time that some policemen be trained as organized crime specialists, and that their training include general studies of the kind now necessary for military leadership.

In this form, Cressey's suggestion appears to head toward the Crime Commission's comments concerning the development of strategic intelligence;[24]

---

20. Cressey, *The Functions and Structure of Criminal Syndicates*, in Crime Commission, *supra* note 1, at 60.

21. *Id.* at 57.

22. D. Cressey, *supra* note 1, at 297.

23. *Id.* at 297-98.

24. Crime Commission, *supra* note 1, at 15.

but it is difficult to imagine how this approach could facilitate the asking of "New questions, different from those traditionally raised by police . . . ."[25]

Second, early in his discussion of the nature of organized crime, Cressey considered "[t]he problem of assigning a name to the American confederation of criminals."[26] He described the discussions that took place at the 1965 Oyster Bay Conferences on Combating Organized Crime, and the conclusion then reached that "Confederation" was the best term to use. Although not perfectly descriptive, it had the advantage, according to the conferees, of being sufficiently free from local terminology to be usable in the interjurisdictional setting. It did not mean that the conferees rejected any ethnic identification of organized crime; undoubtedly, most of them said "Confederation" but thought "Italian." They had in mind a "loosely knit conspiracy, which is Italian dominated . . . ."[27] On the other hand, it is apparent that they wished to leave room for a wider focus on the problem: "Practically all students of organized crime are agreed that this organization does not represent the total or organized crime . . . ."[28] In his paper for the Crime Commission, Cressey adopted this approach. Although clearly describing a structure based on existing theories of "Mafia" and "Cosa Nostra," he referred to it throughout his paper as "Confederation."

With the publication of *Theft of the Nation*, however, a change occurred. His earlier description of the Oyster Bay discussion is recapitulated, with some side observations interpolated;[29] it is followed immediately, however, by a supplemental comment not in the original paper:[30]

> We are satisfied that "Cosa Nostra" is as good as any other term . . . .
> While Cosa Nostra still tolerates some major operations by criminals of ethnic backgrounds which are not Sicilian or Italian, if one understands Cosa Nostra he understands organized crime in the United States.

In the remaining discussion "Confederation" is replaced throughout by "Cosa Nostra."[31] This change in name is unfortunate. It restricts Cressey's later analysis — most of which is quite useful in a speculative sense — to

---

25. Cressey, *supra* note 20, at 60. The development of strategic intelligence resources within the agency responsible for ultimate action is risky. "Intelligence must be close enough to policy, plans, and operations to have the greatest amount of guidance, and must not be so close that it loses its objectivity and integrity of judgment." S. KENT, STRATEGIC INTELLI-GENCE 180 (1951).

26. Cressey, *supra* note 20, at 27.

27. *Id.* at 28.

28. *Id.*

29. D. CRESSEY, *supra* note 1, at 16-20.

30. *Id.* at 20-21.

31. With few exceptions the only significant one of which is noted above, (*see* text accompanying notes 21-23 *supra*), the entire paper is incorporated into the remainder of the book, with the addition of supplemental material based largely on now-public material obtained by law enforcement agencies through wiretap or "overhear" devices. The change in name noted here is the only substantive modification of the earlier Crime Commission material not previously noted.

what can be understood about organized crime if one is limited to previously established notions of the law enforcement community. That perspective contains little room for "new questions."

WHAT SHOULD WE UNDERSTAND ABOUT ORGANIZED CRIME?

Since there has not yet been a sustained, systematic search for new understandings about organized crime, no firm assurances can be given that the lines of inquiry suggested here will turn out, in the long run, to have been correct ones to follow. Nevertheless, some promising starting points can be identified and pursued briefly. The ultimate goal in each case is knowledge that will contribute generally to organized crime control.

What Is the Role of Illicit Enterprise in American Life?

The choice of a name other than "organized crime" is a deliberate effort to escape from a concept so overburdened with stereotyped imagery that it cannot meet the basic requirements of a definition – it does not include all the phenomena that are relevant; it does not exclude all the phenomena that are not relevant; and it does not provide a sufficient framework for taxonomic description.[32] "Enterprise" is preferable to "activity" because the phenomena in question have objectives that are entrepreneurial in nature. "Illicit" is preferable to "criminal" because, in the present discussion, it establishes a less pejorative base for analysis, and because it can be distinguished in an economic sense from "licit." The antonym of "criminal" is the legal alternative "civil" – a less useful distinction for the purposes of the present analysis.

Implicit in the question being posed is an assumption that social and economic behavior can be depicted as a continuous distribution, "ranging from [the] very saintly to the most sinful."[33] If this be the case, there is no clear distinction between so-called "astute business practices" and illicit practices; the entrepreneur faced with the right mix of competetive stresses and undetectable (or at least low risk) opportunity may shift his behavior toward the "bad" or "sinful" end of the scale.

Conventional descriptions of organized crime appear to operate from a different assumption – that activities such as gambling, loansharking, union racketeering and drug trafficking are distinctive in character from "legitimate business" and operate according to different cultural values. The distinction becomes most apparent when the threat of organized crime is found to be its "infiltration of legitimate business,"[34] or its "culture of fraud, corruption, violence, and murder."[35]

---

32. *See* Schelling, *supra* note 12, at 115-17. Schelling attempted such a taxonomic description, to explain "why some underworld business becomes organized and some remains unorganized." *Id.* at 115.
33. L. WILKINS, SOCIAL DEVIANCE 46-47 (1965).
34. CRIME COMMISSION *supra* note 1, at 4.
35. D. CRESSEY, *supra* note 1, at 1.

Is the distinction between the upperworld and underworld that clear, or is there one world in fact, in which illicit enterprises, which have clear and often accepted roles, are linked to licit enterprises by functional similarity and by practices that evidence only the subtlest of distinctions? Is loansharking, for example, really a distinctive enterprise, or is it an extension of the banking business beyond legally permissible rates of interest with functionally identical problems of credit review, collection and default, loan conditions, customer satisfaction? Is the loansharking enterprise based on forcing otherwise reluctant customers to deal with it, or on the opportunity for relatively low-risk profit from individuals or enterprises that cannot obtain credit from legal sources? Is the threat of violence the force that inhibits the borrower from defaulting, or is it the potential loss of a credit line that impels repayment?

It may be somewhat unfair to impute as heavy an emphasis on an upper-under world distinction to contemporary organized crime writings as these questions seem to do. Salerno and Tompkins refer often to the functional and operating "correspondence between United States business and organized crime."[36] At the same time, a distinction is drawn between organized crime and legitimate business that assumes a sharp demarcation between the two:[37]

> The difference between organized crime and a large corporation is that a company may use sharp, and even unfair, business practices in moving ahead of the competition, but it does not try to capture a share of market with a gun or club. It sells by persuasion, competition, service, and ideas rather than extortion. And many companies' violations of antitrust, labor, tax, food and drug and other laws are inadvertant rather than systematic.[38]

When the principal frame of reference shifts from a stereotyped cast of persons operating in a separate world of crime to illicit enterprises at one end of a continuous spectrum of business activity, it becomes clear that more is involved than the events and persons conventionally identified as organized crime. Such activities as price-fixing, "blockbusting," fraudulent sales, and contract payoffs — perhaps even "conflicts of interest . . . in connection with the organization and operation of unregistered investment partnerships"[39] — are also part of illicit enterprise. To make sense of this larger category, a typology, accompanied by a list of distinguishing characteristics, would be required. For example, while all activities properly identified as illicit enterprise apparently entail conspiracy, do they also require corruption? Is violence a common characteristic? Do they all represent the same dangers to society in terms of illegal accumulation of wealth, neutralization

---

36. R. Salerno & J. Tompkins, The Crime Confederation 101 (1969).

37. *Id.* at 203-04.

38. The distinction insisted upon here is a curious one, considering that only two pages earlier the Chicago jukebox industry is described in terms of politeness, service, and persuasion, as an example of how "the soft sell has taken hold in Chicago, the last stronghold for rampant violence." *Id.* at 200-01.

39. Steiger, *Secret Report on Wall St. Abuses*, N.Y. Post, Dec. 8, 1970, at 4, col. 2.

of law enforcement, and subversion of "the very decency and integrity that are the most cherished attributes of a free society"?[40] It may well be that within a correct typology of illicit enterprise, conventional organized crime activities remain clustered and, in the final analysis, they may be the largest single grouping within the larger category. However, other and perhaps unexpected companions will also emerge, and an understanding of the category as a whole may provide a clearer and more convincing explanation of the origins and significance of any of its subjects. From the standpoint of law enforcement, it may also have the practical advantage of providing a clearer relationship between the functions of an Organized Crime and Racketeering Division and other regulatory agencies.

This line of inquiry may provide a better explanation for the vexing problem often characterized as the "fabric of society" question. As Salerno and Tompkins put it: "Organized crime . . . is so thoroughly woven into the fabric of our society that we no longer recognize it as special or different, immensely wealthy or powerful."[41] This statement assumes that organized crime was once a separate entity, not inherent in American life (else, why note that "we *no longer* recognize it as special"). As such, the further assumption is that it can be divorced from American life if the right approach is taken. The essence of the ensuing strategy is to eliminate organized crime by eliminating the group of persons who engage in it. If, on the other hand, illicit enterprises, including those activities usually categorized as organized crime, are a natural outgrowth of our economic structure, then the assumption that an attack on its purveyors will lead to its demise is questionable and an entirely different strategy may be called for.

Another potential advantage of this line of inquiry is that it may lead to a successful search for historic parallels and the insights they may provide. The present-day focus on Italian dominated syndicate crime as synonymous with organized crime assumes that the Prohibition Era gave it birth. Salerno and Tompkins note:[42]

Any list of organized crime's heroes would have to rank Representative Andrew J. Volstead and Benito Mussolini at the top. Unknown to each other, and without conscious intent they set the stage for the organization of crime in the United States.

A second theory, one that never really caught on, traces its history to the early gangs of the 19th century. Tyler enunciated this theory a decade ago:[43]

40. CRIME COMMISSION, *supra* note 1, at 24.
41. R. SALERNO & J. TOMPKINS, *supra* note 36, at 392.
42. *Id.* at 275. Similarly: "[C]rime first got organized along modern business lines during Prohibition. This development has been clearly documented, although the reasons for it have been somewhat confused." Moynihan, *The Private Government of Crime,* 25 THE REPORTER, July 6, 1961, at 15.
43. G. TYLER, ORGANIZED CRIME IN AMERICA 89 (1962). *See also* Tyler, *An Interdisciplinary Attack on Organized Crime,* in *Combating Organized Crime,* 347 ANNALS, May 1963, at 107-08 (special issue).

Contrary to popular belief, organized crime did not begin with Prohibition. . . . Nor did "crime incorporated" begin with the highly publicized Mafia. . . . The line of development from buccaneer to businessmen, from fisticuffs to finance parallels the contour of the American economy. The binding tie from past to present is the very accurate word "gangster."

Tyler's preoccupation with gangs[44] obscured his more penetrating observation concerning parallels in the American economy. Ordinarily, when that possibility is raised, similarities are found in the turn-of-the-century robber barons. Tyler recalls Jay Gould, Daniel Drew, and Commodore Vanderbilt, but only in terms of their relationship (as potential employers) to his gang theory.[45] If the focus is instead on illicit enterprises in the American economy, not simply on figures from the immediate past whose affairs are characterized by dubious business practices and by the use of violence, perhaps more useful referents will emerge. For example: Is the slave trade one of the earliest examples of organized crime in America?

Originally, slavery was a legitimate business in the American Colonies. As DuBois observed: "That the slave trade was the very life of the colonies had, by 1700, become an almost unquestioned axiom in British practical economics."[46] By 1774 under a combination of economic, moral, and patriotic arguments the Continental Congress decided to prohibit the slave trade. In the long run, the result of that action was an increase in demand for new slaves and a rise in prices. During the Revolution, "smugglers made fortunes."[47] Although the trade revived after the Revolutionary War, various states enacted laws against it. The stalemate between Georgia and South Carolina, the only states with a flourishing slave trade,[48] and the rest of the delegates to the Constitutional Convention of 1787 made a national prohibition of the trade impossible. The compromise adopted was a provision that the importation of slaves could not be prohibited nationally before 1808.[49]

In the intervening period, additional state laws were passed and, beginning in 1794, federal legislation was enacted to restrict American engagement in international slave trade. By 1798 even the states that had previously sanctioned slave trade prohibited it. In 1803, however, South Carolina reopened the traffic. One justification for that action was the state's inability to enforce its law:[50]

---

44. This preoccupation with gangs is illustrated by stories from New York, Chicago, Denver, and San Francisco in the mid-1800's, as well as the tale of Wyatt Earp's capture of the Thompson Brothers. G. TYLER, ORGANIZED CRIME IN AMERICA 96-146 (1962).

45. G. TYLER, *supra* note 43, at 90.

46. W. DuBOIS, THE SUPPRESSION OF THE AFRICAN SLAVE TRADE TO THE UNITED STATES OF AMERICA 1638-1870, 4 (1896).

47. *Id.* at 48.

48. The slave trade was also legal in North Carolina, but with a prohibitive duty applied. *Id.* at 69.

49. U. S. CONST. art. V.

50. Speech by Rep. Lowndes of South Carolina, 13 ANNALS OF CONG. 733 (1804); W. DuBOIS, *supra* note 46, at 85-86.

> With navigable rivers running into the heart of [the state], it was impossible, with our means, to prevent our Eastern brethren, who, in some parts of the Union, in defiance of the authority of the General Government, have been engaged in this trade, from introducing them into the country. The law was completely evaded, and, for the last year or two, Africans were introduced into the country in numbers little short, I believe, of what they would have been had the trade been a legal one.

The South Carolina action "led . . . to an irresistible demand for a national prohibitory act at the earliest possible moment;"[51] the Act of 1807 resulted. However, the Act was ineffective because no special machinery had been provided for enforcement, and the appeal of profit was too strong for entrepreneur and sympathetic (or venal) enforcement officer alike. Nor was the appeal of illicit enterprise limited to the South:[52]

> When I was young, the slave trade was still carried on, by Connecticut ship masters and Merchant adventurers, for the supply of Southern ports. This trade was carried on by the consent of the Southern States, under the provisions of the Federal Constitution, until 1808, and, after that time, clandestinely. There was a good deal of conversation on the subject, in private circles.

Supplemental acts for tighter enforcement were passed in 1818 and 1820, but traffic in slaves was not successfully eliminated until slavery itself was ended by the Civil War. In the intervening period, smuggling continued with only sporadic and ineffective efforts to suppress it.

This brief review of circumstances suggests that the slave trade, at least from 1808, was an organized criminal activity. It is also clear that the question of legality had little effect on the operation of the enterprise, other than tactical adjustments (such as registration of vessels under foreign flags) to avoid the unlikely possibility of prosecution. But legality aside, the slave trade remained a force in the American economy even after it was outlawed.

What role did the slave trade play in the economic development of America? How was the illicitly derived development capital of the slave traders absorbed into the economy? How were the slavers themselves, as illicit entrepreneurs, eventually absorbed into American life? Did the slavers attempt to control all "legitimate economic and political activities," or to "influence legislation," as Cressey fears today's organized criminals wish to do?[53] Such exploration of historic parallels may help illuminate effective strategies for today's needs and, equally importantly, point to deficiencies in ineffective strategies.

One cautionary note. It is easy to draw mistaken parallels from history, especially when only some of the details of past events are known. Thus, before drawing too many inferences from the history of illicit slave trading, the valid-

---

51. W. DuBois, *supra* note 46, at 72.

52. W. C. Fowler, LOCAL LAW IN MASSACHUSETTS AND CONNECTICUT, HISTORICALLY CONSIDERED 122-26 (1872) (*quoted by* W. DuBois, *supra* note 46, at 110).

53. D. Cressey, *supra* note 1, at 2-3.

ity of apparent parallels must be considered carefully. Two contradictory conclusions can be drawn. History in this case either demonstrates the futility of prohibitory measures that do not rest on a sufficiently broad public consensus or demonstrates the inexorable threat that immoral but lucrative practices pose to a moral society (the uncompromising stand of the slave traders in the late 1700's did, after all, lay the seeds of the Civil War). Which conclusion should be drawn if the attempted parallel is between the slave trade and gambling? It appears that the slave trade parallel can be used to support either side of the legalized gambling debate.

A focus on illicit enterprise may also justify cross-cultural comparisons. Organized crime is conventionally viewed as an American phenomenon. The growth of gambling casinos in the Bahamas and in Great Britain is generally viewed as an example of American organized criminal activities expanding into overseas ventures.[54] Illicit enterprise is not culturally circumscribed — all it appears to require is entrepreneurial skill and the willingness to exploit for illicit gain.[55] An exploration of the distinctions between illicit enterprise in this country and in others might suggest peculiar vulnerabilities of the American economy that could be remedied.

A final advantage of this line of inquiry is the identification of a category of activities wider than the conventional description of organized crime and more nearly inclusive of the modern-day illicit enterprises that do threaten American life. Activities within the conventional spectrum do not hold a monopoly on organized corrupt practices, extortion, black markets, or racketeering. A concept that is inclusive of such activities will be more appropriate as a base for analysis and understanding.

What Is the Nature of the Task Environment of Illicit Enterprise?

Thompson has formulated an approach to organization theory that combines open system and closed system strategies.[56] He conceives of complex organizations *"as open system, hence indeterminate and faced with uncertainty, but at the same time as subject to criteria of rationality and hence needing determinateness and certainty."*[57] Under these circumstances it is advantageous for an organization to protect its technical core by reducing the number of variables operating on it. Thompson speaks of the "task environment" of an organization as those parts in its environment that are "relevant or potentially relevant to goal setting and goal attainment";[58] its four principal sectors are customers, suppliers, competitors, and regulatory groups. Within the task environment an organization seeks to establish its domain, or the claims that it stakes out for itself in terms of a range of pro-

---

54. *See, e.g.,* H. MESSICK, SYNDICATE ABROAD (1969).

55. An example of non-American organized illicit enterprise is Antonio Moreno who defrauded the French Social Security Administration to the extent of an estimated 30 million francs by registering 3,000 nonexistent children as recipients of family assistance. Albany-Times-Union, Dec. 20, 1970, §A at 10, col. 1.

56. J. THOMPSON, ORGANIZATIONS IN ACTION (1967).

57. *Id.* at 10.

58. *Id.* at 27.

ducts, the population served, and the services rendered. Most significantly, Thompson points out:[59]

> Establishment of domain cannot be an arbitrary, unilateral action. Only if the organization's claims to domain are recognized by those who can provide the necessary support, by the task environment, can a domain be operational. The relationship between an organization and its task environment is essentially one of exchange, and unless the organization is judged by those in contact with it as offering something desirable, it will not receive the inputs necessary for survival . . . . The specific categories of exchange vary from one type of organization to another, but in each case . . . exchange agreements rest upon *prior consensus regarding domain.*

The task environment presents numerous constraints and contingencies against which the core technology must be protected. To deal with such exogenous variables, organizations create boundary-spanning components — units with a principal responsibility of relating to the outside world.

There is a great deal more to Thompson's analysis than this brief introduction suggests. While one can readily concede that it applies to General Motors, does it also apply to organized crime and other illicit enterprises? It may say more about the phenomena under study than the prevailing stereotypes, even though at first glance there appear to be problems with events that are more predatory appearing than exchange appearing.[60] It suggests that there may be more effective routes to the control of organized crime than the "massive attrition" strategy of strike forces. And it raises questions concerning scholarly approaches to the analysis of organized crime that depend too heavily on conventional stereotypes as a starting point.

Is there really a unique position of "corrupter" in the structure of organized crime, or is that simply the name that might be given to a boundary-spanning component that in legitimate businesses would be referred to as a registered lobbyist? The functions are basically similar: to insure that the powers of regulatory groups in the task environment — the legislature, the regulatory agency, and the judiciary — do not interfere unduly with the organization's core technology. The distinctions between them have more to do with the tools of the trade and the circumstances under which they operate than with ultimate objectives. The lobbyist can appeal openly to common values and shared political allegiances, and can offer nonmonetary rewards such as recognition and acceptance in desirable social circles, whereas his counterpart in organized crime apparently must deal surreptitiously and in terms of his only meaningful reward — money.

Recognizing the importance of the consumer in defining the task environment may also be important because it confronts the notion that organized crime is an enterprise that stands by itself. This becomes significant when one considers responses to organized crime. If it were a self-contained, basically

---

59. *Id.* at 28.

60. *See* text accompanying note 10 *supra.* It suggested, for example, that Judge Weintraub's perception of the phenomena at issue may be better than he realizes.

alien entity, it could be erased from the contemporary scene as political leaders have promised to do. But is this possible? Would the "elimination" of the individuals presently associated with organized crime also eliminate the demand for gambling or for unsecured loans at excessive interest rates or for narcotics?

In fairness to a good number of law enforcement personnel it should be noted that the challenge here is to a doctrinaire assumption that is seldom held in its pure form. The consumer's role in creating the demand for organized crime is generally recognized in the better police departments and prosecutors' offices as well as in the serious literature. Cressey devotes the major portion of one chapter to supply and demand, discussing the details of gambling, loansharking, drugs, and black market labor.[61] His attention then shifts to a consideration of how the profits of organized crime activities are reinvested in legitimate businesses, and the dangers that entail without resolving the original question of the role of supply and demand in creating opportunities for illicit enterprises.[62] One can only conclude that prior allegiance to the Mafia Conspiracy theory permitted no interference from contradictory notions that might emerge from a more complete analysis.

What Function Does Violence Perform in Illicit Enterprise, as Distinguished from Its Function in the Economy Generally?

Violence is associated with the conventional view of organized crime, and contemporary literature makes a conspicuous point of it — associating it with extortion, loanshark collection, and the maintenance of order within organized crime groups.[63] Pathological violence, while not entirely passed, is certainly less frequent than in the days of Arthur Flegenheimer ("Dutch Schultz")[64] and indiscriminate violence is not part of the regular organized crime scene.

What is the function of violence? Is the function unique to organized crime, or is it likely to occur in any illicit enterprise? Is there an equivalent function in legitimate business? If there is a functional correspondence, it may suggest new clues as to how violence within illicit enterprises may be met. It would appear that the activities within organized crime that are identified as "violence" might serve three principal functions: maintenance of internal discipline; enforcement of market conditions; and control of competition. The latter function was particularly evident during the 1920's and 1930's, but was largely stabilized by a series of events that culminated in the so-called "Castellammarese War" of 1930-1931.[65]

---

61. D. Cressey, *supra* note 1, at 72-108.

62. *Id.* at 99-107.

63. *See generally id.* for examples of the identification and interpretation of "violence" in the conventional literature of organized crime. *See also* R. Salerno & J. Tompkins, *supra* note 36.

64. *See, e.g.*, Davis, *Things I Couldn't Tell Till Now*, Colliers, July 22, 1939, at 9, *quoted by* D. Cressey, *supra* note 1, at 179 (account of the murder of Jules Martin).

65. D. Cressey, *supra* note 1, at 35-49; R. Salerno & J. Tompkins, *supra* note 36, at

Cressey has suggested that one of the positions within the organization structure of organized crime is that of the Enforcer, who "makes arrangements for injuring or killing members and, occasionally, nonmembers."[66] He has interpreted the function of the Enforcer's violence in political terms. The Enforcer is analogous to the prison official who makes arrangements for imposing the death penalty. The presence of such a position indicates that the code within which Cressey's Cosa Nostra operates "has been designed to minimize the degree of conflict and to maximize the degree of conformity among members."[67] It also indicates that there are legislative and judicial processes through which "regularized expectations" (to use Cressey's phrase) are set concerning the way conflict will be resolved within the organization. The Crime Commission, on the other hand, suggests that violence has a different purpose: enforcement "is necessary for the maintenance of both internal discipline *and the regularity of business transactions.*"[68] In their view, the "law" being applied is both criminal and commercial.

If the enforcer function identified by Cressey is viewed within Thompson's task environment concept described earlier,[69] the business regulation function proposed by the Crime Commission assumes greater importance. If organized crime, as an illicit enterprise, operates by the same rules of organizational dynamics that characterize legitimate enterprises, then its principal internal concern is to protect its technical core from uncertainties in the task environment.[70] Stability in the market place may thus be a stronger motive for controlling individual behavior than political fealty.

That assumption can be tested by considering the kinds of problems that affect businesses of all kinds, both licit and illicit. Such a study indicates that legitimate businesses do have problems similar to those of organized crime. One of the most direct parallels appears between the bank and the loanshark. The bank is an example of what Thompson calls a mediating technology, or "the linking of clients and customers who are or wish to be interdependent."[71] With both multiple suppliers (depositors) and customers (borrowers), the bank requires a high degree of standardization:[72]

> The commercial bank must find and aggregate deposits from diverse depositors; but however diverse the depositors, the transaction must conform to standard terms and to uniform bookkeeping and accounting procedures. It must also find borrowers; but no matter how varied their needs or desires, loans must be made according to standardized criteria and on terms uniformly applied to the category appropriate

---

85-87. The principal historical source is Valachi. *See* P. MAAS, THE VALACHI PAPERS 83-112 (1968).

66. D. CRESSEY, *supra* note 1, at 165. The role of "Enforcer" is described at length at 164-67.

67. *Id.* at 166.

68. CRIME COMMISSION, *supra* note 1, at 8 (emphasis added).

69. *See* text accompanying notes 56-62 *supra*.

70. J. THOMPSON, *supra* note 56, at 19.

71. *Id.* at 16.

72. *Id.* at 16-17.

to the particular borrower. Poor risks who receive favored treatment jeopardize bank solvency.

The bank must be prepared for the borrower who cannot repay a loan. Ultimately, its response will be to claim the collateral posted by the borrower; this may entail foreclosing on personal or business property. The bank's purpose in foreclosing is not simply to recover funds loaned in a particular case, but also to insure that other borrowers will operate within "regularized expectations" of the banking business. The individual defaulter who receives favored treatment is not likely to jeopardize bank solvency by himself; but if his treatment sets an example for other borrowers, solvency might well be endangered. The application of standard criteria for both lending and collecting thus protects the stability of the mediating function (linking lender and borrower) which is the bank's core technology.

The loanshark's task environment is much simpler. For all practical purposes he has only one supplier, either himself or his backer. Since he operates outside banking laws, he has no responsibility to regulatory agencies. His only purpose in maintaining records is to protect the link between his one supplier and multiple customers; he thus avoids the complexities occasioned by the bank's accountability to multiple money suppliers and to the regulators of banking activity. His major problems in protecting his core technology relate to obtaining customers and ensuring loan repayment. The loanshark may foreclose on property, as does a bank; but since he does not have access to judicial authority his methodology is that of becoming a silent partner in a legitimate business.[73] Alternatively, or in the absence of other collateral and the unavailability of judicial remedies, he may resort to violence against the borrower.[74] As with the legitimate banker, his purpose is not simply to recover any particular funds, but to set an example for other borrowers. In this fashion, the long-term stability of the mediating function is protected.

Legitimate businesses and organized crime also have comparable problems in personnel management. Particular parallels concern the overly-ambitious subordinate and the defector. If a legitimate enterprise cannot reach an accommodation with the ambitious subordinate (promotion, transfer, reorganization and reassignment, or even reconciliation to a subordinate role), that individual can be dismissed. He may leave with bitterness sufficiently hostile to push for a public airing of his version of the separation, and his assessment of the company in general.[75] Resulting publicity may be distasteful to the enterprise, but as long as the employee does not reveal information that would affect the enterprise's competitive position, or does not detail illegal practices, the core technology of the enterprise will not be af-

---

73. *See* R. SALERNO & J. TOMPKINS, *supra* note 36, at 235-42.

74. *Id.* at 397-402.

75. The recent litigation between the Hughes Tool Co. and Robert Maheu, former manager of Howard Hughes' Nevada enterprises, while colored by the personal nature of the Hughes' operation, is a case in point.

fected. If necessary, the risks that might accompany such a separation can be anticipated and defensive strategies devised.

A defector poses a more serious problem in a highly competitive industry in which trade secrets lie at the heart of the core technology. Personnel management in such a circumstance may become much more delicate, and individual decisions may reflect the potential vulnerability of the core technology as much as the enterprise's need for a particular individual's competencies. Since stability of the market place (from the standpoint of the enterprise) remains a paramount concern, such an industry may be characterized by active intelligence and counter-intelligence components, aimed in part at reducing dependence of the enterprise on holders of "secrets," and thus minimizing the risks that a defector might pose to its core technology.

The task environment of the illicit enterprise presents different problems. Public revelations by the discharged employee or the defector cannot be tolerated — the enterprise itself would then come under scrutiny by regulatory agencies. Survival of the illicit enterprise may then be at stake in a more critical way than is the case with personnel matters in a legitimate enterprise.

As these examples illustrate, drawing correct comparisons between legitimate businesses and illicit enterprises is a difficult task. The principal barrier lies in the differences in task environments, particularly regarding the relationship between the illicit enterprise and regulatory groups. In the legitimate business, regulating agencies monitor action and assist in applying the "rules of the game" to the remainder of the task environment. To enforce those rules, a range of sanctions exists, many of which are economic in nature. In the illicit enterprise, however, the regulatory agency is unable to maintain the integrity of market activities: enterprises that are proscribed at the outset can hardly be monitored to see that the "rules of the game" are being followed. In these circumstances, the illicit enterprise has limited alternatives.[76] While the core technology must be protected, the available sanctions are personal, rather than economic. The individual, not his property, may be attacked.

Prevailing theories of organized crime interpret such a possibility as entirely "political," rather than "economic." The borrower who does not repay the loanshark appears to be defying the organization's avowed intention to control personal conduct; the employee who threatens stability is presumed to be a political risk to the invisible government. The foundation of this conclusion is an interpretation of the use of violence to serve the same function of protecting the authority of the illicit organization as criminal sanctions perform in maintaining the authority of the state. As noted at the outset of this discussion, the justification for viewing organized crime as a political activity — as a government as well as a business — lies in the

---

76. The limited alternatives of an illicit enterprise may be comparable to the options of a vigilante group. For a discussion of those limitations see J. CAUGHEY, THEIR MAJESTIES THE MOB 13-17 (1960).

role of the Enforcer being analogous to the prison official, a "political" officer, whose function in turn implies legislative and judicial activity within the organization. On the other hand, if the basic decision being made is protection of the business enterprise, not simply survival of an organization and its feudal chief who enunciates and interprets the organization's code of behavior,[77] then perhaps the assumption that organized crime is an "invisible government" should be reassessed. In that reassessment, what would be the relationship between the activities associated conventionally with organized crime, and other illicit enterprises? Is the use of violence common to other enterprises, or is the function of maintaining economic stability carried out in some other fashion? Further investigation might indicate varying alternatives in the application of sanctions, just as there are likely to be variations in the spectrum of illicit enterprise.

Further investigation might also reveal that a shift away from violent self-regulation has been occurring since the end of World War II.[78] If this is the case, it may be useful to consider what has prompted that transition. It may be that violence was necessary in the past because market stability was based on the fear it engendered. Perhaps it is fair to ask today whether illicit enterprises survive because they are feared, or because they are useful, or because they have become necessary. If utility or necessity is replacing fear — and if this change in values is more than just rationalization of a weak power position relative to illicit enterprise — then perhaps grounds exist for a reexamination of the legal distinctions between licit and illicit behavior.

Finally, further investigation might reveal that the so-called position of "Enforcer" has become obsolete. The decrease in violence may be a signal of that. The role of enforcement —monitoring action and assisting in applying the "rules of the game," may be increasingly assumed by law enforcement. Judicial remedies are available to the illicit entrepreneur in at least one significant way — the maintenance of a monopoly position; competitors can be "turned in." One can assume that a law enforcement agency would appreciate information leading to a successful arrest. The continuing competition for the Harlem numbers racket suggests that it may be profitable to eliminate a competitor;[79] the fact that arrests help regulate the illicit market place is incidental, from the standpoint of the arresting agency, to the fact that action is taken against persons who are violating the law. The fact that both the illicit entrepreneur and the law enforcement officer "benefit" from

---

77. *See* D. Cressey, *supra* note 1, at 186: "The code of honor and silence which asks every member of Cosa Nostra to be a 'stand-up guy,' and which underlies the entire structure of the criminal cartel and confederation, performs the same important function that the 'rule of law' once performed for absolute monarchs – it protects the personal power of the rulers."

78. *See, e.g.*, note 38 *supra*.

79. Some of the circumstances of this competition are noticed in Grutzver, *Cubans Here Are Ending Mafia's Monopoly on Numbers Racket, with 20% of City Play*. N.Y. Times, Feb. 22, 1970, at 36, col. 2.

such circumstances suggests that a symbiotic relationship between them may be a more accurate analogy than the conventional view of organized crime as a "malignant parasite."[80]

A further exploration of this alternative might reveal that the violence historically associated with the Italian-dominated syndicate crime of the 1920's and the 1930's was not so much an essential attribute of the enterprise being developed as it was a misreading of the real nature of law enforcement in this country by immigrants from a different law enforcement setting. Once the role of law enforcement as a regulator of the black market was better understood, reliance on self-regulation quickly dropped off. By way of comparison, the success of the illicit slave trade a century earlier certainly seems to have had little need for violence as a means of controlling the market place; the violence associated with trading activities (as distinct from the violence of slavery itself) was directed at the problem of inventory control that was peculiar to an enterprise dealing in human beings as objects of trade.

Judicial remedies may also be available indirectly for control of the customer. The power of the narcotics distributor over the addict-pusher is more than just the junkie's dependence on the narcotics; that dependency is also a potential basis for turning the noncooperative pusher over to the police. A less direct, but equally useful, weapon may be present in some loanshark arrangements. The loanshark is interested in maintaining a hold over his debtor. He may not have access to the courts to enforce the express conditions of his loan; but if the customer is engaged in questionable activities those activities can be the basis for "punishing" or penalizing the uncooperative customer.[81]

It may also be that other means of enforcement are available beyond that of violence or recourse to the courts. The loanshark may be able to use the fear of exposure without the need for other forms of pressure. That "punishment" also need not be related directly to the circumstances of the entrepreneurial arrangement between borrower and lender; other social or economic conditions not directly related to the loan may create a sufficient position of vulnerability.

What Function Does Corruption Perform in Illicit Enterprise, as Distinguished from its Function in the Economy Generally?

To a greater extent than violence, corruption is considered a hallmark of organized crime. The Crime Commission believed it to be an essential attribute: "All available data indicate that organized crime flourishes only

80. "[Organized crime] is a malignant parasite which fattens on human weakness." OYSTER BAY CONFERENCES ON COMBATTING ORGANIZED CRIME, REPORT, COMBATTING ORGANIZED CRIME 19 (1965).

81. For example, the gambler who needs the services of a loanshark may not be reporting his correct income to tax agencies. Threatening to anonymously supply such information to the Internal Revenue Service may impel prompt payment.

where it has corrupted local officials."[82] Corruption can occur in any element of criminal justice administration, and at any level, with public officials "whose legitimate exercise of duties would block organized crime and whose illegal exercise of duties helps it."[83]

Corruption and graft are not exclusive prerogatives of organized crime; consequently, it may be useful to distinguish between organized, sustained, and systematic corruption aimed at creating a favorable climate for illicit enterprise, and individual instances of bribery aimed at obtaining favorable resolution of a particular governmental matter. The latter may have been what Sufrin meant when he wrote that "under some circumstances graft may play a positive role in modifying an administrative structure in line with rationality and, perhaps, even public morality."[84] He observed that practical levels of behavior — despite "deep moral sentiments of society" — do not always present a clear choice between what is morally right and wrong; and that the differing criteria of the political market vis-à-vis the economic market may well lead to conflicts between desirable political behavior (through administrative rulings and legal enactments) and their intended economic effects. The more complex the bureaucracy, the more complex the transactions and the greater the likelihood of incompatibility. Thus, circumstances may arise in which the only effective way to achieve a desirable economic end is through an act of graft. In such circumstances, the most useful question may be: "What would the government or business have done in the absence of graft?"[85]

In contrast, the focus here is on deliberate and continuous efforts to deflect the application of law to illicit enterprises. Once again, the questions to be asked concern the function of corruption in organized crime, its uniqueness, if any, to that form of enterprise, and the functional parallels that may exist with legitimate business. Generally, the function of corruption is to see that legal sanctions that might otherwise stop the illicit enterprise, or penalize the entrepreneur, are not brought into play. In the discussion that ordinarily follows, a semantics problem emerges that may appear precious, but is important in setting the context within which the significance of organized crime is to be assessed: Should the function of corruption be referred to as an effort to *nullify,* or as an effort to *neutralize* law enforcement and the political process? This question arises because the Crime Commission used both words in describing the activities of organized crime. In its introductory statement, the Commission spoke of *nullification:*[86]

> The purpose of organized crime is not competition with visible, legal government but nullification of it. When organized crime places an

---

82. CRIME COMMISSION, *supra* note 1, at 6.
83. *Id.*
84. Sufrin, *Graft: Grease for the Palm and Grease for the Wheels,* CHALLENGE, Oct. 1964, at 30.
85. *Id.* at 31.
86. CRIME COMMISSION, *supra* note 1, at 2.

official in public office, it nullifies the political process. When it bribes
a public official, it nullifies law enforcement.

When it turned to the issue of corruption, the Commission switched its
terminology:[87]

> Neutralizing local law enforcement is central to organized crime's op-
> erations. What can the public do if no one investigates the investiga-
> tors, and the political figures are neutralized by their alliance with
> organized crime?

Cressey noted the problem of corruption by suggesting that "any citizen
purchasing illicit goods and services from organized criminals contributes
to a culture of fraud, corruption, violence, and murder."[88] His analysis of
corruption focused on internal questions of structure and authority, rather
than function; consequently, his concern for the Crime Commission centered on identification of the positions of "Corrupter" and "Corruptee" within organized crime. Their function appears to have been of secondary
importance, noted simply by the observations that corruption is required
to keep illicit businesses in operation, and that "the position of 'Corrupter'
is as essential to an illicit business as the position of 'negotiator' is to a
labor union."[89]

His subsequent book devoted greater attention to corruption.[90] His ex-
position of the problem began with an elaboration of the Crime Commission's orginal statement:[91]

> Cosa Nostra functions as an illegal invisible government. However,
> its political objective is not competition with the established agencies
> of legitimate government. Unlike the Communist Party, it is not in-
> terested in political and economic reform. Its political objective is a
> negative one: nullification of government.

He further asserted that nullification is directed at both the law enforcement process (bribing a policeman) and the political process (bribing a politician), and that potential harm today is greater than ever before "simply
because nullification of government today means nullification of a broader
range of regulatory activity."[92] The method is simple: "Corrupters nullify
the law enforcement and political processes primarily by outright bribery
and other rationally designed forms of 'influence' . . . ."[93] In this fashion,

---

87. *Id.* at 6.

88. D. CRESSEY, *supra* note 1, at 1.

89. Cressey, *The Functions and Structure of Criminal Syndicates*, in CRIME COMMISSION,
supra note 1, at 59.

90. D. CRESSEY, *supra* note 1, at at 248-89.

91. *Id.* at 248. Other observers have taken similar "political" approaches: "[I]n effect
organized crime constitutes a private government whose power rivals and often supplants
that of elected public government." Moynihan, *supra* note 42, at 15 n.39.

92. D. CRESSEY, *supra* note 1, at 250.

93. *Id.* at 271.

Cressey adopted the Crime Commission's line of thought through the consistent use of *nullify* and abandonment of the idea of *neutralize*.

The difference between them, in careful usage, denotes a difference in context. "Nullification" relates to the reversal or abolition of a legal entity, the most famous use of the concept in American history being John Calhoun's efforts to abolish the tariff of 1828 — the "tariff of abominations." Thus, when the Crime Commission observed that "the purpose of organized crime is . . . nullification" of government, it was suggesting an intention to have government void and inoperative. The concept of "neutralization," on the other hand, refers to modification of a process though which policy is implemented. When the Crime Commission observed that "neutralizing local law enforcement is central to organized crime's operation," it was suggesting a mere desire that the law not be enforced in certain circumstances. These are rather different goals for an enterprise to pursue.

If organized crime is viewed within the context of Thompson's task environment,[94] it becomes clear that illicit enterprise would be handicapped by an inoperative government. Strong regulatory agencies can be used effectively to protect or increase one's domain at the expense of potential competitors. From the standpoint of the illicit businessman, the regulatory agency has a useful function to perform in helping to maintain stability in the market place of a black market enterprise. As Schelling put it: "Without the law and some degree of enforcement, there is no presumption that the monopoly organization can survive competition."[95] It may be significant that the major documented efforts to describe organized crime all refer to Commissioner Thom's 1960 testimony before the New York State Investigations Commission:[96]

> [T]he syndicates are particularly happy with the consolidation of the nine police departments into the Suffolk County Police Department, as they feel that protection is easier to arrange through one agency than through many. [An intensive anti-gambling campaign] had the astounding side effect of solving the recruitment problems of the syndicate, as our drive successfully stampeded the independents into the arms of the syndicate for protection and the syndicate can now pick and choose those operators they wish to admit.

This observation illustrates how corruption can take place, and how it may be helpful to the illicit enterprise. However, its deeper significance is usually overlooked. The entrepreneur, whether engaged in organized crime or in more conventional enterprise, may wish to *manipulate* or *use* government to his advantage, but he would much prefer to have *a* government, rather than *no* government.

---

94. *See* text accompanying notes 56-62 *supra*.

95. Schelling, *Economic Analysis of Organized Crime*, in CRIME COMMISSION, *supra* note 1, at 123.

96. Thom, Statement Before the New York Commission of Investigation on April 22, 1960, at 2 (mimeographed). *See also* D. CRESSEY, *supra* note 1, at 76-77; CRIME COMMISSION, *supra* note 1, at 3; R. SALERNO & J. TOMPKINS, THE CRIME CONFEDERATION 244 (1969).

If one wishes to gain a better understanding of the functioning of illicit enterprise in contrast to legitimate business (the objective presumably being better control of the former and better protection of the latter), it may be helpful to understand why the discussion of corruption focuses on nullification. On the surface, nullification may be more useful to the advocate wishing to drive home the magnitude of the organized crime threat, since it is a more threatening word than neutralization. Public support for organized crime control might be strengthened by such an escalation in vocabulary. A more important reason, however, may be the need to differentiate clearly between organized crime and other entrepreneurial activities. As Cressey suggested at the beginning of his analysis: "The threat of organized crime in America is similar to the threat any potential monopolizer poses to a small businessman."[97] This observation poses an immediate question: Why pick on organized crime instead of "potential monopolizers?" Cressey responded by noting two differences: the use of force and the effort to nullify government.[98] But they turn out, even with attention directed at nullification, not to be real differences at all: "[O]rganized crime uses force and threat of force to obtain monopoly, while legitimate firms do not, *at least not as often* . . . organized crime nullifies legitimate government *more directly, and to a greater extent,* than do other forms of monopoly."[99]

The justification for concentrating on eliminating organized crime must rest on a showing that it does undesirable or dangerous things that other enterprises do not. "Nullification" does this in part, by suggesting a level of political competition, rather than simply economic competition. This is the significance of Cressey's reference to the "illegal invisible government;" his assertion that it is only an alternative political approach and not a competitive one (as, he suggests, is the Communist Party) has an appeal that does not hold up under close analysis. If, on the other hand, organized crime is primarily concerned with stabilizing an illicit market place to its advantage, a goal that the neutralization of law enforcement would facilitate, then its character and aspirations are not that different from any other economic enterprise. If its principal motives are more economic than political, the similarities noted earlier between the corrupter and the registered lobbyist may be more useful than the distinctions between them.

When the problem of assessing the basic intent of illicit enterprise vis-à-vis law enforcement is presented in this fashion, a further question emerges as to whether *either* "neutralization" *or* "nullification" is an appropriate view of the matter. In the previous discussion concerning violence in illicit enterprises, it was suggested that the relationship between those enterprises and law enforcement may be symbiotic; if this is correct, the conventional interpretations of corruption may also need to be reassessed. As an indication of the direction that further analysis might take, it may be noted that "co-optation" may be a more useful way to describe the objectives of both

---

97. D. Cressey, *supra* note 1, at 7.
98. *Id.*
99. *Id.* (emphasis added).

law enforcement and the illicit enterprise. One of the implications inherent in this approach is that the initiative for transactions between them — the exchanges of money usually identified as bribery or corruption — may come from either side. The law enforcement officer who proposes or demands a pay-off may be guilty of selfish, venal activity;[100] but there may also be circumstances in which there is a higher social value to be gained by assisting in regulating the illicit market place than could be reached by attempting to suppress that market place entirely. It is this circumstance that Schelling seems to have had in mind when he spoke of "compromising" with organized crime:[101]

> Aside from the approved negotiations by which criminals are induced to testify, to plead guilty, to surrender themselves, and to tip off the police, there is undoubtedly sometimes a degree of accommodation between the police and the criminals — tacit or explicit understandings analogous to what in the military field would be called the limitation of war, the control of armament, and the development of spheres of influence.

The negotiating process need not involve the exchange of money or other items of value. Regardless of the arrangements made, the end result remains a relationship definable as a "corrupt practice." When one looks at corruption, however, rather than looking solely at organized crime, it appears to have a more general utility than simply maintaining the enterprises of organized crime. Is it an attribute of illicit enterprise generally? Is it a function associated only with governmental activities (obviously, it is not limited to the standard grouping of law enforcement agencies), or is it also useful, as Sufrin suggests graft may be, in the "purely private transaction"?[102] Has the focus of organized crime served, in practical terms, as a diversion from the real issue?[103] Perhaps most importantly, what remedies can be adopted to reduce corruption? If it is so vital to illicit enterprise, direct attack on the function itself might be more effective than a direct attack on the enterprise.

Curiously enough, serious contemporary publications say much about controlling organized crime, but little about controlling corruption. The discussion of corruption is extensive; but it is more descriptive than reme-

---

100. "[A]fter a while, the shakedown gets to be part of the everyday budget —going into the mortgage, the car payments, and the dentist bills for the kids — and the greedy few start looking for assignments in those units, like gambling, where they can really rake it in." Burnham, *How Corruption Is Built into the System — and a Few Ideas for what To Do About It.* NEW YORK, Sept. 21, 1970, at 30.

101. Schelling, *supra* note 95, at 123. D. CRESSEY, *supra* note 1, at 322-24, uses this theme as the basis for his concluding comments. *See also* Cressey's comments at 260-63 concerning "the issuing and policing of illegal licenses."

102. Sufrin, *supra* note 84, at 31.

103. Most discussions of this point of view see organized crime as a scapegoat for anger, distress, and anxiety concerning the crime scene. *See* N. MORRIS & G. HAWKINS, THE HONEST POLITICIAN'S GUIDE TO CRIME CONTROL 232-33 (1970). In an earlier vintage, *see* Bell, *Crime as an American Way of Life*, 13 THE ANTIOCH REV. 131, 144 (1953).

28   *UNIVERSITY OF FLORIDA LAW REVIEW*   [Vol. XXIV

dial, and it abounds with case histories, not recommended solutions. For example, the Crime Commission was particularly concerned because it recognized that as governmental regulation expands, the opportunities to corrupt, and corruption's potential effect on the ordinary citizen and the legitimate business, will expand accordingly.[104] The Commission concluded that although the extent of corruption was impossible to measure, it surely existed, and that it needed to be controlled.[105] The problem of corruption was subsequently mentioned only three times in connection with the Commission's twenty-two recommendations, and then almost in passing.[106] It was not mentioned at all in the recommendations emerging from other matters investigated by the Commission. Concerning the formation of organized crime intelligence units in offices of state attorneys general and local police departments, the Commission observed that state-wide agencies might undertake investigation and action in areas "where . . . law enforcement agencies are not adequately combatting organized crime," and that this should be done without local knowledge "if, because of apparent corruption, it is necessary."[107] In connection with the desirability of increased news coverage of organized crime, the Commission recommended that coverage of organized crime activities include reports on "the corruption caused by it . . . ."[108] Concerning regular briefings of government officials about organized crime, the Commission noted that "enforcement against organized crime and accompanying public corruption proceeds with required intensity only when the political leaders in Federal, State, and local governments provide aggressive leadership."[109] It noted further that the reporting process should be sensitive to problems of corruption: "[R]eports should be withheld from jurisdictions where corruption is apparent and knowledge by a corrupt official of the information in the report could compromise enforcement efforts."[110] Additionally:[111]

> Public fears of reporting organized crime conditions to apparently corrupt police and government personnel must also be met directly. If an independent agency for accepting citizen grievances is established, it should be charged with accepting citizen complaints and information about organized crime and corruption.

The Commission's concern for protection of intelligence information is commendable. But if corruption is the *sine qua non* of organized crime, as the Commission asserted at the outset, it is surprising that more direct action against corruption was not suggested. On the other hand, considering the Commission's initial view of organized crime, the absence of recommenda-

---

104. CRIME COMMISSION, *supra* note 1, at 6.
105. *Id.*
106. *Id.* at 24.
107. *Id.* at 20.
108. *Id.* at 24.
109. *Id.*
110. *Id.*
111. *Id.*

tions against corruption may not be surprising. The Commission began by looking at a specified group of enterprises, a particular group of persons held responsible for them, and the quasi-political organization they had apparently created. The enterprises themselves were not the Commission's concern;[112] rather, its focus was on the perpetrators and their organization, which "is dedicated to subverting not only American institutions, but the very decency and integrity that are the most cherished attributes of a free society."[113] Their solution to the problem of organized crime seemed to lie in attacking the organization itself. If the Commission had been concerned instead with illicit enterprise generally, perhaps it would have noted that decency and integrity are under attack from corrupt practices, not simply from organized crime, and that the preservation of American institutions depends on a effective program to control corruption.

If the Commission had not been concerned primarily with the persons who perpetrate organized crime, perhaps the relationship of Corrupter and Corruptee would have been better understood. They require each other, as Cressey pointed out — but at whose initiative? Conventional organized crime theory assumes that organized criminals generally take the initiative in governmental relations; but this may not always be the case. The definition of corruption places initiative on the entrepreneur as destroying integrity, or causing one to be dishonest; with graft, however, attention shifts to the public servant who enriches himself through the abuse of position. In either event, a reciprocal act is undertaken; but conventional strategies of organized crime control emphasize an attack on a limited set of entrepreneurs. One might ask, within the context of the cost-effectiveness approach noted earlier,[114] whether organized crime control would have been further advanced at this time if, for example, the energies of the last five years devoted to obtaining legal sanctions for wiretapping had been directed instead at obtaining better controls over corrupt practices.

CONCLUSION

The questions considered in the previous section do not constitute an entire, integrated theory. In testing the approach they identify, and in suggesting alternative ways of remedying the problems they are intended to explain, other areas of investigation may prove helpful. As a sketch, only, of the nature of such other matters, the following questions can be posed:

What are the forces that have shaped illicit enterprise in America?
Are the "dangers" that might be associated with illicit enterprise located in the enterprise itself, or in the consequences of its activities?

---

112. "It is organized crime's accumulation of money, not the individual transactions by which the money is accumulated, that has a great and threatening impact on America." *Id.* at 2.
113. *Id.* at 24.
114. *See* text accompanying notes 3-7 *supra*.

What are the characteristics of the entrepreneur who concentrates his activities in the illicit sector of the economy?

What has been the relationship between the development of illicit enterprise and economic development generally?

Are the illicit enterprises conventionally associated with "organized crime" more concerned with making maximum, short-range profits, or with perpetuating a stable market place?

The propositions advanced in this article rest on two fundamental assumptions: that enterprise in this country takes place across a continuous range of behavior, from very saintly to very sinful, and that the concept of a "task environment" is applicable to that entire range of behavior. When the phenomena we conventionally categorize as "organized crime" are viewed against those two assumptions, and apart from the stereotyped references to Italian-dominated syndicate crime, it seems plausible that an alternate theoretical base would have validity: a theory of illicit enterprise. Our attention should be directed toward the development of that theory.

[4]
Fact,
fancy,
and
organized crime

PETER REUTER & JONATHAN B. RUBINSTEIN

O RGANIZED crime has become
firmly established on the agenda of national problems requiring
Federal action for control. Since it was made a national issue by the
Kefauver Committee's successful exploitation of the latent power of
the emerging television networks, every President has been required
to make a statement deploring the growth of organized crime and
outlining a program to eliminate it. As an issue, its rise to prominence has not been slowed by the failure of any legislative or administrative body to define adequately what it is, or who is involved.
Lacking such a definition, it is obviously difficult to determine
whether the phenomenon is indeed growing or declining—but this
has not prevented the continued, and successful, demand for increased authority and resources to fight it. The evident lack of any
strategy behind these demands also has had a curiously small impact. Countless government reports are filled with "estimates" of
the degree to which organized crime controls lucrative illegal activities, whose monopoly profits are then used to take over legitimate
industries.

These analytic failures have had serious consequences. Unlike most
bureaucratic puffery which results in inflated and wasteful expenditures, the threats posed by organized crime have been repeatedly

cited to justify a significant expansion of police powers. Legal wire-tapping entered domestic life in order more effectively to pursue organized crime figures; for the same reason, immunity and conspiracy statutes have been greatly expanded, as have been the powers of investigative grand juries. Citing the threats of organized crime to legitimate business, governments are creating numerous licensing and regulatory agencies which permit public officials to meddle with all kinds of business activity. This threat has also been used to justify the creation of state-owned liquor and gambling monopolies, monopolies which would otherwise be deplored.

Each agency has its own definition, ranging from Frank Hogan's famous assertion that "organized crime is two or more persons engaged in criminal activity" to the FBI's careful (we have traced it through seven versions) and meaningless potpourri: "the sum aggregate of the more lucrative, continuing types of racketeering activities, involving some sort of formalized structure and generally requiring graft or corruption to conduct its operations without interference."

But despite strong differences about specifics, there is a consensus about the general characteristics of this social threat. Organized crime is viewed as a set of stable, hierarchically organized gangs which, through violence or its credible threat, have acquired monopoly control of certain major illegal markets. This control has produced enormous profits, which have been used to bribe public officials, thus further protecting the monopolies. These funds have also been invested in acquiring legitimate businesses in which the racketeers continue to use extortion and threats to minimize competition.

The "lifeline" theory

Ever since the Kefauver Committee asserted that racketeers from the larger cities had established a national monopoly in horse racing information, which gave them control over illegal gambling in America, gambling has been viewed as the fountainhead of criminal capital. Every government probe has come to the same conclusion. The absence of any concrete information did not stop the New York State Investigations Commission from concluding that the infamous meeting in November 1957 in Apalachin, New York, was a conclave of gambling operators. Joe Valachi, a long-time government informant and former numbers controller from Harlem, provided the McClellan Committee with "living proof" that the Mafia or La Cosa

Nostra, as he styled it, existed and that gambling and loansharking were the sources of its capital. This notion was raised to the level of orthodoxy by President Johnson's Crime Commission (1967), which estimated that organized crime netted a minimum of $7 billion annually from illegal gambling, a one-third profit from one of the lower estimates of total wagering made available to the Commission. In 1969 President Nixon asserted, using a confused metaphor, that "gambling income is the lifeline of organized crime. If we can cut it or constrict it, we will be striking close to the heart." Congress responded in 1970 by passing the Organized Crime Control Act, which enshrined this notion in statute. In 1974 the Department of Justice summarized government views of illegal gambling:

> It is the unanimous conclusion of the President, the Congress, and law enforcement officials that illegal organized gambling is the largest single source of revenue for organized crime.... [It] provides the initial investment for narcotic trafficking, hijacking operations, prostitution rings, and loan-shark schemes.

These are not just beliefs espoused by agencies and politicians in hearings or when they are asking for money. There is recent evidence that the police themselves hold these beliefs as firmly as Presidents and District Attorneys. In a 1976 survey of police departments throughout the country, some 73 percent of police agreed with the statement that "profits from illegal gambling operations are the main source of income for organized crime."

The belief in the dominance of stable criminal gangs and the centrality of gambling in their continuing control of the rackets extends beyond law enforcement circles. In addition to being continually restated in the daily press, which is almost completely dependent upon police sources for its crime news, these views are also espoused in academic circles—both by those friendly to the views of the police and those who argue for the revocation of prohibitory legislation on gambling, prostitution, and other so-called victimless crimes. Donald Cressey, who is the most respectable academic advocate of the official position, argued in his book *Theft of A Nation* that "the suppliers of illicit goods and services ... accumulate vast wealth which can be used to attain even wider monopolies on illicit activities, and on legal businesses as well." Concerning illegal gambling, Cressey asserted, "the profits are huge enough to make understandable the fact that any given member of La Cosa Nostra is more likely to be a millionaire than not." Herbert Packer, whose book *The Limits of the Criminal Sanction* is the most widely quoted argument for decriminalization, made essentially the same argument as Cressey:

> In gross financial terms, the laws against gambling represent our most generous subsidy to organized crime. . . . By responding to the economic logic of the situation, criminal organizations have arisen that take enormous monopoly profits out of the gambling business. These monopoly profits then become available to sustain the activities of the criminal organization on a wide variety of fronts, including the penetration of legitimate and quasi-legitimate economic markets.

Many such statements from respectable academics could be found, but regardless of the policies they are arguing for, they all share one important feature: They all make assertions about the nature and organization of gambling based entirely on statements from the police, or on legislative reports that are themselves based on police statements.

A systematic analysis

For the last several years, we have been studying the structure and operation of the gambling rackets in metropolitan New York since 1965. With the cooperation of the New York City Police Department and several other departments in the area, as well as local prosecutors' offices, we have examined the financial records of many gambling operations raided by the police. We have been able to obtain numerous official records on gambling operations and investigations, some wiretap transcripts, and also information drawn from lengthy interviews with police gambling specialists and informants active in bookmaking and numbers. Enforcement agencies certainly have more access to all of these sources, but we are certain that no agency has ever analyzed the gambling rackets by the systematic use of such data.

The traditional account asserts that illegal gambling is dominated by a cartel of criminal gangs who are involved in many kinds of racketeering. Their domination of the gambling rackets is maintained by the use of violence and coercion when necessary, but whenever possible they use their corrupt relationships with local officials to make certain that independent operators do not enter the market. "Organized crime brooks no opposition," is a common refrain. The dominant position of these gangs allows them to extract monopoly profits from illegal gambling, further enhanced by the predatory pursuit of gambling debts by mob-licensed loansharks.

The evidence we have obtained makes it clear that illegal gambling in New York does not conform to this grim account. Our research has focused on bookmaking and numbers, the two most important forms of illegal gambling. These are, in fact, two quite distinct trades. They have entirely different operating routines and problems. Their customers come from different segments of society, in terms of both income and ethnic background. Given these fundamental differences, it is not surprising that there are few people who are active in both businesses. Most law and enforcement policy merges these forms of gambling in ways that can be quite misleading, although there is little more relationship between bookmaking and numbers than there is between the insurance industry and supermarkets.

The evidence we have obtained for each of these activities is sharply in conflict with the standard account. We begin with bookmaking. Most bookmakers are just that—bookmakers; perhaps not the worthiest of citizens but certainly not the terrifying mobsters of whom we are told. They have few involvements in other criminal activities such as narcotics trafficking or fencing. It is true that they are involved with loansharks—but as customers themselves, rather than as providers of customers. There is very little use of violence in bookmaking, either for purposes of restricting competition or for disciplining of recalcitrant customers. Given the extent to which bookmakers extend short-term credit, often totaling thousands of dollars for an individual customer, this is quite a striking finding indeed.

Moreover, there are many autonomous bookmaking organizations, all of them small when compared to legitimate firms. The very largest operations, of which there are perhaps five in New York, handle about $500,000 per week in bets. Such an operation would employ only five clerks to record the bets, although it will have as many as 50 commission agents, known as "sheetwriters," directing bets to the central office. The sheetwriters, however, are not employees and may work for several operations simultaneously. There are at least 50 bookmaking operations in the city and near suburbs, each with a high degree of autonomy. Many of them are quite ephemeral. Narrow profit margins, the high cost of credit, difficulty in collecting debts, law enforcement, and poor entrepreneurial judgment (which is characteristic of many bookmakers), all combine to ensure that most of even the largest operations have relatively short lifetimes, although most individual bookmakers stay in the business for many years.

There is nothing to suggest that bookmakers are part of a coercive cartel, and considerable evidence suggests that they are involved in a risky and highly competitive business. We are certain that there is no territoriality or control of entry into the business. Occasional efforts to raise prices have met with no success. Corruption is a minor and episodic feature now, in contrast to the situation prevailing in the 1950's at the time of the Kefauver Committee. While there is a lot of betting between New York and New Jersey, there is nothing to suggest a nationwide "layoff" network; New York bookmakers do not have regular dealings with bettors or bookmakers in other parts of the country.

The "sheetwriter"

Perhaps the easiest way to understand the extent and origins of the fluid nature of this market is through an examination of the role of the sheetwriter. In many instances it is he who brings the customer to the bookmaker in the first place. Because the bets are all telephone transactions, the bettor has very little information about the bookmaker. Generally, all he has is a telephone number, which is changed from time to time. This anonymity provides important security for the bookmaker and his clerks. The bookmaker rarely meets his customers, since it is the sheetwriter who moves money between them.

However, in the current system, it is also true that the customers are generally the "property" of the sheetwriter and not the bookmaker. The sheetwriter has the right, in most operations and under most circumstances, to move his customers to another bookmaker. It is a trivial matter for him to do so; all he has to do is to tell his customers to call a different number. Sheetwriters, in fact, frequently make these shifts and it is extremely rare for a bookmaker to take any effective retaliation against this, even though the shifts always cost him money.

Most shifting of customers by a sheetwriter occurs when he owes a bookmaker money. The sheetwriter is an uninvested partner with the bookmaker, sharing profits and losses. When the sheetwriter's customers, as a group, win money from the bookmaker, half of those winnings are charged against the sheetwriter, although he does not have to provide any of the money paid to the customers. Instead, this "red figure," as it is called, is charged against his future earnings, which are generally 50 percent of what his customers lose. When the red figure becomes large, the sheetwriter has little prospect of receiving any income from the bookmaker for some weeks. His response to this is to shift his customers to another book-maker with whom he has no red figure.

We want to stress that this is not a hypothetical problem. The reports of informants indicate that sheetwriters frequently move when they have accumulated large red figures. Financial records show that these debts owed to the bookmaker do get to be substantial; a red figure of $20,000 is not extraordinary. Indeed, the problem has become acute enough that at least two bookmakers, faced by the loss of sheetwriters with substantial red figures, have offered those particular sheetwriters alternative financial arrangements which give the writer a share of the total wagering, eliminating the red figure.

We take this arrangement to be a critical indicator of the lack of control by any individual or group in the bookmaking market in New York. No cartel would permit agents, such as sheetwriters, to play off one member against another. Indeed, while we find little centralization in the numbers business, it is apparently sufficiently organized so that the controller, who is in that business the equivalent of the sheetwriter, cannot shift to another operation while he owes money to his original employer.

Another important indication of the lack of coordinated control in bookmaking is the failure of occasional efforts to raise prices. The standard terms for betting football and basketball in New York involve the player risking $11 to win $10, giving an expected return to the bookmaker of 4.4 percent of the money wagered.[1] At the beginning of each football season some bookmakers try to persuade their colleagues to change the terms to six-for-five. These repeated efforts have never been successful, and the 11-for-10 bet has persisted for over a decade, despite a high rate of bankruptcy among bookmakers.

Though the expected margin of profit is 4.4 percent, records indicate that the actual gross margin is less than 1 percent. There are at least four factors that explain this difference. First, the book-maker must share profits with his sheetwriters, who probably account for 80 percent of his wagering in a large operation. Second, sheetwriters may leave the operation when it has suffered losses through their accounts. Third, baseball betting, which may total nearly as much as football betting, works on a more complicated formula yielding an expected margin of less than 3 percent even

---

[1] If a bookmaker takes in one bet on each side of a game, he receives $22 in wagers. The winner receives $21, his $11 wager plus $10 in winnings, leaving the bookmaker with a $1 profit.

before the sheetwriters take their share. Finally, cheating by clerks is an endemic problem that has serious consequences for the bookmakers; clerks also make accounting errors which are not caught by any auditing system, and customers only point out errors that favor the bookmaker at their expense.

The fact that cheating is widely acknowledged but goes largely unpunished is frankly puzzling. It is certainly incompatible with the image of bookmakers who rule their organization and customers by the credible threat of violence. In a recent court case in New York, it emerged during pre-trial hearings that the tapes from a wiretap showed the clerks cheating their employer of some hundreds of thousands of dollars. In order to ensure that the tapes were played and that the bookmaker found out how much money was involved, he pleaded not guilty and ended up with a long jail sentence; if he had taken a guilty plea he would have received a shorter sentence, but he would not have found out how much money the clerks had taken. At this writing, some three years later, the clerks are still alive, although they have spent much of the intervening time in jail. And this particular bookmaker has a long-standing reputation for command of violence.

A fragmented market

Why, in fact, is this market fragmented? There are, after all, none of the usual legal constraints against cartel formation or domination through violence. We believe that a key element is the anonymity of everyone in the business. Because all the betting is done by telephone, often through call-back services that prevent the bettor from even knowing the telephone number of the operation, there is no way of determining who is in the business or the scale of their activities. Even bookmakers who command substantial resources and have ready access to "muscle," and there are several in the New York market, cannot prevent others from entering the business or control the terms on which they do business. Because members would have an interest in preserving anonymity, a bookmakers' cartel would have little more success in controlling the market.

This anonymity also bears directly on the role of police corruption. It is undoubtedly true that, at the time of the Kefauver Committee, bookmakers in New York systematically purchased police protection. At that time, though, they were primarily in the business of providing locations to which bettors came mainly to make horse bets; it was only at those "wire rooms" or "pool rooms" that bettors could hear the results of the races more or less immediately. With the shift to sports betting, an activity whose result can be heard over the radio, telephone betting became the dominant mode. The same difficulty facing a potential monopolist also hinders the corrupt policeman. It is not easy for him to locate the bookmakers for the purpose of extortion, and the bookmakers can move easily after the first contact. Bookmakers are still eager to purchase some degree of police cooperation, mainly for insurance (perhaps prior warning of a raid or a wiretap) we believe, but the relationships have become few and strained compared to the situation in earlier decades.

We have also been struck by the lack of violence and coercion in bookmaking.[2] It is a business that depends in large part on short-term credit. The bookmaker usually settles with his customers on a weekly basis in most operations, and the customer may owe several thousand dollars by that time. Yet it is extremely rare for violence to be used to collect that money. In case of any problem in making payment, the bookmaker will generally agree to some partial settlement and limit the betting of the customer until he pays the remainder of his debt. We have only isolated instances of a bookmaker turning over a delinquent account to a loanshark for collection. The bookmaker knows that an angry or frightened customer is the greatest threat to his anonymity and security.

Loansharks are, nonetheless, important to the functioning of the bookmaking business. They frequently provide capital for a bookmaker who is in financial difficulty. Since bookmakers are generally poor businessmen who often assume large risks voluntarily (being bettors themselves at heart), it is not uncommon for them to seek large sums at short notice, $50,000 being the upper end of the range of these loans. Only loansharks can supply this money. We are not in a position to estimate the importance of bookmakers' borrowing to the loansharking industry, but it is probable that a substantial segment of the industry specializes in lending to bookmakers.

The connection between loansharking and bookmaking is critical. Loansharking may well be an activity dominated by organized crime. Certainly a loanshark who does not have a well-established reputation for violence is at considerable risk from customers who believe they can defraud him; at a minimum he will have high collection costs. If it turns out that bookmakers account for a large

---

[2] To some extent this may be explained by the media's fascination with violence and organized crime. Many bookmaking customers, like citizens generally, probably have been convinced by the nightly news of the dire consequences of failing to meet their bookmaker's demands.

share of loanshark borrowing, then it will mean that bookmaking is important to organized crime for reasons almost exactly contrary to the conventional descriptions offered of the relationship between gambling and organized crime. In fact, this suggests that effective enforcement against bookmakers, by creating additional financial difficulties, may increase the market for loansharks—scarcely a blow to organized crime.

Whatever the exact relationship between bookmakers and loansharks, the police appear to be unaware of its importance. We have found no official documents that discuss the financing of gambling. Although the police have assembled much information about many bookmakers, they have almost no information about their financing. It is always assumed in law enforcement circles that gambling is the source of capital for other illegal activities, but our evidence indicates that the flow is in the other direction.

The numbers business

The numbers business, which we have also studied in great detail, is only slightly closer to the standard account of organized crime monopoly. Important racketeers, persons who are known to be involved in a variety of criminal activities and who have recognized status in the underworld, have a more direct involvement in the numbers than in bookmaking, though they are rarely involved in an operating capacity. Corruption also appears to be a more central feature, because numbers is still largely an activity involving face-to-face transactions between the customer and the seller. There is also some evidence of violence in the disciplining of sales agents, when, for example, they are believed to be withholding bets from the numbers "bank."

But it is important not to exaggerate these features. Although efforts have been made from time to time to establish a cartel, they have never had enduring success. Territoriality is slight. There are numbers banks with outlets in all five boroughs of the city. It is common for a single neighborhood to have several outlets, each representing a different bank. A "controller"—the intermediary between the collectors (who have almost exclusive access to customers) and the numbers "bank"—may set up his own bank with little threat of retaliation. Controllers also frequently maintain substantial interest-free balances, which the numbers banker has difficulty collecting.

There is considerably more stability among numbers banks than among bookmaking operations. It is not uncommon to find banks operating for a decade or longer. They also appear to generate larger and more stable flows of profits than bookmaking, but again far less than alleged in official accounts. We have found in New York that a bank doing $10 million annually is relatively large. On the average, we find that a gross profit of 4 percent can be reasonably expected—but from this must be deducted the not insignificant operating expenses of the bank.

It is useful to compare the retailing of illegal numbers in New York with the legal state monopolies that provide the same service in New Jersey and five other states. The state monopolies offer their retailers less than 10 percent of the wagers they process; the illegal operators in New York pay 25 percent and sometimes as much as 30 percent to their retailers. Similarly, the agents, who act in the same capacity as controllers, receive only about 2 percent from the state monopolies, while in New York controllers receive 10 percent of the wagers. The state monopolies restrict the number of outlets, so as to guarantee their agents total wagers of about $5,000 per week. In the illegal system retailers frequently handle less than $500 per week. The inability of numbers banks to coordinate their actions and to prevent new banks from entering or new retailers from starting with some existing bank has led to quite modest returns for the bank when compared to the cartel possibilities.

We can supplement our data in New York with some observations on numbers in the Miami area. Here we also find a large number of small banks, each bidding for the services of retailers and controllers. The recent influx of Cubans has led to a transfer in the control of banks, formerly operating in predominantly black areas but owned by native whites, and an increase in the share of wagering going to the retailers. In this case, despite the presence in Miami of major Italian and Jewish racketeers with a considerable interest in loansharking and narcotics, the Cuban numbers operators appear to have no relationship with any outside groups, though some individuals among them are involved in the drug business. Again, there is general agreement among our informants that violence and coercion are an unimportant part of the business.

The reforms instituted by the New York City Police Department after the Knapp Commission appear to have had a salutary effect on corruption. While there is undoubtedly still some corruption of street police, the systematic "pads," often involving quite senior commanders, appear to have come to an end. This reduction in corruption, which was accomplished essentially by ending aggressive enforcement, has been accompanied by a loosening up of the market. More controllers are branching out on their own, no longer needing to worry about arranging for protection from police they could not reach. The payout rate is rising, suggesting a growth in competition and a reduction in profits. Thus the reduction of enforcement has had three salutary effects. It has reduced police corruption, which may, in the long run, reduce overall access to police by criminals; it has reduced the concentration of the market (although it was not great prior to the reforms); and it has brought a better price to the customer.

It is possible that our findings apply only to New York. It is, after all, a larger metropolitan market than any other and anonymity is easier to achieve in such a large market than in areas served by only a few bookmakers. At this stage we have too little information about other areas, apart from Miami, to make any definite statement, but all of the scattered indications are consistent with our findings in New York. We note also that the Department of Justice estimated in 1974 that organized crime controlled over 50 percent of illegal gambling in New York City, compared to 42 percent in the nation as a whole. We are making our case in a city where the belief in organized crime's control of gambling is well-established.

Convenient errors

If our description of illegal gambling in New York is accurate and holds for other cities, then we must explain the rise and continued hold of the conventional wisdom, which has become the central doctrine of official statements on organized crime. It is not an easy task, for we have used no information or techniques that are not available to police agencies. Indeed, our analytic approach has been almost embarrassingly direct.

Two factors explain existing beliefs. First, these beliefs are bureaucratically and politically convenient. Second, they are produced by agencies whose unusually striking deficiencies in analytic work have gone largely unnoticed because, for a variety of reasons, they have been able to protect themselves from outside scrutiny with great success.

The police are the dominant source of information about organized crime in America. They collect almost all of the available information, do their own analyses of it, and then make the results available to the public and other government agencies. Government statements and legislative committee reports are mainly restatements of police views. The Kefauver Committee undertook no independent investigation or analysis; instead it provided a forum for information and theories advanced by local police and former FBI agents. The McClellan Committee did not "find" Joe Valachi; he was made available to them by the FBI on orders from the Attorney General. Valachi had been a Federal informant for several years and his testimony was the product of extensive debriefing by FBI agents. The President's Crime Commission acknowledged the lack of independent expertise available to it on organized crime.

The difficulty the government has had in obtaining accurate information on the reserves of energy-producing companies in the wake of the 1973 oil boycott should serve as a sober reminder of how difficult it is to collect accurate information even from legitimate organizations operating in a highly regulated environment. The challenges are immeasurably greater in collecting information about people who are consciously involved in illegal activities. The disproportionately large collections of photographs, tag numbers, and automobile descriptions in police files seem like an example of wasted effort until one realizes how difficult it is even to identify participants accurately. People on the street are frequently known only by nicknames, and often they use more than one.

One of our informants recalls being shown a surveillance photo of a suspect in a gambling investigation and being given a nickname for this person by an undercover police officer. On the basis of the nickname, which was familiar to him, he identified the suspect as a particular gambler. The police followed this person for several days before they learned that he was indeed a gambler, but not the person they thought they were following. This is not an uncommon occurrence nor is it evidence of the incompetence of the police. Rather it should be taken as a timely reminder of the difficulties involved in determining who is doing what, when the only sources of information are distant surveillances by people who are not familiar with the environment in which they are operating, informants who have no incentive to be accurate but considerable reason to provide information, and overheard snatches of converation whose meanings are frequently unclear.

The police are the only agents who have the authority and the necessary skills to collect information in this hostile environment. It would be very difficult for researchers to do a study of illegal gambling without the information obtained from police sources. In many areas of the city, people are simply unwilling to discuss these matters with strangers; other areas are too dangerous to wander about in. For some time we have been assembling information on the payout rate paid by numbers banks in various parts of New York and can attest to the difficulty of obtaining accurate, verified accounts from informants even about so simple a matter. It is striking, however, that not only are the police the exclusive suppliers of information to the entire system, they are also sovereign in interpreting what they collect.

Prosecutors are essentially passive receivers of the product of police work. They have almost no independent capacity to collect their own intelligence or to evaluate what the police are providing them. In New York City, under District Attorney Frank Hogan, any information about illegal gambling received by his office was turned over to the police department for investigation. He ordered his own investigators to do no work connected with gambling or narcotics. This division of labor between the police and their lawyers exists at Federal, state, and local levels of the criminal justice system. In responding to criticism over his unwillingness to allow the FBI to work under the direction of Justice Department lawyers in Strike Forces, J. Edgar Hoover wrote to an inquiring Congressman, ". . . as a general rule, we have found it to be true that greater efficiency results and responsibilities become more clearly established when investigators investigate and prosecutors prosecute."

This rigid separation of functions between police and prosecutors is another example of the deference for jurisdictional boundaries that is observable throughout the criminal justice system and is one of its defining characteristics. It is as common among units of the same organization as it is among separate agencies. One reason, certainly, why police and prosecutors are convinced that territoriality is an important characteristic of racketeering is because it is a defining feature of their own work routines. (As a matter of fact, we have found little evidence of territorial control of illegal gambling except where it is protected by the police.) In the processing of routine criminal cases, which is the majority of work done by prosecutors' offices, this separation is understandable; but in the area of organized crime enforcement it means that the police control the prosecutors' access to the critical facts on which decisions are made.

The police monopoly over information places prosecutors at a severe disadvantage in any discussion about tactics and strategy. The police are reluctant to tell a prosecutor very much about their sources of information, because he will most likely soon leave to enter private practice where he may defend people they are arresting. This is symptomatic of more fundamental differences between the police and their lawyers. The district attorney is elected, (that is, is inherently political) while the police view themselves as civil servants. Prosecutors are much better educated than police and have marketable skills, which means that most of them do enter private life after only a few years in public service, while the police, lacking alternative opportunities, tend to remain in their department for many years. The police, uniquely wedded to government, consider themselves to be more trustworthy. It is also true that the senior police involved in rackets investigations have many years of experience while most of the attorneys they deal with are relatively junior. The potential for conflict between them is substantial, and it is largely avoided by prosecutors deferring to the police in deciding how investigations are conducted.

Police sovereignty

The police are not unique in resisting the intrusion of experts into their domain, but they have been more successful than any other bureaucracy. The military resisted civilian control over their operations until the technological base, from which military doctrine and strategy were derived, compelled the inclusion of people in the decision-making process who possessed skills not available within the traditional military system. Although many military bureaucrats have resisted the expansion of civilian influences, the educational requirements of the officer corps have steadily expanded to the point where officers are routinely sent to traditional universities for higher degrees.

Using arguments about the need to keep from the underworld knowledge of informants and law-enforcement techniques, the police have managed to keep out everyone else as well. And since the police are ruled by a rigid civil service system which guarantees that anyone who has climbed high on the promotion ladder will be reluctant to express dissenting views, each force is insulated against external influences. They resist civilian intrusions even into non-sensitive areas such as communications control. This insularity makes it very difficult to have a discussion about organized crime, since the police can rightly claim they have most of the facts. Most discussions end up sounding like debates about UFO's: Those who have seen one are arrayed on one side, and all of those who have never seen one but dispute the validity or interpretation of the observations are on the other.

We know of no other area of public life where the sovereignty of the bureaucracy remains so strong. Like the rest of us, the police generalize from their own experience. Their policies are based primarily on the unanalyzed sum of their experiences, since even the few specialists who have been introduced to the policy-making process in recent years are rarely permitted to participate in the information-collection process, but are again passive recipients of what the street police bring them. A recent national survey of Rackets Bureaus by the Cornell Institute on Organized Crime found only one state or local agency among those sampled in their survey which was making an effort to analyze the information collected by its agents. The Institute concluded, "Put simply, intelligence activity continues essentially as a collection effort." Even the FBI, whose agents are much better educated than are the local police, has resisted outside specialists and sought to train its own people.

Gambling again provides an excellent example of the analytical limitations of the law enforcement community, even at the highest levels of government. The Department of Justice recognized that, since it frequently asserted that organized crime derived its major income from illegal gambling, it would be useful to have some notion of the absolute and relative scale of illegal gambling revenues. The President's Crime Commission, while endorsing the centrality of gambling, noted that estimates of revenues ranged from $7 to $50 billion per annum, and that, in 1967, there were no claims that any systematic study had been done.

In 1974, in testimony before the National Gambling Commission, the Justice Department announced that it had developed an estimate of the total volume of illegal gambling, which in 1973 lay somewhere between $29 and $39 billion. Details of the method used for producing the estimate were not made available for another two years, and even then in a most sketchy form. We cannot go through all the steps of the estimating procedure, but shall describe two of the critical steps which suggest that the estimate was exceptionally crude and designed to guarantee a very large result.

The basic data source was the wagering discovered by the Federal Strike Forces against Organized Crime during their program of intensive gambling enforcement in 1971 and 1972, known as Operation Anvil. It was assumed that all Strike Forces detected the same proportion of illegal wagering as had the Strike Force in New York City. No justification was offered for that assumption, which was unnecessary although it simplified the procedure. In fact, there is reason to believe that the Department had a higher sampling fraction in New York than elsewhere. Operation Anvil had been built around wiretapping, and the rate of surveillances per capita was higher in New York than in other major cities. This fact is by no means conclusive, but it is the only available piece of evidence on the reasonableness of the assumption—and it suggests an upward bias.

More important, the estimate required some measure of the percentage of illegal gambling sampled in each city by Operation Anvil. For this the Department used figures from a survey of gambling in New York carried out by the Oliver Quayle Company in 1973. The technique may be described as either ingenious or arcane.

The Quayle survey

Quayle found that, among *sports bettors who bet on horses*, betting with bookies accounted for 37.8 percent of their total off-track horse betting. The Department of Justice assumed that this was true for all persons who bet on horses, so that bookies accounted for 37.8 percent of all off-track horse betting. Since they had available the figures from the New York Off-Track Betting Corporation on its "handle," they could use this assumption to estimate total horse betting with bookies. They compared this figure with the total volume of illegal horse betting they had detected in New York through Anvil, and assumed that the same sampling fraction held for sports and numbers as well, in New York and all other cities.

There are many problems with this procedure. Most important is that it is unreasonable to assume that all horse bettors use bookmakers to the same extent as horse bettors who are also sports bettors. Because sports betting is the main service of bookmakers, any sports bettor who wants to bet on horses with a bookie is likely to have already established contact with one. Hence we might more reasonably expect that pure horse bettors—and the Quayle figures indicate that they account for most of the horse betting at the track and with OTB—do a smaller percentage of their off-track betting with bookies than does the subgroup on which Quayle obtained data.

It is interesting to compare the Department's estimate of illegal sports betting in New York with that obtained by Quayle—$2.8 billion for the Department, against $428 million for Quayle. It is difficult to see why the Department should have placed such faith in the survey's peculiar 37.8 percent figure, given the discrepancies in the two estimates of total betting.

In truth, we suspect that the real failing of the estimate was that no one really cared precisely how it was developed, but only that it produce a large number.[3] The assumption that the details of the calculations would not be subjected to any scrutiny led to a cavalier use of the available data. Also, the estimate had no possible consequences; it was produced for rhetorical purposes and has served those purposes very well.

This crude and cavalier treatment of information by police agencies is commonplace. It is important only because these agencies use the resulting estimates to provide legislatures with justification for passing statutes which define their tasks. In the case of organized crime, the tasks have been defined so that the police can continue their traditional fight against illegal gambling under a slightly altered rationale—the threat of national rather than local "mobs."

After years of concerted enforcement against gamblers, without any demonstrable results, it is difficult for the civil servants who direct the government's organized crime control program to conceal the fact that they have no policies. A recent study by the General Accounting Office of the Justice Department's Organized Crime Strike Forces elicited this appraisal, "The Chief, Organized Crime and Racketeering Section, does not believe that it is possible to establish overall program goals and then measure progress toward these goals." It is not often that a bureaucrat will admit this, although we suspect that more of them ought to. But the unembarrassed confession of the fact that there are no policies is symptomatic of the extent to which these particular civil servants have been free from outside scrutiny.

The Strike Forces, much heralded at the beginning of the decade as a bold new approach to the endless war on organized crime, are currently out of favor because of objections by U.S. Attorneys who feared the undermining of their autonomy. Despite all the ballyhoo about innovation, the Strike Forces mainly pursued gamblers. Between 1968 and 1974, 72 percent of Federal wiretaps were for gambling. Moreover, their attention was focused primarily on the traditional organized crime groups, the 24 crime families who are the national Mafia. In testimony before the National Gambling Commission, the Justice Department stressed its success in using anti-gambling statutes against senior members of the Mafia. Our interviews with former Strike Force prosecutors indicate that they

---

[3] Indeed, when the Department of Justice first announced the results of Operation Anvil, the range of estimates was far higher, $35-60 billion. No explanation for the later downward revision has ever been given.

felt a strong obligation to focus their efforts on Italian organized crime groups. Most of the press releases issued by the Strike Forces were about the activities of the Mafia.

It is not our intention to deny the existence of a Mafia. In this respect we differ from earlier critics who have had a splendid time demonstrating the inconsistencies of witnesses before legislative committees. Gordon Hawkins, some ten years ago in *The Public Interest*, showed how hard the McClellan and Kefauver Committees had to strain in using the evidence of their witnesses to show the existence of a national criminal conspiracy. Our own research does show that there is a Mafia, and probably more than one, although it is far less distinctive than is normally alleged and its relation to other criminal groups is not clearly defined.

The Mafia

All of our informants who are participants in gambling and other criminal activities firmly believe in the existence of the Mafia, although there are differences in terminology; alas, all have read *The Valachi Papers* or seen *The Godfather*. They also tend to agree about who is a member and who is not, and even about the relative seniority of various members. Though none of them claims to be a member, and no one alleges any of them is, several grew up in families associated with members and have friends they believe to be members. Curiously, none of them claims any knowledge of how members are "made" or what initiation actually involves.

It is clear that membership confers certain rights and obligations, but there is disagreement over whether it is better to be a member or a close associate; associates appear to enjoy most of the rights and incur none of the obligations. Which family one joins has relevance apparently only in case of disputes. There are no restrictions on whom one does business with, but if there is a dispute each member is required to align with his own family.

There may be a "national" Mafia Commission. If there is, it has very limited powers, perhaps only to mediate high-level disputes. The apparent intercity territoriality, whereby racketeers from Detroit are not active in Boston, is almost certainly a consequence of the local nature of the racketeer's power base, rather than any rulings by committees. A more important national function of the Mafia is that it provides a network of contacts in other cities that allows members, who tend to have a range of criminal interests, opportunities for intercity deals.

The Mafia is clearly only a part of the world of stable, hierarchical criminal organizations. There are others, more or less ethnically homogenous (since most racketeering involves core groups of persons who have known each other from childhood), which also exert power in local criminal activities, have an established reputation for the use of violence, and use corrupt relations with public officials to further their goals, as much as does the Mafia. Narcotics trafficking is certainly one activity in which the Mafia exercises control over only a small part of the market. It is not merely a bow to civil rights to suggest that public officials who focus so much attention on one particular ethnic group, Italians, have an obligation to provide some credible evidence that it is truly distinctive. Americans of other ethnic origins should be given their opportunities to enter the pantheon of popular folk heroes, chased by equal opportunity prosecutors.

In fact, there is one distinctive service provided by the Italian Mafia that is apparently not offered by any other group: arbitration. In an economy without conventional written contracts, there is obviously room for frequent disagreements. These are hard to resolve. Many bookmakers make payments to "wise guys" to ensure that when disputes arise they have effective representation. Sometimes these disputes are resolved on their merits. Sometimes they are resolved simply on the basis of the rank of the two arbitrators. It is critical to note that this arbitration is used in only a very restricted set of circumstances.

It is *not* used to collect from delinquent customers who are unable to meet their commitments as a result of either poor planning or over-indulgence. A legitimate bettor may be cut off and mildly harassed, but he will receive no threats from "enforcers." If, however, the dispute is with a "wise guy" or a "connected" person, then the arbitration system will be invoked. In particular, if it appears that there is a deliberate intention by such persons to defraud the bookmaker, then the Mafia man will be called in. This risk insurance is important to the bookmaker because people in the criminal trades are among the largest bettors and are the customers most likely to flout him. There is general, though only moderately well-informed agreement among the police and our informants that no such system of arbitrating disputes exists in other organized crime groups.

These differences between Mafia groups and other racketeers do not seem sufficiently threatening to justify the special attention they receive either in the press or from law enforcement. But in order to make that judgment we must consider the very basis for our concern with organized crime. Though it is true that organized crime control is a matter to which a relatively small percentage of police resources is devoted, certainly less than 5 percent, it has been used to justify giving the police and prosecutors special powers.

Two justifications

Two themes stand out in the legislative justification for organized crime laws. One is the predatory nature of racketeers. The FBI, in particular, is tireless in its reiteration of the notion that gambling is not a victimless crime, because homicides are committed as a result of gambling debts. Others point to the demoralizing nature of heroin addiction, or the inducement that "fences" provide for thieves. In fact, of course, all these are the function of supplying the service rather than of the existence of stable gangs. (By the same reasoning a case can be made for outlawing marriage since it is the principal "cause" of murder.) In other words, if bookies use violence against delinquent customers, it is unlikely that the destruction of the Mafia will reduce that violence. In fact, there is even a credible argument that, by reducing the customer's belief in the power of his bookie to enforce his demands, the actual use of violence will increase. One consequence of the proliferation of numbers banks in New York appears to be an increase in the robberies of runners and collectors by bandits who are not worried about retaliation from organized forces.

Corruption is the other evil that has been used to justify special legislation and action against organized crime. "The inevitable companion of flourishing gambling activity ... is the bribery and corruption of local law enforcement officials," asserted the preamble to the Organized Crime Control Act of 1970. It is certainly true that the historical record shows many cases of widespread and systematic corruption of major city police departments by gamblers. There are, however, two problems with this statement.

First, it assumes that the relation between illegal gambling and corruption is inevitable. Our own research indicates that it is a function of the particular environment and technology rather than inherent in gambling itself. Telephone bookmaking, during a period of low gambling enforcement, flourishes with little direct contact with the police.

Second, it is not clear that gambling does account for a particularly high percentage of police corruption, measured either in money or social impact. For example, narcotics dealing in recent years appears to have generated much larger bribery cases than gambling, as well as instances of police involvement in murder and other aspects of trafficking. And the Chicago Strike Force recently obtained numerous convictions against several networks of precinct police for "shaking down" tavern owners who had no connection with gambling.

More important, though, is the curious obsession with police gambling corruption without any accompanying concern to discover its causes or to find ways to eliminate it. Gambling enforcement has always posed dilemmas for police administrators. Most gambling statutes are designed to enforce prohibition, not to control the activity or to restrict it to certain places. But the police have never been given the political support necessary to achieve this dubious goal. Few judges have ever been willing to give convicted gamblers jail sentences and the fines imposed have usually been trivial. In New York City, gambling cases had so little importance to the District Attorneys' offices that they were used to train new assistants in the routines of criminal procedure.

In New York, at least, the police seem to be resolving this dilemma for themselves. They have abolished aggressive enforcement and replaced it with a policy which is directed at keeping gambling discreet and enforcement honest. There is a relatively small, specialized gambling unit which responds to complaints, maintains an intelligence-gathering apparatus, and conducts raids on those it considers major operators. This policy does not appear to have increased organized crime presence in illegal gambling, although gambling is somewhat more visible on the streets than it once was.

The costs of misinformation

The most important consequence of all the misinformation and inflammatory rhetoric put out by official agencies is to make impossible any realistic discussion about gambling policy. The possibility of legalizing bookmaking, as has been smoothly and successfully done in England, is never discussed. It seems to be assumed that because bookmakers are all working for organized crime, legalization would simply give the Mafia more money. When a state does lurch toward legalization of gambling, as New Jersey has just done with casinos in Atlantic City, there is obsessive concern about who will make money from it. Instead of asking whether there are any Italians who have ever played golf with executives of casino licensees, it would be more sensible to concern ourselves with the fact that one applicant hired as its lobbyists close relatives of the two legislators who chair the committees responsible for drafting casino regulations. Organized crime, in this instance, is clearly a diversion from a far more fundamental and familiar political problem.

It is clear that the campaign against organized crime has been based on myths and misinterpretations. These have led to bad law and even worse policy. We will continue to feel the consequences for a long time to come, as the government monopolies many states have created to regulate gambling become enveloped in the webs of special interests and collusion that afflict government regulation of the liquor and horse-racing industries. The remedies are easy to suggest, if difficult to implement. But a first step certainly is to develop a body of critical expertise based on access to more than statistical reports and conversations with law enforcement officials.

CONTRIBUTORS

DAVID A. STOCKMAN is a Member of the U.S. House of Representatives, where he serves on the Energy and Power subcommittee of the House Interstate and Foreign Commerce Committee and is Chairman of the Republican Economic Policy Task Force. . . . PETER REUTER and JONATHAN B. RUBINSTEIN are associated with The Policy Sciences Center, Inc. Research for their paper has been funded by grants from the National Institute of Law Enforcement and Criminal Justice, Law Enforcement Assistance Administration. The views expressed do not necessarily represent the policies or opinions of L.E.A.A. . . . WILLIAM ALONSO is Saltonstall Professor of Population Policy and Director of the Center for Population Studies at Harvard University. A fuller version of his article is to appear in a volume on the Mature Metropolis, edited by Charles Leven. The research was funded by a National Science Foundation grant. . . . ANN R. MARKUSEN is Assistant Professor of City and Regional Planning at the University of California, Berkeley. JERRY FASTRUP is Staff Economist at the Program Analysis Division of the General Accounting Office. . . . MICHAEL ANDREW SCULLY is Managing Editor of *The Public Interest.* . . . CHRISTINE H. ROSSELL is Assistant Professor of Political Science at Boston University and author of several articles on the community impact of school desegregation based on a longitudinal research study funded by the National Institute of Education of 113 school districts. DIANE RAVITCH is Adjunct Assistant Professor of History and Education at Teachers College, Columbia University, and author of *The Great School Wars: New York City, 1805-1973* and *The Revisionists Revised: A Critique of the Radical Attack on the Schools.* DAVID J. ARMOR is Senior Social Scientist at Rand Corporation.

TABLE 15

Concurrent Relation between Child Rejection of Parent and the Child's Delinquency or Aggression

Study	Subjects	Age	Race	Child Behavior	Respondent	Measurement Mode[a]	Conduct Problem	Strength of Relation[b]
Nye (1958)	780 BG	14–18	White	B-M: Most rejecting	Child	Questionnaire (11)	Self-reported delinquency (most)	RIOC = 17.2
				G-M:				RIOC = 25.5
				B-F:				RIOC = 23.2
				G-F:				RIOC = 22.6
Hirschi (1969)	1,256 B	12–18	Mixed	B-F: No identification	Child	Questionnaire (1)	Self-reported delinquency	RIOC = 24.1
Hindelang (1973)	441 rural B, 445 rural G	11–18	White	B-F: No identification	Child	Questionnaire	High self-reported delinquency	RIOC = 18.6
Gold (1963)	93 del., 93 nondel. B	12–16	White	C-P: No identification (think/sure)	Child	Interview (1)	Recidivism	RIOC = 20.0

Part II
Theoretical Frameworks
and
Interpretations

[5]

Crime as an American Way of Life

By DANIEL BELL

IN THE 1890's, the Reverend Dr. Charles Parkhurst, shocked at the open police protection afforded New York's bordellos, demanded a state inquiry. In the Lexow investigation that followed, the young and dashing William Travers Jerome staged a set of public hearings that created sensation after sensation. He badgered "Clubber" Williams, First Inspector of the Police Department, to account for wealth and property far greater than could have been saved on his salary; it was earned, the Clubber explained laconically, through land speculation "in Japan." Heavy-set Captain Schmittberger, the "collector" for the "Tenderloin precincts"—Broadway's fabulous concentration of hotels, theaters, restaurants, gaming houses, and saloons—related in detail how protection money was distributed among the police force. Crooks, policemen, public officials, businessmen, all paraded across the stage, each adding his chapter to a sordid story of corruption and crime. The upshot of these revelations was reform—the election of William L. Strong, a stalwart businessman, as mayor, and the naming of Theodore Roosevelt as police commissioner.

It did not last, of course, just as previous reform victories had not lasted. Yet the ritual drama was re-enacted. Twenty years ago the Seabury investigation in New York uncovered the tin-box brigade and the thirty-three little MacQuades. Jimmy Walker was ousted as Mayor and in came Fiorello La Guardia. Tom Dewey became district attorney, broke the industrial rackets, sent Lucky Luciano to jail and went to the Governor's chair in Albany. Then reform was again swallowed up

DANIEL BELL is a lecturer in sociology at Columbia University. He has recently written a chapter called "Labor and Public Opinion" to be included in a volume published by the Society for the Psychological Study of Social Issues on Industrial Relations, and a long study of the Longshoresmen's union for a book of union profiles, edited by J. B. S. Hardman.

in the insatiable maw of corruption until Kefauver and the young and dashing Rudolph Halley threw a new beam of light into the seemingly bottomless pit.

How explain this repetitious cycle? Obviously the simple moralistic distinction between "good guys" and "bad guys," so deep at the root of the reform impulse, bears little relation to the role of organized crime in American society. What, then, does?

II

Americans have had an extraordinary talent for compromise in politics and extremism in morality. The most shameless political deals (and "steals") have been rationalized as expedient and realistically necessary. Yet in no other country have there been such spectacular attempts to curb human appetites and brand them as illicit, and nowhere else such glaring failures. From the start America was at one and the same time a frontier community where "everything goes," and the fair country of the Blue Laws. At the turn of the century the cleavage developed between the Big City and the small-town conscience. Crime as a growing business was fed by the revenues from prostitution, liquor and gambling that a wide-open urban society encouraged and which a middle-class Protestant ethos tried to suppress with a ferocity unmatched in any other civilized country. Catholic cultures rarely have imposed such restrictions, and have rarely suffered such excesses. Even in prim and proper Anglican England, prostitution is a commonplace of Piccadilly night life, and gambling one of the largest and most popular industries. In America the enforcement of public morals has been a continuing feature of our history.

Some truth may lie in Svend Ranulf's generalization that moral indignation is a peculiar fact of middle-class psychology and represents a disguised form of repressed envy. The larger truth lies perhaps in the brawling nature of American development and the social character of crime. Crime, in many ways, is a Coney Island mirror, caricaturing the morals and manners of a society. The jungle quality of the American business community, particularly at the turn of the century, was reflected in the mode of "business" practiced by the coarse gangster elements, most of them from new immigrant families, who were "getting ahead," just as Horatio Alger had urged. In the older, Protestant tradition the intense acquisitiveness, such as that of Daniel Drew, was rationalized by a compulsive moral fervor. But the formal obeisance of the ruthless businessman in the workaday world to the church-going pieties of the Sabbath was one that the gangster could not make. Moreover, for the young criminal, hunting in the asphalt jungle of the crowded city, it was not the businessman with his wily manipulation of numbers but the "man with the gun" who was the American hero. "No amount of commercial prosperity," once wrote Teddy Roosevelt, "can supply the lack of the heroic virtues." The American was "the hunter, cowboy, frontiersman, the soldier, the naval hero." And in the crowded slums, the gangster. He was a man with a gun, acquiring by personal merit what was denied to him by complex orderings of a stratified society. And the duel with the law was the morality play *par excellence:* the gangster, with whom rides our own illicit desires, and the prosecutor, representing final judgment and the force of the law.

Yet all this was acted out in a wider context. The desires satisfied in extra-legal fashion were more than a hunger for the "forbidden fruits" of conventional morality. They also involved, in the complex and ever shifting structure of group, class and ethnic stratification, which is the warp and woof of America's "open" society, such "normal" goals as independence through a business of one's own, and such "moral" aspirations as the desire for social advancement and social prestige. For crime, in the language of the sociologists, has a "functional" role in the society, and the urban rackets—the illicit activity organized for continuing profit rather than individual illegal acts—is one of the queer ladders of social mobility in American life. Indeed, it is not too much to say that the whole question of organized crime in America cannot be understood unless one appreciates (1) the distinctive role of organized gambling as a function of a mass consumption economy; (2) the specific role of various immigrant groups as they one after another became involved in marginal business and crime; and (3) the relation of crime to the changing character of the urban political machines.

III

As a society changes, so does, in lagging fashion, its type of crime. As American society became more "organized," as the American businessman became more "civilized" and less "buccaneering," so did the

American racketeer. And just as there were important changes in the structure of business enterprise, so the "institutionalized" criminal enterprise was transformed too.

In the America of the last fifty years the main drift of society has been toward the rationalization of industry, the domestication of the crude self-made captain of industry into the respectable man of manners, and the emergence of a mass-consumption economy. The most significant transformation in the field of "institutionalized" crime was the increasing relative importance of gambling as against other kinds of illegal activity. And, as a multi-billion-dollar business, gambling underwent a transition parallel to the changes in American enterprise as a whole. This parallel was exemplified in many ways: in gambling's industrial organization (e.g., the growth of a complex technology such as the national racing wire service and the minimization of risks by such techniques as lay-off betting); in its respectability, as was evidenced in the opening of smart and popular gambling casinos in resort towns and in "satellite" adjuncts to metropolitan areas; in its functional role in a mass-consumption economy (for sheer volume of money changing hands, nothing has ever surpassed this feverish activity of fifty million American adults); in the social acceptance of the gamblers in the important status world of sport and entertainment, i.e., "café society."

In seeking to "legitimize" itself, gambling had quite often actually become a force against older and more vicious forms of illegal activity. In 1946, for example, when a Chicago mobster, Pat Manno, went down to Dallas, Texas, to take over gambling in the area for the Accardo-Guzik combine, he reassured the sheriff as to his intent as follows: "Something I'm against, that's dope peddlers, pickpockets, hired killers. That's one thing I can't stomach, and that's one thing the fellows up there—the group won't stand for, things like that. They discourage it, they even go to headquarters and ask them why they don't do something about it."

Jimmy Cannon once reported that when the gambling raids started in Chicago, the "combine" protested that, in upsetting existing stable relations, the police were only opening the way for ambitious young punks and hoodlums to start trouble. Nor is there today, as there was twenty or even forty years ago, prostitution of major organized scope in the United States. Aside from the fact that manners and morals have changed, prostitution *as an industry* doesn't pay as well as gambling. Besides, its existence threatened the tacit moral acceptance and quasi-respectability that gamblers and gambling have secured in the American way of life. It was, as any operator in the field might tell you, "bad for business."

The criminal world of the last decade, its tone set by the captains of the gambling industry, is in startling contrast to the state of affairs in the two decades before. If a Kefauver report had been written then, the main "names" would have been Lepke and Gurrah, Dutch Schultz, Jack "Legs" Diamond, Lucky Luciano, and, reaching back a little further, Arnold Rothstein, the czar of the underworld. These men (with the exception of Luciano, who was involved in narcotics and prostitution) were in the main industrial racketeers. Rothstein, it is true, had a larger function: he was, as Frank Costello became later, the financier of the underworld—the pioneer big businessman of crime, who, understanding the logic of co-ordination, sought to *organize* crime as a source of regular income. His main interest in this direction was in industrial racketeering, and his entry was through labor disputes. At one time, employers in the garment trades hired Legs Diamond and his sluggers to break strikes, and the Communists, then in control of the cloakmakers union, hired one Little Orgie to protect the pickets and beat up the scabs; only later did both sides learn that Legs Diamond and Little Orgie were working for the same man, Rothstein.

Rothstein's chief successors, Lepke Buchalter and Gurrah Shapiro, were able, in the early '30's, to dominate sections of the men's and women's clothing industries, of painting, fur dressing, flour trucking, and other fields. In a highly chaotic and cut-throat industry such as clothing, the racketeer, paradoxically, played a stabilizing role by regulating competition and fixing prices. When the NRA came in and assumed this function, the businessman found that what had once been a quasi-economic service was now pure extortion, and he began to demand police action. In other types of racketeering, such as the trucking of perishable foods and water-front loading, where the racketeers entrenched themselves as middlemen—taking up, by default, a service that neither shippers nor truckers wanted to assume—a pattern of accommodation was roughly worked out and the rackets assumed a quasi-legal veneer. On the water-front, old-time racketeers perform the necessary function of loading—but at an exorbitant price, and this monopoly was recognized by both the union and the shippers, and tacitly by government. (See my case study "The Last of the Business Rackets," in the June, 1951 issue of *Fortune.*)

But in the last decade and a half, industrial racketeering has not offered much in the way of opportunity. *Like American capitalism itself, crime shifted its emphasis from production to consumption.* The focus of crime became the direct exploitation of the citizen as consumer, largely through gambling. And while the protection of these huge revenues was inextricably linked to politics, the relation between gambling and "the mobs" became more complicated.

IV

Although it never showed up in the gross national product, gambling in the last decade was one of the largest industries in the United States. The Kefauver Committee estimated it as a twenty-billion-dollar business. This figure has been picked up and widely quoted, but in truth no one knows what the gambling "turnover" and "take" actually is, nor how much is bet legally (pari-mutuel, etc.) and how much illegally. In fact, the figure cited by the committee was arbitrary and arrived at quite sloppily. As one staff member said: "We had no real idea of the money spent. . . . The California crime commission said twelve billion. Virgil Peterson of Chicago estimated thirty billion. We picked twenty billion as a balance between the two."

If comprehensive data are not available, we do know, from specific instances, the magnitude of many of the operations. Some indications can be seen from these items culled at random:

—James Carroll and the M & G syndicate did a 20-million-dollar annual business in St. Louis. This was one of the two large books in the city.

—The S & G syndicate in Miami did a 26-million-dollar volume yearly; the total for all books in the Florida resort reached 40 millions.

—Slot machines were present in 69,786 establishments in 1951 (each paid $100 for a license to the Bureau of Internal Revenue); the usual average is three machines to a license, which would add up to 210,000 slot machines in operation in the United States. In legalized areas, where the betting is higher and more regular, the average gross "take" per machine is $50 a week.

—The largest policy wheel (i.e. "numbers") in Chicago's "Black

Belt" reported taxable net profits for the four-year period from 1946 through 1949, after sizable deductions for "overhead," of $3,656,968. One of the large "white" wheels reported in 1947 a gross income of $2,317,000 and a net profit of $205,000. One CIO official estimated that perhaps 15 per cent of his union's lower echelon officials are involved in the numbers racket (a steward, free to roam a plant, is in a perfect situation for organizing bets).

If one considers the amount of betting on sports alone—an estimated six billion on baseball, a billion on football pools, another billion on basketball, six billion on horse racing—then Elmo Roper's judgment that "only the food, steel, auto, chemical, and machine-tool industries have a greater volume of business" does not seem too far-fetched.

While gambling has long flourished in the United States, the influx of the big mobsters into the industry—and its expansion—started in the '30's when repeal of Prohibition forced them to look about for new avenues of enterprise. Gambling, which had begun to flower under the nourishment of rising incomes, was the most lucrative field in sight. To a large extent the shift from bootlegging to gambling was a mere transfer of business operations. In the East, Frank Costello went into slot machines and the operation of a number of ritzy gambling casinos. He also became the "banker" for the Erickson "book," which "laid off" bets for other bookies. Joe Adonis, similarly, opened up a number of casinos, principally in New Jersey. Across the country, many other mobsters went into bookmaking. As other rackets diminished, and gambling, particularly horse-race betting, flourished in the '40's, a struggle erupted over the control of racing information.

Horse-race betting requires a peculiar industrial organization. The essential component is time. A bookie can operate only if he can get information on odds up to the very last minute before the race, so that he can "hedge" or "lay off" bets. With racing going on simultaneously on many tracks throughout the country, this information has to be obtained speedily and accurately. Thus, the racing wire is the nerve ganglion of race betting.

The racing-wire news service got started in the '20's through the genius of the late Moe Annenberg, who had made a fearful reputation for himself as Hearst's circulation manager in the rough-and-tumble Chicago newspaper wars. Annenberg conceived the idea of a telegraphic news service which would gather information from tracks and shoot it immediately to scratch sheets, horse parlors, and bookie joints. In some instances, track owners gave Annenberg the rights to send news from tracks; more often, the news was simply "stolen" by crews operating inside or near the tracks. So efficient did this news distribution system become, that in 1942, when a plane knocked out a vital telegraph circuit which served an Air Force field as well as the gamblers, the Continental Press managed to get its racing wire service for gamblers resumed in fifteen minutes, while it took the Fourth Army, which was responsible for the defense of the entire West Coast, something like three hours.

Annenberg built up a nationwide racing information chain that not only distributed wire news but controlled sub-outlets as well. In 1939, harassed by the Internal Revenue Bureau on income tax, and chivvied by the Justice Department for "monopolistic" control of the wire service, the tired and aging Annenberg simply walked out of the business. He did not sell his interest, or even seek to salvage some profit; he simply gave up. Yet, like any established and thriving institution, the enterprise continued, though on a decentralized basis. James Ragen, Annenberg's operations manager, and likewise a veteran of the old Chicago circulation wars, took over the national wire service through a dummy friend and renamed it the Continental Press Service.

The salient fact is that in the operation of the Annenberg and Ragen wire service, formally illegal as many of its subsidiary operations may have been (i.e. in "stealing" news, supplying information to bookies, etc.) gangsters played no part. It was a business, illicit, true, but primarily a business. The distinction between gamblers and gangsters, as we shall see, is a relevant one.

In 1946, the Chicago mob, whose main interest was in bookmaking rather than gambling casinos, began to move in on the wire monopoly. Following repeal, the Capone lieutenants had turned, like Lepke, to labor racketeering. Murray ("The Camel") Humphries muscled in on the teamsters, the operating engineers, and the cleaning-and-dyeing, laundry, and linen-supply industries. Through a small-time punk, Willie Bioff, and union official George Browne, Capone's chief successors, Frank ("The Enforcer") Nitti and Paul Ricca, came into control of the motion-picture union and proceeded to shake down the movie industry for fabulous sums in order to "avert strikes." In

1943, when the government moved in and smashed the industrial rackets, the remaining big shots, Charley Fischetti, Jake Guzik, and Tony Accardo decided to concentrate on gambling, and in particular began a drive to take over the racing wire.

In Chicago, the Guzik-Accardo gang, controlling a sub-distributor of the racing news service, began tapping Continental's wires, In Los Angeles, the head of the local distribution agency for Continental was beaten up by hoodlums working for Mickey Cohen and Joe Sica. Out of the blue appeared a new and competitive nationwide racing information and distribution service, known as Trans-American Publishing, the money for which was advanced by the Chicago mobs and Bugsy Siegel, who, at the time, held a monopoly of the bookmaking and wire-news service in Las Vegas. Many books pulled out of Continental and bought information from the new outfit, many hedged by buying from both. At the end of a year, however, the Capone mob's wire had lost about $200,000. Ragen felt that violence would erupt and went to the Cook County district attorney and told him that his life had been threatened by his rivals. Ragen knew his competitors. In June 1946 he was killed by a blast from a shotgun.

Thereafter, the Capone mob abandoned Trans-American and got a "piece" of Continental. Through their new control of the national racing-wire monopoly, the Capone mob began to muscle in on the lucrative Miami gambling business run by the so-called S & G syndicate. For a long time S & G's monopoly over bookmaking had been so complete that when New York gambler Frank Erickson bought a three months' bookmaking concession at the expensive Roney Plaza Hotel, for $45,000, the local police, in a highly publicized raid, swooped down on the hotel; the next year the Roney Plaza was again using local talent. The Capone group, however, was tougher. They demanded an interest in Miami bookmaking, and, when refused, began organizing a syndicate of their own, persuading some bookies at the big hotels to join them. Florida Governor Warren's crime investigator appeared—a friend, it seemed, of old Chicago dog-track operator William Johnston, who had contributed $100,000 to the Governor's campaign fund—and began raiding bookie joints, but only those that were affiliated with S & G. Then S & G, which had been buying its racing news from the local distributor of Continental Press, found its service abruptly shut off. For a few days the syndicate sought to bootleg information from New Orleans, but found itself limping along. After ten days' war of attrition, the five S & G partners found themselves with a sixth partner, who, for a token "investment" of $20,000 entered a Miami business that grossed $26,000,000 in one year.

V

While Americans made gambling illegal, they did not in their hearts think of it as wicked—even the churches benefited from the bingo and lottery crazes. So they gambled—and gamblers flourished. Against this open canvas, the indignant tones of Senator Wiley and the shocked righteousness of Senator Tobey during the Kefauver investigation rang oddly. Yet it was probably this very tone of surprise that gave the activity of the Kefauver Committee its piquant quality. Here were some Senators who seemingly did not know the facts of life, as most Americans did. Here, in the person of Senator Tobey, was the old New England Puritan conscience poking around in industrial America, in a world it had made but never seen. Here was old-fashioned moral indignation, at a time when cynicism was rampant in public life.

Commendable as such moralistic fervor was, it did not make for intelligent discrimination of fact. Throughout the Kefauver hearings, for example, there ran the presumption that all gamblers were invariably gangsters. This was true of Chicago's Accardo-Guzik combine, which in the past had its fingers in many kinds of rackets. It was not nearly so true of many of the large gamblers in America, most of whom had the feeling that they were satisfying a basic American urge for sport and looked upon their calling with no greater sense of guilt than did many bootleggers. After all, Sherman Billingsley did start out as a speakeasy proprietor, as did the Kreindlers of the "21" Club; and today the Stork Club and the former Jack and Charlie's are the most fashionable night and dining spots in America (one prominent patron of the Stork Club: J. Edgar Hoover).

The S & G syndicate in Miami, for example (led by Harold Salvey, Jules Levitt, Charles Friedman, Sam Cohen, and Edward (Eddie Luckey) Rosenbaum was simply a master pool of some two hundred bookies that arranged for telephone service, handled "protection," acted as bankers for those who needed ready cash on hard-hit books, and, in short, functioned somewhat analogously to the large factoring corporations in the textile field or the credit companies in the auto industry. Yet to Kefauver, these S & G men were "slippery and arrogant characters. . . . Salvey, for instance, was an old-time bookie who told us he had done nothing except engage in bookmaking or finance other bookmakers for twenty years." When, as a result of committee publicity and the newly found purity of the Miami police, the S & G syndicate went out of business, it was, as the combine's lawyer told Kefauver, because the "boys" were weary of being painted "the worst monsters in the world." "It is true," Cohen acknowledged, "that they had been law violators." But they had never done anything worse than gambling, and "to fight the world isn't worth it."

Most intriguing of all were the opinions of James J. Carroll, the St. Louis "betting commissioner," who for years had been widely quoted on the sports pages of the country as setting odds on the Kentucky Derby winter book and the baseball pennant races. Senator Wiley, speaking like the prosecutor in Camus's novel, *The Stranger*, became the voice of official morality:

SENATOR WILEY: Have you any children?
MR. CARROLL: Yes, I have a boy.
SENATOR WILEY: How old is he?
MR. CARROLL: Thirty-three.
SENATOR WILEY: Does he gamble?
MR. CARROLL: No.
SENATOR WILEY: Would you like to see him grow up and become a gambler, either professional or amateur?
MR. CARROLL: No . . .
SENATOR WILEY: All right. Is your son interested in your business?
MR. CARROLL: No, he is a manufacturer.
SENATOR WILEY: Why do you not get him into the business?
MR. CARROLL: Well, psychologically a great many people are unsuited for gambling.

Retreating from this gambit, the Senator sought to pin Carroll down on his contributions to political campaigns:

SENATOR WILEY: Now this morning I asked you whether you contributed any money for political candidates or parties, and you said not more than $200 at any one time. I presume that does not indicate the total of your contributions in any one campaign, does it?

MR. CARROLL: Well, it might, might not, Senator. I have been an "againster" in many instances. I am a reader of *The Nation* for fifty years and they have advertisements calling for contributions for different candidates, different causes. . . . They carried an advertisement for George Norris; I contributed, I think, to that, and to the elder La Follette.

Carroll, who admitted to having been in the betting business since 1899, was the sophisticated—but not immoral!—counterpoint to moralist Wiley. Here was a man without the stigmata of the underworld or underground; he was worldly, cynical of official rhetoric, jaundiced about people's motives, he was—an "againster" who believed that "all gambling legislation originates or stems from some group or some individual seeking special interests for himself or his cause."

Asked why people gamble, Carroll distilled his experiences of fifty years with a remark that deserves a place in American social history: "I really don't know how to answer the question," he said. "I think gambling is a biological necessity for certain types. I think it is the quality that gives substance to their daydreams."

In a sense, the entire Kefauver materials, unintentionally, seem to document that remark. For what the Committee revealed time and time again was a picture of gambling as a basic institution in American life, flourishing openly and accepted widely. In many of the small towns, the gambling joint is as open as a liquor establishment. The town of Havana, in Mason County, Illinois, felt miffed when Governor Adlai Stevenson intervened against local gambling. In 1950, the town had raised $15,000 of its $50,000 budget by making friendly raids on the gambling houses every month and having the owners pay fines. "With the gambling fines cut off," grumbled Mayor Clarence Chester, "the next year is going to be tough."

Apart from the gamblers, there were the mobsters. But what Senator Kefauver and company failed to understand was that the mobsters, like the gamblers, and like the entire gangdom generally, were seeking to become quasi-respectable and establish a place for themselves in American life. For the mobsters, by and large, had immigrant roots, and crime, as the pattern showed, was a route of social ascent and place in American life.

VI

The mobsters were able, where they wished, to "muscle in" on the gambling business because the established gamblers were wholly vulnerable, not being able to call on the law for protection. The Senators, however, refusing to make any distinction between a gambler and a gangster, found it convenient to talk loosely of a nationwide conspiracy of "illegal" elements. Senator Kefauver asserted that a "nationwide crime syndicate does exist in the United States, despite the protestations of a strangely assorted company of criminals, self-serving politicians, plain blind fools, and others who may be honestly misguided, that there is no such combine." The Senate Committee report states the matter more dogmatically: "There is a nationwide crime syndicate known as the Mafia. . . . Its leaders are usually found in control of the most lucrative rackets in their cities. There are indications of a centralized direction and control of these rackets. . . . The Mafia is the cement that helps to bind the Costello-Adonis-Lansky syndicate of New York and the Accardo-Guzik-Fischetti syndicate of Chicago. . . . These groups have kept in touch with Luciano since his deportation from the country."

Unfortunately for a good story—and the existence of the Mafia would be a whale of a story—neither the Senate Crime Committee in its testimony, nor Kefauver in his book, presented any real evidence that the Mafia exists as a functioning organization. One finds police officials asserting before the Kefauver committee their *belief* in the Mafia; the Narcotics Bureau *thinks* that a worldwide dope ring allegedly run by Luciano is part of the Mafia; but the only other "evidence" presented—aside from the incredulous responses both of Senator Kefauver and Rudolph Halley when nearly all the Italian gangsters asserted that they didn't know about the Mafia—is that certain crimes bear "the earmarks of the Mafia."

The legend of the Mafia has been fostered in recent years largely by the peephole writing team of Jack Lait and Lee Mortimer. In their *Chicago Confidential*, they rattled off a series of names and titles that made the organization sound like a rival to an Amos and Andy Kingfish society. Few serious reporters, however, give it much credence. Burton Turkus, the Brooklyn prosecutor who broke up the "Murder, Inc." ring, denies the existence of the Mafia. Nor could Senator Kefauver even make out much of a case for his picture of a national crime syndicate. He is forced to admit that "as it exists today [it] is an elusive and furtive but nonetheless tangible thing," and that "its organization and machinations are not always easy to pinpoint." His "evidence" that many gangsters congregate at certain times of the year in such places as Hot Springs, Arkansas, in itself does not prove much; people "in the trade" usually do, and as the loquacious late Willie Moretti of New Jersey said, in explaining how he had met the late Al Capone at a race track, "Listen, well-charactered people you don't need introductions to; you just meet automatically."

Why did the Senate Crime Committee plump so hard for its theory of the Mafia and a national crime syndicate? In part, they may have been misled by their own hearsay. The Senate Committee was not in the position to do original research, and its staff, both legal and investigative, was incredibly small. Senator Kefauver had begun the investigation with the attitude that with so much smoke there must be a raging fire. But smoke can also mean a smoke screen. Mob activities is a field in which busy gossip and exaggeration flourish even more readily than in a radical political sect.

There is, as well, in the American temper, a feeling that "somewhere," "somebody" is pulling all the complicated strings to which this jumbled world dances. In politics the labor image is "Wall Street," or "Big Business"; while the business stereotype was the "New Dealers." In the field of crime, the side-of-the-mouth low-down was "Costello."

The salient reason, perhaps, why the Kefauver Committee was taken in by its own myth of an omnipotent Mafia and a despotic Costello was its failure to assimilate and understand three of the more relevant sociological facts about institutionalized crime in its relation to the political life of large urban communities in America, namely: (1) the rise of the American Italian community, as part of the inevitable process of ethnic succession, to positions of importance in politics, a process that has been occurring independently but almost simultaneously in most cities with large Italian constituencies—New York, Chicago, Kansas City, Los Angeles; (2) the fact that there are individual Italians who play prominent, often leading roles today in gambling and in the mobs; and (3) the fact that Italian gamblers and mobsters often possessed "status" within the Italian community itself and a "pull" in city politics.[1] These three items are indeed related—but not so as to form a "plot."

VII

The Italian community has achieved wealth and political influence much later and in a harder way than previous immigrant groups. Early Jewish wealth, that of the German Jews of the late nineteenth century, was made largely in banking and merchandising. To that extent, the dominant group in the Jewish community was outside of, and independent of, the urban political machines. Later Jewish wealth, among the East European immigrants, was built in the garment trades, though with some involvement with the Jewish gangster, who was typically an industrial racketeer (Arnold Rothstein, Lepke and Gurrah, etc.) Among Jewish lawyers, a small minority, such as the "Tammany lawyer" (like the protagonist of Sam Ornitz's *Haunch, Paunch* and *Jowl*) rose through politics and occasionally touched the fringes of crime. Most of the Jewish lawyers, by and large the communal leaders, climbed rapidly, however, in the opportunities that established and legitimate Jewish wealth provided. Irish immigrant wealth in the northern urban centers, concentrated largely in construction, trucking and the waterfront, has, to a substantial extent, been wealth accumulated in and through political alliance, e.g. favoritism in city contracts.[2]

---

[1]Toward the end of his hearings, Senator Kefauver read a telegram from an indignant citizen of Italian descent, protesting against the impression the committee had created that organized crime in America was a distinctly Italian enterprise. The Senator took the occasion to state the obvious: that there are racketeers who are Italian does not mean that Italians are racketeers. However, it may be argued that to the extent the Kefauver Committee fell for the line about crime in America being organized and controlled by the Mafia, it did foster such a misunderstanding. Perhaps this is also the place to point out that insofar as the relation of ethnic groups and ethnic problems to illicit and quasi-legal activities is piously ignored, the field is left open to the kind of vicious sensationalism practiced by Mortimer and Lait.

[2]A fact which should occasion little shock if one recalls that in the nineteenth century American railroads virtually stole 190,000,000 acres of land by bribing Congressmen, and that more recently such scandals as the Teapot Dome oil grabs during the Harding administration, consummated, as the Supreme Court said, "by means of conspiracy, fraud and bribery," reached to the very doors of the White House.

Control of the politics of the city thus has been crucial for the continuance of Irish political wealth. This alliance of Irish immigrant wealth and politics has been reciprocal; many noted Irish political figures lent their names as important window-dressing for business corporations (Al Smith, for example, who helped form the U.S. Trucking Corporation, whose executive head for many years was William J. McCormack, the alleged "Mr. Big" of the New York waterfront) while Irish businessmen have lent their wealth to further the careers of Irish politicians. Irish mobsters have rarely achieved status in the Irish community, but have served as integral arms of the politicians, as strong-arm men on election day.

The Italians found the more obvious big city paths from rags to riches pre-empted. In part this was due to the character of the early Italian immigration. Most of them were unskilled and from rural stock. Jacob Riis could remark in the '90's, "the Italian comes in at the bottom and stays there." These dispossessed agricultural laborers found jobs as ditch-diggers, on the railroads as section hands, along the docks, in the service occupations, as shoemakers, barbers, garment workers, and stayed there. Many were fleeced by the "padrone" system, a few achieved wealth from truck farming, wine growing, and marketing produce; but this "marginal wealth" was not the source of coherent and stable political power.

Significantly, although the number of Italians in the U.S. is about a third as high as the number of Irish, and of the 30,000,000 Catholic communicants in the United States, about half are of Irish descent and a sixth of Italian, there is not one Italian bishop among the hundred Catholic bishops in this country, or one Italian archbishop among the 21 archbishops. The Irish have a virtual monopoly. This is a factor related to the politics of the American church; but the condition also is possible because there is not significant or sufficient wealth among Italian Americans to force some parity.

The children of the immigrants, the second and third generation, became wise in the ways of the urban slums. Excluded from the political ladder—in the early '30's there were almost no Italians on the city payroll in top jobs, nor in books of the period can one find discussion of Italian political leaders—finding few open routes to wealth, some turned to illicit ways. In the children's court statistics of the 1930's, the largest group of delinquents were the Italian; nor were there any

CRIME 147

Italian communal or social agencies to cope with these problems. Yet it was, oddly enough, the quondam racketeer, seeking to become respectable, who provided one of the major supports for the drive to win a political voice for Italians in the power structure of the urban political machines.

This rise of the Italian political bloc was connected, at least in the major northern urban centers, to another important development which tended to make the traditional relation between the politician and the protected or tolerated illicit operator more close than it had been in the past. This is the fact that the urban political machines had to evolve new forms of fund-raising since the big business contributions, which once went heavily into municipal politics, now—with the shift in the locus of power—go largely into national affairs. (The ensuing corruption in national politics, as recent Congressional investigations show, is no petty matter; the scruples of businessmen do not seem much superior to those of the gamblers.) One way urban political machines raised their money resembled that of the large corporations which are no longer dependent on Wall Street: by self-financing—that is, by "taxing" the large number of municipal employees who bargain collectively with City Hall for their wage increases. So the firemen's union contributed money to O'Dwyer's campaign.

A second method was taxing the gamblers. The classic example, as *Life* reported, was Jersey City, where a top lieutenant of the Hague machine spent his full time screening applicants for unofficial book-making licenses. If found acceptable, the applicant was given a "location," usually the house or store of a loyal precinct worker, who kicked into the machine treasury a high proportion of the large rent exacted. The one thousand bookies and their one thousand landlords in Jersey City formed the hard core of the political machine that sweated and bled to get out the votes for Hague.

A third source for the financing of these machines was the new, and often illegally earned, Italian wealth. This is well illustrated by the career of Costello and his emergence as a political power in New York. Here the ruling motive has been the search for an entrée—for oneself and one's ethnic group—into the ruling circles of the big city.

Frank Costello made his money originally in bootlegging. After repeal, his big break came when Huey Long, desperate for ready cash to fight the old-line political machines, invited Costello to install slot machines in Louisiana. Costello did, and he flourished. Together with Dandy Phil Kastel, he also opened the Beverly Club, an elegant gambling establishment just outside New Orleans, at which have appeared some of the top entertainers in America. Subsequently, Costello invested his money in New York real estate (including 79 Wall Street, which he later sold), the Copacabana night club, and a leading brand of Scotch whiskey.

Costello's political opportunity came when a money-hungry Tammany, starved by lack of patronage from Roosevelt and La Guardia, turned to him for financial support. The Italian community in New York has for years nursed a grievance against the Irish and, to a lesser extent, the Jewish political groups for monopolizing political power. They complained about the lack of judicial jobs, the small number—usually one—of Italian Congressmen, the lack of representation on the state tickets. But the Italians lacked the means to make their ambitions a reality. Although they formed a large voting bloc, there was rarely sufficient wealth to finance political clubs. Italian immigrants, largely poor peasants from Southern Italy and Sicily, lacked the mercantile experience of the Jews, and the political experience gained in the seventy-five-year history of Irish immigration.

During the Prohibition years, the Italian racketeers had made certain political contacts in order to gain protection. Costello, always the compromiser and fixer rather than the muscle-man, was the first to establish relations with Jimmy Hines, the powerful leader of the West Side in Tammany Hall. But his rival, Lucky Luciano, suspicious of the Irish, and seeking more direct power, backed and elected Al Marinelli for district leader on the Lower West Side. Marinelli in 1932 was the only Italian leader inside Tammany Hall. Later, he was joined by Dr. Paul Sarubbi, a partner of Johnny Torrio in a large, legitimate liquor concern. Certainly, Costello and Luciano represented no "unified" move by the Italians as a whole for power; within the Italian community there are as many divisions as in any other group. What is significant is that different Italians, for different reasons, and in various fashions, were achieving influence for the first time. Marinelli became county clerk of New York and a leading power in Tammany. In 1937, after being blasted by Tom Dewey, then running for district attorney, as a "political ally of thieves . . . and big-shot racketeers," Marinelli was removed from office by Governor Lehman. The subsequent conviction by Dewey of Luciano and Hines, and the election of La Guardia, left most of the Tammany clubs financially weak and foundering. This was the moment Costello made his move. In a few years, by judicious financing, he controlled a block of "Italian" leaders in the Hall—as well as some Irish on the upper West Side, and some Jewish leaders on the East Side—and was able to influence the selection of a number of Italian judges. The most notable incident, revealed by a wire tap on Costello's phone, was the "Thank you, Francisco" call in 1943 by Supreme Court nominee Thomas Aurelio, who gave Costello full credit for his nomination.

It was not only Tammany that was eager to accept campaign contributions from newly rich Italians, even though some of these *nouveaux riches* had "arrived" through bootlegging and gambling. Fiorello La Guardia, the wiliest mind that Melting Pot politics has ever produced, understood in the early '30's where much of his covert support came from. (So, too, did Vito Marcantonio, an apt pupil of the master: Marcantonio has consistently made deals with the Italian leaders of Tammany Hall—in 1943 he supported Aurelio, and refused to repudiate him even when the Democratic Party formally did.) Joe Adonis, who had built a political following during the late '20's, when he ran a popular speakeasy, aided La Guardia financially to a considerable extent in 1933. "The Democrats haven't recognized the Italians," Adonis told a friend. "There is no reason for the Italians to support anybody but La Guardia; the Jews have played ball with the Democrats and haven't gotten much out of it. They know it now. They will vote for La Guardia. So will the Italians."

Adonis played his cards shrewdly. He supported La Guardia, but also a number of Democrats for local and judicial posts, and became a power in the Brooklyn area. His restaurant was frequented by Kenny Sutherland, the Coney Island Democratic leader; Irwin Steingut, the Democratic minority leader in Albany; Anthony DiGiovanni, later a Councilman; William O'Dwyer, and Jim Moran. But, in 1937, Adonis made the mistake of supporting Royal Copeland against La Guardia, and the irate Fiorello finally drove Adonis out of New York.[3]

---

[3]Adonis, and associate Willie Moretti, moved across the river to Bergen County, New Jersey, where, together with the quondam racketeer Abner, "Longie" Zwillman, he became one of the political powers in the state. Gambling flourished in

La Guardia later turned his ire against Costello, too. Yet Costello survived and reached the peak of his influence in 1942, when he was instrumental in electing Michael Kennedy leader of Tammany Hall. Despite the Aurelio fiasco, which first brought Costello into notoriety, he still had sufficient power in the Hall to swing votes for Hugo Rogers as Tammany leader in 1945, and had a tight grip on some districts as late as 1948. In those years many a Tammany leader came hat in hand to Costello's apartment, or sought him out on the golf links, to obtain the nomination for a judicial post.

During this period, other Italian political leaders were also coming to the fore. Generoso Pope, whose Colonial Sand and Stone Company began to prosper through political contacts, became an important political figure, especially when his purchase of the two largest Italian-language dailies (later merged into one), and of a radio station, gave him almost a monopoly of channels to Italian-speaking opinion of the city. Through Generoso Pope, and through Costello, the Italians became a major political force in New York.

That the urban machines, largely Democratic, have financed their heavy campaign costs in this fashion rather than having to turn to the "moneyed interests," explains in some part why these machines were able, in part, to support the New and Fair Deals without suffering the pressures they might have been subjected to had their source of money supply been the business groups. Although he has never publicly revealed his political convictions, it is likely that Frank Costello was a fervent admirer of Franklin D. Roosevelt and his efforts to aid the common man. The basic measures of the New Deal, which most Americans today agree were necessary for the public good, would not have been possible without the support of the "corrupt" big-city machines.

VIII

There is little question that men of Italian origin appeared in most of the leading roles in the high drama of gambling and mobs, just as twenty years ago the children of East European Jews were the most

---

Bergen County for almost a decade but after the Kefauver investigation the state was forced to act. A special inquiry in 1953 headed by Nelson Stamler, revealed that Moretti had paid $286,000 to an aide of Governor Driscoll for "protection" and that the Republican state committee had accepted a $25,000 "loan" from gambler Joseph Bozzo, an associate of Zwillman.

prominent figures in organized crime, and before that individuals of Irish descent were similarly prominent. To some extent statistical accident and the tendency of newspapers to emphasize the few sensational figures gives a greater illusion about the domination of illicit activities by a single ethnic group than all the facts warrant. In many cities, particularly in the South and on the West Coast, the mob and gambling fraternity consisted of many other groups, and often, predominantly, native white Protestants. Yet it is clear that in the major northern urban centers there was a distinct ethnic sequence in the modes of obtaining illicit wealth, and that uniquely in the case of the recent Italian elements, the former bootleggers and gamblers provided considerable leverage for the growth of political influence as well. A substantial number of Italian judges sitting on the bench in New York today are indebted in one fashion or another to Costello; so too are many Italian district leaders—as well as some Jewish and Irish politicians. And the motive in establishing Italian political prestige in New York was generous rather than scheming for personal advantage. For Costello it was largely a case of ethnic pride. As in earlier American eras, organized illegality became a stepladder of social ascent.

To the world at large, the news and pictures of Frank Sinatra, for example, mingling with former Italian mobsters could come somewhat as a shock. Yet to Sinatra, and to many Italians, these were men who had grown up in their neighborhoods, and who were, in some instances, bywords in the community for their helpfulness and their charities. The early Italian gangsters were hoodlums—rough, unlettered, and young (Al Capone was only twenty-nine at the height of his power). Those who survived learned to adapt. By now they are men of middle age or older. They learned to dress conservatively. Their homes are in respectable suburbs. They sent their children to good schools and had sought to avoid publicity.[4] Costello even went to a psychiatrist in his efforts to overcome a painful feeling of inferiority in the world of manners.

---

[4]Except at times by being overly neighborly, like Tony Accardo, who, at Yuletide 1949, in his elegant River Forest home, decorated a 40-foot tree on his lawn and beneath it set a wooden Santa and reindeer, while around the yard, on tracks, electrically operated skating figures zipped merrily around while a loud speaker poured out Christmas carols. The next Christmas, the Accardo lawn was darkened; Tony was on the lam from Kefauver.

As happens with all "new" money in American society, the rough and ready contractors, the construction people, trucking entrepreneurs, as well as racketeers, polished up their manners and sought recognition and respectability in their own ethnic as well as in the general community. The "shanty" Irish became the "lace curtain" Irish, and then moved out for wider recognition.[5] Sometimes acceptance came first in established "American" society, and this was a certificate for later recognition by the ethnic community, a process well illustrated by the belated acceptance in established Negro society of such figures as Sugar Ray Robinson and Joe Louis, as well as leading popular entertainers.

Yet, after all, the foundation of many a distinguished older American fortune was laid by sharp practices and morally reprehensible methods. The pioneers of American capitalism were not graduated from Harvard's School of Business Administration. The early settlers and founding fathers, as well as those who "won the west" and built up cattle, mining and other fortunes, often did so by shady speculations and a not inconsiderable amount of violence. They ignored, circumvented or stretched the law when it stood in the way of America's destiny, and their own—or, were themselves the law when it served their purposes. This has not prevented them and their descendants from feeling proper moral outrage when under the changed circumstances of the crowded urban environments later comers pursued equally ruthless tactics.

IX

Ironically, the social development which made possible the rise to political influence sounds, too, the knell of the Italian gangster. For it is the growing number of Italians with professional training and legitimate business success that both prompts and permits the Italian

---

[5] The role of ethnic pride in corralling minority group votes is one of the oldest pieces of wisdom in American politics; but what is more remarkable is the persistence of this identification through second and third generation descendants, a fact which, as Samuel Lubell noted in his *Future of American Politics*, was one of the explanatory keys to political behavior in recent elections. Although the Irish bloc as a solid Democratic bloc is beginning to crack, particularly as middle-class status impels individuals to identify more strongly with the G.O.P., the nomination in Massachusetts of Jack Kennedy for the United States Senate created a tremendous solidarity among Irish voters and Kennedy was elected over Lodge although Eisenhower swept the state.

group to wield increasing political influence; and increasingly it is the professionals and businessmen who provide models for Italian youth today, models that hardly existed twenty years ago. Ironically, the headlines and exposés of "crime" of the Italian "gangsters" came years after the fact. Many of the top "crime" figures long ago had forsworn violence, and even their income, in large part, was derived from legitimate investments (real estate in the case of Costello, motor haulage and auto dealer franchises in the case of Adonis) or from such quasi-legitimate but socially respectable sources as gambling casinos. Hence society's "retribution" in the jail sentences for Costello and Adonis was little more than a trumped-up morality that disguised a social hypocrisy.

Apart from these considerations, what of the larger context of crime and the American way of life? The passing of the Fair Deal signalizes, oddly, the passing of an older pattern of illicit activities. The gambling fever of the past decade and a half was part of the flush and exuberance of rising incomes, and was characteristic largely of new upper-middle class rich having a first fling at conspicuous consumption. This upper-middle class rich, a significant new stratum in American life (not rich in the nineteenth century sense of enormous wealth, but largely middle-sized businessmen and entrepreneurs of the service and luxury trades—the "tertiary economy" in Colin Clark's phrase—who by the tax laws have achieved sizable incomes often much higher than the managers of the super-giant corporations) were the chief patrons of the munificent gambling casinos. During the war decade when travel was difficult, gambling and the lush resorts provided important outlets for this social class. Now they are settling down, learning about Europe and culture. The petty gambling, the betting and bingo which relieve the tedium of small town life, or the expectation among the urban slum dwellers of winning a sizable sum by a "lucky number" or a "lucky horse" goes on. To quote Bernard Baruch: "You can't stop people from gambling on horses. And why should you prohibit a man from backing his own judgment? It's another form of personal initiative." But the lush profits are passing from gambling, as the costs of coordination rise. And in the future it is likely that gambling, like prostitution, winning tacit acceptance as a necessary fact, will continue on a decentralized, small entrepreneur basis.

But passing, too, is a political pattern, the system of political "bosses" which in its reciprocal relation provided "protection" for and was fed revenue from crime. The collapse of the "boss" system was a product of the Roosevelt era. Twenty years ago Jim Farley's task was simple; he had to work only on some key state bosses. Now there is no longer such an animal. New Jersey Democracy was once ruled by Frank Hague; now there are five or six men each top dog, for the moment, in his part of the state or faction of the party. Within the urban centers, the old Irish-dominated political machines in New York, Boston, Newark, and Chicago have fallen apart. The decentralization of the metropolitan centers, the growth of suburbs and satellite towns, the break-up of the old ecological patterns of slum and transient belts, the rise of functional groups, the increasing middle-class character of American life, all contribute to this decline.

With the rationalization and absorption of some illicit activities into the structure of the economy, the passing of an older generation that had established a hegemony over crime, the general rise of minority groups to social position, and the break-up of the urban boss system, the pattern of crime we have discussed is passing as well. Crime, of course, remains as long as passion and the desire for gain remain. But big, organized city crime, as we have known it for the past seventy-five years, was based on more than these universal motives. It was based on certain characteristics of the American economy, American ethnic groups, and American politics. The changes in all these areas means that it too, in the form we have known it, is at an end.

[6]

This article examines some of the American roots of organized crime, and its place within the American culture. The ethnic succession and limited mobility theses are critically examined, and some new perspectives presented regarding the analysis of organized crime. A number of research needs and propositions in need of further testing are presented.

INDIVIDUAL CHOICE, MATERIAL CULTURE, AND ORGANIZED CRIME

PETER A. LUPSHA
University of New Mexico-Albuquerque

the American phenomenon of organized crime has been examined from a variety of perspectives. Donald Cressey (1972) tended to stress organization, hierarchy and structure; Francis Ianni (1972) kinship and familial cultural adaptation; Schelling (1967) and Annelise Anderson's (1979) work stresses economic variables; Daniel Bell (1953) has emphasized social mobility. The major theoretical construct that flows through most of these works is the "ethnic succession thesis." This formulation sees organized crime as simply the adaptation of a deprived group to limitations on upward mobility and opportunities for social status. Immigrant groups accepted crime as an alternative status ladder and rose on it. Or, as Balzac aptly said: "Behind every great fortune is a crime."

In this article we dispute this thesis, and present an alternative perspective on the emergence of organized crime in twentieth-century America. Our thesis is that organized crime as we know it is not based on either (a) a narrow or limited status or mobility ladder for early twentieth-century immigrants; or (b) frustration or anger at thwarting of mobility desires of immigrants by the dominant culture. These are the root arguments of the ethnic

CRIMINOLOGY. Vol. 19 No. 1. May 1981 3-24
© 1981 American Society of Criminology

succession thesis. Instead we suggest that entrance to organized crime life styles was a self-choice based on individual skills and a personal rationalization which perverts traditional American values and culture. In our view the organized criminal does not seek, and has not sought, traditional status and respect values because he has his own world view of our culture which makes him right and the rest of us suckers (Lupsha, 1980). The very openness of our values permits this and supports the rise of different views. From his perspective the organized criminal is correct, and success has replaced respect or deference as a value. Power wealth and the fear it can generate replaces the positive deference of any "good society." Yet organized crime is a true product of American values and American culture. It is an American crime. It has simply taken the very openness of those values and placed them in a "fun house" perspective of its own.

Dwight C. Smith, Jr. and Richard Alba (1979) have recognized this. They see through the unilinear development from Mafia in Sicily, to Black-Handers, to Cosa Nostra. They see the role of American values and enterprise culture on organized crime. They, however, do not accept the testimony of Joseph Valachi (U.S. Senate, 1965), Vincent Teresa (1973), or the array of FBI wire taps now available, and tend, in this author's view, to throw out the baby of organized crime along with the bath water of "alien conspiracy" theory. Our view is less sanguine. The author agrees with Smith both on the need for data, testable conceptualization, and analytical rigor, as well as on the point of the key role of economics. We find, however, that Valachi and Teresa are supported by later empirical data from wiretaps in New Jersey, Rhode Island, Kansas City, Missouri, and Chicago (Volz and Bridge, 1969; Zeiger, 1975).

Even when Valachi and Teresa are placed in perspective as limited and parochial period pieces, shaped by specific situational variables, there is enough pattern between them and wiretap data from the 1960s, and now the 1970s, to suggest a pattern of events, attitudes and association that underscore the existence of Italian-American organized crime groups. And, importantly, these groups appear to have historic associational and social network patterns that go back to the period of Prohibition. Thus, while La Cosa Nostra (LCN) may not be the perfect term, we find it a useful descriptor of Italian-American organized crime groups.

It is our contention that while there are many other groups—Colombian, Cuban, Mexican, Syrian, Chinese, Afro-American, and WASP—active in organized crime (Cordesco, 1977; Light, 1974; Lupsha and Schlegel, 1979; Ianni, 1974a), the Italian-American groups, while withdrawing from street and direct front-line operations, remain as leading members in the orchestration of organized crime enterprises in the United States. While we want to avoid any misleading structural analogies, conceptually it appears that traditional Italian-American organized crime members have not left the business, but simply moved to upper management positions. With capital and efficient associates, fewer people can carry out these director functions while there is ethnic succession in certain functions and enterprises and on the street.

Smith in his more recent writings (1980) has performed an important service of pressing toward enterprise conceptions of organized crime. There, it is hoped that any difference we have will be resolved in the crucible of research, data, and the needed empirical testing of various conceptualizations.

John Landesco (1929) first pointed to the American roots of organized crime. Also, Fredrick Thrasher (1927: 153) noted the multiethnic nature of street gangs as well as their process of Americanization. Italian-American groups are but one group involved in organized crime. Law enforcement and press accounts have, historically, skewed our vision and understanding as Smith (1975), among others (Nelli, 1976; Ianni, 1972; Hawkins, 1969), has pointed out. Yet there is a grain of truth to the vision. It is skewed, not false, and we should not forget that. However, now is not the time for conclusions; it is for conceptualization, hypothesis formation, and propositional testing. Now we must move, as Smith and others have advised, beyond image to argument.

6   CRIMINOLOGY / MAY 1981

In order to move beyond image to argument, we need first to define the values which make up the taproots of American culture. They are the Lockeian values embodied in the writings and documents and declarations of our Founding Fathers and their interpreters, as well as the social and technological shifts in that value continuum over time. These values are based in beliefs in: (a) individualism, (b) property or "materialism," (c) competitiveness, and (d) freedom of action or independence. From the interplay of these values comes our perceptions of opportunity, procedural equality, substantive equality, material success, acquisitiveness, and a belief in right vested in the individual rather than the community. As these values have shaped our political and economic system, so, too, they have shaped the rise and development of organized crime.

By organized crime we refer to those crimes involving ongoing criminal conspiracies and interactions over time, which therefore may be thought of as organized or syndicated. While there are many ways to define organized crime, this broad definition should be suitable for this article.[1]

Organized criminal groups have operated in the United States from its very beginnings. Whenever there is an opportunity to enhance profit, or create wealth; whenever there are imbalances in the market system or government has through its actions created scarcity and "black markets"; or whenever local culture and mores make for illicit actions or behaviors against which there are no universal taboos, enterprising individuals will appear to take advantage of the opportunity and risk possible sanction in order to accrue potential windfall profits. The boundaries of such fields of illicit action are delineated only by culture, precedent, opportunity, and the swiftness and certainty of sanction. If the balance of this behavioral equation swings in the direction of large profits from criminal action and relatively little certain, or immediate, sanction, the potential for criminal enterprise and entrepreneurship is enhanced.

To say organized crime is rooted in the "Jungle" quality of American business traditions is not new. Daniel Bell (1953) said it in his classic, "Crime as an American Way of Life," in the

Antioch Review. To say that organized crime is based in "a frontier ethic which justifies an individual taking the law into his own hands," or in "the struggle under our value system of every ethnic group to achieve greater social and economic status" is not new. Gus Tyler (1971) said that in his "Sociodynamics of Organized Crime," in the *Journal of Public Law.* Along with Bell's theme of organized crime as a "queer ladder of social mobility," this notion of "ethnic succession" is repeated as orthodoxy by every student in the field (Ianni, 1972). Thus, these works must be given close scrutiny.

Francis A. J. Ianni is perhaps the best known exponent of these views. He developed them first in 1972 in his *A Family Business,* an examination of the "Luppolo" crime family and its mixed generational shifts into legitimate businesses and illegal ones. This movement of the Luppolo sons into noncriminal entrepreneurship, Ianni tells us, is the indicator of the queer ladder of social mobility in action. In more recent work he goes further (Ianni, 1974a), noting

> that organized crime provides an easy and swift route for social and economic mobility, and that there is a certain ethnic succession whereby a group that has already achieved some measure of socio-economic status need no longer utilize that route.

In saying this, Ianni succinctly summarizes the modern orthodoxy. We feel, however, this view fails to recognize certain basic truths regarding power and power relations, as well as certain rigidification in our culture. Organized crime is an American phenomenon but it does not function in precisely the manner Ianni (1972), Tyler (1971), Bell (1953), and other exponents of the "queer ladder" and "ethnic succession models" suggest.

Organized crime had its beginnings in the late nineteenth-century neighborhood street gangs (Thrasher, 1927; Nelli, 1976). These gangs defended the ethnic neighborhood from outside influences while preying on it themselves. They did the bidding of the local political machine, turning out the vote and dampening the opposition. One of the largest New York City gangs was

the "Paul Kelly Political Association," better known as the
"Five Points Gang." Kelly, whose real name was Paolo Vac-
carelli, would later become a leader of New York's waterfront
and vice-president of the International Longshoremen's Association (Nelli, 1976). He helped raise to manhood such future
leaders of organized crime as Charles "Lucky" Luciano, John
Torrio, and Al Capone; and through loose local contacts he
influenced others, such as Benjamin "Bugsy" Siegel, Jacob
"Gurrah" Shapiro, Lepke Buchalter, and Meyer Lansky, all
Lower East Side youths. Thrasher's (1927) work noted parallel
lines of development.

One important proposition which can be made about the
nature of organized crime is that it is American—its leadership
was, for the most part, American born or raised. Volumes have
been written on the Sicilian roots of organized crime and also
on peer influence on adult development; we need not repeat them
here. We only note, with Smith and Alba (1979), that organized
crime is a product of America. It is not Italian, Sicilian, Jewish,
German, Polish, or Russian. Its leaders were American born
or socialized, and the context of the American economic and
political system affected them.

Table 1 shows that the major organized crime figures who
have been identified by law enforcement, federal government
hearings, and the media, were overwhelmingly American born
or raised. Only "Joe the Boss" Masseria and Salvatore Maranzano were adults (i.e., not teenagers or younger) when they
entered the United States, and their leadership period was brief,
as the young Americans took over the organization in the wake
of the Castellammarese War (1928-1931). Torrio, Luciano, Capone, Costello, Lansky, Lucchese, Anastasia, Genovese, Schultz,
and their Prohibition associates around the country—Boo Huff,
King Solomon, Nig Rosen, Moe Dalitz, Jacob Guzik, Lou
Rothkopf, Nucky Johnson, Chuck Polizzi (born Leo Berkowitz),
Abe Bernstein, John Lazia, Lepke Buchalter, Frank Erickson,
Bill Duffey, and others—were all young Americans and as-
similators.[2]

TABLE 1

Place of Birth, Origin and Approximate Age at Time of Entry into the
United States of Major Reputed Crime "Leaders" and Their Associates

NAME	Place of Birth or Origin	Approximate Age at Time of Entry
John Torrio	Naples, Italy	2 yrs.
Giuseppe Masseria	Sicily	26 yrs.
Salvatore Maranzano	Castellammarse, Sicily	43 yrs.
Charles "Lucky" Luciano	Lercara Friddi, Sicily	10 yrs.
Vito Genovese	Naples, Italy	15 yrs.
Albert Anastasia	Sicily	13 yrs.
Frank Costello (Castiglia)	Calabria, Italy	4 yrs.
Thomas Lucchese	Sicily	11 yrs.
Joseph Bonanno	Castellammarese, Sicily	(1-6)[a], 19 yrs.
Meyer Lansky	Grodino, Russia	9 yrs.
Willie Moretti	New York, New York	NA[b]
Joe Doto (Adonis)	Naples, Italy	6 yrs.
Carlo Gambino	Palermo, Sicily	19 yrs.
Carlos Marcello (Minacore)	Tunis, N.Africa	8 months
Al Capone	Brooklyn, New York	NA
Jerry Catena	Newark, New Jersey	NA
Dutch Schultz	New York, New York	NA
Angleo Bruno	Villabe, Sicily	2 yrs.
Johnny Dio (Dioguardi)	New York, New York	NA
Carmine Galante	East Harlem, New York	NA
John Roselli (Sacco)	Esteria, Italy	6 yrs.
Peter Licavoli	St. Louis, Missouri	NA
John "Sonny" Franzese	New York, New York	NA
Anthony Spilotro	Chicago, Illinois	NA
Raymond Patriarca	Worcester, Massachusetts	NA

a. Bonanno was brought to the USA at age one, returned to Sicily at age seven and
returned to the United States at nineteen.
b. NA = Not Applicable. Born in the USA.

Evidence of assimilation into the American culture can be
seen, in part, in the numerous name changes and anglicizations
that were common. Some of this was obviously for convenience
and duplicity, but it is at least symbolically indicative of assimi-

lationist tendencies, and separation from the homeland and its culture. Maier Suchowljansky to Meyer Lansky, Francesco Castiglia to Frank Costello, Salvatore Luciana to Charles Luciano and Charles Ross, Joseph Doto to Joe Adonis, Arnold Flegenheimer to "Dutch" Schultz; these changes are acts of simplification, vanity, and cover, but all suggest assimilation, openness to adaptation, and change (Nelli, 1976; Cressey, 1969; Salerno and Tompkins, 1969; Talese, 1971; Maas, 1968). This can also be seen in the adaptations and "democratization" that occurred in the Italian-American organized crime groups after the Castellammarese War.

Salvatore Maranzano, after the murder of Joe "the Boss" Masseria, continued a rigid autocratic structure in Italian-American organized crime groups in the New York metropolitan area. The "Capo di tutti Capi" (Boss of all Bosses) was absolute ruler. There were five family Bosses beneath him: a sottocapo (underboss) beneath the boss; the capodecina, or caporegime (lieutenants) below them; and the mass of soldati (soldiers) making up the bottom tier of the pyramid, but all subject to the Boss (Cressey, 1969). This rigid authoritarian model fitted Maranzano's European background and tastes. It did not, however, fit with the attitudes and values of the young Italian-Americans he was attempting to lead. His murder, six months after he acquired leadership, brought not only young Americans, but also some Americanized "democratic" tendencies, to the leadership and organizational structure of LCN organized crime. Charles "Lucky" Luciano and his associates, first, abolished the position of Boss of all Bosses. They replaced it with a national Commission (9-12 members), which served as a quasi-judicial body and board of arbitration (Maas, 1968). The local borgata ("village-family" or "community") bosses were to be relatively autonomous within their jurisdictions, while the Commission provided this loose confederation with a communication and coordination mechanism, when needed, and a means of arbitrating differences. Thus it helped eliminate rancorous conflict and stabilized operations. It was quite similar to the "Combination," created in the 1928 Prohibition days, that Torrio,

Luciano, Lansky, and others worked with to coordinate distribution of illegal alcohol and eliminate disruptive conflicts. It was probably this loose working relationship that served as the model for the Commission. When Prohibition ended, the Commission helped to coordinate the regional and national linkages needed to maintain a lay-off book and wire systems to coordinate race track and sports gambling enterprises, and other organized crime endeavors.

The second democratizing innovation of Luciano's was the establishment of the Consigliere, or Counselor position, a practice which soon became common to all Italian-American organized crime groups (Maas, 1968). The consigliere served in two capacities. One, as an elder statesman, justifying and legitimating the executive decisions of the Boss. Thus, he acted as an internal arbitrator smoothing internal (intraorganizational) conflicts, the way the Commission acted to dampen conflict and legitimate lethal sanctions at a national level. Two, as an area or regional board or court of last resort, hearing the charges and arguments for the death of a particular soldier, before his execution could be authorized. In legitimating sanctions, removing the appearance of capricious action, smoothing differences and limiting conflict, the consigliere, like the Commission, opened the organization for discussion, the airing of grievances, communication, and at least the appearance of a democratic, fair hearing for the soldiers at the bottom of the organization, as well as among the leaders at the top. While such openness to discussion and group arbitration may not appear to be much of a democratic change, compared to the complete autocracy of the earlier Capo di tutti Capi period (when a soldier might be murdered so the Boss could take his wife) it certainly was.

The third major change that the Italian-American leaders brought to their groups was a willingness to use and associate with non-Italian criminal elements in carrying out organized crime operations. While both Masseria and Maranzano were reluctant to develop ties to non-Italian criminal associates and crime groups (although Maranzano used a non-Italian as a principal "hit man"), the Luciano group was quite open to active association with non-Italian mobsters in furthering mutual ends. Thus, the Kefauver Committee could legitimately talk of the Costello-Adonis-Lansky gambling syndicate in New York, and the Accardo-Guzik-Fishetti axis in Chicago (U.S. Justice Department, 1967).

Daniel Bell (1953), Dwight Smith (1975), and others (Hawkins, 1969) are properly skeptical of the existence of a tightly organized, singular conspiratorial group called the "Mafia." Yet, it is equally foolish to be so closed-minded as to fail to recognize that loose interactions, and associational and goal commonalities do exist among organized criminals and organized criminal groups. Certainly changes are taking place among the different organized crime groups, but this does not constitute "ethnic succession," nor a loss of the preeminent position of the Italian-American leadership among these groups. This is an area in need of long term research. The typical law enforcement conceptualizations of the major changes in LCN groups are: (a) the increased diversification into legitimate business areas, complex crime schemes, and political corruption matrices; (b) the use of multiple individual and corporate "fronts" and "buffers" staffed by non-Italian associates; (c) a shift away from "line" activities in some of the traditional crime matrices, such as drug trafficking and bookmaking, while maintaining a financing, franchising, and licensing role; (d) dispersion of blood relatives into widely diverse career paths, but always maintaining a controlling family influence in the crime side of the business; (e) increased age, death, and retirement among well-known LCN leadership; but their replacement by kin, relatives, and "greenies" from Sicily; (f) increasing use of non-Italian nonmember associates in management, professional, and high risk line activities.[3] Such changes may suggest to some that ethnic succession is taking place, but close examination of control and paper flow, particularly profits, shows the continuing premier influence of the Italian-American LCN groups.

To focus in on this we must first look to the Bell (1953) article, "The American Way of Crime," which, while dated, still represents the classic formulation of the "queer ladder of mobility" thesis. Bell (1953: 141-143) presents the argument for the Italian-American groups as follows:

> The Italian community has achieved wealth and political influence much later and in a harder way than previous immigrant groups. The Italians found the more obvious big city paths from rags to riches preempted. . . . The children of the [Italian] immigrants, the second and third generations became wise in the ways of the urban slums. Excluded from the political ladder . . . finding few open routes to wealth, some turned to illicit ways.

Here we have the basic tenets of the "queer ladder" thesis. The second half of the argument, "ethnic succession," comes about as one group replaces another on the "queer ladder" of crime, and the earlier group moves on to respectability, and legitimate status and livelihood. Thus, according to the argument, Jews replaced the Irish in crime, Italians replaced the Jews, and now the Blacks, Cubans, Puerto Ricans, and Mexicans are replacing the Italians.

This argument seems neat and facile and superficially sound, but Bell presents no hard data. Were the legitimate avenues of mobility and advancement blocked for the Italian-American immigrants? Did their "slum wise" children, frustrated by "finding few open routes to wealth," thus turn to crime?

We do not find the picture as bleak as the thesis presents, and most importantly, we do not find that those who chose the "queer ladder" did so because of frustration or because few legitimate routes to wealth were open to them. They did it because they—Luciano, Teresa, Lansky, and the others—saw in American values and culture an alternative easy, exciting, and romantic route to wealth. Namely, "something for nothing, there's a sucker born every minute," lawlessness. Plus, they were good at crime and depersonalized violence, and received peer and material reinforcement from it. Equally important, they arrived at adulthood as Prohibition began. Thus, serendipity provided opportunity, capital, and organization to routinize nationwide syndicated crime. At the time of the enactment of national Prohibition legislation, "Lucky" Luciano was 20, Vito Genovese

14   CRIMINOLOGY / MAY 1981

19, Carlo Gambino 17, Joseph Profaci 20, Al Capone 18, Thomas
Lucchese 18, Frank Costello 26. By the time it went into effect,
on January 16, 1920, other teenagers were becoming of an age
to make a name in crime: Meyer Lansky 17, Peter Licavoli 16,
Jerry Catena 17, Joe Adonis 17, Albert Anastasia 15. By March
1933, when legislation repealing Prohibition was enacted, these
teenagers had grown to manhood, and had capital, organizational skills, and influence. Prohibition and personal choice,
not career blockage or frustration with legitimate mobility paths,
provided the opportunity structure to move these small-time
hoodlums into nationally syndicated confederations of crime.

Let's look at other data. Nelli (1976: 129) cites a 1909 study
which showed:

> Today in New York City alone the estimated material value of
> the property in the Italian colonies is $120,000,000, aside from
> $100,000,000 invested by Italians in commerce, $50,000,000 in
> real estate, and $20,000,000 on deposit in the banks.

While comparative data with other groups is called for, these data
do suggest that there was considerable wealth in the Italian
colonies at that time. It is unlikely that this wealth was brought
into the United States, and so suggests that the ladder of socio-
economic opportunity for an ambitious, hardworking immigrant
was not as narrow or blocked as has been suggested.

When discussing the occurrence of the Mano Nera (Black
Hand), Nelli (1976) notes that between 1901 and 1903, extortion
gangs "reaped a harvest from hundreds of wealthy Italians," and
gives the estimated wealth of one victim, Nicola Cappiello, a
Brooklyn contractor, at $100,000. He also cites a New York
Herald article which "recounts that prominent Italian bankers,
merchants, and physicians have corroborated accounts of blackmail." Given that this was 1903, it shows the Italian colonies had
their own elite and professional leadership and suggests exaggeration when Bell (1953) says, "the Italian community achieved
wealth much later" or "the more obvious paths from rags to
riches were preempted." Nelli's (1976) analysis of Italian colonies

in the first decade of the twentieth century clearly shows that while there was much poverty and crime, the bulk of the Italian community was hardworking, seeking both education and opportunity.

Nelli (1976: 105) also notes:

> To slum area youngsters like Salvatore Lucania (Charles "Lucky" Luciano), John Torrio and Alphonse Caponi (Al Capone), excitement and economic opportunity seemed to be out in the streets rather than in the classroom. As soon as they reached the legal withdrawal age of fourteen, they left school.

As this was a period when "education began to emerge as an increasingly important qualification for . . . employment," we can only interpret "economic opportunity" to mean criminal or delinquent activity. Lucky Luciano worked at a "straight" job approximately one week before deciding work was for "crumbs" and chose life in the pool halls and street gangs, taking and pushing drugs instead. As Nelli (1976: 106) states:

> Unlike most of their contemporaries, who also belonged to street gangs and were involved in occasional mischief-making, the criminals-in-the-making had little or nothing to do with legitimate labor, which they believed was only for "suckers," men who worked long hours for low play and lived in overcrowded tenements with their families.

This picture of the opportunity pattern and choices sounds somewhat different than the "queer ladder" thesis. Yes, some turned to crime, but not from frustration, or any long struggle of being excluded from the political ladder, or blocked from avenues for advancement. They turned to crime because they felt the legitimate opportunity structure was for "suckers."

They were "wiseguys"—a term still used to denote organized crime soldiers—and could make an easy buck without working. They could have economic mobility without ever climbing the status ladder. Their choice was an individual decision, a self-choice, reinforced by peers, experience, and a talent for violence. They were not more frustrated, nor deprived (relatively or ab-

solutely), than their classroom peers and fellow street gang
members who chose to be "straights" and "suckers," following
the legitimate socioeconomic mobility ladder, narrow and
crowded as it may have been.

Meyer Lansky, for example, graduated from eight grade, and
was a promising apprentice tool and die maker, running crap
games on the side. He then decided to become an automobile
mechanic, stealing and altering cars and trucks for thieves, and,
with Prohibition, entered the alcohol hauling and hijacking business. His opportunity path in the legitimate world was never
blocked or frustrated, he simply preferred the "fast track" of
crime (Messick, 1971) to the less exciting and, for him, less remunerative legitimate world of work.

The second half of the thesis is the concept of "ethnic succession." In order for this to take place, the group that has been
successful in crime must leave it and be replaced by some new
immigrant group that is lower on the status ladder. The model
assumes that with increased wealth, the organized criminal will
move into the legitimate sector of the economy and his children
will live lives of honesty and respectability. The basic assumtion
(Bell, 1953: 147-150) is that the organized criminal desired respectability all along:

> Yet it was, oddly enough the quondam racketeer, seeking to
> become respectable, who provided one of the major supports for
> a drive to win a political voice for Italians. . . .
>
> The early Italian gangsters were hoodlums—rough unlettered
> and young (Al Capone was only twenty-nine at the height of his
> power). Those who survived learned to adapt. By now they are
> men of middle age or older. They learned to dress conservatively.
> Their homes are in respectable suburbs. They sent their children
> to good schools and had sought to avoid publicity.
>
> As happens with all "new" money in American society the . . .
> racketeers polished up their manners and sought recognition and
> respectability in their own ethnic community.
>
> Many of the top "crime" figures long ago had forsworn violence,
> and even their income, in large part, was derived from legitimate
> investments . . . or from such quasi-legitimate but socially accept-
> able sources as gambling casinos.

These statements are all from Bell's classic article, yet today they seem naive.

Of course organized criminals bought homes in respectable suburbs and sent their children to good schools. Such actions are common to anyone of affluence in our society, criminal or college professor. That they dressed conservatively and avoided publicity likewise tells us nothing about either their respectability or having left crime. Such comments focus on the trappings and appearance of a noncriminal lifestyle, they show nothing of the substance. These comments also seem to reflect little understanding of the use of "fronts," "buffers," and political connections for criminal purposes.

Did Costello and others in organized crime seek political links with Franklin Roosevelt, Huey Long, Tammany leader James Hines, Mayor Jimmie Walker, and numerous judges and political appointees because they were seeking respectability, or because they understood, as did Paul Kelly and Arnold Rothstein before them, that it was useful to have friends in high places? Nelli (1976) notes that at the 1932 Democratic Convention Costello shared a suite with Tammany leader James Hines, and Luciano shared one with Albert Marinelli (leader of New York's Second Assembly District). This arrangement was not based on some "quondam racketeer's" desire for respectability; it was mainly business. Nelli (1976: 195) puts it this way: "This sharing of quarters was of symbolic as well as practical significance for it demonstrated that criminal syndicate leaders from New York had achieved . . . power and influence equal to that of local party bosses."

Bell himself (1953) notes that Tammany Hall had to turn to Costello and others for support and funds, yet he does not note the evidence in the court trial of James Hines, in the Marinelli resignation, as well as in the movement of slot machines to Long's Louisiana, that these were business trade-offs and that status or respectability was not the main consideration. Some search for respectability cannot entirely be discounted. Frank Costello's attempt to hire a public relations man, and pressure from wives, particularly as intermarriage across ethnic lines occurs, must be noted. This is another area of much needed research.

18   CRIMINOLOGY / MAY 1981

The use of business "fronts" as laundries to wash illegally gained wealth, and for purposes of creating a basis for taxable income, as well as the penetration of legitimate business by organized crime has been well documented (Bers, 1970; Kwitny, 1979). The use of gambling casinos to skim millions of dollars in cash, as well as fronts for acts of corruption and blackmail is also well documented and is a common reason for organized crime's interest and hidden ownership in such enterprises (Reid and Demaris, 1963; Messick, 1971). Perhaps these facts were not widely known in 1953, but they are today, and they suggest goals other than respectability.

If the ethnic succession thesis is to stand the test of evidence, we must find: (a) Italian organized crime figures who, once they had economic status, sought social status by getting out of the business of crime; or (b) that intergenerationally the sons, nephews, and relations of organized crime figures are not entering the business of crime; or (c) that the new ethnic groups— Black, Mexican, Puerto Rican—are succeeding not only to control crime markets that the LCN groups have discarded as having poor risk-to-profit ratios, such as prostitution or street level narcotics dealing and bookmaking, but that they are moving up to positions of real influence. In short, if the ethnic succession model is working, we must be able to show that Italian-American organized criminals are leaving the business of crime, and not simply using their capital and influence to buffer themselves while they license and franchise the new ethnics in the high risk-lower profit aspects of the business.

To do a proper empirical study to prove, or disprove, this is very difficult. The needed data is hard to collect; it is scattered and fragmentary. A proper study will take years of effort, but the initial work is underway. In the meantime, enough bits and pieces of data are around to suggest that ethnic succession is not taking place. New elites are emerging, particularly in the high risk crime markets (Ianni, 1974b). New ethnics are forming successful crime elites within their own ethnic communities, and in the street level retailing of crime. The part of the proposition that remains to be proven is that the Italian organized criminal families who chose the business of crime early in this century are giving up their premier positions and choosing legitimate lifestyles and revenue sources—not as fronts and laundries—instead of crime. We do not find that ethnic succession has been proven on this latter point.

One can show the increased age of Italian organized crime figures, the problems of recruitment, and promotion of "the best and the brightest" of relatives in the family (Lupsha, 1979). Yet, disturbing contrary evidence and data remains, and suggests that the Italian groups are not giving up control, they are simply engaging in wider use of non-Italian criminal associates, entering new and more complex crime matrices, and licensing the new ethnics to operate the more traditional, more risky, and lower profit organized crime markets. Let us briefly turn to this, before concluding.

First, what evidence is there that any of the major leaders of Italian American organized crime have made an obvious break with the past, to live a life outside of crime? There appears to be very little. Frank Costello retired after being shot, but simply lived off the proceeds of his earlier life, as did John Torrio. Meyer Lansky and Joseph Bonanno claim to be in retirement, yet information regularly surfaces to suggest they are still active in controlling their interests in criminal enterprises. Recent FBI searches of Bonanno's Tucson home confirm this. Meanwhile, a 1978 New Jersey Department of Law and Public Safety report cites Lansky interests in the development of Resorts International Inc., the Atlantic City Casino Company (New Jersey Department of Law and Public Safety, 1978). Tony Accardo lives in retirement in Palm Springs, as Moe Dalitz does at "La Costa" in California; both, however, maintain active contacts with Las Vegas, Chicago, the Teamster pension fund, and other organized crime interests and personalities. In all we find little evidence of people leaving successful careers in organized crime except when death intervenes. Second, what evidence is there that children and relatives of Italian-American organized crime figures are getting out of the business? While there is evidence that some of the children and relatives choose not to follow the criminal side of family business, there appears to be equal evidence that a sufficient number of family members and relatives do stay in the business that family control is maintained.

The Kansas City "Family" of Nick Civella, which in 1980 is an active and aggressive organized crime family, for example, has the ongoing participation of a brother, Carl "Corky" Civella, a nephew, Anthony Civella, relatives by marriage, and another nephew, Anthony Chiavola, a Chicago police lieutenant who hosted meetings for Chicago crime boss Joseph Aiuppa and Nick Civella (Federal Bureau of Investigation, 1979). This was not a social meeting; it involved organized crime group interests in Las Vegas, Teamster pension fund loans, and skimming of casinos. Joseph Bonanno's sons Salvatore (Bill) and Joe, Jr., both currently in prison, appear to be following in the family tradition. Carmine Galante was chauffeured by his nephew, James, the day he was murdered in Brooklyn (July 12, 1979). Johnny Dio was the nephew of James "Jimmy Doyle" Plumeri, and Dio's brother, Thomas, is still active in the business. Carlo Gambino's relatives, Paul Castellano and Joseph Gambino, Jr., have not separated themselves from the family's past activities; nor has Anthony Zerrilli, son of the late Detroit Don, who in 1972 was convicted in a Las Vegas skim and hidden ownership. So where are we? There is evidence that some of the children leave the family business. There is other evidence that enough remain in the business to maintain, manage, and control it. The answer is we need more data and more research. However, for now we can say there is no clear empirical evidence that the Italian families who became active in organized crime early in this century have left the business. Perhaps one reason for this has to do with our material culture and the way we handle inheritance of legitimate versus illegitimate fortunes. Annelise Anderson (1979) suggests this as a proposition relating to organized crime penetrations of legitimate economic sectors and organizational continuity. It deserves further thought and research.

What is American about American organized crime? Precisely that it is such a reflection of American economic and political institutions. Bell (1953) has noted the parallel between the "robber barons" of business and the early organized crime entrepreneurs, and the way organized crime, like business, has moved from production to consumer services, although one could argue the specifics of this point. He did note that, like the corporation—moving from direct family participation in all phases of the enterprise to indirect, diversified manager control—organized crime has evolved into a similar buffered position where the organized crime family can sit on the Board and still control the company, without dirtying their hands in the line tasks. Are the Italian-Americans, or the members of any other ethnic group who have made millions in organized crime, going to abandon this queer, but successful, ladder of economic success? Given our thesis that organized crime in America is deeply imbedded in our Lockeian values and beliefs, we can predict this will occur when the Rockefellers give up their interest in banking and Standard Oil; the Mellons their interest in Gulf Oil; and all others who have gained a dominant place in our socioeconomic system willing to step aside for new elites. The new ethnics have a rung of the "queer ladder of crime" to stand on. They have the dirty, dangerous line jobs in crime, the less profitable and higher risk crime markets, they even have some limited autonomy within their own communities and enclaves, but it is doubtful that the old elites of organized crime will simply give them their empire.

In making these observations about the implications of the general American culture, its values, and attitudes, we do not mean to ignore or deny that ethnic, racial, and religious factors also influence organized crime groups. These groups depend on trust and loyalty to operate and survive. Cultural bases for that trusts are usually in the primary "blood" culture, not the overall social, political, and economic culture. Thus for Italian-American, Mexican-American, and Chinese-American organized crime groups, kinship patterns, place of family origin, and birth are important factors. For Black-Americans and WASP-Americans engaged in organized crime, racial ties, prison association, neighborhood and cohort associations are important. These cultural factors affect organizational life, as does the overall social, economic, and political values of the culture. By choosing to emphasize the latter in this article, we in no way intended to dismiss the former.

To sum up, in this essay we have attempted to look at what is American about American crime by focusing on the evolution of organized crime, and particularly Italian-American organized crime groups. We have argued that organized crime is rooted in our values and culture, and that its development mirrors our economic and political institutions. Rather than being a forced option because of limited choice or opportunities for mobility, it is a chosen career path, a rational choice, rooted in one perverse aspect of our values: namely, that only "suckers" work, and that in our society, one is at liberty to take "suckers" and seek easy money, just as one is at liberty to be one. Like American values, organized crime is flexible, practical, and adaptive. It is an American institution, not a Sicilian by-product. It has moved from prostitution to pornography in film and home video cassettes as smoothly as our technology and corporations. Like corporate evolution it has evolved into a diversified multinational conglomerate, franchising criminal markets and firms. In a society that has always had a place for lawlessness, sharp practice, easy money, a disdain for suckers, and an idolatry of mammon and lucre, organized crime is as American as McDonald's.

NOTES

1. Definitions of organized crime range widely from Frank Hogan's dictum that organized crime consists "of two or more persons engaged in criminal activity," to the State of California's inclusion of prison gangs and terrorist groups. The author's own working definition is as follows: Organized crime consists of activity by a group of individuals who consciously develop roles and specializations, patterns of interaction, spheres of responsibility and accountability, and who, with continuity over time, engage in a variety of illegal and illicit endeavors (enterprises) involving the use of large amounts of capital, nonmember associates, and the corruption of public officials and their agents, directed toward the achievement of greater capital accumulation in the form of untaxed

monies and goods of value which are then processed through legitimate "fronts" and "buffers" to "launder" this black income into white (legitimate economic) earnings.

2. The purpose of this table is to reinforce the view of nonlinear development stated by Smith and Alba (1979) and to set down some facts about major Italian-American reputed organized crime figures. Facts are badly needed to construct testable hypotheses and propositions. This table is based on data that the author was able to uncover. It is non-random material that I came across in research work. This search for three simple facts— (a) dates of birth; (b) place of birth; (c) approximate year of arrival in the United States so entry socialization age could be computed—took more than four and one-half months of searching.

3. It is important to recognize that these statements are, for the most part, propositions that have only fragmentary verification, and badly need empirical testing on a large enough data base as to allow hard confirmation.

REFERENCES

ANDERSON, A. G. (1979) The Business of Organized Crime. Stanford, CA: Hoover Institution Press.

BELL, D. (1953) "Crime as an American way of life." Antioch Rev. 13 (Summer): 131-154.

BERS, M. (1970) The Penetration of Legitimate Business by Organized Crime. Washington, DC: U.S. Government Printing Office.

CORDESCO, B. (1977) "The Golden Dragon Labor Day massacre." New Times (October 28).

CRESSEY, D. (1972) Criminal Organization: Its Elementary Forms. New York: Harper & Row.

——— (1969) Theft of the Nation. New York: Harper & Row.

Federal Bureau of Investigation (1979) Affidavits for Kansas City wiretaps—23 volumes transcript. Released Kansas City, MO. (Xerox)

HAWKINS, G. (1969) "God and the Mafia." Public Interest 14 (Winter): 24-51.

IANNI, F.A.J. (1978) Ethnic Succession in Organized Crime: Summary Report. Washington, DC: National Institute of Law Enforcement and Criminal Justice.

——— (1974a) "New Mafia: Black, Hispanic and Italian styles." Society 2 (March-April): 23-36.

——— (1974b) Black Mafia: Ethnic Succession in Organized Crime. New York: Simon & Schuster.

——— (1972) A Family Business. New York: Russell Sage.

KWITNY, J. (1979) Vicious Circles: The Mafia in the Marketplace. New York: Norton.

LANDESCO, J. (1929) Organized Crime in Chicago. Part III, The Illinois Crime Survey. Reprinted Chicago: The Univ. of Chicago Press.

LIGHT, I. (1974) "From vice district to tourist attraction: the moral career of American Chinatowns, 1880-1940." Pacific Historical Rev. 43: 367-394.

LUPSHA, P. (1980) "American values and organized crime: suckers and wiseguys," in S. Girgus (ed.) Myth, Popular Culture and American Ideology. Albuquerque: Univ. of New Mexico Press.

24   CRIMINOLOGY / MAY 1981

——— (1979) "Mobs and myths: a requiem for La Cosa Nostra?" Presented at the Western Social Science Association, Lake Tahoe, CA.

——— and K. SCHLEGEL (1979) "The political economy of drug trafficking: the Herrera organization (Mexico and the United States)." Presented at the Latin American Studies Association, Philadelphia.

MAAS, P. (1968) The Valachi Papers. New York. G. P. Putnam.

MESSICK, H. (1971) Lansky. New York: G. P. Putnam.

NELLI, H. (1976) The Business of Crime. New York: Oxford Univ. Press.

New Jersey Department of Law and Public Safety (1978) Report to the Casino Control Commission with Reference to the Casino License Application of Resorts International Hotel, Inc. Trenton, NJ: Division of Gaming Enforcement.

REID, E. and O. DEMARIS (1963) The Green Felt Jungle. New York: Trident Press.

SALERNO, R. and J. S. TOMPKINS (1969) The Crime Confederation. New York: Popular Library.

SCHELLING, T. (1967) "Economic analysis of organized crime." Appendix D. Organized Crime Task Force Report. Washington, DC: President's Commission on Law Enforcement and Organized Crime.

SMITH, D. C., Jr. (forthcoming) "Paragons, pariahs, and pirates: a spectrum-based theory of enterprise." Crime and Delinquency.

——— (1978) "Organized crime and entrepreneurship." J. of Criminology and Penology 6 (May): 161-177.

——— (1975) The Mafia Mystique. New York: Basic Books.

——— and R. ALBA (1979) "Organized crime and American life." Society 16 (March-April): 32-38.

TALESE, G. (1971) Honor Thy Father. New York: World Publishing.

TERESA, V. (1973) My Life in the Mafia. Greenwich, CT: Fawcett Publications.

THRASHER, F. M. (1927) The Gang. A Study of 1,313 Gangs in Chicago. Chicago: The Univ. of Chicago Press.

TYLER, G. (1971) "Sociodynamics of organized crime." J. of Public Law 20, 3: 487-498.

——— (ed.) (1962) Organized Crime in America. Ann Arbor: Univ. of Michigan Press.

U.S. Justice Department (1967) Task Force Report: Organized Crime. Appendix A: 25-60. Washington, DC: U.S. Government Printing Office.

U.S. Senate (1965) Organized Crime and the Illicit Traffic in Narcotics. 89th Congress, 1st Session. Washington, DC: U.S. Government Printing Office.

VOLZ, J. and P. J. BRIDGE (1969) The Mafia Talks. Greenwich, CT: Fawcett Publications.

ZEIGER, H. A. (1975) The Jersey Mob. New York: Signet.

Peter A. Lupsha is an Associate Professor of Political Science at the University of New Mexico—Albuquerque. He teaches Political Corruption and Organized Crime, is working on a book, Organized Crime in America: A Text and Analysis (Prentice-Hall, forthcoming), and is engaged in research on organized crime in the Southwest. He is consultant to the Governor's Organized Crime Prevention Commission in New Mexico. He would appreciate opportunities for correspondence with anyone interested in organized crime research.

[7]

Paragons, Pariahs, and Pirates:
A Spectrum-Based Theory of Enterprise

Dwight C. Smith, Jr.

Americans have traditionally treated white-collar crime and organized crime as if they were two independent phenomena, but there is a growing awareness that they may not be that distinct and that a better appreciation of both problems would be possible if we had a single conceptual perspective through which to view them. Our alien conspiracy notions about organized crime are a major barrier to that understanding; they proceed from five underlying assumptions about the differences between business and crime. If instead of those differences we recognize a common thread of enterprise, and understand that it takes place across a spectrum including legal and criminal businesses, then a single, unifying perspective can take shape. The distinctions along that spectrum are exemplified by three kinds of businessmen: the paragon, the pariah, and the pirate.

The original paradigm of white-collar crime was Edwin Sutherland's theory of differential association, an effort to explain both white-collar and lower-class criminality by an overarching concept. The two forms of criminality were of similar character, Sutherland argued, and differed from each other primarily in how criminal laws were enforced against them. His theory was intended to supplant other theories of crime causation (especially those maintaining that poverty or psychopathic or sociopathic conditions were the primary causes), which were based on invalid samples (i.e., they excluded the white-collar class) and did not, in any event, fully explain the lower-class crime at which they were directed. Subsequent research, however, focused on differential association in other settings, and not on white-collar crime, perhaps because Sutherland himself had never precisely defined white-collar crime. It is not a particular crime, nor is there a cluster of crimes with which it could be linked, as organized crime has been linked with narcotics, gambling, and loansharking. This lack of specificity is illustrated by Donald Newman's later observation that the primary criterion of white-collar crime is simply that "it occurs as a part of, or a deviation from, the violator's occupational role."[1] There is no etiological explanation of white-collar crime; standard methods of correlative research have not been useful; information is fragmentary, impressionistic, and seldom available. But operat-

---

DWIGHT C. SMITH, JR.: Associate Professor, School of Criminal Justice, Rutgers University, Newark, New Jersey.

1. Donald H. Newman, "White-Collar Crime: An Overview and Analysis," *Law and Contemporary Problems*, Autumn 1958, p. 737.

A Spectrum-Based Theory of Enterprise   359

ing "on the pragmatic view that everybody pretty much knows what is meant by white-collar crime,"[2] research has proceeded in near-random fashion, directed at a wide range of targets, including corporations, businesses, commercial activities, the professions, and politics. This pragmatic focus has allowed work to be done, but its lack of rigorous definition has hampered cumulative, integrated research—which, in turn, has hampered an effective public response. Some definitional advances have been made, but little new theory has been proposed in the last decade.

The prevailing paradigm of organized crime, on the other hand, is based on an assumption about the alien nature of crime groups and their sole responsibility for the existence of organized crime. This assumption is best expressed by reference to "Mafia" and "Cosa Nostra." Its exemplars rely heavily on the 1963 testimony of Joseph Valachi, reinforced in 1969 and 1970 by publication of the so-called De Cavalcante and De Carlo transcripts. It should be noted that this is not the paradigm presented by John Landesco and Frederick Thrasher when they discussed organized crime in the late 1920s. Rather than an alien phenomenon, they perceived a social and economic structure in which the gangster emerged as "a product of his surroundings in the same way in which the good citizen is a product of his environment."[3] Little subsequent research was undertaken to pursue that clue, however, and their conclusions regarding the indigenous nature of organized crime dropped from view. When organized crime reappeared in 1944 as a topic of public attention, it was as an alien phenomenon, associated particularly with drug smuggling, and that assumption has remained paramount.[4] Its elaboration a decade ago, by the President's Crime Commission in 1967 and by Donald Cressey in 1969, has been the formal base for subsequent theory, research, and public policy.[5]

There is a growing sense that organized and white-collar crime are not that distinct, and that parallel, separate theoretical approaches are inadequate for continued research and subsequent public policy.[6] Questions as to theory have been evident in academic research for some time. The limitations of

2. Gilbert Geis and Robert F. Meier, eds., *White-Collar Crime: Offenses in Business, Politics, and the Professions*, 2d ed. (New York: Free Press, 1977), p. 254.

3. John Landesco, "Organized Crime in Chicago," Part III, in Illinois Association for Criminal Justice, *Illinois Crime Survey* (Chicago: IACJ, 1929), p. 1057; see also Frederick M. Thrasher, *The Gang* (Chicago: University of Chicago Press, 1927), esp. pp. 409–51.

4. For an extended analysis of the narcotics-focused roots of organized crime theory, see Dwight C. Smith, Jr., *The Mafia Mystique* (New York: Basic Books, 1975), pp. 121–27.

5. President's Commission on Law Enforcement and Administration of Justice, *Task Force Report: Organized Crime* (Washington, D.C.: Govt. Printing Office, 1967); and Donald R. Cressey, *Theft of the Nation: The Structure and Operations of Organized Crime in America* (New York: Harper & Row, 1969).

6. It is not a new idea; even Sutherland made the connection in 1948, observing, "Businessmen . . . are participants in organized crime." See "Crime of Corporations," in *The Sutherland Papers*, Albert Cohen, Alfred Lindesmith, and Karl Schuessler, eds. (Bloomington: Indiana University Press, 1956), p. 96. He meant the connection as Landesco had before him, but he did not pursue the point.

white-collar crime theory have been voiced almost from its origins. Although Gilbert Geis and Robert Meier concluded recently that a clearer conceptual base is developing, they add that "there is a pressing need for accumulation of case studies, for hypothesis development and testing, and for the kind of research that moves forward by careful, additive processes."[7] There is also growing evidence of decreasing confidence in (and decreasing reliance upon) existing organized crime theory. These concerns have been reflected to a limited extent in recent government investigations, although they remain largely the property of investigators from outside law enforcement. But, despite the new element of doubt, existing theory is still dominant in some quarters, as evidenced by the 1976 report of the National Gambling Commission.[8] Still, the General Accounting Office showed in its 1977 report that within the Justice Department there is a clear absence of consensus on the fundamental question of a definition of organized crime, making control programs less effective.[9]

With particular reference to organized crime theory but with obvious implications for white-collar crime theory as well, there is an increasing belief that there are significant limits to prevailing paradigms, that their anomalies are growing in number and importance, and that the necessity of better explanations requires development of a new and wider conceptual base. That wider base is clearly interdisciplinary in its potential, making use of knowledge from sociology, history, business, psychology, and economics. Its economic aspects are most evident at the present time; the common thread in current research, around which a new paradigm appears to be forming (as a substitute for both differential association and the alien phenomenon paradigm) is the effort to relate concepts of enterprise and entrepreneurship to existing knowledge about crime. The potential significance of a firm theoretical relationship is best indicated by the policy shift inherent in former Attorney General Bell's comment that organized crime investigations of the Justice Department "would in the future concentrate on activities *in a particular industry or enterprise* and [would] move away from the practice of picking syndicate families or individuals as targets" (emphasis added),[10] and implicitly reaffirmed in Assistant Attorney General Philip Heymann's recent comment that the Justice Department was now "trying to focus on the type of crime committed rather than worrying about the name of the organization involved."[11]

7. Geis and Meier, *White-Collar Crime*, p. 4.

8. U.S. Commission on the Review of the National Policy toward Gambling, *Gambling in America* (Washington, D.C.: Govt. Printing Office, 1967), p. 171.

9. General Accounting Office, "War on Organized Crime Faltering—Federal Strike Forces Not Getting the Job Done," in *Comptroller General's Report to the Congress* (Mar. 17, 1977).

10. Nicholas M. Horrock, "Government to Mount an Attack on Organized Crime," *New York Times*, Oct. 5, 1977, p. A25.

11. "Justice Dept. Reports 'Impact' on Organized Crime," *New York Times*, Dec. 19, 1979, p. A13.

The phenomena of organized and white-collar crime deserve a more sustained and active program of empirical research. The absence of an adequate theoretical base is an important barrier to it. As Daniel Glaser noted earlier in this decade, "The primary cause of a poor yield from criminal justice research . . . is more often a poverty of theory than of methodological skills."[12] If the ordinary course of theoretical development in the social sciences were to be followed, a number of researchers would continue to work relatively independently, using their own slightly varying conceptual models to pursue particular lines of substantive inquiry. In time, their findings might suggest the potential of a wider body of formal theory that could be derived from their separate studies, though the variances of original conceptual models might create barriers to the integrative process. It is a slow-paced process, but it is also the inevitable process unless a deliberate effort is made to pursue the wider theory itself. Without it, studies that could (and should, for their ultimate value to public policy) be more structured and interrelated will continue to develop slowly, erratically, and independently.

As a mechanism for initiating and stimulating a more focused discussion and debate, a tentative conceptual approach to a spectrum-based theory of enterprise is set forth here.

THE ALIEN CONSPIRACY PERSPECTIVE

The significance and implications of an enterprise perspective will become clearer if some attention is given first to the context in which the alien conspiracy perspective emerged. As it took shape in the mid- to late 1960s, that perspective was molded by some assumptions about crime and business that had nothing to do with organized crime, but which set some basic understandings about commercial life and economic activity in general. Five assumptions have been particularly important in that process: that business and crime are distinct, and totally separate, categories of behavior; that business is most appropriately understood in terms that encompass legitimate and legal products or services; that beyond such product classification, size and ownership are the major distinctions within business (which is to suggest by their omission that shades of legality and legitimacy are not); that the professionally managed corporation is the predominant model of business; and that if any area of criminal activity is to be seen as the equivalent of business, the structure of the professionally managed corporation will provide the most useful parallels. To be sure, these assumptions have begun to erode in some circles, particularly over the last decade, as the anomalies of organized crime theory began to surface to plague the alien conspiracy perspective. Some important research on the criminal firm has been done by persons whose underlying

12. Daniel Glaser, "The State of the Art of Criminal Justice Evaluation" (Keynote speech at the second annual meeting of the Association for Criminal Justice Research, Los Angeles, Nov. 9, 1973).

perspective has been that of the business community: the initial work of
Thomas Schelling on "Economic Analysis and Organized Crime" for the
Crime Commission; the dissertations of John Seidl and Louis Gasper on the
illegal markets of loansharking and cigarette bootlegging, respectively; the
recently published dissertation of Annelise Anderson on the economics of a
particular conspiratorial group; and the gambling study of Peter Reuter and
Jonathan Rubinstein.[13] Their insights have gone well beyond the alien conspiracy view, but their business colleagues are few and tend in their work to
show that there is a considerable difference between the ability to manipulate
old tools in new workshops—as when the economist's techniques are applied
to traditional views of crime—and the ability to think in new ways about old
problems. The assumptions of the 1960s about business and crime remain
strong. If an enterprise perspective is to emerge, the prior assumptions themselves must be challenged.

Assumption: Business and Crime Are Distinct Categories

Business theorists and criminologists traditionally have worked and studied
independently. For example, there is no such category in business literature
(excepting the few studies just mentioned) as the theory of the criminal firm.
One of the major historical business journals, *Explorations in Entrepreneurial
History*, published 250 articles from 1963 to 1976 on enterprise in its historical setting; not one of them even hints at the existence of enterprise in an
illegal market. When business schools offer courses in business ethics, they
are most likely to cover bribery, corporate spying, and price fixing as dysfunctional aberrations from the model of business as a legal activity.

Criminologists might like to think they are more broad-minded, but even
when they have looked at criminal activity in the business sphere it has been
as a distinctive category not to be confused with crime in general, or with
general business practices. Attempts to classify white-collar crime as criminality (beginning with Sutherland's original argument in 1940) have been limited to the assumption that the perpetrator is "a businessman who went
wrong." Even when Marshall Clinard and Richard Quinney described organized crime as "business enterprises organized for the purpose of making
economic gain through illegal activities"[14] and implied that such a meaning
was common among criminologists, they classified it as one category in a

13. Thomas C. Schelling, "Economic Analysis and Organized Crime," in President's Commis-
sion, *Organized Crime*, pp. 114–26; John M. Seidl, "Upon the Hip—A Study of the Criminal
Loanshark Industry" (Ph.D. diss., Harvard University, 1968); Louis C. Gasper, "Organized
Crime: An Economic Analysis" (Ph.D. diss., Duke University, 1969); Annelise G. Anderson, *The
Business of Organized Crime: A Cosa Nostra Family* (Stanford, Calif.: Hoover Institution Press,
1979); and Peter Reuter and Jonathan Rubinstein, "Fact, Fancy and Organized Crime," *Public
Interest* (1978), pp. 45–67.

14. Marshall B. Clinard and Richard Quinney, *Criminal Behavior Systems: A Typology* (New
York: Holt, Rinehart and Winston, 1967), p. 382.

typology of crime, not one of business. Until the 1970s, the only notable exception to this general tendency was Landesco's 1929 analysis, "Organized Crime in Chicago," in which he described organized crime as the manner in which the cooperative arrangements of good citizens, characterized as business enterprises, were mirrored in the life of the gangster; but his study went out of print within a year and was forgotten or ignored until it was revived in the late 1960s. Partly because of that revival, the past decade has seen increased interest in the concept of crime as business.[15] There are signs—more from criminologists than from business theorists—that some theoretical links are not only desirable but also necessary in order to remove the anomalies that an alien conspiracy approach cannot handle. Nevertheless, despite occasional cynicism about business, the prevailing sense among both criminal justice practitioners and the general public remains close to that of the mid-1960s— that business and crime come from entirely separate and incommensurable roots.

Assumption: Business Is Best Described by the Labels of Legal Undertakings

The generally accepted taxonomy of business is detailed in the federal government's *Standard Industrial Classification (SIC) Manual*, the most recent edition of which was published in 1972.[16] The manual begins by asserting that it "is intended to cover the entire field of economic activities. . . ." Ten major categories are identified (plus a "nonclassifiable" catchall), from agriculture, forestry, and fishing to public administration; these categories are divided again into ninety-four major groups which are, in turn, subdivided more finely into specific industries or fields. The descriptions in each case are exclusively those of legitimate undertakings. To illustrate: Category H, finance, insurance, and real estate, includes eight major groups, one of which (Code 61) is "credit agencies other than banks." Its definition instructs the user that "this major group includes establishments engaged in extending credit in the form of loans but not engaged in deposit banking," and then lists six subgroups, including "personal credit institutions" (Code 614), which consists of "establishments primarily engaged in extending credit to individuals," and "business credit institutions" (Code 615), consisting of "establishments primarily engaged in making loans to business enterprises." Among

15. See, for example, Francis A. Ianni, *A Family Business: Kinship and Social Control in Organized Crime* (New York: Russell Sage Foundation, 1972); Humbert S. Nelli, *The Business of Crime* (New York: Oxford University Press, 1976); Marilyn E. Walsh, *The Fence: A New Look at the World of Property Theft* (Westport, Conn.: Greenwood Press, 1977); Ivan T. Light, "The Ethnic Vice Industry, 1880–1944," *American Sociological Review* (1977), pp. 464–79; and Peter K. Manning, "Resources, Information and Strategy: The Open Systems Perspective on Narcotics Law Enforcement" (1977, unpub.).

16. United States Bureau of the Budget, *Standard Industrial Classification Manual* (Washington, D.C.: Govt. Printing Office, 1972).

the eight industries specified within these two subgroups, thirty-three distinct kinds of establishments are listed, including licensed small lenders, personal finance companies, factors, and purchasers of accounts receivable—but nowhere is there mention of a loanshark. Or take Category G, retail trade, which also includes eight major groups. The final group, "miscellaneous retail" (Code 59), includes an activity (593) "used merchandise stores," which includes a single industry code, 5931. The manual lists twenty-three establishments, including second-hand stores of wide variety and pawnshops—but not a fence.[17]

It is obvious that the SIC taxonomy could be used to denote illegal business activities, if one wished to expand its descriptors. "Loanshark" could be an establishment within either personal or business credit institutions, and "fence" could be an alternative kind of used merchandise store. It is also clear, however, that the designers of the SIC manual had only legitimate businesses in mind. "Establishment," as the entity through which economic activity takes place, may be the critical semantic turning point, as it conveys strong overtones of institutional authority and sanction. An industry is recognized in the manual if its collection of establishments is "statistically significant in the number of persons employed, the volume of business done, and other measures of economic activity."[18] An establishment within an industry is defined as "an economic unit, generally at a single physical location where business is conducted or where services or industrial operations are performed."[19] It need not be large or commercially significant ("singing societies" is an example of an establishment within the industry, Code 8641, of "civic, social, and fraternal organizations"), and thus the only reason for excluding the fence and loanshark, among other illegal businesses, is that they are not sanctioned or licensed—"established." If what we are told about the power and scope of organized crime is true, however, then the SIC manual should either list its establishments or admit that the taxonomy is intended to cover *only legitimate* economic activities. Meanwhile, the metaphors of business serve to reinforce the conceptual distinction between business and crime.

*Assumption: Within an Industrial Classification,
the Principal Distinctions Are Size and Ownership*

The SIC manual does not distinguish among establishments beyond its taxonomy by product or service. Implicit in our general understanding of business, however, is the expectation that within an industry the principal distinc-

17. For those particularly interested in organized crime, Major Group 86, "membership organizations," includes "organizations operating on a membership basis for the promotion of the interests of its [sic] members." Its seven groups range from business, professional, and labor through civic, political, and religious—and even a group of organizations "not elsewhere classified"—but its fifty-eight establishment examples do not include La Cosa Nostra.
18. Bureau of the Budget, *Standard Industrial Classification Manual*, p. 9.
19. Ibid., p. 10.

tions are size and ownership. An enterprise may be a small business, in which case it is eligible for certain tax and financing benefits; otherwise it is Big Business. It may be publicly or privately owned, it may be a partnership or a corporation, it may be a government-run business, or it may have some mixed form of ownership. But once the product or service of the industry has been specified, and its ownership and size described, there is no further distinction regarding the manner in which the business is organized and managed. That is to say, a continuum of legality is not acknowledged—the descriptor "legal" is always implicit and always unequivocal. That some firms may be more willing, say, to engage in marginally deceptive advertising, or that some establishments or industries may be more vulnerable to cutting corners or legal hairsplitting (one's attention is drawn quickly within the manual to burlesque companies, racetrack operations, and shooting galleries, all of which are establishments within Major Group 79, "amusement and recreation services except motion pictures") is of no concern to systems that classify businesses.

Assumption: Business = the Professionally Managed Corporation

In the mid-twentieth century, the ultimate dominant force within the "capitalist engine" was perceived to be the large corporation. The entrepreneur, who had been the mainspring of classic capitalism, would be swallowed up because the large corporation had such a natural superiority in organization and capitalization. The entrepreneurial function would inevitably be taken over by the salaried staffs of research and development units; innovation would become routine. Joseph Schumpeter forecast this state of affairs in *Capitalism, Socialism and Democracy*,[20] and his and others' Darwinian analyses of natural selection and survival of the fittest in the marketplace had a major influence on the way business was perceived until around the mid-1960s. As Edwin Harwood wrote recently,

> By the time *Capitalism, Socialism and Democracy* was published (1942), the large bureaucratic corporation had truly come into its own. As the new institutional reality on the American economic scene, it could easily be assumed to be the dominant reality. It had revolutionalized methods of production and had also broken new ground in the fields of marketing and distribution. One is reminded in this connection of the marketing superiority of General Motors under professional management over the Ford Motor Company which, though also a large firm, was trapped by the idiosyncracies of its entrepreneur-founder, Henry Ford, and as a result suffered losses in market share during the 1930s and 1940s. Also, the beginning of corporate research and development, an organizational innovation of Thomas Edison's, had undoubtedly strengthened corporate balance sheets and earning statements. Thus, the corporate monoliths of the 1930s seemed well-nigh invulnerable.[21]

20. Joseph Schumpeter, *Capitalism, Socialism and Democracy* (New York: Harper, 1942).

21. Edwin Harwood, "The Entrepreneurial Renaissance and Its Promoters," *Society*, March/April, 1979, p. 28.

Dwight C. Smith, Jr.

The established large firm is still a dominant object on the economic landscape, but one of the surprises of the postwar years was the survival—indeed, the critical importance—of entrepreneurship, contrary to Schumpeter's prediction. As Harwood adds,

> The economy's cutting edge has ... moved to firms that were hardly known to the public in the 1930s or didn't as yet exist, among them firms such as Xerox, Hewlitt-Packard, Texas Instruments, Analog Devices, Digital Equipment, Control Data, most founded ... by solo entrepreneurs or entrepreneurial teams, many working out of now legendary garage and basement industries.[22]

The small entrepreneurial firm survived among the giants, even in the face of greatly increased regulation, because it could move faster; it had a natural champion (the entrepreneur himself) who was freer to take risks than a corporate manager; and it was not burdened by heavy investments in a previous product line. It took a while for observers to realize that Schumpeter's predictions had not come to pass, but by the mid-1960s the postwar entrepreneurial renaissance had been joined by an emerging sense of the continuing profession of entrepreneurship.

We now can turn to two coexistent models of business activity, and their respective business personalities, the entrepreneur and the corporate hierarch. When one thought of business in the early 1960s, however, the hierarch was the only recognized and appropriate style. William H. Whyte, Jr., portrayed one side of him in 1957, in *The Organization Man*[23]: His success was measured by his ability to manage the tasks of business—planning and forecasting, goal and priority setting, financial allocation and control—in a setting dominated by an established social structure, channels, rational design and decision making, and calculation of profit and loss in corporate, long-range terms rather than on a short-term, individual basis.

Assumption: The Corporate Model
Can Be Projected onto Organized Crime

When organized crime was first perceived as a national problem, during the Kefauver Committee inquiry of 1950–51, its structure was of little interest, and it was not well defined. Its historical analogy was the gang, particularly gangs associated with Prohibition. Its principal operating characteristic was syndication, which implied some kind of status and power system, but no one bothered to describe it. There was no firm organizational evidence on which to draw. But, even if there had been, the focus of investigation was on organized crime's apparent principal activity, illegal gambling (particularly bookmaking and long-distance horse-race betting), and not on its organization.

22. Ibid.
23. William H. Whyte, Jr., *The Organization Man* (New York: Simon & Schuster, 1956).

Seven years later, organized crime returned to center stage, under the probing eye of the McClellan Committee. The committee's main interest had been labor racketeering, particularly as practiced by the Teamsters Union, and organized crime gained a place on its agenda largely as a result of the so-called gangland conclave at Joseph Barbara's house in Apalachin, New York, in November 1957. Three characteristics of that meeting seemed particularly important to the committee: conspiracy (which replaced syndication as organized crime's operating mechanism), because none of Barbara's guests would give a sufficiently credible explanation for his presence; a tie-in, in some fashion, to business activities (which superseded gambling as organized crime's principal activity), some of which, like the narcotics trade, were illegal while others were legitimate; and ethnicity. The Barbara gathering was tangible evidence of considerably more organization than in the popular notion of gangs; and since common ethnic ties seemed to be a major clue, investigators began charting family and marriage relationships as the basis of "organization." The results, which on paper looked more like a depiction of spaghetti and meatballs, hardly deserved to be called "organized."

But then Joseph Valachi's stories of Cosa Nostra surfaced in 1963, and organization came into its own. Valachi described a hierarchical arrangement that appeared to reflect a conscious effort to manage and control; he told how it had survived changes in leadership, which suggested not only continuity but also a stable structure ("permanency of form" was the quality later ascribed to it); and he described a process of decision making and supervision that suggested a considerably higher level of rationality than in the impermanent, loosely structured gang. Even though crime and business were still perceived as separate entities, it was obvious that the old criminal metaphor was insufficient. Some other analogy was needed, around which new shared mental pictures could be constructed. To some, it was the military: "In the Cosa Nostra's paramilitary organization, he was on the order of a master sergeant, working out of headquarters" was the way Peter Maas referred to Valachi at one point.[24] The business analogy became the primary one, however, with Cosa Nostra appearing as the IBM of crime. When Meyer Lansky was credited (apocryphally?) as boasting that "we're bigger than U.S. Steel," the business/organized crime parallel was complete.[25]

Valachi's testimony was reinforced for the law enforcement community by a mass of data that the FBI collected between 1961 and 1965 through the use of illegal electronic eavesdropping. The transcripts of that material are said to comprise more than 300 volumes. Only a minor portion (principally the so-called De Cavalcante and De Carlo transcripts, which were released in New Jersey in 1969 and 1970) has ever been made public. It is reasonably clear,

24. Peter Maas, *The Valachi Papers* (New York: G. P. Putnam's Sons, 1969), p. 59.
25. The claim appeared in both Cressey, *Theft of the Nation*, p. 243, and Ralph Salerno and John S. Tompkins, *The Crime Confederation* (Garden City, N.Y.: Doubleday, 1969), p. 225, but neither source documented the quote.

however, that Valachi's credibility in the eyes of his interrogators rested on his confirmation of their interpretation of what had been overheard on those illegal bugs. But what had been heard, and how had it been interpreted? A conservative estimate would be that the transcripts total something like 70,000 pages. It is unlikely that they were (or ever have been) studied in detail. Rather, analysts and investigators with access to them have skimmed the material, looking for clues to conversations that should be studied with greater care. The criteria for such skimming reflected prior expectations of what would be important—expectations influenced, we can guess, by the available analogies from business that emphasized the structural formality of the large corporation.

Even though the structural imagery of large business was adopted, accompanying understandings of business operations were ignored. Crime and business were still separate entities; the business model was merely an overlay. Under it, the operating style and objectives of organized crime were those of a conspiracy, motivated by alien forces intent upon subverting legitimate society with techniques previously unknown to (or at least not practiced by) legal businesses. Resources that could have supplied operating analogies were left generally untapped. Clues that businesses sometimes operate in questionable ways were ignored or downplayed. And late 1960s perceptions of organized crime were frozen in place, despite the publication of new material[26] that could have provided exceedingly useful insights into the operations and significance of criminal enterprise.[27]

While conventional theories of organized crime were never generalized beyond a specific organization, Cosa Nostra, it is possible to reconstruct the process by which analysts would differentiate evidence, and determine whether it was applicable to organized crime, to other forms of crime, or to legitimate business. The process is shown in Figure 1, a taxonomic tree through which all economic activity can be categorized.[28] As the foregoing

26. See, for example, James D. Thompson, *Organizations in Action: Social Science Bases of Administrative Theory* (New York: McGraw-Hill, 1967); and William Copulsky and Herbert W. McNulty, *Entrepreneurship and the Corporation* (New York: American Management Association, 1974).

27. I do not mean to imply that a conscious decision was made not to elaborate further. I reflect rather the process by which now-conventional theory was derived. Its triggering mechanism was the 1967 Crime Commission, which provided a forum and research resources for Cressey and others. The absence of continuing theoretical advance is a result of the absence of a subsequent forum plus the general unavailability to researchers of the organized crime data that have been in the possession of law enforcement agencies. The research of Reuter and Rubinstein and Anderson, referred to previously, demonstrates that there is a great deal to be learned from these sources, and that significant theoretical advances could emerge from the right forum.

28. I do not mean to imply that all crime is economically motivated. I do not presume to have accounted for all criminal behavior on the "illegal" side of economic activity. How non-economically motivated criminality relates to this description is a potential anomaly that I consider unimportant to this discussion.

Figure 1.   *A Taxonomy of All Economic Activity*[a]

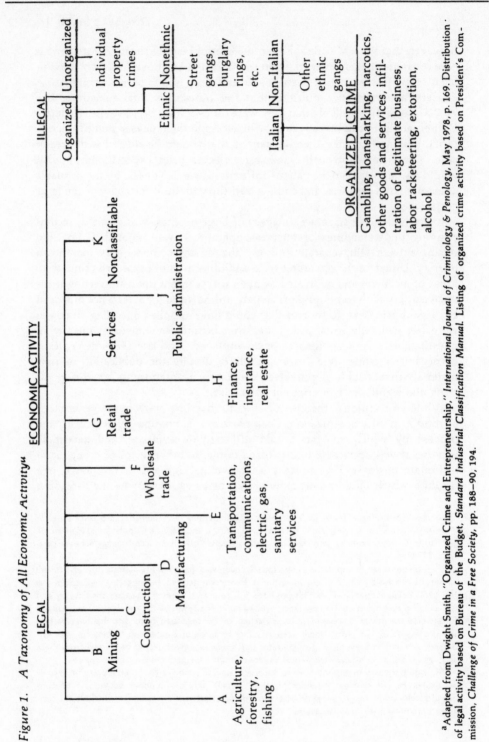

[a] Adapted from Dwight Smith, "Organized Crime and Entrepreneurship," *International Journal of Criminology & Penology*, May 1978, p. 169. Distribution of legal activity based on Bureau of the Budget, *Standard Industrial Classification Manual*. Listing of organized crime activity based on President's Commission, *Challenge of Crime in a Free Society*, pp. 188–90, 194.

Dwight C. Smith, Jr.

observations have suggested, the first branch occurs when activities are separated by the question of legality. On the legal side of the tree, the SIC taxonomy can be easily portrayed. (In this diagram, I have ignored the choice sequence by which that classification was constructed—product versus service, sales versus manufacture, etc.—and have simply reproduced the major categories as a result.) On the illegal side, distinctions take on a different character, as issues of organized versus unorganized and of ethnic coloration are used to measure the potential significance of a piece of evidence or information.

To the traditional organized crime specialist of the late 1960s, this chart would have made sense. The activities grouped as organized crime were bound by the glue of conspiracy. Gambling, loansharking, narcotics, and the rest had significance because an alien, ethnically identifiable group, working together secretly, had brought them to pass. They made sense in relation to each other without reference to entertainment establishments, finance, wholesale and retail trade, and other categories of activity in the legitimate business world. Today's organized crime specialist might not hold this view as strongly as his predecessor, because its internal anomalies have been hard to ignore. When Cressey referred to "illegal goods and services" in 1967 (and again in 1969),[29] he stimulated—inadvertently, it would seem—competing trains of thought. The ethnic conspiracy commands less attention now, as it must compete with a growing recognition of and concern about white-collar crime. The underlying theory still persists, however; and when a person previously linked with organized crime is observed in an apparently legitimate business deal, the immediate inference is drawn, as in 1967, that he is "infiltrating legitimate business," where he will (in Cressey's words) "start to undermine basic economic and political traditions and institutions."[30]

THE ENTERPRISE PERSPECTIVE

Can we still assume that loansharking bears no relationship to banking, or that fencing bears no relationship to retailing, or that narcotics importation and the wholesale trade have nothing in common until an "infiltrator" starts to undermine? It is at this point that an enterprise perspective begins to make sense. It starts from three basic assumptions that replace those undergirding the alien conspiracy view: that enterprise takes place across a spectrum that includes both business and certain kinds of crime; that behavioral theory regarding organizations in general and business in particular can be applied to the entire spectrum; and that, while theories about conspiracy and ethnicity have some pertinence to organized crime, they are clearly subordinate to a theory of enterprise.

29. Donald R. Cressey, "The Functions and Structure of Criminal Syndicates," in President's Commission, *Organized Crime*, pp. 25–60; and Cressey, *Theft of the Nation*.

30. Cressey, *Theft of the Nation*, p. 1.

A Spectrum-Based Theory of Enterprise 371

A Spectrum of Enterprise

There is a range of economic activity that is continuous," from the very saintly to the most sinful," as Leslie Wilkins has put it.[31] There is a range of behavior along which any business can be conducted; legality—the litmus test that traditionally has separated business from crime—is an arbitrary point on that range. Its placement varies by industry (and, in some cases, by establishment type), and it can be relocated if new laws are passed. It is one variable factor in the business environment, not an intrinsic characteristic of a process by which legal goods and services are produced differently from illegal ones.

Behind these assertions lies a fundamental philosophical issue that cannot be ignored: the relationship between Good and Evil. The traditional alien conspiracy perspective is premised, knowingly or not, on assumptions about good and evil, and the reality of "criminality" as a master trait that distinguishes between them in some absolute and irrevocable way. These beliefs have enabled some theorists to view organized criminals as a class apart. That is probably why theories of white-collar crime are so popular—they provide a rationalization for not applying the master trait distinction in all cases (i.e., the "white-collar criminal" remains a businessman). In contrast, I am contending that good and evil are not absolute determinants according to which behavioral theories can be constructed. Existing theories of enterprise and crime have perceived bankers, retailers, importers, and other businessmen as conforming to a set of behavioral rules having nothing to do with loansharking, fencing, smuggling, and other forms of criminal behavior that conform to their own set of rules. A spectrum of enterprise enables the analyst to perceive instead that the businessman of impeccable standards, the sharp or questionable operator, and the underworld supplier are all entrepreneurs who must be distinguished on grounds other than a master trait of "criminal." The loanshark *is* a credit establishment; the fence *is* a retailer.

The initial task in describing that spectrum is to identify the characteristics of business or enterprise that will permit a useful classification of economic activity. The consequent categories should group businesses that reflect similar problems of manufacture and share common products or services. The SIC system is perhaps the most widely recognized answer. There are obvious differences between mining and retailing, for example, and the spectrum of enterprise in each category will reflect different criteria of legitimacy. But the SIC system by itself may not be sufficient. By focusing on the establishment, it does not deal with the multifunction business or multiproduct conglomerate, whose operations require different kinds of entrepreneurial behavior and a more complex matrix of business decisions.[32] By

31. Leslie T. Wilkins, *Social Deviance* (Englewood Cliffs, N.J.: Prentice-Hall, 1965), pp. 46–47.

32. One alternative is to list a business under multiple codes, reflecting the variety of establishments it operates or controls. The Dun and Bradstreet *Million Dollar Directory* resolves the problem of identifying multiple products or services in this way, but its schema ignores the higher

distinguishing between governmental and private establishments, it cannot accommodate the marketplace that contains a mixture of governmental and private entrepreneurs. (For example, Industry 7393, "detective agencies and protective services," which covers "establishments primarily engaged in providing personnel for detective, investigative, patrolling, night watching, or personal protection services," is totally separate from Industry 9221, "police protection," which comes under the major group of public administration.) And by focusing on the end product or service, it offers few clues as to entrepreneurial or business behavior, which may be more important in describing a spectrum of legitimacy. James Thompson recognized the behavioral aspect of business in his *Organizations in Action*, maintaining that the appropriate distinction would be by the technology of production as well as its end result.[33] Technologies range widely in form, from the assembly line of the large manufacturer to the double-entry bookkeeping processes of the banker and the professional knowledge and licensure of the lawyer or doctor; but, whatever their form, entrepreneurial behavior revolves around them. Thompson described three primary forms: *long-linked technology*, as when a cigarette manufacturer directs a sequence of activities from tobacco growing to the case lot distribution of packaged cigarettes; *intensive technology*, as when a nursing home brings a variety of services to bear upon the needs of a patient; and *mediating technology*, as when bankers serve as middlemen in the transfer of funds between lenders and borrowers. A fourth category would be *service technology*, as when the Wells Fargo or Burns organization markets private security services. As far as mediating and service technologies are concerned, Thompson's approach parallels the SIC system, but long-linked and intensive technologies cut across an establishment classification. They reflect some but not all of the elements of a multifunction enterprise or a multiproduct conglomerate. No two-dimensional classification system can be comprehensive, however, and the problems encountered in reconciling these two systems suggest that ultimately a multidimensional classification approach may be required.

For our present purposes, a definitive resolution of this issue is unnecessary. If we assume a reasonably consistent and complete classification system and assume that a spectrum of enterprise is present throughout the system and reflects legal and illegal ways of operating, then there must be some scale by which behavior can be ranked according to criteria that define legal business practices. For example, when the city police department, the private security organization, the posse, neighborhood vigilantes, a lynch mob, and an "enforcer" are perceived as belonging to the same entrepreneurial marketplace of security and enforcement services that cuts across a governmental/private ownership distinction, it becomes evident that criteria

---

levels of business ownership and operation, and thus could not be an adequate structure for understanding business behavior.

33. Thompson, *Organizations in Action*.

are at work through which some of these mechanisms are defined as illegal and others as legal. Furthermore, some of the latter are "more legal" than others, in the sense that they possess more authority and power. The extent of their legitimacy would be defined in terms of practices that are either sanctioned or forbidden. In this instance, differences appear to have something to do with the ability to arrest or detain, and with the use of deadly force. It becomes evident that, as laws governing detention and force are changed, the point of legitimacy on the spectrum may shift; but the continuum of entrepreneurial behaviors will remain essentially the same. The scale of measurement would also have changed, but the ability to measure would remain.

(One might predict that not all forms of enterprise are as amenable to scaling. As regulations increase in a marketplace, flexibility of operations is diminished, and the scale of legitimacy may be reduced to a few discrete points —or perhaps only one. One value of a scale of legitimacy then becomes clear; it enables us to describe and measure the ways in which regulation reduces the options of legitimate behavior as well as the ways in which it defines illegal behavior.)

A Focus on Organizational Behavior

However formally (or informally) constructed, organizations enable entrepreneurs to deal with the dynamics of the marketplace. They emerge and function as they do in response to the challenges posed by their environments. It is essential to understand how they behave in order to appreciate the dynamics of the environment and to understand, from a public policy standpoint, how modifications in the environment can affect and limit illegal behavior. Thompson sets the stage for that understanding in the following terms:

> Most of our beliefs about . . . organizations follow from one or the other of two distinct strategies. The closed-system strategy seeks certainty by incorporating only those variables positively associated with goal achievement and subjecting them to a monolithic control network. The open-system strategy shifts attention from goal achievement to survival, and incorporates uncertainty by recognizing organizational interdependence with environment. A newer tradition enables us to conceive of the organization as an open system, indeterminate and faced with uncertainty, but subject to criteria of rationality and hence needing certainty.[34]

The sociology of organizations has produced a large body of literature on organizations in action, but has focused on the legitimate firm. Left to their own devices, analysts of organized crime in the mid-1960s adopted the closed system as their operating model. An open-system model was obviously inappropriate: A monolithic organization like Cosa Nostra, operating under rules of absolute obedience, could hardly be described as governed by uncertainty. The third alternative of combining open- and closed-system models came to

34. Ibid., p. 13.

flower after organized crime theory had been established, and was not available at the right time. As a result, traditional theory ignored (or missed) the crucial concept of interdependence and its operating principle, the necessity of exchange agreements between organization and environment as a precondition to survival and growth.

The need for a concept of interdependence is evident in two related aspects of conventional organized crime control programs and strategies: coming to terms with a dynamic environment where—unlike the case of the solitary, predatory lawbreaker, whose career is interrupted or terminated by arrest and incarceration—environmental pressures, such as increased regulation, stimulate protective modifications in the ongoing enterprise; and recognizing that initiative is not always the property of the organized criminal. The latter problem is illustrated particularly in Cressey's notion of "corrupter" and "corruptee" to describe the process (translated here into enterprise terms) by which an entrepreneur seeks through exchange agreements to modify or gain power over a restrictive aspect of his task environment. Cressey's choice of terms made it clear that his organized criminal occupies an active role while the person with whom that criminal deals remains in a passive role. The limitation of this set of labels in describing interdependent economic activity becomes evident when we recognize the person receiving a bribe as a broker operating in a marketplace that facilitates access to power, either corporate or governmental. The power broker is himself an entrepreneur (who may, as the ombudsman illustrates, be entirely legal) to whom the illicit entrepreneur comes as a customer. When, for example, Prince Bernhardt received funds from the Lockheed Aircraft Corporation to help the sale of airplanes in Europe, he was not a passive "corruptee" responding to the blandishments of the corporation, but an active power broker with whom Lockheed had to deal in order to protect its position in the international marketplace.

Primacy of Enterprise Theory

Organized crime has been a recognized American phenomenon for fifty years, the past twenty-five of which have been noteworthy for a continuing debate over its significance and origins. The three competing schools in this debate have been the adherents of enterprise as the key to understanding organized crime, the adherents of conspiracy, and the adherents of ethnicity. As noted previously, Landesco, with Thrasher's assistance, founded the enterprise school with his description of Chicago's organized crime milieu as a mirror of the legitimate business world. His analysis was soon forgotten, and in the period immediately following World War II, when the narcotics problem appeared to many to be the most troublesome aspect of organized crime, the Federal Narcotics Bureau began promoting its view of an alien Mafia conspiracy as the cause and explanation. The bureau's view gained limited headway when the Kefauver Committee described the Mafia as a "sinister criminal organization," loosely knit (a description quickly discarded by hard-line pro-

A Spectrum-Based Theory of Enterprise   375

ponents of the conspiracy perspective) and serving as a "binder" tying together the major criminal syndicates in the country. The committee did not accept the entire conspiracy view—syndication remained organized crime's principal operating technique—but its quasi-endorsement of the Narcotics Bureau's theories prompted a rejoinder from those who saw ethnicity as a more significant piece in the organized crime puzzle. Their spokesman, Daniel Bell, argued that ethnic stratification was a better explanation for the contemporary presence of so many Italian-Americans at the juncture of "compromise in politics and extremism in morality" in which gambling and other vices were nurtured; in that context, organized crime was "one of the queer ladders of social mobility" in American life.[35] His rejection of the Mafia as organized crime's touchstone did not sit well with conspiracy adherents; in the decade from 1957 to 1967 (marked by the "Apalachin conclave," the testimony of Valachi, and the reports of the Crime Commission and its consultants), they perfected an alien conspiracy view that was institutionalized in federal legislation of 1968 and 1970 (i.e., Omnibus Crime Control and Safe Streets Act of 1968 and Organized Crime Control Act of 1970). Subsequent observers have continued to push the ethnicity view, or a rediscovered enterprise alternative, but with little success against an entrenched, formally accepted conspiracy theory.

The three-way debate of the past decade has tended, mistakenly, to flirt with exclusivity. Conspiracy, ethnicity, or enterprise is the explanation for organized crime—to the exclusion of the other two. On further reflection, however, it is clear that each contains some truth, and that a complete explanation for organized crime must call on each theory in some integrated way. The problem then becomes one of establishing a useful relationship among them.

It is my contention that enterprise is the principal but not exclusive explanation for the events we identify as organized crime. Market dynamics operating past the point of legitimacy establish the primary context for the illicit entrepreneur, regardless of his organizational style or ethnic roots. An entrepreneur's task environment (a concept to which I will return shortly) is markedly different on the illegal side of the spectrum, primarily because of the absence of regulation to ensure order and protect property rights. An operating strategy is required, as is a mechanism through which order and stability can be maintained. The former is explained in part by conspiracy theory, since the device of conspiracy may be the best way to further outlawed economic activity. The latter is best explained by ethnicity, since ethnic ties provide the strongest possibility of ensuring trust among persons who cannot rely on the law to protect their rights and obligations within cooperative but outlawed economic activity.[36]

35. Daniel Bell, "Crime as an American Way of Life," *Antioch Review*, June 1953, pp. 131–54.
36. For a more extensive commentary on the problem of trust, see Dwight Smith and Richard Alba, "Organized Crime and American Life," *Society*, March/April 1979, esp. pp. 36–38.

A number of analytic advantages are gained by such a linkage among enterprise, ethnicity, and conspiracy. It is possible to see then that ethnicity is not a characteristic peculiar to one group or to illicit businesses; a marketplace may be stratified in a number of ways, and ethnicity is a potential factor in that stratification across the entire spectrum. Similarly, conspiracy is not peculiar to illicit business, since it is an important aspect of white-collar crime activities of otherwise legitimate businessmen. (For that matter, there may well be conspiratorial behavior in the marketplace that is not part of an illegal act but which needs to be understood in the context of illegal conspiracies across the market spectrum.) Conspiracy theory benefits from a linkage with enterprise theory in two ways: The static limitations of its closed-system origins can be replaced by the dynamics of continuing economic activity, and the reification that results from the association of conspiracy-as-a-concept with conspiracy-as-a-criminal-act can be reduced to manageable proportions.

THE ENTERPRISE SPECTRUM IN OPERATION

The heart of any enterprise is its core technology, the technical functions by which it is able to create and dispose of its end product or services. That core technology exists in a task environment, a set of external conditions that enable it to function but simultaneously offer hazards to its continuance. In very general terms the task environment for any business consists of four primary forces: suppliers, customers, competitors, and regulators.

The core technology of an enterprise is the area of activity that responds to closed-system strategies aimed at maximum goal achievement within bounded rationality; the task environment is the area of entrepreneurial activity that responds to open-system strategies aimed at survival in an arena characterized by uncertainty. The function of enterprise is, through risk taking, to direct an activity in such a way that both open- and closed-system requirements are met in a balanced fashion.

The core technology of an enterprise works most efficiently when it is protected by some form of buffering from the uncertainties of the task environment. Internally, those devices commonly take the form of inventory controls and market forecasting; externally, they take the form of legal representation and trade associations. The objective of such buffers is to protect against crucial contingencies that threaten certainty and determinateness.

The result of efforts to protect an enterprise's core technology is the creation of a territory, or domain: a set of claims staked out in terms of a range of products, population served, or services rendered. Establishment of domain takes place within the task environment of the enterprise. Because domain produces stability, efficiency, and increased profits, the focus of the entrepreneur is on protecting and expanding his domain. It is not an arbitrary or unilateral task; the entrepreneur interacts with his environment, a large part of which will be other entrepreneurs who are equally intent upon establishing their own domains as suppliers, customers, or competitors—and, in some instances, as regulators. As Thompson notes,

> Only if the organization's claims to domain are recognized by those who can provide the necessary support, by the task environment, can a domain be operational. The relationship between an organization and its task environment is essentially one of exchange, and unless the organization is judged by those in contact with it as offering something desirable, it will not receive the inputs necessary for survival. . . . The specific categories of exchange vary from one type of organization to another, but in each case . . . exchange agreements rest upon *prior consensus regarding domain.*[37]

Earlier, I argued that there are two models of organization and operating style—the professionally managed corporation with its hierarch and the enterprise with its entrepreneur—but in this summary of organizational dynamics I have referred exclusively to "enterprise." In doing so, I have subsumed two considerably different operating concepts under the label of one. The corporate hierarch can be identified primarily as the person concerned with long-range organizational stability, with the stewardship of an owner's investment, and with a focus on management and the coordination of both production and higher-level administrative activities. The entrepreneur, on the other hand, is the person more concerned with innovation, with personal risk taking, and with a focus on doing a productive task. They are not mutually exclusive roles; one can perceive the necessary interaction of both in the preceding summary of organizational behavior. On the other hand, the two roles are likely to be occupied by very different people. William Copulsky and Herbert McNulty commented on this difference, even as they pressed for the encouragement of entrepreneurial ventures within the large firm:

> The entrepreneur and the hierarch must inevitably clash because their perspectives on business and their role in it are poles apart. The hierarch in the large organization spends a great deal of time jockeying for position and playing politics. What is more, he is always asking himself of any action he contemplates: "How will it affect me and my position in the organization?" rather than: "How will this contribute to the goal?" To the entrepreneur, in contrast, politics, poor communication, and basic defects in company structure can be the cause of intolerable friction.[38]

Despite these differences, I chose one role to serve as the reference for both. The choice was partly for the sake of simplicity, and partly a means of establishing the idea of entrepreneurship in an area of investigation that previously has perceived only the large corporation and the hierarch. More important, I mean to emphasize the risk-taking and growth aspects of economic activity, particularly as they occur near or beyond the demarcation of legitimacy.

37. Thompson, *Organizations in Action*, p. 28.
38. Copulsky and McNulty, *Entrepreneurship and the Corporation*, p. 40.

Whether one speaks of the corporation or the enterprise, however, the previously described conditions of organizational activity govern any establishment, without respect to its technological processes, the nature of its product, or the legality of either product or process. Opportunities for initiating an enterprise and the methods used in establishing its domain may necessarily reflect differences in product or process, but the basic entrepreneurial obligation remains the same. There are other differences, however, that reflect the entrepreneur's place on a spectrum of legitimacy. These differences are most notable at the demarcation of legitimacy, but that point is not always precise. A variety of behaviors may emerge in a surrounding gray area. An area of ambiguity and controversy may well develop, to which a large body of litigation may adhere; its scope may be a function of the level of detail at which the technology is regulated.

The nature of legality both creates uncertainty at the boundary and limits regulation as a force to control the search for domain at the illicit end of the market. Regulation as a device for defining the entrepreneurial rules of the game applies only to legal activities. The only regulatory response to illegality is suppression. If domain for the illicit entrepreneur is to be modified in any fashion other than the traditional "headhunting" strategy of arrest, conviction, and incarceration, pressure must be applied elsewhere in the task environment. A further complication in the role of regulation derives from the fact that in a political environment—which is to say an environment that takes into account more than the direct power dynamics of the marketplace—regulation may be the only means of protecting social values that are not inherent in the market economy. Consumer protection, environmental protection, and equal employment opportunities are three examples. The debates between their proponents and entrepreneurs who maintain that such regulation is inappropriate to market control add further ambiguity to the demarcation between legitimate and illicit enterprises.

Even as one approaches the boundary of legitimacy, however, the task environment changes. Different competitors and customers may be more prominent, and the entrepreneur's response will differ accordingly. Consider the circumstances in which customers apply for loans. On the legitimate side of the market spectrum, their choices range from the commercial bank to the pawnbroker. They deal with different mixes of risk and collateral, but for all, the significant issues of legality have to do with permissible rates of interest and conditions governing loans and their repayments. A simple measure of the spectrum for this industry would be the interest rate, which increases (with risk and, inversely, with decreasing collateral) toward the boundary point of legitimacy and beyond—that is, to the province of the loanshark. These three establishments occupy different points on the market spectrum. Because their customers come from different points in the market, they will compete less with each other than with like-minded lending establishments. They will also fall under different degrees and forms of regulation (even though the common rubric of "standard auditing practices" is applied to the legal establishments); and they will respond differently to prospective borrowers.

This illustration suggests four important aspects of a spectrum-based theory of enterprise: entrepreneurs, customers, stratification, and power. First, enterprise itself may reflect a spectrum of legitimacy. To some, the idea of producing an illegal product, or of producing a legal product in an illegal way, might never occur; to others, the thought alone might be offensive. From their perspective, the premise of a continuum including illicit entrepreneurs would not be real. But there are other ways of doing business, buttressed by such mental processes as a fear of failure greater than a fear of illegality, a lack of respect for the niceties of the law, a high tolerance for rationalizing questionable behavior, a desire for profit at any cost, a principled disagreement with certain legal restrictions, or a contempt for the law and/or its minions. Specific motives are obviously difficult to classify and probably harder to measure, in either frequency or intensity; but they exist, and will explain why a spectrum of legitimacy for the market may be met by the willingness of entrepreneurs to spread themselves across it.

Second, just as there is a spectrum of entrepreneurship, there is a spectrum of customers. There are four major categories: the customer who has legitimate needs that are met legally, the customer with legitimate needs for whom the legal market is, for some reason, unresponsive, the customer with illicit needs who cannot risk dealing with the legitimate entrepreneur (who would keep business records that could subsequently be subpoenaed by an enforcement agency), and, at the end of the spectrum, the extortionist or pirate, who is intent simply upon exploiting the domains of other entrepreneurs.

Third, the ways in which customers and establishments relate across a spectrum of legitimacy produces a stratified marketplace. Certain kinds of customers deal with certain kinds of businessmen. The established businessman who suddenly experiences a minor personal cash-flow problem is more likely to go to a commercial bank where he is known and where his reputation helps the transaction than to go to a pawnbroker, or even a small-loan company. (The exception is the businessman whose cash-flow problem has questionable origins—a gambling debt, for example—and whose word alone might not gain a legitimate loan; he is more likely to become the loanshark's customer.) Such stratification is seldom a problem for the established business, but it can create real problems for the small businessman forced to operate close to the margin of legitimacy. His peers in a stratified market—the company he keeps—may be a handicap in his efforts to achieve standing and reputation. Even more troublesome is the fact that in an interdependent economy—where a businessman is at once the supplier of some, the customer of others, and the competitor of still others—stratification tends to carry over from one market to another. The marginal entrepreneur seeking supplies (including financial support) or customers must seek those willing to tolerate him as their customer or supplier.

Dwight C. Smith, Jr.

Such stratified interdependence creates problems for regulators who find that a simple-appearing enforcement situation may rapidly become intertwined with other simple-appearing circumstances. It also provides a partial explanation other than the likelihood of conspiracy for the fact that the same "suspicious characters" (to the investigator) are likely to reappear in each other's company.

Fourth, the demarcation of domain represents the point at which an entrepreneur's power over his task environment is balanced with his dependence on it. An enterprise and its environment are in a continuing state of tension, with the environment presenting a recurring series of problems to which the entrepreneur must respond in order to protect his domain. His weakness is dependency; his strength is power. Each is relative to some element in the task environment (i.e., a firm may be dependent on a bank for financial support while possessing considerable power over a particular supplier for which the firm is a principal customer), and domain ultimately represents a net balance among a number of relationships in a complex environment. That is, power is not some generalized attribute of an organization, but the sum of complex interdependence. A firm that is relatively powerless in all of its task environment must cater to fleeting interests and scrounge for resources. A firm that is powerless in one area may compensate by increasing power elsewhere (e.g., a firm might agree with its competitors to establish a trade organization that could indirectly put pressure on a regulating body). A firm may have considerable power and yet choose not to use it (e.g., a natural price leader may shun that role in order not to prompt regulatory control). Whatever its circumstances, a rational enterprise will seek, in Thompson's words, "to avoid becoming subservient to elements of the task environment."[39] There are a variety of strategies for reducing dependency: maintaining alternatives, seeking prestige, contracting, coopting, coalescing. Each has its price, which is a relative increase in the amount of power that must be given up in return. The crucial task of the entrepreneur, in sorting out these power-dependency relationships, is to avoid the crucial contingency —the environmental condition that must be met for survival.

Most business writings (Thompson's included) address power-dependency problems of the large firm. Little has been written (before the relatively recent literature on the profession of entrepreneurship) about the problems of the small business that is near or beyond the point demarking legitimacy. The large firm will have a wide range of resources with which to respond; the repertoire of the small firm is limited. The case of the illegal firm is relatively clear. In a simpler era, the ultimate crucial contingency of the illegal operator would have been the threat of identification and apprehension by the police. He might cope with (or adjust to) anything else, but his schemes could work only if he evaded the law. In today's marketplace, however, arrest may be a

39. Thompson, *Organizations in Action*, p. 32.

relatively simple variable that can be controlled by a mix of payoffs, quick bail, plea bargaining, and clever legal assistance; meanwhile, the new crucial contingency may have become the operator's need for capitalization.

The problem of the legitimate but small firm is not markedly different. There, the entrepreneur must contend with crucial contingencies which may involve the other side of regulation (e.g., the new restaurant that must struggle on a tight budget to meet local sanitary rules), or perhaps capitalization. The chances are that both may spend a great deal of effort working out domain problems in that gray, often ambiguous area around the legality border. It is not an easy task, as Copulsky and McNulty suggest:

> In contrast (to the managerial enterprise), the owner of a small business has all he can do to survive. He must scratch and scramble for enough business to keep him going tomorrow, next month, next year. He is the owner, the manager—everything. With little reputation, he has to compete by offering his product at a lower price. He cannot control the market or his environment. He has constant battles with suppliers and customers. He has no staff services or support. He is reluctant to put out the money for accounting and legal services. When he consults with his market research department he is talking to himself. He has no long-term budgets, no quotas, no reserves. If he shows a profit, he's happy; if he doesn't, he's out of business.[40]

The terminology and metaphors of normal business theory are obvious and essential characteristics of a spectrum-based theory of enterprise: Equally obvious is the fact that this theory covers ground that has been mined previously by sociologists and criminologists. That entrepreneurs and customers occasionally behave legally and occasionally behave illegally needs little proof; that motivation and opportunity are critical factors in that choice of behavior is also beyond argument. The significance of a spectrum-based theory of enterprise is that it provides a new framework within which to consider and evaluate "legitimate and illegitimate opportunity structures," as Richard Cloward and Lloyd Ohlin once put it.[41] The new elements that argue for reexamination of older theoretical constructs are embodied in the assumption that opportunity relates to a spectrum of behavioral possibilities and that the decisive factors in determining opportunity relate to the dynamics of the marketplace as it changes character across that spectrum.

PARAGONS, PARIAHS, AND PIRATES

If some points on a market spectrum are perceived to be "more legitimate" than others, there must be criteria by which comparisons are made. At our present state of sophistication, that perception may be akin to the "I know

---

40. Copulsky and McNulty, *Entrepreneurship and the Corporation,* pp. 8–9.
41. Richard A. Cloward and Lloyd E. Ohlin, *Delinquency and Opportunity: A Theory of Delinquent Gangs* (Glencoe, Ill.: Free Press, 1960), p. 150.

good art when I see it" school of analysis, rather than a well-defined and measured process of evaluation; but one candidate criterion is available. It is summed up by the notion of standing and reputation, an assessment that can govern access to respectable lending sources and favorable financing, or more respectful interchange with competitors and regulators, or greater acceptance by preferred customers. A firm with standing is likely to be perceived as more legitimate than one without.

If standing and reputation are limited to economics, comparative judgments entail an assessment of business reliability that reflects past performance and predictions about the future. How promptly are bills paid? How closely are delivery schedules upheld? Are contract obligations honored? Is collateral sufficiently secured? Do the firm's experience and skill augur well for larger undertakings? Experience and skill may be the critical requirements for standing; the smaller and less experienced firm may find capitalization difficult even though it pays the bills. There is a spectrum of lending institutions, however, and the small, unproven firm will seek a lender prepared to deal with borrowers of its limited standing and reputation. The weight of stratification may extend beyond finances, as the small firm is further constrained to an operating level at which survival bears a higher priority than growth and development, and at which its choices of suppliers, customers, and operating strategies are limited.

But standing involves more than economics: It may reflect a qualitative measure of the firm and its products. Is the company run by the "right" people? Is it a "nice" business, and a "clean" operation? Size can have an effect on this calculation as well, because of its relationship to the issue of power. A large corporation with reliable assets may have the power to influence its reputation despite uncertainty or ambiguity over the way it conducts its business or the value of its products. Current debates over the anti-union policies of the J. P. Stevens Company or the overseas marketing strategies of the Nestle Corporation illustrate how a powerful firm tries to cope with such contingencies in its task environment, in order to protect its domain. Neither controversy would have lasted as long if Stevens and Nestle were small, struggling, less powerful enterprises.

Size, financial standing, management reputation, and product-process legitimacy thus combine to produce a spectrum of economic activities. With a broader view of standing and reputation thus taken into account, three images appear clearly on that spectrum: the paragon, the pirate, and the pariah. The first two need little explanation; they mark the "saintly" and "sinful" poles of the spectrum. The pariah firm is a more complex matter, reflecting in the American experience those enterprises whose products or processes cannot pass ordinary tests of standing and reputation but for which demand is such that they cannot be rejected or dismissed into the deep-water social exile of the pirate.

I do not mean to suggest that every small firm having difficulty establishing

A Spectrum-Based Theory of Enterprise   383

its reputation is a pariah. The term applies to certain sets of enterprises only. They tend to cluster at the margin of legitimacy, some recognizably illegal and trying to evade regulations and others trying hard to maintain a newly won or problematic measure of legality. In most business respects, they resemble other small entrepreneurial establishments; the most obvious difference has to do with the product or service.

Economic activity is dynamic, and reputations, or standing, can change. An industry (or an establishment) may in time escape from the pariah label; another may have the label forced upon it. Two areas of inquiry, then, are worth mentioning. First, what conditions create and control a pariah industry? Second, what historical precedents may illuminate the special role of the pariah in the American economy?

As Jerome Skolnick pointed out, pariah industries are most closely associated with the notion of commercial vice.[42] The combination of pleasure and immorality that vice represents produces criminal behavior; "even when such conduct is outlawed, the laws are widely violated."[43] The result is so-called victimless crime, in which customers replace prey, and in which the illegal act is more socially opprobrious than seriously harmful.

Some kinds of vice have commercial potential, because their product (or service) can be organized and managed profitably on behalf of a continuing supply of customers. If law enforcement can be evaded, through ignorance, indifference, legal ambiguity, or corrupt influence, a commercial enterprise can establish its roots, create a clear domain, and begin to accumulate power over its task environment despite its underlying illegality. The principles of a free market economy provide fertile soil for the establishment of commercial vice, even though many citizens may still perceive it to be deviant behavior. But as de facto establishment takes place, the pressure is likely to increase for legal establishment as well. That pressure reflects a changing sense of values. As long as vice activities are recognized as being naturally bad, their social support will be limited. Once "badness" is seen as culturally defined rather than as a matter of fact, however, the issue of deviance or immorality becomes a political question in which observers (and participants) can choose sides. Some may argue that the vice in question isn't all that bad, while others continue to maintain its essential depravity. The conflict between them, quickly becoming a combination of political and ideological issues, creates a continuing moral dualism that influences the way we come to see and interpret the vice in both social and economic terms.

As the pressure increases for acceptance of a vice despite its deviancy, the conflict between libertarians and traditionalists is likely to focus on the issue of hypocrisy. Is it fair and consistent for society to continue to condemn activities that many people seem to enjoy, that others are willing to provide, and

---

42. Jerome Skolnick, *House of Cards* (Boston: Little, Brown, 1978).
43. Ibid., p. 8.

in which no one is really being hurt? Skolnick notes that "human beings appear to be limited in their capacity to endure an inconsistency easily susceptible to the label of hypocrisy."[44] The libertarian in the debate presses forward, expecting ultimate success, "not because libertarianism represents the unfolding of a preordained historical process, but because of the difficulty of sustaining parochial conceptions of sin in an increasingly differentiated and secular society."[45] The traditionalist, on the other hand, will continue to argue the sinful nature of the vice.

American experience demonstrates that in any given case the outcome of this conflict can go either way. The debates over Prohibition, gambling, commercial sex, pornography, and marijuana each illustrate different mixes of traditional morality and more modern (and more secular) ideas, and different degrees of success or failure for either side.[46]

The pariah entrepreneur in the United States is the purveyor of goods and services that nontraditionalists find good, or at least acceptable. Standing in opposition to them is the moral traditionalist, faced with developing patterns of behavior perceived as unacceptable, if not evil. The dynamics of how they press their respective cases, and the consequent tension between them, may only be possible in an open, democratic society. The formal policies of law enforcement are nearly always associated with the traditionalists; together, they may be able to proscribe but they can never fully suppress activities that nontraditionalists accept. The consequent gray area of social control is the territory of the pariah.

If the debate over commercial vice were less heavily influenced by moral overtones and more strictly limited to questions of economic and technical development, we would probably find it easier to refer to the process of change as "progress" or "development." We have done this consistently in observing and analyzing the way traditional agricultural societies become technologically advanced economies. The traditionalists in those societies may feel very differently; the old ways can have moral value that the capitalist observer—the nontraditionalist—either cannot see or rejects as old-fashioned irrelevancies. If we set aside the value-laden assumptions usually accompanying development, morality, and vice, some useful insights into the pariah entrepreneur can be gleaned from the literature on economic development.

One such source is the work of Nicolas Spulber, who demonstrated several years ago the significance of the nonindigenous and unassimilable risk taker in the transformation of a traditionalist economy into a technologically advanced economy.[47] An agricultural society does not become a mechanized,

---

44. Ibid., p. 25.

45. Ibid., pp. 26–27.

46. The continuing national debate over cigarette smoking may turn out to be an interesting illustration of the way an established industry can be turned into a pariah.

47. Nicolas Spulber, *The State and Economic Development in Eastern Europe* (New York: Random House, 1966).

commercial society overnight; there is likely to be a period of "technological dualism," Spulber notes, as modern methods of production are gradually introduced. A commercial middleman is needed, usually one whose skills and resources were gained elsewhere, and whose cultural traditions permit and encourage entrepreneurial risk taking in ways the traditional society would have not permitted. Once the formerly traditionalist society has generated its own competence in banking and trading, however, the foreign middleman is replaced.

Spulber's analysis was based on a comparison of two historical examples: the alien, unassimilable Jewish entrepreneur in Rumania from the middle of the nineteenth century to the beginning of World War II and the alien, unassimilable Chinese trader in Indonesia from the final quarter of the nineteenth century into the early 1960s. The historical American policy of welcoming and assimilating alien, immigrant entrepreneurs was an alternate approach, and the "foreign" middleman in our economic development was not, generally, forced to give way to indigenous successors. But that may reflect the lack of strong traditionalist sentiment regarding agriculture versus commerce. The comparable traditionalist sentiment in this country was concentrated instead on the morality-dominated question of vice. Consequently, traditionalist hostility toward entrepreneurial risk takers has been reflected in the attitudes and behavior of law enforcement agencies contending with the "development" of commercial vice. And that hostility may explain some of the attractiveness and strength of the alien conspiracy view of organized crime.

To return to the pariah entrepreneur, once the moral significance of a vice becomes problematic rather than matter of fact and pressure increases for its legalization, its character becomes negotiable. Is it still "evil" conduct? In the case of the gambling industry, such pressure has been fostered by a growing desire to capitalize on its commercial opportunities. As that has occurred, the debate over legalization has taken a new course. Previously, the issue was dominated by the voices of potential customers on the one hand, and the voices of tradition and moral order on the other. Now a new voice can be heard, that of the entrepreneur for whom morality is a secondary question at best. Sinfulness and morality aside, says the entrepreneur, an opportunity exists for making a legitimate profit under acceptable and competitive risk conditions. Furthermore, the profit can be taxed for the benefit of the community at large, which in a sense atones for any residual ambiguity over the morality of the enterprise. (The appropriate response of the traditionalist may be to shift from moral grounds to a cost-benefit argument: The activity in question may be appealing, but the community will have to bear new costs as a by-product of its operation.)

It is a significant shift in focus, leading to important changes in the roles of entrepreneur, regulator, and customer. The entrepreneur's principal concern had been to evade enforcement and suppression; his new role is to begin a struggle for standing and reputation that would be made possible by legal-

Dwight C. Smith, Jr.

ization. The regulator's new role is to determine how to control, rather than suppress, especially as arguments for legalization have cut the ground from under the "harmful" possibilities that justified enforcement efforts. The customer must adjust to a less powerful role in the marketplace, since his assistance (or connivance) is no longer as important to the entrepreneur's survival.

The industry's equivocal, still-pariah status is bound up in the new relationship between entrepreneur and regulator. Legalizing a vice is not sufficient to erase the pariah label. As Skolnick points out, decriminalization and consequent regulation produce a new conflict between control (because the activity is still "bad," even if not technically a "vice") and industrial expansion (because profit, not simply survival, is now a legitimate objective, with its side benefit of increased tax revenues): "Once an activity has been made licit, those who pursue it come to regard themselves as legitimate businessmen, and both resent and resist the state's attempt to exercise control."[48] The economic and cultural imperatives of capitalism follow. Profit requires growth; growth requires capital; capital requires social legitimacy. The entrepreneur's fundamental problem is to generate "the social legitimacy needed to acquire the economic capital for operation and expansion of the industry."[49]

Social legitimacy makes it possible to achieve standing and reputation. As a pariah establishment works toward this goal, the primacy of the entrepreneur gives way to the emerging power of the corporate hierarch. The shift is an important one to note, not only because of the changing style of leadership it represents. Behind it lies a change in the character of the organization. No matter how much profit a pariah may earn, it remains entrepreneurial, not a managed firm, because the open-system uncertainties of the gray area of social control dominate its task environment. After standing and reputation become possible, the enterprise can look beyond survival and begin to act more consistently like a legitimate, rationally directed firm.

48. Skolnick, *House of Cards*, p. 11.
49. Ibid.

Part III
Structure and Networks of Criminal Enterprises

[8]

FORMAL AND SOCIAL ORGANIZATION IN AN ORGANIZED CRIME "FAMILY": A CASE STUDY

FRANCIS A. J. IANNI*

Of all the charges made against the Italo-American criminal "families" collectively described as the *Mafia* or *Cosa Nostra*, few are as disturbing as the allegation that criminal elements are infiltrating and taking over large areas of legal business enterprise. While the vast majority of the public appears to tolerate organized crime's control of such "harmless" areas of illicit profit as gambling, many people are worried by reports connecting underworld figures with the ownership of a wide range of businesses such as food processing, construction, trucking, importing, restaurants, bars, race tracks, and slot machines.[1]

One reason for public and governmental concern, of course, is the idea that the syndicates will use the profits for their legitimate enterprises to expand their illegal activities. Another more important cause for concern is the fear that criminal elements, by operating their legal business with illegal methods, will make it impossible for legitimate businessmen to compete with them. The belief, held by virtually all government law enforcement officials, that Italo-American syndicates are allied in a nationwide criminal conspiracy makes the movement into legitimate business seem even more sinister.[2] Obviously, criminal organizations pose the greatest threat to legitimate business when they act in concert. The mere allegation of conspiracy suggests that criminal syndicates do have a subversive purpose in mind when entering legitimate business fields.

Though it is easy to expose the legitimate business portfolios of many known underworld figures, it is less simple to uncover the reasons behind their movement into lawful enterprise. The seemingly obvious answer, espoused by criminologists,[3] is that the rich criminal organizations need new areas in which to reinvest illicit profits. Buying, starting, or "muscling" into legitimate business also permits the underworld figures to evade income tax prosecutions and provides a respectable front behind which they can discreetly continue their illicit operations.[4] The assumption behind this theory is that criminal syndicates operate just like any other business corporation. Rationally designed to achieve maximum profits, the expanding criminal organization will naturally diversify its activities. Hence, moving into legal

---

*Professor and Director, Horace Mann-Lincoln Institute Teachers College, Columbia University, New York.

1. *See, e.g.,* D. CRESSEY, THEFT OF THE NATION 100 (1969) [hereinafter cited as D. CRESSEY].

2. THE PRESIDENT'S COMMISSION ON LAW ENFORCEMENT AND ADMINISTRATION OF JUSTICE, THE CHALLENGE OF CRIME IN A FREE SOCIETY 192-95 (1967) [hereinafter cited as PRESIDENT'S COMMISSION].

3. PRESIDENT'S COMMISSION, *supra* note 2, at 189-90.

4. D. CRESSEY, *supra* note 1, at 99-100.

business is nothing more than a sensible decision by which more profits can be accrued while the original investment in crime is protected.

A different, though not entirely incompatible, explanation for organized crime's entry into legitimate enterprise is offered by sociologist Daniel Bell. For Bell, organized crime is a "queer ladder of social mobility," through which successive ethnic groups — the Irish, the Jews, and now the Italo-Americans — have sought to move out of the poverty and powerlessness of the ghetto.[5] In this view, the move into legitimate business can be seen not only as a rational business decision, but as a natural step up the social ladder by which the next generation of Italo-Americans might gain acceptance and status in the wider American community.

While the motivation for organized crime's movement into legitimate business has been much discussed, little is known in detail about the legitimate business activities of a typical criminal syndicate or about the relationship between a syndicate's legal and illegal business activities. Recently, I had the opportunity to investigate these questions in the course of a study of one Italo-American organized crime "family" in the New York area.[6] This article presents field data collected on the organization of the legitimate and illegitimate enterprises of this syndicate's family business. An additional purpose of this study was an attempt to discover how the family's business en-

---

5. *See* D. BELL, THE END OF IDEOLOGY 141-49 (1960).

6. The data presented in this article is the result of two years of close observation of the activities and behavior of an Italo-American organized crime family. Originally, contacts with this family were the result of a personal friendship with one of its members. Hence, in a sense, observations of family patterns had commenced before the study formally began. Over the two-year period I was able to observe behavior in settings that varied from large-scale family events, such as weddings and christenings, to more intimate situations such as dinners with one or more family members in their homes or in the social clubs to which everyone belonged. It should be added that members of the family were aware of my role as an anthropologist.

In order to validate data acquired by observation, family members and other persons knowledgeable and familiar with the family businesses were interviewed. The data on the legitimate business structure of the family were gathered from interviews with family members, substantiated by checking business listings and by subsequent interviews with other family members or persons involved in business operations with the family. Providing the same kinds of control for data on illegal activities was, of course, more difficult since there are no record forms for factual checking. All of the data presented on the operation of the family gambling and loansharking activities were, however, checked for internal consistency and constantly compared with what is known about the operation of these areas in organized crime in general.

There are, of course, many pieces of data and some large areas of information that were simply unavailable. I could surmise just how the legal and illegal enterprises are integrated only on the basis of what was seen and heard and what members of the family were willing to tell. The exact relationship between the gambling operations and loansharking, precisely how much money is involved, how much of it must be used to buy protection, and the relationship between the family operation and any larger syndicate were not discovered. The data is particularly thin regarding the relationship between the subject family and other families involved in organized crime. There was no evidence that would indicate that the family is part of a national or international syndicate. Neither, of course, was there any conclusive evidence that they are not.

terprises related to patterns that have traditionally structured family behavior, and how social and cultural change affected the family as a business organization. In the process, a rather startling fact emerged: rather than being a recent step, the family's involvement with legitimate business began with its founding almost seventy years ago. And its movement toward increased legitimization seems to be a steady trend that has been going on for four decades.

The research, conducted under a grant from the Russell Sage Foundation, has followed the approach of an anthropologist rather than that of a criminologist. By and large, the approach of criminologists to the study of organized crime families has focused on a formal organization model of analysis.[7] That is, the criminal organization has been studied not primarily as a social system but rather as a business empire deliberately constructed to achieve specific goals. Elaborate charts have been developed showing the organization of model criminal families staffed by a hierarchy of members whose titles and functions are sometimes borrowed from the Sicilian Mafia and analogized to positions in an American business corporation.[8]

While such a structuralist approach has its advantages, it also has major drawbacks. The most serious of these is that it views the criminal organization primarily as a hierarchy of jobs to be filled and carried out, a blueprint that can be used to construct and reconstruct organizations everywhere. The findings, however, cast doubt upon this approach — secret societies such as the Sicilian Mafia and the Italo-American criminal families are not consciously constructed formal organizations. Rather, they are traditional social systems, products of culture, and responsive to cultural change. Far from being hierarchies of organizational positions, which can be diagrammed and then changed by recasting the organization chart, they are patterns of relationship among individuals, which have the force of kinship, and which can be changed only by drastic, often fatal, action.

THE LUPOLLO[9] "FAMILY"

Italo-American criminal syndicates are justly called "families" because the relationships established within them produce kinship-like ties among members, ties that are given even greater power when they are legitimated through marriage or godparenthood. Every family member knows that every other member has some duties toward him and some claim on him. Whether the relationships are based on blood or marriage, as they often are, or are fictive as in the intricate pattern of ritual alliances through godparenthood, it is kinship of some form that ties generations together and allies lineages

---

7. D. Cressey, *supra* note 1, at 141.

8. For example, *capo*—president, *sottocapo*—vice president, *caporegima*—plant supervisor. *See, e.g.,* D. Cressey, *supra* note 1, at 111-15; R. Salerno, & J. Tompkins, The Crime Confederation 85-93 (1969); President's Commission, *supra* note 2, at 193.

9. "Lupollo" is a pseudonym.

and families. It is the feature that sets Italo-American crime families off from other ethnic gangs involved in organized crime.

In this and most other respects, the Lupollo family is no different from any other Italo-American criminal syndicate. In it, as in others, the association of members are a kinship group and their alliance as a business organization are one and inseparable. Functional roles in the family's business enterprises — whether legal or illegal — are almost always a function of kinship relationships, and the power hierarchy usually parallels generational position. A member of the Lupollo family may have other "outside" business activities and even a profession of his own, but these are completely separate and have little or no effect on his functional role within the Lupollo family business.

ORGANIZATIONAL STRUCTURE OF THE LUPOLLO FAMILY BUSINESS

The patriarch and founder of this family empire, Giuseppe Lupollo, was born of peasant parents in the district of Camporeale in western Sicily. Coming to New York's Lower East Side in 1902, he began the family business by using his nest egg to set up two small enterprises. One of these, a grocery-importing business, was legitimate; the other, a private storefront "Italian bank," was also apparently legitimate, but seems related, by the interest charged and the collection methods used, to the family's future loansharking activities.

Soon thereafter, by shrewd management of these original enterprises, Giuseppe established himself as partial or complete owner of several other legitimate enterprises including a small combination bar-and-card parlor. He also began the family gambling interest by setting up a branch of the "Italian lottery," the precursor of the policy or numbers racket.

By 1915 Giuseppe Lupollo was an established and feared "man of respect" in the Italo-American community. He had achieved considerable financial success, and while his loanshark and gambling activities were well known in the community his status there was that of a banker and businessman.

Over subsequent decades, both the family business and the family itself continued to expand. Through marriage and other kinship ties, three other lineages entered the family business.

The consolidation of the Lupollo family's legitimate business began after World War II when family members began to pare off some of the less profitable enterprises and to "shore up" and combine some of the more profitable ones. The businesses were combined into eleven interconnected enterprises forming the legitimate base for the Lupollo family.[10]

---

10. The legitimate businesses include such diverse enterprises as a real estate and management corporation, Italian foods producing company, baking company, food processing company, catering service, trucking company, fuel company, garbage and refuse hauling company, limousine service, and a public relations firm.

Illegal Operations: Gambling

The legitimate business structure of the family is complimented by a similar structure of illegal enterprises. Since the time that Giuseppe Lupollo established his first bar-and-card parlor, gambling has formed the financial base for the Luppolo family organization. The choice of this area of concentration was not accidental. While gambling is, of course, an illegal activity, it is characterized by both low visibility and high societal tolerance. With the exception of ultramoralists, no one is really concerned about the prevalence of gambling, including the authorities.[11] In the New York area where the Lupollo family operates, the police tend to look upon gambling as a minor social vice that, whether carried on in the stock exchange or the horse parlor, does not hurt anyone. People gamble by their own choice and the gambler is merely providing a service for a population that demands to be served. Exposure of gambling syndicates, no matter how large, seldom produces any widespread indignation, and the penalties usually assigned by courts for gambling violations reflect this lenient attitude.[12]

The family's involvement in gambling began soon after old Giuseppe came to the United States when he opened the bar-and-card parlor. Immigrant laborers would come to the card parlor to play *ziganetta*, an Italian card game that involved betting in much the same manner as the game of poker. Sometime during the First World War, Giuseppe Lupollo began operating an "Italian lottery" out of the same bar-and-card parlor. The Italian lottery was the forerunner of the policy or numbers game.[13] In this form of lottery the player must successfully guess which three digit number will result from some previously agreed upon tabulation, such as the final digits of the United States Treasury cash balance or the total amount bet on the horse races at a given track on that day. The New York Stock Exchange is also a popular source for the daily number. While the odds are 1,000 to 1 in favor of the "house," if the gambler does guess the proper three digit number, he is paid at odds that run as high as 600 to 1.

The lottery is operated out of a storefront "bank" in Brooklyn that is known in the family as the regional office, the bank, or the main office. The actual gambling operations take place at a number of distinct and separate district offices in Brooklyn, Queens, and Long Island. Each of these districts is referred to as a "wheel" and has a franchised manager who has territorial and functional control over organized gambling in that particular district.

Each of the district wheels is fully guaranteed and protected by the family and for this service each pays a stipulated percentage of the gross back to the regional bank. As far as it could be determined, each district wheel funds its own local operations, although the regional bank will supply emergency funds on a loan basis if there is a "run" as where there are too many winners on a particular day. Each wheel is completely autonomous

---

11. D. Cressey, *supra* note 1, at 283-87.
12. *Id.*
13. This is the most prevalent form of illegal lottery in large cities at the present time.

from the others — there is no functional relationship between them nor is there any comingling of the receipts from each of the different wheels.

Each district manager establishes and operates his own organization. Runners pick up the bets on the street or in "numbers drops" located in small business establishments or large industrial concerns. The money and the bet slips are picked up from the runners by collectors. The collector turns the funds and slips over to a controller who operates out of one of a number of branch banks of the district wheel. The money and numbers slips from each of the branch banks are turned over to the district controller who operates the lottery in that district. The district controller is not the same person as the manager. The manager is the entrepreneur who owns and finances the district wheel while the controller is his employee who actually operates the enterprise. Payoffs on winning numbers follow the reverse of the route for the cash inflow.

Illegal Operations: Loansharking

The loansharking or usury operations of the Lupollo family have grown considerably from old Giuseppe's "Italian bank." This bank, which he started soon after his arrival in the United States, was actually an unchartered lending service operating on the basis of Giuseppe's relationship with specific borrowers. Since there was no regulatory body to set rates of interest or conditions under which loans could be made, Giuseppe could obtain whatever interest the traffic would bear. Because most of the immigrants either distrusted American banks or were unable to obtain credit there, and since they usually needed extra money, Giuseppe's business was brisk. With the money he obtained through his door-to-door selling of imported goods he was able to capitalize a substantial enterprise. There is no way of knowing what his rates of interest were, but people in the community who borrowed money from him now consider it to have been quite high.[14] Whatever his rates of interest, or his ethics, Giuseppe operated his bank as a private enterprise. He was known as a banker in the community, and as a result of the independence with which he could operate he was able to use the bank as a means of partial ownership in a number of businesses when businessmen defaulted on loans.

Today, loansharking or "Shylocking" is a major part of the family's illegal empire. Like gambling, it sustains little risk vis-à-vis the police and courts, and is viewed with tolerance by society. Except for the widespread belief that loansharks kill or maim defaulters, few really condemn the individual who lends the money even at exorbitant rates; rather they suspect the improvident who must borrow.

The organizational structure of the loansharking operations roughly parallels that of the numbers game. The "street" portion of the business is

---

14. No loan seems to have been too small for Giuseppe's consideration in the early days. One informant reports that he always borrowed $2.00 from Giuseppe on Wednesdays and repaid $2.50 every Saturday. Loans as low as $0.50 were heard of in the pre-1920 days.

carried on by a number of bankers who are similar to the controllers in the numbers operation.[15] Money is supplied to the bankers at a two per cent per week rate of interest. The banker then makes the loans directly to the borrower or, in some cases, through a street man, who like the runner in the numbers operation is the person actually in closest contact with small borrowers. The bank charges the street man three per cent interest, and the rate paid by the borrower is usually five per cent per week.

Unlike gambling, the loansharking activities of the family seem to be prospering and growing. While the gambling operations are under strong pressure from Blacks, Puerto Ricans, and Cubans whose mobility in organized crime is gradually forcing the Lupollo family either to accommodate through franchises or to move out, there does not seem to be much pressure from the insurgent Blacks and Puerto Ricans in the loanshark business.

Relationships Between Legal and Illegal Business Enterprises

Tracing the relationship between the illegal activities of the Lupollo family and their legitimate business enterprises is a difficult and uncertain task. In the first place, all of the data on these relationships comes from observation, inferences drawn from patterns of business, social, and personal interaction among family members, and some sketchy interview data obtained from non-family members.

A second problem is that the motivation for movement from illegal into legal business enterprise is a complex one. Unquestionably, some of it develops from the interrelated needs of legitimating the money that is received in illegal activities and finding a variety of legitimate ways to put this money to good use. Some of the movement, however, is the result of the normal process of social and occupational mobility, which characterizes all ethnic groups in the United States.[16] The social motivation to move ahead of one's own social and occupational world, as well as the urge to have one's children reach the American dream, operate just as potently for the Lupollo family as for other American ethnics. There is an old Sicilian adage that admonishes the peasant not to make his children better than he because this can only earn ingratitude and sorrow. The proverb, however, seems to have been left behind in Sicily along with the closed social system that made social mobility difficult if not impossible.

A third difficulty in describing the relationship between illegal activities and legitimate enterprises is that the nature of that relationship has changed over time. Over the course of the family's history, there has been a gradual movement toward legitimation — an increasing acquisition of legitimate businesses, and an increasing separation of legitimate and illegitimate activities.

---

15. *See* text following subheading *Illegal Operations: Gambling.*
16. *See* Ianni, *Residential and Occupational Mobility as Indices of the Acculturation of an Ethnic Group*, 36 Social Forces, Oct. 1957, No. 1.

When Giuseppe first came to the United States in the pre-World War I period, he personally operated and controlled both the legal and illegal activities as part of one organization. During this period in the development of the family business structure, the distinction between the legitimate and illegitimate portions of the organization were minimal since Giuseppe ran all of the activities as the visible and sole owner. Profits from illegal activities were placed directly into legitimate activities, such as the purchase of real estate or movement into business enterprises such as baking and grocery stores. As a matter of fact, Giuseppe used the "Italian bank" as a means of gaining control of these businesses. Default on loans resulted in his taking over an increasing amount of control of numerous small businesses, and in each case the pattern was the same. Illegal and legal business activities, no matter how small, were centered in Giuseppe himself who linked the two areas together.

Sometime after 1920 the first of two transformations of the Lupollo family business began. As Giuseppe's business enterprises grew and prospered, it became necessary to delegate responsibility for various segments to someone else. In this phase, Giuseppe began to diffuse control, but always with two organizational guidelines uppermost. Whether as a result of the familial orientation of the southern Italian culture from which he came, or because of his own inherent shrewdness, he built his business empire — legal and illegal — on kinship. During his lifetime, no position of importance was ever assigned to anyone who was not a relative. Moreover, the higher the position in the organization the closer the relationship. The second organizational imperative led Giuseppe to begin the process of dividing the family members into those who would operate the legitimate businesses and those who would perform in the illegal world. He seems to have taken a very pragmatic approach in deciding who should go where. When the illegal gambling and banking activities became large enough, he employed a distant cousin of his wife to work for him in the gambling enterprises, but kept the bank for himself.

Giuseppe's eldest son began his career working in the Italian lottery. Later, however, when the legitimate businesses became large enough, he moved out of the illegal area and gradually gained control of the various legal business enterprises, eventually being designated by his father as the head of the family business organization. Thus, Giuseppe's eldest son has had experience in both the legal and illegal aspects of the business. On the other hand, Giuseppe's second son seemed by inclination and training always destined to move into the respectable areas of business. From the outset, the younger son operated, at least as far as his visibility was concerned, only in the area of legitimate businesses. Whether or not old Giuseppe designed it deliberately, this division with the eldest son more in control of illegal areas and the younger son controlling the legitimate front for the family continues to this day.

In the post-World War II years, the Lupollo family moved out of the ghetto into the mainstream of American business and social life. The various family companies gradually began to take shape as related but distinct corporations.[17] Illegal activities continued also, but now that the family's legitimate enterprises operated outside the protective walls of the ghetto in the relatively open world of American business, it was important that the legitimate businesses be insulated from unlawful activities. This was the aim of the second transformation of the family business. This insulation was achieved through a system by which monies and services were tranferred from person to person, rather than from company to company. In Giuseppe's day, services had been rendered by one company to another, and some illegal activities were serviced by legal enterprises. Cash was also transferred from activity to activity regardless of distinctions of legality. Now, however, cash and services flow only through individuals.

Legal and illegal activities seem to be further insulated from each other by the use of two companies as centers for the transfer of funds. The money from gambling is invested in a family controlled realty company. Then, after money is "cleansed" by reinvestment in legal activities, it is reinvested in loansharking.

THE FUTURE OF THE LUPOLLO FAMILY BUSINESS

The successful blend of illegal and legal enterprises that constitutes the Lupollo business empire has been seventy years in the making. Over this period, its constantly increasing prosperity has enabled heads of the family's various lineages to provide their relatives — from children and grandchildren to distant cousins — with jobs, financial security, and a lavish lifestyle. In this sense it could be said that the kinship-based organization of the Lupollo family empire has enabled family members to preserve a type of extended family system that the counterpressures of American life could otherwise have easily destroyed.

Yet while the family business is flourishing today, a number of sociocultural developments cast a shadow over its future. Most important of these is the disappearance of the kinship model on which such families are based. This model is drawn from the culture of southern Italy, where the extended family has always eclipsed social institutions in importance; where, in fact, there has been almost no social structure outside the family.[18] In the old country, the extended family embraced an individual's whole life and demanded his total loyalty. Within its confines family members learned a common set of roles, norms, and values, which not only regulated their behavior within the family but structured their relationships with the outside world as well. In his relations with outsiders, a man never acts simply as an individual, but rather as a representative of his clan. Highly moral and self-sacrificing within his family, the southern Italian could not conceive of any moral or social force outside it. Family roles were structured to insure that he learned this lesson early and well.[19]

17. *See* note 10 *supra.*
18. A. PARSONS, BELIEF, MAGIC AND ANOMIE 96-97 (1969).
19. L. BARZINI, THE ITALIANS 193-94 (1964).

40   *UNIVERSITY OF FLORIDA LAW REVIEW*   [Vol. XXIV

Immigrants such as Giuseppe Lupollo brought this pattern with them to America where, for a long time, the fact that extra-familial institutions were alien reinforced the reliance on the family-centered moral system. Ultimately, since men like Giuseppe knew of no other way to organize their world, the southern Italian kinship-based moral code was used to organize roles and behavior within criminal syndicates, which fittingly became known as "families." Thus the southern Italian's filial respect and obedience toward parents was expanded to include the head of his criminal family (who was usually a relative anyway). His obligation to be loyal to his kin before outsiders became the famous "Mafia code of silence." And the collective amorality toward extra-familial authority structures traditionally felt by southern Italians became a powerful force binding criminal families to each other.

After three generations of acculturation, this powerful pattern of organization is finally losing its hold on Italo-Americans generally — and on the crime families as well. In the Lupollo family, the change can be seen in many ways. The old authoritarian structure, in which generational position, the closeness of kinship relations, and traditional personal qualities (ruthlessness, a high sense of honor, et cetera) determined a man's role in the family is being challenged by new conditions.

As the Lupollo family's legitimate businesses continue to move into the American mainstream, political influence, the ability to work outside the Italo-American community, and technical expertise will become more important for the continued success of the family empire. Ultimately, the family's businesses will become more bureaucracized and more like other American business corporations. When this transformation is completed, ability rather than kinship will be the criteria for determining positions and rewards, and the family business structure will no longer be coterminous with the family's social organization.

The effect of acculturation on the Lupollo family can be seen in another, more direct way — increasingly the younger generation is disengaging itself from the family business. The movement of the younger generation of the Lupollo family into independent mainstream careers would seem to support the thesis that for Italo-Americans, as for other ethnic groups, organized crime has been a way station to ultimately respectable roles in American society. If the Lupollo family is a fair example, it is predictable that fewer and fewer young Italo-Americans will be recruited for membership in criminal syndicates of the future. Instead, like the Irish and the Jews before them, they will continue to advance into mainstream politics, professions, and corporate businesses. Only one obstacle would seem to stand in the way of this trend: with public interest in organized crime's infiltration of business and politics at its height, it is possible that the younger generation of Italo-Americans will be penalized for the sins of some of their elders, and that the Mafia stigma will act, temporarily at least, as a brake on this natural movement.

As American culture continues to erode the strength of family and kinship in the Italo-American community, the criminal families will weaken too. Eventually, they will disappear, or at least change their present form so much as to be unrecognizable. As they do, they will give way to the next wave of aspiring ethnics.

The evidence of this displacement is already apparent. In New York City, for example, Blacks, Puerto Ricans, and Cubans are now displacing Italo-Americans in the control and operation of the policy or numbers racket. In some cases, as with the Lupollo family, this is a peaceful succession in which the Italo-American families literally lease the rackets on a concession basis. In this arrangement, the family supplies money and protection while the Blacks or Puerto Ricans run the operation. In other cases, however, the transition is not as peaceful and the syndicate members are actually pushed out. Current estimates are that upward to one-fourth of the policy racket in New York has already changed hands.[20]

An era of Italo-American crime seems to be passing in large measure due to the changing character of the Italo-American community and to the ability of American society to absorb and transform immigrant cultures. What remains to be seen is whether the "myth of the Mafia" — the image of a nationwide conspiracy to control all organized crime and to subvert legitimate business and political life — will die out too, or whether it will linger to haunt the next generation of Italo-Americans.

---

20. Information gathered from interviewing.

[9]

DIEGO GAMBETTA

Fragments of an economic theory of the mafia

WE KNOW MUCH and understand little about the Italian mafia. The amount of factual information surrounding it—whatever that 'it' may be—is disproportionately and dramatically greater than our theoretical understanding of this elusive entity. We do not know everything it might be interesting to know, of course, yet in the monumental quantity of scholarly and judicial sources devoted to the mafia, we can find far more information than scholars have been able to make good, cogent sense of. Facts and anecdotes are not only numerous, but of the most diverse and seemingly irreconcilable kinds, and theoretical and analytical shortcomings have made it impossible to accomplish two fundamental and related operations: first, to discriminate between relevant information and contingent ethnographical detail, and between reliable and distorted evidence; second, to find a coherent thread linking whatever disparate pieces of information remain after the first screening operation.

In this paper I shall first outline some theoretical assumptions which represent a preliminary attempt to reduce the gap between knowledge and understanding. They belong to what could ultimately evolve into an economic theory of private protection. However, I shall not elaborate such a theory here. I shall instead proceed to show how, by simple inference from those assumptions, forms of behaviour traditionally associated with the mafia, such as *omertà*, violence, honour, myth, and also other forms more loosely associated with the Mediterranean world at large, such as hospitality and religious festivals, can all be explained in a more coherent and economic fashion than has so far been the case. Thus, in this essay, the theory will not be tested on empirical evidence, but indirectly, on some of its conceptual and explanatory consequences.

Arch. europ. sociol., XXIX (1988), 127-145   0003-9756 88/0000-539 $02.50 © 1988 *A.E.S.*

DIEGO GAMBETTA

I

The central theoretical assumption of this paper is that the most specific activity of *mafiosi* consists in producing and selling a very special commodity, intangible, yet indispensable in a majority of economic transactions. Rather than producing cars, beer, nuts and bolts, or books, they produce and sell *trust*. Alternative, yet analytically equivalent, names for this commodity might be *protection* or *guarantees*. In historical terms, the mafia can therefore be seen as the particular form in which the supply of private protection has developed in southern Italy (1): like 'organized crime' in general, it consists of a set of firms—not necessarily tightly organized among themselves—which aim to produce, advertize and sell protection in conflict with the state. The market for protection, as for that of any other commodity, can be—even if it seldom has been—usefully subjected to economic analysis (2).

In essence, mafiosi operate in those economic transactions and agreements where trust, while of paramount importance, is nevertheless fragile, and where it is either inefficiently supplied or cannot be supplied at all by the state: typically, in illegal transactions in otherwise legal goods, or in all transactions in *il*legal goods. Depending on a number of conditions, mafiosi may protect all parties of a transaction against each other—they may, that is, enforce agreements and prevent cheating—or alternatively, they may protect just one party against the others, deterring competition or occasional crime, for instance, on behalf of specific dealers. Similarly, they may either watch over every transaction in a market (as in the example below) or intervene *ex post* only to settle disputes.

To make my argument less abstract, consider the following example, in which the absence of a *mafioso* who used to act as a guarantor in the second-hand horse market is bitterly regretted by a

---

(1) Here I shall not consider the historical reasons why Sicily in particular and southern Italy in general have developed those conditions and skills which have sustained the growth and persistence of a pervasive private protection market (on this see Blok 1974, Pizzorno 1987, Pagden 1988, Gambetta 1988a).

(2) Attempts to analyze trust and protection as commodities in themselves are rare. On trust as a commodity see Dasgupta

(1988) and on trust more generally see Gambetta (1988); on protection applied to interstate trade and warfare see the illuminating essays by Lane (1966: part 3). Such analysis has never been applied to 'organized crime' in southern Italy and seldom to its counterpart in the U.S. With regard to the latter see Buchanan (1973), Schelling (1984: chs. 7 and 8), and especially the work of Reuter (1983).

FRAGMENTS OF AN ECONOMIC THEORY OF THE MAFIA

coachman who has to buy a horse without his protection. This ethnographical detail dates from Naples in 1863. I have chosen this passage because, from an analytical point of view, everything the mafia does can be interpreted as a set of variations on this core theme. Three different events are described here: (i) the mafioso protects both buyers and sellers from mutual cheating and both pay him for his protection; (ii) he protects the coachman only and helps him to sell an equine *lemon* to, presumably, an unprotected buyer, and (iii) as the mafioso ends up in jail, it is the coachman's turn to be saddled with a bad horse (3).

I am a murdered man. I bought a *dead* horse who does not know his way around, wants to follow only the roads he likes, slips and falls on slopes, fears squibs and bells, and yesterday he reared and crashed into a flock of sheep that was barring the way. A *camorrista* [the Neapolitan version of a mafioso] who protects me and used to control the horse market, would have spared me from this theft. He used to check on the sales and get his tip from both buyers and sellers. Last year I wanted to get rid of a blind horse and he helped me to sell it as a good one, for he protected me. Now he is in jail and I was forced to buy this bad horse without him. He was a great gentleman! (quoted by Monnier [1863] 1965: 73-74).

The approach briefly presented above runs counter to a number of established views on the mafia. One such view sees the mafia as dealing first and foremost in the supply of illegal goods and services. But one might claim that the reason the mafia has become involved in protecting criminal as well as non-criminal markets is not the result of a first order aim (4). It derives rather from the fact that illegal transactions take place in a market in which the threat of law enforcement, the fear of deception, the absence of written contracts, the uncertainty concerning property rights, the largely imperfect flow of information, all contribute to make the demand for protection significantly higher than in legal markets (cf. Reuter 1983, esp. chs. 5 and 7). From an analytical viewpoint, to confuse the mafiosi who protect with the dealers whose goods are protected is analogous to

(3) For a discussion of the theoretical implications of this piece and other more recent exemples see Gambetta 1988a. For an interesting list of settled disputes in the U.S. see Reuter (1983: 160-165).

(4) Recent historical research indicates that, contrary to a more established view (Blok 1974) which holds that the mafia emerged in the large country estate (*latifondi*), the mafia has been active since the nineteenth century in rich agricultural markets such as olives (Piselli and Arrighi 1985) and oranges (Lupo 1984: ch. 5), and was

protecting the oligopolies of water suppliers and milling (Franchetti [1876] 1974). Whatever the case, the mafia began by protecting the transaction of legal rather than illegal goods in an almost lawless world. Somewhat different is the history of the Neapolitan twin of the mafia, 'la camorra'; although it operated in legal markets too, such as the horse market, by the mid-nineteenth century it was already involved in the protection of illegal gambling and loansharking in the city of Naples (Monnier [1863] 1965).

DIEGO GAMBETTA

confusing those who sell weapons with those who wage wars. The seller may simply not care what the buyer does with his weapons (or protection), so long as he buys them.

In other words, my contention is that, analytically, the mafiosi are entrepreneurs only of that particular commodity *trust* and that this is their defining characteristic, the feature which distinguishes them from simple criminals, simple entrepreneurs, or criminal entrepreneurs. Their relatives, friends, and friends of friends may at times be criminals, inasmuch as they deal with illegal goods, but they may equally be quite ordinary entrepreneurs of legal goods. In both these cases, however, these agents should be seen not as mafiosi but as customers, as buyers and not as suppliers of protection. Even in those instances where the mafiosi themselves are involved in some other economic activity they should be considered as their own customers.

An entrepreneur who trades in heroin or second-hand cars may purchase the protection of a mafioso. Alternatively, under certain conditions the mafioso himself may deal in drugs or used cars, but this in itself does not make him a mafioso, merely a drug dealer or second-hand car salesman. What makes him a mafioso is the fact that he is capable of protecting himself against cheats and competitors. The fact that, say, the owner of Fiat buys a car from himself does not make him just a driver; similarly, the fact that a mafioso who is involved in drug or second-hand car dealing 'buys' his own protection does not make him either just a drug or a used car dealer. This has been perhaps the most regrettable of the several confusions (5) which have inhibited a proper understanding of the mafia, as it has systematically conflated the market of whatever legal or illegal good is being protected, with the market of protection itself. As each, on the contrary, is subject to sharply differing constraints and opportunities, any successful analysis must preserve a clear conceptual distinction between protected commodities and protection as a commodity.

The second view contradicted by my approach is that which sees the mafia as offering protection from dangers, threats, and distrust which the mafia itself creates (6). It would not, in other words, supply

---

(5) For a recent, bold, and opaque example of this cf. Arlacchi 1983.

(6) Among the very few to take the view that the protection services supplied by the mafia tend to be real rather than bogus is Reuter (1983). Much more common, however, is the view that, among its various

activities, the mafia practises extortion. There are some similarities between this discussion, in which I undertake to show that *mafiosi* do not simply take advantage of their customers, and the discussion by Korovkin(1988) in this same issue of *Archives européennes de sociologie*, in which he likewise

FRAGMENTS OF AN ECONOMIC THEORY OF THE MAFIA

a *real* service but merely practise extortion. A proper answer to this very important question would require a far more elaborate set of arguments than I can develop here. There are, however, four fundamental points to be made which suggest that extortion is not necessarily the primary concern of the market for private protection.

The first of these has to do with a possible informational bias which may exaggerate the importance of extortion as opposed to those transactions—such as that involving the Neapolitan coachman —in which the likelihood of being cheated (or being caught cheating) is truly reduced thanks to protection. We are more likely to hear about the former simply because dealers are more likely to talk to the police in this case than in the latter.

The second point concerns the fact that protection is one of those commodities which is likely to have both positive and negative externalities. Let us consider first the negative case. Imagine that in a given area there is a small and constant proportion of cheats or thieves who are independent of the mafia and that the probability of being cheated or robbed by them is on average low enough for dealers in that area not to really worry about buying protection. Assume, however, that some do nevertheless begin to buy it. This may be because some worry more than others (jewellers, for example, who stand to lose more), or because in an area densely populated by protection firms they enjoy protection as the open credit of kin or friendship, or again, because they yield more readily than others to the threats of the protection firms. Only in the latter case would we be justified in considering the first dealers to yield as victims of extortion. Even so, as more and more dealers buy protection, the risk to those who do not increases, because cheats and thieves are more likely to concentrate their efforts on the unprotected. As a result there will be a progressively more *genuine* incentive to buy protection which could act as a catalyst to a chain reaction in which everyone ends up buying protection simply because everyone else is already

seeks to demonstrate that patrons are not merely exploiting their clients. I am not entirely clear, analytically, as to what exactly patrons do; according to Korovkin 'most authors agree that "security" and "insurance" are the key terms that ultimately describe the resources that clients demand from their patrons'. This invites useful comparison with the mafiosi, and no doubt the two roles may on occasion be performed by the same person. My impression, however, is that patrons are perhaps concerned with related yet somehow different commodities more akin to *mediation*, between clients and higher authorities, and the privileged supply of useful *information*. The features of the commodities dealt with by patrons in relation to those of mafiosi should indeed be explored in further depth; however, I think they differ considerably from many forms of protection which mafiosi supply. In Blok's (1974) analysis the two roles are kept together. Cf. also Pizzorno's (1987) comments on Blok's study.

DIEGO GAMBETTA

doing so. The greater the number of people buying private protection the greater the need for others to buy it too. In other words, even if the process is initially triggered by threats and intimidation and can thus be seen as a form of extortion, when it is once underway it soon becomes very difficult to claim that the remaining dealers are buying bogus protection (7). This claim could legitimately be made only if the efficiency of the police in preventing stealing and cheating was such that the efficiency of private protection did not significantly reduce the risk.

The above example refers to the case in which, if some buy protection, this causes a negative externality on those who do not. Consider now the case in which there is a positive externality and protection is a kind of public good. The local garage, for instance, is protected and this means that others may enjoy some derived protection by virtue of the fact that thieves are afraid to enter the street. If this were the case then the protection firm would clearly have an interest in exacting a tax from the neighbouring dealers too, for providing them with protection would entail no more cost than that already incurred in providing protection to the garage. But the garage owner too would rather everybody else in the neighbourhood paid his share. The interests of the protection firm and its customers would thus coincide, and we would then arrive at the apparent paradox whereby the standard piece of evidence from which we would infer that a dealer is being forced to pay extortion money—for example, a shop window blowing up—might simply mean that he is being punished for free-riding at the expense of those around him, who are paying for a commodity—protection—from which he benefits without bearing his share of the cost.

The third point to be made about the relationship of protection to extortion does not suggest that protection firms are not practising extortion, but simply that, even if they were, this would not be technically different from comparable forms of behaviour widespread in legal business. Imagine that the blowing up of the shop window was in fact an act of intimidation to extort money from an innocent dealer. In abstract economic terms one might say that those who committed this act were trying to increase demand for their product

(7) If we were to consider this as extortion we would then also have to consider as extortion several other goods which we buy simply to avoid the externalities that are dumped on us by the fact that others are already buying them. Cars and publicity may serve as examples. In a city where everyone goes by car the pollution is likely to encourage more people to buy cars too, so as to be among the 'gassers' rather than the 'gassed'. Similarly, if all firms in an industry pay for publicity then every new firm planning to enter that industry must take publicity costs into account.

FRAGMENTS OF AN ECONOMIC THEORY OF THE MAFIA

by unfair means. Consider now a company producing cars which puts covert pressure on the government, or, more probably, on individual politicians, to encourage them to spend more money on motorways and less on railways irrespective of whether this is in the public interest. The latter event—which the *legal* world of business has no doubt witnessed countless times—is, in economic terms, exactly analogous to the former case of the shop window: the car company was 'trying to increase demand for its product by unfair means'. The fact that one person commits a crime does not, of course, excuse anyone else from committing that same crime. Nevertheless, this parallel serves to demonstrate that whatever the commodity, the temptation to influence demand by improper means exists, and is sometimes acted upon, and that the extortion perpetrated by 'organized crime' is not necessarily more common than that perpetrated, on a much lager scale, by big business, distinguished only by the outwards forms of convention from the less socially acceptable groups running protection firms. The dubious taste of the latter should not of itself make one's moral judgement more severe.

. The fourth and final point I want to make here further emphasizes the ambiguity between real and bogus protection. Perhaps the most refined expression of the view that organized crime is essentially about extortion was put forward by Schelling (1983: ch. 7). He claims that the victim of the mafia in the *U.S.* is 'the man who sells illicit services to the public. And the crime of which he is the victim is extortion. *He pays to stay in business*' (p. 185, my italics). Schelling agrees that illegal dealers 'may find the [protection racket] useful as many small businessmen find trade associations and lobbies and even public relations offices useful' (p. 185). However, dealers in illicit services do not really need the 'services' of organized crime: rather it is the latter which needs and lives off the former. The only real protection organized crime offers, apart from 'protection' against itself, is against other rival extortionists; and this is because it is only possible to tax people successfully if one holds a monopoly over taxation, if nobody else is taxing them at the same time (8).

The crucial point in Schelling's argument would seem to be that dealers are willing to pay for protection *just* in order to stay in business. But one might challenge this as evidence of extortion by reasoning in the following way: in a protected market a potential dealer aiming to enter that market would face a cost of entry higher than the cost which would be strictly necessary were the market not

(8) Schelling's last point is also proposed by Buchanan (1973) in more detail.

DIEGO GAMBETTA

protected. Thus, from the point of view of the new entrant, that cost
may appear as extortion. (Incidentally, a new dealer would feel
exactly the same if the entry cost was that of publicity). However,
from the point of view of those dealers who are already buying
protection, the extra cost imposed on the new entrant can be seen as
precisely one of the reasons they pay for protection in the first place:
to deter new competitors. Oligopolies of dealers may simply enjoy
this benefit knowingly but unintentionally, yet nothing prevents
them from hiring a protection firm precisely in order to obtain
protection from competition. There is only one case, which may not
be infrequent, in which the whole process would still savour of
extortion, and that is when the protection firm reaps all the benefits
that dealers derive from being able to set prices above competition
level. Yet, especially in Sicily, where the persistence and the popular
support of the mafia are particularly marked, it is more plausible to
suppose that protection firms, even assuming they could bully
dealers, might prefer to refrain from doing so and to let them share in
the oligolopolistic profits for the sake of 'social peace' and complicity.

The four arguments outlined above make the borderline between
extortion and genuine protection less well defined than would at first
appear. They do not, however, exclude the possibility that private
protection may often turn into extortion, although for quite different
reasons than are generally assumed. Perhaps the reason protection so
often resembles extortion is not so much that buyers may not need it,
but rather that the peculiarities of protection as a commodity are
likely to foster the growth of monopolies in the protection market (9).
In this case, as in countless other cases concerning legal as well as
illegal goods, customers would pay monopoly prices and be subject to
the whims and greed of the protectors.

II

It cannot be just anyone who goes around and succeeds in selling
guarantees and protection to others. There may of course be cases in
which a protection firm may just live off its past reputation (Reuter
1983), or even cases (I know of only one in Sicily) in which there are

(9) For some of the reasons why this is the   tion as a commodity cf. below where I
case cf. Schelling 1983: ch. 7; for reasons   discuss violence.
more specific to the peculiarities of protec-

FRAGMENTS OF AN ECONOMIC THEORY OF THE MAFIA

cheats who try to sell faulty protection and non-existent guarantees. Yet, as for the production and sale of any other commodity, to perform the mafioso's role credibly there is a need for specific resources: some of these are *structural*, in that they do not depend on the particular kind of transaction which is being guaranteed, while others are *conditional* on the latter. Here I shall consider only the former; I shall not, that is, enter into any specific protected market. My aim is to undertake a purely preliminary test and to check whether, by simply reasoning theoretically on the requirements and peculiarities of the commodity 'protection', the rich, colourful, and sometimes horrifying array of facts, notions and anecdotes which simply the word *mafia* evokes, may, while losing some of their literary and mythical connotations, begin to gain a better understanding.

Let us conduct a mental experiment and ask ourselves how *we* would go about producing and selling guarantees and protection and try to take a preliminary look at how much of what we would do seems to be really part of the business. Assume therefore that among our options for a career, not necessarily a dashing one, is the possibility of becoming a mafioso. (We do not need to do just that but we may start it as a second job. Better still if some of the features of our first job are such as to enhance our ability to perform the second and vice versa). By far the greatest asset we need to build is *reputation*—or *honour* as it is usually called in this field—and here, rather than discussing reputation as such, I shall consider its constitutive elements.

A business of any kind requires information. But it also, for a variety of more or less obvious reasons, needs to withhold information. But the business of protection needs these things in a very special sense. This, then, is the point from which I shall start.

Intelligence and secrecy

Omertá, although etymologically related to being a man, to being strong, has come to mean the capacity for silence and secrecy even under compelling conditions. More precisely, the meaning spread by scholars and journalists refers to the silence that a large section of Sicilians would be capable of maintaining when facing public enquiries concerning crime, and, more generically, their reluctance to talk to even vaguely threatening strangers. The mafia represents the quintessential embodiment of the code of secrecy, having an almost

DIEGO GAMBETTA

mythical capacity for it, which, together with the capacity for violence, is usually set at the top of the list of its specific attributes.

Here, against this standard view, I want to argue that (a) secrecy towards public authorities is but one—and perhaps not the most important—of several forms of secrecy required by protection firms and (b) that at the top of the list of important attributes, together with secrecy, we must consider intelligence, a side of the business which, while of fundamental importance, has been virtually ignored. The reasons for both statements can be understood once we reflect on the coachman's account of his troubles (see above). I shall consider statement (b) first.

If we want to offer protection to the second-hand horse dealer and to the coachman, to seller and buyer, and we want to be convincing about the fact that what we offer is itself a reliable commodity, the first and foremost resource we need is information. We must make sure we know enough about both of them—how their business is going, what their children are doing, how their wives are behaving, whether any debt or credit has been opened, who their friends are, and so on—and that we keep such information updated. The reasons for this are straightforward: we need to have some idea of the objective constraints they are facing so as to be able to assess their reliability. We may need to know their private affairs too, not only to the extent that they impinge directly on the economic side, but also in order to hold potentially blackmailing weapons should either party entertain the idea of cheating the other and, if we protect the latter, of cheating us too as a result. (Note that being cheated, for somebody who sells guarantees and protection, is an event which could have devastating consequences, just as if the owner of, say, Fiat were seen to be driving a Fiat car which frequently broke down). And if we protect just one party of the transaction, we still need to know whether the other party is harmless, or whether, on the contrary, he is—or is protected by—an equally tough or even tougher fellow.

The parties to the transaction too need to know that we know something about them, or *they* would not take us as credible guarantors. Our ability to obtain information is part of our reputation. However, they must not know *what* we know about the other party, for if our position as monopolist of information is weakened, the parties may learn to exchange without our guarantees or they may even step in as potential guarantors themselves. What they must believe is that we know enough—or that we can easily know if we wish—to be able to keep the other party in line. The possibility for retaliation is based on information. Even if we could easily resort to

FRAGMENTS OF AN ECONOMIC THEORY OF THE MAFIA

violence as a deterrent and discounted weaker forms of threat and retaliation—based, for instance, on the potential bargaining force of threatening to reveal the information we possess—we would still need to know something about the parties' property and whereabouts to know where to direct our violence.

Building and managing an intelligence network may be difficult, time-consuming, and treacherous, but still it would be one of our first tasks should we aim to become successful mafiosi. The task becomes more complicated as the number of people we have to monitor increases, for we would have to subcontract part of the work. It is not just a matter of scale, though, but of the types of market we have the opportunity to protect: we may protect large estates in the countryside or the shops of an urban district; we may watch over international drug exchange deals or oligopolies of sub-contractors in public works; we may be ready to punish the defectors of corrupt political coalitions or to monopolize the sale of guarantees in a specific market such as that of horses, cows, or oranges. For each of these cases our need for information gathering is bound to vary widely and affect the way in which we may go about creating and running an intelligence network.

Initially, we can realistically expect to be better at protecting *all* transactions over a small territory rather than *some* transactions over different territories. The place where we were born or where we lived for a long time is obviously the best suited in which to begin our operations, for there we know everyone and every corner. Simply hanging about in the right spots—bars, shops, banks, churches—brings useful information to our attention.

We can monitor directly and check more easily the reliability of the information received. We are more likely to have a higher concentration of friends and kin than elsewhere, and they represent cheaper and more reliable sources. Women talk to each other, children hear from other children, and both may report back to us. In small enough territories new faces are noticed immediately and, often under the traditional guise of hospitality, strangers are rapidly questioned and their business, roles, accents, common acquaintances defined. In small territories the network of active intelligence can be so dense that even the most anonymous of thieves can be easily traced, and the reported cases of stolen property recovered thanks to the good offices of the local mafiosi are literally countless: they begin in the sixteenth century (Cancila 1984) and are still common in Palermo today.

(One thing most travellers notice when they visit southern Italy is

DIEGO GAMBETTA

the conspicuously large number of people congregating in social gatherings of various kinds even during normal working hours: the standard explanation of this 'local custom' is to invoke typical Mediterranean laziness fuelled by high rates of unemployment. I would not deny that these may play some part in accounting for this phenomenon, but I suspect that information gathering could provide a somewhat less depressing hypothesis. Even in those areas of the Mediterranean countries where 'policing' has not taken on the features of specialized production as with the mafia, the well known reciprocity which is the basis of the equilibrium of the traditional community is not maintained just by the visible exchange of gifts and feasts, but also by the in-house production of less visible mutual 'policing' based on curiosity, gossip and the frequent exchanging of visits. Consider, for a classical analogy, the accounts of how Ulysses was received by his numerous hosts. Lavish hospitality is provided, especially wine, and subsequently, when his hosts consider him to be in a warm and relaxed mood, they usually subject him to detailed interrogation (10)).

A similar line of reasoning can be applied to secrecy. While secrecy is the most elementary form of self-protection, both from rivals and the state, it is first of all required for selling protection to others: if our customers knew anything about *us* which could be used against us, our position as guarantor would be weakened as we would find it difficult to retaliate against someone who can fight back. Leading a discreet life, out of the public eye, and letting only honourable information filter out: these are no more than the essential requirements of the product we sell. *Omertà* is not just a traditional style which has matured over long periods of foreign domination and is now retained through inertia, nor is it simply necessary in order to keep the hands of the state off our business, as the standard argument runs: it is a crucial part of our ability as entrepreneurs of protection. This is one of the specific differences between selling protection and selling cars. For while our private life is not necessarily a sign of how good our cars will be, in the case of protection—although what is considered honourable may be historically mutable—what *we* are—or what others believe we are—counts as the foremost sign (11).

(10) I am indebted for this analogy to Chris Prendergast.

(11) Cf. Reuter (1983) who suggests very convincing reasons as to why illegal enterprises in general find it hard to evolve more impersonal forms of organization and tend to keep their identity and reputation strongly related to specific persons (esp. pp. 119-123).

FRAGMENTS OF AN ECONOMIC THEORY OF THE MAFIA

Violence

In addition to intelligence and secrecy, if we want to supply credible protection, we also need a certain strength, not just physical but psychological as well, a kind of charisma or leadership-ability. We need to be stronger than either party or possibly than both simultaneously, and both parties must know that in case of 'misbehaviour' punishment is a feasible option and not so costly that we would prefer to refrain from it. Otherwise, either party could fight back and protect itself effectively from the consequences of whatever action it might wish to undertake. The capacity to command respect, even to inspire awe, has often been attributed to mafiosi of some standing. The knowledge that mafiosi can and will, if necessary, resort to violence comes as no surprise, and once the theoretical assumptions are taken into account, it is not difficult to understand that mafiosi must show some convincing skill in this field if they want to stand a chance in the protection business. However, in spite of this, and in spite of the fact that most writers on the subject take the use of violence for granted, descriptively that is, if we ask why and under what conditions the mafioso really does use violence the answer is not as self-evident as might first appear.

On the whole, there may be four general reasons that make sense of the use of violence.

(a) As we have just seen, violence, or more generally the capacity to inflict costly punishments, would seem to be a crucial part of the role of guarantor: the protected party pays to be protected from the potential cheating to which it exposes itself in transaction with another party, and it therefore needs to be able to count on our ability to deter the other party from cheating. And violence, or the credible threat of violence, seem to represent effective forms of deterrence, not just, of course, in the world of the mafia.

There is something unconvincing about the seemingly cogent argument in (a), and it concerns the apparent weakness of options other than violence. Why is it, in other words, that violence has to feature so prominently in the career and reputation of a mafioso? Why are mafioso groups so heavily militarized and, allowing for changes in arms technology, not just in recent years (12)? The range

___

(12) Cf. Reuter (1983) who claims that the mafia in the U.S. is likely to have been more militarized in the past than now. I very much doubt that this applies to the Sicilian mafia, whose recent internecine wars were by far the worst they have ever experienced. For a quantitative idea of the exceptionally high level of violence in Sicily in recent years cf. Chinnici and Santino (1986).

DIEGO GAMBETTA

of effective punishments which in business fall short of violence
would seem to be wide enough to push the use of violence, as well as
its symbolic manifestations, quite far into the background and still
allow one to supply protection effectively. If any evolution can be
detected in the handling of (legal) economic affairs, at least in those
of an ordinary scale, it is towards subtler contractual forms which
exclude the threat of violence to deter defectors. Physical defeat and
commercial defeat appear as increasingly divergent events. If the
mafia were able to offer protection whilst generally avoiding violence
it would seem rational to do so, as the corresponding risks would be
smaller. But in the case of the Sicilian mafia all evidence, on the
contrary, is against subtlety. Of course, not all punishment takes
violent forms, and often violence is merely threatened with a view to
bargaining. However, the instances in which conflict escalates into
violence are surprisingly frequent. Surprising, not by reference to
what one reads of mafia practices in the daily paper, but with respect
to theoretical expectations.

(b) If, in spite of these reservations, we provisionally take (a)
above as a convincing argument, then it is natural to suppose that
competition among guarantors would also take violent forms. Sustaining competition is in fact the second reason for using violence. Cars
compete on the basis of speed, safety, durability, and comfort.
Protection, in the absence of milder retaliatory options, competes
also on the basis of toughness: he who beats hardest not only does
away with the beaten competitors, but advertizes himself as an
adequate protector.

There are several accounts in the literature describing how honour
among mafiosi represents a variable attribute having nothing to do
with the fixed quantity of honour acquired by birth (e.g. Hess 1973):
by winning violent conflicts with potential or established competitors
a mafioso increases his quota of *honour*—the old fashioned synonym
for reputation—at the expense of the losers in what amounts to a
zero-sum game. These accounts are invariably descriptive, presenting the conflict as a phenomenological oddity and stopping short of
explaining in depth what brings it about. In contrast, if we consider
the special characteristics of the commodity sold by the mafiosi,
conflict follows almost automatically whenever competition emerges:
if one of the structural—rather than merely optional—features of
protection is the toughness of the supplier, then it is part of the logic
of the commodity itself to invite toughness comparisons. Holding
price constant, we can expect a car that performs better to be bought
by more customers. Likewise, a mafioso who hits harder can be

FRAGMENTS OF AN ECONOMIC THEORY OF THE MAFIA

expected to be a more reliable protector. The most credible proof he can offer, in fact, consists in eliminating his competitors altogether. Toughness is a quality that ostensibly lacks fine-tuning, for either you have it or you do not: there is no coming second, but only winning or losing. These aspects of violence are very telling, for they also suggest one reason why the protection market tends to evolve as a succession of territorial monopolies much more frequently than other commodity-markets: while most other commodities can be traded in terms of continuous quantities and prices, because protection relies heavily on violence it tends to be measured as a dychotomous variable, i.e. if not you then me. Imagine that in a given area there are two potential *mafiosi*, A and B, competing for the protection market and that A gains a reputation for being just a fraction tougher than B. Then, without A even having to try to gain a monopoly, all customers would fling themselves under his protection regardless of the lower prices that B might offer, for B's protection would be irredeemably unreliable and vulnerable to A's greater physical clout.

(c) The third reason the mafia may find to use violence is at once more contingent than the two preceding ones and more immediately plausible: if and when the state—which could be seen as just another monopoly trying to impose its rules—acts forcibly against it, then violence enters the scene as a means of self-protection. The catalogue of cases of public officials murdered for this reason is tragically long and needs little comment. Bearing in mind the doubts expressed above, of course, one might object that if the mafia had less recourse to violence, there would also be less incentive for the state to fight it.

(d) But there is at least one further reason why violence is required, and I believe it is the most important. It also explains our doubt as to why should violence be so widespread. It follows directly from argument (a) above when applied to criminal markets and not just to a generic commodity market, and it has nothing to do with inter-mafioso competition or protection from state intervention.

It still concerns the state though, for, to the extent to which it defines certain goods as illegal, it generates two relevant consequences from a mafioso point of view: first, it opens up a market which is in particular need of guarantees and protection, those of the state being by definition unavailable. If a new market opens up there will be a strong incentive for mafiosi, as for any other economic agent, to enter into it. It is the good they sell that makes the mafiosi enter illegal markets as they are those markets which by definition are not protected by the state. Second, by declaring a good illegal, the state

DIEGO GAMBETTA

indicates that those who, despite this illegality, still choose to deal in
such a good, will be chased and punished. Thus, if the mafioso aims
to handle and protect these daring entrepreneurs he will have to
equip himself accordingly.

In order to be a credible protector, the mafioso must be stronger
than his clients. He thus encounters at least two reasons for
militarizing his firm. First, the illegal dealers—given that they
challenge the state prohibition—are likely to be selected from among
individuals who are not easily deterred, and so the punishment they
respect tends to be more rigorous than that to which legal businessmen may be sensitive. Next, they themselves are likely to be more
militarized than the average dealer, in order both to perform their
criminal activities and to protect themselves from official retribution.
Both are powerful reasons for the mafioso to become exceptionally
ruthless and to escalate the militarization of his firm.

This latter argument, which explains the frequent use of violence
in the protection of criminal markets, can also help to explain why
violence is also employed in other contexts with equally impressive
ease. First, economies of scale make violence a relatively cheap
strategy even when it comes to 'settling' conflicts with state officials
and to protecting legal markets which would not of themselves
demand such high levels of violence. Second, the need to sell
protection to criminal dealers, themselves potentially violent, increases the importance of a reputation for extreme violence in the
competition for the protection market and fuels in turn the mafioso
wars.

Saints, advertizing, and myth

By way of conclusion, I shall try to show that protection treated as
a good can also make sense of some folklore. An old man, who used
to be a farmer in a village on the outskirts of Palermo, told me the
story of his step-brother—he repeatedly stressed that he was only a
step-brother—who became a mafioso and of whom he thought very
badly. 'Don Peppe' (let this be his name) among his restless activities
counted one that was very peculiar. Although no one in the village
had ever shown any reverence for Sant'Antonino (a forgotten saint,
protector of the *lagnusi*, the rather disreputable set of lazy people),
'Don Peppe' had salvaged him from the dust—other more reputable
saints already being 'taken'—and organized an annual feast in his
honour. He went around the village collecting money for the feast

FRAGMENTS OF AN ECONOMIC THEORY OF THE MAFIA

and kindly invited the local electrician to arrange, free of charge, coloured street lamps. I know little of the particular organization of the feast, but the old man's recollection was of a thoroughly pleasing occasion. Don Peppe became mayor of the village after the war and when he died (in his bed) the feast no longer took place and Sant'Antonino was promptly forgotten once again. This story is representative of a common pattern of behaviour among mafiosi, who, especially in the past, used to associate their names with that of a saint whom they honoured with their personal protection.

Ethnologists may shudder in disagreement at what follows, but it is my conviction that, viewed with an austere economic eye and stripped of its entertaining folklore, what Don Peppe was doing belongs in essence under the heading of *advertizing*. This very peculiar form of sponsorship, in which the sponsor is the mafioso, while the saint—perhaps unbeknown to himself—is the sponsored party, relies, as all publicity does, on people's current beliefs and exploits the saint's attributes, both the general attributes related to sanctity and those specific to the saint in question. In this case, the sponsorship informs the world at large that not only is 'Don Peppe's protection firm' itself protected by an entity whose main job is, after all, to protect, but, more subtly, that the firm is so powerful as to offer freely its earthly protection even to a protector *par excellence*, whose virtues, by the very definition of sanctity, are beyond doubt. In this case, the implied power of the sponsor is even greater as, in order to protect the *lagnusi*, a saint presumably needs a particularly robust dose of sanctity.

Korovkin (1988), in this same issue of *Archives européennes de sociologie*, describes how patrons too sponsor festivals and processions. In doing so, it seems reasonable to suppose that patrons, like mafiosi, are also advertizing themselves and the goods they sell. If their activity is more akin to brokerage (see fn. 6 above) between people and higher authorities than to protection in the mafioso sense, it may be that they are exploiting a different attribute of saintliness (cf. Blok 1974: 214, fn 2). In addition to protecting different categories of people, popular Catholic belief also holds that saints are the mediators between men and the highest authority of all, namely God Himself. Saints have a privileged access to God as they are trusted by Him and share the same heavenly lodgings: they can thus transmit the demands of the faithful and make a good case to the Lord, attracting his benevolent and prompt attention—if one prays hard enough one may even jump the queue. As for the fact that patrons, as Korovkin informs us, do not themselves participate in the

DIEGO GAMBETTA

procession, it would scarcely be proper, after all, for one who proposes himself as protector, guarantor, and mediator, to walk with the flock of his potential customers: if he can sponsor on earth such powerful people as saints he does not need to and to do so would generate unprofitable confusion.

All this to make a very simple point: that, like other commodities once again, but with its own peculiarities, the sale of protection needs to be promoted, publicized, made attractive, and presented to potential customers in a credible language. In the appropriate circumstances the language of Catholic religious belief—which also concerns the worldly if unreliable *protection* of people by saints—may serve just as well as or even better than any other in enhancing the reputation of the mafioso firm.

Here anthropologists would talk not about reputation but *myth*: Korovkin writes about patronage as myth and many scholars have noticed how mafiosi tend to be surrounded, even more so than patrons, by mythical beliefs. Yet, once again, if one thinks about it in economic terms, the possible interpretation is considerably simpler and less obscure than is normally the case: myth is in fact the only possible form reputation can take for those selling protection and related commodities. In the *mafioso* case, reputation, like violence, is a dychotomous variable: one either has it or is just a common mortal, as untrustworthy as anyone else. Imagine, in fact, what it means to trust someone in a world where trust, as in southern Italy, is truly scarce (Pagden 1988, Gambetta 1988a). Why should people trust mafiosi, or patrons, to be able to protect them at all? There is a cognitive discontinuity between the threatening world outside and those one trusts which must somehow be bridged; the pressure to trust at least someone generates a tension between desirable action and pessimistic belief. And, of all human constructs, myth is perhaps the most likely form to serve as that bridge(13)*.

* I wish to thank for their comments and suggestions Partha Dasgupta, Jon Elster, Geoffrey Hawthorn, and Alessandro Pizzorno. I also wish to thank John Davis and his colleagues at the Department of Anthropology at Kent University for subjecting me to a rather trying and helpful discussion. My gratitude goes to Heather Pratt for her usual ability and care in editing my English.

(13) See Gambetta (1988b) for a more general discussion of this case.

FRAGMENTS OF AN ECONOMIC THEORY OF THE MAFIA

REFERENCES

ARLACCHI, P., 1983. *La mafia imprenditrice* (Bologne, Il Mulino).

BLOK, A., 1974. *The mafia of a Sicilian village, 1860-1960* (Oxford, Basil Blackwell).

BUCHANAN, J., 1973. A defense of organized crime?, *in* S. ROTTENBERG (ed.), *The economics of crime and punishment* (Washington D.C., the American Enterprise Institute).

CANCILA, O., 1984. *Come andavano le cose nel sedicesimo secolo* (Palermo, Sellerio).

CHINNICI, G., *and* U., SANTINO, 1986. L'omicidio a Palermo e provincia negli anni 1960-1966 e 1978-1984 (Palermo, Stass).

DASGUPTA, P., 1988. Trust as a commodity, *in* D. GAMBETTA (ed.), 1988.

FRANCHETTI, L., [1876] 1974. *Condizioni politiche ed amministrative della Sicilia* (Firenze, Vallecchi).

GAMBETTA, D. (ed.), 1988. *Trust. Making and breaking cooperative relations* (Oxford, Basil Blackwell).

—, 1988a. Mafia: the price of distrust, *in* D. GAMBETTA (ed.), 1988.

—, 1988b. Can we trust trust?, *in* D. GAMBETTA (ed.), 1988.

HESS, H., 1973. *Mafia and mafiosi: the structure of power* (Lexington, Mass., Lexington Books).

LANE, F., 1966. *Venice and history* (Baltimore, John Hopkins Press).

LUPO, S., 1987. *Agricoltura ricca nel sottosviluppo* (Catania, società di storia patria per la Sicilia orientale).

MONNIER, M., [1863] 1965. *La Camorra* (Napoli, Arturo Berisio Editore).

PAGDEN, A., 1988. The destruction of trust and its economic consequences in the case of eighteenth-century Naples, *in* D. GAMBETTA 1988.

PISELLI F., *and* G. ARRIGHI, 1985. Parentela, clientela e comunità, *in* Storia d'Italia: *Le Regioni dall'Unità ad oggi: la Calabria* (Torino, Einaudi).

PIZZORNO, A., 1987. I mafiosi come classe media violenta, *Polis*, 1, 195-204.

REUTER, P., 1983. *Disorganized crime. The economics of the visible hand* (Cambridge, Mass., MIT Press).

SCHELLING, T., 1984. *Choice and consequences* (Harvard, Harvard University Press).

[10]

NUMBERS GAMBLING AMONG BLACKS:
A FINANCIAL INSTITUTION*

IVAN LIGHT

University of California, Los Angeles

American Sociological Review 1977, Vol. 42 (December):892–904

Mainstream financial institutions have never been able to provide generally prevailing service levels in poor communities. In the resulting partial-service vacuum, blacks invented numbers gambling. Numbers-gambling banks became sources of capital and a major savings device of urban black communities. In conjunction with the usury industry, numbers banks framed an alternative institutional system for the savings-investment cycle in the slum. Numbers banking illustrates the conjoint contribution of institutional and cultural causes in analysis of poverty.

CULTURAL AND INSTITUTIONAL
EXPLANATIONS OF POVERTY

The literature on poverty conventionally distinguishes institutional and cultural explanations (Light and Wong, 1975; Elesh, 1977). The distinction hangs upon whether an explanation identifies social institutions or the culturally-induced behavior of the poor as the cause of poverty. Although this taxonomy satisfactorily encompasses the structures of explanation, two intervening processes always precipitate poverty. These two are low income and wasteful and/or destructive consumption.

Low income is the most obvious cause of poverty, but the balance between income and consumption is always the technical issue. Even where disposable family incomes are above the poverty level, wasteful or destructive expenditures may deplete a family's reserve until income is no longer adequate. In this case, wasteful consumption—not low income—actually caused a family's poverty. Naturally, when incomes are inadequate, low income becomes the immediate cause of poverty but, even here, wasteful or destructive consumption can exacerbate it.

The intervening processes of low income and wasteful/destructive consumption are compatible in principle with either institutional or cultural explanations of poverty. For example, institutional explanations of income-induced poverty have stressed external barriers imposed by racial discrimination, structural unemployment, minimum wage laws, labor exploitation, the split labor market, and so forth. Cultural explanations of low income-induced poverty have stressed unfavorable work habits (absenteeism, soldiering, tardiness) which reduced employability, attributing these variously to the lack of a Protestant ethic, or the presence of employment and earning-inhibiting cultural residues (Banfield, 1974).

On the neglected consumption side, cultural explanations have emphasized the adverse consequences of wasteful/destructive consumption habits allegedly characteristic of the "disreputable poor" (Matza, 1966). For example, in the decades of temperance agitation preceding the Prohibition Era in the United States, much social research concerned insobriety among the working class and the putative connection of drinking and pauperism (Koren, 1899: 64–99). Many other consumption habits have been linked to poverty, among them: unsophisticated shopping, purchase of luxuries, big families, unhealthy diet, excessive use of installment purchase, failure to save and gambling (Glazer and Moynihan, 1970: 33; Foxall, 1974).

* The author gratefully acknowledges a grant from the University of California Academic Senate, Los Angeles Division. The American Bankers Association permitted inspection and reproduction of their unpublished research findings. The author also wishes to thank Oscar Grusky, Robert Herman, Joan Huber and Lynne Zucker for advice.

NUMBERS GAMBLING

One institutional response to this catalogue of wasteful consumption practices has been to question the scope of culturally-induced consumption differences between the poor and nonpoor. This issue produced a complex and contradictory literature which permits no easy encapsulation (Alexis, 1962; Nixon, 1963; Simon and Simon, 1968; Stafford et al., 1968; Sturdivant, 1969; Cicarelli, 1974). In some cases, undeniable income-linked differences have appeared—for example, lower rates of life insurance purchase by the poor. Even here, institutional writers have insisted that poverty produces situational pressures which require the poor to seek irregular and often more expensive alternatives to those prevailing elsewhere in the market (Light, 1972: 152–69; Ferman and Ferman, 1973; Wong, 1977). In a memorable phrase, Caplovitz (1963) observed that "the poor pay more" because the retail stores of the slum compel it. Similarly, successive studies of pawnbrokers and loan sharks have concluded that poor people turn to high-priced lenders because they are unable to obtain credit in cheaper institutions (Forman, 1906: 622; Seidl, 1968: 88–9). In all of these cases, the poor are making unwise, destructive or wasteful purchases, but circumstances rather than improvidence necessitates the waste.

The ideological implications of any simply cultural or simply institutional explanation of poverty are mutually repugnant (see Huber, 1974), and a spirit of dogmatism often has characterized social science discussion as a result. The source of this dogmatism is the insistence that cultural and institutional theories of poverty must exclude one another. This insistence is fallacious because cultural and institutional explanations can produce poverty jointly as well as singly. Recognizing this possibility of conjoint causality, Valentine (1968: 117) nonetheless condemned it as "eclectic," and social scientists have been dismayingly willing to accept this unwarranted constraint.

The treatment of Lewis' (1968) "culture of poverty" thesis is a case in point. Lewis' detractors as well as his defenders accepted the premise that his thesis is a cultural theory (Leacock, 1971). Yet, the premise is strictly untrue for, in Lewis' view, historic institutions gave rise to contemporary cultures of poverty. His total explanation actually included both institutional and cultural components so it was never a purely institutional nor a purely cultural explanation. The controversial Moynihan report was only a specific application of Lewis' formula to American blacks (Rainwater, 1967). Moynihan asserted that slavery, a bygone institution, had engendered a matriarchal cultural tradition among blacks. The female-headed family, a cultural survival of the bygone institution, had become the principal cause of poverty among American blacks today. Moynihan's thesis contained cultural and institutional components; it was never a purely cultural explanation.

True, a purely cultural phase succeeded a purely institutional phase in both the Lewis and Moynihan versions. (The sequence might, in principle, have been reversed.) On the other hand, no barrier prevents institutional-income and/or institutional-consumption causes from coexisting in time with cultural-income and/or cultural-consumption causes. Numbers gambling offers empirical confirmation of this logical possibility. Numbers gambling is a wasteful consumption practice of the poor. Existing literature attributes this wasteful consumption to cultural causes. This cultural-consumption orthodoxy is simplistic. Actually, numbers gambling combines institutional and cultural causes in the same time span. Therefore, this empirical case supports the conclusion that institutional and cultural causes of poverty may operate conjointly in a situation, and that empirical determination of preponderance is necessary in every case.

NUMBERS GAMBLING: A FINANCIAL INSTITUTION

In the late nineteenth century and until roughly 1940, policy wheels were the prevailing type of lottery among urban blacks and whites of the lower class. Although policy gambling persisted in Chicago and Detroit until 1940, numbers gambling by now has replaced policy in all major American cities. In numbers gambling, a "gig" bettor stakes a small sum on three digits, 000 to 999. Instead of a wheel or drum, the house takes its winning number from published numbers such as bank clearing totals, volume on the New York Stock Exchange, or parimutuel totals. The published figures eliminate the possibility of a rigged outcome, a decisive technical advantage over the policy format (Light, 1974). Beale and Goldman (1974: 541; cf. Roebuck, 1967: 136; Black Enterprise, 1973: 12) estimate that numbers gamblers in the United States wagered 2.5 billion dollars in 1973, roughly ten percent of all illegal gambling revenue.

Discursive evidence claims that blacks were overrepresented among policy gamblers, but the implications of these statements are unclear (Crapsey, 1872: 104; Martin, 1868: 517; Du Bois, 1899: 265). There is no evidence that blacks were overrepresented relative to poor nonblacks; in addition, white ethnics commonly had their own lotteries which may have been functional equivalents of policy gambling (Ianni, 1972: 67; Carlson, 1940: 24). However, Caribbean blacks invented and popularized numbers in this country during the 1920s. As a result, numbers gambling was still 60 percent black in 1934 (Light, 1974: 55). Carlson (1940: 3–4; see also Caldwell, 1940:2) noted that although "white people of the lower economic classes" had begun to bet on numbers, this form of gambling remained "predominantly an urban negro [sic] activity." Currently, Marcum and Rowen (1974: 31) observe that numbers gambling is "concentrated among blacks and ethnic groups in the older cities, especially in the East and Midwest." The Fund for the City of New York (1972) found that blacks represented 30 percent of numbers bettors, but only 20 percent of the city's population. This progression indicates that numbers began as an exclusively black lottery, but diffused to nonblacks.

Studies of lottery gambling, even those most sympathetic to blacks, have always regarded the betting as superstitious nonsense justifying a prodigal waste of money (Riis, 1892: 155; Peterson, 1952: 194; Drake and Cayton, 1962: II, 491). The amount wasted is substantial. Drake and Cayton (1962: II, 481; cf. Warner and Junker, 1941: 19) concluded that the policy syndicate on Chicago's South Side employed 5,000 persons and grossed at least 18 million dollars in 1938. This sum would represent $64 for every black person in Chicago and $256 for a family of four. The median income of all families in Chicago was $1,463 in 1940, so numbers gambling of blacks accounted for about 17.5 percent of family income. More recently, the Fund for the City of New York (1972: 9) concluded that New Yorkers wagered 600 million dollars a year on numbers bets. Blacks represented 30 percent of New York's numbers bettors, so the city's black population presumably laid 180 million dollars on numbers in that year. This sum represents $87 for every black person in New York City. Since the median family income of blacks in New York was $7,309 in 1969, nearly five percent of black family income went for numbers gambling. This estimate is conservative. Director of Political Affairs for the Congress of Racial Equality, Ed Brown (1973) has claimed that in Harlem alone blacks wager "at least" 300 to 500 million dollars a year on numbers. If only 300 million dollars were wagered yearly, this betting gross would represent about $300 for every black person in Harlem or 16 percent of family income. In the 94 percent black Bedford-Stuyvesant section of Brooklyn, Lasswell and McKenna (1972: 55–62) examined numbers gambling between 1963 and 1970. Their estimates are the most reliable of any. They found that impoverished residents spent between 2.5 and 5.1 percent of per capita income on numbers bets. Admittedly, these estimates of betting volume are crude and vary widely. Nonetheless, even the lower estimates indicate that numbers betting represents a significant waste of money by poor people.

Why do poor blacks waste money on numbers? The sociological literature on gambling is scanty (Scimecca, 1971: 56; Tec, 1964: 105) and it offers only two efforts to explain numbers gambling as opposed to gambling in general, the usual focus. The two offer exclusively cultural explanations. Carlson (1940) called attention to "the culture complex" underlying the numbers gambling of Detroit blacks. This complex included dream interpretation, folklore and music, social roles, spiritualism, ceremonial festivities, fad and fashion in playing style, and an extensive gambling jargon. McCall (1963) stressed the "symbiotic" relationship between spiritualist cults and numbers gambling, claiming that the superstitions mutually reinforced each other. The cultural source of the superstition McCall identified as animistic religions of West Africa and Caribbean "hoodoo." In view of the heavy folklore surrounding the numbers complex, cultural explanations have an undeniable plausibility. Moreover, the metropolitan black press continues to depict numbers gambling as a "soul" preoccupation (E. Brown, 1973) while reminding readers that blacks invented the game. In all cases, what is evoked is a specifically black cultural heritage rather than a generalized "culture of poverty." Nonetheless, the prevailing cultural interpretation of numbers gambling among blacks comes down to a cultural-consumption interpretation of poverty among this group.

The evidence supporting the cultural side of black numbers gambling is too strong to deny, but a close look at numbers gambling turns up three telling anomalies. First, of cultural theories of gambling in general, the preeminent is Devereaux (1968; see also Thurner, 1956) who stresses the incompatibility between gambling and the Protestant work ethic. The obvious difficulty is that black numbers gamblers are predominantly Protestant fundamentalists whose gambling can only occur despite the restraint of this religious tradition. Hence, the cultural baggage of blacks does not provide unmixed support for numbers gambling. Second, a cultural explanation of black numbers gambling cannot account for the 70–80 percent of numbers gamblers who are now nonblack. This objection was less serious when numbers was an exclusively black preoccupation, but the subsequent diffusion of the game to nonblacks compels the conclusion that cultural continuities originating in the black heritage cannot give the whole explanation. The supposed improvidence of the lower class

offers a class cultural explanation for numbers gambling by the black and nonblack poor. However, the actual distribution of gambling among social classes lends little evidentiary support. Li and Smith (1976) reported national survey data which show that the propensity to gamble is positively associated with socioeconomic status, a result repugnant to any class cultural theory. The best evidence cited in support of a negative relationship between socioeconomic status and gambling is Tec (1964; see also Newman, 1972: 85). However, Tec concentrated only on football pool gambling, an admitted preoccupation of the working class. Numerous studies (Bloch, 1951: 218; Commission, 1975: 13) report that identifiable social groups have favorite gambling activities. For example, the Fund for the City of New York (1972) reported that low-income gamblers preferred numbers, but high-income gamblers preferred casino games; at middle-income levels, sports and race track betting prevailed. This mosaic of gambling preferences implies that the correlation between social-economic status and gambling depends upon which gambling game is under scrutiny.

Third, a fundamental assumption of any cultural theory of gambling is the expectation that rates should remain stable over long periods of time in reflection of cultural divergences. But the history of lottery gambling in general (Light, 1974: 52–3) and numbers gambling in particular (Carlson, 1940: 4, 138, 158; Caldwell, 1940: 30) shows abrupt shifts in participation: lottery gambling increases in frequency in economic hard times and declines in periods of prosperity. Cultural theory cannot account for cyclical fluctuation.

On the other hand, the increase in numbers gambling in periods of business depression immediately suggests the anomie theory (Durkheim, 1951: 241–46). Merton (1957: 149) also identifies the numbers gambling of blacks as a form of "innovative deviance." Big prize lotteries offer the possibility of immense wealth to winners, and sociological treatments of these have commonly asserted that working-class bettors hope to strike it rich (Stocking, 1932: 558; Marcum and Rowen, 1974: 30; Ianni, 1974: 110), a conclusion congenial to anomie theory (Tec, 1964: 62; Zetterberg, 1962: 122). A related view has developed in economics since the analysis of Friedman and Savage (1948) reversed the economists' long-standing belief that gambling is always irrational. Even the enemies of gambling within the economics profession now acknowledge that gambling is "rational when a person's wish to obtain an otherwise unattainable large prize is very large" (Rubner, 1966: 52). Eadington (1972: 24; see also Off Track Betting Corporation, 1973: II) assumes that numbers gambling satisfies this condition and, thus, justifies its economic rationality.

Anomie theory fits big prize lotteries, but it does not fit numbers gambling because numbers bettors do not expect to change life-style when they win. On an average bet of one dollar, a numbers winner receives a pot which may range from $500 to $600. Players are expected to tip the runner ten percent of winnings, a practice which reduces net gain to $450–$540. In the depressed Bedford Stuyvesant sector of Brooklyn, slum dwellers averaged only 50 cents a numbers wager, so their expected return was only $225 to $270 in 1970. These calcualtions exaggerate expected return because the game permits less radical bets than the three-digit gig. In "single action," for example, a bettor selects only one digit at odds of 10 to 1. The maximum return in this popular bet is only $6, less the runner's tip. These returns fall far short of riches permitting a change in life-style.

Personal Saving

Sellin (1963:19; see also Ianni, 1974; 110) supposes that numbers gambling thrives because a "segment of the population enjoys betting" and does not regard it as harmful. But the entertainment theory does not correspond with the bettors' understanding of the numbers game. On the contrary, they vigorously disclaim betting for the thrill, fun or sport of it. Numbers gamblers view the game as a rational economic activity and characteristically

refer to their numbers bets as "investments" (Carlson, 1940: 138–9).

Most gamblers understand their numbers betting as a means of personal saving. This ubiquitous self-justification is the crucial prop for the entire gambling order (Eadington, 1972: 29; Ianni, 1974: 78). The bettor's justification for this seemingly preposterous misconception arises from unsatisfactory experiences with depository savings techniques. Once a numbers collector has a man's quarter, they aver, there is no getting it back in a moment of weakness. If, on the other hand, the quarter were stashed at home, a saver would have to live with the continuing clamor of unmet needs. In a moment of weakness, he might spend the quarter. Therefore, in the bettor's view, the most providential employment of small change is to bet it on a number (Grow, 1939: 213; see also Whyte, 1943: 41). "The dime or quarter which one bets is scarcely missed," writes R. Brown (1973), "but when one 'hits' the payoff is a chunk of money large enough to be really useful to the winner." Bettors do win (Johnson, 1971: 42). On an average day, the betting public receives back in "hits" fifty percent of its total wager. From the bettors' perspective, numbers gambling is a means of converting change into lump sums; in effect, a savings method (see Samuelson, 1973: 423; Commission, 1975: 17).

The methodical style of numbers gambling also indicates that bettors have adopted a long-range perspective, suggesting a rational savings strategy. The Fund for the City of New York (1972: Appendix 15) found that 72 percent of numbers bettors placed a bet "two or three times a week" and 42 percent bet every day. The Off Track Betting Corporation (1973) concluded that: "The typical numbers player currently wagers on the game between 2 and 4 times a week." Even more strikingly, the Fund for the City of New York (1972: Appendix 25) found that 41 percent of numbers bettors had been betting on the game for ten years or more, and 59 percent for six to ten years. Indeed, the largest bettors were those who had been playing the longest. The frequency of wagering and the decades-long perseverance of numbers gamblers outlines an average

NUMBERS GAMBLING

playing career which encompasses 1,300 trials. In a decade of gambling at this rate, a gambler confidently can expect to hit at least once (for $550) against his total investment of $1,300. Viewed from a decade's perspective, the expected return of a numbers gambling career approaches the expected value of the game (Ignatin and Smith, 1976; Ianni, 1974: 78; Eadington, 1972: 205).

Numbers games attract funds which would not otherwise be saved in depository accounts (cf. Rubner, 1966: 36). First, numbers gambling is convenient. Numbers runners make a regular circuit of their customers who thus do not have to go out of their way to bet. In addition, numbers stations are located in newsstands, pool halls, cigar stores and groceries which people visit on an average day. Therefore, even people who have savings accounts find it convenient to lay a dollar on a number while at the barber shop rather than risk making no "investment" at all in the day. The fund for the City of New York (1972: 57; see also Haller, 1970: 623) concluded that a legalized numbers game would require seven to ten thousand outlets to compete with the illegal game in convenience. In 1970, Bedford-Stuyvesant alone contained 1,345 numbers runners whose business was making it easy to bet (Lasswell and McKenna, 1972: 111).

The friendly atmosphere of numbers gambling encourages "saving." People choose to deal with a numbers runner whom they trust and like (McKay, 1940: 112–3). Therefore, interactions with this person are enjoyable. An established numbers station is usually operated in a small grocery store, candy shop or beauty parlor. Stores of this sort often serve as neighborhood hangouts as well as retail outlets (cf. Whyte, 1943: 143; Firey, 1947: 190). When placing a bet, a gambler has an opportunity for a few moments of sociable interaction with whomever is hanging around. The sociable atmosphere of a numbers station thus stimulates to "saving" these persons who would otherwise simply have spent all small change.

Numbers gambling also appeals to the race pride and community spirit of the ghetto public. The real extent of altruistic motivations is unclear, but the experience of state lotteries suggests that altruistic motives do induce some people to gamble. When asked why they purchased Connecticut state lottery tickets, 82 percent of bettors mentioned financial reasons and 33 percent the benefit to the state.[1] In some cases, blacks have actually gotten together in order to set up an unemployed friend as their numbers runner (McKay, 1940: 112–3). However, even in cases where the direct support of a friend is not involved, blacks understand their numbers gambling as a local form of work-relief (Drake and Cayton, 1962: II, 493; Ottley, 1943: 155; Black Enterprise, 1973: 44; Ofari, 1970: 44–5). Numbers gambling syndicates do provide a lot of employment in black communities. Lasswell and McKenna (1972: 168) found that numbers gambling syndicates were the largest employers in the slum, second only to the federal government. Numbers collectors frequently double as town criers and fund raisers on their rounds. One black informant, an experienced collector in Detroit, observes that passing the hat for hard-luck cases was a regular function of his daily rounds. In this manner, the people who regularly dealt with him put themselves into a loose federation for mutual assistance in time of need.

Consumer Credit

In addition to drawing savings out of an impoverished population which finds saving difficult, numbers-gambling banks also make credit available to poor people who would otherwise be unable to obtain it (Dominguez, 1976: 38). The capital fund from which this credit derives is the gambling play of the neighborhood. The methods by which this capital returns as credit to the local economy are sometimes circuitous and sometimes direct.

Numbers runners make direct loans to customers. These direct loans are of two sorts. First, numbers runners sometimes permit the needy to borrow the where-

---

[1] I am grateful to John T. Macdonald and Fillis W. Stober, State of Connecticut, Commission on Special Revenue, for showing me these unpublished tabulations.

withal to bet. Eighteen percent of numbers players in New York City acknowledged placing bets on credit (Fund for the City of New York, 1972: Appendix 29). Among those who bet a dollar or more per day, this percentage increased to 23. Second, some runners lend cash to steady customers. Nine percent of numbers players in New York City had borrowed cash from their numbers runner for some purpose other than betting. Among persons who usually bet a dollar or more per day, this percentage increased to 15 percent. These percentages are modest, and there is no indication of how recourse to credit varies with income or color. On the other hand, a 1970 sample of California households (Day and Brandt, 1972: Table 6.2) found that eight percent of white and 15 percent of minority households with annual incomes less than $7,500 reported borrowing money from a credit union. Therefore, the direct credit service of numbers gamblers is roughly comparable to credit unions in a low income population.

A wider credit conduit is the return to the local community of numbers gambling profits as loan shark's capital. This return is the standard underworld employment of numbers gambling profits (Seidl, 1968: 32–3; Kaplan and Matteis, 1968). Consumers and small businessmen are the principal customers of slum loan sharks who actually frequent banks in order to approach disappointed loan applicants, sometimes being waved or pointed out to these by the platform official (Seidl, 1968: 16–7; 109–19, 139; Congressional Record, 1967). In many cases, numbers gamblers and loan sharks are the same individual, who simply transfers money from one pocket to another when he changes roles (Anderson, 1974: 25, 127, 130–1; Ianni, 1974: 80, 136; Knudten, 1970: 140).

Business Investment

Numbers racketeers have been the largest investors in black-owned business or ghetto real estate and the chief source of business capital in the ghetto (Roebuck, 1967: 142; Drake and Cayton, 1962: II, 487; Caldwell, 1940: 153; Strong, 1940: 133; see also Whyte, 1943: 145; cf. Ofari, 1970: 46). In addition, numbers bankers

have been virtually the only sources of business capitalization available to local blacks lacking collateral or credit rating (Cook, 1971). As a result of these loans, black-owned businesses not actually owned by numbers bankers were often in debt to them (Drake and Cayton, 1962: II, 469). Finally, numbers bankers have been leading philanthropists in depressed black neighborhoods, making donations to churches and athletic teams, and providing Christmas and Easter baskets for the poor (cf. Perucci, 1969; Whyte, 1943: 142–5).

MAINSTREAM FINANCIAL INSTITUTIONS: MALFUNCTION

One way to appraise the importance of numbers gambling in the financial life of the slum is to compare this subterranean financial system with the saving and investment services of mainstream financial institutions, such as banks. Even a casual review of relevant literature proves that mainstream institutions do not now, nor have they ever in the past (U.S. Immigration Commission, 1911: 216) been able to provide the same standard of financial service in depressed communities which they routinely provide in affluent ones (Hiltz, 1971; Dominguez, 1976: 18). The chronic malfunction of mainstream financial institutions in the slum leaves an enormous service gap in which a diversity of popular financial institutions— including the numbers racket—plausibly may flourish.

Saving

Poor people in general and nonwhites in particular make less use of banks for savings or checking accounts than do nonpoor (Lewis, 1968: 190–2; Irons, 1971: 420). Low income is the most obvious cause: the less money people earn, the less they have to deposit in banks. National survey data confirm this expectation (see Table 1). The consumption of banking services declines as income declines. Of those who own no savings account, 75 percent (1972) and 80 percent (1970) explained that lack of "money left over" after paying bills was the reason

NUMBERS GAMBLING   899

Table 1. Usage of Banking Services by Color and Family Income, 1966 and 1972

	Have a Savings Account (%)		Have a Regular Checking Account (%)	
	1966	1972	1966	1972
All Persons	52	73	56	76
Family Income:				
$15,000 & over	⎫ 74	84	⎫ 84 ª	85
10–14,999	⎭	81	⎭	83
6–9,999	68	72	78 ª	76
4–5,999	47	⎫ 58	63 ª	⎫ 62
Under 4,000	28	⎭	38 ª	⎭
Color:				
White	60	74	71 ª	80
Nonwhite	30	61	23 ª	48

Sources: Opinion Research, 1966: 33, 71; Harris, 1972: 49, 55.
ª Regular and/or special checking account.

(Harris, 1972: 73; Opinion Research, 1966: 39). Among those who had no checking account, 45 percent (1962) and 46 percent (1966) blamed lack of money, the modal explanation.

Investment

A result of nondepositing in banks is noncreation of capital funds in them. This shortage begins the "capital gap" in the inner city, a condition which strangles consumer, mortgage and business credit alike (Garvin, 1971: 445). Moreover, such funds as do make their way into deposit accounts in low-income areas do not, in general, find local investment outlets. Because they lack collateral and have irregular and low income, poor residents make bad risks for bank loans (King, 1929: 18–9; Neifeld, 1939: 169; Dominguez, 1976: 19). In addition, the sums poor people borrow are normally too small to permit profitable lending (U.S. Senate, 1970: 89, 160; 1968: 404). Even credit unions require federal subsidies to offer loans to the poor at legally permissible rates of interest (Cargill, 1973). Therefore, consumer finance companies, like banks, also avoid poor families (Booth, 1973: 71).

Small business loans in poverty areas are more risky than investments in corporate or government securities (Cross, 1969: 45, 46; U.S. Senate, 1970: 148). Adverse profit considerations also have shaped mortgage lending policies in inner cities. Savings and loan associations

routinely refuse to issue mortgages in "red-lined" areas deemed to be in deterioration (U.S. Senate, 1975). The undesirability of consumer, business or mortgage investment opportunities has resulted in a flight of capital from the inner city to more profitable suburban locations (see Orren, 1974: 145–78). A source of interracial tension, this flight of capital owes more to economic calculation than to color prejudice. In 1971, for example, all U.S. banks had 13 percent of total assets in government securities whereas the nation's 20 black-owned banks had 30 percent of their assets so invested. The ultra-conservative investment policies of the black-owned banks led Brimmer (1971) to observe that the black banks were "diverting resources from the black community into the financing of the national debt." This investment policy contributes to the "almost total void of low cost credit and capital" in the inner city (U.S. Senate, 1968: 408).

Bank-Community Relations

Nonfinancial barriers to the normal operation of depository institutions arise from the mutual lack of sympathy of bankers and the poor. The cultural ethos of a bourgeois society provides bankers with no basis for an indulgent view of poor people, and the problem is more acute when the poor are also nonwhite. Blacks have complained for over 200 years that white bankers discriminate against them (Light, 1972: 19). This persistent complaint turned up in Harris' (1972: 94) research for the banking industry. In this survey, 43 percent of nonwhites but only 18 percent of whites agreed that banks made it "too difficult" for nonwhites to obtain loans.

Banking industry research (Harris, 1970: 97–8) confirms that the loan turndown rate "has been highest among lower income groups and nonwhites." Bankers also have acknowledged the interpersonal problems which arise when white credit managers refuse nonwhite customers (U.S. Senate, 1970: 195–6). However, banking industry spokesmen have denied that bankers' race prejudices were the source of the problem (Haugen, 1968: 103; U.S. Senate, 1970: 160; see also Marsh, 1971). The practical line between prejudice and an adverse but impartial bank decision is difficult to draw because of the connection of color characteristics with economic marginality. A U.S. Senate (1968) investigation addressed allegations that the racism of white bankers was responsible for the inner city financial gap. However, the extensive hearings provided no evidence of more than a clash of cultural standards; and subsequent research also has unearthed no evidence that the color antipathies of bankers distort their business judgment.

Nonetheless, poor minorities fervently believe that bankers discriminate against them and discourage their patronage (Day and Brandt. 1972: 102). This belief nourishes the antipathy of these people to banks (Cross, 1969: 51, 54, 66; Kurtz, 1973: 55). Banking industry research shows a decline of confidence in banks as family income declines (Harris, 1972: 28; 1970: 46), but color makes an autonomous contribution. Black people are more alienated from banks than would be expected on the basis of income or educational attainment alone (Root, 1966: 65). Selby and Lindley (1973) found that Atlanta blacks were less prone than whites to maintain a checking account, even holding constant the blacks' generally lower income and educational level. Similarly, banking industry research (Harris, 1972: 49) found that among families

with incomes under $6,000 a year, the poorest class, 62 percent had checking accounts but only 48 percent of nonwhites did (Table 1). More generally, surveys record a level of disenchantment with business and banks which is higher among nonwhites than among the poor. For example, Harris (1972: 131) found that among families with annual incomes less than $6,000, 37 percent rated banks "very high" in their concern for helping the local community, but only 28 percent of nonwhites agreed. Harris (1970: 130) also found that among families with annual incomes less than $6,000, 34 percent perceived bankers as "highly concerned" with helping their community, but only 16 percent of nonwhites made this friendly rating.

Naturally, many expressions of mistrust reflect hostile stereotypes rather than harsh experience. Harris (1970: 46; also Hiltz, 1971: 996) reported that nonwhites indicated less familiarity than whites with every type of financial institution except the sales finance company. Ignorance and public image in principle are open to change through "education" which bankers now view as the key to extending their market in black and low-income areas. The banks' record of recent extensions in response to "advertising and promotional activities" proves that poor people's unfavorable attitudes are open to suasion (Opinion Research, 1966: 74).

However, the malfunction of mainstream service in inner cities is neither epiphenomenal, nor easily rectified within a profit system. To extend service markets in low-income neighborhoods, depository institutions must surmount the barriers posed by the residents' poverty as well as their ignorance of and antipathy toward banks. Although the record of recent extensions proves these barriers are not insuperable, the dollar costs of attracting new bank customers increase as the income of the new customers decreases, but marginal revenues decline. Hence, profit-making institutions cannot provide normal service levels in poverty areas. As a result, the private burden of supporting the savings-investment cycle in such localities falls upon whatever financial institutions the poor improvise.

NUMBERS GAMBLING

CONCLUSIONS

Banks combine the savings of depositors to create a capital fund for business, mortgage and consumer investments. Numbers banks mimic this rhythm, first taking in the "savings" of the poor, then returning capital to the poor community in the form of usurious loans, free loans, philanthropy and direct business investments by racketeers. Therefore, numbers gambling banks are an irregular financial institution.

Prevailing economic conditions in black neighborhoods mutely suggest that numbers banks have not provided a level of financial service sufficient to sustain economic development, even though they helped to close a gap left by the chronic malfunction of mainstream financial institutions. Numbers banking did not, therefore, represent a "sensible, strong, and adequate response to environment" (Glazer, 1971: 42). From the point of view of local economic development and collective social mobility, the numbers-loan shark system is less efficient than rotating credit associations, another financial improvisation of urban blacks (Light, 1972; Bonnett, 1976).

This explanation extends and amplifies the strictly cultural view of numbers gambling which has hitherto prevailed in sociological literature. Numbers gambling of blacks actually reflects the conjoint influence of institutional as well as cultural causes. On the institutional side, the malfunction of mainstream financial communities in low-income communities creates a financial problem. Residents reach into their cultural repertoires for solutions. The solutions they extract have consequences for the rate and character of local economic development.

The case of numbers gambling suggests that cultural and institutional causes may operate in tandem, and their segregation in sequential all-cultural or all-institutional historical phases is not an adequate resolution of their tension. Cultural repertoires offer whole or partial solutions for institutionally-induced disabilities. Therefore, the institutional disability and the cultural solution coexist. When institutions obstruct, victims cope. There is no reason to suppose that all victims' cultural repertoires contain the same remedies nor that all remedies have identical consequences. True, numbers gambling is a remedy, but a wasteful one; and the chronic malfunction of financial institutions which encouraged this remedy does not render numbers gambling a fully satisfactory alternative.

REFERENCES

Alexis, M.
1962 "Some Negro-white differences in consumption." American Journal of Economics and Sociology:11–28.
Anderson, Annelise G.
1974 The Economics of Organized Crime. Ph.D. dissertation, Columbia University.
Banfield, Edward
1974 The Unheavenly City Revisited. Boston and Toronto: Little, Brown.
Beale, David and Clifford Goldman
1974 "Background paper." Pp. 27–88 in Easy Money: Report of the Task Force on Legalized Gambling. New York: Twentieth Century Fund.
Black Enterprise
1973 "Legalized numbers." 3 (April): 41–5.
Bonnett, Aubrey W.
1976 Rotating Credit Associations among Black West Indian Immigrants in Brooklyn: An Exploratory Study. Ph.D. dissertation, City University of New York.
Booth, S. Lees (ed.)
1973 1973 Finance Facts Year Book. Washington, D.C.: National Consumer Finance Association.
Bloch, Herbert A.
1951 "The sociology of gambling." American Journal of Sociology 57:215–21.
Brimmer, Andrew F.
1971 "Small business and economic development in the Negro community." Pp. 164–72 in R. Bailey (ed.), Black Business Enterprise. New York: Basic Books.
Brown, Ed
1973 "CORE warns Harlem: beware of OTB and Howard Samuels." N. Y. Amsterdam News (March 31): A-5.
Brown, Robert
1973 "A black economist looks at the proposal." N. Y. Amsterdam News (March 31): A-5.
Caldwell, Lewis A. H.
1940 The Policy Game in Chicago. M. A. thesis, Northwestern University.
Caplovitz, David
1963 The Poor Pay More. Glencoe, Il.: Free Press.
Cargill, Thomas
1973 "Credit unions and the low-income consumer." The Journal of Consumer Affairs 7: 69–76.

Carlson, Gustav G.
  1940 Number Gambling: A Study of a Culture
        Complex. Ph.D. dissertation, University of
        Michigan.
Cicarelli, James
  1974 "On income, race, and consumer be-
        havior." American Journal of Economics
        and Sociology 33:243–7.
Commission on the Review of National Policy
    toward Gambling
  1975 First Interim Report. Washington, D.C.:
        U.S. Government Printing Office.
Congressional Record
  1967 "Study of organized crime and the urban
        poor." 113: 24460–4.
Cook, Fred J.
  1971 "The black mafia moves into the numbers
        racket." New York Times Magazine (April
        4): 26ff.
Crapsey, Edward
  1872 The Nether Side of New York. New York:
        Sheldon.
Cross, Theodore
  1969 Black Capitalism. New York: Atheneum.
Day, George S. and William K. Brandt
  1972 A Study of Consumer Credit Decisions:
        Implications for Present and Prospective
        Legislation. National Commission on Con-
        sumer Finance, Technical Studies, Vol. I.
Devereaux, Edward C., Jr.
  1968 "Gambling." International Encyclopedia of
        the Social Sciences 6:53–62.
Dominguez, John R.
  1976 Capital Flows in Minority Areas.
        Lexington, Ma.: Heath.
Drake, St. Clair and Horace R. Cayton
  1962 Black Metropolis, 2nd ed. New York:
        Harper and Row, Harper Torchbooks.
Du Bois, W. E. B.
  1899 The Philadelphia Negro. Philadelphia: Uni-
        versity of Pennsylvania Publications, Series
        in Political Economy and Public Law.
Durkheim, Emile
  [1897] Suicide. Glencoe, Il.: Free Press.
  1951
Eadington, William R.
  1972 The Economics of Gambling Behavior: An
        Economic Analysis of Nevada's Tourist In-
        dustry. PhD. dissertation, Claremont
        Graduate School.
Elesh, David
  1977 "Poverty theory and income maintenance:
        validity and policy relevance." Pp. 156–71
        in Maurice Zeitlin (ed.), American Society,
        Inc. (2nd ed.). Chicago: Rand McNally
Ferman, Patricia R. and Louis A. Ferman
  1973 "The structural underpinnings of the irregu-
        lar economy." Poverty and Human Re-
        sources Abstracts 8:3–17.
Firey, Walter
  1947 Land Use in Central Boston. Cambridge,
        Ma.: Harvard University Press.
Forman, S. E.
  1906 "Conditions of living among the poor."
        U.S. Bureau of Labor Bulletin 64:593–698.

Foxall, G. R.
  1974 "Sociology and the study of consumer be-
        havior." American Journal of Economics
        and Sociology 33:127–36.
Friedman, Milton and Leonard J. Savage
  1948 "The utility analysis of choices involving
        risk." Journal of Political Economy
        16:279–304.
Fund for the City of New York
  1972 Legal Gambling in New York: Discussion
        of Numbers and Sports Betting. New York:
        Fund for the City of New York.
Garvin, W. J.
  1971 "The small business capital gap: the special
        case of minority enterprise." Journal of Fi-
        nance 26:445–57.
Glazer, Nathan
  1971 "The culture of poverty: the view from
        New York City." In J. Alan Winter (ed.),
        The Poor: A Culture of Poverty or a Pov-
        erty of Culture? Grand Rapids, Mi.:
        William B. Eerdamns.
Glazer, Nathan and Daniel P. Moynihan
  1970 Beyond the Melting Pot, 2nd ed. (rev.).
        Cambridge: Massachusetts Institute of
        Technology Press.
Grow, Raymond
  1939 "De king is daid." American Mercury
        48:212–5.
Haller, Mark H.
  1970 "Urban crime and criminal justice: the
        Chicago case." Journal of American His-
        tory 57: 619–35.
Harris, Louis and Associates, Inc.
  1970 The American Public's View of Banks and
        Bankers in 1970: The Findings of a Survey
        Conducted for the Foundation for Full
        Service Banks. Unpublished manuscript,
        Library of the Federal Deposit Insurance
        Corporation, Washington, D.C.
  1972 The American Public's and Community
        Opinion Leaders' Views of Banks and
        Bankers in 1972. Philadelphia: Foundation
        for Full Service Banks.
Haugen, Carl E.
  1968 "Short term financing." Pp. 95–105 in Eli
        Ginzberg (ed.), Business Leadership in the
        Negro Crisis. New York: McGraw-Hill.
Hiltz, S. Roxanne
  1971 "Black and white in the consumer financial
        system." American Journal of Sociology
        76:987–98.
Huber, Joan
  1974 "Poverty, stratification, and ideology." Pp.
        1–16 in Joan Huber and Peter Chalfant
        (eds.), The Sociology of American Poverty.
        Cambridge: Schenkman.
Ianni, Francis A. J.
  1972 A Family Business. New York: Russell
        Sage.
  1974 Black Mafia. New York: Simon and Schus-
        ter.
Ignatin, George and Robert Smith.
  1976 "Economics of gambling." Pp. 69–91 in
        William Eadington (ed.), Gambling and
        Society. Springfield, Il.: Thomas.

NUMBERS GAMBLING

Irons, Edward D.
1971 "Black banking—problems and pros-
      pects." Journal of Finance 26:407–25.
Johnson, Thomas A.
1971 "Numbers called Harlem's balm." New
      York Times (March 1): 1.
Kaplan, Lawrence J. and Salvatore Matteis
1968 "The economics of loan sharking." Ameri-
      can Journal of Economics and Sociology
      27:239–52.
King, Willford Isbell
1929 The Small Loan Situation in New Jersey in
      1929. Trenton: New Jersey Industrial Len-
      ders' Association.
Knudten, Richard D.
1970 Crime in a Complex Society. Homewood,
      Il.: Dorsey.
Koren, John
1899 Economic Aspects of the Liquor Problem.
      Boston and New York: Houghton Mifflin.
Kurtz, Donald V
1973 "The rotating credit association: an adapta-
      tion to poverty." Human Organization
      32:49–58.
Lasswell, Harold D. and Jeremiah B. McKenna
1972 The Impact of Organized Crime on an Inner
      City. Springfield, Va.: U.S. Department of
      Commerce, National Technical Information
      Service.
Leacock, Eleanor B. (ed.)
1971 The Culture of Poverty: A Critique. New
      York: Simon and Schuster.
Lewis, Oscar
1968 "The culture of poverty." Pp. 187–200 in
      Daniel P. Moynihan (ed.), On Understand-
      ing Poverty. New York: Basic Books.
Li, Wen Lang and Martin H. Smith
1976 "The propensity to gamble: some structural
      determinants." Pp. 189–206 in William
      Eadington (ed.), Gambling and Society.
      Springfield, Il.: Thomas.
Light, Ivan
1972 Ethnic Enterprise in America. Berkeley and
      Los Angeles: University of California
      Press.
1974 Number and Policy Gambling in New York
      City, 1872–1973: Guide to New York Times
      with Annotations. Monticello, Il.: Council
      of Planning Librarians.
Light, Ivan and Charles Wong
1975 "Protest or work: dilemmas of the tourist
      industry in American Chinatowns." Ameri-
      can Journal of Sociology 80: 1342–68.
McCall, George J.
1963 "Symbiosis: the case of hoodoo and the
      numbers racket." Social Problems
      10:361–7.
McKay, Claude
1940 Harlem: Negro Metropolis. New York:
      Dutton.
Marcum, Jess and Henry Rowen
1974 "How many games in town? The pros and
      cons of legalized gambling." The Public
      Interest 36:25–54.
Marsh, James
1971 "Viewing the loss experience in minority

enterprise loans." The Bankers' Magazine
      154:84–7.
Martin, Edward Winslow (James McCabe, pseud.)
1868 The Secrets of the Great City. Philadelphia:
      n.p.
Matza, David
1966 "The disreputable poor." Pp. 289–302 in
      Reinhard Bendix and Seymour Martin Lip-
      set (eds.), Class, Status, and Power, 2nd ed.
      New York: Free Press.
Merton, Robert K.
1957 Social Theory and Social Structure (rev.
      ed.). New York: Free Press.
Neifeld, M. R.
1939 Personal Finance Comes of Age. New York
      and London: Harper.
Newman, Otto
1972 Gambling: Hazard and Reward. London:
      Athlone Press.
Nixon, Julian H.
1963 "The changing status of the Negro—some
      implications for savings and life insur-
      ance." The American Behavioral Scientist
      6:80–2.
Ofari, Earl
1970 The Myth of Black Capitalism. New York:
      Monthly Review Press.
Off Track Betting Corporation (N.Y.)
1973 Legalized Numbers: A Plan to Operate a
      Legal Numbers Game Now. New York: Off
      Track Betting Corporation.
Opinion Research Corporation
1966 New Dimensions in Full Service Banking.
      Princeton: Foundation for Commercial
      Banks.
Orren, Karen
1974 Corporate Power and Social Change. Bal-
      timore: Johns Hopkins University Press.
Ottley, Roi
1943 New World A-Coming. New York:
      World.
Perucci, Robert
1969 "The neighborhood 'Bookmaker': entre-
      preneur and mobility model." Pp. 302–11 in
      Paul Meadows and Ephraim H. Mizruchi
      (eds.), Urbanism, Urbanization, and
      Change: Comparative Perspectives. Read-
      ing, Ma.: Addison-Wesley.
Peterson, Virgil W.
1952 Barbarians in Our Midst. Boston: Little,
      Brown.
Rainwater, Lee
1967 The Moynihan Report and the Politics of
      Controversy. Cambridge: Masachusetts In-
      stitute of Technology Press.
Riis, Jacob A.
1892 How the Other Half Lives. New York:
      Scribner's.
Roebuck, Julian B.
1967 Criminal Typology. Springfield, Il.:
      Thomas.
Root, Anthony
1966 "On banking the social conscience." The
      Bankers' Magazine 155:64–6.
Rubner, Alex
1966 The Economics of Gambling, London:
      Macmillan.

Samuelson, Paul A.
1973 Economics. 95th ed. New York: McGraw-Hill.

Scimecca, Joseph A.
1971 "A typology of the gambler." International Journal of Contemporary Sociology 8:56–72.

Seidl, John
1968 Upon The Hip—A Study of the Criminal Loan Shark Industry. Ph.D. dissertation, Harvard University.

Selby, Edward B. and James T. Lindley
1973 "Black customers—hidden market potential." The Bankers' Magazine 156:84–7.

Sellin, Thorsten
1963 "Organized crime: a business enterprise." Annals of the American Academy of Political and Social Science 347:12–9.

Simon, Julian and Rita Simon
1968 "Class, status, and savings of Negroes." American Sociologist 3:218–9.

Stafford, James, Keith Cox and James Higginbotham
1968 "Some consumption pattern differences between urban whites and Negroes." Social Science Quarterly 49:619–30.

Stocking, Collis
1932 "Gambling." Encyclopedia of the Social Sciences, Vol. 6. London: Macmillan.

Strong, Samuel M.
1940 Social Types of the Negro Community of Chicago: An Example of the Social Type Method. Ph.D. dissertation, University of Chicago.

Sturdivant, Frederick D. (ed.)
1969 The Ghetto Marketplace. New York: Free Press.

Tec, Nechama
1964 Gambling in Sweden. Totowa, N.J.: Bedminster.

Thurner, Isidore
1956 "Ascetic Protestantism, gambling and the one-price system." American Journal of Economics and Sociology 15:161–72.

U.S. Immigration Commission
1911 Reports of the Immigration Commission. U.S. Senate, 61st Congress, 2nd Session, Document 753. Immigrant Banks. Vol. 37. Washington, D.C.: U.S. Government Printing Office.

U.S. Senate, Ninetieth Congress, 2nd Session. Committee on Banking and Currency
1968 Financial Institutions and the Urban Crisis. Washington, D.C.: U.S. Government Printing Office.
1970 Credit in Low-Income Areas. Washington, D. C.: U.S. Government Printing Office.

U.S. Senate, Ninety-Fourth Congress, 1st Session. Committee on Banking, Housing, and Urban Affairs
1975 Home Mortgage Disclosure Act of 1975, Parts 1 and 2. Washington, D.C.: U.S. Government Printing Office.

Valentine, Charles A.
1968 Culture and Poverty. Chicago: University of Chicago Press.

Warner, W. Lloyd and Buford H. Junker
1941 Color and Human Nature. Washington, D. C.: American Council on Education.

Whyte, William Foote
1943 Street Corner Society. Chicago: University of Chicago Press.

Wong, Charles
1977 "Black and Chinese grocery stores in Los Angeles' black ghetto." Urban Life 5:439 - 64.

Zetterberg, Hans
1962 Social Theory and Social Practice. New York: Bedminster.

[11]

Appendix B

WINCANTON: THE POLITICS OF CORRUPTION

by John A. Gardiner, with the assistance of David J. Olson

Contents

INTRODUCTION [1]

This study focuses upon the politics of vice and corruption in a town we have chosen to call Wincanton, U.S.A. Although the facts and events of this report are true, every attempt has been made to hide the identity of actual people by the use of fictitious names, descriptions and dates.

Following a brief description of the people of Wincanton and the structure of its government and law enforcement agencies, a section outlines the structure of the Wincanton gambling syndicate and the system of protection under which it operated. A second section looks at the corrupt activities of Wincanton officials apart from the protection of vice and gambling.

The latter part of this report considers gambling and corruption as social forces and as political issues. First, they are analyzed in terms of their functions in the community—satisfying social and psychological needs declared by the State to be improper; supplementing the income of

JOHN A. GARDINER, A.B., Princeton University, 1959; M.A., Yale University, 1962; LL.B., Harvard University, 1963; Ph. D., Harvard University, 1966. In 1965, while finishing his doctoral dissertation, "Traffic Law Enforcement in Massachusetts," Professor Gardiner was appointed to his current position of assistant professor of Political Science at the University of Wisconsin. Professor Gardiner was a member of Phi Beta Kappa at Princeton and graduated Magna Cum Laude in public affairs. He has been an honorary Woodrow Wilson Fellow and Falk Fellow in Political Science at Yale; V. O. Key, Jr., Fellow of the Joint Center for Urban Studies of M.I.T. and Harvard; and Woodrow Wilson Dissertation Research Fellow and Honorary Social Science Research Council Fellow at Harvard.

DAVID J. OLSON, B.A., Concordia College, 1963; M.A., University of Wisconsin, 1965. David J. Olson teaches Political Science at the University of Wisconsin, where he is also a candidate for a Ph. D. degree. Under a grant from the Rockefeller Foundation he did independent research at Union Theological Seminary in New York for one year. Mr. Olson is a member of the American Political Science Association. He formerly served as a community planner II and as a consultant to the Redevelopment Authority of Madison, Wis.

the participants, including underpaid city officials and policemen, and of related legitimate businesses; providing speed and certainty in the transaction of municipal business. Second, popular attitudes toward gambling and corruption are studied, as manifested in both local elections and a survey of a cross-section of the city's population. Finally, an attempt will be made to explain why Wincanton, more than other cities, has had this marked history of lawbreaking and official malfeasance, and several suggestions will be made regarding legal changes that might make its continuation more difficult.

WINCANTON

In general, Wincanton represents a city that has toyed with the problem of corruption for many years. No mayor in the history of the city of Wincanton has ever succeeded himself in office. Some mayors have been corrupt and have allowed the city to become a wide-open center for gambling and prostitution; Wincanton voters have regularly rejected those corrupt mayors who dared to seek re-election. Some mayors have been scrupulously honest and have closed down all vice operations in the city; these men have been generally disliked for being too straitlaced. Other mayors, fearing one form of resentment or the other, have chosen quietly to retire from public life. The questions of official corruption and policy toward vice and gambling, it seems, have been paramount issues in Wincanton elections since the days of Prohibition. Any mayor who is known to be controlled by the gambling syndicates will lose office, but so will any mayor who tries completely to clean up the city. The people of Wincanton apparently want both easily accessible gambling and freedom from racket domination.

Probably more than most cities in the United States, Wincanton has known a high degree of gambling, vice (sexual immorality, including prostitution), and corruption (official malfeasance, misfeasance and nonfeasance of duties). With the exception of two reform administrations, one in the early 1950's and the one elected in the early 1960's, Wincanton has been wide open since the 1920's. Bookies taking bets on horses took in several

[1] This study, part of a larger investigation of the politics of law enforcement and corruption, was financed by a grant from the Russell Sage Foundation. All responsibility for the contents of this report remains with the senior author. The authors wish gratefully to acknowledge the assistance of the people and officials of Wincanton who will, at their request, remain anonymous. The authors wish particularly to acknowledge the assistance of the newspapers of Wincanton; Prof. Harry Sharp and the staff of the Wisconsin Survey Research Laboratory; Henry S. Ruth, Jr., Lloyd E. Ohlin, and Charles H. Rogovin

of the President's Commission on Law Enforcement and Administration of Justice; and many National, State, and local law enforcement personnel. The authors shared equally in the research upon which this report is based; because of the teaching duties of Mr. Olson, Mr. Gardiner assumed the primary role in writing this report. Joel Margolis and Keith Billingsley, graduate students in the Department of Political Science, University of Wisconsin, assisted in the preparation of the data used in this report.

62

millions of dollars each year. With writers at most newsstands, cigar counters, and corner grocery stores, a numbers bank did an annual business in excess of $1,300,000 during some years. Over 200 pinball machines, equipped to pay off like slot machines, bore $250 Federal gambling stamps. A high stakes dice game attracted professional gamblers from more than 100 miles away; $25,000 was found on the table during one Federal raid. For a short period of time in the 1950's (until raided by U.S. Treasury Department agents), a still, capable of manufacturing $4 million in illegal alcohol each year, operated on the banks of the Wincanton River. Finally, prostitution flourished openly in the city, with at least 5 large houses (about 10 girls apiece) and countless smaller houses catering to men from a large portion of the State.

As in all cities in which gambling and vice had flourished openly, these illegal activities were protected by local officials. Mayors, police chiefs, and many lesser officials were on the payroll of the gambling syndicate, while others received periodic "gifts" or aid during political campaigns. A number of Wincanton officials added to their revenue from the syndicate by extorting kickbacks on the sale or purchase of city equipment or by selling licenses, permits, zoning variances, etc. As the city officials made possible the operations of the racketeers, so frequently the racketeers facilitated the corrupt endeavors of officials by providing liaison men to arrange the deals or "enforcers" to insure that the deals were carried out.

The visitor to Wincanton is struck by the beauty of the surrounding countryside and the drabness of a tired, old central city. Looking down on the city from Mount Prospect, the city seems packed in upon itself, with long streets of red brick row houses pushing up against old railroad yards and factories; 93 percent of the housing units were built before 1940.

Wincanton had its largest population in 1930 and has been losing residents slowly ever since.[2] The people who remained—those who didn't move to the suburbs or to the other parts of the United States—are the lower middle class, the less well educated: they seem old and often have an Old World feeling about them. The median age in Wincanton is 37 years (compared with a national median of 29 years). While unemployment is low (2.5 percent of the labor force in April 1965), there are few professional or white collar workers; only 11 percent of the families had incomes over $10,000, and the median family income was $5,453. As is common in many cities with an older, largely working class population, the level of education is low—only 27 percent of the adults have completed high school, and the median number of school years completed is 8.9.

While most migration into Wincanton took place before 1930, the various nationality groups in Wincanton seem to have retained their separate identities. The Germans, the Poles, the Italians, and the Negroes each have their own neighborhoods, stores, restaurants, clubs and politicians. Having immigrated earlier, the Germans are more assimilated into the middle and upper middle classes; the other groups still frequently live in the neighborhoods in which they first settled; and Italian and Polish politicians openly appeal to Old World loyalties. Club life adds to the ethnic groupings by giving a definite neighborhood quality to various parts of the city and their politics; every politician is expected to visit the ethnic associations, ward clubs, and voluntary firemen's associations during campaign time—buying a round of drinks for all present and leaving money with the club stewards to hire poll watchers to advertise the candidates and guard the voting booths.

In part, the flight from Wincanton of the young and the more educated can be explained by the character of the local economy. While there have been no serious depressions in Wincanton during the last 30 years, there has been little growth either, and most of the factories in the city were built 30 to 50 years ago and rely primarily upon semiskilled workers. A few textile mills have moved out of the region, to be balanced by the construction in the last 5 years of several electronics assembly plants. No one employer dominates the economy, although seven employed more than 1,000 persons. Major industries today include steel fabrication and heavy machinery, textiles and food products.

With the exception of 2 years (one in the early 1950's; the other 12 years later) in which investigations of corruption led to the election of Republican reformers, Wincanton politics have been heavily Democratic in recent years. Registered Democrats in the city outnumber Republicans by a margin of 2 to 1; in Alsace County as a whole, including the heavily Republican middle class suburbs, the Democratic margin is reduced to 3 to 2. Despite this margin of control, or possibly because of it, Democratic politics in Wincanton have always been somewhat chaotic—candidates appeal to the ethnic groups, clubs, and neighborhoods, and no machine or organization has been able to dominate the party for very long (although a few men have been able to build a personal following lasting for 10 years or so). Incumbent mayors have been defeated in the primaries by other Democrats, and voting in city council sessions has crossed party lines more often than it has respected them.

To a great extent, party voting in Wincanton follows a business-labor cleavage. Two newspapers (both owned by a group of local businessmen) and the Chamber of Commerce support Republican candidates; the unions usually endorse Democrats. It would be unwise, however, to overestimate either the solidarity or the interest in local politics of Wincanton business and labor groups. Frequently two or more union leaders may be opposing each other in a Democratic primary (the steelworkers frequently endorse liberal or reform candidates, while the retail clerks have been more tied to "organization" men); or ethnic allegiances and hostilities may cause union members to vote for Republicans, or simply sit on their hands. Furthermore, both business and labor leaders express greater interest in State and National issues—taxation, wage and hour laws, collective bargaining policies, etc.—than in local issues. (The attitude of both business and labor toward Wincanton gambling and corruption will be examined in detail later.)

Many people feel that, apart from the perennial issue

---

[2] To preserve the anonymity of the city, it will only be stated that Wincanton's 1960 population was between 75,000 and 200,000.

of corruption, there really are not any issues in Wincanton politics and that personalities are the only things that matter in city elections. Officials assume that the voters are generally opposed to a high level of public services. Houses are tidy, but the city has no public trash collection, or fire protection either, for that matter. While the city buys firetrucks and pays their drivers, firefighting is done solely by volunteers—in a city with more than 75,000 residents. (Fortunately, most of the houses are built of brick or stone.) Urban renewal has been slow, master planning nonexistent, and a major railroad line still crosses the heart of the shopping district, bringing traffic to a halt as trains grind past. Some people complain, but no mayor has ever been able to do anything about it. For years, people have been talking about rebuilding City Hall (constructed as a high school 75 years ago), modernizing mass transportation, and ending pollution of the Wincanton River, but nothing much has been done about any of these issues, or even seriously considered. Some people explain this by saying that Wincantonites are interested in everything—up to and including, but not extending beyond, their front porch.

If the voters of Wincanton were to prefer an active rather than passive city government, they would find the municipal structure well equipped to frustrate their desires. Many governmental functions are handled by independent boards and commissions, each able to veto proposals of the mayor and councilmen. Until about 10 years ago, State law required all middle-sized cities to operate under a modification of the commission form of government. (In the early 1960's, Wincanton voters narrowly—by a margin of 16 votes out of 30,000—rejected a proposal to set up a council-manager plan.) The city council is composed of five men—a mayor and four councilmen. Every odd-numbered year, two councilmen are elected to 4-year terms. The mayor also has a 4-year term of office, but has a few powers not held by the councilmen; he presides at council sessions but has no veto power over council legislation. State law requires that city affairs be divided among five named departments, each to be headed by a member of the council, but the council members are free to decide among themselves what functions will be handled by which departments (with the proviso that the mayor must control the police deparment). Thus the city's work can be split equally among five men, or a three-man majority can control all important posts. In a not atypical recent occurrence, one councilman, disliked by his colleagues, found himself supervising only garbage collection and the Main Street comfort station! Each department head (mayor and councilmen) has almost complete control over his own department. Until 1960, when a $2,500 raise became effective, the mayor received an annual salary of $7,000, and each councilman received $6,000. The mayor and city councilmen have traditionally been permitted to hold other jobs while in office.

To understand law enforcement in Wincanton, it is necessary to look at the activities of local, county, State, and Federal agencies. State law requires that each mayor select his police chief and officers "from the force" and "exercise a constant supervision and control over their conduct." Applicants for the police force are chosen on the basis of a civil service examination and have tenure "during good behavior," but promotions and demotions are entirely at the discretion of the mayor and council. Each new administration in Wincanton has made wholesale changes in police ranks—patrolmen have been named chief, and former chiefs have been reduced to walking a beat. (When one period of reform came to an end in the mid-1950's, the incoming mayor summoned the old chief into his office. "You can stay on as an officer," the mayor said, "but you'll have to go along with my policies regarding gambling." "Mr. Mayor," the chief said, "I'm going to keep on arresting gamblers no matter where you put me." The mayor assigned the former chief to the position of "Keeper of the Lockup," permanently stationed in the basement of police headquarters.) Promotions must be made from within the department. This policy has continued even though the present reform mayor created the post of police commissioner and brought in an outsider to take command. For cities of its size, Wincanton police salaries have been quite low—the top pay for patrolmen was $4,856—in the lowest quartile of middle-sized cities in the Nation. Since 1964 the commissioner has received $10,200 and patrolmen $5,400 each year.

While the police department is the prime law enforcement agency within Wincanton, it receives help (and occasional embarrassment) from other groups. Three county detectives work under the district attorney, primarily in rural parts of Alsace County, but they are occasionally called upon to assist in city investigations. The State Police, working out of a barracks in suburban Wincanton Hills, have generally taken a "hands off" or "local option" attitude toward city crime, working only in rural areas unless invited into a city by the mayor, district attorney, or county judge. Reform mayors have welcomed the superior manpower and investigative powers of the State officers; corrupt mayors have usually been able to thumb their noses at State policemen trying to uncover Wincanton gambling. Agents of the State's Alcoholic Beverages Commission suffer from no such limitations and enter Wincanton at will in search of liquor violations. They have seldom been a serious threat to Wincanton corruption, however, since their numbers are quite limited (and thus the agents are dependent upon the local police for information and assistance in making arrests). Their mandate extends to gambling and prostitution only when encountered in the course of a liquor investigation.

Under most circumstances, the operative level of law enforcement in Wincanton has been set by local political decisions, and the local police (acting under instructions from the mayor) have been able to determine whether or not Wincanton should have open gambling and prostitution. The State Police, with their "hands off" policy, have simply reenforced the local decision. From time to time, however, Federal agencies have become interested in conditions in Wincanton and, as will be seen throughout this study, have played as important a role as the local police in cleaning up the city. Internal Revenue Service

64

agents have succeeded in prosecuting Wincanton gamblers for failure to hold gambling occupation stamps, pay the special excise taxes on gambling receipts, or report income. Federal Bureau of Investigation agents have acted against violations of the Federal laws against extortion and interstate gambling. Finally, special attorneys from the Organized Crime and Racketeering Section of the Justice Department were able to convict leading members of the syndicate controlling Wincanton gambling. While Federal prosecutions in Wincanton have often been spectacular, it should also be noted that they have been somewhat sporadic and limited in scope. The Internal Revenue Service, for example, was quite successful in seizing gaming devices and gamblers lacking the Federal gambling occupation stamps, but it was helpless after Wincantonites began to purchase the stamps, since local officials refused to prosecute them for violations of the State antigambling laws.

The court system in Wincanton, as in all cities in the State, still has many of the 18th century features which have been rejected in other States. At the lowest level, elected magistrates (without legal training) hear petty civil and criminal cases in each ward of the city. The magistrates also issue warrants and decide whether persons arrested by the police shall be held for trial. Magistrates are paid only by fees. usually at the expense of convicted defendants. All serious criminal cases, and all contested petty cases. are tried in the county court. The three judges of the Alsace County court are elected (on a partisan ballot) for 10-year terms, and receive an annual salary of $25,000.

GAMBLING AND CORRUPTION: THE INSIDERS

THE STERN EMPIRE

The history of Wincanton gambling and corruption since World War II centers around the career of Irving Stern. Stern is an immigrant who came to the United States and settled in Wincanton at the turn of the century. He started as a fruit peddler, but when Prohibition came along, Stern became a bootlegger for Heinz Glickman, then the beer baron of the State. When Glickman was murdered in the waning days of Prohibition, Stern took over Glickman's business and continued to sell untaxed liquor after repeal of Prohibition in 1933. Several times during the 1930's. Stern was convicted in Federal court on liquor charges and spent over a year in Federal prison.

Around 1940, Stern announced to the world that he had reformed and went into his family's wholesale produce business. While Stern was in fact leaving the bootlegging trade. he was also moving into the field of gambling, for even at that time Wincanton had a "wide-open" reputation, and the police were ignoring gamblers. With the technical assistance of his bootlegging friends, Stern started with a numbers bank and soon added horse betting. a dice game. and slot machines to his organization. During World War II. officers from a nearby Army training base insisted that all brothels be closed,

but this did not affect Stern. He had already concluded that public hostility and violence, caused by the houses. were, as a side effect, threatening his more profitable gambling operations. Although Irv Stern controlled the the lion's share of Wincanton gambling throughout the 1940's, he had to share the slot machine trade with Klaus Braun. Braun, unlike Stern. was a Wincanton native and a Gentile, and thus had easier access to the frequently anti-Semitic club stewards. restaurant owners, and bartenders who decided which machines would be placed in their buildings. Legislative investigations in the early 1950's estimated that Wincanton gambling was an industry with gross receipts of $5 million each year; at that time Stern was receiving $40,000 per week from bookmaking, and Braun took in $75,000 to $100,000 per year from slot machines alone.

Irv Stern's empire in Wincanton collapsed abruptly when legislative investigations brought about the election of a reform Republican administration. Mayor Hal Craig decided to seek what he termed "pearl gray purity"—to tolerate isolated prostitutes. bookies, and numbers writers—but to drive out all forms of organized crime, all activities lucrative enough to make it worth someone's while to try bribing Craig's police officials. Within 6 weeks after taking office. Craig and District Attorney Henry Weiss had raided enough of Stern's gambling parlors and seized enough of Braun's slot machines to convince both men that business was over—for 4 years at least. The Internal Revenue Service was able to convict Braun and Stern's nephew, Dave Feinman, on tax evasion charges; both were sent to jail. From 1952 to 1955 it was still possible to place a bet or find a girl. But you had to know someone to do it, and no one was getting very rich in the process.

By 1955 it was apparent to everyone that reform sentiment was dead and that the Democrats would soon be back in office. In the summer of that year, Stern met with representatives of the east coast syndicates and arranged for the rebuilding of his empire. He decided to change his method of operations in several ways; one way was by centralizing all Wincanton vice and gambling under his control. But he also decided to turn the actual operation of most enterprises over to others. From the mid-1950's until the next wave of reform hit Wincanton after elections in the early 1960's. Irv Stern generally succeeded in reaching these goals.

The financial keystone of Stern's gambling empire was numbers betting. Records seized by the Internal Revenue Service in the late 1950's and early 1960's indicated that gross receipts from numbers amounted to more than $100,000 each month, or $1.3 million annually. Since the numbers are a poor man's form of gambling (bets range from a penny to a dime or quarter), a large number of men and a high degree of organization are required. The organizational goals are three: have the maximum possible number of men on the streets seeking bettors, be sure that they are reporting honestly. and yet strive so to decentralize the organization that no one, if arrested, will be able to identify many of the others. During the "pearl gray purity" of Hal Craig, numbers writing was completely unorganized—many isolated writers took bets from their friends and frequently had to renege if an unusually popular number came up; no one writer was big enough to guard against such possibilities. When a new mayor took office in the mid-1950's, however, Stern's lieutenants notified each of the small writers that they were now working for Stern—or else. Those who objected were "persuaded" by Stern's men, or else arrested by the police, as were any of the others who were suspected of holding out on their receipts. Few objected for very long. After Stern completed the reorganization of the numbers business, its structure was roughly something like this: 11 subbanks reported to Stern's central accounting office. Each subbank employed from 5 to 30 numbers writers. Thirty-five percent of the gross receipts went to the writers. After deducting for winnings and expenses (mostly protection payoffs), Stern divided the net profits equally with the operators of the subbanks. In return for his cut, Stern provided protection from the police and "laid off" the subbanks, covering winnings whenever a popular number "broke" one of the smaller operators.

Stern also shared with out-of-State syndicates in the profits and operation of two enterprises—a large dice game and the largest still found by the Treasury Department since Prohibition. The dice game employed over 50 men—drivers to "lug" players into town from as far as 100 miles away, doormen to check players' identities, loan sharks who "faded" the losers, croupiers, food servers, guards, etc. The 1960 payroll for these employees was over $350,000. While no estimate of the gross receipts from the game is available, some indication of its size can be obtained from the fact that $50,000 was found on the tables and in the safe when the FBI raided the game in 1962. Over 100 players were arrested during the raid; one businessman had lost over $75,000 at the tables. Stern received a share of the game's profits plus a $1,000 weekly fee to provide protection from the police.

Stern also provided protection (for a fee) and shared in the profits of a still, erected in an old warehouse on the banks of the Wincanton River and tied into the city's water and sewer systems. Stern arranged for clearance by the city council and provided protection from the local police after the $200,000 worth of equipment was set up. The still was capable of producing $4 million worth of alcohol each year, and served a five-State area, until Treasury agents raided it after it had been in operation for less than 1 year.

The dice game and the still raise questions regarding the relationship of Irv Stern to out-of-State syndicates. Republican politicians in Wincanton frequently claimed that Stern was simply the local agent of the Cosa Nostra. While Stern was regularly sending money to the syndicates, the evidence suggests that Stern was much more than an agent for outsiders. It would be more accurate to regard these payments as profit sharing with coinvestors and as charges for services rendered. The east coasters provided technical services in the operation of the dice game and still and "enforcement" service for the Wincanton gambling operation. When deviants had to be persuaded to accept Stern's domination, Stern called upon outsiders for "muscle"—strong-arm men who could not be traced by local police if the victim chose to protest. In the early 1940's, for example, Stern asked for help in destroying a competing dice game; six gunmen came in and held it up, robbing and terrifying the players. While a few murders took place in the struggle for supremacy in the 1930's and 1940's, only a few people were roughed up in the 1950's and no one was killed.

After the mid-1950's, Irv Stern controlled prostitution and several forms of gambling on a "franchise" basis. Stern took no part in the conduct of these businesses and received no share of the profits, but exacted a fee for protection from the police. Several horse books, for example, operated regularly; the largest of these paid Stern $600 per week. While slot machines had permanently disappeared from the Wincanton scene after the legislative investigations of the early 1950's, a number of men began to distribute pinball machines, which paid off players for games won. As was the case with numbers writers, these pinball distributors had been unorganized during the Craig administration. When Democratic Mayor Gene Donnelly succeeded Craig, he immediately announced that all pinball machines were illegal and would be confiscated by the police. A Stern agent then contacted the pinball distributors and notified them that if they employed Dave Feinman (Irv Stern's nephew) as a "public relations consultant," there would be no interference from the police. Several rebellious distributors formed an Alsace County Amusement Operators Association, only to see Feinman appear with two thugs from New York. After the association president was roughed up, all resistance collapsed, and Feinman collected $2,000 each week to promote the "public relations" of the distributors. (Stern, of course, was able to offer no protection against Federal action. After the Internal Revenue Service began seizing the pinball machines in 1956, the owners were forced to purchase the $250 Federal gambling stamps as well as paying Feinman. Over 200 Wincanton machines bore these stamps in the early 1960's, and thus were secure from Federal as well as local action.)

After the period of reform in the early 1950's, Irv Stern was able to establish a centralized empire in which he alone determined which rackets would operate and who would operate them (he never, it might be noted, permitted narcotics traffic in the city while he controlled it). What were the bases of his control within the criminal world? Basically, they were three: First, as a business matter, Stern controlled access to several very lucrative operations, and could quickly deprive an uncooperative gambler or numbers writer of his source of income. Second, since he controlled the police department he could arrest any gamblers or bookies who were not paying tribute. (Some of the local gambling and prostitution arrests which took place during the Stern era served another purpose—to placate newspaper demands for a crackdown. As one police chief from this era phrased it, "Hollywood should have given us an Oscar for some of our performances when we had to pull a phony raid to keep the papers happy.") Finally, if the mechanisms of fear of financial loss and fear of police

66

arrest failed to command obedience, Stern was always able to keep alive a fear of physical violence. As we have seen, numbers writers, pinball distributors, and competing gamblers were brought into line after outside enforcers put in an appearance. Stern's regular collection agent, a local tough who had been convicted of murder in the 1940's, was a constant reminder of the virtues of cooperation. Several witnesses who told grand juries or Federal agents of extortion attempts by Stern, received visits from Stern enforcers and tended to "forget" when called to testify against the boss.

Protection.   An essential ingredient in Irv Stern's Wincanton operations was protection against law enforcement agencies. While he was never able to arrange freedom from Federal intervention (although, as in the case of purchasing excise stamps for the pinball machines, he was occasionally able to satisfy Federal requirements without disrupting his activities), Stern was able in the 1940's and again from the mid-1950's through the early 1960's to secure freedom from State and local action. The precise extent of Stern's network of protection payments is unknown, but the method of operations can be reconstructed.

Two basic principles were involved in the Wincanton protection system—pay top personnel as much as necessary to keep them happy (and quiet), and pay something to as many others as possible to implicate them in the system and to keep them from talking. The range of payoffs thus went from a weekly salary for some public officials to a Christmas turkey for the patrolman on the beat. Records from the numbers bank listed payments totaling $2,400 each week to some local elected officials, State legislators, the police chief, a captain in charge of detectives, and persons mysteriously labeled "county" and "State." While the list of persons to be paid remained fairly constant, the amounts paid varied according to the gambling activities in operation at the time; payoff figures dropped sharply when the FBI put the dice game out of business. When the dice game was running, one official was receiving $750 per week, the chief $100, and a few captains, lieutenants, and detectives lesser amounts.

While the number of officials receiving regular "salary" payoffs was quite restricted (only 15 names were on the payroll found at the numbers bank), many other officials were paid off in different ways. (Some men were also silenced without charge—low-ranking policemen, for example, kept quiet after they learned that men who reported gambling or prostitution were ignored or transferred to the midnight shift; they didn't have to be paid.) Stern was a major (if undisclosed) contributor during political campaigns—sometimes giving money to all candidates, not caring who won, sometimes supporting a "regular" to defeat a possible reformer, sometimes paying a candidate not to oppose a preferred man. Since there were few legitimate sources of large contributions for Democratic candidates, Stern's money was frequently regarded as essential for victory, for the costs of buying radio and television time and paying pollwatchers were high. When popular sentiment was running strongly

in favor of reform, however, even Stern's contributions could not guarantee victory. Bob Walasek, later to be as corrupt as any Wincanton mayor, ran as a reform candidate in the Democratic primary and defeated Stern-financed incumbent Gene Donnelly. Never a man to bear grudges, Stern financed Walasek in the general election that year and put him on the "payroll" when he took office.

Even when local officials were not on the regular payroll, Stern was careful to remind them of his friendship (and their debts). A legislative investigating committee found that Stern had given mortgage loans to a police lieutenant and the police chief's son. County Court Judge Ralph Vaughan recalled that shortly after being elected (with Stern support), he received a call from Dave Feinman, Stern's nephew. "Congratulations, judge. When do you think you and your wife would like a vacation in Florida?"

"Florida? Why on earth would I want to go there?"

"But all the other judges and the guys in City Hall—Irv takes them all to Florida whenever they want to get away."

"Thanks anyway, but I'm not interested."

"Well, how about a mink coat instead. What size coat does your wife wear? * * *"

In another instance an assistant district attorney told of Feinman's arriving at his front door with a large basket from Stern's supermarket just before Christmas. "My minister suggested a needy family that could use the food," the assistant district attorney recalled, "but I returned the liquor to Feinman. How could I ask a minister if he knew someone that could use three bottles of scotch?"

Campaign contributions, regular payments to higher officials, holiday and birthday gifts—these were the bases of the system by which Irv Stern bought protection from the law. The campaign contributions usually ensured that complacent mayors, councilmen, district attorneys, and judges were elected; payoffs in some instances usually kept their loyalty. In a number of ways, Stern was also able to reward the corrupt officials at no financial cost to himself. Just as the officials, being in control of the instruments of law enforcement, were able to facilitate Stern's gambling enterprises, so Stern, in control of a network of men operating outside the law, was able to facilitate the officials' corrupt enterprises. As will be seen later, many local officials were not satisfied with their legal salaries from the city and their illegal salaries from Stern and decided to demand payments from prostitutes, kickbacks from salesmen. etc. Stern, while seldom receiving any money from these transactions, became a broker: bringing politicians into contact with salesmen, merchants, and lawyers willing to offer bribes to get city business; setting up middlemen who could handle the money without jeopardizing the officials' reputations; and providing enforcers who could bring delinquents into line.

From the corrupt activities of Wincanton officials, Irv Stern received little in contrast to his receipts from his gambling operations. Why then did he get involved in them? The major virtue, from Stern's point of view, of the system of extortion that flourished in Wincanton was that it kept down the officials' demands for payoffs directly from Stern. If a councilman was able to pick up $1,000 on the purchase of city equipment, he would demand a lower payment for the protection of gambling. Furthermore, since Stern knew the facts of extortion in each instance, the officials would be further implicated in the system and less able to back out on the arrangements regarding gambling. Finally, as Stern discovered to his chagrin, it became necessary to supervise official extortion to protect the officials against their own stupidity. Mayor Gene Donnelly was cooperative and remained satisfied with his regular "salary." Bob Walasek, however, was a greedy man, and seized every opportunity to profit from a city contract. Soon Stern found himself supervising many of Walasek's deals to keep the mayor from blowing the whole arrangement wide open. When Walasek tried to double the "take" on a purchase of parking meters, Stern had to step in and set the contract price, provide an untraceable middleman, and see the deal through to completion. "I told Irv," Police Chief Phillips later testified, "that Walasek wanted $12 on each meter instead of the $6 we got on the last meter deal. He became furious. He said, 'Walasek is going to fool around and wind up in jail. You come and see me. I'll tell Walasek what he's going to buy.' "

Protection, it was stated earlier, was an essential ingredient in Irv Stern's gambling empire. In the end, Stern's downfall came not from a flaw in the organization of the gambling enterprises but from public exposure of the corruption of Mayor Walasek and other officials. In the early 1960's Stern was sent to jail for 4 years on tax evasion charges, but the gambling empire continued to operate smoothly in his absence. A year later, however, Chief Phillips was caught perjuring himself in grand jury testimony concerning kickbacks on city towing contracts. Phillips "blew the whistle" on Stern, Walasek, and members of the city council, and a reform administration was swept into office. Irv Stern's gambling empire had been worth several million dollars each year; kickbacks on the towing contracts brought Bob Walasek a paltry $50 to $75 each week.

OFFICIAL CORRUPTION

Textbooks on municipal corporation law speak of at least three varieties of official corruption. The major categories are nonfeasance (failing to perform a required duty at all), malfeasance (the commission of some act which is positively unlawful), and misfeasance (the improper performance of some act which a man may properly do). During the years in which Irv Stern was running his gambling operations, Wincanton officials were guilty of all of these. Some residents say that Bob Walasek came to regard the mayor's office as a brokerage, levying a tariff on every item that came across his desk. Sometimes a request for simple municipal services turned into a game of cat and mouse, with Walasek sitting on the request, waiting to see how much would be offered, and the petitioner waiting to see if he could obtain his rights without having to pay for them. Corruption was not as lucrative an enterprise as gambling, but it offered a tempting supplement to low official salaries.

NONFEASANCE

As was detailed earlier, Irv Stern saw to it that Wincanton officials would ignore at least one of their statutory duties, enforcement of the State's gambling laws. Bob Walasek and his cohorts also agreed to overlook other illegal activities. Stern, we noted earlier, preferred not to get directly involved in prostitution; Walasek and Police Chief Dave Phillips tolerated all prostitutes who kept up their protection payments. One madam, controlling more than 20 girls, gave Phillips et al. $500 each week; one woman employing only one girl paid $75 each week that she was in business. Operators of a carnival in rural Alsace County paid a public official $5,000 for the privilege of operating gambling tents for 5 nights each summer. A burlesque theater manager, under attack by high school teachers, was ordered to pay $25 each week for the privilege of keeping his strip show open.

Many other city and county officials must be termed guilty of nonfeasance, although there is no evidence that they received payoffs, and although they could present reasonable excuses for their inaction. Most policemen, as we have noted earlier, began to ignore prostitution and gambling completely after their reports of offenses were ignored or superior officers told them to mind their own business. State policemen, well informed about city vice and gambling conditions, did nothing unless called upon to act by local officials. Finally, the judges of the Alsace County Court failed to exercise their power to call for State Police investigations. In 1957, following Federal raids on horse bookies, the judges did request an investigation by the State Attorney General, but refused to approve his suggestion that a grand jury be convened to continue the investigation. For each of these instances of inaction, a tenable excuse might be offered—the beat patrolman should not be expected to endure harassment from his superior officers, State police gambling raids in a hostile city might jeopardize State-local cooperation on more serious crimes, and a grand jury probe might easily be turned into a "whitewash" in the hands of a corrupt district attorney. In any event, powers available to these law enforcement agencies for the prevention of gambling and corruption were not utilized.

MALFEASANCE

In fixing parking and speeding tickets, Wincanton politicians and policemen committed malfeasance, or committed an act they were forbidden to do, by illegally compromising valid civil and criminal actions. Similarly, while State law provides no particular standards by which the mayor is to make promotions within his police department, it was obviously improper for Mayor Walasek to demand a "political contribution" of $10,000 from Dave Phillips before he was appointed chief in 1960.

The term "political contribution" raises a serious legal and analytical problem in classifying the malfeasance of Wincanton officials, and indeed of politicians in many cities. Political campaigns cost money; citizens have a right to support the candidates of their choice; and officials have a right to appoint their backers to noncivil service positions. At some point, however, threats or oppression convert legitimate requests for political contributions into extortion. Shortly after taking office in the mid-1950's, Mayor Gene Donnelly notified city hall employees that they would be expected "voluntarily" to contribute 2 percent of their salary to the Democratic Party. (It might be noted that Donnelly never forwarded any of these "political contributions" to the party treasurer.) A number of salesmen doing business with the city were notified that companies which had supported the party would receive favored treatment; Donnelly notified one salesman that in light of a proposed $81,000 contract for the purchase of fire engines, a "political contribution" of $2,000 might not be inappropriate. While neither the city hall employees nor the salesmen had rights to their positions or their contracts, the "voluntary" quality of their contributions seems questionable.

One final, in the end almost ludicrous, example of malfeasance came with Mayor Donnelly's abortive "War on the Press." Following a series of gambling raids by the Internal Revenue Service, the newspapers began asking why the local police had not participated in the raids. The mayor lost his temper and threw a reporter in jail. Policemen were instructed to harass newspaper delivery trucks, and 73 tickets were written over a 48-hour period for supposed parking and traffic violations. Donnelly soon backed down after national news services picked up the story, since press coverage made him look ridiculous. Charges against the reporter were dropped, and the newspapers continued to expose gambling and corruption.

MISFEASANCE

Misfeasance in office, says the common law, is the improper performance of some act which a man may properly do. City officials must buy and sell equipment, contract for services, and allocate licenses, privileges, etc. These actions can be improperly performed if either the results are improper (e.g., if a building inspector were to approve a home with defective wiring or a zoning board to authorize a variance which had no justification in terms of land usage) or a result is achieved by improper procedures (e.g., if the city purchased an acceptable automobile in consideration of a bribe paid to the purchasing agent). In the latter case, we can usually assume an improper result as well—while the automobile will be satisfactory, the bribe giver will probably have inflated the sale price to cover the costs of the bribe.

In Wincanton, it was rather easy for city officials to demand kickbacks, for State law frequently does not demand competitive bidding or permits the city to ignore the lowest bid. The city council is not required to advertise or take bids on purchases under $1,000, contracts for maintenance of streets and other public works, personal or professional services, or patented or copyrighted products. Even when bids must be sought, the council is only required to award the contract to the lowest responsible bidder. Given these permissive provisions, it was relatively easy for council members to justify or disguise contracts in fact based upon bribes. The exemption for patented products facilitated bribe taking on the purchase of two emergency trucks for the police department (with a $500 campaign contribution on a $7,500 deal), three fire engines ($2,000 was allegedly paid on an $81,000 contract), and 1,500 parking meters (involving payments of $10,500 plus an $880 clock for Mayor Walasek's home). Similar fees were allegedly exacted in connection with the purchase of a city fire alarm system and police uniforms and firearms. A former mayor and other officials also profited on the sale of city property, allegedly dividing $500 on the sale of a crane and $20,000 for approving the sale, for $22,000, of a piece of land immediately resold for $75,000.

When contracts involved services to the city, the provisions in the State law regarding the lowest responsible bidder and excluding "professional services" from competitive bidding provided convenient loopholes. One internationally known engineering firm refused to agree to kickback in order to secure a contract to design a $4.5 million sewage disposal plant for the city; a local firm was then appointed, which paid $10,700 of its $225,000 fee to an associate of Irv Stern and Mayor Donnelly as a "finder's fee." Since the State law also excludes public works maintenance contracts from the competitive bidding requirements, many city paving and street repair contracts during the Donnelly-Walasek era were given to a contributor to the Democratic Party. Finally, the franchise for towing illegally parked cars and cars involved in accidents was awarded to two garages which were then required to kickback $1 for each car towed.

The handling of graft on the towing contracts illustrates the way in which minor violence and the "lowest responsible bidder" clause could be used to keep bribe payers in line. After Federal investigators began to look into Wincanton corruption, the owner of one of the garages with a towing franchise testified before the grand jury. Mayor Walasek immediately withdrew his franchise, citing "health violations" at the garage. The garageman was also "encouraged" not to testify by a series of "accidents"—wheels would fall off towtrucks on the highway, steering cables were cut, and so forth. Newspaper satirization of the "health violations" forced the restoration of the towing franchise, and the "accidents" ceased.

Lest the reader infer that the "lowest responsible bidder" clause was used as an escape valve only for corrupt purposes, one incident might be noted which took place under the present reform administration. In 1964, the Wincanton School Board sought bids for the renovation of an athletic field. The lowest bid came from a construction company owned by Dave Phillips, the corrupt police chief who had served formerly under Mayor Walasek. While the company was presumably competent to carry out the assignment, the board rejected Phillips' bid "because of a question as to his moral responsibility." The board did not specify whether this referred to his prior corruption as chief or his present status as an informer in testifying against Walasek and Stern.

One final area of city power, which was abused by Walasek et al., covered discretionary acts, such as granting permits and allowing zoning variances. On taking office, Walasek took the unusual step of asking that the bureaus of building and plumbing inspection be put under the mayor's control. With this power to approve or deny building permits, Walasek "sat on" applications, waiting until the petitioner contributed $50 or $75, or threatened to sue to get his permit. Some building designs were not approved until a favored architect was retained as a "consultant." (It is not known whether this involved kickbacks to Walasek or simply patronage for a friend.) At least three instances are known in which developers were forced to pay for zoning variances before apartment buildings or supermarkets could be erected. Businessmen who wanted to encourage rapid turnover of the curb space in front of their stores were told to pay a police sergeant to erect "10-minute parking" signs. To repeat a caveat stated earlier, it is impossible to tell whether these kickbacks were demanded to expedite legitimate requests or to approve improper demands, such as a variance that would hurt a neighborhood or a certificate approving improper electrical work.

All of the activities detailed thus far involve fairly clear violations of the law. To complete the picture of the abuse of office by Wincanton officials, we might briefly mention "honest graft." This term was best defined by one of its earlier practitioners, State Senator George Washington Plunkitt who loyally served Tammany Hall at the turn of the century.

> There's all the difference in the world between [honest and dishonest graft]. Yes, many of our men have grown rich in politics. I have myself.
>
> I've made a big fortune out of the game, and I'm gettin' richer every day, but I've not gone in for dishonest graft—blackmailin' gamblers, saloonkeepers, disorderly people, etc.—and neither has any of the men who have made big fortunes in politics.
>
> There's an honest graft, and I'm an example of how it works. I might sum up the whole thing by sayin': "I seen my opportunities and I took 'em."
>
> Let me explain by examples. My party's in power in the city, and it's goin' to undertake a lot of public improvements. Well, I'm tipped off, say, that they're going to lay out a new park at a certain place.
>
> I see my opportunity and I take it. I go to that place, and I buy up all the land I can in the neighborhood. Then the board of this or that makes its plan public, and there is a rush to get my land, which nobody cared particular for before.
>
> Ain't it perfectly honest to charge a good price and make a profit on my investment and foresight? Of course, it is. Well, that's honest graft.[3]

While there was little in the way of land purchasing—either honest or dishonest—going on in Wincanton during this period, several officials who carried on their own businesses while in office were able to pick up some "honest graft." One city councilman with an accounting office served as bookkeeper for Irv Stern and the major bookies and prostitutes in the city.

Police Chief Phillips' construction firm received a contract to remodel the exterior of the largest brothel in town. Finally one councilman serving in the present reform administration received a contract to construct all gasoline stations built in the city by a major petroleum company; skeptics say that the contract was the quid pro quo for the councilman's vote to give the company the contract to sell gasoline to the city.

How Far Did It Go?   This cataloging of acts of nonfeasance, malfeasance, and misfeasance by Wincanton officials raises a danger of confusing variety with universality, of assuming that every employee of the city was either engaged in corrupt activities or was being paid to ignore the corruption of others. On the contrary, both official investigations and private research lead to the conclusion that there is no reason whatsoever to question the honesty of the vast majority of the employees of the city of Wincanton. Certainly no more than 10 of the 155 members of the Wincanton police force were on Irv Stern's payroll (although as many as half of them may have accepted petty Christmas presents—turkeys or liquor.) In each department, there were a few employees who objected actively to the misdeeds of their superiors, and the only charge that can justly be leveled against the mass of employees is that they were unwilling to jeopardize their employment by publicly exposing what was going on. When Federal investigators showed that an honest (and possibly successful) attempt was being made to expose Stern-Walasek corruption, a number of city employees cooperated with the grand jury in aggregating evidence which could be used to convict the corrupt officials.

Before these Federal investigations began, however, it could reasonably appear to an individual employee that the entire machinery of law enforcement in the city was controlled by Stern, Walasek, et al., and that an individual protest would be silenced quickly. This can be illustrated by the momentary crusade conducted by First Assistant District Attorney Phil Roper in the summer of 1962. When the district attorney left for a short vacation, Roper decided to act against the gamblers and madams in the city. With the help of the State Police, Roper raided several large brothels. Apprehending on the street the city's largest distributor of punchboards and lotteries, Roper effected a citizen's arrest and drove him to police headquarters for proper detention and questioning. "I'm sorry, Mr. Roper," said the desk sergeant, "we're under orders not to arrest persons brought in by you." Roper was forced to call upon the State Police for aid in confining the gambler. When the district attorney returned from his vacation, he quickly fired Roper "for introducing politics into the district attorney's office."

³ William L. Riordan, "Plunkitt of Tammany Hall" (New York: E. P. Dutton, 1963), p. 3.

70

If it is incorrect to say that Wincanton corruption extended very far vertically—into the rank and file of the various departments of the city—how far did it extend horizontally? How many branches and levels of government were affected? With the exception of the local Congressman and the city treasurer, it seems that a few personnel at each level (city, county, and State) and in most offices in city hall can be identified either with Stern or with some form of free-lance corruption. A number of local judges received campaign financing from Stern, although there is no evidence that they were on his payroll after they were elected. Several State legislators were on Stern's payroll, and one Republican councilman charged that a high-ranking State Democratic official promised Stern first choice of all Alsace County patronage. The county chairman. he claimed, was only to receive the jobs that Stern did not want. While they were later to play an active role in disrupting Wincanton gambling, the district attorney in Hal Craig's reform administration feared that the State Police were on Stern's payroll, and thus refused to use them in city gambling raids.

Within the city administration, the evidence is fairly clear that some mayors and councilmen received regular payments from Stern and divided kickbacks on city purchases and sales. Some key subcouncil personnel frequently shared in payoffs affecting their particular departments—the police chief shared in the gambling and prostitution payoffs and received $300 of the $10,500 kickback on parking meter purchases. A councilman controlling one department. for example, might get a higher percentage of kickbacks than the other councilmen in contracts involving that department.

LEGAL PROTECTION AGAINST CORRUPTION

Later in this report, Wincanton's gambling and corruption will be tied into a context of social and political attitudes. At this point. however. concluding the study of official corruption. it might be appropriate to consider legal reforms which might make future corruption more difficult. Many of the corrupt activities of Wincanton officials are already covered sufficiently by State law—it is clearly spelled out, for example, that city officials must enforce State gambling and prostitution laws, and no further legislation is needed to clarify this duty. The legal mandate of the State Police to enforce State laws in all parts of the State is equally clear. but it has been nullified by their informal practice of entering cities only when invited: this policy only facilitates local corruption.

The first major reform that might minimize corruption would involve a drastic increase in the salaries of public officials and law enforcement personnel. During the 1950's Wincanton police salaries were in the lowest quartile for middle-sized cities in the Nation. and were well below the median family income ($5,453) in the city. City councilmen then were receiving only slightly more than the median. Since that time, police salaries have been raised to $5.400 (only slightly below the median) and council salaries to $8.500. Under these circum-

stances, many honest officials and employees were forced to "moonlight" with second jobs; potentially dishonest men were likely to view Stern payoffs or extortionate kickbacks as a simpler means of improving their financial status. Raising police salaries to $7.000 or $8,000 would attract men of higher quality, permit them to forego second jobs, and make corrupt payoffs seem less tempting. The same considerations apply to a recommendation that the salaries of elected officials be increased to levels similar to those received in private industry. A recent budget for the city of Wincanton called for expenditures of $6 million; no private corporation of that size would be headed by a chief executive whose salary was $9,500 per year.

A second type of recommendation would reduce the opportunities available to officials to extort illegal payoffs or conceal corruption. First, the civil service system should be expanded. At the time this report was written, Wincanton policemen could not be discharged from the force unless formal charges were brought, but they could be demoted from command positions or transferred to "punishment" details at the discretion of the chief or mayor. The latter option is probably a proper disciplinary tool, but the former invites policemen to seek alliances with political leaders and to avoid unpopular actions. Promotions within the force (with the possible exception of the chief's position) should be made by competitive examination, and demotions should be made only for proven cause. (While research for this report was being conducted. a full 18 months before the next local election. police officers reported that politicking had already begun. Men on the force had already begun making friends with possible candidates for the 1967 elections. and police discipline was beginning to slip. Command officers reported that the sergeants were becoming unwilling to criticize or discipline patrolmen. "How can I tell someone off?" one captain asked. "I'll probably be walking a beat when the Democrats come back into power, and he may be my boss.") A comprehensive civil service system would also give command officers control over informal rewards and punishments, so that they could encourage "hustlers" and harass slackers, but formal review of promotions and demotions is essential to guard against the politicking, which has been characteristic of the Wincanton police force.

Second, opportunities for corruption could be reduced by closing the loopholes in State laws on bidding for municipal contracts. While a city should be free to disregard a low bid received from a company judged financially or technically unable to perform a contract. the phrase "lowest responsible bidder" simply opens the door to misfeasance—either to accepting under-the-table kickbacks or to rewarding political friends. In this regard. the decision to ignore the bid of former Police Chief Phillips is just as reprehensible as the decision to give paving contracts to a major party contributor. Furthermore, there is no reason why service contracts should be excluded from the competitive bidding: while the professions regard it as undignified to compete for clients. there is no reason why road repair or building maintenance contracts could not be judged on the basis of bids (with a proviso regarding some level of competence). Finally, the exclusion of "patented or copyrighted products" is untenable—it is well known that distributors of say, automobiles, vary widely in their profit margins, or allowances for trade-ins, etc. City officials should be forced therefore to seek the best possible deal.

One mechanism, which is often suggested to guard against official misconduct, is an annual audit of city books by a higher governmental agency, such as those conducted of local agencies (e.g., urban renewal authorities) administering Federal programs. The evidence in Wincanton, however, seems to indicate that even while official corruption was taking place, the city's books were in perfect order. When a kickback was received on a city purchase, for example, the minutes of council meetings would indicate that X was the "lowest responsible bidder," if bids were required, and X would slip the payoff money to a "bagman," or contactman, on a dark street corner. The books looked proper and auditors would have had no authority to force acceptance of other bids. It would seem that revision of the bidding laws would be more significant than an outside audit.

Finally, the problem of campaign contributions must be considered. As was stressed earlier, contributions to political candidates are regarded in this country as both a manifestation of free speech and the best alternative to government sponsorship of campaigns. The use of political contributions as a disguise for extortion and bribery could be curtailed, however, by active enforcement of the "full reporting of receipts" provision of State campaign laws (in Wincanton, candidates filed reports of receipts, but, of course, neglected to mention the money received from Irv Stern). Second, city hall employees should be protected against the type of voluntary assessment imposed by Mayor Donnelly. Third, State and local laws might more clearly prohibit contributions, from persons doing business with the city, which can be identified as payoffs for past or future preferment on city contracts. (Tightening of bidding requirements, of course, would make such activities less profitable to the contractors.) [4]

GAMBLING AND CORRUPTION: THE GENERAL PUBLIC

THE LATENT FUNCTIONS OF GAMBLING AND CORRUPTION

I feel as though I am sending Santa Claus to jail. Although this man dealt in gambling devices, it appears that he is a religious man having no bad habits and is an unmeasurably charitable man.
—a Federal judge sentencing slot machine king Klaus Braun to jail in 1948.

When I was a kid, the man in the corner grocery wrote numbers. His salary was about $20 a week and he made $25 more on book.
—a reform candidate for the Wincanton City Council, early 1960's.

The instances of wrongdoing cataloged in earlier sections seem to paint an easily censurable picture. Irv Stern, Gene Donnelly, Bob Walasek—these names conjure up an image of such total iniquity that one wonders why they were ever allowed to operate as they did. While gambling and corruption are easy to judge in the abstract, however, they, like sin, are never encountered in the abstract—they are encountered in the form of a slot machine which is helping to pay off your club's mortgage, or a chance to fix your son's speeding ticket, or an opportunity to hasten the completion of your new building by "overlooking" a few violations of the building code. In these forms, the choices seem less clear. Furthermore, to obtain a final appraisal of what took place in Wincanton one must weigh the manifest functions served—providing income for the participants, recreation for the consumers of vice and gambling, etc.—against the latent functions, the unintended or unrecognized consequences of these events.[5] The automobile, as Thorstein Veblen noted, has both a manifest function, transportation, and a latent function, affirming the owner's social status. To balance the picture presented in earlier sections, and thus to give a partial explanation of why Wincanton has had its unusual history, this section explores the latent functions, the unintended and unexpected consequences, of gambling and corruption.

Latent Social Functions. The social life of Wincanton is organized around clubs, lodges, and other voluntary associations. Labor unions have union halls. Businessmen have luncheon groups, country clubs, and service organizations, such as the Rotary, Kiwanis, the Lions, etc. Each nationality group has its own meetinghouse—the Ancient Order of Hibernians, the Liederkranz, the Colored Political Club, the Cristoforo Colombo Society, etc. In each neighborhood, a PTA-type group is organized around the local playground. Each firehall is the nightly gathering place of a volunteer firemen's association. Each church has the usual assortment of men's, women's, and children's groups.

A large proportion of these groups profited in one way or another from some form of gambling. Churches sponsored lotteries, bingo, and "Las Vegas nights." Weekly bingo games sponsored by the playground associations paid for new equipment, Little League uniforms, etc. Business groups would use lotteries to advertise "Downtown Wincanton Days." Finally, depending upon the current policy of law enforcement agencies, most of the clubs had slot machines, payoff pinball machines, punchboards, lotteries, bingo, poker games, etc. For many of these groups, profits from gambling meant the difference between financial success and failure. Clubs with large and affluent membership lists could survive with only fees and profits from meals and drinks served. Clubs with few or impecunious members, however, had to rely on other sources of revenue, and gambling was both lucrative and attractive to nonmembers.

The clubs therefore welcomed slots, pinball machines, punchboards, and so forth, both to entertain members and to bring in outside funds. The clubs usually divided

[4] See the excellent discussion of political campaign contributions in Alexander Heard, "The Costs of Democracy" (Chapel Hill: University of North Carolina Press, 1960), and Herbert Alexander, "Regulation of Political Finance" (Berkeley: Institute of Governmental Studies, and Princeton: Citizens' Research Foundation, 1966).

[5] See the classic examination of manifest and latent functions in Robert K. Merton, "Social Theory and Social Structures", revised edition (New York: Free Press, 1957), pp. 19-87.

gambling profits equally with machine distributors such as Stern or Klaus Braun. Some clubs owed even more to gamblers; if Braun heard that a group of men wanted to start a new volunteer firemen's association, he would lend them mortgage money simply for the opportunity to put his slot machines in the firehall. It is not surprising, therefore, to find that the clubs actively defended Stern, Braun, and the political candidates who favored open gambling.

Gambling in Wincanton also provided direct and indirect benefits to churches and other charitable organizations. First, like the other private groups, a number of these churches and charities sponsored bingo, lotteries, etc., and shared in the profits. Second, leading gamblers and racketeers have been generous supporters of Wincanton charities. Klaus Braun gave away literally most of his gambling income, aiding churches, hospitals, and the underprivileged. In the late 1940's, Braun provided 7,000 Christmas turkeys to the poor, and frequently chartered buses to take slum children to ball games. Braun's Prospect Mountain Park offered free rides and games for local children while their parents were in other tents patronizing the slot machines). Irv Stern gave a $10,000 stained glass window to his synagogue, and aided welfare groups and hospitals in Wincanton and other cities. (Since the residents of Wincanton refuse to be cared for in the room that Stern gave to Community Hospital, it is now used only for the storage of bandages.) When Stern came into Federal court in the early 1960's to be sentenced on tax evasion charges, he was given character references by Protestant, Catholic, and Jewish clergy, and by the staff of two hospitals and a home for the aged. Critics charge that Stern never gave away a dime that wasn't well publicized; nevertheless, his contributions benefited worthwhile community institutions.

(Lest this description of the direct and indirect benefits of gambling be misleading, it should also be stressed that many ministers protested violently against gambling and corruption, led reform movements and launched pulpit tirades against Stern, Walasek, et al.)

One final social function of Wincanton gambling might be termed the moderation of the demands of the criminal law. Bluntly stated, Irv Stern was providing the people with what at least a large portion of them wanted, whether or not State lawmakers felt they should want it. It is, of course, axiomatic that no one has the right to disobey the law, but in fairness to local officials it should be remembered that they were generally only tolerating what most residents of the city had grown up with—easily accessible numbers, horsebetting, and bingo. When reform mayor Ed Whitton ordered bingo parlors closed in 1964, he was ending the standard form of evening recreation of literally thousands of elderly men and women. One housewife interviewed recently expressed relief that her mother had died before Whitton's edict took effect: "It would have killed her to live without bingo," she said.

In another sense, Wincanton law enforcement was also moderated by the aid that the gambling syndicates gave, at no cost to the public, to persons arrested by the police

for gambling activity. Stern provided bail and legal counsel during trials, and often supported families of men sent to jail. A large portion of the payments that Stern sent to the east coast syndicates (as discussed earlier) was earmarked for pensions to the widows of men who had earlier served in the Stern organization. In light of the present interest in the quality of legal services available to the poor, this aspect of Wincanton gambling must be regarded as a worthy social function.

In these ways, Wincanton gambling provided the financial basis for a network of private groups, filling social service, and quasi-governmental functions. Leading the list of latent functions of gambling, therefore, we must put the support of neighborhood and other group social life and the provision of such important services as recreation and fire protection. Providing these services through private rather than public mechanisms not only reduced tax burdens but also integrated the services into the social structure of the neighborhood served. While it is hard to give profits from gambling sole credit for maintaining these clubs, it must be noted that a number of firemen's and political associations were forced to close their doors when law enforcement agencies seized slot and pinball machines.

Latent Economic Functions. Just as the proceeds from gambling made possible, or at least less expensive, an extensive series of social relationships and quasi-public services, so also did gambling and corruption affect the local economy, aiding some businesses while hindering others. Their manifest function, of course, was to increase the incomes of the providers of illicit services (members of the Stern syndicate, individual number writers and pinball machine distributors, madams, prostitutes, etc.), the recipients of payoffs (elected officials and policemen, for whom these payments were a welcome addition to low salaries), and the businessmen who secured unwarranted contracts, permits, variances, etc. On the other hand, these arrangements provided entertainment for the consumers of gambling and prostitution.

In describing the latent functions of Wincanton illegality, we can begin with two broad phenomena. First, gambling permitted a number of outmoded businesses to survive technological change. As a quotation at the beginning of this chapter indicated, a "mom and pop" grocery store or a candy or cigar store could make more from writing numbers or taking horse bets than they did from their nominal source of support. When reform mayors cracked down on betting, many of these marginal shops went out of business, not being able to compete with the larger, more efficient operations solely on the basis of sales. Second, the system provided an alternate ladder of social mobility for persons who lacked the educational or status prerequisites for success in the legitimate world. Irv Stern came to this country as a fruit peddler's son and is believed by the Internal Revenue Service to be worth several millions of dollars. Gene Donnelly was a bartender's son; Bob Walasek grew up in a slum, although he was able to attend college on an athletic scholarship. Many Wincantonites believe that each of these men collected at least a quarter of a million dollars during his 4 years in city hall. As Daniel Bell has pointed out,[6] and as these men illustrate. organized crime in America has provided a quick route out of the slums. a means of realizing the Horatio Alger dream.

A number of legitimate enterprises in Wincanton profited directly or indirectly when gambling was wide open. Eight or ten major bingo halls provided a large nighttime business for the local bus company. In one year, for example, 272,000 persons paid to play bingo, and most of them were elderly men and women who were brought to the games on regular or chartered buses. Prizes for the bingo games were purchased locally; one department store executive admitted that bingo gift certificates brought "a sizable amount" of business into his store. Several drugstores sold large quantities of cosmetics to the prostitutes. As in Las Vegas, one Wincanton hotel offered special weekend rates for the gamblers at the dice game, who would gamble at night and sleep during the daytime. Finally, several landlords rented space to Stern for his bookie parlors and accounting offices. Worried that legislative investigations might terminate a profitable arrangement. one landlord asked the investigating committee, "Who else would pay $150 a month for that basement?" Being the center of gambling and prostitution for a wide area also meant increased business for the city's restaurants, bars. and theaters. One man declared that business at his Main Street restaurant was never as good as when gamblers and bingo players were flocking to the downtown area. Many of these restaurants and bars, of course, provided gambling as well as food and drink for their customers. ᵢ

Corruption, like gambling, offered some businessmen opportunities to increase sales and profits. If minor building code violations could be overlooked. houses and office buildings could be erected more cheaply. Zoning variances, secured for a price, opened up new areas in which developers could build high-rise apartment buildings and shopping centers. In selling to the city, businessmen could increase profits either by selling inferior goods or by charging high prices on standard goods when bidding was rigged or avoided. Finally, corruptible officials could aid profits simply by speeding up decisions on city contracts, or by forcing rapid turnover of city-owned curb space through either "10-minute parking" signs or strict enforcement of parking laws. (Owners of large stores. however, sought to maximize profits by asking the police to ignore parking violations, feeling that customers who worried about their meters would be less likely to stay and buy.)

This listing of the latent benefits of gambling and corruption must be juxtaposed against the fact that many Wincanton businessmen were injured by the Stern-Walasek method of operations and fought vigorously against it. Leaders of the Wincanton business community—the bankers. industrialists. Chamber of Commerce, etc.—fought Walasek and Stern. refusing to kickback on anything. and regularly called upon State and Federal agencies to investigate local corruption.

It is somewhat misleading, however, to use the single term "business" in analysing responses to corruption. It will be more fruitful to classify businesses according to the nature of their contact with the city of Wincanton. Some industries had a national market. and only called upon the city for labor and basic services—water, sewage, police and fire protection, etc. Other companies such as sales agencies or construction firms did business directly with city hall and thus were intimately concerned with the terms upon which the city government did business. Because of the looseness of State bidding procedures, these businesses had to be careful, however, not to alienate officials. A third group, while not doing business with the city, had primarily a local clientele. Under these conditions, businesses in this group were frequently interested in corruption and gambling policies.

Official corruption affected each of these groups differently. Businesses whose markets lay primarily outside the city usually had to be concerned only with the possibility that Walasek might force them to pay for building permits. Companies dealing with City Hall, however, were exposed to every extortionate demand that the mayor might impose. As an example, agencies usually able to underbid their competitors were ignored if they refused to abide by the unofficial "conditions" added to contracts. Businessmen in the third category were in an intermediate position. both in terms of their freedom to act against the system and in terms of the impact that it had upon them. Like the others, they suffered when forced to pay for permits or variances. Legitimate businesses, such as liquor stores, taverns, and restaurants, whose functions paralleled those of the clubs, lost revenue when the clubs were licensed to have gambling and slot machines. Those businesses, such as banks, whose success depended upon community growth, suffered when the community's reputation for corruption and gambling drove away potential investors and developers. (Interestingly, businessmen disagree as to whether it is the reputation for corruption or for gambling that discourages new industry. Several Wincanton bankers stated that no investor would run the risk of having to bribe officials to have building plans approved, permits issued. and so forth. One architect. however, argued that businessmen assume municipal corruption, but will not move into a "sin town," for their employees will not want to raise children in such circumstances.)

The last detrimental aspect of gambling and corruption seems trivial in comparison with the factors already mentioned. but it was cited by most of the business leaders interviewed. Simply stated, it was embarrassing to have one's hometown known throughout the country for its vice and corruption. "I'd go to a convention on the west coast," one textile manufacturer recalled, "and everyone I'd meet would say, 'You're from Wincanton? Boy, have I heard stories about that place!' I would try to talk about textiles or opportunities for industrial development, but they'd keep asking about the girls and the gambling." An Air Force veteran recalled being ridiculed about his hometown while in boot camp. Finally, some insiders feel that a Wincanton judge was persuaded

---

[6] Daniel Bell. "The End of Ideology" (New York: Free Press, 1960), ch. 7, "Crime as an American Way of Life".

74

to act against Irv Stern when he found that his daughter was being laughed at by her college friends for being related to a Wincanton official.

PUBLIC ATTITUDES TOWARD GAMBLING AND CORRUPTION

A clean city, a city free of gambling, vice, and corruption, requires at least two things—active law enforcement and elected officials who oppose organized crime. Over the last 20 years, Federal agents have been successful in prosecuting most of the leaders of Wincanton gambling operations. Slot machine king Klaus Braun was twice sent to jail for income tax evasion. Federal agents were also able to secure convictions against Irv Stern for income tax evasion (a 4-year sentence), gambling tax evasion (a 2-year sentence running concurrently with the income tax sentence), and extortion on a city contract to purchase parking meters (a 30-day concurrent sentence). Federal men also sent to jail lesser members of the Stern syndicate and closed down a still and an interstate dice game.

These Federal actions, however, had very little effect upon Wincanton gambling. Lieutenants carried on while Stern was in jail, and local police, at the direction of city officials, continued to ignore numbers writers, bookies, and prostitutes. As one Federal agent put it, "Even though we were able to apprehend and convict the chief racketeers, we were never able to solve the political problem—city officials were always against us." On the two occasions when Wincanton voters did solve the political problem by electing reform officials, however, organized crime was quickly put out of business. Mayor Hal Craig chose to tolerate isolated bookies, numbers writers, and prostitutes, but Stern and Braun were effectively silenced. Mayor Ed Whitton, in office since the early 1960's, has gone even further, and the only gamblers and prostitutes still operating in Wincanton are those whom the police have been unable to catch for reasons of limited manpower, lack of evidence, etc. The American Social Hygiene Association reported after a recent study that Wincanton has fewer prostitutes today than at any time since the 1930's. The police acknowledge that there are still a few gamblers and prostitutes in town, but they have been driven underground, and a potential patron must have a contact before he can do business.

If the level of law enforcement in a community is so directly tied to local voting patterns, we must look more closely at the attitudes and values of Wincanton residents. First, how much did residents know about what was going on? Were the events which have been discussed previously matters of common knowledge or were they perceived by only a few residents? Second, were they voting for open gambling and corruption: were they being duped by seemingly honest candidates who became corrupt after taking office; or were these issues irrelevant to the average voter, who was thinking about other issues entirely? Our conclusions about these questions will indicate whether long-range reform can be attained through legal changes

(closing loopholes in the city's bidding practices, expanding civil service in the police department, ending the "home rule" policy of the State Police, etc.) or whether reform must await a change in popular mores.

PUBLIC AWARENESS OF GAMBLING AND CORRUPTION

In a survey of Wincanton residents conducted recently,[7] 90 percent of the respondents were able correctly to identify the present mayor, 63 percent recognized the name of their Congressman, and 36 percent knew the Alsace County district attorney. Seventy percent identified Irv Stern correctly, and 62 percent admitted that they did recognize the name of the largest madam in town. But how much did the people of Wincanton know about what had been going on—the extent and organization of Irv Stern's empire, the payoffs to city hall and the police, or the malfeasance and misfeasance of Bob Walasek and other city officials? Instead of thinking about simply "knowing" or "not knowing," we might subdivide public awareness into several categories—a general awareness that gambling and prostitution were present in the city, some perception that city officials were protecting these enterprises, and finally a specific knowledge that officials X and Y were being paid off. These categories vary, it will be noticed, in the specificity of knowledge and in the linkage between the result (e.g., presence of gambling or corruption) and an official's action.

While there is no way of knowing exactly how many Wincantonites had access to each type of knowledge about gambling and corruption during the period they were taking place, we can form some ideas on the basis of the newspaper coverage they received and the geographical distribution of each form of illegality. The dice game, for example, was in only one location (hidden and shifted periodically to escape Federal attention) and relied primarily on out-of-town gamblers. The newspapers said little about it, and it was probably safe to say that few residents knew of its existence until it was raided by the FBI in the early 1960's.

Prostitutes were generally found only in two four-block areas in the city—semi-slum areas that no outsider was likely to visit unless he was specifically looking for the girls. The newspapers, however, gave extensive coverage to every prostitution arrest and every report by the American Social Hygiene Association which detailed the extent of prostitution and venereal disease in the city. A series of newspaper articles, with photographs, forced the police to close (for a short period of time) several of the larger brothels. With regard to prostitution, therefore, it is likely that a majority of the adult population knew of the existence of commercialized vice: but, apart from innuendoes in the papers, there was little awareness of payoffs to the police. It was not until after the election of a reform administration, that Stern and Walasek were indicted for extorting payments from a madam.

In contrast to the dice games and prostitution, public awareness of the existence of pinball machines, horsebooks, and numbers writing must have been far more widespread. These mass-consumption forms of gambling

[7] This survey was conducted by eight female interviewers from the Wisconsin Survey Research Laboratory, using a schedule of questions requiring 45 to 75 minutes to complete. Respondents were selected from among the adults residing in housing units selected at random from the Wincanton "City Directory". One hundred eighty-three completed interviews were obtained.

depended upon accessibility to large numbers of persons. Bets could be placed in most corner grocery stores, candy shops, and cigar counters: payoff pinball machines were placed in most clubs and firehalls, as well as in bars and restaurants. Apart from knowing that these things were openly available, and thus not subject to police interference, there was no way for the average citizen to know specifically that Irv Stern was paying to protect these gambling interests until Police Chief Phillips began to testify—again after the election of reformer Whitton.

Public awareness of wrongdoing was probably least widespread in regard to corruption—kickbacks on contracts, extortion, etc. Direct involvement was generally limited to officials and businessmen, and probably few of them knew anything other than that they personally had been asked to pay. Either from shame or from fear of being prosecuted on bribery charges or out of unwillingness to jeopardize a profitable contract, those who did pay did not want to talk. Those who refused to pay usually were unable to substantiate charges made against bribes so that exposure of the attempt led only to libel suits or official harassment. As we have seen, the newspapers and one garage with a towing contract did talk about what was going on. The garageman lost his franchise and suffered a series of "accidents": the newspapers found a reporter in jail and their trucks harassed by the police. Peter French, the district attorney under Walasek and Donnelly, won a libel suit (since reversed on appeal and dismissed) against the papers after they stated that he was protecting gamblers. Except for an unsuccessful citizen suit in the mid-1950's seeking to void the purchase of fire trucks (for the purchase of which Donnelly received a $2,000 "political contribution") and a newspaper article in the early 1960's implying that Donnelly and his council had received $500 on the sale of a city crane, no evidence—no specific facts—of corruption was available to the public until Phillips was indicted several years later for perjury in connection with the towing contracts.

Returning then to the three categories of public knowledge, we can say that even at the lowest level—general perception of some form of wrongdoing—awareness was quite limited (except among the businessmen, most of whom, as we noted in the "Introduction," live and vote in the suburbs). Specific knowledge—this official received this much to approve that contract—was only available after legislative hearings in the early 1950's and the indictment of Phillips in the early 1960's: on both occasions the voters turned to reform candidates.

If, therefore, it is unlikely that many residents of Wincanton had the second or third type of knowledge about local gambling or corruption (while many more had the first type) during the time it was taking place, how much do they know now—after several years of reform and a series of trials—all well-covered in the newspapers revealing the nature of Stern-Donnelly-Walasek operations? To test the extent of specific knowledge about local officials and events, respondents in a recent survey were asked to identify past and present officials and racketeers and to compare the Walasek and Whitton administrations on a number of points.

Earlier, we noted that 90 percent of the 183 respondents recognized the name of the present mayor, 63 percent knew their Congressman (who had been in office more than 10 years), and 36 percent knew the district attorney. How many members of the Stern organization were known to the public? Seventy percent recognized Stern's name, 63 percent knew the head of the numbers bank, 40 percent identified the "bagman" or collector for Stern, and 31 percent knew the operator of the largest horsebook in town. With regard to many of these questions, it must be kept in mind that since many respondents may subconsciously have felt that to admit recognition of a name would have implied personal contact with or sympathy for a criminal or a criminal act, these results probably understate the extent of public knowledge. When 100 of the respondents were asked "What things did Mr. Walasek do that were illegal?", 59 mentioned extortion regarding vice and gambling, 2 mentioned extortion on city contracts, 7 stated that he stole from the city, 8 that he fixed parking and speeding tickets, 4 that he was "controlled by rackets," and 20 simply stated that Walasek was corrupt, not listing specific acts.

Even if Wincantonites do not remember too many specific misdeeds, they clearly perceive that the present Whitton administration has run a cleaner town than did Walasek or Donnelly. When asked to comment on the statement, "Some people say that the present city administration under Mayor Whitton is about the same as when Mayor Walasek was in office," 10 percent said it was the same, 74 percent said it was different, and 14 percent didn't know. When asked why, 75 respondents cited "better law enforcement" and the end of corruption: only 7 of 183 felt that the city had been better run by Walasek. Fifty-eight percent felt the police force was better now, 22 percent thought that it was about the same as when Walasek controlled the force, and only 7 percent thought it was worse now. Those who felt that the police department was better run now stressed "honesty" and "better law enforcement," or thought that it was valuable to have an outsider as commissioner. Those who thought it was worse now cited "inefficiency," "loafing," or "unfriendliness." It was impossible to tell whether the comments of "unfriendliness" refer simply to the present refusal to tolerate gambling or whether they signify a more remote police-public contact resulting from the "professionalism" of the commissioner. (In this regard, we might note that a number of policemen and lawyers felt that it had been easier to secure information regarding major crimes when prostitution and gambling were tolerated. As one former captain put it, "If I found out that some gangster was in town that I didn't know about, I raised hell with the prostitutes for not telling me.")

Comparing perceptions of the present and former district attorneys, we also find a clear preference for the present man, Thomas Hendricks, over Peter French, but there is a surprising increase in "Don't knows." Thirty-five percent felt the district attorney's office is run "differently" now, 13 percent said it is run in the same way, but 50 percent did not know. Paralleling this lack of attitudes toward the office, we can recall that only 36 percent of the respondents were able to identify the present incumbent's name, while 55 percent knew his more flamboyant predecessor. Of those respondents who saw a difference between the two men, 51 percent cited "better law enforcement" and "no more rackets control over law enforcement."

In addition to recognizing these differences between past and present officials, the respondents in the recent survey felt that there were clear differences in the extent of corruption and gambling. Sixty-nine percent disagreed with the statement, "Underworld elements and racketeers had very little say in what the Wincanton city government did when Mr. Walasek was mayor;" only 13 percent disagreed with the same statement as applied to reform Mayor Whitton. When asked, "As compared with 5 years ago, do you think it's easier now, about the same, or harder to find a dice game in Wincanton?"; only one respondent felt it was easier, 8 percent felt it was about the same, 56 percent felt it was harder, and 34 percent didn't know. The respondents were almost as sure that Whitton had closed down horse betting; 51 percent felt it was harder to bet on horses now than it was 5 years ago, 11 percent felt it was about the same, and three respondents thought it was easier now than before. Again, 34 percent did not know.

PUBLIC ATTITUDES TOWARD CRIME AND LAW ENFORCEMENT

Earlier, we asked whether Wincanton's long history of gambling and corruption was based on a few bad officials and formal, structural defects such as the absence of civil service or low pay scales, or whether it was rooted in the values of the populace. The evidence on "public awareness" indicates that most Wincantonites probably knew of the existence of widespread gambling, but they probably had little idea of the payoffs involved. When we turn to public attitudes, we find a similar split—many citizens wanted to consume the services offered by Irv Stern, but they were against official corruption: few residents think that one produces the other. But in thinking about "public attitudes," several problems of definition arise. For one thing, "attitudes" depend on the way in which a question is phrased—a respondent would be likely to answer "no" if he were asked, "Are you in favor of gambling?", but he might also answer "yes" if he were asked whether it was all right to flip a coin to see who would buy the next round of drinks. As we will shortly see, it is very difficult to conclude that because a Wincantonite voted for candidate X, he was voting "for corruption"— in his mind, he might have been voting for a fellow Pole, or a workingman, or an athletic hero, etc., and the decision did not involve "corruption" or "reform."

Second, we have to ask whether "attitude," in the sense of a conscious preference for X over Y, is an appropriate concept. We must keep in mind that for Wincantonites, "reform" has been the exception rather than the rule. The vast majority of local citizens have lived with wide-open gambling all their lives, and the reform administrations of Craig and Whitton add up to only 7 of the last 40 years. As one lawyer said, "When I was

a little kid, my dad would lift me up so I could put a dime in the slot machine at his club. We never saw anything wrong in it." In addition to knowing about gambling in Wincanton, the residents knew of other cities in the State in which gambling was equally wide open, and they believe that Wincanton is similar to most cities in the country. Fifty-four percent of the respondents in the survey agreed with the statement, "There is not much difference between politics in Wincanton and politics in other American cities." (Nineteen percent were undecided and only 25 percent disagreed.) Because of this specific history of gambling and this general perception that Wincanton is like other cities, it may be more accurate to speak of latent acceptance of gambling and petty corruption as "facts of life" rather than thinking of conscious choices, e.g., "I prefer gambling and corruption to a clean city and honest officials." Under most circumstances, the question has not come up.

In a series of questions included in the recent attitude survey, Wincantonites indicated a general approval or tolerance of gambling, but they frequently distinguished between organized and unorganized operations. Eighty percent felt that the State legislature should legalize bingo. Fifty-eight percent felt that a State-operated lottery would be a good idea. Fifty-four percent agreed with the general statement, "The State should legalize gambling." When asked *why* the State should legalize gambling, 42 percent of those favoring the idea felt that gambling was harmless or that people would gamble anyway; 44 percent thought that the State should control it and receive the profits; 8 percent felt that legalization would keep out racketeers. Forty-nine percent agreed that "gambling is all right so long as local people, not outsiders, run the game;" 35 percent disagreed; and 11 percent were uncertain. Forty-six percent felt that "the police should not break up a friendly poker game, even if there is betting." Here, 37 percent disagreed and 14 percent were uncertain.

If Wincanton residents are tolerant of gambling, they show little tolerance of official corruption: 72 percent of the respondents disagreed with a statement that, "A city official who receives $10 in cash from a company that does business with the city should not be prosecuted;" only 13 percent agreed. Sixty-one percent were unwilling to agree that, "It's all right for the mayor of a city to make a profit when the city buys some land so long as only a fair price is charged." Thirty-four percent agreed that, "It's all right for a city official to accept presents from companies so long as the taxpayers don't suffer," but 47 percent disagreed and 13 percent were undecided. Fifty-four percent did not believe that, "The mayor and police chief should be able to cancel parking and speeding tickets in some cases," but 36 percent thought it might be a good idea.

The intensity of feelings against corruption was brought out most strongly when the respondents were asked about the 30-day jail sentences imposed on Irv Stern and Bob Walasek for extorting $10,500 on city purchases of parking meters. Eighty-six percent felt that the sentences were too light; seven respondents felt that they were too severe.

generally feeling that publicity arising from the trial had hurt Walasek's family. When asked why they felt as they did, 32 percent felt that Walasek had "betrayed a public trust;" 18 percent gave an answer such as, "If it had been a little guy like me instead of a guy with pull like Walasek, I'd still be in jail."

In light of the mixed feelings about gambling and corruption, we might wonder whether Wincantonites are hostile toward the police department's present antigambling policy. This does not appear to be the case: 55 percent of the respondents disagreed with the statement, "The Wincanton police today are concentrating on gambling too much"; only 17 percent agreed, and 21 percent were undecided. Further support for the local police was indicated by the respondents when asked to comment on the statement, "If there is any gambling going on in Wincanton, it should be handled by the local police rather than the FBI"; 57 percent agreed and 19 percent disagreed. The preference for local action was slightly stronger—58 percent—when the question stated "* * * the local police rather than State Police."

We have frequently mentioned that Walasek and Stern were convicted on the basis of testimony given by former Police Chief Dave Phillips. Phillips was given immunity from Federal prosecution, and perjury charges against him were dropped. What was the public response to Phillips having testified? Was he regarded as a "fink" or a hero? Fifty-nine percent of the respondents felt that it was right for Phillips to testify. Only 15 percent felt that he should have received immunity, 40 percent felt the grant of immunity was wrong, and 40 percent did not know whether it was right or wrong. The most common reaction was that Phillips was as guilty as the others, or "he only testified to save his own skin."

Finally, to ascertain how much citizens know about law enforcement agencies. the survey respondents were asked. first, "As you remember it, who was it who decided that bingo should not be played in Wincanton?". Five percent attributed the ban to the legislature. Forty-three percent correctly stated that a joint decision of Mayor Whitton and District Attorney Hendricks (declaring that the State gambling law included bingo) had led to the current crackdown. Thirty-four percent didn't know. Ironically, 13 respondents believed that Walasek, Donnelly, Police Chief Phillips, or District Attorney French had ended bingo (all had been out of office for at least 6 months and opposed the ban)! Second, respondents [8] were asked. "Which of the Federal investigative agencies would you say was primarily responsible for most of the prosecutions of Wincanton people in the past 10 years?". Thirty-one percent correctly cited the Internal Revenue Service, 20 percent mentioned the Federal Bureau of Investigation (whose only major involvement had been in raiding the dice game), and 46 percent did not know.

The Politics of Reform. In every local election in Wincanton, it seems that some candidates are running on "reform" platforms. charging their opponents with corruption or at least tolerating gamblers and prostitutes.

Usually, we see Republicans attacking Democratic corruption. But Democratic primary candidates also attack the records of Democratic incumbents, and in 1955, Democrats promised the voters that they would rid the town of the prostitutes and bookies that "pearl gray" Hal Craig had tolerated. Frequently, officials have become corrupt after they were elected, but Wincanton voters have never returned a known criminal to office. Following legislative investigations in the early 1950's, Mayor Watts lost the general election, receiving only 39 percent of the vote. After the Federal indictment of Police Chief Phillips in the early 1960's, Bob Walasek was defeated in the Democratic primary, running a poor third, with only 19 percent of the vote. Even with Walasek out of the running, the voters selected Republican Whitton over his Democratic opponent, a councilman in the Walasek administration. While the Republicans were able to elect councilmen in two elections, they were unable to make inroads in the off-year council elections despite wholesale Federal gambling raids in the months just prior to the elections in these years.

Looking at these voting figures, two questions arise—why corruption and why reform? As we have seen, Wincantonites have never voted for corruption, although they may have voted for men tolerant of the gambling citizens demanded. While the newspapers and the reformers have warned of the necessary connection between gambling and corruption, their impact has been deadened by repetition—Wincanton voters have acquired a "ho-hum" attitude, saying to themselves. "That's just the Gazette sounding off again." or "The Republicans are 'crying wolf' just like they did 4 years ago." As Lord Bryce said of Americans 80 years ago:

> The people see little and they believe less. True, the party newspapers accuse their opponents of such offenses. but the newspapers are always reviling somebody; and it is because the words are so strong that the tale has little meaning * * *.
> The habit of hearing charges promiscuously bandied to and fro, but seldom probed to the bottom, makes men heedless.[9]

If the Democrats have dominated Wincanton elections so consistently, why did they lose in two important elections? Those years were different because official corruption was being documented by Federal investigators; in other years investigations were only showing widespread gambling, and only newspaper inferences suggested that officials were being paid off. It is equally, perhaps more. significant to note that Federal investigations attracted national attention—instead of seeing allusions of corruption in the Wincanton Gazette, city voters were beginning to read about themselves and their city in *The New York Times* and the papers of the larger cities within the State. Just as national media coverage of the "War on the Press" may have forced Mayor Donnelly to back down. so the national interest during the two elections may have shamed local voters into deserting the Democratic Party. The years when the Republicans

---

8 This question was inserted in the schedule after the survey was underway; only 87 respondents were asked this question.

9 James Bryce, "The American Commonwealth", vol. II (London: MacMillan, 1889), p. 204.

78

won were different because the voters were forced to
recognize the conflict between their norms (honesty in
government, no corruption, etc.) and the actions of local
Democratic officials. Their "active sense of outrage" [10]
produced a crisis leading to a readjustment of their normal patterns of behavior. Furthermore, even though
the voters had been willing to tolerate petty corruption
on the part of past officials, the national investigations
indicated that officials were now going too far. As Irv
Stern had predicted, Bob Walasek, unlike his predecessor,
got "greedy," and pushed the voters too far, tolerating
too much vice and gambling and demanding kickbacks
on too many contracts and licenses. For the voters, the
"price" of Democratic control had gotten too high. [11]

A city where the government has for its subjects
acquaintances, whose interests and passions it knows
and can at pleasure thwart or forward, can hardly
expect a neutral government.

—Sir Ernest Barker,
"Greek Political Theory" [12]

THE FUTURE OF REFORM IN WINCANTON

When Wincantonites are asked what kind of law enforcement they want, they are likely to say that it is all
right to tolerate petty gambling and prostitution, but
that "you've got to keep out racketeers and corrupt politicians." Whenever they come to feel that the city is being
controlled by these racketeers, they "throw the rascals
out." This policy of "throwing the rascals out," however, illustrates the dilemma facing reformers in Wincanton. Irv Stern, recently released from Federal prison,
has probably, in fact, retired from the rackets; he is ill
and plans to move to Arizona. Bob Walasek, having
been twice convicted on extortion charges, is finished
politically. Therefore? Therefore, the people of Wincanton firmly believe that "the problem" has been
solved—"the rascals" have been thrown out. When
asked, recently, what issues would be important in the
next local elections, only 9 of 183 respondents felt that
clean government or keeping out vice and gambling
might be an issue. (Fifty-five percent had no opinion.
15 percent felt that the ban on bingo might be an issue,
and 12 percent cited urban renewal, a subject frequently
mentioned in the papers preceding the survey.) Since,
under Ed Whitton, the city is being honestly run and is free
from gambling and prostitution, there is no problem to
worry about.

On balance, it seems far more likely to conclude that
gambling and corruption will soon return to Wincanton
(although possibly in less blatant forms) for two reasons—
first, a significant number of people want to be able to
gamble or make improper deals with the city government.
(This assumes, of course, that racketeers will be available
to provide gambling if a complacent city administration
permits it.) Second, and numerically far more important, most voters think that the problem has been perma-

nently solved, and thus they will not be choosing candidates based on these issues, in future elections.

Throughout this report, a number of specific recommendations have been made to minimize opportunities
for wide-open gambling and corruption—active State
Police intervention in city affairs, modification of the
city's contract bidding policies, extending civil service protection to police officers, etc. On balance, we could probably also state that the commission form of government
has been a hindrance to progressive government; a
"strong mayor" form of government would probably handle the city's affairs more efficiently. Fundamentally,
however, all of these suggestions are irrelevant. When
the voters have called for clean government, they have
gotten it, in spite of loose bidding laws, limited civil service, etc. The critical factor has been voter preference.
Until the voters of Wincanton come to believe that illegal
gambling produces the corruption they have known, the
type of government we have documented will continue.
Four-year periods of reform do little to change the habits
instilled over 40 years of gambling and corruption.

RESEARCH ON THE POLITICS OF
CORRUPTION [13]

Reviewing the literature on the politics of corruption,
one is tempted to conclude that while everyone is writing
about it, no one is saying very much about it. Most of
the material in the field can be classified as simple reports
of wrongdoing or official investigations. Both tend to
come in waves coinciding with popular interest in reform, [14] and are written with a strongly moralistic bias.
The classic exposés of municipal corruption are, of course,
the works of the muckrakers—Steffans, Sinclair, Tarbell,
etc.—written at the turn of the century. [15] More recently,
issues of the "National Civic Review" (known as the
"National Municipal Review" until 1958), have presented
reports of specific cases of corruption, graft, or bribery;
titles such as "Indianapolis Mayor Faces Jail Sentence,"
"Election Frauds in Philadelphia," and "Eliminating
California Bosses" indicate the specific and reforming
quality of most "Review" articles. Their authors generally view the world in black and white terms—a conflict between the good guys (the average, basically honest
but put-upon citizenry) and the bad guys ("politicans"
and "bosses"). The typical "Review" solution to the
problem of corruption calls for both structural changes—
nonpartisan elections, city manager government, etc.—
and citizen action—the uprising of an alert, informed,
and indignant public against evil machines. Local politics
is represented as a morality play: an example is the story
of municipal reform in Des Moines in the 1920's:

A remarkable story * * * one in which taxpayers
were arrayed against politicians, prosecuting attorneys against slick lawyers, and municipal graft
against good government. It is the story of how an

---

10 Arnold A. Rogow and Harold D. Lasswell, "Power, Corruption and Rectitude"
(Englewood Cliffs: Prentice-Hall, 1963), p. 72.
11 Cf. Eric L. McKitrick, "The Study of Corruption", 72 Political Science
Quarterly 507 (December 1957).
12 Sir Ernest Barker, "Greek Political Theory" (London: Methuen, 1918), p. 13.
13 Joel Margolis, a graduate student in the Department of Political Science,
University of Wisconsin, performed the research upon which this review of the
literature is based.
14 Ironically, there has been a strong interest in corruption in the years since

World War II, even though ethics in government have probably been at a higher
level than at most other periods in our history. For a brief overview of American
corruption which puts recent misdeeds in their proper historical perspective, see
Sidney Warren, "Corruption in Politics", 22 Current History 65-69, 211-215, 285-
289, and 348-354 (1952).
15 The ideas and work of the major muckrakers are summarized in David Mark
Chalmers, "The Social and Political Ideas of the Muckrakers" (New York: Citadel
Press, 1964).

American city cleaned house, lodged a number of public servants * * * in the State's penal institutions * * * placed an increased value on its tax dollar, and put its public affairs on a plane of decency and efficiency all in the last two years * * *

The people * * * who have been looted see the dawn of a new day in popular self-government.[16]

The official investigations of political corruption display a similar degree of specificity and simplicity. Both Federal (e.g., the Wickersham Commission and the Kefauver and McClellan committee hearings) and State (e.g., the Massachusetts Crime Commission and the Illinois Crime Investigating Commission reports) agencies hold hearings, report that crime and corruption were found in city X or department Y, and then call for prosecutions and new legislation to correct these situations. Little time or space is devoted to analysis of the social or political causes of the events portrayed.

In contrast with these numerous but superficial journalistic and official investigations and reports, social scientists have had an infrequent but somewhat more analytical interest in corruption. Corruption has seldom been the direct focus of their work, but has often been discussed in connection with other phenomena. Generally using the "functional" approach [17] applied earlier in this report, students of political parties, for example, have argued that corruption can serve as an important supplement to legal patronage [18] as a means of financing and holding together a political machine.[19] More broadly, it has been argued that corrupt practices may be necessary to overcome the decentralization of government brought about by the separation of executive, legislative, and judicial processes, the creation of independent boards and commissions, etc.[20] Finally, corrupt distribution of governmental jobs and services has been viewed as a mechanism for instilling a feeling of national identity in new immigrant populations, as well as providing for their social welfare.[21]

From another point of view, political corruption has been considered functional to the business community in offering protection against aggressive competition, speed in finalizing contracts with government, and freedom from cumbersome codes and regulations.[22] In underdeveloped nations, Nathaniel Leff feels that corruption can be a vital catalyst in inclining political leaders toward economic development, mobilizing the state bureaucracy to aid entrepreneurs, and paying off the existing "power elite" to tolerate economic and social change.[23] The benefits that corruption offers to legitimate businessmen accrue also to illegitimate enterprises; as we have seen in Wincanton, corruptly procured protection allowed Irv Stern to stabilize the gambling industry and assign contracts with the city, while landowners and businessmen were able to buy immunity from building and zoning regulations.

A third group of studies has served to break down any false notions that corruption and criminality are sharply distinct from the values and way of life of "law-abiding" members of society. A number of studies have shown that to a certain extent criminal careers mirror the approved values of seeking social advancement, prestige, and having one's own business; furthermore, gamblers and racketeers are frequently respected and emulated members of immigrant and lower class social groups.[24] Finally, as law enforcement officers know all too well, some members of all social classes condone or approve gambling and corruption, although many citizens may also, either ambivalently or hypocritically, demand strict law enforcement.[25] Because of these conflicts between legal norms and actual popular attitudes, several political scientists have concluded that corruption can perform the valuable function of permitting the continued existence of the society. Instead of a direct confrontation between the norm and the fact, corrupt enforcement of the laws can permit quiet fulfillment of both sets of values, e.g., through a territorial arrangement in which "good neighborhoods" are kept free of gambling and prostitution while other areas of the city or metropolitan area are "wide open."[26] Until legal norms coincide with popular values, these corruptly induced adjustments allow the society to run more smoothly.[27]

[16] Merze Marvin, "Des Moines Cleans House," 14 National Municipal Review 539 (September, 1925).

[17] See Robert K. Merton, "Social Theory and Social Structure," revised edition (New York: Free Press, 1957), pp. 19-87; Eric L. McKitrick, "The Study of Corruption," 72 Political Science Quarterly 502-514 (December, 1957); Don Martindale, editor, "Functionalism in the Social Sciences" (Philadelphia: American Academy of Political and Social Sciences, 1965).

[18] On the role of patronage in the party system, see V. O. Key, Jr., "Politics, Parties and Pressure Groups," 4th ed. (New York: Thomas Y. Crowell, 1958), ch. 13; and James Q. Wilson, "The Economy of Patronage," 69 Journal of Political Economy 369-380 (August, 1961).

[19] For a general description of city machines, see Edward C. Banfield and James Q. Wilson, "City Politics" (Cambridge: Harvard University Press, 1963), ch. 9. Literature on some of our more famous city bosses is listed in Charles R. Adrian, "Governing Urban America" (New York: McGraw-Hill, 1961) pp. 498-499.

[20] Henry Jones Ford, "Municipal Corruption," 19 Political Science Quarterly 673-686 (1904).

[21] V. O. Key, Jr., "The Techniques of Political Graft in the United States," unpublished Ph. D. dissertation, Department of Political Science, University of Chicago, 1934.

[22] Ibid.; McKitrick. op. cit. supra. n. 5.

[23] Nathaniel H. Leff, "Economic Development through Bureaucratic Corruption," 8 American Behavioral Scientist 8-14 (November, 1964).

[24] Daniel Bell, "Crime as an American Way of Life," in "The End of Ideology" (New York: Free Press, 1960); William Foote Whyte, "Street Corner Society" (Chicago: University of Chicago Press, 1943), pp. 111-193; David Matza, "Delinquency and Drift" (New York: John Wiley, 1964); Donald R. Cressey, "The Functions and Structure of Criminal Syndicates," a report to the President's Commission on Law Enforcement and Administration of Justice, 1966.

[25] Charles E. Merriam, "Chicago: A More Intimate View of Urban Politics" (New York: MacMillan, 1929), pp. 54-60; Virgil W. Peterson, "Obstacles to Enforcement of Gambling Laws," 269 Annals 9-20 (May, 1950).

[26] Merriam, op. cit. supra. n. 13.

[27] Harold D. Lasswell, "Bribery," 2 Encyclopedia of the Social Sciences 690-692 (New York: MacMillan, 1930); M. McMullan, "A Theory of Corruption," 9 Sociological Review 181-201 (July 1961); Key, op. cit. supra, n. 9.

[12]

ILLEGAL ENTERPRISE: A THEORETICAL AND HISTORICAL INTERPRETATION*

MARK H. HALLER
Temple University

Illegal enterprise—defined as the sale of illegal goods and services to customers who know that the goods or services are illegal—has long been a central part of the American underworld, but it has received little attention as a separate criminological category. Although such activities are often relatively short term and small scale when compared with legal businesses, three major factors explain the cooperation that sometimes emerges among illegal entrepreneurs. The first factor is systematic corruption, which often permits police or politicians to bring order to illegal activities within a political subdivision. A second factor is overlapping partnerships by which entrepreneurs often launch and maintain illegal businesses. A third factor is the internal economic characteristics of illegal businesses, which shape the manner in which they operate. The paper explores the implications of each factor through historical examples and suggests hypotheses concerning the changing structure of illegal enterprises in American cities.

A broad range of criminal activities might logically be called "illegal enterprise." Such activities ultimately entail the sale of illegal goods or services to customers who know that the goods or services are illegal. In recent American history, examples of illegal goods have included bootleg liquor in the 1920s, pornography, and a variety of forbidden drugs. Without much thought, however, the list might be considerably expanded: quack medicines like "laetrile," unlicensed weapons, even bald eagle feathers or illegally imported exotic pets. Examples of illegal services include prostitution, loan-sharking, and, most important, various forms of gambling. Again, the list can be greatly expanded. Less than 20 years ago illegal abortions were common. Other examples range from murder for hire to the operation of gypsy cabs in the ghettoes of many American cities.

In much of the standard criminological literature, those involved in gambling, narcotics, or loan-sharking are classified as part of "organized crime."

---

* I am grateful for a series of grants from the Center for Studies in Criminal Justice in the Law School of the University of Chicago, which made possible the early stages of the research for this paper. A Visiting Fellowship at the National Institute of Justice in 1975–1976 gave me an opportunity to examine files in the National Archives. Franklin E. Zimring and Norval Morris provided helpful comments on early versions of this paper; Frederick Frey, John Goldkamp, Jack Greene, Terry Parssinen, and Peter Reuter improved the paper through their comments at a later stage.

208 HALLER

As a result, discussion of illegal enterprise has often been subsumed under "organized crime" and has not, in itself, been a central concern of criminological theory and research.[1] Yet illegal enterprises shaped the underworld of American cities long before the rise of Italian-American crime families. Even with the emergence of crime families in a number of cities, most illegal enterprises continue to operate independently of them. It is important, then, that illegal enterprise be made a subject of study in its own right. One purpose of this paper is to provide a theoretical and historical framework for the analysis of illegal enterprise in American cities.

The advantage of recognizing illegal enterprise as a criminological category is that such activities have common characteristics that provide a basis for analysis. Because they ultimately involve the retailing of goods or services, they can be studied as businesses, and the same questions can be asked that would be asked of analogous legal businesses. What are the sources of capital for starting or expanding the operations? What factors influence locational decisions? How are the goods or services advertised to customers? How are prices set? What financial arrangements exist between the entrepreneur and others who participate in the enterprise? One can, in short, ask all the questions that would be asked of a legal enterprise. But, for enterprises that are illegal, there is an additional question: What difference does it make that the enterprise is illegal? More specifically, how do various law enforcement strategies shape the operations of illegal businesses? How, for instance, do enforcement policies influence sources of capital, recruitment of personnel, location of retail outlets, advertising, pricing, and the internal structure of the enterprise?

Most of those involved in illegal enterprises have operated on a small scale. In American cities, there have been free-lance prostitutes, street-corner drug dealers, and neighborhood bookmakers. As Peter Reuter (1983:ch. 5) has argued convincingly, illegal enterprises are likely to have lower capitalization, fewer personnel, and less formal management than comparable legal enterprises. Nevertheless, illegal enterprises do sometimes bring together a number of entrepreneurs for cooperative ventures that involve some degree of coordination. Such cooperation is worth exploring because it reveals crucial aspects of illegal enterprise.

Historically, three important factors have underlain cooperation among those involved in illegal enterprise. The most important factor has been the oversight of illegal activities by local politicians or police. In a political ward

---

1. Smith (1971, 1975) has developed the concept of "illicit enterprise," which probably includes what I have called "illegal enterprise" but also includes a much wider range of activities. For discussions of the illegal enterprises of "organized crime" from a variety of perspectives, see Albini (1971:Ch. 7); Cressey (1969: Ch. 5); Ianni (1972:Ch. 5, 1974:Pt. III); Lasswell and McKenna (n.d.:Ch. 4); Rubin (1973); Schelling (1967); and especially Anderson (1979) and Reuter (1983).

ILLEGAL ENTERPRISE 209

or even in an entire city, corrupt relations between criminals and politicians (or police) have often resulted in informal licensing and coordination. A second factor is the use of partnership arrangements in promoting illegal enterprises. Through participation in overlapping partnerships, some entrepreneurs have exerted influence over a range of activities. A third factor leading to cooperation has been the internal economics of some types of criminal enterprise. Such enterprises—numbers banks would be an example—require coordination for economic success and, as a result, have traditionally been operated as syndicates in various cities over many years. The paper examines each of the three factors in turn.

POLICE AND POLITICAL CORRUPTION

American cities have a long history of corrupt relations between some illegal enterprises and local police or politicians. For criminal entrepreneurs, payments to politicians or police can be viewed either as normal business expenses in return for services to the enterprise or as extortionate demands that eat into the profits of the enterprise. For police and politicians, levying regular assessments on illegal entrepreneurs has provided a source of extra income as well as a way to oversee neighborhood enterprises that could not be legally controlled. Historically, oversight by local political organizations (or the police) has been the most important source of coordination for illegal enterprises in American cities.

The process of regularizing payoffs, whether to politicians or to the police, almost inevitably results in some level of coordination or regulation. Indeed, restraint of competition may be in the interest of both the entrepreneurs and political (or police) officials. Those involved in illegal enterprise are often interested in moderating competition, and this can be one of the advantages that they hope to gain through payments to officials. But, to the extent that payments by criminals are regularized, officials have a stake in the economic success of the enterprises and may also see advantages in limiting competition. Furthermore, by arresting outsiders, officials can present the appearance of serious enforcement and reduce the probability that corruption will become a public issue (see, e.g., Chambliss, 1978:91–92; Whyte, 1955:123–46).

Similarly, both sides may be interested in regulation. For obvious reasons, public officials hope to avoid scandals that call attention to tolerated underworld activities. Likewise, those who regard themselves as "honest" criminal entrepreneurs may desire regulation. If a fly-by-night numbers bank fails to pay winners, for instance, this can lessen the popularity of betting on the numbers. If some houses of prostitution rob customers, this may discourage customers from patronizing other prostitutes. Regularized corruption, then,

210   HALLER

has sometimes created a social structure within which the police, often guided by local politicians, use the law as a lever for enforcing informal regulations.

Although corrupt relations between politicians and the underworld have been the subject of a number of scholarly studies (Chambliss, 1978; Fox, 1989:Ch. 6; Gardiner, 1970; Haller, 1988; Landesco, 1968:Ch. 8; Reuter, 1984), little attention has been given to historical trends in the impact of corruption on criminal enterprise. In American cities at the turn of the century, a number of factors combined to facilitate corruption. First was the general expectation that urban political organizations (called political "machines" by their opponents) would accept payments to do favors for various interests within a fragmented metropolis (Merton, 1957:71–82; Tarr, 1967). Second, certain structural characteristics of city government enhanced the role of local politicians. In the nineteenth century, wards were not simply electoral units but also administrative units. It was common for ward boundaries and police precincts to overlap and also for each ward to have its own police court. Because ward politicians often selected the local police captain and because police justices were cogs in the ward's political machine, the criminal justice system was a major resource available to politicians for doing favors that might strengthen the political organization (Fogelson, 1977:Ch. 1; Haller, 1976b; Reppetto, 1978; Richardson, 1970:Ch. 8).

With the passage of time, control by local politicians, particularly in large cities, has weakened, so that regularized corruption has declined as a factor in coordination of illegal activities. To understand the decline, it is first necessary to understand the use of corruption to limit competition and regulate enterprise at the turn of the century.

POLITICS AND GAMBLING

An example of the use of corruption to limit competition was the role of Chicago ward politicians in allocating bookmaking and other gambling rights during the mayoralty of Carter H. Harrison II from 1897 to 1905.[2] By that time Irish–Americans dominated gambling in the city and were disproportionately represented among local politicians and police. Within this Irish gambling/politics complex, a number of patterns existed by which politicians oversaw and, in effect, licensed important gambling activity.

One pattern was for a local gambler to become the ward leader and thereby combine his political and economic interests. On the West Side, for example, William (Billy) Skidmore started selling racing programs at tracks around the city while still a teenager in the 1890s. Soon he opened a saloon with gambling in the back room, entered politics, and became ward committeeman of

---

2. Information on Chicago gambling is chiefly from the Herman F. Schuettler Scrapbooks of Newspaper Clippings, in Chicago Historical Society; also Citizens Association of Chicago, *Bulletin* No. 13 (June 10, 1904). Secondary sources are cited in the text.

ILLEGAL ENTERPRISE   211

the Thirteenth Ward. In 1912 he was sergeant at arms at the Democratic National Convention and later assisted in the presidential campaign of Woodrow Wilson (Murray, 1965:366–374). By 1905, in partnership with Patrick J. (Patsy) King, he operated a horse parlor at 189 West Madison Street, as well as a major policy gambling syndicate. For nearly four decades, until his conviction in 1939 for income tax evasion, he was a Democratic power and leading gambler in Chicago.

Another pattern was for close relations to develop between an important gambler and local political figures. James O'Leary—just two years old in 1871 when the Chicago fire started in his mother's barn—bore a famous Chicago name. In the 1890s he built a saloon and gambling emporium across from the business headquarters of the thriving Chicago stockyards. His three-story building housed bowling alleys, a barbershop, restaurant, turkish bath, gambling rooms, and a horse parlor—everything that might fulfill the dreams of a cattleman who wanted to celebrate after selling his stock for slaughter. From his gambling house, O'Leary also backed the bookmakers who serviced the stockyard workers in saloons west of the stockyards. He maintained his gambling interests through close connections with ward politicians and with Police Inspector Nicholas Hunt, reputed to be the city's wealthiest cop and a political power in his own right. (His son served as a Democratic member of the state legislature from 1901 to 1904.) Inspector Hunt enjoyed horse racing and frequented the tracks, where, standing by the betting ring, he assured reporters that he saw no gambling.

A final pattern was for local ward leaders, although not themselves major gamblers, to license and oversee a range of gambling activities by political supporters. Those two famous Chicago aldermen, Michael (Hinky Dink) Kenna and "Bathhouse" John Coughlin, were prime examples. Large, gregarious, and a gaudy dresser, Bathhouse was well known in gambling circles before entering politics. Hinky Dink, by contrast, was small and quiet and operated a famous saloon in the First Ward. From 1892 until the early 1940s, either Bathhouse John, Hinky Dink, or both served on the city council and oversaw vice and entertainment in the Loop and the Lively Levee entertainment district south of the Loop (Wendt and Kogan, 1943). In the early twentieth century, Tom McGinnis, a saloonkeeper and gambler, coordinated gambling for the two aldermen. He received a cut from poker games in the downtown hotels and accepted payoffs from bookmakers and gambling house owners. Among his associates was John (Mushmouth) Johnson, a black who owned one of the largest gambling houses in the Levee, supported Democratic candidates among black voters, and collected payments from Chinese gambling house operators in Chicago's Chinatown (Haller, 1988; Wooldridge, 1901:191–195). In addition, Johnson and McGinnis were partners in the largest policy gambling syndicate in the ward.

212   HALLER

REGULATING THE RED-LIGHT DISTRICTS

If gambling in Chicago displayed the patterns by which politicians informally licensed illegal enterprise, the red-light districts of American cities exemplified the role of politicians and police in the regulation of vice. The red-light districts, which emerged in American cities between the 1870s and World War I and were located on the edge of the central business districts, contained the disreputable nightlife entertainment of the city. Crammed together with houses of prostitution were burlesque theaters, concert saloons (night clubs), dance halls, and gambling houses. Within the districts, drug dealers hawked morphine and cocaine, thieves fenced stolen goods, and pimps and other outcasts carried on their social life and hustling activities.[3] Often the districts abutted skid row and the local Chinatown (Blumberg et al., 1978:Ch. 1–3; Light, 1974, 1977; Rosen, 1982:Ch. 5, 6; Woolston, 1969:Ch. 4, 5).

By 1900 the red-light districts—San Francisco's Barbary Coast, New Orleans's French Quarter, Chicago's Levee, or the Tenderloins of Philadelphia and New York—were integrated within the local political machines. Those who participated in local politics expected to be allowed to operate a saloon, gambling house, or parlor house in the district. Often the local political club was a social center where pimps and politicians hung out, gambled, and plotted political strategy. There was, in short, an overlap between the political organizations and the economic activities of the districts.

In this context, local officials instituted informal and formal regulation. Regulation had a variety of goals: to minimize the spread of venereal diseases, to prevent scandals that often erupted from the forcible recruitment of prostitutes or the employment of young girls, or to shield respectable citizens from the shock of observing the city's sinful underside (see, for instance, Best, 1987). In Chicago in 1910, although prostitution was illegal, written police regulations prescribed that "no house of ill-fame shall be permitted outside of certain restricted districts, or to be established within two blocks of any school, church, hospital, or public institution, or upon any street car line." No "under age" girls were to work in the houses, and no woman was to be detained against her will. Even decorum within the houses was ostensibly regulated by rules that "short skirts, transparent gowns or other improper attire shall not be permitted in the parlors, or public rooms," and "obscene exhibitions or pictures shall not be permitted" (Vice Commission of Chicago,

---

3. For a description of the varied criminal activities within a red-light district, see investigative reports of the Bureau of Social Morals in New York City, found in the Judah L. Magnes Archives, Central Archives of the Jewish People, Jerusalem, Israel; see also, Block (1979).

ILLEGAL ENTERPRISE 213

1911:329–330). In Houston, where city leaders attempted to establish regulated prostitution in 1907, a major issue was whether to require racially segregated bordellos (Mackey, 1987:Ch. 6).

A few cities, to stem the spread of venereal diseases, tried medical regulation, modeled on the European system (Flexner, 1969). An early attempt was a "Social Evil Ordinance," which was backed by the St. Louis Board of Health and passed by the city council in 1870. The ordinance required that prostitutes register with the city, that they undergo weekly examination by a city physician, and that women diagnosed to have a venereal disease be hospitalized until cured. Although the ordinance lasted just four years before outraged opponents persuaded the state legislature to nullify it, health officials in other cities looked favorably on the St. Louis experiment (Burnham, 1971a, 1971b). In 1911, some 40 years later, San Francisco established through its Board of Public Health a system requiring all prostitutes in the city to undergo a medical examination twice weekly at the municipal clinic. Women free of venereal disease received a card that permitted them to practice prostitution in the prescribed red-light district. Despite charges of corruption, the system lasted two years before being abandoned (Shumsky, 1980).

The regulation of red-light districts can, of course, be regarded with cynicism. Generally the regulations were only haphazardly enforced; often they were intended, in part, to assure the public that the problem was under control in order to head off demands that the laws against prostitution be seriously enforced. But the rules also reflected what police leaders and many politicians believed to be sensible public policy. Convinced that prostitution was inevitable, they argued that it was better to regulate it in recognized sections of the city rather than to have it dispersed throughout the city. In Milwaukee, for instance, although there was no evidence of police corruption, police policies mirrored the policies in other cities. Any woman intending to practice prostitution had to register with the police, listing her age and place of previous work. This was to prevent "white slavery" and the recruitment of underage girls. Milwaukee police also banned the sale of alcoholic beverages in houses of prostitution in the belief that alcohol and sex were a volatile mixture.[4]

The regulation of prostitution within a system of corruption, then, represented an attempt by local authorities to deal with vice activities that, while illegal, were also regarded as inevitable. Systematic corruption had multiple functions: to organize politics and voting within the entertainment district, to supplement the income of police and local politicians, but also to introduce regulations that dominant groups favored as strategies to deal with the shadier entertainment activities of the city.

---

4. Teasdale Commission Papers, Series No. 2/3/1/3–8, Box 19, Wisconsin State Historical Society, Madison.

214   HALLER

DISCUSSION OF CORRUPTION

To the extent that politicians or the police coordinate illegal enterprise, the coordination generally reflects the structure of local politics and law enforcement. Because law enforcement at the turn of the century was highly decentralized, coordination was decentralized; each ward (and police district) tended to coordinate gambling and vice within its area. On the other hand, to the extent that law enforcement was sometimes centralized, coordination might be centralized. The formation of a citywide gambling squad, for instance, introduced the possibility of citywide coordination of gambling activities and the potential breakdown of local arrangements.

During the twentieth century, the role of institutionalized corruption in the control of illegal enterprise has undergone two important changes. One change has been a relative decline in the importance of corruption as a factor underlying coordination (Haller, 1976b). To the extent that corruption continues to coordinate illegal activities, however, a second change is that the police are now more likely to act on their own rather than under the control of local politicians.

Many factors have reduced systematic corruption and undercut the control of local politicians over the police. These factors include civil service reform, police unionization, centralization of police communication and command functions, and the redrawing of local police districts so that they no longer correspond with political wards (Fogelson, 1977:Ch. 6–9; Walker, 1980:Ch. 9). Particularly since the 1960s, in addition, new laws and policies have empowered state and especially federal law enforcement agencies to investigate local corruption and prosecute criminal entrepreneurs (see, e.g., Carlisle, 1976; Johnson, 1981:Ch. 10, 11; Mollenhoff, 1972).

Local politicians, as a result, have less ability to set local police policy or to protect criminal activities within their bailiwicks. This can be seen, for instance, in the Knapp Commission investigation of the New York City police in the early 1970s. Unlike earlier studies of police corruption in New York, the Knapp Commission found that police acted independently of politicians in establishing corrupt relations for the regulation of gambling or prostitution.[5]

---

5. Committee to Investigate Allegations of Corruption (1972). For an interesting discussion of the relation between police and gambling before and after the Knapp Commission, see Rubinstein and Reuter (1982:60–93) and Reuter (1984). For a situation in Philadelphia similar to that found by Knapp in New York, see Pennsylvania Crime Commission (1974:166–216). On the other hand, the continuation of the traditional system of corrupt political control over the police is documented for the town of Chester in Pennsylvania Crime Commission (1989); see also Bellis (1985). Sherman (1978) provides a general discussion of police corruption and reform in recent years. The corruption from recent drug enforcement has generally not resulted in systematic licensing or regulation but has chiefly consisted of opportunistic shakedowns by police (McCormack, 1988).

BUSINESS PARTNERSHIPS

Partnership arrangements have long been a common method for launching various illegal enterprises. Partnerships have the same advantages for illegal entrepreneurs as for legal entrepreneurs. First, partnerships allow several entrepreneurs to share risks, particularly the risk of business failure. Second, partnerships enable persons with different resources to pool their resources in a single enterprise. For those involved in illegal businesses, partnerships permit persons with political influence, capital, and managerial skills to cooperate so that each has a direct economic stake in the enterprise. The possibility of coordination arises when some partners, through participation in multiple and overlapping partnerships, can ensure that the different enterprises act cooperatively. The best way to clarify the use of partnerships is by examples.

COLONIAL INN

The Colonial Inn, a posh illegal casino that opened in December 1945 in Hallandale, Florida, near Miami, was an example of a partnership that brought together a variety of entrepreneurs in a complex joint venture. Meyer Lansky was the chief entrepreneur. He arranged political protection, oversaw the remodeling of a mansion into a casino with a fine restaurant and elegant gaming rooms, and called on long-time business associates in New York and Florida to provide the necessary capital. Investors included Frank Erickson and Frank Costello (already cooperating in numerous New York and Florida gambling enterprises), Vincent "Jimmy Blue Eyes" Alo, and Joe Adonis. To ensure success, however, the casino needed an expert manager (see Figure 1).[6]

Mert Wertheimer had run gambling enterprises in Detroit since the 1920s. Within the American gambling fraternity, he enjoyed a reputation as a skilled operator with important contacts in the world of sports and entertainment. In 1944, after he and his partners—Reuben Mathis, Danny Sullivan, and Lincoln Fitzgerald—were indicted for gambling, they left Michigan to evade prosecution. In October 1945, while attending the World Series in Chicago,

---

6. The section on the Colonial Inn is based on a variety of sources. Investments are discussed in testimony before the Kefauver Committee; see U.S. Congress, Senate, Special Committee to Investigate Organized Crime in Interstate Commerce, *Investigation of Organized Crime in Interstate Commerce*, Hearings 81st Cong., 2nd Sess., 1950, and 82nd Cong., 1951, Part I:9–10, 115, 154–155, 480–481. Wertheimer's role is described in a memorandum from James E. Anderson to Special Agent in Charge, September 19, 1951, in the Guzik–Accardo income tax investigation file, File No. 42739–FR, Internal Revenue Service (IRS), Washington, D.C. The Colonial Inn is also mentioned in several secondary sources: Conrad (1982:7–14); Eisenberg et al. (1979:280, 292, 319); Fox (1989:314); Messick (1971:139-114). According to testimony before the Kefauver Committee (Part I:155), the Detroit group had a one-third interest in the Colonial Inn rather than the 50% interest claimed by Wertheimer.

216   HALLER

Figure 1.

Casino Partnership, 1945-1946

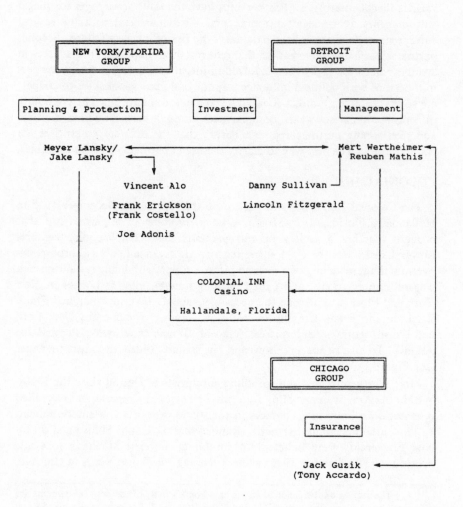

Wertheimer ran into Jake Lansky, Meyer's brother. Jake asked Wertheimer to manage the casino in the Colonial Inn. Indeed, so eager was Jake to secure Wertheimer's services that he offered him a 50% partnership. Although Wertheimer was not required to invest money in the casino, he was expected to cover 50% of any losses that might occur. Wertheimer agreed, but insisted that his partners also participate. As a result, Sullivan and Fitzgerald each invested $50,000, and Mathis became the assistant manager.

As opening day approached, however, Wertheimer was troubled by his commitment to cover half the casino's losses. He therefore approached Jack Guzik, once Al Capone's bootlegging partner and now a partner with Tony Accardo in various gambling enterprises in Chicago, downstate Illinois, and Florida. Over the years, Guzik had invested in several Wertheimer ventures. Wertheimer now offered Guzik 50% of his profits from the Colonial Inn if Guzik would agree to cover 50% of his losses. Guzik (and Accardo) agreed and thereby assumed a 25% interest in the casino.

The Colonial Inn opened on schedule, with Xavier Cugat's band on hand to entertain and deputy sheriffs as attendants to park customers' cars. It was probably the largest and most successful illegal casino in the country. In March 1946 Wertheimer, having earned nearly a quarter of a million dollars, quit as partner. He gave Guzik some $92,000.

The Colonial Inn, then, was a complex partnership that united the skills and resources of diverse entrepreneurs. Geographically, the partners came from Detroit, Chicago, New York, and Florida. In ethnic background, they were Jewish, Italian, and Irish. Together they provided planning, capital, political protection, managerial ability, and insurance against financial loss. Lansky, by combining his entrepreneurial skills and political influence with Wertheimer's managerial competence, ensured the casino's success.

CICERO ENTERPRISES

If the Colonial Inn demonstrated the use of partnerships to pool resources, Cicero, Illinois, in the late 1920s revealed, in exaggerated form, the use of partnerships to provide the structure for coordinating diverse enterprises. Before prohibition, Cicero was a respectable blue-collar town, just five miles west of downtown Chicago. The major employer was Bell Telephone's Western Electric Company. Like many blue-collar towns, Cicero had long been a place where small gambling houses and saloons operated openly.

By 1923 the bootlegging organizations of John Torrio and Dion O'Banion peddled liquor to the speakeasies there, and the two men became jointly involved in local gambling houses. Louis Alterie represented the O'Banion group in the gambling ventures. During the elections in spring 1924, Torrio sent Al (Snorky) Capone and his gunmen into Cicero to seize the polling places and ensure the victory of a friendly slate. Although Chicago police

218 HALLER

entered the city late in the day and drove the gunmen out, the Torrio slate won, and his group thereafter exercised significant political influence. Then a series of events upset relationships in Cicero. Torrio was arrested at one of his Chicago breweries and soon afterwards was shot and wounded by an O'Banion gunman. In the ensuing gang warfare, O'Banion himself was assassinated, and his allies were ousted from Cicero. A further result of the warfare was that Torrio, after serving a brief jail term, decided that Chicago was dangerous to his health and returned to New York. His associates, including Capone, inherited his business interests. Because Capone was a media celebrity who fascinated both investigative reporters and law enforcement agencies, it is possible to reconstruct the coordination of illegal activities in Cicero from 1925 to 1930 (see Figure 2).[7]

The group known to history as the Capone gang is best understood not as a hierarchy directed by Al Capone but as a complex set of partnerships. Four men might be called "senior partners"—Al and his older brother Ralph Capone, their cousin Frank Nitti, and Jack Guzik. They shared more or less equally in their joint income and acted as equals in looking after their varied business interests.[8] The senior partners, in turn, formed partnerships with others to launch numerous bootlegging, gambling, and vice activities in the Chicago Loop, South Side, and several suburbs. Cicero, because of their political influence there, was an important arena for their operations.

The senior partners had an interest in several of the gambling houses in Cicero. Because of periodic police raids or newspaper exposés, gambling houses often closed, moved, merged, or changed their names, and the history of the various houses is too complicated for this paper. By 1925, however, the largest of the gambling houses was the Hawthorne Smoke Shop. To manage bookmaking at the Smoke Shop, the senior partners entered into partnership with Frankie Pope; to run gambling games, they entered into partnership

---

7. Analysis of the Capone group businesses in Cicero is based on a number of sources: raw data in Capone income tax investigation, IRS File No. SI 7085-F; extensive newspaper clippings and investigative reports at Chicago Crime Commission, File Nos. 65, 65-50A, 3482-2, 8685, and 11654; also *Transcript of Record* in U.S. Circuit Court of Appeals for the Seventh Circuit, Oct. Term 1930, in Central Files of Department of Justice, No. 5-23-283, in National Archives; and Lipschultz income tax prosecution file, No. 5-23-11, in National Archives. See also two recent and careful journalistic biographies: Kobler (1971) and McPhaul (1970).

8. Capone's attorney estimated that each of the four senior partners received one-sixth of their joint profits, while one-third went to cover overhead expenses (rent on a headquarters, payment to bodyguards and entourage, etc.); see Lawrence P. Mattingly to C.W. Herrick, September 20, 1930, in IRS File No. SI 7085-F. In the IRS files there are different estimates of how profits from the Cicero operations were split but everyone—intelligence agents and crooks—agreed that the structure involved partnerships; see memorandum of Frank J. Wilson, December 21, 1933, in Env. No. 1 of the above file.

ILLEGAL ENTERPRISE 219

Figure 2.

Cicero Enterprises, 1925-1930

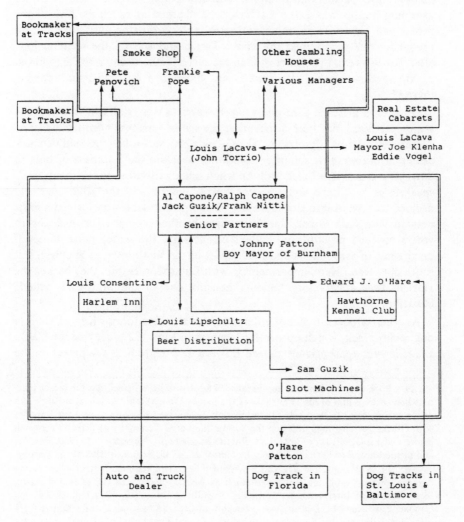

220   HALLER

with Pete Penovich.[9] Each of their other gambling houses in Cicero was a separate, relatively small operation, in which the senior partners and a local manager had partnership interests. Another person with a stake in Cicero gambling houses was Louis LaCava, who claimed as much as 20% of the profits and served as an important gambling coordinator until 1927. In all probability, he represented the absent Torrio and was on the scene to look after Torrio's remaining interests. In the early 1930s, at any rate, he followed Torrio to New York and served as an officer in a major Torrio company there.[10]

Other enterprises in Cicero and nearby suburbs were similarly linked to the senior partners. For beer distribution the senior partners negotiated a partnership with Louis Lipschultz, Jack Guzik's brother-in-law. Already a truck dealer in the western suburbs, Lipschultz oversaw the purchase of beer in downstate cities, like Joliet, and the wholesale distribution to the many small speakeasies in Cicero and adjacent towns. Eventually the senior partners decided to expand into slot machines. For this business, they formed a partnership with Sam Guzik, Jack's younger brother. Finally, because Cicero voters opposed prostitution in their community, the senior partners developed a line of vice resorts and roadhouses in the small town of Stickney, just south of Cicero. Here, in partnership with Louis Consentino, they backed the Harlem Inn, a two-story building housing one of the Midwest's notable bordellos.[11]

Another important Cicero enterprise was the Hawthorne Kennel Club, a dog racing track, which opened for business in May 1927. At that time, a St. Louis lawyer appropriately named Edward J. O'Hare held the patent on the

---

9. Pope quit the Smoke Shop in late 1926 because he believed that the senior partners had cheated him of his 18% share of the money ($84,000) in the safe at the time of a police raid in April of that year. Later, though, he engaged in various gambling activities with Guzik. Among documents on the Smoke Shop are "Testimony of Peter P. Penovich before Federal Grand Jury" in U.S. vs. Ralph Capone et al., November 25, 1930, Env. 76, and memorandum of Frank J. Wilson, December 21, 1933, Env. 1, in IRS file on Capone.

10. In 1923 Louis LaCava and his brother Rocco represented Torrio when Torrio began setting up gambling in Cicero, much as Alterie represented the O'Banion group. (See "Record of Interview with Cornelius J. Sullivan, March 9, 1931," in IRS file on Capone, Env. No. 29.) LaCava was ostensibly in Chicago as a sales representative for a New York lithographer. In appearance before a federal grand jury, he claimed that, in his gambling activities, he had fronted for various deceased leaders of the Unione Siciliana. This story was presumably to protect Torrio. ("Testimony of Louis LaCava before the Federal Grand Jury, March 5, 1931," in IRS file on Capone, Env. No. 79.) On his activities with Torrio in New York in the 1930s, see McPhaul (1970:274, 311, 320).

11. For descriptions of the Harlem Inn and other Stickney resorts, see Russell (1931:Ch. 2); also K.B. Alwood and J.L. Munday, "Stickney," student term paper (March 1930), in Ernest W. Burgess papers, University of Chicago Library. On involvement of the senior partners, see "Memorandum Relative to Houses of Prostitution under Control of the Capone Organization," June 29, 1931, and other materials in IRS file on Capone.

mechanical rabbit used for dog racing. (The Chicago airport is named after his son, who died a hero in World War II.) Because dog tracks derived their profits from illegal betting, O'Hare searched in various cities for local partners with political connections and a willingness to risk money in an enterprise of questionable legitimacy. Often he turned to bootleggers, because they were likely to have both capital and political influence. In Chicago he entered into an agreement with the senior partners, under which they probably held a 49% interest in the Kennel Club. For this enterprise, the senior partners were joined by Johnny Patton, known as the "Boy Mayor of Burnham." Elected mayor of that small Illinois town while still a teenager before World War I, Patton encouraged Chicago vice entrepreneurs to open resorts there and, in the process, met Torrio and Guzik. Because O'Hare had dog tracks in other states and was often out of town, Patton took on important management responsibilities at the Kennel Club.[12]

In short, the various enterprises of the so-called "Capone gang" were not controlled bureaucratically. Each, instead, was a separate enterprise of small or relatively small scale. Most had managers who were also partners. Coordination was possible because the senior partners, with an interest in each of the enterprises, exerted influence across a range of activities.

The partnerships in Cicero were not a disguise for an essentially hierarchical structure. Many of the partners were themselves businessmen who carried on other business activities, legal and illegal, independently of the senior partners. Penovich and Pope, for instance, in addition to their partnership in the Smoke Shop, were illegal bookmakers at several Chicago dog or horse tracks and pursued other gambling interests around the city. Lipschultz, as already mentioned, was not only a partner in beer distribution with the senior partners but also a truck dealer in the Chicago suburbs. LaCava, in addition to his share in the various gambling houses of Cicero, conducted a real estate business with Cicero Mayor Joe Klenha and two other local politicians. As realtors, they owned picnic grounds and cabarets. Finally, O'Hare not only joined with Patton and the senior partners in the Hawthorne Kennel Club, but also promoted dog tracks in St. Louis, Baltimore, Pennsylvania, and Florida.[13]

Cicero was unusual in terms of the degree of coordination exercised by the

---

12. For a description of Burnham under Mayor Patton, see Mezzrow and Wolfe (1946:Ch. 5). The story of the Hawthorne Kennel Club is based on "Memorandum of Interview with Mae Baker, November 24, 1930," unnumbered envelope; memorandum of Frank J. Wilson, June 22, 1930; and correspondence in Env. No. 68 and two unnumbered envelopes, in IRS file on Capone; also typewritten report (1930) in Chicago Law and Order League papers, Chicago Historical Society. For a somewhat different version, see Kobler (1971:236–238, 331–332). O'Hare was killed, gangland style, in November 1939.

13. Since Patton was a partner with O'Hare in the Florida track, it is probable that some of the senior partners were also involved.

222   HALLER

senior partners. Nevertheless, the coordination was exerted through a series of deals with relatively independent businessmen to operate separate, small-scale enterprises.

PARTNERSHIPS: A DISCUSSION

The structure of criminal partnerships differs from that often imputed to those involved in such activities—especially if the activities are thought of as "organized crime." Yet the structure makes sense theoretically. The "organized crime" model stresses hierarchy and centralized control, but a partnership model posits that each enterprise is a separate enterprise that pools resources and provides local management. Such decentralization, of course, renders a business less vulnerable to law enforcement. By spreading the risks among separate partnerships, entrepreneurs minimize losses from bankruptcy or police raids of any single enterprise. But decentralization also makes sense for another important reason: Criminal entrepreneurs generally have had neither the skills nor the personalities for the detailed, bureaucratic oversight of large organizations. They are, instead, hustlers and dealers, for whom partnership arrangements are ideally suited. They enjoy the give and take of personal negotiations, risk-taking, and moving from deal to deal. Adler (1985:148), in her study of drug dealers, captured this well: "In contrast to the bureaucratization of most conventional forms of work, drug dealing and smuggling were flexible, creative, exciting, and personal enterprises."

An emphasis on decentralization through partnerships is not, however, an argument that all participants are equal. An analysis of partnerships permits, instead, clearer understanding of the mechanisms by which some persons exert more influence than others. Those with political influence, for instance, will be attractive partners because they can supply a critical need. Indeed, they can often insist on being given a share of the profits. Similarly, since enterprises often require capital, wealthy entrepreneurs can invest in a range of enterprises and thereby extend their influence. Partnerships, then, constitute a structure within which some entrepreneurs exercise more influence than others because they have political or economic resources to participate in a number of partnerships simultaneously.

The study of partnerships, therefore, should be given greater attention within criminology. How, for instance, do partners enforce partnership arrangements? One factor is that reliability as a partner (or, at least, the appearance of reliability) is important for career success. Smart entrepreneurs fulfill their obligations in order to be offered future opportunities. Johnny Patton, by being a reliable partner with the Capone/Guzik group in the Hawthorne Kennel Club and other enterprises, established his credentials. In the 1930s and into the 1940s, he was an important figure in several Florida racing ventures. His successful early cooperation was the key to more lucrative opportunities in subsequent years.

ILLEGAL ENTERPRISE 223

Violence or the threat of violence, of course, can also shape partnership behavior. But the importance of violence can easily be exaggerated. Violence is destabilizing and not an effective method for partnership enforcement. A person with a reputation for violence is less likely to be accepted as a partner by successful entrepreneurs. Who, after all, would wish to jeopardize his life or health if he could pursue a successful career without doing so? Furthermore, violence can be used to cheat a partner as easily as it can be used to ensure honesty. A person who is violent can, and often does, take money from an enterprise and dare the partners to do something about it. Although many criminal entrepreneurs, especially since the 1920s, have had reputations for violence, factors other than violence better explain the enforcement of partnership agreements.

INTERNAL ECONOMIC FACTORS

Numerous economic factors also shape the structure of illegal enterprise, some working to bring about forms of cooperation and others tending to reduce the scale of cooperation. This paper focuses on two quite different types of economic relationships that have been important in providing structure to illegal enterprises. One relationship is that between buyers and sellers in moving illegal goods from manufacture or import to the ultimate consumer. The other relationship is that which develops within gambling syndicates to handle the problem of economic risk that gamblers face when bettors have lucky streaks.

Enterprises that involve illegal goods often have at least three levels of operation. First, the goods must be manufactured or imported; then they may be processed and wholesaled; and finally, they are peddled to consumers. Both the distribution of bootleg liquor in the 1920s and the distribution of illegal drugs in more recent years have generally involved entrepreneurs who specialize at different levels; rarely has a single group been engaged at all three levels. Indeed, recent heroin or cocaine networks have often involved several levels of wholesalers between importation and the final sale, so that the price to the user may be 10 times the price at import (Adler, 1985; Lasswell and McKenna, n.d.:Ch. 3, 4; Moore, 1977; Reuter and Kleiman, 1986). The fact that entrepreneurs have generally operated at separate levels, then, has necessarily required continued business dealings among persons with different specializations.

In the 1920s bootleg liquor importers in the New York region sold their goods not only in the Northeast corridor but also to Midwestern cities. By the late 1920s, when the Coast Guard had considerably reduced smuggling into the Northeast, Florida and New Orleans became major centers of importation, selling to wholesalers in as far away as New York and Chicago. Similarly, wholesalers who serviced a metropolitan market required a broad range

224   HALLER

of products for sale to the speakeasies and other retail outlets. A group specializing in wholesale activities, such as the Capone/Guzik partnership in Chicago, purchased imported liquor from Detroit, New York, and Florida; obtained alcohol from Midwest distilleries; sometimes secured industrial alcohol from Philadelphia; and trucked beer from Racine, Wisconsin, or from blue-collar cities in downstate Illinois. The fact that liquor was a bulky product and that it often required fairly complicated manufacture or processing forced bootleggers, depending on their position in the network of distribution, to invest in ships, trucks, breweries, distilleries, and bottling companies. Nevertheless, although the range of regional and even international cooperation in bootlegging was impressive, the scale of individual firms was relatively small when compared with the legal liquor industry in the period before or after Prohibition. Crucially important were the sometimes temporary and sometimes regular deals among numerous firms, rather than the creation of large, bureaucratic organizations for trafficking in bootleg liquor.[14]

Among illegal services, the history of policy gambling syndicates in American cities, dating from at least the 1860s, and the history of numbers syndicates, dating from the 1920s, indicate that certain inherent economic factors lead to syndication. (A syndicate is here defined as a system of cooperation so that many retailers are backed by the same group of entrepreneurs.) The primary reason for the 120-year history of policy and numbers syndicates is the desire of small-time operators to limit economic risk.

Policy gambling, which has existed in American cities from at least the late eighteenth century, is a betting game using the numbers 1 to 78. Those operating the game draw 12 numbers, and the bettors normally choose 1 to 5 numbers that they hope will be among the 12 drawn. In the 1920s, numbers gambling replaced policy in most cities, in part because it was a simpler game. In numbers, bettors normally select a single three-digit number between 000 and 999. The odds are 1 in 1,000 of winning, but the payoff has traditionally ranged from 500:1 to 650:1. Both policy and numbers have the same crucial characteristic: because the customers select the numbers, there is the risk that, on any given day, a heavily played number may win and the entrepreneur will be unable to cover the losses. For someone selling policy or numbers as an adjunct to operating a barbershop, saloon, or newspaper kiosk, failure to pay will not only lose bettors but legitimate customers as well. What the retailer needs, then, is for someone to assume the risks (Asbury, 1938:Ch. 6; Carlson, 1940:Pt. II; Haller, 1976a:104–105, 117–121).

---

14. The discussion of the economics of bootlegging is based on a number of sources: Coast Guard Intelligence files, National Archives, Washington, D.C.; clippings and investigative reports in files of Chicago Crime Commission, Chicago. See also Haller (1976a, 1985b); Mormino (1986); Nelli (1976:Ch. 6); and Vyhnanek (1979:Ch. 3).

ILLEGAL ENTERPRISE   225

As a result, policy and numbers have typically been coordinated by syndicates in which there is a division of function. Retailers cultivate customers in the neighborhoods and take the bets. They keep a set percentage of the money bet with them (typically 15 to 20%) and pass on the rest of the money, along with the betting slips, to syndicate backers. The important economic function of the syndicate is to assume the risk by paying the winners. Syndicate backers often furnish other services: They arrange for the daily collection of money and slips, provide notification of the winning numbers, and, when possible, negotiate political and police protection (Haller, 1976a; Lasswell and McKenna, n.d.:Ch. 3, 4; Reuter, 1983:Ch. 3).[15]

Both retailers and backers benefit from syndication. Retailers enjoy a steady income, based on the amount bet each day by their customers, without assuming the risk of paying winning bettors. Syndicate backers, in turn, receive money from a large number of retailers. Because retailers keep a percentage of the money and because there are the expenses of collecting from retailers, making payments to winners, administering a headquarters, and providing protection, backers may have a small profit margin. Their hope is that the syndicate can clear a small percentage from a large gross income and thus earn a profit commensurate with the investment in the enterprise. Syndication of policy or numbers gambling has meant that dozens or even hundreds of retailers may have the same backers, offer similar odds, and pay off on the same winning numbers. Syndication obviously involves a significant degree of coordination. The hierarchical or bureaucratic nature of that coordination should not be exaggerated, however. To a considerable extent, retailers have remained independent sellers working on a commission. If they operate a barbershop or bar, the numbers or policy selling is a service provided to customers within the context of a legitimate business. The daily contact of retailers with customers is as important to the syndicate backers as the syndicate backers' assumption of risk is to the sellers. In Chicago in the 1930s, the major retailers (or "policy stations," as they were called) advertised that they sold policy slips for all of the major policy wheels. Like independent insurance agents who represent several companies, the policy stations were commission agents for a number of policy syndicates (Caldwell, 1940). In New York in the early 1930s, when a group of partners including Arthur ("Dutch") Schultz muscled in on many of the Harlem numbers syndicates and then reduced the retailers' commission, retailers ceased writing numbers until the previous commission was restored (Block, 1983:Ch. 6). An important recent study of numbers in New York City found that retailers (collectors) sometimes retained small bets (keeping the full profits and paying the losses), that some collectors made payoffs on winning numbers at a rate

---

15. For analyses of similar problems of risk among bookmakers, see Reuter (1983:Ch. 2) and Scott (1968:Ch. 7).

226   HALLER

lower or higher than that of the syndicate, and that individual collectors, on occasion, moved their business from one syndicate to another (Reuter, 1983:Ch. 3). Thus, although syndicate backers typically enjoy greater economic and political resources than retailers, retailers nevertheless may act as relatively independent operators in their dealings with both customers and backers.

Because so much of the research dealing with illegal enterprise uses an "organized crime" model, too little attention has been given to the impact of economics in determining the structure and methods of cooperation within illegal enterprise. Yet, as Reuter (1983) has shown, the internal economics of numbers gambling, sports bookmaking, and loan-sharking are similar whether or not the entrepreneurs are members of an Italian–American crime family. Even in New York, with its five families, the families have little measurable impact in shaping the structure of an enterprise or in limiting competition among enterprises. Furthermore, an understanding of the economics of illegal enterprise has important implications for understanding the intended and unintended consequences of various law enforcement strategies (see, e.g., Ekland–Olson et al., 1984; Kleiman, 1985). Because the economic decisions of criminal entrepreneurs occur within an environment formed by diverse law enforcement policies, an analysis of the interaction between the legal environment and entrepreneurial decisions provides the most promising strategy for understanding the economic relationships within illegal enterprise.

DISCUSSION AND CONCLUSION

This analysis has implications for understanding the relationship of illegal enterprise to the Cosa Nostra outfits formed by Italian–American criminals and emerging in some American cities during the past 40 to 60 years. If the underworld of illegal enterprise consists typically of entrepreneurs involved in numerous short-term and long-term legal and illegal money-making activities, then one way to understand the functions and durability of Cosa Nostra groups is to examine how they serve their members' business interests.[16] Such an analysis would recognize the separation between the Cosa Nostra family, on the one hand, and the members' independent business activities, on

---

16. Of course, Italian–American crime families have served a number of functions, in addition to aiding the members' business interests. They are also like benevolent societies, such as the Elks or Masonic lodges, in having (more or less) secret memberships and rituals. And, since membership is by invitation only, members enjoy the prestige on the street from having been selected to join the elite of their profession. Thus, the place of the crime family in the lives of many members goes well beyond a consideration of rational business interest.

ILLEGAL ENTERPRISE 227

the other.[17] Like the Chamber of Commerce or Rotary Club for legal busi-nessmen, Cosa Nostra group would be seen, not as an organization that oper-ates illegal (or legal) businesses, but as an association that businessmen join partly to further their business careers. This notion was captured in a conver-sation in 1962 between Angelo Bruno, then leader of the Philadelphia outfit, and Sam DeCavalcante, soon-to-be head of a northern New Jersey mob. Bruno complained: "Look, Sam, I got people, they want to go partners with me. I don't want to go partners with them. When a man is hard to get along with, Sam, you should not go partners with him."[18] The statement recog-nized that he and other individuals within his outfit were independent busi-nessmen whose business relations with each other were mediated chiefly through independent partnerships.

As with legal businessmen in a Rotary club, a major reason to join a Costa Nostra group is to cultivate business contacts. Those who are beginners hope that more experienced entrepreneurs will throw opportunities their way and perhaps offer attractive partnership opportunities. More successful business-men will wish to wheel and deal among their equals, make selective invest-ments in the enterprises of younger men, and have access to information that will aid their business decision making. Members may also be aided by other members who can provide specific services. Bookmakers, who cannot borrow from legitimate lenders when they suffer loses, can gain access to a loan shark. Or, at a more general level, members who encounter problems with law enforcement anticipate that politically influential members will come to their assistance.

Another function of Cosa Nostra outfits is to provide norms of behavior and a system for resolving business disputes. Those who pursue careers in illegal activities have a need for understood rules for interacting with others in the same culture (Anderson, 1979:44–47; Best and Luckenbill, 1982:Ch. 10) but often lack groups that can define the rules. Beyond this, as many scholars have noted, those in illegal operations generally cannot turn to the legal system to settle disputes that arise out of violations of norms in their business dealings. In earlier years, politicians and police, in order to avoid violence and the attendant scandal, often mediated disputes within the under-world, but their ability to resolve disputes has been weakened in recent years.

---

17. This distinction between independent businesses and the Cosa Nostra outfit is the same as the distinction that Anderson (1979:2) makes between "the firm" and the "organ-ized crime group." I believe it also parallels the distinction made by Ianni (1988:89) between "two different systems of organization. One is an informal system in which people have prestige. The other is business."

18. Conversation of Bruno and DeCavalcante, February 11, 1962, in "Transcripts of Organized Crime Phone Taps," Papers of Citizens Crime Commission of Philadelphia, in Urban Archives, Temple University Library, Vol. 13:14.

228   HALLER

Under these circumstances, dispute settlement can be a significant activity by
Cosa Nostra leaders (Abadinsky, 1983:Ch. 11; Reuter, 1983:Ch. 7).

Although the perspective outlined here offers insight into the relationship
of Italian–American outfits to the illegal enterprises of the city, the chief purpose is to explore illegal enterprise as a criminal activity in its own right. In
this respect, a number of generalizations can be made.

First, of course, although illegal enterprises may sometimes develop stability through corruption of officials or through skillful and clandestine management, most such activities are relatively small scale and short term. Even
activities involving large sums of money and substantial profits are often carried out by relatively small and informally structured groups. A major drug
deal, for instance, may involve a few persons who pool resources to purchase
drugs from an importer and then sell at a considerable markup to one or
more buyers. Although the individuals may remain active in drug trafficking,
the particular group may never deal with each other again. And, if groups do
develop regular relations, buying or selling on credit, they will generally operate in an informal and unstructured manner. (See, e.g., Adler, 1985:Ch. 4;
Reuter, 1988; Reuter and Haaga, 1989:Ch. 3; for an earlier period, see Block,
1979, and Vyhnanek, 1981.)

Careers in illegal enterprise vary considerably. Some operators may specialize and stick to a single illegal activity. A few bookmakers, with a love of
sports and sports gambling, will attempt to make a career in bookmaking.
Even when a bookmaker goes bankrupt, his next step may be to work for
another bookmaker (Pledge, 1956; Reuter, 1983:Ch. 2). Other entrepreneurs,
though, may spend their time looking for varied opportunities to turn a profit.
Street-level entrepreneurs—the blue-collar workers of illegal enterprise—seek
ventures that require street smarts and muscle: selling a van of stolen televisions, bringing in a truckload of untaxed cigarettes from the Carolinas, or
helping to collect a delinquent loan for a loan shark (Pileggi, 1985). At a
middle level, Joseph Valachi, for example, after his apprenticeship period, ran
a numbers bank, dabbled in loan-sharking, and eventually sold counterfeit
ration stamps during World War II (Maas, 1968). Top entrepreneurs like
Meyer Lansky had sufficient resources of money and entrepreneurial skills
that they operated in regional and even international markets. Such persons
might have interests in casinos, race tracks, and hotels in Miami, Havana,
and Las Vegas (Haller, 1985a; Messick, 1967, 1971).

For many illegal entrepreneurs, the distinction between legal and illegal
business activities is blurred. Their own careers move from one to the other,
and their ventures often bridge the two worlds. Furthermore, illegal entrepreneurs often deal with "legitimate" businessmen. They know that many
retailers will buy stolen goods, that some bankers will make loans with stolen

ILLEGAL ENTERPRISE 229

securities as collateral (Teresa, 1973), that businesses ranging from the garment industry to antique dealers borrow regularly from loan sharks (Goldstock and Coenen, 1980:157–159; Haller and Alviti, 1977; Seidle, 1968:Ch. 2, 3), and that various legitimate businessmen will make investments in shady deals or help launder the funds from illegal enterprises (President's Commission on Organized Crime, 1984; Karchmer, 1985).[19] Illegal entrepreneurs may also have ongoing political contacts, ranging from a prostitute's bribery of a policeman on the beat to the linkage of international drug traffickers with the Central Intelligence Agency and the foreign policy establishment (Cockburn, 1987; Kwitney, 1987; Sharkey, 1988). Criminal entrepreneurs act within a world of money-making, deals, and favors; all the "wise guys" have rackets, and they see little difference between their rackets and the rackets of those who look down on them (Haller, 1971–72).

Finally, as this paper has argued, the cooperation that sometimes emerges within illegal enterprise is seldom based on hierarchy or bureaucratic specialization. The urban underworld of small firms, hustling, and deal-making has a structure that reflects the necessity to avoid prosecution and to find a niche within the interstices of a larger and more bureaucratic society. Especially in the late nineteenth and early twentieth centuries, local ward leaders and local police often intervened to bring a certain amount of order to the illegal activities of a neighborhood or a ward. Seldom did that order extend even to an entire city. Furthermore, particularly since World War II, the ability of police and politicians to coordinate at the local level has weakened as a result of changes in both police and politics. Another source of coordination has derived from those entrepreneurs with the resources to participate in multiple and overlapping partnerships. In the nineteenth century, partnerships provided a structure for coordination primarily at the local level. But the experience of dealing bootleg liquor within an international market in the 1920s and the improvements in communication and transportation of the twentieth century have increasingly meant that some entrepreneurs used partnerships to exercise influence within regional and even international operations. Finally, economic factors within some illegal activities—whether the networks that transferred alcohol from foreign countries to the streets of American cities or the syndicates that assumed the risks in policy and numbers gambling—have resulted in a variety of cooperative relationships. The internal economic characteristics of such activities have led to cooperation at the same time that their illegality has worked against formal or bureaucratic solutions to the need for cooperation.

---

19. The same merging of illegal and legal activities can occur in fencing; see Klockars (1974) and Steffensmeier (1986). These two studies of fences provide models for the types of studies that should be done for illegal enterprises.

230 HALLER

REFERENCES

Abadinsky, Howard
1983 The Criminal Elite: Professional and Organized Crime. Westport, Conn.: Greenwood Press.

Adler, Patricia A.
1985 Wheeling and Dealing: An Ethnography of an Upper-Level Drug Dealing and Smuggling Community. New York: Columbia University Press.

Albini, Joseph L.
1971 The American Mafia: Genesis of a Legend. New York: Appleton–Century Crofts.

Anderson, Annelise
1979 The Business of Organized Crime: A Cosa Nostra Family. Stanford, Calif.: Hoover Institution Press.

Asbury, Herbert
1938 Sucker's Progress: An Informal History of Gambling in America from the Colonies to Canfield. New York: Dodd, Mead.

Bellis, David J.
1985 Political corruption in small, machine-run cities. In Herbert E. Alexander and Gerald E. Caiden (eds.), the Politics and Economics of Organized Crime. Lexington, Mass.: Lexington Books.

Best, Joel
1987 Business is business: Regulating brothel prostitution through arrests, St. Paul 1865–83. Research in Social Policy 1:1–20.

Best, Joel and David S. Luckenbill
1982 Organizing Deviance. Englewood Cliffs, N.J.: Prentice–Hall.

Block, Alan A.
1979 The snowman cometh: Coke in progressive New York. Criminology 17:75–99.
1983 East Side—West Side: Organising Crime in New York, 1930–1950. New Brunswick, N.J.: Transaction.

Blumberg, Leonard U., Thomas E. Shipley, and Stephen F. Barsky
1978 Liquor and Poverty: Skid Row as a Human Condition. New Brunswick, N.J.: Rutgers Center for Alcohol Studies.

Burnham, John
1971a Medical inspection of prostitutes in America in the nineteenth century: The St. Louis experiment and its sequel. Bulletin of the History of Medicine 45:203–218.
1971b The social evil ordinance—A social experiment in nineteenth century St. Louis. The Bulletin of the Missouri Historical Society 27:203–217.

Caldwell, Lewis A.H.
1940 The policy game—Chicago. Master's thesis, Northwestern University, Evanston, Ill.

Carlisle, Jack
1976 Gambling in Detroit: An informal history. In Commission on the Review of National Policy Toward Gambling, Gambling in America. Washington, D.C.: Government Printing Office. Appendix I.

ILLEGAL ENTERPRISE 231

Carlson, Gustav G.
  1940   Number gambling: A study of a culture complex. Ph.D. dissertation,
          University of Michigan, Ann Arbor.

Chambliss, William J.
  1978   On the Take: From Paltry Crooks to Presidents. Bloomington: Indiana
          University Press.

Cockburn, Leslie
  1987   Out of Control. New York: Atlantic Monthly Press.

Commission to Investigate Allegations of Police Corruption and the City's Anti-
Corruption Procedures
  1972   Commission Report. New York: George Braziller.

Conrad, Harold
  1982   Dear Muffo: 35 Years in the Fast Lane. New York: Stein and Day.

Cressey, Donald R.
  1969   Theft of the Nation: The Structure and Operations of Organized Crime in
          America. New York: Harper & Row.

Eisenberg, Dennis, Dan Uri and Eli Landau
  1979   Meyer Lansky, Mogul of the Mob. New York: Paddington Press.

Ekland–Olson, Sheldon, John Lieb and Louis Zurcher
  1984   The paradoxical impact of criminal sanctions: Some microstructural
          findings. Law & Society Review 18:160–178.

Flexner, Abraham
  1969   Prostitution in Europe. Montclair, N.J.: Patterson Smith.

Fogelson, Robert M.
  1977   Big-City Police. Cambridge: Harvard University Press.

Fox, Stephen
  1989   Blood and Power: Organized Crime in Twentieth-Century America. New
          York: William Morrow.

Gardiner, John A.
  1970   The Politics of Corruption: Organized Crime in an American City. Beverly
          Hills, Calif.: Russell Sage Foundation.

Goldstock, Ronald and Dan T. Coenen
  1980   Controlling the contemporary loanshark: The law of illicit lending and the
          problem of witness fear. Cornell Law Review 65:127–185.

Haller, Mark H.
  1971–72 Organized crime in urban society: Chicago in the twentieth century.
          Journal of Social History 5:210–234.
  1976a   Bootleggers and American gambling, 1920–1950. In Commission on the
          Review of National Policy Toward Gambling, Gambling in America.
          Washington, D.C.: Government Printing Office. Appendix I.
  1976b   Historical roots of police behavior: Chicago, 1890–1925. Law & Society
          Review 10:303–324.
  1985a   Bootleggers as businessmen: From city slums to city builders. In David E.
          Kyvig (ed.), Law, Alcohol, and Order: Perspectives on National Prohibition.
          Westport, Conn.: Greenwood Press.

232 HALLER

1985b   Philadelphia bootlegging and the report of the Special August Grand Jury. Pennsylvania Magazine of History and Biography 104:215–233.

1988   Policy gambling, entertainment, and the emergence of black politics: Chicago, 1900 to 1940. Unpublished paper.

Haller, Mark H. and John V. Alviti
1977   Loansharking in American cities: Historical analysis of a marginal enterprise. American Journal of Legal History 21:125–156.

Ianni, Francis A.J.
1972   A Family Business: Kinship and Social Control in Organized Crime. New York: Russell Sage Foundation.

1974   Black Mafia: Ethnic Succession in Organized Crime. New York: Simon & Schuster.

1988   Ethnic factors in drug networks. In Pennsylvania Crime Commission, Organized Crime Narcotics Enforcement Seminar. Conshohocken: Pennsylvania Crime Commission.

Johnson, David R.
1981   American Law Enforcement: A History. St. Louis: Forum Press.

Karchmer, Clifford L.
1985   Money laundering and the organized underworld. In Herbert E. Alexander and Gerald E. Caiden (eds.), The Politics and Economics of Organized Crime. Lexington, Mass.: Lexington Books.

Kleiman, Mark
1985   Drug enforcement and organized crime. In Herbert E. Alexander and Gerald E. Caiden (eds.), The Politics and Economics of Organized Crime. Lexington, Mass.: Lexington Books.

Klockars, Carl B.
1974   The Professional Fence. New York: Free Press.

Kobler, John
1971   Capone: The Life and World of Al Capone. New York: G.P. Putnam's Sons.

Kwitney, Jonathan
1987   The Crimes of Patriots: A True Tale of Dope, Dirty Money, and the CIA. New York: W.W. Norton.

Landesco, John
1968   Organized Crime in Chicago. Chicago: University of Chicago Press.

Lasswell, Harold D. and Jeremiah B. McKenna
n.d.   The Impact of Organized Crime on an Inner City Community. New York: Policy Sciences Center.

Light, Ivan
1974   From vice district to tourist attraction: The moral career of American Chinatowns, 1880–1940. Pacific Historical Review 43:367–394.

1977   The ethnic vice industry, 1880–1944. American Sociological Review 42:464–479.

Maas, Peter
1968   The Valachi Papers. New York: G.P. Putnam's Sons.

Mackey, Thomas C.
1987   Red Lights Out: A Legal History of Prostitution, Disorderly Houses, and Vice Districts, 1870–1917. New York: Garland.

McCormack, Robert
1988   Perspectives on police corruption. In Pennsylvania Crime Commission, Organized Crime Narcotics Enforcement Seminar. Conshohocken: Pennsylvania Crime Commission.

McPhaul, Jack
1970   Johnny Torrio: First of the Gang Lords. New Rochelle, N.Y.: Arlington House.

Merton, Robert K.
1957   Social Theory and Social Structure. New York: Free Press.

Messick, Hank
1967   The Silent Syndicate. New York: Macmillan.
1971   Lansky. New York: G.P. Putnam's Sons.

Mezzrow, Mezz and Bernard Wolfe
1946   Really the Blues. Garden City, N.Y.: Doubleday.

Mollenhoff, Clark R.
1972   Strike Force: Organized Crime and the Government. Englewood Cliffs, N.J.: Prentice-Hall.

Moore, Mark
1977   Buy and Bust. Lexington, Mass.: Lexington Books.

Mormino, Gary
1986   A still on the hill: Prohibition and cottage industry. Gateway Heritage 7:2–13.

Murray, George
1965   The Madhouse on Madison Street. Chicago: Follett.

Nelli, Humbert J.
1976   The Business of Crime: Italians and Syndicate Crime in the United States. New York: Oxford University Press.

Pennsylvania Crime Commission
1974   Report on Police Corruption and the Quality of Law Enforcement in Philadelphia. St. Davids: Pennsylvania Crime Commission.
1989   The Limits of the Criminal Sanction: The Case of John Nacrelli. Public Hearings Re: Chester, Pa. Conshohocken: Pennsylvania Crime Commission.

Pileggi, Nicholas
1985   Wise Guy: A Life in a Mafia Family. New York: Simon & Schuster.

Pledge, Joe
1956   Bombshell: From Boxer to Bookmaker. New York.

President's Commission on Organized Crime
1984   The Cash Connection: Organized Crime, Financial Institutions, Money Laundering. Interim report to the President and Attorney General. Washington, D.C.: Government Printing Office.

Reppetto, Thomas A.
1978   The Blue Parade. New York: Free Press.

234   HALLER

Reuter, Peter
    1983   Disorganized Crime: The Economics of the Visible Hand. Cambridge,
            Mass.: MIT Press.
    1984   Police regulation of illegal gambling: Frustrations of symbolic enforcement.
            Annals of the American Academy of Political and Social Sciences 474:36–47.
    1988   A profile of major drug traffickers. In Pennsylvania Crime Commission,
            Organized Crime Narcotics Enforcement Seminar. Conshohocken: Penn-
            sylvania Crime Commission.

Reuter, Peter and John Haaga
    1989   The Organization of High-Level Drug Markets: An Exploratory Study.
            Santa Monica, Calif.: Rand.

Reuter, Peter and Mark Kleiman
    1986   Risks and prices: An economic analysis of drug enforcement. In Michael
            Tonry and Norval Morris (eds.), Crime and Justice: An Annual Review of
            Research. Vol. 7. Chicago: University of Chicago Press.

Richardson, James F.
    1970   The New York Police: Colonial Times to 1901. New York: Oxford
            University Press.

Rosen, Ruth
    1982   The Lost Sisterhood: Prostitution in America, 1900–1918. Baltimore: Johns
            Hopkins University Press.

Rubin, Paul H.
    1973   The economic theory of the criminal firm. In Simon Rottenberg (ed.), The
            Economics of Crime and Punishment. Washington, D.C.: American
            Enterprise Institute.

Rubinstein, Jonathan and Peter Reuter
    1982   Illegal Gambling in New York: A Case Study in the Operation, Structure,
            and Regulation of an Illegal Market. Washington, D.C.: Government
            Printing Office.

Russell, Daniel
    1931   The road house: A study of commercialized amusements in the environs of
            Chicago. Master's thesis, University of Chicago.

Schelling, Thomas C.
    1967   Economic analysis of organized crime. In President's Commission on Law
            Enforcement and Administration of Justice, Task Force Report: Organized
            Crime. Washington, D.C.: Government Printing Office.

Scott, Marvin B.
    1968   The Racing Game. Chicago: Aldine.

Seidl, John Michael
    1968   "Upon the hip"—A study of the criminal loan-shark industry. Ph.D.
            dissertation, Harvard University, Cambridge, Mass.

Sharkey, Jacqueline
    1988   The Contra-drug trade off. Common Cause Magazine 14:23–33.

Sherman, Lawrence W.
    1978   Scandal and Reform: Controlling Police Corruption. Berkeley: University
            of California Press.

ILLEGAL ENTERPRISE 235

Shumsky, Neil Larry
1980   Vice responds to reform: San Francisco, 1910–1914. Journal of Urban
History 7:31–47.

Smith, Dwight C., Jr.
1971   Some things that may be more important to understand about organized
crime than Cosa Nostra. University of Florida Law Review 24:1–30.
1975   The Mafia Mystique. New York: Basic Books.

Steffensmeier, Darrell J.
1986   The Fence: In the Shadow of Two Worlds. Totowa, N.J.: Rowman &
Littlefield.

Tarr, Joel A.
1967   The urban politician as entrepreneur. Mid-America 49:55–67.

Teresa, Vincent with Thomas C. Renner
1973   My Life in the Mafia. Garden City, N.Y.: Doubleday.

Vice Commission of Chicago
1911   The Social Evil in Chicago. Chicago: City of Chicago.

Vyhnanek, Louis A.
1979   The seamier side of life: Criminal activity in New Orleans during the 1920s.
Ph.D. dissertation, University of South Florida, Tampa.
1981   "Muggles," "inchy," and "mud": Illegal drugs in New Orleans during the
1920s. Louisiana History 22:253–279.

Walker, Samuel
1980   Popular Justice: A History of American Criminal Justice. New York:
Oxford University Press.

Wendt, Lloyd and Herman Kogan
1943   Lords of the Levee: The Story of Bathhouse John and Hinky Dink.
Indianapolis: Bobbs–Merrill.

Whyte, William Foote
1955   Streetcorner Society. Chicago: University of Chicago Press.

Wooldridge, Clifton R.
1901   Hands Up! In the World of Crime, Or 12 Years a Detective. Chicago:
Charles C. Thompson.

Woolston, Howard B.
1969   Prostitution in the United States. Montclair, N.J.: Patterson Smith.

Mark H. Haller is a Professor of History and Criminal Justice at Temple University. His research focuses on the history of crime in American cities since the Civil War. He has published numerous articles on the development of police, gambling, bootlegging, loan-sharking, and vice activities.

[13]

STATE-ORGANIZED CRIME—The American Society of Criminology, 1988 Presidential Address*

WILLIAM J. CHAMBLISS

There is a form of crime that has heretofore escaped criminological inquiry, yet its persistence and omnipresence raise theoretical and methodological issues crucial to the development of criminology as a science. I am referring to what I call "state-organized crime."

THE PROBLEM

Twenty-five years ago I began researching the relationship among organized crime, politics, and law enforcement in Seattle, Washington (Chambliss, 1968, 1971, 1975a, 1975b, 1977, 1980, 1988a). At the outset I concentrated on understanding the political, economic, and social relations of those immediately involved in organizing and financing vice in the local area. It became clear to me, however, that to understand the larger picture I had to extend my research to the United States and, eventually, to international connections between organized criminal activities and political and economic forces. This quest led me to research in Sweden (Block and Chambliss, 1981), Nigeria (Chambliss, 1975b), Thailand (Chambliss, 1977), and of course, the Americas.

My methods were adapted to meet the demands of the various situations I encountered. Interviews with people at all levels of criminal, political, and law enforcement agencies provided the primary data base, but they were supplemented always with data from official records, government reports, congressional hearings, newspaper accounts (when they could be checked for accuracy), archives, and special reports.

While continuing to research organized crime, I began a historical study of piracy and smuggling. In the process of analyzing and beginning to write on these subjects, I came to realize that I was, in essence, studying the same thing in different time periods: Some of the piracy of the sixteenth and seventeenth centuries was sociologically the same as some of the organized criminal relations of today—both are examples of state-organized crime.

At the root of the inquiry is the question of the relationship among criminality, social structure, and political economy (Petras, 1977; Schwendinger and Schwendinger, 1975; Tilly, 1985). In what follows, I (1) describe the characteristics of state-organized crime that bind acts that are unconnected by time and space but are connected sociologically, (2) suggest a theoretical

---

* Portions of this paper are based on William J. Chambliss, *Exploring Criminology* (New York: Macmillan, 1988).

184   CHAMBLISS

framework for understanding those relationships, and (3) give specific examples of state-organized crime.

STATE-ORGANIZED CRIME DEFINED

The most important type of criminality organized by the state consists of acts defined by law as criminal and committed by state officials in the pursuit of their job as representatives of the state. Examples include a state's complicity in piracy, smuggling, assasinations, criminal conspiracies, acting as an accessory before or after the fact, and violating laws that limit their activities. In the latter category would be included the use of illegal methods of spying on citizens, diverting funds in ways prohibited by law (e.g., illegal campaign contributions, selling arms to countries prohibited by law, and supporting terrorist activities).

State-organized crime does not include criminal acts that benefit only individual officeholders, such as the acceptance of bribes or the illegal use of violence by the police against individuals, unless such acts violate existing criminal law and are official policy. For example, the current policies of torture and random violence by the police in South Africa are incorporated under the category of state-organized crime because, apparently, those practices are both state policy and in violation of existing South African law. On the other hand, the excessive use of violence by the police in urban ghettoes is not state-organized crime for it lacks the necessary institutionalized policy of the state.

PIRACY

In the history of criminality, the state-supported piracy that occurred between the sixteenth and nineteenth centuries is an outstanding example of state-organized crime (Andrews, 1959, 1971).

When Christopher Columbus came to the Americas in search of wealth and spices in 1492, he sailed under the flag of Spain although he himself was from Genoa. Vasco da Gama followed Columbus 6 years later, sailing under the Portuguese flag. Between Spain and Portugal, a vast new world was conquered and quickly colonized. The wealth of silver and gold was beyond their wildest dreams. A large, poorly armed native American population made the creation of a slave labor force for mining and transporting the precious metals an easy task for the better armed Spanish and Portuguese settlers willing to sacrifice human life for wealth. Buttressed by the unflagging belief that they were not only enriching their motherland and themselves but also converting the heathens to Christianity, Spanish and Portuguese colonists seized the opportunity to denude the newly found lands of their wealth and their people (Lane–Poole, 1890). Portugal, as a result of Vasco da Gama's voyages, also established trade routes with India that gave it a franchise on

STATE-ORGANIZED CRIME 185

spices and tea. Portuguese kings thus became the "royal grocers of Europe" (Howes, 1615; Collins, 1955).

In Europe during the sixteenth and seventeenth centuries, nation–states were embroiled in intense competition for control of territory and resources. Then, as now, military power was the basis for expansion and the means by which nation–states protected their borders. Military might, in turn, depended on labor and mineral resources, especially gold and silver. The wealthier nations could afford to invest in more powerful military weapons, especially larger and faster ships, and to hire mercenaries for the army and navy. Explorations cost money as well. When Spain and Portugal laid claim to the Americas, they also refused other nations the right to trade with their colonies (Mainwaring, 1616). Almost immediately, conflict developed between Spain and Portugal, but the pope intervened and drew a line dividing the New World into Spanish and Portuguese sectors, thereby ameliorating the conflict. But the British, French, and Dutch were not included in the pope's peace. They were forced to settle for less desirable lands or areas not yet claimed by the Spanish and Portuguese.

Although they lacked the vision to finance explorers such as Christopher Columbus and Vasco da Gama, France, England, and Holland nonetheless possessed powerful navies. They were also the home of some of the world's more adventurous pirates, who heretofore had limited their escapades to the European and African coasts.

With the advent of Spain and Portugal's discovery of vast new sources of wealth, other European nations were faced with a dilemma: They could sit idly by and watch the center of power tip inexorably toward the Iberian Peninsula, or they could seek ways to interfere with the growing wealth of their neighbors to the south. One alternative, of course, was to go to war. Another, less risky for the moment but promising some of the same results, was to enter into an alliance with pirates. France, England, and Holland chose the less risky course.

To transport the gold and silver from the Spanish Main (the Caribbean coast of South America) to Bilbao and from Brazil to Lisbon required masterful navigational feats. A ship laden with gold and silver could not travel fast and was easy prey for marauders (Exquemling, 1670). To complicate matters, ships were forced by the prevailing winds and currents to travel in a predictable direction. These conditions provided an open invitation for pirates to exploit the weaknesses of the transporting ships to their advantage. Poverty and a lack of alternatives drove many young men to sea in search of a better life. Some came to the New World as convicts or indentured slaves. The lure of the pirate's life was an alternative that for all its hardships was more appealing than the conditions of serfdom and indentured servitude.

The French government was the first to seize the opportunity offered by engaging in piracy (Ritchie, 1986). It saw in piracy a source of wealth and a

186   CHAMBLISS

way of neutralizing some of the power of Spain and Portugal. Although
piracy was an act second to none in seriousness in French law (summary
execution was the punishment), the French government nonetheless
instructed the governors of its islands to allow pirate ships safe portage in
exchange for a share of the stolen merchandise. Thus, the state became complicitous in the most horrific sprees of criminality in history.

The pirate culture condoned violence on a scale seldom seen. There was no
mercy for the victims of the pirates' attacks. Borgnefesse, a French pirate
who wrote his memoirs after retiring to a gentleman's life in rural France,
was an articulate chronicler of these traits. He wrote, for example, of how he
once saved a young girl "not yet into puberty" from being raped by two
"beastly filibusters" who were chasing her out of a house in a village that he
and his men had attacked (LeGolif, 1680). Borgnefesse wrote of being
embarrassed that on that occasion he felt "pity" for the young girl and violated one of the ironclad laws of the pirate's world: that women were prizes
for whoever found them in the course of a raid. The would-be rapists resisted
his effort to save the girl and "told me I was interfering in a matter which was
none of my business, that pillage was permitted in the forcing of the women
as well as the coffers."

It was commonplace among pirates to "take no prisoners" unless, of
course, they could be useful to the victors. Borgnefesse described how he cut
off the heads of everyone on board a Spanish "prize" because the enemy
angered him by injuring his arm during the battle. Another time he and his
men took all the people on a captured ship, tied them up in the mainsail,
threw them in the water, and then drank rum while listening to the screams
of the slowly drowning men. For all his criminal exploits, however,
Borgnefesse was well protected by French ships and French colonies.

England and Holland were quick to join the French. Sir Richard Hawkins
and his apprentice, Francis Drake, were issued "letters of marque" from the
Admiralty directing governors of British colonies and captains of British war-
ships to give safe passage and every possible assistance to Hawkins and Drake
as they were acting "under orders of the Crown" (British Museum, 1977).
Their "orders" were to engage in piracy against Spanish and Portuguese
ships. Thus, the state specifically instructed selected individuals to engage in
criminal acts. The law, it must be emphasized, did not change. Piracy
remained a crime punishable by death, but some pirates were given license to
murder, rape, plunder, destroy, and steal.

The state's complicity in piracy was more successful, one suspects, than
even the most avaricious monarchs expected. On one voyage (between 1572
and 1573), Drake returned to England with enough gold and silver to support
the government and all its expenses for a period of 7 years (Corbett, 1898a,
1898b). Most of this wealth came from Drake's attack on the town of Nom-
bre de Dios, which was a storage depot for Spanish gold and silver. In this

STATE-ORGANIZED CRIME 187

venture Drake joined forces with some French pirates and ambushed a treasure train.

Drake was knighted for his efforts, but the Spanish were not silent. They formally challenged Britain's policies, but the queen of England denied that Drake was operating with her blessing (after, of course, taking the gold and silver that he brought home) and Drake was tried as a criminal. He was publicly exiled, but privately he was sent to Ireland, where he reemerged several years later (in 1575) serving under the first Earl of Essex in Ireland.

Borgnefesse and Sir Francis Drake are only two of hundreds of pirates who plied their trade between 1400 and 1800 (Senior, 1976). Their crimes were supported by, and their proceeds shared with, whatever nation–state offered them protection and supplies. In theory, each nation–state only protected its own pirates, but in practice, they all protected any pirates willing to share their gains.

To rationalize the fundamental contradiction between the law and the interests of the state, European nations created a legal fiction. Issued either directly from the monarch or the Admiralty, the letters of marque gave pirates a sort of license, but with specific limitations on the kinds of acts that were permissible. One restriction was that the pirates were not to (a) attack ships of the country issuing the letter, (b) plunder villages or towns, or (c) open the captured cargo until they returned to port.

The reality of piracy was quite at odds with all of these limitations. Much of the success of piracy depended on attacking towns and villages, during which raping, plundering, and razing the town were accepted practices. Pirates sometimes kept one or more officers from captured ships along with their letters of marque and identifying flags in order to show them in case of attack by a ship from another country. This also enabled a pirate ship from France, say, to raise an English flag and attack a French ship. For the pirates loyalty to the nation came second to the search for gold.

At one time or another virtually every European nation, and the United States as well, between 1500 and 1800 was complicitous in piracy. In the United States, Charleston, South Carolina, several New England towns, and New York were safe harbors for pirates. In return for sharing in the prize, these towns provided safety from capture by foreign authorities and a safe place for pirates to celebrate their victories.

John Paul Jones became an American hero through his success as a pirate and was even given a commission in the navy (de la Croix, 1962; MacIntyre, 1975). Jean and Pierre Lafitte were the toast of New Orleans society while they enriched themselves by organizing and aiding pirates and smugglers at the mouth of the Mississippi River. Their status was considerably enhanced when the federal government enlisted their aid in the war against England and made Jean an officer of the U.S. Navy in return for helping to defeat the

188   CHAMBLISS

British Navy that was gathering its forces for an attack on New Orleans (Ver-rill, 1924) In time of war, nations enlisted pirates to serve in their navy. In time of peace, they shared in the profits.

During the period from 1600 to 1900, capitalism was becoming firmly established as the dominant economic system of the world. The essential determinant of a nation's ability to industrialize and to protect its borders was the accumulation of capital. Not only was another nation's wealth a threat to the autonomy of neighboring states, one nation's gain was invariably another's loss. Piracy helped to equalize the balance and reduce the tendency toward the monopolization of capital accumulation. The need for capital accumulation does not end with the emergence of capitalism; it continues so long as the economy and a nation's military and economic strength depend on it. When piracy ceased to be a viable method for accumulating capital, other forms of illegality were employed. In today's world, there is evidence that some small city–states in the Far East (especially in Indonesia) still pursue a policy of supporting pirates and sharing in their profits. But piracy no longer plays a major role in state–organized crime; today, the role is filled by smuggling.

SMUGGLING

Smuggling occurs when a government has successfully cornered the market on some commodity or when it seeks to keep a commodity of another nation from crossing its borders. In the annals of crime, everything from sheep to people, wool to wine, gold to drugs, and even ideas, have been prohibited for either export of import. Paradoxically, whatever is prohibited, it is at the expense of one group of people for the benefit of another. Thus, the laws that prohibit the import or export of a commodity inevitably face a built–in resistance. Some part of the population will always want to either possess or to distribute the prohibited goods. At times, the state finds itself in the position of having its own interests served by violating precisely the same laws passed to prohibit the export or import of the goods it has defined as illegal.

NARCOTICS AND THE VIETNAM WAR

Sometime around the eighth century, Turkish traders discovered a market for opium in Southeast Asia (Chambliss, 1977; McCoy, 1973). Portuguese traders several centuries later found a thriving business in opium trafficking conducted by small ships sailing between trading ports in the area. One of the prizes of Portuguese piracy was the opium that was taken from local traders and exchanged for tea, spices, and pottery. Several centuries later, when the French colonized Indochina, the traffic in opium was a thriving business. The French joined the drug traffickers and licensed opium dens throughout

STATE-ORGANIZED CRIME 189

Indochina. With the profits from those licenses, the French supported 50% of the cost of their colonial government (McCoy, 1973: 27).

When the Communists began threatening French rule in Indochina, the French government used the opium profits to finance the war. It also used cooperation with the hill tribes who controlled opium production as a means of ensuring the allegiance of the hill tribes in the war against the Communists (McCoy, 1973).

The French were defeated in Vietnam and withdrew, only to be replaced by the United States. The United States inherited the dependence on opium profits and the cooperation of the hill tribes, who in turn depended on being allowed to continue growing and shipping opium. The CIA went a step further than the French and provided the opium-growing feudal lords in the mountains of Vietnam, Laos, Cambodia, and Thailand with transportation for their opium via Air America, the CIA airline in Vietnam.

Air America regularly transported bundles of opium from airstrips in Laos, Cambodia, and Burma to Saigon and Hong Kong (Chambliss, 1977: 56). An American stationed at Long Cheng, the secret CIA military base in northern Laos during the war, observed:

> . . . so long as the Meo leadership could keep their wards in the boon-docks fighting and dying in the name of, for these unfortunates anyway, some nebulous cause . . . the Meo leadership [was paid off] in the form of a carte-blanch to exploit U.S.-supplied airplanes and communication gear to the end of greatly streamlining the opium operations . . . . (Chambliss, 1977: 56).

This report was confirmed by Laotian Army General Ouane Rattikone, who told me in an interview in 1974 that he was the principal overseer of the shipment of opium out of the Golden Triangle via Air America. U.S. law did not permit the CIA or any of its agents to engage in the smuggling of opium.

After France withdrew from Vietnam and left the protection of democracy to the United States, the French intelligence service that preceded the CIA in managing the opium smuggling in Asia continued to support part of its clandestine operations through drug trafficking (Kruger, 1980). Although those operations are shrouded in secrecy, the evidence is very strong that the French intelligence agencies helped to organize the movement of opium through the Middle East (especially Morocco) after their revenue from opium from Southeast Asia was cut off.

In 1969 Michael Hand, a former Green Beret and one of the CIA agents stationed at Long Cheng when Air America was shipping opium, moved to Australia, ostensibly as a private citizen. On arriving in Australia, Hand entered into a business partnership with an Australian national, Frank Nugan. In 1976 they established the Nugan Hand Bank in Sydney (Commonwealth of New South Wales, 1982a, 1982b). The Nugan Hand Bank

190   CHAMBLISS

began as a storefront operation with minimal capital investment, but almost immediately it boasted deposits of over $25 million. The rapid growth of the bank resulted from large deposits of secret funds made by narcotics and arms smugglers and large deposits from the CIA (Nihill, 1982).

In addition to the records from the bank that suggest the CIA was using the bank as a conduit for its funds, the bank's connection to the CIA and other U.S. intelligence agencies is evidenced by the people who formed the directors and principal officers of the bank, including the following:

- Admiral Earl F. Yates, president of the Nugan Hand Bank was, during the Vietnam War, chief of staff for strategic planning of U.S. forces in Asia and the Pacific.
- General Edwin F. Black, president of Nugan Hand's Hawaii branch, was commander of U.S. troops in Thailand during the Vietnam War and, after the war, assistant army chief of staff for the Pacific.
- General Erle Cocke, Jr., head of the Nugan Hand Washington, D.C., office.
- George Farris, worked in the Nugan Hand Hong Kong and Washington, D.C. offices. Farris was a military intelligence specialist who worked in a special forces training base in the Pacific.
- Bernie Houghton, Nugan Hand's representative in Saudi Arabia. Houghton was also a U.S. naval intelligence undercover agent.
- Thomas Clines, director of training in the CIA's clandestine service, was a London operative for Nugan Hand who helped in the takeover of a London-based bank and was stationed at Long Cheng with Michael Hand and Theodore S. Shackley during the Vietnam War.
- Dale Holmgreen, former flight service manager in Vietnam for Civil Air Transport, which became Air America. He was on the board of directors of Nugan Hand and ran the bank's Taiwan office.
- Walter McDonald, an economist and former deputy director of CIA for economic research, was a specialist in petroleum. He became a consultant to Nugan Hand and served as head of its Annapolis, Maryland, branch.
- General Roy Manor, who ran the Nugan Hand Philippine office, was a Vietnam veteran who helped coordinate the aborted attempt to rescue the Iranian hostages, chief of staff for the U.S. Pacific command, and the U.S. government's liaison officer to Philippine President Ferdinand Marcos.

On the board of directors of the parent company formed by Michael Hand that preceded the Nugan Hand Bank were Grant Walters, Robert Peterson, David M. Houton, and Spencer Smith, all of whom listed their address as c/o Air America, Army Post Office, San Francisco, California.

STATE-ORGANIZED CRIME 191

Also working through the Nugan Hand Bank was Edwin F. Wilson, a CIA agent involved in smuggling arms to the Middle East and later sentenced to prison by a U.S. court for smuggling illegal arms to Libya. Edwin Wilson's associate in Mideast arms shipments was Theodore Shackley, head of the Miami, Florida, CIA station.[1] In 1973, when William Colby was made director of Central Intelligence, Shackley replaced him as head of covert operations for the Far East; on his retirement from the CIA William Colby became Nugan Hand's lawyer.

In the late 1970s the bank experienced financial difficulties, which led to the death of Frank Nugan. He was found dead of a shotgun blast in his Mercedes Benz on a remote road outside Sydney. The official explanation was suicide, but some investigators speculated that he might have been murdered. In any event, Nugan's death created a major banking scandal and culminated in a government investigation. The investigation revealed that millions of dollars were unaccounted for in the bank's records and that the bank was serving as a money-laundering operation for narcotics smugglers and as a conduit through which the CIA was financing gun smuggling and other illegal operations throughout the world. These operations included illegally smuggling arms to South Africa and the Middle East. There was also evidence that the CIA used the Nugan Hand Bank to pay for political campaigns that slandered politicians, including Australia's Prime Minister Witham (Kwitny, 1977).

Michael Hand tried desperately to cover up the operations of the bank. Hundreds of documents were destroyed before investigators could get into the bank. Despite Hand's efforts, the scandal mushroomed and eventually Hand was forced to flee Australia. He managed this, while under indictment for a rash of felonies, with the aid of a CIA official who flew to Australia with a false passport and accompanied him out of the country. Hand's father, who lives in New York, denies knowing anything about his son's whereabouts.

Thus, the evidence uncovered by the government investigation in Australia linked high-level CIA officials to a bank in Sydney that was responsible for financing and laundering money for a significant part of the narcotics trafficking originating in Southeast Asia (Commonwealth of New South Wales, 1982b; Owen, 1983). It also linked the CIA to arms smuggling and illegal involvement in the democratic processes of a friendly nation. Other investigations reveal that the events in Australia were but part of a worldwide involvement in narcotics and arms smuggling by the CIA and French intelligence (Hougan, 1978; Kruger, 1980; Owen, 1983).

---

1. It was Shackley who, along with Rafael "Chi Chi" Quintero, a Cuban–American, forged the plot to assassinate Fidel Castro by using organized–crime figures Santo Traficante, Jr., John Roselli, and Sam Giancana.

192   CHAMBLISS

ARMS SMUGGLING

One of the most important forms of state-organized crime today is arms smuggling. To a significant extent, U.S. involvement in narcotics smuggling after the Vietnam War can be understood as a means of funding the purchase of military weapons for nations and insurgent groups that could not be funded legally through congressional allocations or for which U.S. law prohibited support (NARMIC, 1984).

In violation of U.S. law, members of the National Security Council (NSC), the Department of Defense, and the CIA carried out a plan to sell millions of dollars worth of arms to Iran and use profits from those sales to support the Contras in Nicaragua (Senate Hearings, 1986). The Boland amendment, effective in 1985, prohibited any U.S. official from directly or indirectly assisting the Contras. To circumvent the law, a group of intelligence and military officials established a "secret team" of U.S. operatives, including Lt. Colonel Oliver North, Theodore Shackley, Thomas Clines, and Maj. General Richard Secord, among others (testimony before U.S. Senate, 1986). Shackley and Clines, as noted, were CIA agents in Long Cheng; along with Michael Hand they ran the secret war in Laos, which was financed in part from profits from opium smuggling. Shackley and Clines had also been involved in the 1961 invasion of Cuba and were instrumental in hiring organized-crime figures in an attempt to assassinate Fidel Castro.

Senator Daniel Inouye of Hawaii claims that this "secret government within our government" waging war in Third World countries was part of the Reagan doctrine (the *Guardian*, July 29, 1987). Whether President Reagan or then Vice President Bush were aware of the operations is yet to be established. What cannot be doubted in the face of overwhelming evidence in testimony before the Senate and from court documents is that this group of officials of the state oversaw and coordinated the distribution and sale of weapons to Iran and to the Contras in Nicaragua. These acts were in direct violation of the Illegal Arms Export Control Act, which made the sale of arms to Iran unlawful, and the Boland amendment, which made it a criminal act to supply the Contras with arms or funds.

The weapons that were sold to Iran were obtained by the CIA through the Pentagon. Secretary of Defense Caspar Weinberger ordered the transfer of weapons from Army stocks to the CIA without the knowledge of Congress four times in 1986. The arms were then transferred to middlemen, such as Iranian arms dealer Yaacov Nimrodi, exiled Iranian arms dealer Manucher Ghorbanifar, and Saudi Arabian businessman Adman Khashoggi. Weapons were also flown directly to the Contras, and funds from the sale of weapons were diverted to support Contra warfare. There is also considerable evidence

STATE-ORGANIZED CRIME 193

that this "secret team," along with other military and CIA officials, cooperated with narcotics smuggling in Latin America in order to fund the Contras in Nicaragua.

In 1986, the Reagan administration admitted that Adolfo Chamorro's Contra group, which was supported by the CIA, was helping a Colombian drug trafficker transport drugs into the United States. Chamorro was arrested in April 1986 for his involvement (Potter and Bullington, 1987: 54). Testimony in several trials of major drug traffickers in the past 5 years has revealed innumerable instances in which drugs were flown from Central America into the United States with the cooperation of military and CIA personnel. These reports have also been confirmed by military personnel and private citizens who testified that they saw drugs being loaded on planes in Central America and unloaded at military bases in the United States. Pilots who flew planes with arms to the Contras report returning with planes carrying drugs.

At the same time that the United States was illegally supplying the Nicaraguan Contras with arms purchased, at least in part, with profits from the sale of illegal drugs, the administration launched a campaign against the Sandanistas for their alleged involvement in drug trafficking. Twice during his weekly radio shows in 1986, President Reagan accused the Sandanistas of smuggling drugs. Barry Seal, an informant and pilot for the Drug Enforcement Administration (DEA) was ordered by members of the CIA and DEA to photograph the Sandanistas loading a plane. During a televised speech in March 1986, Reagan showed the picture that Seal took and said that it showed Sandinista officials loading a plane with drugs for shipment to the United States. After the photo was displayed, Congress appropriated $100 million in aid for the Contras. Seal later admitted to reporters that the photograph he took was a plane being loaded with crates that did not contain drugs. He also told reporters that he was aware of the drug smuggling activities of the Contra network and a Colombian cocaine syndicate. For his candor, Seal was murdered in February 1987. Shortly after his murder, the DEA issued a "low key clarification" regarding the validity of the photograph, admitting that there was no evidence that the plane was being loaded with drugs.

Other testimony linking the CIA and U.S. military officials to complicity in drug trafficking includes the testimony of John Stockwell, a former high-ranking CIA official, who claims that drug smuggling and the CIA were essential components in the private campaign for the Contras. Corroboration for these assertions comes also from George Morales, one of the largest drug traffickers in South America, who testified that he was approached by the CIA in 1984 to fly weapons into Nicaragua. Morales claims that the CIA opened up an airstrip in Costa Rica and gave the pilots information on how to avoid radar traps. According to Morales, he flew 20 shipments of weapons

194   CHAMBLISS

into Costa Rica in 1984 and 1985. In return, the CIA helped him to smuggle thousands of kilos of cocaine into the United States. Morales alone channeled $250,000 quarterly to Contra leader Adolfo Chamorro from his trafficking activity. A pilot for Morales, Gary Betzner, substantiated Morales's claims and admitted flying 4,000 pounds of arms into Costa Rica and 500 kilos of cocaine to Lakeland, Florida, on his return trips. From 1985 to 1987, the CIA arranged 50 to 100 flights using U.S. airports that did not undergo inspection.

The destination of the flights by Morales and Betzner was a hidden airstrip on the ranch of John Hull. Hull, an admitted CIA agent, was a primary player in Oliver North's plan to aid the Contras. Hull's activities were closely monitored by Robert Owen, a key player in the Contra Supply network. Owen established the Institute for Democracy, Education, and Assistance, which raised money to buy arms for the Contras and which, in October 1985, was asked by Congress to distribute $50,000 in "humanitarian aid" to the Contras. Owen worked for Oliver North in coordinating illegal aid to the Contras and setting up the airstrip on the ranch of John Hull.

According to an article in the *Nation*, Oliver North's network of operatives and mercenaries had been linked to the largest drug cartel in South America since 1983. The DEA estimates that Colombian Jorge Ochoa Vasquez, the "kingpin" of the Medellin drug empire, is responsible for supplying 70% to 80% of the cocaine that enters the United States every year. Ochoa was taken into custody by Spanish police in October 1984 when a verbal order was sent by the U.S. Embassy in Madrid for his arrest. The embassy specified that Officer Cos–Gayon, who had undergone training with the DEA, should make the arrest. Other members of the Madrid Judicial Police were connected to the DEA and North's arms smuggling network. Ochoa's lawyers informed him that the United States would alter his extradition if he agreed to implicate the Sandanista government in drug trafficking. Ochoa refused and spent 20 months in jail before returning to Colombia. The Spanish courts ruled that the United States was trying to use Ochoa to discredit Nicaragua and released him. (The *Nation*, September 5, 1987.)

There are other links between the U.S. government and the Medellin cartel. Jose Blandon, General Noriega's former chief advisor, claims that DEA operations have protected the drug empire in the past and that the DEA paid Noriega $4.7 million for his silence. Blandon also testified in Senate committee hearings that Panama's bases were used as training camps for the Contras in exchange for "economic" support from the United States. Finally, Blandon contends that the CIA gave Panamanian leaders intelligence documents about U.S. senators and aides; the CIA denies these charges. (The *Christian Science Monitor*, February 11, 1988: 3.)

Other evidence of the interrelationship among drug trafficking, the CIA, the NSC, and aid to the Contras includes the following:

STATE-ORGANIZED CRIME 195

- In January 1983, two Contra leaders in Costa Rica persuaded the Justice Department to return over $36,000 in drug profits to drug dealers Julio Zavala and Carlos Cabezas for aid to the Contras (Potter and Bullington, 1987: 22).
- Michael Palmer, a drug dealer in Miami, testified that the State Department's Nicaraguan humanitarian assistance office contracted with his company, Vortex Sales and Leasing, to take humanitarian aid to the Contras. Palmer claims that he smuggled $40 million in marijuana to the United States between 1977 and 1985 (The *Guardian*, March 20, 1988: 3).
- During House and Senate hearings in 1986, it was revealed that a major DEA investigation of the Medellin drug cartel of Colombia, which was expected to culminate in the arrest of several leaders of the cartel, was compromised when someone in the White House leaked the story of the investigation to the *Washington Times* (a conservative newspaper in Washington, D.C.), which published the story on July 17, 1984. According to DEA Administrator John Lawn, the leak destroyed what was "probably one of the most significant operations in DEA history" (Sharkey, 1988: 24).
- When Honduran General Jose Buseo, who was described by the Justice Department as an "international terrorist," was indicted for conspiring to murder the president of Honduras in a plot financed by profits from cocaine smuggling, Oliver North and officials from the Department of Defense and the CIA pressured the Justice Department to be lenient with General Buseo. In a memo disclosed by the Iran-Contra committee, North stated that if Buseo was not protected "he will break his longstanding silence about the Nic[araguan] resistance and other sensitive operations" (Sharkey, 1988: 27).

On first blush, it seems odd that government agencies and officials would engage in such wholesale disregard of the law. As a first step in building an explanation for these and other forms of state-organized crime, let us try to understand why officials of the CIA, the NSC, and the Department of Defense would be willing to commit criminal acts in pursuit of other goals.

WHY?

Why would government officials from the NSC, the Defense Department, the State Department, and the CIA become involved in smuggling arms and narcotics, money laundering, assassinations, and other criminal activities? The answer lies in the structural contradictions that inhere in nation–states (Chambliss, 1980).

As Weber, Marx, and Gramsci pointed out, no state can survive without

196   CHAMBLISS

establishing legitimacy. The law is a fundamental cornerstone in creating legitimacy and an illusion (at least) of social order. It claims universal principles that demand some behaviors and prohibit others. The protection of property and personal security are obligations assumed by states everywhere both as a means of legitimizing the state's franchise on violence and as a means of protecting commercial interests (Chambliss and Seidman, 1982).

The threat posed by smuggling to both personal security and property interests makes laws prohibiting smuggling essential. Under some circumstances, however, such laws contradict other interests of the state. This contradiction prepares the ground for state-organized crime as a solution to the conflicts and dilemmas posed by the simultaneous existence of contradictory "legitimate" goals.

The military–intelligence establishment in the United States is resolutely committed to fighting the spread of "communism" throughout the world. This mission is not new but has prevailed since the 1800s. Congress and the presidency are not consistent in their support for the money and policies thought by the frontline warriors to be necessary to accomplish their lofty goals. As a result, programs under way are sometimes undermined by a lack of funding and even by laws that prohibit their continuation (such as the passage of laws prohibiting support for the Contras). Officials of government agencies adversely affected by political changes are thus placed squarely in a dilemma: If they comply with the legal limitations on their activities they sacrifice their mission. The dilemma is heightened by the fact that they can anticipate future policy changes that will reinstate their resources and their freedom. When that time comes, however, programs adversely affected will be difficult if not impossible to re-create.

A number of events that occurred between 1960 and 1980 left the military and the CIA with badly tarnished images. Those events and political changes underscored their vulnerability. The CIA lost considerable political clout with elected officials when its planned invasion of Cuba (the infamous Bay of Pigs invasion) was a complete disaster. Perhaps as never before in its history, the United States showed itself vulnerable to the resistance of a small nation. The CIA was blamed for this fiasco even though it was President Kennedy's decision to go ahead with the plans that he inherited from the previous administration. To add to the agency's problems, the complicity between it and ITT to invade Chile and overthrow the Allende government was yet another scar (see below), as was the involvement of the CIA in narcotics smuggling in Vietnam.

These and other political realities led to a serious breach between Presidents Kennedy, Johnson, Nixon, and Carter and the CIA. During President Nixon's tenure in the White House, one of the CIA's top men, James Angleton, referred to Nixon's national security advisor, Henry Kissinger (who became secretary of state) as "objectively, a Soviet Agent" (Hougan,

STATE-ORGANIZED CRIME 197

1984: 75). Another top agent of the CIA, James McCord (later implicated in the Watergate burglary) wrote a secret letter to his superior, General Paul Gaynor, in January 1973 in which he said:

> When the hundreds of dedicated fine men and women of the CIA no longer write intelligence summaries and reports with integrity, without fear of political recrimination—when their fine Director [Richard Helms] is being summarily discharged in order to make way for a politician who will write or rewrite intelligence the way the politicians want them written, instead of the way truth and best judgment dictates, our nation is in the deepest of trouble and freedom itself was never so imperiled. Nazi Germany rose and fell under exactly the same philosophy of governmental operation. (Hougan, 1984: 26–27)

McCord (1974: 60) spoke for many of the top military and intelligence officers in the United States when he wrote in his autobiography: "I believed that the whole future of the nation was at stake." These views show the depth of feeling toward the dangers of political "interference" with what is generally accepted in the military–intelligence establishment as their mission (Goulden, 1984).

When Jimmy Carter was elected president, he appointed Admiral Stansfield Turner as director of Central Intelligence. At the outset, Turner made it clear that he and the president did not share the agency's view that they were conducting their mission properly (Goulden, 1984; Turner, 1985). Turner insisted on centralizing power in the director's office and on overseeing clandestine and covert operations. He met with a great deal of resistance. Against considerable opposition from within the agency, he reduced the size of the covert operation section from 1,200 to 400 agents. Agency people still refer to this as the "Halloween massacre."

Old hands at the CIA do not think their work is dispensable. They believe zealously, protectively, and one is tempted to say, with religious fervor, that the work they are doing is essential for the salvation of humankind. With threats from both Republican and Democratic administrations, the agency sought alternative sources of revenue to carry out its mission. The alternative was already in place with the connections to the international narcotics traffic, arms smuggling, the existence of secret corporations incorporated in foreign countries (such as Panama), and the established links to banks for the laundering of money for covert operations.

STATE-ORGANIZED ASSASSINATIONS AND MURDER

Assassination plots and political murders are usually associated in people's minds with military dictatorships and European monarchies. The practice of assassination, however, is not limited to unique historical events but has

198   CHAMBLISS

become a tool of international politics that involves modern nation–states of many different types.

In the 1960s a French intelligence agency hired Christian David to assassinate the Moroccan leader Ben Barka (Hougan, 1978: 204–207). Christian David was one of those international "spooks" with connections to the DEA, the CIA, and international arms smugglers, such as Robert Vesco.

In 1953 the CIA organized and supervised a coup d'etat in Iran that overthrew the democratically elected government of Mohammed Mossadegh, who had become unpopular with the United States when he nationalized foreign–owned oil companies. The CIA's coup replaced Mossadegh with Reza Shah Pahlevi, who denationalized the oil companies and with CIA guidance established one of the most vicious secret intelligence organizations in the world: SAVAK. In the years to follow, the shah and CIA–trained agents of SAVAK murdered thousands of Iranian citizens. They arrested almost 1,500 people monthly, most of whom were subjected to inhuman torture and punishments without trial. Not only were SAVAK agents trained by the CIA, but there is evidence that they were instructed in techniques of torture (Hersh, 1979: 13).

In 1970 the CIA repeated the practice of overthrowing democratically elected governments that were not completely favorable to U.S. investments. When Salvador Allende was elected president of Chile, the CIA organized a coup that overthrew Allende, during which he was murdered, along with the head of the military, General Rene Schneider. Following Allende's overthrow, the CIA trained agents for the Chilean secret service (DINA). DINA set up a team of assassins who could "travel anywhere in the world . . . to carry out sanctions including assassinations" (Dinges and Landau, 1980: 239). One of the assassinations carried out by DINA was the murder of Orlando Letellier, Allende's ambassador to the United States and his former minister of defense. Letellier was killed when a car bomb blew up his car on Embassy Row in Washington, D.C. (Dinges and Landau, 1982).

Other bloody coups known to have been planned, organized, and executed by U.S. agents include coups in Guatemala, Nicaragua, the Dominican Republic, and Vietnam. American involvement in those coups was never legally authorized. The murders, assassinations, and terrorist acts that accompany coups are criminal acts by law, both in the United States and in the country in which they take place.

More recent examples of murder and assassination for which government officials are responsible include the death of 80 people in Beirut, Lebanon, when a car bomb exploded on May 8, 1985. The bomb was set by a Lebanese counterterrorist unit working with the CIA. Senator Daniel Moynihan has said that when he was vice president of the Senate Intelligence Committee, President Reagan ordered the CIA to form a small antiterrorist effort in the Mideast. Two sources said that the CIA was working with the group that

STATE-ORGANIZED CRIME   199

planted the bomb to kill the Shiite leader Hussein Fadallah (the *New York Times*, May 13, 1985).

A host of terrorist plans and activities connected with the attempt to overthrow the Nicaraguan government, including several murders and assassinations, were exposed in an affidavit filed by free–lance reporters Tony Avirgan and Martha Honey. They began investigating Contra activities after Avirgan was injured in an attempt on the life of Contra leader Eden Pastora. In 1986, Honey and Avirgan filed a complaint with the U.S. District Court in Miami charging John Hull, Robert Owen, Theodore Shackley, Thomas Clines, Chi Chi Quintero, Maj. General Richard Secord, and others working for the CIA in Central America with criminal conspiracy and the smuggling of cocaine to aid the Nicaraguan rebels.

A criminal conspiracy in which the CIA admits participating is the publication of a manual, *Psychological Operation in Guerrilla Warfare*, which was distributed to the people of Nicaragua. The manual describes how the people should proceed to commit murder, sabotage, vandalism, and violent acts in order to undermine the government. Encouraging or instigating such crimes is not only a violation of U.S. law, it was also prohibited by Reagan's executive order of 1981, which forbade any U.S. participation in foreign assassinations.

The CIA is not alone in hatching criminal conspiracies. The DEA organized a "Special Operations Group," which was responsible for working out plans to assassinate political and business leaders in foreign countries who were involved in drug trafficking. The head of this group was a former CIA agent, Lou Conein (also known as "Black Luigi"). George Crile wrote in the *Washington Post* (June 13, 1976):

> When you get down to it, Conein was organizing an assassination program. He was frustrated by the big–time operators who were just too insulated to get to . . . Meetings were held to decide whom to target and what method of assassination to employ.

Crile's findings were also supported by the investigative journalist Jim Hougan (1978: 132).

It is a crime to conspire to commit murder. The official record, including testimony by participants in three conspiracies before the U.S. Congress and in court, make it abundantly clear that the crime of conspiring to commit murder is not infrequent in the intelligence agencies of the United States and other countries.

It is also a crime to cover up criminal acts, but there are innumerable examples of instances in which the CIA and the FBI conspired to interfere with the criminal prosecution of drug dealers, murderers, and assassins. In the death of Letellier, mentioned earlier, the FBI and the CIA refused to cooperate with the prosecution of the DINA agents who murdered Letellier

200   CHAMBLISS

(Dinges and Landau, 1980: 208–209). Those agencies were also involved in the cover–up of the criminal activities of a Cuban exile, Ricardo (Monkey) Morales. While an employee of the FBI and the CIA, Morales planted a bomb on an Air Cubana flight from Venezuela, which killed 73 people. The Miami police confirmed Morales's claim that he was acting under orders from the CIA (Lernoux, 1984: 188). In fact, Morales, who was arrested for overseeing the shipment of 10 tons of marijuana, admitting to being a CIA contract agent who conducted bombings, murders, and assassinations. He was himself killed in a bar after he made public his work with the CIA and the FBI.

Colonel Muammar Qaddafi, like Fidel Castro, has been the target of a number of assassination attempts and conspiracies by the U.S. government. One plot, the *Washington Post* reported, included an effort to "lure [Qaddafi] into some foreign adventure of terrorist exploit that would give a growing number of Qaddafi opponents in the Libyan military a chance to seize power, or such a foreign adventure might give one of Qaddafi's neighbors, such as Algeria or Egypt, a justification for responding to Qaddafi militarily" (the *Washington Post*, April 14, 1986). The CIA recommended "stimulating" Qaddafi's fall "by encouraging disaffected elements in the Libyan army who could be spurred to assassination attempts" (the *Guardian*, November 20, 1985: 6).

Opposition to government policies can be a very risky business, as the ecology group Greenpeace discovered when it opposed French nuclear testing in the Pacific. In the fall of 1985 the French government planned a series of atomic tests in the South Pacific. Greenpeace sent its flagship to New Zealand with instructions to sail into the area where the atomic testing was scheduled to occur. Before the ship could arrive at the scene, however, the French secret service located the ship in the harbor and blew it up. The blast from the bomb killed one of the crew.

OTHER STATE–ORGANIZED CRIMES

Every agency of government is restricted by law in certain fundamental ways. Yet structural pressures exist that can push agencies to go beyond their legal limits. The CIA, for example, is not permitted to engage in domestic intelligence. Despite this, the CIA has opened and photographed the mail of over 1 million private citizens (Rockefeller Report, 1975: 101–115), illegally entered people's homes, and conducted domestic surveillance through electronic devices (Parenti, 1983: 170–171).

Agencies of the government also cannot legally conduct experiments on human subjects that violate civil rights or endanger the lives of the subjects. But the CIA conducted experiments on unknowing subjects by hiring prostitutes to administer drugs to their clients. CIA–trained medical doctors and

STATE-ORGANIZED CRIME 201

psychologists observed the effects of the drugs through a two–way mirror in expensive apartments furnished to the prostitutes by the CIA. At least one of the victims of these experiments died and others suffered considerable trauma (Anderson and Whitten, 1976; Crewdson and Thomas, 1977; Jacobs 1977a, 1977b).

The most flagrant violation of civil rights by federal agencies is the FBI's counterintelligence program, known as COINTELPRO. This program was designed to disrupt, harass, and discredit groups that the FBI decided were in some way "un-American." Such groups included the American Civil Liberties Union, antiwar movements, civil rights organizations, and a host of other legally constituted political groups whose views opposed some of the policies of the United States (Church Committee, 1976). With the exposure of COINTELPRO, the group was disbanded. There is evidence, however, that the illegal surveillance of U.S. citizens did not stop with the abolition of COINTELPRO but continues today (Klein, 1988).

DISCUSSION

Elsewhere I have suggested a general theory to account for variations in types and frequency of crime (Chambliss, 1988a). The starting point for that theory is the assumption that in every era political, economic, and social relations contain certain inherent *contradictions*, which produce *conflicts* and *dilemmas* that people struggle to resolve. The study of state-organized crime brings into sharp relief the necessity of understanding the role of contradictions in the formation and implementation of law.

Contradictions inherent in the formation of states create conditions under which there will be a tendency for state officials to violate the criminal law. State officials inherit from the past laws that were not of their making and that were the result of earlier efforts to resolve conflicts wrought by structural contradictions (Chambliss, 1980; Chambliss and Seidman, 1982). The inherited laws nonetheless represent the foundation on which the legitimacy of the state's authority depends. These laws also provide a basis for attempts by the state to control the acts of others and to justify the use of violence to that end.

For England in the sixteenth century, passing laws to legitimize piracy for English pirates while condemning as criminal the piracy of others against England would have been an untenable solution, just as it would undermine the legitimacy of America's ideological and political position to pass legislation allowing for terrorist acts on the part of U.S. officials while condemning and punishing the terrorism of others.

Law is a two–edged sword; it creates one set of conflicts while it attempts to resolve another. The passage of a particular law or set of laws may resolve conflicts and enhance state control, but it also limits the legal activities of the state. State officials are thus often caught between conflicting demands as they find themselves constrained by laws that interfere with other goals demanded of them by their roles or their perception of what is in the interests of the state. There is a contradiction, then, between the legal prescriptions and the agreed goals of state agencies. Not everyone caught in this dilemma will opt for violating the law, but some will. Those who do are the perpetrators, but not the cause, of the persistence of state-organized crime.

When Spain and Portugal began exploiting the labor and natural resources of the Americas and Asia, other European nations were quick to realize the implications for their own power and sovereignty. France, England, and Holland were powerful nations, but not powerful enough at the time to challenge Spain and Portugal directly. The dilemma for those nations was how to share in the wealth and curtail the power of Spain and Portugal without going to war. A resolution to the dilemma was forged through cooperation with pirates. Cooperating with pirates, however, required violating their own laws as well as the laws of other countries. In this way, the states organized criminality for their own ends without undermining their claim to legitimacy or their ability to condemn and punish piracy committed against them.

It should be noted that some monarchs in the sixteenth and seventeenth centuries (James I of England, for example) refused to cooperate with pirates no matter how profitable it would have been for the Crown. So, too, not all CIA or NSC personnel organize criminal activities in pursuit of state goals.

The impetus for the criminality of European states that engaged in piracy was the need to accumulate capital in the early stages of capitalist formation. State–organized criminality did not disappear, however, with the emergence of capitalism as the dominant economic system of the world. Rather, contemporary state–organized crime also has its roots in the ongoing need for capital accumulation of modern nation–states, whether the states be socialist, capitalist, or mixed economies.

Sociologically, then, the most important characteristics of state–organized crime in the modern world are at one with characteristics of state–organized crime in the early stages of capitalist development. Today, states organize smuggling, assassinations, covert operations, and conspiracies to criminally assault citizens, political activists, and political leaders perceived to be a threat. These acts are as criminal in the laws of the nations perpetrating them as were the acts of piracy in which European nations were complicitous.

At the most general level, the contradictions that are the force behind state-organized crime today are the same as those that were the impetus for piracy in sixteenth-century Europe. The accumulation of capital determines a nation's power, wealth, and survival today, as it did 300 years ago. The state must provide a climate and a set of international relations that facilitate this accumulation if it is to succeed. State officials will be judged in accordance with their ability to create these conditions.

STATE-ORGANIZED CRIME 203

But contradictory ideologies and demands are the very essence of state formations. The laws of every nation–state inhibit officials from maximizing conditions conducive to capital accumulation at the same time that they facilitate the process. Laws prohibiting assassination and arms smuggling enable a government to control such acts when they are inimical to their interests. When such acts serve the interests of the state, however, then there are pressures that lead some officials to behave criminally. Speaking of the relationship among the NSC, the CIA, and drug trafficking, Senator John Kerry, chairman of the Senate Foreign Relations Subcommittee on Terrorism, Narcotics and International Operations, pinpointed the dilemma when he said "stopping drug trafficking to the United States has been a secondary U.S. foreign policy objective. It has been sacrificed repeatedly for other political goals" (Senate Hearings, 1986). He might have added that engaging in drug trafficking and arms smuggling has been a price government agencies have been willing to pay "for other political goals."

These contradictions create conflicts between nation–states as well as internally among the branches of government. Today, we see nations such as Turkey, Bolivia, Colombia, Peru, Panama, and the Bahamas encouraging the export of illegal drugs while condemning them publicly. At the same time, other government agencies cooperate in the export and import of illegal arms and drugs to finance subversive and terrorist activities. Governments plot and carry out assassinations and illegal acts against their own citizens in order to "preserve democracy" while supporting the most undemocratic institutions imaginable. In the process, the contradictions that create the conflicts and dilemmas remain untouched and the process goes on indefinitely.

A U.S. State Department report (1985) illustrates, perhaps, the logical outcome of the institutionalization of state–organized crime in the modern world. In this report the State Department offered to stop criminal acts against the Nicaraguan government in return for concessions from Nicaragua. Three hundred years earlier England, France, and Spain signed a treaty by which each agreed to suppress its piracy against the others in return for certain guarantees of economic and political sovereignty.

CONCLUSION

My concern here is to point out the importance of studying state-organized crime. Although I have suggested some theoretical notions that appear to me to be promising, the more important goal is to raise the issue for further study. The theoretical and empirical problems raised by advocating the study of state–organized crime are, however, formidable.

Data on contemporary examples of state–organized crime are difficult to obtain. The data I have been able to gather depend on sources that must be used cautiously. Government hearings, court trials, interviews, newspaper

204   CHAMBLISS

accounts, and historical documents are replete with problems of validity and reliability. In my view they are no more so than conventional research methods in the social sciences, but that does not alter the fact that there is room for error in interpreting the findings. It will require considerable imagination and diligence for others to pursue research on this topic and add to the empirical base from which theoretical propositions can be tested and elaborated.

We need to explore different political, economic, and social systems in varying historical periods to discover why some forms of social organization are more likely to create state-organized crimes than others. We need to explore the possibility that some types of state agencies are more prone to engaging in criminality than others. It seems likely, for example, that state agencies whose activities can be hidden from scrutiny are more likely to engage in criminal acts than those whose record is public. This principle may also apply to whole nation–states: the more open the society, the less likely it is that state-organized crime will become institutionalized.

There are also important parallels between state-organized criminality and the criminality of police and law enforcement agencies generally. Local police departments that find it more useful to cooperate with criminal syndicates than to combat them are responding to their own particular contradictions, conflicts, and dilemmas (Chambliss, 1988b). An exploration of the theoretical implications of these similarities could yield some important findings.

The issue of state–organized crime raises again the question of how crime should be defined to be scientifically useful. For the purposes of this analysis, I have accepted the conventional criminological definition of crime as acts that are in violation of the criminal law. This definition has obvious limitations (see Schwendinger and Schwendinger, 1975), and the study of state–organized crime may facilitate the development of a more useful definition by underlying the interrelationship between crime and the legal process. At the very least, the study of state-organized crime serves as a reminder that crime is a political phenomenon and must be analyzed accordingly.

REFERENCES

Anderson, Jack, and Lee Whitten
   1976   The CIA's "sex squad." The Washington Post, June 22:B13.

Andrews, K.R.
   1959   English Privateering Voyages to the West Indies 1598–1695. Ser. 11., vol.
           111. London: Hakluyt Society.
   1971   The Last Voyage of Drake and Hawkins. New York: Cambridge University
           Press.

Block, Alan A., and William J. Chambliss
   1981   Organizing Crime. New York: Elsevier.

STATE-ORGANIZED CRIME   205

British Museum
  1977   Sir Francis Drake. London: British Museum Publications.

Chambliss, William J.
  1968   The tolerance policy: An invitation to organized crime. Seattle October:
          23–31.
  1971   Vice, corruption, bureaucracy and power. Wisconsin Law Review
          4:1,150–1,173.
  1975a   On the paucity of original research on organized crime: A footnote to
          Galliher and Cain. The American Sociologist 10:36–39.
  1975b   Toward a political economy of crime. Theory and Society 2:149–170.
  1977   Markets, profits, labor and smack. Contemporary Crises 1:53–57.
  1980   On lawmaking. British Journal of Law and Society 6:149–172.
  1988a   Exploring Criminology. New York: Macmillan.
  1988b   On the Take: From Petty Crooks to Presidents. Revised ed. Bloomington:
          Indiana University Press.

Chambliss, William J., and Robert B. Seidman
  1982   Law, Order and Power. Rev. ed. Reading, Mass.: Addison–Wesley.

Church Committee
  1976   Intelligence Activities and the Rights of Americans. Washington, D.C.:
          Government Printing Office.

Commonwealth of New South Wales
  1982a   New South Wales Joint Task Force on Drug Trafficking. Federal
          Parliament Report. Sydney: Government of New South Wales.
  1982b   Preliminary Report of the Royal Commission to Investigate the Nugan
          Hand Bank Failure. Federal Parliament Report. Sydney: Government of
          New South Wales.

Corbett, Julian S.
  1898a   Drake and the Tudor Army. 2 vols. London: Longmans, Green.
  1898b   Paper Relating to the Navy during the Spanish War, 1585–1587. Vol. 11.
          London: Navy Records Society.

Crewdson, John M., and Jo Thomas
  1977   Abuses in testing of drugs by CIA to be panel focus. The New York Times,
          September 20.

de La Croix, Robert
  1962   John Paul Jones. London: Frederik Muller.

Dinges, John, and Saul Landau
  1980   Assassination on Embassy Row. New York: McGraw–Hill.
  1982   The CIA's link to Chile's plot. The Nation, June 12:712–713.

Exquemling, A.O.
  1670   De Americanaenshe Zee-Roovers. MS. 301. London, British Museum.

Goulden, Joseph C.
  1984   Death Merchant: The Brutal True Story of Edwin P. Wilson. New York:
          Simon and Schuster.

Hersh, Seymour
  1979   Ex-analyst says CIA rejected warning on Shah. The New York Times,
          January 7:A10. Cited in Piers Beirne and James Messerschmidt, Criminol-
          ogy. New York: Harcourt Brace Jovanovich, forthcoming.

206   CHAMBLISS

Hougan, Jim
    1978   Spooks: The Haunting of America—The Private Use of Secret Agents. New
            York: William Morrow.
    1984   Secret Agenda: Watergate, Deep Throat, and the CIA. New York:
            Random House.

Jacobs, John
    1977a   The diaries of a CIA operative. The Washington Post, September 5:1.
    1977b   Turner cites 149 drug-test projects. The Washington Post, August 4:1.

Klein, Lloyd
    1988   Big Brother Is Still Watching You. Paper presented at the annual meetings
            of the American Society of Criminology, Chicago, November 12.

Kruger, Henrik
    1980   The Great Heroin Coup. Boston: South End Press.

Kwitny, Jonathan
    1987   The Crimes of Patriots. New York: W.W. Norton.

Lane-Poole
    1890   The Barbary Corsairs. London: T. Fisher Unwin.

LeGolif, Louis
    1680   The Manuscripts of Louis LeGolif alias Borgnefesse. London, British
            Museum.

Lernoux, Penny
    1984   The Miami connection. The Nation, February 18:186–198.

MacIntyre, Donald
    1975   The Privateers. London: Paul Elek.

Mainwaring, Henry
    1616   Of the Beginnings, Practices, and Suppression of Pirates. No publisher
            acknowledged.

McCord, James W., Jr.
    1974   A Piece of Tape. Rockville, Md.: Washington Media Services.

McCoy, Alfred W.
    1973   The Politics of Heroin in Southeast Asia. New York: Harper & Row.

NARMIC
    1984   Military Exports to South Africa: A Research Report on the Arms
            Embargo. Philadelphia: American Friends Service Committee.

Nihill, Grant
    1982   Bank links to spies, drugs. The Advertiser, November 10:1.

Owen, John
    1983   Sleight of Hand: The $25 Million Nugan Hand Bank Scandal. Sydney:
            Calporteur Press.

Parenti, Michael
    1983   Democracy for the Few. New York: St. Martin's.

Petras, James
    1977   Chile: Crime, class consciousness and the bourgeoisie. Crime and Social
            Justice 7:14–22.

STATE-ORGANIZED CRIME 207

Potter, Gary W., and Bruce Bullington
1987   Drug Trafficking and the Contras: A Case Study of State-Organized Crime. Paper presented at annual meeting of the American Society of Criminology, Montreal.

Ritchie, Robert C.
1986   Captain Kidd and the War Against the Pirates. Cambridge, Mass.: Harvard University Press.

Rockefeller Report
1975   Report to the President by the Commission on CIA Activities within the United States. Washington, D.C.: Government Printing Office.

Schwendinger, Herman, and Julia Schwendinger
1975   Defenders of order or guardians of human rights. Issue in Criminology 7:72-81.

Senate Hearings
1986   Senate Select Committee on Assassination, Alleged Assassination Plots Involving Foreign Leaders. Interim Report of the Senate Select Committee to Study Governmental Operations with Respect to Intelligence Activities. 94th Cong., 1st sess., November 20. Washington, D.C.: Government Printing Office.

Senior, C.M.
1976   A Nation of Pirates: English Piracy in its Heyday. London: David and Charles Newton Abbot.

Sharkey, Jacqueline
1988   The Contra-drug trade eff. Common Cause Magazine, September-October: 23-33.

Tilly, Charles
1985   War making and state making as organized crime. In P. Evans, D. Rueschemeyer, and T. Skocpol (eds.), Bringing the State Back In. Cambridge: Cambridge University Press.

Turner, Stansfield
1985   Secrecy and Democracy: The CIA in Transition. New York: Houghton Miflin.

U.S. Department of State
1985   Revolution Beyond Our Border: Information on Central America. State Department Report N 132. Washington, D.C.: U.S. Department of State.

Verrill, A. Hyatt
1924   Smugglers and Smuggling. New York: Duffield.

AUTHOR'S NOTE

The historical documents used for the research on piracy were provided by the British Museum Library, the Franklin D. Roosevelt Library in New York, Columbia University Library, and the Naval Archives. For the more recent happenings and machinations of the CIA, DEA, and other government agencies, the primary data bases are confidential interviews with people involved in the events described, or people closely associated with the events, and information obtained through Freedom of Information requests. Attribution to people who generously gave their time and in some cases took risks for the sake of providing a better understanding of the world we live in is, of course, impossible. Where possible

208 CHAMBLISS

the information forthcoming from the interviews has been supplemented by reference to published government documents, newspaper reports, and verifiable research.

ACKNOWLEDGMENTS

This research owes a debt to so many people it is impossible to acknowledge them all. The many informants and officials who cooperated with various parts of the research and the librarians who helped uncover essential historical documents must come first. I am also deeply indebted to Raquel Kennedy, Pernille Baadsager, Richard Appelbaum, Marjorie Zatz, Alan Block, Jim Petras, Ray Michalowski, Stan Cohen, Hi Schwendinger, Tony Platt, and Martha Huggins for their insights and help at many stages in the development of the research. I am also indebted to a confidential donor who helped support the research effort in Thailand during 1974.

[14]

Crime, Law and Social Change **16**: 3–39, 1991.
© 1991 *Kluwer Academic Publishers. Printed in the Netherlands.*

Colombia's cocaine syndicates

RENSSELAER W. LEE III
Global Advisory Services, Alexandria, VA 22314, U.S.A.

Abstract. Colombia's main drug trafficking coalitions – the Medellín and Cali syndicates – constitute powerful illegitimate interest groups. Traffickers (especially the Medellín coalition) exert political influence partly through violence and intimidation; yet the drug lords' political arsenal also includes non-coercive means – bribery, contributions to political campaigns and even open lobbying in the media. Conventional law enforcement strategies have been ineffective against the cocaine mafia, which is well entrenched in Colombian society. Wide domestic opposition to the drug war has prompted Colombia to opt for an unconventional strategy – to negotiate the voluntary withdrawal of major traffickers for the cocaine trade. A negotiation approach is extremely risky; yet, under tightly-controlled conditions, such an approach could allow U.S. and Colombian authorities to make significant progress in disrupting the cocaine multinationals and reducing the flow of Colombian cocaine into international markets.

Introduction

The cocaine industry constitutes a powerful, well-entrenched, and ruthless interest group in Colombia. The cocaine lords apparently have successfully coopted parts of the power structure and intimidated many of their enemies. This article:

- describes the organization, tactics, operation, and political behavior of Colombia's cocaine syndicates – especially the coalitions of trafficking groups centered in Medellín and Cali;
- discusses the internal structure of these coalitions, their organizational and financial resources, and their military and logistical capabilities;
- analyzes the sources and dynamics of conflict in the Colombian cocaine establishment, especially the dispute between the Medellín and Cali coalitions;
- depicts the behavior of traffickers in Colombian society today, their penetration of legitimate economic and political institutions, and their complex relations with Marxist guerrilla groups.

This article emphasizes that recent anti-drug strategies in Colombia – strategies that rely on intensified repression in Colombia and on significant inflows

Pages 21 to 35 of this article appeared in a slightly different form in *ORRIS*, Volume 35, Number 2, Spring 1991, under the title: "Making the Most of Colombia's Drug Negotiations."

4

of U.S. military and law enforcement assistance – have not substantially disrupted the Colombian cocaine trade. Perhaps more important, such strategies have failed politically – they no longer enjoy the support of the Colombian population. Attention in Colombia is now focused on the possibility of a negotiated settlement of the drug war. A major group of Colombian drug dealers is currently trying to negotiate its surrender to the authorities and its collective withdrawal from the cocaine business. In return, the traffickers are demanding an end to extraditions to the United States, recognition of their political status by the authorities, and the opportunity for amnesty.

Today, most Colombians favor a peaceful resolution of the drug problem, in no small part because of the violence that is shredding the fabric of their society. Washington has consistently maintained that a deal with drug traffickers is unacceptable, but such a deal may in fact be in the making. The past year has witnessed considerable bargaining by communique as the Colombian government and the Medellín drug lords relayed their respective positions to the media. Moreover, three important Medellín traffickers – Fabio, Jorge Luis, and Juan David Ochoa Vasquez – recently turned themselves in, taking advantage of lenient terms offered by the Colombian authorities.

This article argues that negotiations with traffickers represent one possible supply-side strategy, a tool of political warfare against the powerful cocaine multinationals. A negotiated settlement clearly would be worthwhile if it crippled existing drug businesses and elicited the knowledge necessary to improve the fight against future cocaine operations. However, Colombia's interests center more on ending mafia-inspired violence than on terminating the drug trade per se. To ensure that a peace settlement furthers U.S. narcotics control objectives – especially the objective of reducing the annual flood of 400 to 700 tons of Colombian cocaine into U.S. markets – Washington will have to participate at some level in Colombia's narco-dialogues. Such participation undoubtedly will require (1) abandoning long-standing objections to negotiating with criminals and (2) coming to terms with the now obviously ongoing process of accommodation in Colombia.

Structure of the cocaine industry

Organizational issues

Colombia accounts for 10 to 15 percent of the world's coca-leaf production, making it the third largest cultivator. Colombia, on the other hand, is by far the most significant producer of refined cocaine (cocaine hydrochloride) in the world. In 1989–1990 at least 70 percent of the cocaine sold in international markets originated from refineries in Colombia.[1]

5

The cocaine business in Colombia is very highly organized. Two loosely articulated coalitions of criminal families – centered in the cities of Medellín and Cali – account for 70 to 80 percent of Colombian cocaine production. The remaining 20 to 30 percent lies mostly in the hands of independent trafficking groups based in Pereira, Bogotá, and the north coast of Colombia; however, Colombia's most important guerrilla group – the Revolutionary Armed Forces of Colombia (FARC) – also may control some refining facilities. The Medellín and Cali coalitions, often somewhat misleadingly called cartels, exported at least 350 tons of cocaine from Colombia in 1990; some of those exports comprised cocaine transshipped from Bolivia and Peru.[2] The majority of those exports – perhaps 80 percent – went to the United States, and most of the rest was shipped to Western Europe. The syndicates' 1990 earnings from international cocaine sales are estimated at more than $8 billion; that year, Colombia's legal exports were valued at almost $7 billion.

Production and price-setting mechanisms within the Medellín and Cali coalitions are not clearly understood.[3] However, there is evidence that the cartels' distributors in the U.S. receive direct orders (often via Fax) from Cali or Medellín on how much to charge different customers for different kilo quantities of cocaine. Also, considerable business collaboration occurs within each coalition – traffickers co-insure cocaine shipments, engage in joint smuggling or production ventures, exchange loads, and jointly plan assassinations. Moreover, cocaine barons share a common agenda that includes blocking the extradition of drug traffickers and immobilizing the criminal justice system.

From a law enforcement standpoint, the narcotraficante organizations represent a major challenge. According to one report, the Medellín cartel consists of "approximately 200 individual trafficking groups" that engage in different phases of cocaine production, transportation, and distribution.[4] Many groups or organizations operate cocaine refining facilities. Available information suggests that production within the Medellín and Cali coalitions seems relatively dispersed – many cocaine trafficking organizations (or families) own and operate cocaine hydrochloride facilities. Of course, a single organization may own more than one laboratory. In addition, several trafficking groups may jointly own a large laboratory complex. For example, Tranquilandia, a large complex of 14 cocaine laboratories discovered in Caqueta in 1984, apparently was the property of at least three major Medellín traffickers – Jorge Ochoa Vasquez, Jose Gonzalo Rodriguez Gacha, and Pablo Escobar Gaviria.

On the other hand, downstream operations are relatively centralized – leadership of the cartels is equivalent to control over distribution and marketing. Colombia's major drug lords – the men at the apex of the trafficking pyramid – apparently coordinate the smuggling of cocaine to the United States and other overseas markets. For many years, the kingpin list included Cali traffickers Gilberto Rodriguez Orejuela, his brother Miguel Angel Rodri-

6

guez, and Jose Santa Cruz Londoño; and Medellín traffickers Pablo Escobar Gaviria, Jose Gonzalo Rodriguez Gacha (now deceased), and the three Ochoa brothers (Jorge, Fabio, and Juan David). These traffickers operate vertically integrated enterprises that procure cocaine paste or base in Peru or Bolivia, refine their product in Colombia, ship the refined cocaine to foreign markets, and maintain networks of wholesalers in the United States. Such enterprises also export and distribute cocaine produced by other trafficking groups in the Medellín and Cali coalitions. The leading traffickers control their export and distribution networks in part by offering suitable suppliers an insurance package for their shipments. That is, the traffickers guarantee 100-percent replacement of any cocaine shipments that are lost or seized.[5] Moreover, Pablo Escobar and Gonzalo Rodriguez Gacha reportedly have ordered the murders of Medellín traffickers who tried to market their cocaine independently in the United States. The transportation network maintained by the drug kingpins furnishes cocaine paste and base (imported primarily from Peru and Bolivia) to the small refiners in the coalitions. Medium-size organizations, however, may operate their own procurement and transportation systems.

Cocaine trafficking requires a range of specialized personnel, including buyers of paste or base, chemists, chemical engineers (some modern labs are equipped with their own chemical recycling plants), pilots, wholesalers, money launderers, accountants, lawyers, security guards, and professional assassins. The large and vertically integrated organizations – such as those of Escobar, the Ochoas, and Rodriguez Orejuela – maintain a full complement of such personnel. As the U.S. end, these organizations employ a number of regional managers, and each one "oversees the distribution of cocaine and the collection of money for a particular area of the United States".[6] Some emerging evidence documents professionalism in the syndicate's operations. Although the leading Medellín and Cali traffickers conform somewhat to the "Miami Vice" stereotype of Colombian drug lords, the traffickers can and do hire high-power legal and managerial talent. At least four former members of the Colombian Supreme Court are on the Ochoa family's payroll. A former money launderer for the Medellín cartel, Ramon Milian Rodriguez, testified before a Senate committee that all of the members of the cartel's management hold advanced degrees in their specialty.[7]

The Medellín-Cali syndicates have a well-deserved reputation for violence. With a gross income of more than $ 8 billion a year, traffickers can easily afford to stockpile large arsenals of automatic weapons (such as AK 47s, Uzis, AR-15 and Galil rifles, and M-16 machine guns), grenades, rocket launchers, and ground-to-ground missiles. They also may have purchased ground-to-air missiles, but there is no evidence that those missiles have been deployed. (In April 1990, Colombians allegedly working for the Medellín cartel tried to buy 120 Stinger anti-aircraft missiles and other U.S. military hardware in Florida, but were foiled by the FBI and Florida police.[8]) The Medellín mafia, at least until recently, ran several training schools for paramilitary operatives – essentially for drug traffickers' private armies – in the Middle Magdalena Valley. Former Israeli Army and British Strategic Air Services (SAS) personnel were hired as instructors, and courses covered topics such as camouflage, self-defense, weapons, intelligence and counterintelligence, and communications.

The syndicates, especially the Medellín mafia, also support standing bands of trained contract assassins, including the Medellín groups "Los Quesitos" and "Los Priscos", recruited by Pablo Escobar. Some of these assassins may be former FARC or April 19th Movement (M-19) guerrillas who have deserted or retired from those organizations. Outside talent can be enlisted for specific act of violence. For example, the 1,100-pound bomb that exploded in front of the Colombian Department of Administrative Security (DAS) building in Bogotá in early December 1989, killing 63 people, apparently was fabricated by a Spanish terrorist who was a member of the "Basque Fatherland and Liberty" group.[9] The Medellín mafia also reportedly hired M-19 guerrillas to raid Colombia's Palace of Justice in November 1988, kill a number of Colombian Supreme Court justices in the building, and destroy extradition files. That attack probably was not the product of a consensus decision by the entire Medellín mafia, which in general holds a basic aversion to Colombian revolutionaries. Moreover, at that time, the mafia's modus operandi stressed assassinations of carefully selected targets, not messy high-profile terrorist actions. Yet, a loose cannon in the syndicate could conceivably have financed the Palace takeover. Suspicion fell on Carlos Lehder (now imprisoned in the United States), a radical and a revolutionary who apparently maintained close ties with the M-19's leaders.

The syndicates also incorporate the most modern forms of air transportation and the best state-of-the-art communication networks that money can buy (including, for example, satellite radios). Traffickers possess encryption devices and voice-privacy mechanisms and, according to all reports, regularly intercept messages from – and even use for their own purposes – the Colombian government's communication system. Retired Colombian Army General Paul Gorman observed:

> The Colombian Armed Forces are well aware that the narcotraficantes can track the movements of Colombian armed forces and aircraft better than their respective commanders, know more surely where they are and where they are going.[10]

Overall, the Medellín and Cali trafficking syndicates apparently wield immense financial, organizational, and military-logistical resources. Furthermore, they represent a difficult target for law enforcement agencies. The

8

cartels are relatively decentralized and amorphous, not bureaucracies in the Weberian sense, but rather coalitions or confederations. No single heart or head drives these syndicates. Key figures in the trafficking groups that compose these coalitions "traditionally are close relations, childhood friends, or neighbors from hometowns in Colombia".[11] Consequently, DEA and the Colombian police find it difficult to infiltrate these organizations. Moreover, even the elimination of a prominent trafficker is unlikely to have a sustained effect on the syndicates' cocaine exports. For instance, Rodriguez Gacha's smuggling and distribution networks, which were built up over a period of 10 or more years, will almost certainly survive his death – they will either be managed by the trafficker's immediate associates or absorbed by the Escobar or Ochoa organizations.

In addition, the Medellín and Cali syndicates exercise substantial influence in Colombian society. Part of this power undoubtedly stems from the syndicates' capacity for violence. According to a high-ranking DEA official, Medellín and Cali traffickers have been responsible for more than 4,000 murders in Colombia. The victims include hundreds of law enforcement officials, more than 50 judges, and numerous prominent politicians, journalists, and government officials. The DEA source notes that traffickers have "stymied DEA's efforts in Bogotá by threatening any police officer that cooperates with DEA and by killing any informant that can be identified".[12] The syndicates, however, do not rely only on violence or the threat of violence to pursue their aims. For example, traffickers invest in the economy; bribe or coopt government officials, politicians, and judges; and donate vast sums of money to the poor. The drug lords' dual personalities – operating both outside and inside the Colombian system – make them a particularly powerful and elusive enemy.

Cracks in the firmament

Colombia's cocaine establishment has endured its fair share of internal conflicts. Although the early 1980s constituted a period of relative cooperation among the major cocaine bosses, significant disputes began emerging in the mid- and late 1980s. These disputes focused on issues such as political ideology, economic competition (turf wars), and differences in operating philosophy. For example, a radical-conservative split occurred between Carlos Lehder (a violently anti-establishment trafficker) and his colleagues in the Medellín cartel. A more important dispute between the Medellín and Cali coalitions arose largely from economic factors, but also reflected differences in tactics – the Cali syndicate always preferred a lower profile than the Medellín syndicate and consequently maintained smoother relations with the Colombian government. By late 1989, however, the Medellín-Cali split had healed in part. Perhaps the most significant division in the Colombian cocaine establishment lies between those traffickers who are addicted to political violence (roughly the Rodriguez Gacha-Escobar wing of the Medellín coalition) and those who favor a more conciliatory approach toward the authorities.

The story of Carlos Lehder is instructive. Lehder, a trafficker from Armenia, the capital of Quindío department, had earned several hundred million dollars in the late 1970s by running a smuggling operation on the Bahamas island of Norman's Key, which served as a refueling stop and a staging area for Colombian traffickers flying loads of cocaine and marijuana to the southern United States. Lehder collected a percentage fee on each kilo of drugs shipped through the island. Lehder left Norman's Key in 1981, but continued his association with the Medellín syndicates in various trafficking-smuggling ventures during the 1980s. Lehder's forte was setting up and running drug transportation networks – according to U.S. attorney Robert Merkle, who prosecuted Lehder in Florida, the trafficker "was to cocaine transportation what Henry Ford was to automobiles".[13]

In 1982 and 1983, Lehder took advantage of a tax amnesty declared by then-President of Colombia, Belisario Betancur, and repatriated much of his ill-gotten fortune to Colombia. Lehder's interests, it turned out, lay more in politics than in business. His political philosophy approximated a bizarre combination of nationalism and populism (he professed to be an admirer of Adolf Hitler, but dallied with Colombia's Marxist guerrillas) and probably was his undoing. Lehder used his cocaine profits to found a political movement in his native Quindío, the Movimiento Latino Nacional (MLN). The MLN's raison d'être was campaigning against the extradition treaty with the United States, but the party also managed a full-blown international political program that included the struggle against "communism, imperialism, neo-colonialism, and Zionism". Lehder attacked what he called Colombia's monarchical oligarchy (which he viewed as a slave to U.S. imperialism) and favored the replacement of Colombia's traditional parties with mass popular organizations. Lehder was, however, ideologically ambidextrous. In the 1986 presidential elections, his party supported the extreme leftist UP candidate, while Lehder himself maintained ties with several Colombian revolutionary organizations, including the Quintin Lamé, the FARC, and the M-19. As already noted, he may even has helped finance the M-19's raid on Colombia's Palace of Justice in November 1985, which culminated in a virtual holocaust that killed 11 Colombian Supreme Court justices and scores of other people.

Lehder's extreme radicalism, however, was not shared by his colleagues, who generally prefer to work within the system. Many Colombian observers believe that the Medellín syndicates viewed Lehder as an embarrassment, were eager to cultivate a pro-establishment image, and consequently betrayed

10

the trafficker to authorities. Lehder himself blames Pablo Escobar for tipping off the Colombian police to his whereabouts. Lehder was captured at a ranch near Medellín in February 1987 and subsequently was extradited to the United States, where he was tried and sentenced to life imprisonment plus 135 years.[14]

In contrast, the war between the Medellín and Cali coalitions was rooted in economic competition, which in time was accentuated by an apparent overproduction of cocaine. The average U.S. wholesale price of cocaine fell 70 to 80 percent between 1983 and 1989, precipitating increased competition for markets. New York City, which accounts for as much as 35 percent of the entire U.S. cocaine market, constituted the focal point of this rivalry. The Cali group traditionally had dominated the New York City market, but Medellín was attempting with some success to muscle in on Cali's sales territory.

The opening shot in the Medellín-Cali war was fired in January 1988, when a huge car bomb was detonated in front of a Medellín apartment building, "Monaco", owned by Pablo Escobar. A group calling itself "Death to the Mafia" claimed credit for the blast, which largely destroyed the upper floors of the building. However, a Colombian Army investigation established that Cali leader Gilberto Rodriguez Orejuela had commissioned and paid for the bombing. A series of reprisals and counter-reprisals was set in motion, and by August 1989, the Medellín cartel had bombed in various Colombian cities 47 outlets of Orejuela's "Drogas de Rebaja" drug store chain and 6 radio station's in Orejuela's Grupo Radial Colombiano network. During 1988 and 1989, the two coalitions' enforcers engaged in frequent shootouts. By mid-August 1989, an estimated 200 Colombians had lost their lives in the "adjustment of accounts" between Medellín and Cali.[15]

Factors beyond mere competition must be considered to explain the depth of hostility between the two syndicates. Although both Medellín and Cali traffickers crave social acceptability and have sought to buy into the system, the Medellín style is far more confrontational. Unlike their Cali counterparts, Medellín traffickers are addicted to using violence as a political tool; as one Colombian official remarked, "The problem is their attacks against the establishment".[16] Two leading Medellín drug lords, Pablo Escobar and Gonzalo Rodriguez Gacha, were implicated in every major assassination in Colombia, from the murder of Justice Minister Rodrigo Lara Bonilla in April 1984 to the assassination of Luis Carlos Galan in August 1989. The subsequent rash of terrorist bombings in Colombia was also attributed largely to those two traffickers and their close associates. In contrast, the Cali group abhors political violence, favoring bribes over gunplay, and in general tries not to embarrass the Colombian authorities. The authorities have responded by not persecuting the Cali drug lords – by "defending the interests of certain citizens of the Valle de Cauca", as one Medellín cartel communique put it.[17] Persistent rumors suggest that the Cali traffickers gave the Colombian government

11

intelligence information on Pablo Escobar. (In December 1990, Escobar accused a Cali kingpins of being an informer and a hypocrite.)[18] In sum, the Cali-Medellín split has acquired political and economic overtones, and the factions are unlikely to reconcile anytime soon.

Political behavior

Introduction

In Washington and in South American capitals, public debate about cocaine often seems to revolve around two competing models of the cocaine industry, the participation model and the insurgency model. The participation model stresses cocaine traffickers' ties to the power structure – that is, their penetration of established economic and political institutions. According to this model, the cocaine mafia's overriding objectives are protecting trafficking networks and legitimate business assets and keeping the industry's chief executives out of jail. Given these aims, traffickers are not revolutionaries, because they seek to coexist with and manipulate the political status quo. The model therefore implies that cocaine trafficking, if left unchecked, will produce serious and lasting corruption, but not fundamental change in the political system.

The insurgency model highlights confrontation between the cocaine industry and South American governments. In this model, the industry represents a direct threat to democratic institutions and values and in general constitutes a force that creates instability in the hemisphere. By extension, cocaine traffickers and Marxist guerrillas are allied or at least coordinate informally, and cocaine traffickers tacitly or actively cooperate with communist countries in fomenting revolution in Latin America and derailing the lives of American youth. The insurgency model categorizes the cocaine industry as anti-system, anti-government, and anti-democracy. Of course, the idea of a narco-guerrilla alliance plays well in Washington, Bogotá, and Lima because of the convenience and political expedience of depicting two such detestable groups as somehow operating in tandem.

Evidence can be cited in support of each model, because drug traffickers operate both inside and outside of existing political systems. Nowhere is this ambivalence more excruciatingly clear than in Colombia. The Colombia mafia (the cartels) clearly poses a danger to public order. The cartels possess the tools of violence: private armies, sophisticated armaments, foreign mercenaries, and teams of highly-trained contract assassins. Moreover, the cartels have not hesitated to use violence or the threat of violence against the Colombian government and the private citizens who support the government's anti-drug

12

policies. Violence constitutes just one of the weapons in the mafia's protectionist arsenal, which also includes bribery of officials and a variety of public relations activities, but violence performs two essential functions. First, violence is the first line of defense for trafficking operations – laboratories, supply routes, and distribution networks – and a buffer between the cartels' chief executives and Colombian jails. Hundreds of Colombian police officers, judges, prosecutors, and other officials have died in the Colombian government's war against drugs. Mafia-sponsored violence produces devastating effects in the Colombian criminal justice system: Police are afraid to make arrests, and judges are reluctant to preside over drug trafficking cases. Reportedly only 1 percent of those charged with narcotics offenses in Colombia are actually convicted.[19]

A second function of mafia violence is modifying or undermining national enforcement policies for drug laws. Specifically, the mafia's aim is demoralizing the Colombian government, halting the extradition of traffickers to the United States, discouraging high-level investigations of criminal operations and official corruption, and creating a public consensus against the war on drugs. Such policy-directed violence has gone through two stages. Stage one, roughly from April 1984 to August 1989, relied on selectively targeting and murdering high-level combatants, prominent Colombians who supported the extradition of Colombian drug lords to the United States or who otherwise crusaded against the cocaine industry. Such victims included:
- A justice minister
- A supreme court justice
- Superior court judges from Medellín and Bogotá
- An attorney general
- A former head of Colombia's anti-narcotics police, who was preparing a black book on the mafia's criminal activities
- The police chief of Antioquia department
- The leading Liberal Party candidate for president

The Medellín mafia has been implicated in every one of the above deaths. The killing on August 18, 1989, of Luis Carlos Galan provoked a wide-ranging crackdown by the Colombian government on the cocaine industry. The government invoked an emergency decree, which paved the way for the administrative extradition of drug dealers – that is, extradition not authorized by a prior court decision or by a functioning international treaty. (In June 1987, Colombia's Supreme Court had effectively invalidated a 1979 extradition treaty between the United States and Colombia.) Between August 1989 and December 1990, the government sent 24 suspected drug traffickers to the United States for prosecution. Another emergency decree enabled the government to confiscate drug traffickers' real estate, aircraft, money, weapons, and other assets. At least $ 125 million of drug trafficking assets – including 400

13

ranches. 470 planes, and 600 vehicles – that belonged mostly to the leaders of the Medellín cartel and to their associates were seized under this decree.[20]

The Medellín mafia responded by escalating the level of violence. In a communique issued on August 23, the Extraditables (the collective name adopted by members of the Medellín coalition) declared "a widespread and total war" against the government, the "industrial and political oligarchy", unfriendly journalists, magistrates who extradited drug dealers, and other who "have persecuted us in the past".[21] Unlike the strategy pursued in stage one, the mafia's total war strategy relied on broadly-based attacks on the civilian population. During the next 16 months, the Extraditables unleashed a wave of bombings, murders, and kidnappings that rocked Colombian society and seemingly undermined the anti-drug effort. This campaign of narcoterrorism claimed the lives of more than 1,000 Colombians, including many civilians, and imposed millions of dollars in economic losses.

Perhaps most demoralizing to Colombia's leaders was the traffickers' decision in late 1989 to begin taking members of the oligarchy as hostages. Among the kidnap victims were members of families – Santos, Turbay, Montoya, and Echevarria – that also had close ties with the Liberal Party elites. As of this writing, the government is still conducting behind-the-scenes negotiations to free Diana Turbay, the daughter of a former Colombian president; Maria Montoya, the daughter of Colombia's ambassador to Canada, German Montoya, who formerly was the secretary to the president in the Barco administration); and Francisco Santos, the news editor of Colombia's most important newspaper, *El Tiempo*, and the son of the newspaper's owner.

The new stage of mafia-inspired violence conformed in part to the pattern of terrorist groups in South America, the Middle East, Western Europe, and elsewhere. Yet, for all their hostility toward the so-called oligarchy, the Medellín Extraditables are not revolutionaries and are not bent on destroying Colombia's political order or on implementing radical social change. In fact, their political agenda is relatively modest: an end to extradition, a dialogue with the government, and an opportunity to assimilate into Colombian society. (Ironically and tragically, the traffickers' violence against the state is in part designed to win them acceptance as a political group, a tactic exemplified by the M-19 guerrillas, who recently received a pardon from the government.) Some cartel leaders conceivably would be willing to abandon the cocaine trade in return for a more tranquil life. Indeed, in the last 6 years, the drug lords have made four offers, all contingent on an end to extradition and various other guarantees, to withdraw entirely from the cocaine business. Whether the cocaine lords are serious or not in their offers, clearly their main quarrel is with the government's anti-drug policy, not with the Colombian system per se. In important respects, they are already part of the system, as the following discussion illustrates.

14

The cocaine industry as interest group

Both Medellín and Cali traffickers participate significantly in Colombian economic and political life. In effect, the cocaine industry constitutes an influential if illegal interest group, one that produces widespread multiplier effects and generates visible and invisible constituencies. Colombia's war against drugs resembles a peculiar form of civil war in which the "South" not only occupies territory and maintains its own armed forces, but also controls part of the government, economy, and military institutions of the "North".

What are the dimensions and components of drug traffickers' influence in Colombian society? First, cocaine profits exert significant influence over the Colombian economy. The cocaine trade procures an estimated $800 million to $1 billion a year in foreign exchange and probably another $1.0–1.5 billion in contraband or unregistered imports (legal imports totaled $6.2 billion in 1989).[22] The effect of the cocaine economy is highly visible in Medellín, the Middle Magdalena Valley, Cordoba department, the Urabá region of Antioquia, and other drug trafficking strongholds.

In Medellín, for instance, the influx of cocaine dollars compensates in part for the deteriorating fortunes of the city's main industry, textiles. The multiplier effect of these earnings helped lower the unemployment rate in Medellín from about 17 percent in 1983 to 12 percent in 1987 (nationally, the rate increased during that period). Similarly, the Barco administration's crackdown on the Medellín cartel – initiated in August 1989 after the murder of Luis Carlos Galan – particularly devastated the economy of Medellín. Many restaurants and discotheques shut down, some because they were confiscated by the authorities; hotel occupancy rates plunged to less than 10 percent; and licensed building construction, which declined about 10 percent nationally between 1988 and 1989, dropped an estimated 37 percent in Medellín.[23]

Yet, cocaine's most dramatic inroads came in the legal agricultural sector. In the past decade, for economic or strategic reasons, Colombian drug lords (mainly those associated with the Medellín coalition) bought an estimated 1 million hectares of land – or roughly 0.87 percent of the total land area of Colombia – and an estimated 4.3 percent of the total productive (cultivatable and pastoral) land. Some of these estates house cocaine laboratories, but the traffickers sometimes take their new role as landed gentry seriously, bringing electricity to remote regions of the countryside, modernizing stables and other livestock facilities, importing new strains of cattle, and introducing new breeding techniques. Just as important, the capos' private armies have brought a measure of security to guerrilla-infested regions such as Cordoba and the Middle Magdalena Valley, concomitantly boosting agriculture. In Cordoba, for instance, the acquisition of arable land by traffickers during the 1980s

15

correlated with that department's more than doubling its share of national crop yields from 1983 to 1988.[24]

Second, cocaine traffickers have penetrated the power structure at all levels. Cocaine money finances extensive protection and intelligence networks, including accomplices and informants in key national institutions such as the military, the various police forces, the court system, the government bureaucracy, the legislature, the church, the news media, and the national telephone system. Corrupt officials in key government ministries (Justice, Foreign Affairs, Defense, Government) furnish the cocaine lords with strategic intelligence on major anti-drug plans and initiatives. On an operational level, traffickers pay the military and police to overlook cocaine refineries and drug smuggling. Informants supply advance information on exact plans for raids, checkpoints, and attacks on traffickers' bastions. The financial inducements to cooperate with the drug lords are enormous by Colombian standards: For instance, a police private on the trafficker's payroll may receive $ 255 a month and a police captain $ 5,000; the official monthly salaries earned in their ranks are, respectively, $ 128 and $ 180.[25]

Third, cocaine lords function as power brokers, funneling large sums of money to the major political parties and electoral campaigns. In Colombia, where political campaigns are not funded from the state treasury, drug money represents an important underpinning for the entire democratic process. One Colombian senator from Antioquia, Ivan Marulanda, estimates that 40 percent of the legislators in the Colombian Congress have accepted contributions for their political campaigns from drug dealers.[26] Traffickers contribute indiscriminately to aspiring politicians – often through front organizations – to hedge their bets. Pablo Escobar and Gonzalo Rodriguez Gacha, for example, contributed money to both candidates in the 1982 Colombian presidential campaign. The influence of cocaine traffickers on Colombia's political system has long been a concern of that country's reformist politicians, such as the recently assassinated Luis Carlos Galan, and now constitutes a target of U.S. anti-drug policy as well. The United States reportedly has blacklisted approximately 25 Colombian congressmen, forbidding their entry into this country, because of alleged links to drug dealers. The list reputedly contains five senators, including Alberto Santofimio Botero, a Liberal Party candidate for president.[27]

Fourth, Colombian cocaine traffickers have merged with or supplanted the power structure in some parts of Colombia, especially in the northwest. Traffickers' purchases of land, their enormous wealth, their logistical resources, and their private armies have enabled them to build a large regional power base. This power base was developed in part at the expense of rural guerrilla groups, particularly the FARC and the Ejercito Popular de Liber-

16

ación (EPL), and includes much of the Middle Magdalena Valley and parts of Córdoba, Antioquia (outside of the Magdalena Valley), Meta, Magdalena, Cundinamarca, and other Colombian departments. Mafia influence also extends to cities such as Medellín, Cali, and the Amazon port of Leticia. In such islands of power, the traffickers' protection networks and early-warning systems are especially well-developed. (Again, witness the failure of the government's massive manhunt for Escobar in Medellín.) Unless a major government crackdown is in progress, traffickers can walk the streets and conduct their business operations almost with impunity. When traffickers leave their base areas, however – as Rodriguez Gacha did when he supervised a shipment of cocaine from Colombia's north coast – they become vulnerable to capture by the government.

Fifth, drug lords in Colombia, like their counterparts elsewhere, have generated political support in the general populace by underwriting the cost of public works and social services that benefit poor communities. Pablo Escobar, for example, built between 450 and 500 two-bedroom cementblock houses in a Medellín slum now rechristened as the Barrio Pablo Escobar. Escobar reportedly has constructed more public housing in Medellín than the government has. Escobar also financed many other Medellín projects, including sewer repair, educational facilities, clinics, and sports plazas. Similarly, Gonzalo Rodriguez Gacha donated an outdoor basketball court to his native town of Pacho, Cundinamarca; repaired the facade of Pacha's town hall; and showered money on the town's residents (reputedly giving away as much as $7,500 a day during 1989).[28] Although the cost of such projects represented a tiny fraction of all cocaine resources – the personal fortunes of Rodriguez Gacha and Escobar totaled well in excess of $1 billion – rewards in terms of status and good will have been incalculable.

Relations with guerrillas

General axioms[29]
Perhaps because of the cocaine industry's multi-front challenges to the Colombian government's authority, Washington expressed concern about a connection between the cocaine industry and Marxist guerrilla groups. Indeed, the Reagan administration analyzed the drug problem within the framework of the East-West conflict. Administration officials spoke publicly and privately about a "deadly connection" and an "unholy alliance" between cocaine kings and guerrillas. A 1985 U.S. government report on Soviet influence in Latin America warned of an "alliance between drug smugglers and arms dealers in support of terrorists and guerrillas".[30] In effect, the Reagan Administration's

17

rhetoric and, to a lesser extent, its policies were governed by the insurgency model of the cocaine industry. The idea of a narco-guerrilla alliance still plays very well in Washington, Bogotá, and Lima. In general, governments find it expedient to depict cocaine traffickers as hostile to the political order – working outside of the system – and the narco-guerrilla label serves that purpose admirably.

The label, however, does not stick very well to the Colombian cocaine cartels. The cocaine elites in Medellín and Cali basically constitute a conservative political force. Their values reflect (in an exaggerated form) those of the establishment that they emulate. As landowners, ranchers, and businessmen, traffickers are far more closely aligned with the traditional power structure than with the revolutionary left. Indeed, the cocaine mafia is strategically at odds with Colombia's insurgent movements. Guerrillas increase the cocaine industry's overhead costs, because traffickers must either pay protection money (war taxes) to guerrillas or make large outlays to guard their drug shipments, laboratories, supply routes, clandestine airfields, and exports. The Colombian cocaine leadership – which invests much of its new-found wealth in farms, ranches, and landed estates in Colombia's relatively unprotected hinterland – is vulnerable to extortion by the FARC and other guerrilla predators. Consequently, Colombia's large cocaine syndicates have emerged as determined foes of the Marxist revolutionary movements. Colombian traffickers sit on the cutting edge of the dirty war being waged between the property-owning classes and the revolutionary leftist groups – a struggle that may have substantial implications for the future evolution of Colombia's political system.

Significant emphasis has been placed on the financial nexus between the cocaine trade and insurgent groups. Substantial documentation supports the contention that FARC guerrillas tax and in certain cases directly manage coca cultivation and cocaine processing facilities (the majority of such laboratories produce cocaine base rather than cocaine hydrochloride). Yet, the Medellín-Cali syndicates – which obtain most of their crude cocaine from Bolivia and Peru and which account for most of Colombia's refined cocaine production – probably maintain few ties with the FARC. Most cocaine hydrochloride laboratories in Colombia are not protected (i.e., taxed) by the guerrillas. Many are located deep in the Amazon jungles along the Peru-Colombia-Brazil border, where virtually no guerrillas can be detected. Many other laboratories are located in regions such as the Middle Magdalena Valley, where traffickers hold a preponderance of power. To put the point somewhat differently, if Colombia halted coca cultivation tomorrow, the FARC's financial base would shrink considerably, and some independent cocaine operators would go out of business; however, the Medellín and Cali operations would not be greatly affected.

18

In sum, the narco-guerrilla connection has been exaggerated in Washington and in South American capitals. This is not to say that the connection is nonexistent, but it does depend on three determining factors.

First, the strength of the relationship is inversely proportional to (1) the economic, logistical, and military resources of the trafficking networks and (2) the strength of cooperative links among their members. The organizations based in Medellín and Cali, for example, have demonstrated their capabilities for joint actions, albeit primarily on an intra-city basis. Medellín and Cali have the wherewithal to defend most of their laboratories, supply routes, and cocaine shipments against predatory guerrilla groups. They maintain close ties with the power structure in some regions and can buy additional protection as necessary from local army units. Finally, the cartels' leaders and probably many of their members share the values of the property-owning classes and consequently detest the guerrillas on ideological grounds.

Colombian syndicates are archetypical mature criminal organizations. The structure of the Colombian cocaine industry differs from that of Peru, the other major cocaine-producing country with a guerrilla problem. Peruvian trafficking groups are relatively weak, disorganized, and dependent on Colombian groups for leadership, technical advice, and armed support. Peru harbors no self-conscious bourgeois narco-class comparable to that in Colombia or Bolivia. Cocaine traffickers have not yet developed a common anti-leftist agenda, nor have they established a close alliance with the propertied classes and the military. Considerable evidence documents turf disputes between Peruvian (and Colombian) traffickers and the Sendero Luminoso (Shining Path) guerrillas. However, Sendero has made inroads into the cocaine paste and base industry in the Upper Huallaga Valley by exploiting both conflicts between Peruvian traffickers and their sense of nationalism (i.e., their hostility toward the Colombian buyers). The trafficker-Sendero balance of power in the Upper Huallaga Valley now seemingly favors Sendero, which reportedly collects an estimated $5 million to $30 million each year by taxing the cocaine trade, largely shipments rather than laboratories. The significance of such payments must be viewed in context, however: Traffickers sometimes pay off local military commanders, the anti-narcotics police, and Sendero for the same planeloads of cocaine leaving the Valley. An informed U.S. source in Lima reports that for one shipment of cocaine flown out of the Uchiza district in mid-1988, traffickers paid bribes totaling $12,000: $5,000 to the local military command, $5,000 to the Uchiza branch of the Guardia Civil (national police), and $2,000 to Sendero front organizations.

A second and related axiom holds that the narco-guerrilla nexus is much stronger in the upstream phases of the industry (cultivation and low-level processing) than in the downstream phases (refining and distribution). Guerrillas in both Colombia and Peru provide political guidance and armed protection for coca-growing peasants who must contend with government eradication programs and exploitation by drug dealers. In Peru, for example, Sendero has established a high floor price for coca leaves in those areas under its control.

In Colombia, the FARC administered vast coca cultivation zones in several Colombian departments – Meta, Vichada, Vaupes, Guaviare, Caqueta, Putumayo, and Magdalena. The FARC probably controls or at least taxes most of the cocaine-base laboratories in these zones.[31] However, the FARC's presence in Colombian production of refined cocaine and export operations is still small; as already noted, the structure of the industry is dominated by two major coalitions that have little use for insurgents, and most hydrochloride laboratories do not seem top be located in FARC strongholds. Moreover, guerrillas tend to perceive traffickers, even low-level cocaine processors, as ideological enemies, as part of the bourgeois class (of course, this view does not preclude periodic opportunistic cooperation). For instance, some Peruvian traffickers have cut deals with Sendero, providing money to the guerrillas in return for the exclusive right to operate in a particular territory. However, the ideological split also precipitates conflicts, because traffickers resent paying extortion money to guerrillas and high prices to peasants for coca leaves.

The relationship between guerrillas and the cocaine industry obviously is complex, but a deep and murderous hostility undoubtedly exists between the primary refining-exporting coalitions and the Colombian revolutionary left. The evidence of such hostility is examined in more detail below.

Paramilitaries and the Dirty War
From a strategic standpoint, no clearer evidence of narco-guerrilla confrontation can be cited than the emerging Colombian paramilitary movement, which serves as an instrument for combatting guerrilla influence in certain regions of the country. The paramilitary movement also offers cocaine traffickers a vehicle for acquiring a modicum of social legitimacy. By supporting such paramilitary activities, cocaine dealers have cemented their ties with established groups in Colombian society, especially with the land-owning classes and right-wing military factions.

Armed self-defense organizations have operated in Colombia for some time, seeking to protect local communities against extortion, kidnapping, and other guerrilla practices. However, the self-defense movement suffered from a lack of equipment, training, and resources, so local landlords often had no alternative but to pay taxes to guerrillas.

Yet, this situation apparently changed to some degree, as Colombian cocaine barons invested some of their profits in acquiring vast tracts of land in the countryside – reportedly at least one million hectares of land in the past 5 years in Cordoba, Antioquia, Meta, and other Colombian departments. Many of

20

the recently purchased tracts of land lie in *zonas rojas* – areas where predatory guerrillas maintain a strong presence. Traffickers' *fincas*, ranches, and farms may house cocaine laboratories or may be purely legitimate operations; regardless, the new landed narco-gentry has found itself on the cutting edge of Colombia's guerrilla conflict.

This historically significant process has precipitated the revival and overhaul of the local self-defense forces or has created such forces where none previously existed. Cocaine barons or their representatives assumed the leadership of, and most of the financial responsibility for, such forces. Giving the devil his due, the narco-backed self-defense movement has been instrumental in dislodging communist guerrillas from certain regions of Colombia. As one Colombian official put it, "The truth is, where there are paramilitary with money from narcotrafficking, there are no guerrillas. The paramilitary forces are well-trained, well-paid, and bloodthirsty, and the guerrillas respect that."[32] Perhaps the clearest success story is the Puerto Boyacá, Puerto Triunfo, and Puerto Berrió region of the Middle Magdalena Valley, where the FARC maintained a strong presence in the early 1980s. The region has been progressively sanitized by paramilitary squads, with the tacit or active support of local landowners, politicians, businessmen, and military commanders. As a clandestine broadcast of Radio Patria Libra (a guerrilla radio station) plaintively noted in November 1988, "The narco-military republic of the Middle Magdalena region has control over the mayor's offices in nine municipalities and covers more than 20,000 square kilometers, equal in size to the Guajira department."[33]

By early 1989, reportedly some 13 paramilitary networks extended over eight Colombian departments[34] – in light of the traffickers' extensive land purchases in insecure rural areas, many networks were probably backed by drug money. Furthermore, the paramilitary movement is acquiring a political face. Puerto Boyacá, which calls itself the "anti-subversion capital of Colombia", is the center of a new political phenomenon, the so-called "Movement for National Restoration" (MORENA). As the ideological expression of the self-defense groups that operate in the Middle Magdalena Valley, MORENA aspires to "free our beloved country of the infamous communist guerrillas". MORENA is seeking status as a nationwide political party and plans to field its own presidential candidate in 1990 – such a strategy would accord MORENA roughly the same relationship to the paramilitary movement in Colombia as the Unión Patriótica has to the FARC. MORENA is not simply a front for cocaine traffickers, because legitimate landowners and businessmen also support it. (MORENA's leaders deny any connection with the cocaine trade.) Yet, the influence of cocaine traffickers, who have been prime movers in establishing the Middle Magdalena's self-defense network, almost certainly pervades MO-

RENA. Needless to say, traffickers could acquire substantial political legitimacy in Colombia if MORENA achieves the status of a nationwide political party.[35]

As the preceding discussion suggests, the cocaine industry has penetrated Colombian society on many levels, producing benefits of various kinds for a significant number of Colombians. To deliver a single mortal blow, a *gran golpe*, to the industry is probably next to impossible under the circumstances. Yet, although Colombia's cocaine multinationals possess formidable strengths, they are not indestructible; moreover, strategies can be fashioned that exploit the weaknesses of these organizations. Such strategies, however, will need to be more flexible and more sophisticated than those employed in Colombia in the past. A successful anti-cocaine strategy in the Colombian context will have to include elements of bargaining and diplomacy – elements that depart significantly from traditional U.S. concepts of drug law enforcement. The possible benefits of employing political approaches to fight the drug lords – and the possible risks associated with such approaches – will be assessed in the following section.

Dealing with the drug lords

Background

U.S. and Colombian anti-drug strategies to date have failed to restrict the flow of cocaine into international markets. An estimated 400 to 700 tons of refined cocaine still are exported annually from Colombia. An increasing percentage of these exports apparently is moving to Western Europe, where cocaine prices per kilo are two to three times what they are in the United States.[36] Meanwhile, the cocaine industry has amassed substantial economic, political, and military clout in the Andean countries – sometimes challenging the authority of governments and sometimes performing quasi-governmental functions in regions where the authority of the state is weak or nonexistent. In Colombia, the so-called cocaine cartels established in Medellín and Cali represent one of three major power aggregates in Colombia: The others are the Colombian government and the approximately 10,000 members of Colombia's two major guerrilla groups, the Revolutionary Armed Forces of Colombia (FARC) and the National Liberation Army (ELN).

Yet, despite its formidable power, the cocaine industry is not invulnerable. Recognizable choke points include the high level of geographic and organizational concentration of refining and exporting functions. The Medellín and Cali coalitions handle the vast majority of the cocaine sold on world markets. The people essential to the cartels' operation – suppliers, managers,

22

laboratory operators, transporters, money launderers, and the like – probably number no more than 500 to 1,000, compared to an estimated 200,000 to 300,000 cultivators of coca fields in South America and 20,000 to 30,000 proprietors of coca-paste laboratories (that is, first-stage processors of cocaine). Furthermore, most Colombian drug lords, even the violent Medellín Extraditables, aspire to the middle class, and many would abandon the cocaine business if given the opportunity – witness the insistent pressure by the Extraditables for negotiations with the government. Despite the occasional belligerence of their public statements, the drug lords espouse clearly evident political aims: accommodation with the government, an end to extradition to the United States, and the chance for reintegration into Colombian society. (In contrast, Colombia's Marxist guerrillas seek to overthrow the government and fundamentally change Colombian society.) As a former Colombian cabinet minister who served as an intermediary between the government and the Medellín cartel noted, "They have much money, but they are not free men. They are capable of anything, even retirement, provided they can get their freedom."[37]

Conventional law enforcement strategies can exploit such vulnerabilities – the concentration of downstream trafficking functions and the bourgeois intentions of the drug kingpins themselves – only so far. Since the assassination of Luis Carlos Galan in August 1989, the Colombian government has unleashed a wide-ranging crackdown on the Medellín cartel, including resuming extraditions to the United States; seizing traffickers' estates, laboratories, and aircraft; confiscating their bank accounts; and mounting a massive manhunt to capture Medellín kingpin Pablo Escobar and his key associates. Such hard-line policies were initially successful in disrupting the Medellín cartel's trafficking operations, and they doubtless made a high-level career in cocaine trafficking less attractive to many Colombians. These same policies, however, are producing diminishing returns and may well harbor pitfalls that are only beginning to materialize.

For example, by the fall of 1990, Colombian cocaine production had returned to an estimated 90 percent or more of pre-August 1989 levels, and some of the cartel's refining capacity had been relocated to less-restrictive neighboring countries, such as Brazil, Ecuador, and Peru. By the fall of 1990, coca leaf prices in Peru's Upper Huallaga Valley and the Bolivian Chapare had rebounded significantly, a sign that Colombian traffickers were revamping their supply network. (The price for coca leaves in the Andes ranged between 10 cents and 15 cents a pound in the winter and spring of 1990; by September and October, the price had risen to between 50 cents and 70 cents per pound.[38]) Such trends suggest two possible explanations: either the Medellín cartel is succesfully reconfiguring its operations, or – perhaps more likely – the Medellín cartel's clashes with the authorities are opening the door for the rival Cali coalition to capture a larger share of the cocaine business. (According to U.S. narcotics experts in Bogotá, the two cartels today hold roughly equal percentages of the world cocaine market; the percentage ratio before the crackdown reportedly was 75 to 25 in favor of Medellín.) Also worrisome is the Colombian government's failure to apprehend Pablo Escobar, despite a series of encirclement campaigns coordinated by thousands of Colombian soldiers, the Department of Administrative Security (DAS), and public troops. This continuing fiasco suggests that the traffickers have established an extensive informant network by infiltrating the command and control systems of the military and the national police.

Furthermore, from Colombia's perspective, the current drug war is a losing proposition politically, economically, and militarily. Many ordinary Colombians, weary of the violence that is shredding their society, believe that the government should reach an accommodation with the drug lords. According to a February 1990 ABC-Washington Post-Harris poll, 49 percent of Colombians favor negotiations with traffickers, although 43 percent are opposed. A poll conducted in 20 cities for the Bogotá newspaper *Semana* in November 1990 showed that a majority of Colombian's (61.8 percent) favored granting amnesty to traffickers; according to the same survey, an even larger majority (81.3 percent) would accept an Extraditable as a cabinet minister if such a step would bring peace to Colombia.[38]

In addition, Colombia's economic prosperity is fragile. Colombia's economic growth rate dropped from 3.7 percent in 1988 to 3.2 percent in 1989. (The economy is expected to grow slightly faster in 1990, largely because of significantly higher prices for oil, Colombia's chief export.) Between January and September 1990, foreign investment in Colombia plummeted by 68 percent compared to the same period in 1989. Tourism also suffered – restaurant sales, passenger air traffic, and hotel occupancy rates registered steep declines from 1989 to 1990. Such losses are largely attributable to the tremendous rise in narcoterrorism during the government's 16-month crackdown on the Medellín cartel.[40]

Moreover, the drug war probably has invigorated Colombia's various insurgent groups. This year, the FARC and the ELN launched major offensives to expand their power base in the Middle Magdalena Valley, northern Antioquia, the Peru-Ecuador border region (Putumayo department), and elsewhere. The deteriorating state of Colombia's internal security is partly explained by the assignment of at least one-fifth of Colombia's 125,000-man army to occupying narcotraficante estates, performing housekeeping functions such as feeding the animals in Pablo Escobar's zoo.[41] Thousands more undoubtedly are dedicated to chasing Escobar and his colleagues and to guarding people and installations targeted by the narcoterrorists. The government's crackdown also helped the guerrillas by undermining some of the

24

anti-communist paramilitary groups organized and funded by Medellín drug lords. Since the early 1980s, such paramilitary organizations have been instrumental in crippling guerrilla infrastructures in areas where traffickers maintain landed estates, but the paramilitaries lack leadership and funds now that their patrons are dead or in hiding. A few paramilitary groups have actually disbanded, creating a power vacuum of sorts and enabling guerrillas to return to their former strongholds.

Such worrisome trends suggest two conclusions. First, current strategies for controlling the cocaine traffic pose a high risk of failure. Second, curtailing the cocaine trade could inflict significant damage on Colombian society. For Washington and Bogotá, the challenge is crafting a mixed strategy that weakens and disrupts the cocaine multinationals without doing violence to Colombia's other needs and priorities. Such a policy mix must go beyond controversial law enforcement – or militarized law enforcement supported by U.S. helicopters, weapons, and advisers – to incorporate political tools for battling the drug traffic. Such political measures arguably can produce results where frontal assault on the cocaine industry have failed.

Broadly defined, the concept of political solutions encompasses a range of options from incarcerating or obliterating the drug lords to outright legalizing the narcotics industry. More specifically, political options include (1) measures that encourage key traffickers to withdraw voluntarily from the cocaine business and (2) the concurrent elimination of cocaine refining capacity and international trafficking networks. Effecting the retirement of traffickers might require using both tools that are relatively common in U.S. crime fighting, such as plea bargaining and witness protection programs, and other instruments that are relatively unfamiliar, such as grants of amnesty to major criminal figures. In any case, a peaceful solution would be characterized by a degree of negotiation between the government (usually represented by the law enforcement branch) and the criminal underworld.

Under the leadership of the new president, Cesar Gaviria Trujillo, the Colombian government clearly is moving toward more flexible treatment of drug dealers. For instance, in September 1990, the government offered drug dealers the option of accepting sentences reduced by one-third and guarantees against extradition to the United States on the condition that they surrender to the authorities and confess to all their crimes in Colombia and abroad. (These conditions were stipulated in government decree 2047, issued in early September.) If they implicated other participants in their crimes – that is, turned state's evidence – their sentences would be cut in half. However, the traffickers showed little initial interest in this offer. One sticking point arose from the government's offering an olive branch to Marxist guerrilla groups while categorizing traffickers and rightist paramilitary groups as ordinary criminals who are subject to prosecution and incarceration. Until very recently, the Extradit-

25

ables apparently were demanding the same political treatment accorded to guerrilla groups – in short, a general amnesty (total immunity from prosecution). However, in an offer published in the Colombian news media on November 23, the traffickers expressed their willingness to settle for a surrender formula that would differentiate them from common criminals – their communique defined drug trafficking and narcoterrorism as collective rather than individual crimes – but still require them to submit to trial by Colombian courts.[42]

Granting formal amnesty to drug dealers clearly would be politically difficult for the Colombian government: International pressure, particularly from the United States, certainly would prevent Colombia from unilaterally taking such as step. In addition, the government legally and morally could not offer the same treatment to an arch-villain such as Pablo Escobar – the intellectual author of numerous bombings and assassinations – that it would accord to a lower-profile trafficker such as the Cali cartel's Gilberto Rodriguez Orejuela.

Still, realizing a collective withdrawal of traffickers from the cocaine business will require more attractive terms than those thus far proposed by the Colombian government. Because the leaders of the cocaine industry are not currently imprisoned and because they are in many cases protected by members of the police and the military, the government cannot militarily impose a settlement. A negotiated solution represents the only recourse.

In fact, the government apparently is willing to meet the traffickers halfway. In a letter published on November 23, the same day that the traffickers' communique was issued, the Colombian Justice Minister reported that traffickers need only "confess to one of any crimes committed inside or outside of the country" to receive reduced sentences and guarantees against extradition. Moreover, he reassured the traffickers that they would not be required to inform on their accomplices to obtain such benefits. In other words, a kingpin such as Pablo Escobar might plead guilty to, say, transporting a few kilograms of cocaine inside Colombia, be sentenced for that crime, and never face trial on more serious charges, for example, masterminding numerous murders and kidnappings or arranging the export of hundreds of tons of cocaine to the United States.[43] In addition, under the proposed deal, the traffickers would not have to reveal even the most basic information about their organizations, such as who the members are and what roles they perform. Responding to the Extraditables" demand that they be housed in a special compound, the Colombian Justice Minister offered to provide "decent accommodations". According to a recent account in the *Philadelphia Inquirer*, the government is building a deluxe prison in which "apartments with balconies and sculptured archways would be available", and prisoners would be allowed to furnish them with televisions, videocassette recorders, and other luxuries.[44] In yet another benevolent gesture, the government announced on January 27, 1991, that its

26

offer of shorter jail terms and immunity from extradition extended until the moment of a drug trafficker's surrender. (The original offer only covered crimes committed before September 5, 1990.) Thus, the government provided the strongest assurance yet that traffickers who surrender and confess can escape extradition, the fate they fear most.

The negotiation option

On four occasions – in May 1984, September 1988, January 1990, and November 1990 – a major group of Colombian traffickers made formal offers to abandon the narcotics business and relinquish assets used in the industry (such as laboratories, planes, and airstrips) to the Colombian government. In exchange, the traffickers sought concessions from the authorities – for example, revisions in the U.S.-Colombian extradition treaty, an outright end to extradition, and a general amnesty. The first offer, a written statement addressed directly to President Belisario Betancur, was presented to Colombian Attorney General Carlos Jimenez Gomez in Panama in May 1984. Jimenez met in Panama City's Hotel Soloy with Jorge Ochoa, Pablo Escobar, and Gonzalo Rodriguez Gacha, who purportedly represented 100 of Colombia's top narco-mafiosi. At that time, the traffickers were on the run because of the massive government crackdown mounted after the April 1984 assassination of Rodrigo Lara Bonilla, Colombia's Justice Minister. The document proposed "to eliminate once and forever any drug trafficking in our country" and asked the president to "consider the possibility of our reinstatement in Colombian society in the near future". In the "Suggestions" section of the document, the traffickers requested revisions in the extradition section of the document, the traffickers requested revisions in the extradition treaty, an exemption for crimes committed before the revision, and the right to appeal extradition decisions to the Colombian State Court, the country's supreme administrative court.[45] Nothing ever came of the traffickers' proposal, in part because of the overwhelmingly negative reaction of Colombia's political establishment. Political leaders from every political party – liberals, new liberals, and conservatives – virtually unanimously expressed open and categorical opposition to a dialogue with drug traffickers. Carlos Holguin Sardi, the conservative president of the Colombian Senate, summarized the view of the majority when he observed, "[Negotiations] where criminal law is concerned . . . would mean the total disintegration of our legal order and institutions."[46] Furthermore, the U.S. Embassy in Bogotá and the U.S. Department of State were unsympathetic to the idea of negotiation with traffickers. According to the Bogotá newspaper *Semana*, Jimenez Gomez informally communicated the substance of the drug lords' offer to Alexander Watson, then the deputy chief of mission, who replied, "I will send the mesage [to Washington], but I see no possibility of an arrangement." Several days later, Jimenez received via the Embassy a State Department telex outlining U.S. objections to the proposal. The Betancur government in effect capitulated to this strong domestic and international pressure, and in July the president announced that there never would be "any kind of understanding" between the government and the signers of the Panama memorandum.[47]

The second proposal by the traffickers was drafted in response to a September 1988 speech by President Virgilio Barco outlining a peace initiative that seemingly held out the possibility of a government-trafficker accord. The initiative called for "resolving all of the different forms and manifestations of violence, not only those generated by guerrillas". However, the government later denied that this message was directed at the Medellín cartel. For about a year, from Mid-September 1988 until Galan's funeral on August 20, 1989, the Colombian government conducted an indirect dialogue with the leaders of the Medellín cartel. German Montoya, the secretary of the presidency, and Joaquin Vallejo Arbelaez, a former cabinet minister who represented the drug lords, reputedly held 10 meetings during that year to discuss the traffickers' proposals, which had hardened perceptibly since 1984. By the end of the decade, the traffickers were demanding an end to extradition and a pardon as the quid pro quo for their retirement from drug trafficking.[48]

These talks did not progress very far, partly because of Montoya's insistence that the United States must be a party to any substantive negotiations or peace agreement with the drug dealers. Montoya may have been stalling his adversaries: While the conversations with Vallejo were proceeding, the Colombian army and police were conducting a highly effective campaign ("Operation Primavera") against the Medellín cartel's cocaine infrastructure. That operation destroyed hundreds of cocaine laboratories and netted seizures of more than 30 tons of cocaine hydrochloride and more than 2 million gallons of chemicals – such as ether, acetone, and methyl ethyl ketone – that are essential to manufacturing cocaine.[49] Some Colombian observers believe that the Medellín drug lords arranged the murder of Galan because of what they perceived as the government's insincerity during the Montoya-Vallejo dialogue the preceding year.

The third and fourth offers from the traffickers came during the bloodiest phase of Colombia's drug war. The government was applying intense pressure to the Medellín mafia, and the traffickers were escalating their campaign of violence against the state. (After August, the traffickers began committing acts of terrorism – bombings and kidnappings – that were hitherto primarily the province of leftist guerrillas.) The Extraditables delivered both offers to the government after consultations via intermediaries with a group of Colombian political figures, the so-called Los Notables (see Table 1). Ex-presi-

28

dent Alfonso Lopez Michelsen apparently played a leading role in these discussions. Michelsen had met with Jorge Ochoa and Pablo Escobar in Panama in May 1984, several days before their meetings with Carlos Jimenez Gomez. In both cases, the Notables, apparently with the government's blessing, were trying to accomplish two tasks: negotiating terms for the Extraditables' surrender and effecting the release of a number of hostages, among them sons and daughters of prominent Colombian families, held hostage by the traffickers. Such hostages included Alvaro Diego Montoya, the son of the president's secretary; Francisco Santos, the news editor of *El Tiempo*; the son of that paper's publisher; and Diana Turbay, the daughter of former president Julio Cesar Turbay Ayala. Most Colombian observers believe that these hostages were seized to strengthen the traffickers' negotiating position – to give substance to their demands for special political treatment by the government.

In their January 1990 peace initiative, the traffickers announced acceptance of "the triumph of the state and of the existing legal order" and promised to end drug shipments and turn over their weapons and laboratories in return for unspecified "constitutional and legal guarantees".[50] They declared a unilateral truce (which lasted about 2 months), and released several hostages, including Alvaro Montoya. The Barco Administration, however, did not respond favorably to this initiative, although it did suspend extraditions of drug criminals for roughly the period that the traffickers halted their campaign of bombings, kidnappings, and assassinations. The drug peace broke down in late March because of the murder of a leftist presidential candidate and the government's decision to resume extraditions. Narcoterrorism again plagued Colombia for several months. In August and September, the Extraditables kidnapped more members of the Colombian elite, including Diana Turbay and Francisco Santos. In October, the Notables once again offered to serve as intermediaries, effectively unofficial negotiators, on behalf of the Colombian government. In November, the Extraditables delivered a new offer: Approximately 200 to 300 Medellín traffickers would surrender to the authorities and would cease their trafficking and terrorist activities. In return, the traffickers made

Table 1. Los Notables.

Alfonso Lopez Michelsen	Ex-President of the Republic
Misael Pastrana Borrero	Ex-President of the Republic
Julio Cesar Turbay Ayala[1]	Ex-President of the Republic
Monseñor Mario Revollo Bravo	First Archbishop of Colombia
Diego Montaña Cuéllar	Leader, Unión Patriótica

[1] Turbay, whose daughter Diana was kidnapped by the Extraditables in August 1990, did not participate in the round of negotiations leading to the Extraditables' offer of November 23.

several demands: (1) trial by appropriate Colombian courts (in effect, no extradition to the United States), (2) no requirement for traffickers to confess to their crimes or to denounce one another, (3) a special detention center where they could be protected against revenge or reprisals, relying on third parties, the Colombian army or navy, Medellín municipal police, or an international human rights agency.[51] In another communique published just a day later, the Extraditables promised to release their hostages if the government respected their human rights and the rights of their families. The demands of the Extraditables for special treatment stemmed from a novel legal argument: Drug trafficking and narcoterrorism are collective concerns, similar to political acts such as rebellion, so traffickers cannot be punished as ordinary criminals.[52]

The traffickers' new proposals produced a state of near-euphoria in Colombia. Lopez Michelson observed in a radio interview, "The country had never been so close to peace." The Colombian Justice Minister declared, "I believe we are at the threshold of a transcendental occurrence that will bring peace to Colombia."[53] Such optimism seemed partly justified: On December 18, Fabio Ochoa Vasquez, a member of the notorious Ochoa clan and one of the DEA's 12 most wanted traffickers turned himself in to the Colombian authorities, saying:

I have decided to surrender on my own, in the hope that this action will contribute to finding the path that Colombians of all stations in life demand. I hope that this path will be broader, more understanding, more conciliatory, and more Christian.[54]

Fabio's two brothers – Jorge Luis and Juan David – surrendered in early 1991. However, other important Extraditables, including Pablo Escobar – reputedly the leader of the Medellín cartel – are still at large and apparently are trying to negotiate with the Colombian government for more generous terms. In addition, the murders in late January 1991 of two prominent hostages held by the Extraditables – Diana Turbay, a daughter of a former Colombian president, and Marina Montoya, sister of a former presidential aide – represent a grim reminder that the Extraditables are still willing to employ violence as a political tool.[55]

The Colombian government's increasingly flexible stance vis-a-vis the drug dealers reflects a significant shift in the attitudes of Colombia's political establishment. For instance, Joaquin Vallejo, who represented the Medellín cartel in the 1988–1989 conversations with the government, wrote about the Panama discussions in a column in *El Tiempo* in May 1989, observing that "no possible justification" could be cited for a dialogue with traffickers. "Apart from the problems of moral principles," he said, "there remains doubt about

30

whether they [the narcotraficantes] would keep their promises."[56] Similarly,
Juan Gomez Martinez, the former mayor of Medellín, wrote as the director of
El Colombiano in July 1984:

> Colombia is shuddering to learn about the proposal for a dialogue between
> the lords of vice and the government. This is an insolent, immoral, and
> destructive proposal. The entire society repudiates the possibility [of such a
> dialogue].[57]

By late 1989 and early 1990, most polls documented that Colombians were
increasingly disenchanted with the Barco government's hard-line policies. A
consistent two-thirds of all respondents opposed extradition, for example, and
were increasingly open to the possibility of a negotiated solution to the drug
war. In the 1990 presidential elections, Cesar Gaviria apparently was the only
candidate who definitely ruled out the option of negotiating with trafficker,
and Gaviria won by a less-than-overwhelming 47.5 percent of the vote. Now
the government seemingly is ready to abandon extradition – for years, a staple
of U.S.-Colombian anti-drug policy – and to make further concessions to halt
the narcoterrorist violence that is ravaging Colombian society. The United
States obviously cannot continue to ignore these important political shifts. The
question may no longer be whether an accommodation will be reached with
the drug lords, but rather how, when, and on what terms. Washington should
not be debating the merits of negotiating with traffickers – the United States
must actively engage the issue or risk being overtaken by events.

Defining the U.S. role

Negotiating with drug dealers is an abhorrent concept to most North Americans. Yet, if the United States excludes itself for moral or political reasons
from what is now an ongoing if indirect process in Colombia, the result is likely
to be counterproductive. Rather, Washington should seek to insert its own
priorities into Colombia's narco-dialogue. Washington's drug-fighting objectives are not the same as Bogotá's. For the United States, the chief goal is
reducing the flow of Colombian cocaine into North American markets. For
Colombia, as President Cesar Gaviria reportedly emphasizes, ending narcoterrorism – "the principal threat against our democracy"[58] – constitutes a much
higher priority than terminating the drug traffic per se, which Colombia
defines as an international problem that will abate as the consuming countries
lower their demand for narcotics. Consequently, Colombia views the dialogue
with drug traffickers more as a means of reducing societal violence than a tool
for controlling the production and export of cocaine. The United States thus

31

should actively guide and shape the negotiating agenda to ensure that a final settlement will significantly undermine Colombia's trafficking syndicates and simultaneously disrupt the long-term viability of the world cocaine market.

What provisions would be included in such a settlement? Ideally, the accord would be far-reaching, encompassing not only the Medellín Extraditables, now the most vocal proponent of a drug peace, but also the Cali coalition and other smaller quasi-independent trafficking groups based in Bogotá and Pereria and on the north coast. The recent government crackdown has largely disregarded the relatively low-profile Cali cartel, which, unlike its Medellín cousin, has generally avoided attacking the establishment. No manhunts dogged the Cali leaders, no rewards were posted for their capture (compared to $ 625,000 in rewards offered in 1989 for information leading to the arrest of Pablo Escobar and Gonzalo Rodriguez Gacha), and relatively few of their assets were seized by the Colombian authorities. This selective persecution of the Medellín mafia enabled the Cali group to flourish by expanding production and establishing new distribution networks, especially in western Europe. The Cali model, which fosters official tolerance for traffickers who do not threaten the state, obviously must not prevail in any peace settlement. Like their Medellín counterparts, the Cali leaders must be forced or negotiated out of the cocaine business.

In addition, a negotiated solution should exhibit depth as well as breadth, addressing most of the 500 to 1,000 middle managers of the main Colombian cartels, because such people have extensive experience in cocaine production, smuggling, transportation, marketing, and money laundering. Moreover, the cartels' private armies and teams of assassins must be disbanded. Obviously, measures such as terminating extraditions to the United States and granting amnesty or some other political options to drug dealers would serve little purpose if they only enabled the chief executives of the cocaine industry to return ot their homes, spend their fortunes, and live openly in Colombia. Of course, important uncertainties abound: Can a relatively small number of leading traffickers shut down a significant percentage of Colombia's cocaine-refining capacity, or is the industry too balkanized for a negotiated settlement to have much effect? The proposed surrender of 200 to 300 Extraditables is an encouraging sign, but the actual roles that these traffickers play in managing cocaine operations remain to be seen.

Furthermore, a negotiated settlement that is designed to inflict substantial long-term damage on the Colombian cocaine industry would have to incorporate the following conditions.

First, traffickers would need to furnish U.S. and Colombian authorities with information on cocaine suppliers, laboratory sites, smuggling networks, transportation systems, cocaine distribution centers in the United States and western Europe, and overseas bank accounts. Narcotraffickers also would have to

32

describe the inner workings of their organizations, such as the drug cartels' techniques for recruiting members, paying off public officials, making business decisions, and planning acts of violence such as major bombings, kidnappings, and assassinations. Unfortunately, these objectives would not be accommodated by the Extraditables' new offer, which explicitly rejects confessing to crimes and implicating colleagues. Moreover, the government has opted to accept these terms in large measure. In other words, the traffickers do not intend to supply testimony that would produce a more comprehensive picture of cocaine trafficking organizations and their allied enterprises. Even the organizational composition and trafficking functions of the surrendering group would not be known with any certainty.

Second, traffickers would have no relinquish most of the estimated $10 billion to $20 billion that they have stashed in foreign banks. The most appropriate use of this money would be repairing the damage caused by their illicit trade, for example, by funding crop substitution programs and drug rehabilitation projects and by compensating the families of the victims of the Extraditables. In their 1984 proposal, the traffickers offered the "return of our capital to Colombia as soon as formulas enabling this to be done have been worked out".[59] Unfortunately, this provision was not included in subsequent offers. If their huge caches of money abroad are preserved, traffickers could continue funding cocaine laboratories (perhaps locating most new refining operations outside of Colombia), managing distribution networks, and purchasing lethal weapons.

Third, a system of verification would be essential, because the United States and Colombia have no basis for believing that the traffickers would keep their promises. A newly established international commission of law enforcement and intelligence experts would need to monitor the dismantling of cocaine laboratories and transportation systems, document the transfer of traffickers' capital from foreign tax havens, and oversee the surrender of arms caches. Sustaining the drug peace would depend largely on the effectiveness of new technologies – applied with the newly acquired knowledge of drug trade operations – in detecting hidden jungle laboratories, drug-smuggling aircraft, cocaine in cargo containers, flow of narcodollars, and the like. Unfortunately, Colombia's narco-dialogue so far has virtually ignored the verification issue, which is a very serious – and for the United States an unacceptable – omission.

A negotiated settlement of the type outlined above would be inconceivable without U.S. participation and support. The verification and compliance provisions, for instance, would depend substantially on U.S. advice, funds, and technological expertise. The United States already has or is rapidly developing technical tools that could support a monitoring regime – for example, remote sensors that can detect cocaine laboratories, heat-sensitive laser readers that can pick out the chemical signatures of chemicals used in cocaine laboratories, techniques for chemically tagging shipments of specific chemicals, vapor sniffers that can help detect cocaine in cargo, computer programs that can analyze bank records for dirty money, and various radar devices that can monitor air traffic in Colombia's vast plains and jungles.[60] Obviously, drug control verification will parallel arms control verification in the raising of sensitive issues of sovereignty. For example, Colombia might have to concede to overflights of its territory, inspections of suspected laboratory sites, and other intrusive practices. The United States and Colombia will have to craft appropriate arrangements for sharing verification technologies.

In addition, the United States should help Colombia enforce a drug peace by continuing to strengthen that country's criminal justice institutions, which currently are no match for the cocaine industry, probably the most powerful criminal enterprise in the world. As many arms control specialists have argued, verification is essentially meaningless without a policy that punishes significant cheating by the adversary.[61] Such support would include continuing assistance programs for drug law enforcement – supplying training, equipment, intelligence support, and the like to organizations that have proved especially successful in anti-narcotics operations, such as (1) the DAS and the F-2 department of the national police, which are charged with investigating criminal groups, and (2) the elite corps (Cuerpo Elite) of the national police, a paramilitary force of 2,500 hand-picked men that conducted the December 1989 raid that killed Medellín kingpin Gonzalo Rodriguez Gacha. At the same time, the United States can scale back its aid to Andean military establishments. Despite massive infusions of U.S. assistance (about $100 million in 1988 and 1989), the Colombian military is not a particularly effective instrument for enforcing drug laws. Indeed, in Colombia and Peru, the military's counterinsurgency measures often interfere with the prosecution of drug dealers. Furthermore, such demilitarization of U.S. aid probably would create a more conducive atmosphere for negotiating and implementing a formal settlement with the traffickers.

In the same vein, the United States whould take decisive steps to fortify Colombia's beleaguered judiciary. "Antiquated, undertrained, underpaid, and unprotected, the system is in an acknowledged state of collapse," noted a U.S. Congressional report in August 1990.[62] Only about 1 percent of those charged with narcotics offenses in Colombia are ever convicted.[63] Colombia needs help in drafting more effective anti-drug legislation, which might include stronger conspiracy statutes, stiffer penalties for drug trafficking, and laws (in contrast to government decrees) that permit seizures of criminally obtained assets. The judiciary must be professionalized by establishing special cadres of judges who hear only drug cases, compensating such judges adequately, and furnishing sufficient clerical support. Court systems will require modern word processing and data processing equipment and improved statistical procedures

34

to manage their huge backlog of cases effectively. Furthermore, shielding judges and their families against syndicate hit squads obviously ranks as a first-order priority that, in the view of the government, would require secure underground bunkers for both the judges and their dependents. (Such facilities are furnished for magistrates trying mafia cases in Italy.) To accomplish these tasks, U.S. aid to the Colombian judiciary, which now amounts to only about $3 million a year, would have to expand considerably.

Finally, the United States must encourage the Colombian government not to yield the prerogative to extradite drug traffickers to the United States. Extradition is an important weapon in the struggle against drug trafficking – and probably constitutes the sanction that the drug lords fear most. The new Constituent Assembly, a body elected in December 1990 that is charged with revising Colombia's constitution, will seek to impose a constitutional ban on extradition – a revision that should not be allowed. If Colombia's intention is to achieve a negotiated settlement with the traffickers, the loss of the extradition tool will seriously undermine the government's bargaining position.

Political issues

The sheer novelty of the negotiation option makes it politically indigestible. Governments frequently cut deals of various kinds with criminals – such as plea bargains and witness protection arrangements – to advance specific law enforcement and intelligence objectives. However, few if any real precedents apply to dealing with a powerful criminal class such as the Colombian cocaine mafia or to negotiating with criminals to end a specific illegal activity. Yet, Colombia's shadow dialogue with the Medellín cartel and the Gaviria government's willingness to abandon the extradition of acknowledged drug dealers to the United States apparently enjoy broad political support. In contrast to 1984, few Colombian political figures now contend that a deal with the traffickers is immoral, outrageous, or unworkable. Moreover, Colombia's successful negotiations with the M-19 guerrillas earlier this year raised Colombian expectations for a political settlement of the drug issue and intensified fears that if the government does not grant amnesty to the Medellín Extraditables as it did to the M-19, the traffickers will be motivated to earn comparable political treatment by emulating insurgents and continuing their campaign of violence against the state.

At the same time, a successful accord with Colombian drug dealers must satisfy a number of different objectives: ending narcoterrorist violence against the state, enticing a sufficient proportion of the skilled echelons of the Medellín and Cali coalitions to defect from the cocaine business, and ensuring the state's prerogative to dispense justice. These goals are to some extent in-

35

compatible. Even if traffickers do surrender – and to date only the Ochoa brothers have taken this step – they are unlikely to confess their crimes, divulge their organizational secrets, repatriate their capital, and disband their private armies unless the government grants them some kind of amnesty. The Cali leaders probably would not even contemplate surrendering to the government without a full pardon. So far the government has offered only to cease extraditions and reduce prison sentences. If the government raised the ante and offered traffickers the opportunity to escape jail sentences, the political risks would escalate: Quite apart from the reaction of world opinion, many Colombians would question a peace settlement that allowed traffickers to get off scot free.

The case of Pablo Escobar highlights this dilemma. Traffickers allegedly masterminded (1) the assassination of several prominent Colombian leaders, from Colombian Justice Minister Rodrigo Lara Bonilla in 1984 to the Liberal party's 1989 presidential candidate Luis Carlos Galan, and (2) the recent campaigns of bombings and kidnappings in Colombia's major cities. A deal with Escobar would be a controversial and even dangerous political maneuver. On the other hand, not pardoning Escobar, generally acknowledged as the most prominent figure in the Medellín coalition, would complicate the authorities' attempts to destroy the cocaine networks and military groups that Escobar controls. In effect, the more just a settlement is in moral and legal terms, the less effective it is as an instrument for combatting the cocaine trade.

To resolve this dilemma, the Colombian government might opt for a negotiating formula that distinguishes pardonables from unpardonables. If the political calculus of a successful deal with Escobar may be unfavorable, but negotiating with other key actors in the Colombian cocaine trade, such as the Cali kingpins and possibly the Ochoa brothers, is more palatable. The government also might grant leniency, up to and including a pardon, to those Medellín Extraditables who have distanced themselves from the violent tactics of Escobar and his key associates. The split within the Medellín cartel is now well documented. As a dissident factor of the Extraditables wrote in an April 1990 letter to *El Tiempo*:

> We dealers ourselves are in complete disagreement with the terrorist acts ordered presumably by Pablo Escobar – we reject publicly before the Colombian people the conduct of Pablo Escobar, which harms the goals of our struggle.[64]

Pressure from the conservative members of the cocaine establishment might compel Escobar to withdraw from the cocaine business and perhaps even to surrender himself to justice.

To give traffickers amnesty might require a change in Colombia's constitu-

36

tion. According to Article 119 of the current constitution, the president has the power to grant pardons for "political crimes". Yet, Colombian law and jurisprudence still define drug trafficking and narcoterrorism as conventional crimes. Perhaps a broader formula – comparable to the one in the U.S. Constitution (Article 2 , Section 2) that empowers the President to "grant reprieves and pardons for offenses against the United States" – might be adapted to the Colombian case.

From the U.S. perspective, the recent history of the Colombian drug war permits several conclusions. First, conventional law enforcement strategies are not winning the war against cocaine. Second, such strategies no longer have the support of the Colombian public. Third, under certain circumstances, a negotiated settlement might precipitate significant long-term disruptions in the cocaine industry. Fourth, the United States must participate in the cocaine industry. Fourth, the United States must participate in shaping and defining the terms of such a settlement. For the United States, blocking the extradition of the 80 to 100 Colombians wanted in the United States for drug offenses and granting conditional amnesty to most drug kingpins would sacrifice certain U.S. objectives in the drug war. Yet, such steps would be a relatively small price to pay for reducing the 400 or more tons of cocaine that annually stream into American streets, schools, homes, and workplaces. Granted, as long as the demand for drugs remains, other suppliers will eventually satisfy that market, but the key word is eventually. The sophisticated drug networks now in place were built over the course of a decade or more. If successfully dismantled, the business could not be reestablished overnight. Moreover, a major reduction in Colombian refining capacity would wreak havoc with the cocaine industry upstream, forcing a massive shift of peasants away from coca cultivation: The market for coca leaves would, of course, shrink drastically, and prices would fall through the floor, inducing many of the 250,000 or more coca-farming families to switch to legal cash crops or to enter legitimate non-agricultural occupations. In other words, the cocaine production-logistics chain would be seriously ruptured. In the meantime, U.S. and Andean law enforcement officials, educators, and health care workers would have unprecedented opportunities and resources (including billions of dollars in illegal profits) for attacking the remaining drug suppliers, reducing demand, and in general making the narcotics business less attractive to dealers and users alike.

Notes

1. On cultivation, see: U.S. Department of State. *International Narcotics Control Strategy Report*. Washington, D.C.: U.S. Government Printing Office. March 1, 1991, p. 22.
2. The State Department's Bureau of International Narcotics Matters estimates that potential

37

cocaine production in South America was 700 to 890 tons in 1990. Ibid., p. 10. Subtracting 200 tons, which represents worldwide seizures, from the lower-bound estimate of 700 tons leaves 500 tons, a conservative estimate of South America's net exports of cocaine. Assuming that the cartels produce or handle at least 70 percent of this volume – assuming that 80 percent of the cartels' product is sold in the United States for $ 20,000 a kilo and the remaining 20 percent is sold in Europe for $ 40,000 a kilo – the cartels would gross $ 8.4 billion from international cocaine sales.

3. U.S. Senate, Permanent Subcommittee on Investigations, *Structure of International Drug Cartels*. Hearings: Staff Statement. (Washington, D.C.: U.S. Government Printing Office, September 12, 1989), p. 14.

4. Ibid., p. 19.

5. Ibid., p. 24.

6. Ibid., p. 28.

7. Tina Rosenberg, "The Kingdom of Cocaine," *The New Republic*, November 27, 1989, p. 28. U.S. Senate Committee on Foreign Relations, Subcommittee on Terrorism, Narcotics, and International Communications. *Drugs, Law Enforcement, and Foreign Policy*. Hearings, Part. 2 (Washington, D.C.: U.S. Government Printing Office, April 4–7, 1988), p. 177.

8. Michael Isikoff, "2 Colombians Held in Missile Scheme," *The Washington Post*, May 8, 1990, p. 00 A.

9. "Basque Terrorist Group Directed Car Bomb Attack," Hamburg DPA 1859 GMT, December 8, 1989.

10. U.S. Senate Committee on Foreign Relations, Subcommittee on Terrorism, Narcotics, and International Communications. *Drugs, Law Enforcement, and Foreign Policy: Panama*. Hearings, Part 2. (Washington, D.C.: U.S. Government Printing Office, February 8–11, 1988), p. 33.

11. "Opening Statement of William M. Baker," *Structure of International Drug Cartels*, op. cit., p. 7.

12. "Statement of David L. Westrate," *Structure of International Drug Cartels*, op. cit., p. 3.

13. Guy Gugliotta and Jeff Leen. *Kings of Cocaine* (New York: Simon and Schuster, 1989), p. 322.

14. Rensselaer W. Lee. *The White Labyrinth: Cocaine and Political Power* (New Brunswick: Transaction Publishers, 1989), pp. 113–117. See also: *Kings of Cocaine*, op. cit., p. 320.

15. William R. Long, "Unlike Their Medellín Brethren, They Shun Open Violence; The Cali Cartel: Colombia's Gentlemen Traffickers," *The Los Angeles Times*, August 17, 1989, p. 12. "No hay militares metidos en la guerra de los carteles," *La Prensa*, August 18, 1989, p. 13.

16. Joseph Treaster, "The Cali Cartel: Colombia's Smoother Drug Gang," *The New York Times*, September 19, 1989, p. A18.

17. "Extraditables Issue Communique on Murders, Truce," NOTIMEX, Mexico City, 0112 GMT, August 14, 1990.

18. "War Between Medellín, Cali Bosses Renewed," NOTIMEX, Mexico City, 2326 GMT, December 22, 1990.

19. William Roy Surrett. *The International Narcotics Trade: An Overview of Its Dimensions, Production Sources, and Organizations* (Washington, D.C.: Congressional Research Service Report, October 3, 1988), p. 11.

20. Mary Cooper. *The Business of Drugs* (Washington, D.C.: Congressional Quarterly, Inc. 1990), p. 18.

21. "Traffickers Declare War," Bogotá Emisorias Caracol (in Spanish), 1216 GMT, August 24, 1989.

22. Salomon Kalmanovitz, "La economia del narcotráfico en Colombia," *Economia Colombiana*, February–March 1990, pp. 25–26.

38

23. Fabio Giraldo Isaza, "Narcotráfico y construcción," ibid., p. 43.
24. Libardo Sarmiento Auzola and Carlos Moreno Ospina, "Narcotráfico y sector agropecurario en Colombia," ibid., pp. 30–37.
25. Joseph Treaster, "Colombian Policemen and Soldiers are Reportedly Tipping Off Drug Figures," *The New York Times*, September 4, 1989, p. 3.
26. Jose de Cordóba, "Colombia's Narcos Find Brute Force Yields Little Entree," *The Wall Street Journal*, October 5, 1989, pp. A1, A14.
27. "U.S. Blacklist Disclosed; Reaction Noted," Bogotá Inrivision Television, Cardena 1, 0010 GMT, September 21, 1989.
28. James M. Dorsey, "Drug Lord's Hometown Misses Aim," *The Washington Post*, September 4, 1989, pp. A1, A10.
29. Much of the discussion in this section is drawn from: *The White Labyrinth*, op. cit., chapter 4.
30. Rensselaer Lee, "Why the U.S. Cannot Stop South American Cocaine," *Orbis*, Fall 1988, p. 509.
31. "¿El tercer cartel?" *Semana*, February 20, 1989, pp. 22–27.
32. Douglas Farah, "Cartel Enforcer Linked to Massacre," *The Washington Post*, May 6, 1990, p. A21.
33. "Military-Drug Trafficking Link Alleged," Radio Patria Libre (clandestine) to Colombia, November 15, 1988. See also: "El dossier paramilitar," *Semana*, April 11, 1989, pp. 23–29.
34. "El dossier paramilitar," ibid., p. 29.
35. "Morena se destapa," *Semana*, August 21, 1989, pp. 22–29.
36. "Cocaine Exports to Europe Reportedly Double in 1990," *The Times of the Americas*, November 28, 1990, p. 16.
37. "La bomba del diálogo," *Semana*, Bogotá, October 10, 1989, p. 25.
38. "Prepared Statement of Peter Reuter," Subcommittee on Western Hemisphere Affairs, Committee on Foreign Affairs, U.S. House of Representatives, Washington, D.C. February 26, 1991. Figure 2. Interviews AID mission.
39. "Sobre amnista a narcos," *Semana*, January 8, 1991, p. 13. "La gran encuesta," *Semana*, January 8, 1991, p. 29.
40. On foreign investments, see: "Inversión Foranea Cae 68 por ciento," *El Tiempo*, Bogotá, October 12, 1990, p. 1A. On declining tourism, see: "Los platos rojos," *Semana*, August 28 to September 4, 1990, pp. 54–62.
41. U.S. House of Representatives, Committee on Government Operations, "Stopping the Flood of Cocaine With Operation Snowcap: Is It Working," Report of August 15, 1990 (Washington, D.C.: U.S. Government Printing Office, 1990), p. 79.
42. "Narcos: Entrega con reservas," *El Tiempo*, November 23, 1990, p. 8A.
43. Ibid.
44. Ibid. Mark Faziollah, "Tired of Violence, Colombia May Meet Drug Lords' Terms," *The Philadelphia Inquirer*, December 9, 1990, pp. 1A, 8A.
45. "Text of Drug Traffickers' Terms for Ending Activities," *El Tiempo*, July 7, 1984, pp. 1A, 11C.
46. "Political Parties Reject Dialogue," *El Tiempo*, July 6, 1984, p. 8A.
47. "Diálogo: Que ha pasado," *Semana*, October 17–23, 1989, pp. 27–30. "No habra diálogo con los narcotraficantes," *El Siglo*, Bogotá, July 20, 1984, p. 1.
48. "La Bomba del diálogo," op cit., pp. 24–29.
49. "Stopping the Flood of Cocaine," op. cit., pp. 73–74.
50. "Text of Communique Issued by the Extraditables," Bogotá, Inravision Television, Cadeña 1, 1736 GMT, January 17, 1990. For a discussion of the Notables' role, see: "Cumplirá Pablo Escobar?" *Semana*, January 23–30, 1990, pp. 22–27.

51. "Narcos: Entrega con reservas," op cit. On the Notables, see: "Sigue la espera," *Semana*, November 6–13, 1990, p. 38.

52. Ibid. "Comunicado de Los Extraditables," *El Tiempo*, November 24, 1990, p. 8A.

53. Twig Mowatt, "Colombian Kingpins May Surrender: Hundreds in Cartel Offer Deal," *USA Today*, November 26, 1990, p. 4A. Henry Goethals, "Medellín Cartel Offer Poses Dilemma," *The Times of the Americas*, December 12, 1990, p. 14.

54. "Comunicado de Fabio Ochoa Vasquez," *El Tiempo*, December 19, 1990, p. 8A.

55. Escobar and other Colombian traffickers are probably awaiting the outcomes of current debates in Colombia's new constituent assembly on whether or not to outlaw extraditions and on whether or not to grant pardons to drug dealers.

56. "Diálogo: que a pasado," op cit., p. 28.

57. Ibid., p. 26.

58. "La paz del pais es mi retohistórico," *El Tiempo*, August 8, 1990, p. 8A.

59. "Text of Drug Traffickers' Terms. . . ." op cit.

60. On this issue, see, for example: Gordon Witkin, "New Drug Warriors: Lasers, Labs, and Coke-Eating Bugs," *U.S. News and World Report*, February 19, 1990, pp. 20–21.

61. For an excellent statement of this position, see: Colin Grey, "Does Verification Really Matter? Facing Political Facts About Arms Control Non-Compliance," *Strategic Review*, Spring 1990, pp. 32–41.

62. "Stopping the Flood of Cocaine," op. cit., p. 87.

63. William Roy Surrett, "The International Narcotics Trade: An Overview of Its Dimension, Production Sources, and Organizations," *Congressional Research Service*, October 3, 1988, pp. 11–12.

64. "Escobar, abandonado por Los Extraditables," *El Tiempo*, April 16, 1990, p. 8A.

[15]

Crime, Law and Social Change **19**: 245–269, 1993.
© 1993 *Kluwer Academic Publishers. Printed in the Netherlands.*

The dragon breathes fire: Chinese organized crime in New York City

ROBERT J. KELLY,[1] KO-LIN CHIN[2] and JEFFREY A. FAGAN[2]
[1] *Brooklyn College and The Graduate School, City University of New York, Bellmore, NY 11 710, USA;* [2] *Rutgers University, University Heights, Newark, NJ, USA*

Abstract. Although it is widely acknowledged that Chinese businesses are victims of extortion by Asian youth gangs, there is no reliable information to examine the patterns and social processes of the problem. This paper explores the structure of extortion and other forms of victimization based on surveys of (N = 603) Chinese-owned businesses in three Chinatown neighborhoods in New York City. It focuses on the nature of Chinese crime groups, social contexts of gang extortion, social processes of victimization, and merchants' compliance or resistance to gang demands. Finally, the paper discusses the problems and prospects of Chinese criminality in America.

Introduction

Before 1965, except for the "Tong Wars" among adult associations in the late nineteenth and early twentieth century,[1] Chinese communities in the United States had relatively low crime rates. Chinese people in general, and Chinese youths in particular, were viewed as law-abiding, hard-working, and peaceful.[2] The most common crimes among Chinese were victimless offenses such as prostitution, opium smoking, drunkenness, and disorderly conduct.[3] Offenders were primarily adult sojourners who indulged in these culturally sanctioned recreational activities as a respite from work.

The year 1965 was a turning point in the history of Asian immigration. The Immigration and Naturalization Act of 1965 not only placed Asian immigration on an equal footing with that of "preferred" nations, but also established priorities or "preferences" for admissions based largely on family relationships. These preferences permitted those Asian immigrants already living in the United States to initiate documents for visas for their families overseas. As a result, the number of Chinese people in the United States has increased dramatically from 236,084 in 1960 to 1.6 million in 1990.[4]

New York City's Chinatown in Manhattan is an established social, political,

Support for this research was provided by Grant 89-IJ-CX-0021 from the National Institute of Justice. The opinions are those of the authors and do not reflect the policies or views of the U.S. Department of Justice.

246

and commercial center. It is located in the lower east side of Manhattan, surrounded by City Hall, "Little Italy", and the East River.[5] Established in the 1850s, it developed from a few Chinese stores on Mott Street to one of the largest Chinese communities in the world. Approximately 125,000 Chinese residents now live in the vicinity, and the population is growing rapidly as a result of China's open-door policy and the political instability affecting Hong Kong. Residents are mostly working-class, Cantonese-speaking immigrants from China or Hong Kong.[6]

Three types of businesses dominate its economy: restaurants, garment factories, and small stores that sell Chinese groceries, meat, and vegetables. Rents are very high for both commercial and residential property,[7] with costs per square foot for the most expensive retail space in Chinatown about 275 dollars, compared to 400 dollars for "Fifth Avenue"[8] and 255 dollars for "Madison Avenue" addresses.[9] A one-bedroom apartment is 700 dollars monthly, on top of a five to eight thousand dollars so-called *fong tai chin* (Key Money) payment upfront for obtaining the lease. Despite the high rents, apartments in Chinatown are small and poorly-maintained. A substantial number of them have neither bathrooms nor living rooms.[10] Since the decision by the British to concede Hong Kong to China in 1977, huge amounts of investment dollars from the colony have poured into the community over the past several years, further energizing the community's economy and inflating costs in every dimension of the local economy.[11]

Voluntary associations play an important role in Chinatown. Family associations are organized by people with the same family name. A district association comprises people who came from the same district of China. For a Chinese immigrant, family name and province are as important a means of identification as driver license or social security card.[12] Another type of organization, the tong, recruits members without regard to surname or district affiliation. There are also professional groupings such as the Association of Oriental Garment, Chinese American Restaurant Association, and the National Chinese American Jewelry Association which broaden the grip of community social organization.

Politically, community organizations can be divided into three groups with distinctive political orientations. The first group, lead by the Chinese Consolidated Benevolent Associations (CCBA), consists of pro-Koumintang (Taiwan) politically conservative traditional associations and the tongs. A second group includes a small number of traditional associations and many newly established ones that support the government in China. The third coalition is made up of emerging professional organizations that take a politically neutral position between the two governments in Taiwan and China and represent the upwardly mobile Chinese already able to work successfully in the mainstream white economy.[13]

247

The "Chinatown" in New York City's borough of Queens is located in the Flushing section, where 60,000 Chinese have settled along Main Street and the No. 7 subway train through Jackson Heights and Elmhurst. Residents are predominantly new immigrants from Taiwan or Korea, and Mandarin is the most popular dialect in the community.[14]

Brooklyn's "Chinatown" is situated along Eighth Avenue in the Sunset Park section, shoulder to shoulder with working class Bay Ridge and Borough Park. It is connected to Manhattan's Chinatown by the N and B subway trains that serve as social and economic lifelines between the two communities. It is estimated that there are also some 60,000 Chinese in all of Brooklyn, most of whom are immigrants from Hong Kong.[15]

In comparison to Manhattan's Chinatown, residents in the new Chinese communities in Queens and Brooklyn are better educated, wealthier, and more able to adjust to, and identify with, American society. Within these communities, professionals and businessmen are active in community leadership roles. Thus, the power and influence of the traditional organizations such as the tongs, family and district associations in the newly emerging communities of more upwardly mobile Chinese is comparatively weaker.

Contrary to the myth depicting Chinese Americans as the hard-working, intelligent, nose to the grindstone "model minority", some 71 percent Chinatown residents never finished high school, and 55 percent either do not speak English well or at all.[16] Almost 25 percent of families in Chinatown live below the poverty line compared with 17 percent citywide. And then there is the ignominious fate of 5,000 yearly immigrants in low paying jobs in non-union "sweat shops" (garment factories that litter the small-scale economy of Chinatown). Chinese immigrants are easily exploited primarily because most are reluctant to apply for government benefits in housing, food stamps, health care and occupational training for fear of jeopardizing immigration prospects for relatives. In an environment of relentless poverty and limited economic opportunities for large number of residents, it is little wonder that the traditional organizations that have been historically sensitive to this segment of the population, even though they exploit it, retain their power.

Also, in contrast to popular impression, Chinese communities in the United States are culturally and structurally fragmented and disorganized. The inhabitants of these communities are generally isolated from mainstream American society. The neighborhoods often consist of many incompatible subcultural norms and values, with little cohesion among subcultural, communal, and societal values. Community institutions are divided by political ideology or provincial cultural values and are often in conflict. Because of inadequate resources, poor or callous leadership, and social and economic isolation, most local social institutions are inefficient in meeting the basic needs of the inhabitants.[17]

248

With the growth of the Chinese population, a corresponding increase in the crime rates occurred among Chinese people. The Federal Bureau of Investigation's *Uniform Crime Reports* show that, nationwide from 1965 to 1975, Chinese youths had the fastest growing crime rate of all racial groups. Chinese crime groups were alleged to be involved in gambling, extortion, prostitution, burglary, robbery, heroin trafficking and violence.[18] Gang shootouts erupted often within the communities, and innocent bystanders were being hurt or killed.

Immigrants youths are "transplanted children".[19] According to Sung, they are uprooted from their childhood environments and transplanted in a completely different, and sometimes hostile, American society. These adolescents grow up in disorganized and fragmented Chinese communities that lack cohesion and both formal and informal social controls. Accordingly, these youths are likely to experience alienation from both the community and the society. Being detached from the community and adrift in society, they have to rely heavily on school and family for support. However, instead of functioning as institutions of socialization and bonding, both school and family in socially disorganized areas become sources of frustration and disappointment for the immigrant youths. These processes are not unlike the socialization of youths in inner city neighborhoods that are characterized by high rates of residential mobility, social and economic isolation, and in turn, a concentration of youth gangs and high rates of non-gang serious juvenile crime.[20]

Etiological factors related to Chinese gang delinquency can be categorized into causative and intervening factors. The causative factors appears to be: (1) loss of control by school; (2) loss of control by family; and (3) the lack of opportunity structure. Coupled with the isolation and disorganization of the community, immigrant youths detached and alienated from communal and societal norms and values, might easily drift into delinquency. These processes are similar to the experiences of adolescents in other socially isolated areas that in the past have led to gang formation and activity.[21]

However, as we describe below, affiliation with and internalization of Triad norms and values are indispensable intervening stages in the processes of becoming a gang member. Thus, the social processes that have spawned youth gang activity in other inner city social milieux are intensified by a reciprocal relationship with unique social entities in the Chinese community that are involved in criminal activities. These processes legitimate the youth gangs, shield them from other formal and informal neighborhood social controls, create economic and social reciprocity between youth gangs and social groups.

The development of Chinese street gangs in New York City may be divided into five structural stages, i.e., the emergent stage from 1960–68; the symbiotic period between 1969–73; the gang war era of 1974–82; and last, a diffusive cycle marking their differentiation and dispersion between 1983–90.

During the emergent stage, street gangs were formed by native-born or fore-ing-born Chinese (predominantly Cantonese-speaking) students as non-utilitarian self-help groups to protect themselves from other ethnic students, or the community from racist visitors. The gangs were neither associated with the community's adult criminal subculture nor involved in profit-making criminal activities. At this stage, Chinese youth gangs were similar in social process and criminal activities to other youth gangs of that era.[22]

During the symbiotic stage,[23] Chinese gangs became deeply embedded in the community's political and social affairs. Gang members began to victimize the community through extortion, robbery, burglary, and violence. In order to bring the gangs under control, the tongs (voluntary associations formed by Chinese workers in the mid-nineteenth century) recruited gang members to guard the gambling establishments in the community. Triad norms and values were transmitted to the gangs by the tongs. As a result, the gangs transformed into paraprofessional criminal organizations.

After the symbiotic stage, the gangs went through a period of conflict and war in order to determine which of them would control various areas within the community. When intergang conflicts subsided after territories had been established, intragang power struggles broke out when the leaders treated their members unfairly in the distribution of illegal gains. At this point, the tongs lost control of the gangs, and gang members achieved status within the Chinatown (adult) criminal underworld.

With the influx of new immigrants from Taiwan, China, Vietnam, and Korea, coupled with the complex political situations in these Asian regions, the gangs now appear to be in a stage of diffusion. Spatially, they are active not only in the traditional Chinese community, but also in the newly established Chinese ethnic communities. There is also evidence that the gangs are increasingly tied to Chinese crime groups outside of the United States. The ethnic composition of the gangs also changed as non-Cantonese Chinese, Vietnamese, Korean, and Taiwanese criminal elements became prominent in the Chinese underworld. As gang members of the 1960s matured, they shifted their activities from predatory crimes to heroin trafficking or investment in legal businesses such as restaurants and night clubs.[24]

Extortion is considered one of the most prevalent forms of crime in the Chinese communities.[25] Police estimate that at least 80 to 90 percent of Chinese businesses have to pay one or more extortion gangs regularly or occasionally.[26] When retail businesses refuse to pay, their shops may be vandalized, burglarized, robbed, or set on fire. In some instances, businessmen and retail store owners have been beaten, shot at, or killed. When businessmen are no longer able to meet the gang's demand, they simply close down their businesses.

With steady income from extortion, Chinese crime groups are able to recruit new members. Through extortion, the gangs express their firm control on certain territories. When two or more gangs claim control of a specific territory,

250

not only store owners within that territory have to pay more than one gang, but street violence erupts as a result of the power struggle among the competing gangs.

Although merchants are extorted heavily by the gangs, law enforcement authorities are frustrated because few victims file complaints. Most victims would like to be protected by law enforcement, but they are reluctant to report the crime because they fear gang reprisals; or, they are too cynical about the American criminal justice system to trust it. The fear of the gangs, coupled with cynicism and ignorance about the criminal justice system, has exacerbated the victimization of the Chinese commercial community.

No comprehensive data are available to validate claims about the structure and criminal patterns of Chinese crime groups. What is not known beyond anecdotal and impressionistic data from law enforcement sources, community workers and journalists is the proportion of Chinese merchants who are regularly or occasionally extorted; how much they pay; to whom, and what the impact of this criminal activity means in the social and economic life of the communities. Basic information on the organization of extortion is not available. Little is known with any reliability about the characteristics of victims, offenders, their interrelationships and why some businesses are, or seem to be, more susceptible and vulnerable than others.

This study was initiated in October 1989 to examine patterns of extortion and victimization of Chinese business persons by Chinese gangs in New York City, and to determine the unique social processes in Chinese immigrant communities that may contribute or mitigate these offenses. Ethnographic data were collected from face-to-face interviews with business owners (N = 603), community leaders (N = 12), and law enforcement authorities (N = 23).

This article first explains the methodology we used in collecting data pertaining to crime in the Chinese community. It then describes the development and structure of Chinese crime groups; and the patterns of gang victimization. Finally, it discusses the problems and prospects of Chinese criminality in America.

Research methods

Samples

Interviews were conducted with (N = 603) Chinese business owners in the New York Metropolitan area. The sample was drawn from a bilingual directory of Chinese-owned businesses.[27] This comprehensive directory, published annually, is widely circulated free of charge among Chinese businesses and residences.

It lists 4.290 firms. mostly businesses located in the Manhattan. Queens. and Brooklyn boroughs of New York City. Except for large international firms and a few take-out restaurants located far away from the Chinese residential areas, nearly all Chinese-owned businesses are included. Some firms that are owned by non-Chinese but cater to Asian customers are also included in the directory. Accordingly, the directory approximates the universe of Chinese-owned businesses with virtually no biases.

A multi-stage cluster sampling strategy was adopted to ensure adequate representation of the variety of Chinese-owned businesses. Businesses were classified into 11 categories representing the range of commercial business activities. Because certain professional offices and heavily guarded businesses (e.g., health clinics and banks) seem to be rarely victimized by Chinese gangs, they were excluded from the population of Chinese-owned businesses. Illicit businesses such as prostitution houses and gambling clubs that deal directly in cash are extremely vulnerable to extortion. We excluded them, anticipating insurmountable difficulties in gaining entry and unacceptably high risks to the interviewers in these settings.

Sample quotas were set within the 11 business categories to ensure minimal representation among highly vulnerable categories of business, and to permit comparisons of categories across the three Chinese neighborhoods. Businesses that deal directly in cash, that serve primarily Asian customers, that locate at the street level. that have heavy frequent customers' visits are more vulnerable to extortion attempts.

Business also were oversampled by locale. The research focused on three socio-economically different "Chinatowns" in the Manhattan, Queens, and Brooklyn boroughs of New York City. We hypothesized that the symbiotic relationship between the gangs and the ethnic community would lead to higher victimization rates in areas where Chinese populations and commercial activity were concentrated. Accordingly, businesses in those communities were oversampled compared to businesses located in other neighborhoods. Nevertheless, Chinese merchants in other parts of the three selected boroughs were also included to compare victimization rates in Chinese communities with those who do business elsewhere in New York City.

Procedures

To initiate contact, a bilingual letter was sent to the business addresses of potential respondents (N = 888) describing the purpose of the study, how the business was chosen, the confidentiality of the study, that participation was voluntary, and that a stipend of $20 would be paid after the interview. Sensitive terms such as "extortion" and "gangs" were not mentioned. To reassure business owners

252

of the legitimacy of the study, a bilingual letter of support from the director of the sponsoring agency (the National Institute of Justice) was included with our letter.

After the letters were mailed, interviewers contacted business owners by telephone, reminding them of the letter and asking for an appointment for an interview. Because most of the subjects were located in the three Chinese communities, it was more effective to have the interviewers simply visit the store a few days after notification letters were mailed. Interviewers were issued identification cards indicating their affiliation with Rutgers University.

Most (six of seven) interviewers were female college students or social workers. Females were consciously chosen over males because female interviewers to assure respondents that the interviewer was a not gang member. All the interviewers were familiar with the Chinese communities and spoke one or more Chinese dialects. Interviews were conducted in the language or dialect that the respondent was most comfortable with, usually either Cantonese or Mandarin. Interview sessions lasted up to one and a half hours. Questions were read aloud to the respondents, who were encouraged to respond in their own words. Responses were recorded in Chinese and summarized later by bilingual analysts. For categorical responses, coding occurred after the interview. Interviews took place from April–September 1990.

Response rates

Response rates were high: 580 out of the selected 888 subjects (65.3 percent) were interviewed. The refusal rate was 11.0 percent (N = 98). The remainder (23.6 percent) were not interviewed because they could not be found: either the businesses were moved or closed (N = 101), the owner could not be located (N = 19), or the owners were non-Asian (N = 38).[28] In other cases, businesses could not be reached by telephone or the business was located quite far from residential areas (N = 52). With these 210 locations excluded from the original sample, 580 of 678 subjects (85.5 percent) were interviewed, well beyond our best expectations of a 50 percent response rate at the outset of the field work.

To supplement the relatively small number of business owners on the sample list for Brooklyn's Chinatown, 23 business owners in that area that were not part of the target sample were interviewed. Interviewers went door-to-door along Eighth Avenue in Brooklyn and interviewed any Chinese business owner who was willing to participate. Accordingly, the final sample was N = 603 interviews.

Response rates and cooperation were influenced by the victimization experiences of the respondents. Most (85 percent) respondents identified themselves as owners, the rest indicated that they were either "managers" or "employees".

253

During the interviews, respondents often appeared understandably uneasy with questions about Chinese gangs and extortion. Some merchants warily kept an eye on the entrance all the time, as if they expected gang members to walk in at any moment. Other owners were ambivalent about being interviewed, fearing that their participation would somehow become known to gang members who had asked for money. These validity threats were tempered by relief expressed by respondents at the opportunity to discuss their fears and victimization experiences with interested and neutral parties.

In general, garment factory owners were the least cooperative, and often appeared as if they had something to hide. Their reluctance may stem from their illegal hiring practices (many workers in these garment manufacturing businesses do not have legal status or working permits), or failure to file appropriate tax returns. Geographical location also influenced response rates and cooperation: store owners on Bayard Street, one of the core areas of Chinatown and the scene of much gunfire in the past, were also less cooperative. No other business characteristics distinguished between those who were interviewed and those who refused.

Measures

The interview protocol was written in both English and Chinese and was pretested with a small number of business owners. The protocol included both open- and closed-ended items, organized into three categories of information. First, respondents reported background information and described their businesses. Next, respondents were asked to describe the social processes of gang extortion, including robbery, burglary, and other types of victimization. They discussed their interactions with gangs and others who extorted money from them. Data were also collected on whether the victims reported the crime to the police and their experiences in dealing with legal institutions. The third section asked about their perceptions of crime in the Chinese community and the responses of the criminal justice system. Interviewer observations generated data on the physical size of the business and the respondent's honesty and cooperativeness.

Validity and reliability

Interviewer ratings provided assessments of the respondents' honesty in answering the questions. Only 8 respondents (1.3 percent) were rated as not very honest in answering questions on personal and business background questions. Interviewers estimated that 27 respondents (4.5 percent) withheld information, and nine subjects (1.5 percent) were considered to have poor memory. Also, some respondents may have denied their victimization out of fear of reprisal from gang members, while others may have minimized their victimization experiences.

However, respondents who acknowledged their victimization consistently provided detailed information on the frequency or dollar costs. Because most of the stores were relatively new and they reported either rare or regular victimization, the owners were able to recall incidents in great detail. Moreover, many owners kept records of extortion payments or received a receipt from the gang members after each payment. These records or receipts help the owners to keep track of their payments and, for our purposes, their victimization interactions. Thus, estimates of the prevalence, frequency and the financial costs of gang victimizations had high face validity.

The subjects

Most respondents are young, educated Cantonese or Toisanese males from Hong Kong or Taiwan who have been living in the United States for about 10 years. There are 13 Koreans and 15 neither Korean nor Chinese (mostly Whites) in the sample. The sample firms are mainly restaurants or food or non-food retail stores located in the Manhattan or Queens Chinatowns. In comparison, restaurants and retail stores comprise only 20 percent of the small businesses in New York City.[29] The sample firms are relatively new in comparison to a sample of New York City small businesses that are, on average, 19 years old.[30] Most firms are considered small or medium, and were owned by more than one person. More than four out of five proprietors do not own the property where the business is located.

The data also indicate that subjects from Hong Kong dominate business activities in Manhattan and Brooklyn Chinatown, whereas merchants from Taiwan are most active in Queens Chinatown and mid- or upper-Manhattan. Respondents from China, the newest group among the three, tend to congregate in other areas of Brooklyn. In comparison with subjects from Hong Kong and China, business owners from Taiwan are better educated and speak better English. Owners of restaurants and wholesale-retail supply firms are significantly less educated than owners of professional offices. Most factory and wholesale/retail supply firms are located in Manhattan Chinatown, and there is a high concentration of professional offices in Queens Chinatown. Female respondents were predominantly involved in either service-oriented businesses or the garment industry.

Triads, tongs, and street gangs

"Triad" means a "triangle of heaven, earth, and man".[31] Triad societies began as secret societies formed by patriotic Chinese three centuries ago to fight the oppressive and corrupt Ch'ing dynasty. When the Ch'ing government collapsed and the Republic of China was established in 1912, some societies degenerated into crime groups.[32] Most Triad societies now have their headquarters in Hong Kong, but their criminal operations have not national boundaries.[33]

Though often referred to inaccurately as the "Chinese Mafia", Triads differ considerably from Sicilian criminal organizations and Italian-American La Cosa Nostra crime families.[34] Both criminal organizations have much in common, nonetheless. Mafia is structured around families and patron/client networks; Triads, on the other hand, when they are criminally oriented – and not all of them are – consists of initiated members positioned in a hierarchy of power, authority and obedience. Their criminal enterprises include extortion, labor racketeering, drug trafficking, gambling, protection rackets in construction, and control of certain legitimate industries like film and music. Wherever there are Chinese communities throughout the world, it is very likely that a Triad society will make a criminal living from it, surviving parasitically by taking advantage of every illicit opportunity for profit.

The tongs emerged more than a century ago among immigrant Chinese laborers in the gold fields of California.[35] At first they functioned as operators of opium and gambling dens for the migrant male Chinese labor force and then over time expanded their roles as community organizations in San Francisco and New York.[36] The term, "Tong", loosely means "meeting hall".

Apart from their chief, historic role in vice, tong organizations did indeed help immigrants to adapt to their new culture, and while they insist on their legality, law enforcement officials identify them as exerting strong influence on crime in Chinatown from New York to San Francisco.[37]

Power in Chinatown appears to be concentrated in an interlock of family associations, district associations and the tongs. Tongs may therefore be seen, or as many law enforcement agencies choose to see them as semi-secret societies enacting roles respectable people cannot openly undertake. Although the modern tongs are not outwardly and explicitly engaged in criminal activities, they still function as an informal, hidden directorate of street gangs who, in turn, operate like mafia commandos when the need arises. And like mafiosi, the tongs have divided things into sinister spheres of influence.

The tongs are interculturally isomorphic with a bifurcated hierarchy in precisely those operations of the organization that permit it to function as a bridge between two worlds, the English-speaking white community and the Chinese. This shrewd arrangement enables the tongs to adroitly maneuver as "middleman", as cultural entrepreneurs that span the chasm between the dominant

256

white society and the minority Chinese community. The tong serves a dual function: as an agent of the Chinese community and, equally, as an emissary and power broker for the white community that gains entry through the auspices of the tongs into the subculture of Chinatown.

Membership in a tong is, of course, not meant to imply that a person is guilty of illegal activity. And, of course, tong officials routinely and ardently protest against allegations that they are fronts for Chinese rackets. Government officials outline a more sinister aspect of the tongs, however. Tongs do more than deflect attention from criminal enterprises: they seem to be actively involved in managing and directing the bulk of the vice activities in Chinatown. They utilize street gangs to protect their gambling establishments and benefit from the extortion rackets the gangs conduct. One of the largest, the On Leong, has chapters in 20 U.S. cities with approximately 40,000 members. Precisely because the majority of tong members are law-abiding, criminal elements within them enjoy added protection.

While no structural tie between the American tongs and the Hong Kong Triads is evident, tong members swear the same 36 oaths of loyalty that Triad initiates do, and bow to the god of the Triad societies. It is further believed that certain powerful tong members belong to the Triads so there may be a kind of spiritual relationship based on shared values. The tongs follow the norms and values of the Triads. It is well to remember that both tongs and Triads have non-criminal functions and members. They serve as central repositories of money and manpower and as such are good covers for criminal activities.

Gang members are all male, their ages range from thirteen to thirty-seven.[38] Most members are in their late teens or early twenties. Generally, the leaders are in their late twenties or early thirties; street bosses are in their eraly twenties; and ordinary members are teenagers.

In the late 1960s and 1970s, most gang members were young immigrants from Hong Kong, with a few American-born or Taiwan-born member. Since the late 1970s, the Ghost Shadows and the Flying Dragons have recruited many Vietnamese-Chinese.[39] In the 1980s, many young immigrants from Fujian (Fukien), China, are being recruited by gangs such as the Fook Ching, the Tung On, and the Green Dragons. Recently, some Korean youths were inducted into the Queens-based White Tigers and Green Dragons.

Most gang members are school dropouts, although some remain in school while maintaining active membership in a gang. Chinese gang members do not have dress codes, although some prefer to wear black leather jackets, black shirts, black pants, and casual shoes without socks. Most of them spike their hair, have tattoos on their arms or chests, and carry beepers.

Gang size varies. Each gang has, on average, about twenty to fifty hard-core members, a few inactive members, and some peripheral associates. When gang conflicts become intense, reinforcements may be recruited from other cities.

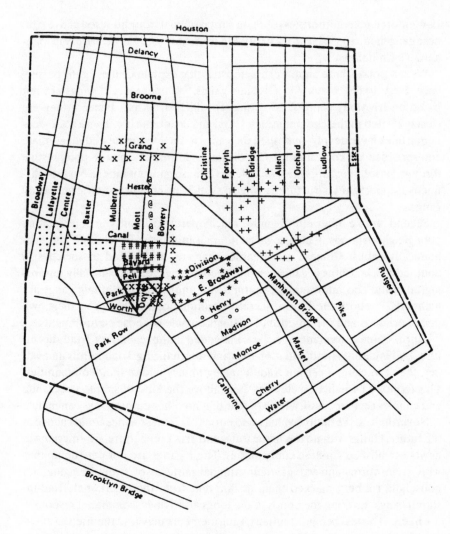

Born to Kill

Ghost Shadows

Golden Star

Flying Dragons

Tung On

Fook Ching

White Tigers

Figure 1. The Archipelago of Crime: Gang Territories in New York City's Chinatown.

258

Law enforcement authorities estimate a total of up to four hundred active Chinese gang members in New York City. Figure 1 shows the gang territory in Manhattan's Chinatown.

We can isolate three unique characteristics that explain Chinese gang persistence. First, unlike black and Hispanic gangs,[40] Chinese street gangs are not based on frivolous youth fads or itinerant illicit drug use. Instead, they are closely related to their communities' social and economic life. These socio-economic links have deeply enmeshed the gangs in the legitimate and illegitimate enterprises of the communities. Opportunities for money, power, and prestige through various ventures are available to Chinese gang members. No such distinctive opportunity structure is able to sustain or encourage other minority gangs.

Second, unlike other ethnic gangs, which operate primarily in deteriorating poor neighborhoods, Chinese gangs flourish in rapidly developing and economically robust Chinese communities that are closely tied to societies in Southeast Asia. Chinese gangs can thus become engaged in financially rewarding domestic and international ventures. In contrast, other ethnic gangs are hampered by both the lack of lucrative criminal opportunities in their own neighborhoods and the absence of contacts outside of those environments.

Third, Chinese gang members are embedded in the legendary Triad subculture. By emulating Triad initiation rites and internalizing Triad norms and values, they can claim a certain traditional legitimacy within their communities. This folkloric benediction elevates them above the kind of simple street thug and enables them to instill a level of fear that no other ethnic gangs can match.

Nevertheless, the nature, values, and norms of Chinese gangs could change in the future. Gangs with no ties to the tongs and Triad subculture are emerging in newly established Chinese communities. These gangs are not only unfamiliar with Triad norms and values, their criminal patterns of street mugging and household robbery marked them as different from the traditional Triad-inspired gangs. Lacking the bonds to the tongs and Triads, communal responses are likely to be less benign: "outlaw" gang members may find themselves alienated from their communities and more likely subjected to arrests and prosecution.

The micro-imperialism of the street gangs:
Gang extortion in the Chinese community

To measure the forms of gang extortion[41] that were evident in previous studies[42] and in our early discussions with business owners, we developed four types of victimization that are unique to gang precipitated crime in the Chinese community. The first type is protection. "Protection" denotes the demand for a fixed amount of money from the owner by gang members to ensure that the business will not be disturbed either by themselves or other gangs. When the amount of protection money is negotiated between the owner and the gang member, the money will be paid by the owner regularly, normally on a weekly, monthly basis or on major holidays. Sometimes, the owners are asked to make one large payment of money for protection.

The second type, "extortion", describes the sporadic demand for money from business owners by gang members.[43] The amount of payment is negotiated on each occasion, and the perpetrators do not promise to provide any service in return. The third type of victimization involves gang members selling items such as plants, cakes, or firecrackers to business owners for prices higher than their market values. The last type of victimization are the gangs' practices of refusing to pay for, or asking for heavy discounts for food and services.

Table 1 shows the number and percent of respondents who have never been approached, approached but not victimized, and victimized by Chinese gangs. About seven out of ten merchants have been approached by gang members, and at least one out of two have been exploited. Among the four types of gang extortion, forced sales is the most prevalent, follow by extortion itself, theft of goods or services, and protection.

The prevalence of victimization is not evenly distributed across business types or gang territories. For example, whereas 74% of the restaurants were victimized, only 9% of the professional offices were exploited. About 82% of the business within the territory of the Tung On gang were targeted by the gangs but only 24% of the stores at the outskirts of Manhattan Chinatown were "shaken down". Restaurants in Manhattan Chinatown were most vulnerable to Chinese gangs. About 85% of the restaurants in the area were extorted, and every restaurateur on Mott Street and Bayard Street (the territory of the Ghost Shadows), Division and East Broadway (the turf of the Tung On), and the southern part of Chinatown (the area of the Fook Ching) indicated that they were victimized by Chinese gangs (data not shown). A study on extortion activ-

Table 1. Prevalence of gang extortion.

	Never approached		Approached but not victimized		Victimized	
	N	%	N	%	N	%
Protection	473	78	60	10	70	12
Extortion	357	59	82	14	158	26
Forced sales	295	49	62	10	246	41
Free goods/services	500	83	4	1	94	16
Total	187	31	86	14	320	55

260

ities in Hawaii also found that, among various types of firms surveyed, bars and restaurants were most likely to be coerced to pay.[44]

Some gangs are more active than other gangs in extortion activities. Among Chinese gangs in New York City, the Tung On is the most heavily involved in criminal activities against business owners. A high proportion of the store owners within the Tung On's territory revealed that they were repeatedly abused by members of the Tung On. The other gangs that were most often mentioned by the respondents are the Ghost Shadows and the Fook Ching. These three gangs not only victimized merchants within their respective territory but also were very active in extorting business owners in Queens and Brooklyn. Although the Flying Dragons are considered to be one of the most powerful gangs and exert tight control over Pell Street and Doyers Street, business owners within the gang's turf were relatively immune to gang extortion. This suggests that the gang is well-controlled by the affiliated Hip Sing Tong, whose members may not tolerate gang activities against business owners within the territory.

The data also show that Chinese gang members did not confine their criminal activities to Manhattan's Chinatown. Businesses in the Chinese community of Queens and Brooklyn were as likely to be victimized as stores in Manhattan's Chinatown, and stores outside the three communities were often approached by "free lancing" Chinese gang members as well.

Table 1 also suggests that there is little resistance from Chinese business owners against the gangs. Only 86 out of 406 proprietors (22%) who have been approached by the gangs indicated that they resisted the gang demands. Business owners were least likely to refuse gang demands for free food or services, followed by forced sales, extortion, and protection. Business owners may be reluctant to succumb to gang demands for protection money because, unlike other types of victimization, once the victim agrees to comply, the victim may have to pay the gang regularly for a prolonged period of time. For example, some stores on the core areas of Manhattan Chinatown have been paying the gangs monthly for more than 10 years.

Besides prevalence, it is important to examine the frequency of gang victimization in assessing its seriousness. Table 2 shows the frequency of gang victimization by type of extortion. Most protection payments are made either at the opening ceremony as a one time payment or paid monthly. More than half the victims paid not more than twice a year. Four out of ten victims who were asked to purchase items from gang members bought only once a year, most likely during the Chinese New Year. The rest had to buy items two to four times a year, mainly firecrackers or orange plants during Chinese New Year, mooncakes on Moon Festival, and liquor on Thanksgiving. Gang members also sell other items such as paper fans for decoration, greeting cards, and oranges whenever they need money. The data suggest that the selling of items to businesspeople is more of a situational expedient than a routine practice as are protection demands.

Businesses forced to provide free or discounted foods, goods or services are mostly restaurants, bakery shops, barber shops, video tapes rental stores, and other retail stores such as grocery and optical stores. Again, restaurants and video rental stores are most likely to be frequently victimized under this category because gang members need to eat and watch video tapes more often than purchasing certain personal items.

In sum, except for paying protection money either weekly or monthly, most victims are exploited not more than three to four times a year. Thus, it is fair to say that most victims in the sample were shaken down only occasionally each year. However, for some large restaurants or retail stores located in the gang territories, the frequency of victimization by gang members could be very often because these businesses were exploitable in many ways. For example, a well-established and successful restaurant in Manhattan Chinatown was forced to pay protection money weekly to at least three gang leaders. It was also extorted frequently by gang members, intimidated into buying items from many gangs on all major holidays, and forced to accommodate many gang members who came to eat for free at least twice a week. For the restaurateur, dealing with gang members is almost a daily harrowing experience.

Although the frequency of victimization is relatively low for most merchants, the frequency of contacts between the victims and the offenders is much higher, because most merchants refuse to and defer meeting gang demands on every attempt. The store owners might ask gang members to come back another time, or they might pretend that they are not the owners and therefore could not therefore make the decision to pay. As a result of this process, merchants are harassed more often by the gangs then the data in Table 2 suggests.

Table 3 shows the mean, median, mode, maximum, and minimum amount of payment or loss per incident. On the average, the victims paid $129 for protection and $76 for extortion on each payment. They also bought an average of $51

Table 2. Annual frequency of gang extortion (in percent).

| | Number of times each year | | | |
	1	2	3	4 or more
Protection	29.5	4.4	5.7	60.3
Extortion	38.9	17.5	17.5	26.1
Forced sales	44.6	28.0	17.9	9.5
Theft of goods/services	19.9	13.3	13.3	53.5

262

worth of items from gang members per incident, and lost an average of $116 due to theft of goods or services. Usually, the victims paid $100 for protection, $20 for extortion, $50 for forced sales, and lost $30 when gang members demanded free or discount foods or services. For most victims, the annual financial loss attributable to gang victimization is estimated to be less than $1,000. A study conducted in Hawaii also found that one third of the victims of extortion indicated that they paid less than $500 a year to the extortionists.

The data show that Chinese entrepreneurs were not significantly hurt by gang members in strictly financial terms. For most businesses in the Chinese communities where rents may run as high as several thousands dollars a year, the loss of approximately a thousand dollars annually to the gangs cannot be considered a serious threat to their financial solvency. Some small business owners probably lost not more than a couple of hundred of dollars due to gang extortion. However, there are also some business owners who have to pay the gangs dearly for operating businesses in the Chinese community. For example, a large restaurant owner indicated that he paid several hundred dollars a month to more than one gang, was extorted for a few hundred dollars more a month by gang members, and was left with the unpaid bills of gang members that added up to a thousand dollars a month.

In the past, police have alleged that Chinese merchants are forced to pay the gangs may thousands of dollars a year.[45] The discrepancy between police estimates and our findings may be due to the fact that business owners rarely pay the gangs the asking price. In most cases, the offenders will ask the owner for a few hundred dollars. For example, a gang member may approach a store owner and demand $360 per week for protection. The owner may tell the gang member that business is slow and the store has just opened and negotiate the price down to $100 a month. Also, a group of gang members may show up during the Moon Festival and try to coerce a store owner into buying a box of mooncakes for $360. After negotiation, the owner may able to persuade the gang members to sell it for $50. Thus, it is important not to base our estimation of the seriousness of extortion on the initial demand price but the actual amount negotiated and paid by the victim.

Table 3. Costs of crime per incident (dollars).

	Mean	Median	Mode	Max.	Min.
Protection	$129	$70	$100	$1,000	$3
Extortion	76	30	20	1,300	2
Forced sales	51	40	50	200	5
Theft of goods/services	116	40	30	3,000	1

263

The social context of Chinese gangs

What the interviews reveal is that there is no centralized management of criminal territories and activities. Criminal diversity seems prevalent. Also, for many commercial enterprises, the extortion practices are but mildly parasitic: the money paid is not ruinous only a nuisance; refusal to pay, however, could generate damaging consequences to the business and personal injury to proprietors.

Other business people resist even token payments and often develop astute defenses against gang intrusions. A Chinese shop owner on Lafayette Street where Vietnamese gangs are active said that no one had approached him in ten years for protection money. It's not that he had connections with the tongs or street gangs or the police. He exploited a social taboo that the ruthless Vietnamese gangs respect. The businessman employed many non-Chinese, that is to say, whites in his business. Apparently, business with white participation enjoys some immunity from extortion. Why this is so, given the collective perceptions of police passivity towards crime in the communities, seems sensible. Perhaps criminal elements believe that victimization of whites may arouse the police to act vigorously and engage in widespread crackdowns on all kinds of vice activities. The shop owner on Lafayette Street exploited the perceived racism in law enforcement towards non-whites to his personal advantage.

A fairly large number of retail businesses with cash flow are the targets of street gangs. Proprietors seemed cynical about police anti-crime control tactics. A sixty-eight year old immigrant from Hong Kong who has been in the United States for 40 years expressed the feelings of many elderly people.

> Tongs support gangs ... that's why gangs are a problem. And the law protects the criminal ... A waste of time to go to the police: the 5th, 7th and 13th precincts (police districts covering Manhattan's Chinatown) all stink! (Case number 20, interviewed on May 3, 1990).

A restaurant in Queens – the city county with a rapidly growing Chinese population outside of traditional Chinatown in Manhattan – was approached for protection money. The Ghost Shadows, a powerful street gang in Manhattan, asked for 30 dollars per month and said, "If anyone bothers you, you call the beeper number; we'll be there." Eventually payments climbed to 100 dollars per month as business volume increased. When asked why he did not go to the police who established an office (the Chinatown Project) to help the Chinese in particular, amid much publicity, the owner replied wistfully: "I think the Chinatown Project is a good idea but if I don't pay to the Ghost Shadows, somebody else will come for it" (Case number 76, interviewed on May 25, 1990).

Joining a tong as a shield against gang predators does not seem to help either. A sixty year old beauty parlor operator did just that to her dismay. She joined the On Leong Association thinking that they could keep the Ghost Shadows at bay. Within Chinatown, the On Leong reputedly use Ghost Shadows to protect their gambling establishments and they therefore are believed to have some influence with them. When the Ghost Shadows visited the shop, the owner proudly displayed her On Leong membership plague and told the gang members to go to the On Leong to check out its authenticity. "It's a good deal", the beautician announces. "I only pay the On Leong 12 dollars a year" (Case number 55, interviewed on May 4, 1990). Nonetheless, Ghost Shadows periodically came to her shop to sell various items.

Among business people who seem untouched by the protection rackets and the ancillary businesses around them, those known to have criminal affiliations with the street gangs, former gang members themselves, and entrepreneurs with visible connections with city Hall, may be successful in evading the gangs. But even the most powerful and well-known relax their resistance to the gangs on Chinese New Year. Buying mooncakes, firecrackers, fruits, and so on at outrageous prices is a local custom. As the operator of a famous restaurant averred: "I pay no protection, but once a year everybody pays. Also, I buy whisky during Christmas from the Ghost Shadows" (Case number 128, interviewed on June 1, 1990).

For the largely non-Chinese police force in Chinatown, the community's collective nervous system must seem utterly mysterious. The police appear at times claustrophobic, dependent upon a handful of community workers who translate, interpret and generally explain the apparent contradictions in the community's cultural system. The Chinatown Project is actually more helpful to the police as a cultural wedge into Chinatown than it is to the Chinese for whom it was purportedly devised. The police are not a formidable presence in the rhythms of everyday life in Chinatown, Manhattan, Flushing, Queens or Sunset Park, Brooklyn – areas where the Chinese population density is making a difference in the racial and ethnic composition of these communities.

The police are something of a benign occupying force which quickly gets absorbed into the armophous social body. The community itself is so richly variegated that it is like a giant amoeba capable of digesting many discrete entities that enter into its mass.

Within the communities, the enforcement of behavioral norms is in the hands of local organizations and influential individuals associated with the powerful and prestigious groups that make up the Chinese Consolidated Benevolent Association. The police themselves recognize this fact and act accordingly but quietly. A police investigator with close ties to community organizations and leaders admitted that the gangs often act as enforcement groups at the behest of community organizations. Ironically, the street gangs linked to the unofficial "government" of Chinatown may perform useful police functions and control as much crime and violence as they produce.

Crime in New York City's Chinese community: Problems and prospects

The crime problem in the Chinese communities is as varied and complex as it is in other neighborhoods.[46] Most of the crime is perpetrated by Chinese against Chinese: non-Chinese are rarely the victims of assaults, robberies or thefts – though on occasion indiscriminate gunfire between street gangs takes its toll among innocent bystanders.

The gangs exercise street power on their turfs. They are not, however, pathological departures from social norms; rather they act often shrewdly and resourcefully and strive to take advantage of the opportunities they encounter. The gangs percolate throughout the business community, and as "spatialists" they establish a habitat as turf which they simultaneously defend and exploit and seek to expand. And if they fail to cultivate a mature relationship with the socio-economic environment which means knowing the limits of tolerance of the community, and being sensitive to the informal rules governing street decorum, they will disappear.

In the period of the research work, there seemed to be a subterranean war of succession between the established gangs and some newcomers who challenged their power. In this fluid situation gang leadership came to mean several things not necessarily interrelated. For those bold enough to resort to open violence and risk disapproval of the community which meant close surveillance and investigation by the police, a group would form and coalesce around a charismatic street boss; at the same time, small groups would cluster around a core network that had access to money sources form both legal and illegal businesses. The latter group proved more durable. The ability to prey cleverly upon the community is a talent requiring delicate sociological instincts. Bluster, gratuitous violence and street mayhem spelled the end for those who irritated the tongs and influential business people in the community. It became apparent that the victims and the victimizers in the Chinese community are neither physically separate nor morally disconnected.

In the United States, the palace coup of street gang leaders against tong authority may continue as street gangs proliferate with the growth of the Chinese population and as immigration keeps apace with the expansion of the community. Because the tongs cannot possibly absorb all the newcomers, street gangs of "FOBs" (Fresh off the Boat) have and will assume more independence and power. As power accrues they are unlikely to surrender it to anyone let alone the doddering old tongs in the gambling dens playing Fan Tan and Mah-jong. With maturation and adjustments to the social and economic realities of New York City, with immigration flows replenishing their ranks, more sophisticated and dangerous organizations with few ties to the wider non-Asian community may emerge to challenge the tongs and their janissaries for power. The outcome of these developments does not bode well: more gangs means more vio-

266

lence and crime in a social and political environment apparently unable to cope with current problems.

Since 1965, Chinese organized criminal groups in New York City have evolved and transformed themselves from predatory street gangs composed of youths battling over the control of turfs into powerful extortionate rings that terrorize local commerce and have established a secure foothold in the illegitimate economy of the community. It is noteworthy that these gangs developed in almost complete isolation from the larger non-Asian community during their tumultuous growth period in New York. They illustrate the universality of the phenomenon of organized criminality.

This paper is part of a study that seeks to describe and understand the dynamics of some aspects of the criminality within the Chinese community. The larger research effort is attempting to examine the nature and organization of extortionate activities among businesses in New York City's Chinese communities. Extortion is a type of crime that is especially pernicious because it preys upon the small retail businessperson as well as the large commercial enterprise.

It is extortion more than prostitution, narcotics trafficking or handling illegal goods that affects the community most directly and palpably. Compared to robbery, burglary and muggings where locals residents are also the prime victims, extortion activities seem especially resistant to law enforcement control measures. Moreover, the pervasiveness of extortion and lack of police success in containing it, has produced a climate of tolerance in the community. The prevalence of extortion gangs in the community makes their criminality particularly worrisome in that they may diversify and venture into a wider range of crime centered in the local communities enervating even more the quality of life there. Weakening and frustrating extortion enterprises by controlling their criminal offending requires a detailed inventory of the extent of extortion activities, how it is organized, and how it sustains the criminal groups in the community. Police and community responses to crime are dependent upon reliable measures of the level of this organized criminality.

Notes and references

1. Dillon, R.H., *The Hatchet Men* (New York: Coward/McCann, 1962); Gong E.Y. and B. Grant., *Tong War!* (New York: N.L. Brown, 1930).
2. Beach, W.G., *Oriental Crime in California* (Stanford, Calif.: Stanford University Press, 1932); MacGill, H.G. "The Oriental Delinquent in the Vancouver Juvenile Court," *Sociology and Social Research* 1938 (12), 428–438.
3. Tracy, C.A., "Race, Crime, and Social Policy: The Chinese in Oregon, 1871–1885," *Crime and Social Justice* 1980, 11–25.
4. Barringer, F., "Immigration Brings New Diversity to Asian Population in the U.S.," *New York Times* June 12, 1991, A1.

267

5. Chinatown and its offshoots – or rivals – now have 10 newspapers, 25 bank branches with a total population of some 300,000. Throughout the United States, the Asian population has grown from 3 million in 1974 to 10 million in 1990. In New York City, the growth pattern has encroached upon "Little Italy", the traditional immigrant settlement and now more of a tourist attraction than an ethnic enclave or habitat. The Chinese people living adjacent to Little Italy have continually moved north absorbing more and more of the neighborhoods that made up the Italian ethnic community.

6. Kwong, P., *The New Chinatown* (New York: Hill and Wang, 1987).

7. Scardino, A., "Commercial Rents in Chinatown Soar as Hong Kong Exodus Grows," *New York Times* December 25, 1986, A1.

8. The commercial neighborhoods between 51st and 59th Streets, at the southern end of Central Park.

9. Between 42nd Street, near Grand Central Station, and the residential neighborhoods that begin at about 59th Street.

10. Chan, Y., "Riding the Dragon," *Village Voice* October 31, 1989.

11. The combination of population expansion and real estate investment monies from Hong Kong are effecting property values in those sections of New York where the Chinese rub shoulders with Italians and Latinos. The communities in southern Manhattan are going through a "transition" phase where tensions are exacerbated and the racial environments have become increasingly hostile. Latinos have vented their anger indiscriminately against all Chinese with regrettable results. The low-income Chinese take the brunt of the antagonism and are wrongly blamed for the Hong Kong inspired gentrification projects intruding into Puerto Rican neighborhoods. Frictions between Latino and Chinese adolescents play a role in strengthening youth gangs in the area. The situation is made worse by the underrepresentation of Chinese in the political system of the city. Chinese do not sit on school boards in any significant numbers in their districts; and they tend to be neglected by the patronage machine where only two persons occupy senior decision-making positions in the city government. The mix of these factors creates a climate conducive to organized criminality in the community.

12. Sung, B., *Mountain of Gold* (New York: Macmillan, 1967).

13. Kuo, C., *Social and Political Change in New York's Chinatown* (New York: Praeger, 1977).

14. Chen, H. and J. Tchen, "Towards a History of Chinese in Queens," Queens College, City Univeristy of New York, 1989.

15. Howe, M., "City's Third Chinatown is Emerging in Brooklyn," *New York Times* September 13, 1987, 74.

16. Chan, op cit.

17. Chin, Ko-lin. *Chinese Subculture and Criminality* (Westport, CT: Greenwood Press, 1990).

18. Attorney General of California. California Organized Crime and Criminal Intelligence Branch. *Proceedings of the Conference on Chinese Gang Problems* (California, Sacramento, 1972); Baridon, B., *Report on Asian Organized Crime* (U.S. Department of Justice, Criminal Division, Washington, D.C., 1988); Booth, M., *The Triads* (New York: St. Martins Press, 1990); Bresler, F., *The Chinese Mafia* (New York: Stein and Day, 1981); Kaplan D.E. and A. Durbo *Yakuza* (New York: MacMillan Publishing Co., 1986); Kaplan, D.E., Goldberg and L. Jue "Enter the Dragon: How Hong Kong notorious underworld syndicates are becoming the number one organized crime problem in California," *San Francisco Focus* December, 1986, 68–84; Loo, C.K., *The Emergence of San Francisco Chinese Juvenile Gangs from the 1950s to the Present* M.A. thesis, San Jose State University 1976; Posner, G., *Warlords of Crimes: Chinese Secret Societies – The New Mafia* (New York: McGraw-Hill, 1988); President's Commission on Organized Crime. Organized Crime of Asian Origin: Record of Hearing III – October 23–25, 1984, New York, New York. (Washington, D.C.; U.S. Government Printing Office, 1985); Ragelman, K.R., Slaying the Dragon: Attacking Chinese Organized Crime in Hong Kong and San Francis-

268

co. A Senior Thesis presented to the Faculty of the Woodrow Wilson School of Public and International Affairs, Princeton University, 1989); Rice, B., "The New Gangs of Chinatown," *Psychology Today* 1977 (10), 60–69; Robertson, F., *Triangle of Death: The Inside Story of the Triads – the Chinese Mafia* (London: Routledge and Kegan Paul, 1977); Robinson, N. and D. Joe "Gangs in Chinatown: The New Young Warrior Class," *McGill Journal of Education* 1980 (15) 149–162; Sheu, C., *Delinquency and Identity* (New York: Harrow and Heston, 1986); U.S. Department of Justice. Oriental Organized Crime: A Report on a Research Project of the Organized Crime Section. Federal Bureau of Investigation, Criminal Investigation Division, Washington, D.C., 1985; U.S. Senate. *Asian Organized Crime* (Washington, D.C.: U.S. Government Printing Office, 1992); Van de Kamp, J.K., *Organized Crime in California*. Annual Report to the California Legislature. State of California, Department of Justice. Sacramento, California, 1986.

19. Sung, B., *Transplanted Chinese Children* (New York: Department of Asian Studies, City Univeristy of New York, 1979).

20. Curry, G.D. and I.A. Spergel, "Gang Homicide, Delinquency and Community," *Criminology*, *1988 (26), 381–405; Weis, J.G. and J. Sederstrom, The Prevention of Serious Delinquency: What to Do? (Washington D.C.: U.S. Government Printing Office, 1981)*.

21. *Cloward, R. and L. Ohlin, Delinquency and Opportunity: A Theory of Delinquent Gangs* (New York: Free Press, 1960); Spergel, I.A., "Youth Gangs: Continuity and Change," in N. Morris and M. (eds), *Crime and Justice: An Annual Review of Research*, Vol. 12 (Chicago: University of Chicago Press, 1989).

22. See for example: Cloward and Ohlin. op. cit.; Klein, M., *Street Gangs and Street Workers* (Englewood Cliffs, N.J.: Prentice-Hall, 1971).

23. Stier, E.H. and P.R. Richards, "Strategic Decision Making in Organized Crime Control," in H. Edelhertz (ed), *Major Issues in Organized Crime Control* (Washington, D.C.: U.S. Government Printing Office, 1987).

24. U.S. Senate, *Asian Organized Crime* (Washington, D.C: U.S. Government Printing Office, 1992).

25. Allen, G and L. Thomas, "Orphans of War," *The Globe and Mail Toronto*, 1987, 1 (12); G. Kinkead, *Chinatown* (New York: Harper Collins, 1992).

26. Bresler, op. cit.

27. Key Publications, Inc., *Chinese Business Guide and Directory* (New York: New York, 1990).

28. After interviewing 15 non-Asian merchants and finding that the respondents were not victimized by Chinese gangs, we decided to exclude non-Asian store owners from the study.

29. Callagher, D., *Small Business, Big Problem: Small Business and Crime in New York City* (New York: INTERFACE, 1989).

30. Callagher, op. cit.

31. Chesneaux, J., *Popular Movements and Secret Societies in China, 1840–1950* (Stanford, Calif.: Stanford University Press, 1972).

32. Morgan, W.P., *Triad Societies in Hong Kong* (Hong Kong: The Government Printer, 1960).

33. Booth, op. cit.

34. Booth, op. cit.

35. Ashbury, H., *The Gangs of New York* (New York: A. Knopf, 1927).

36. Dillon, op. cit.

37. President's Commission on Organized Crime, op. cit.

38. New York City Police Department, Fifth Precinct, 1983. Gang Intelligence Information.

39. President's Commission on Organized Crime, op. cit.

40. Hagedorn, J.M., *People and Folks* (Chicago: Lakeview Press, 1988); Moore, J., *Homeboys* (Philadelphia: Temple University Press, 1978).

41. Money or the provision of goods and services paid to avoid explicit or implicit threats of vio-

lence is the working definition of extortion adopted in the study. Whatever the type of extortion method used, all involve the use of threats of violence or mayhem to obtain money, services and other things of value. The definition of extortion closely follows that contained in the New York State Penal Law (Law & 155.05 (2)(e) (McKinney. 1988)

42. Posner, op. cit.
43. The respondents in the sample make a distinction between "extortion" and "protection" which the New York State Penal Code does not. For the sake of consistency in reporting on criminal behavior and consequences, the differences in defining the crime the community makes about extortionate activity neither violates the spirit of the law nor does it distort the reporting of results. Such community distinctions without significant differences and legal consequences do not confuse the descriptions of crime patterns and their prevalence in these communities.
44. Hawaii Crime Commission, *Extortion* (Honolulu. HI: Hawaii Crime Commission, 1980).
45. Bresler, op. cit.
46. Brennan. P., Interview. Commanding Officer, 5th Precinct. New York City Police Department (April 5, 1991).

Part IV
Organized Crime
and
Economic Structures

[16]

MINERS, TAILORS AND TEAMSTERS: BUSINESS RACKETEERING AND TRADE UNIONISM*

Alan A. Block** and William J. Chambliss***

The sociological literature makes frequent allusion to, but little systematic analysis of corruption in labor unions. The one major exception is the classic study by Daniel Bell of the "Racket-Ridden Longshoremen" (Bell, 1962). Bell's analysis has, for the most part, been uncritically accepted in the sociological literature as the definitive statement on the subject. While Bell's analysis is unquestionably insightful and imaginative, it is seriously flawed because of its uncritical acceptance of the functional paradigm as the lens through which racketeering in the Longshoremen's Union is viewed. From the perspective of functionalism it is sufficient to seek an explanation for any phenomenon simply in terms of the "function" or "consequences" the phenomenon has for maintaining order and stability at a particular point in time. From this starting point it then makes perfectly good sense to seek an explanation for the pervasiveness of racketeering in the Longshoremen's Union in terms of the contribution racketeering makes to smooth-functioning, to the stability, the predictability of the tasks to be accomplished: in this case, the loading and unloading of ships in the New York Harbor. Accepting the legitimacy of this starting point, then Bell's "explanation" for the pervasiveness of racketeering in the Longshoremen's Union, which stresses how racketeering solves the problem of getting ships loaded and unloaded rapidly in a harbor fraught with physical-geographical problems magnified by the unpredictable nature of shipping, is quite logical. The problem is that this interpretation is not only misleading it is quite untenable when viewed from a broader perspective. Rather than tracing the historical development of racketeering in the New York Longshoremen's Union, Bell seeks to "explain" the phenomenon solely in terms of the "functions" served by the existence of racketeering at the time of his study. As is characteristic of research employing the functional paradigm, Bell also

fails to ask: functional for whom? He is therefore misled into believing that "what is good for shippers is good for everyone."

Looking at only one harbor in New York and the activities of one union distorts even a generalization about racketeering in New York's Longshoremen's Union. For instance, by concentrating on Manhattan's West Side piers as the "hub of the port" (p. 161), Bell commits a serious mistake which is compounded when he goes on to discuss aspects of racketeering resulting from the peculiar physical layout of Manhattan's dock area. It was not Manhattan but Brooklyn which contained the "premier port" in America at the time (District Attorney of Kings County and the December 1949 Grand Jury, February 1, 1955). Brooklyn's piers handled "54 percent of all the seaboard traffic of the entire port of New York" (Grand Jury: 99), which included all the docks on the New Jersey side of the Metropolitan region. And the Brooklyn waterfront was more completely dominated by racketeers and their collaborationists in the shipping and stevedoring companies than Manhattan ever was (Block, 1979). Needless to add, the configuration of Manhattan's streets can tell us nothing about the structure and functions of racketeering on the Brooklyn waterfront, and therefore of New York waterfront racketeering, much less of labor racketeering in general.

It is our intention in this paper to trace the social relations that were responsible for the institutionalization of racketeering and other forms of criminality in some labor unions in the United States. To accomplish this we will look in detail at the historical roots of corruption and racketeering among garment industry unions in New York and less intensely, but nevertheless suggestively, at the same phenomenon in the Teamsters and the United Mine Workers.

THE SCOPE OF RACKETEERING

Consider the following list of industries in New York City which were pervaded by "racketeers": bead, cinder, cloth shrinking, clothing, construction, flower shops, Fulton Market, funeral, fur dressing, grape, hod carriers, ice, Kosher butchers, laundry, leather, live poultry, master

* An earlier version of this essay was presented at the annual conference of the European Group for the Study of Deviance and Social Control, September 1977, Barcelona, Spain.

** Alan Block is presently teaching at University College, Cardiff, Wales. He is on leave from the University of Delaware.

*** William Chambliss teaches in the Department of Sociology, University of Delaware.

barbers, milk, millinery, musical, night patrol, neckwear, newsstand, operating engineers, overall, paper box, paper hangers, shirt makers, taxicabs, waterfront workers and window cleaners. All of these industries and trades as well as others were subject in one fashion or another to racketeering which was well defined in the 1930's as organized extortion, the forte of power syndicates (see *New York Times*, September 1, 1931: 14; this is the full report of Samuel Seabury's investigation of racketeering).

The question for researchers, obviously, is how to account for such an extraordinary development in which so many of New York's and indeed America's key trades became the province of power syndicates. The general answer to such an inquiry lies in the often violently antagonistic relations between labor and capital, workers and bosses, in the modern era. The history of trade unionism in the United States reveals the violent methodologies adopted by employers to prevent, contain and destroy unions (Lens, 1973; Dubofsky, 1969; Yellen, 1936; Boyer and Morais, 1955; Huberman, 1937; Foner, 1965; Jeffreys-Jones, 1974; Bernstein, 1966). Among the methodologies was the use of hired thugs to engage in strikebreaking. Very often, the services of strikebreakers were purchased from a burgeoning industry known as the private detective trade, dominated by such agencies as Pinkerton, Burns and Farley. Agencies engaged in strikebreaking were not timorous in announcing their services. For example, *the Journal of the National Association of Manufacturers* in 1906 carried an announcement of the Joy Detective Service of Cleveland which stated: "WE BREAK STRIKES .... We guard property during strikes, employ non-union men to fill places of strikers" (Jeffreys-Jones: 524). Many of the individuals recruited by private detective agencies were local gangsters, some of whom because of their "ethnic and community identification" were doubly useful to employers. Quoting a complaint from a New York trade union official, Jeffreys-Jones comments: "The private detectives employed by these agencies are recruited from East Side gangs, the same gangs that support the politicians ..., with the result that politicians persuaded the police to side with employers" (p. 525).

Within the general social situation in which employers resorted to local power syndicates masquerading as private detective agencies for strikebreaking and labor mediation, there was room for duplicity and the double-cross. Jeffreys-Jones reports on a meeting between David Silverman, an executive board member of the Neck Wear Makers' Union, and Max Schlansky, of the United Secret Service Agency in 1914:

Schlansky entered into conversation with Silverman about the strike in progress against the business of Oppenheimer, Franc and Langsdorf. The guard business arising out of the dispute was being handled for the notorious Val O'Farrell Agency by its chief agent, Schultz. The engagement was yielding $300 weekly for Schultz, but was now coming to an end. Schlansky averred that Schultz did not know his business, for he had let slip by

many opportunities to prolong the strike. Perceiving an opportunity to extract some money from the situation, Schlansky proposed to Silverman that the union leader hire some of his plug uglies to beat up Schultz' men. Schlansky pointed out that in this event, Oppenheimer and partners would probably fire Schultz, and engage Schlansky. Then, presumably for a further fee, Schlansky would ensure that the union won the strike (p. 534).

Having created an arena of violence by their intransigence, employers soon found that extortion could be a double-edged sword. Nevertheless, even with the machinations of some power syndicates who turned their violence against employers, it is clear that the one consistent victim throughout all this turmoil was rank and file workers. Control of workers through violence and the threat of violence lined the pockets of employers first and foremost, and then professional criminals and corrupt union officials. The ends to which this private violence was employed besides the immediate pecuniary ones included strikebreaking, sweetheart contracts, price-fixing, monopoly and oligopoly.

THE NEEDLE TRADES

Among the most significant racketeers to work in the garment industry in the United States was Louis "Lepke" Buchalter who, along with his partner Jacob "Gurrah" Shapiro, had virtual control of the clothing industry in Manhattan from the late 1920's through most of the following decade (Block, 1979). Their dominance of the field of criminal labor relations was not seriously challenged until the fall of 1936 when the federal government tried them on charges of extortion in New York's almost Byzantine fur dressing industry, one of the garment trades. To understand the roles played by Buchalter and Shapiro, and in whose interests they acted, it is important to relate something of the history of the garment industries and their corresponding trade union movements.

The clothing industry provided a place for the Jewish immigrant, according to Moses Rischin, "where the initial shock of contact with a bewildering world was tempered by a familiar milieu" (Rischin, 1962: 61). Although the manufacture of men's clothing was already an important segment of New York's economy, the arrival of the East European immigrant Jews drastically changed the ready-made clothing industry's organizational pattern. Revived was the contractor who had been ousted in the 1870's as factories had replaced outside manufacture. This time, however, the contractor introduced a unique type of production, known as section work, which exploited new recruits through a minute and deplorable division of labor. Because loft and factory rents were so high, the contractor supplied the perfect solution to the destructively competitive economics of seasonal manufacture. Upon the contractor was placed the burdens of manufacture production risks and the responsibility for supervising and recruiting a labor force. In return, contractors attempting to lower production costs developed the task system. This system, Rischin notes. was described as "'the most ingenious and effective system of overexertion known to modern industry'" (Rischin: 64-66).

The changes in the labor process went hand-in-hand with technical improvements and innovations and the influx of cheap immigrant labor which all together were responsible for the exceptional growth of the garment trades which began in the 1880's. Most of this growth was in the area of men's clothing. The phenomenal expansion of women's ready-made clothing had to wait until the turn of the century when "labor costs fell, techniques of design improved, and women gradually emancipated themselves from the home" (Rischin: 62-66). The fur industry, in turn, emerged in conjunction with the women's clothing industry. Rischin concludes that by 1910 around 75 percent of the workers as well as the majority of manufacturers in the fur trades were immigrant Jews (Rischin: 62-66).

Commenting on the overall importance of the garment trades, Rischin states that from 1880 to 1910, the social economy of New York was reshaped by the clothing industry. He notes that in 1880 almost 10 percent of Manhattan's factories were engaged in manufacturing clothing and that they employed over 28 percent of the industrial labor force. By 1910, the figures had changed to 47 percent of the factories manufacturing clothing and employing 46 percent of the industrial labor force. In a study of the demography of the American Jew based on the 1900 census, Ben B. Seligman finds that 36 percent of the 143,337 employed persons described as Russian, almost all of whom were Jewish, living in New York, Chicago, Philadelphia, Detroit, Boston, Pittsburgh and St. Louis, were employed in the needle trades (Seligman, 1950: 56). Remarking on the economic and occupational status of American Jews between the two world wars, Seligman states that "three-fourths of the New York City Jews engaged in manufacturing in 1937 were in the clothing and headwear industries, where they constituted more than one-half of the total number employed in these industries" (Seligman: 57). It is also estimated for 1937 that "6 percent of the New York City Jews in industry were furriers, and they constituted about four-fifths of those in the fur industry" (Seligman: 57). Along with the spectacular and increasing Jewish domination of the needle trades went pitiful wages, extended hours, innumerable slack seasons, contracting and subcontracting, home work, and the lack of even rudimentary safeguards of health and decency which made the needle trades infamous as a "sweated" industry.

As a consequence of conditions like these, and a number of other factors, a dynamic trade union movement developed. The founding institution for the Jewish labor movement was the United Hebrew Trades begun in 1888. The major purpose of this group was obviously organization of Jewish workers into trade unions. In a large number of cases. the unions which were formed either with the initiative or help of the UHT were local or regional bodies that had next to be affiliated with an existing national organization. In the garment trades, however, there were no national organizations until 1891 when the United

Garment workers on the march, 1909

Garment Workers was started for the men's clothing industry. Will Herberg describes this group as "at bottom a coalition of men's tailors, largely radical-minded immigrant Jews and Italians, on the one hand, and conservative American overall and work clothes makers, on the other" (Herberg, 1952: 9-10).

Workers in the women's garment industry waited until 1900 for their national organization – the International Ladies Garment Workers Union (ILGWU). Although the ILGWU started well, the 1903 business depression halted its growth. Subsequently, the ILGWU suffered through a difficult period which ended in 1909 when an economic upswing provided the most important surge of trade unionism that Jewish labor experienced until 1933. In the next five years, (1909-1914) there developed what Herberg calls "a tremendous transformation in the power and status of the Jewish labor movement" (Herberg: 16). The major events during this period in the women's garment industry were the "uprising of the twenty thousand" and the "great revolt."

In the fall of 1909, a spontaneous rebellion of almost 20,000 shirtwaist makers in New York, mostly women, was enormously successful. At the time of the strike, the entire membership of the ILGWU was only 2,000; while at the end, the shirtwaist makers union itself had over 10,000 members (Herberg: 17-18). Closely following the rebellion of shirtwaist makers was the strike of the New York cloak makers known as the "great revolt." Unlike the earlier action, this strike took place in an industry employing primarily men and in which there was a strong and deep tradition of trade unionism. The strike was called for July 10, 1910, and about 60,000 workers responded. Like the earlier strike, this one was a victory with most of the workers' demands granted. Following the example of the women's garment workers, the furriers called a general strike which was successful and led to the formation in 1913 of the International Fur Workers Union.

The trade union movement among the men's clothing workers during these years was hampered by a serious conflict between the leaders of the United Garment Workers and the rank and file tailors. One of the primary differences was found in the extreme reluctance of the UGW leaders to become involved in labor struggles, especially strikes. The militant tailors, however, had great faith in the power of the strike. Increasingly, the tailors viewed their national leaders as indifferent to their problems, primarily interested in containing their militancy. The rift in the United Garment Workers widened in 1910 and again in 1912 when a general strike was called at the instigation of the New York Brotherhood of Tailors. At first, the leaders of the UGW refused to recognize the action. Later, "behind the backs of the workers and even many of the strike leaders, the UGW officials . . . tried to bring the strike to an end with an agreement that enraged the strikers because it ignored the question of recognition and other essential demands" (Herberg: 23-24). In 1914, the conflict between the tailors, who represented a majority of the unionists, and the conservative leadership resulted in the formation of the Amalgamated Clothing Workers of America, an independent union under the leadership of Sidney Hillman and Joseph Schlossberg. The Amalgamated was almost immediately called a "dual union" and therefore a betrayal of labor solidarity by the AFL. The other Jewish unions, however, ignored the slander and viewed it as a bona fide union. The Amalgamated soon established itself as both an integral and significant element of the labor movement wherever men's clothing was manufactured.

So-called racketeering, which in its simplest form is direct extortion by the imposition of union sanctions, originally developed in the needle trade unions out of the necessity to fight scabs and thugs hired by employers. In the early part of this century prior to World War I, known criminals such as Benjamin Fein and Irving Wexler fought employer goons and became semipermanent fixtures in a number of needle trade locals and the United Hebrew Trades.[1] From policing strikes it was a short step to helping in organizing workers and to domination of key locals. Continuing labor-management and internal union struggles throughout the 1920's enabled others such as Buchalter and Shapiro to attain positions of influence.

Their first labor-management efforts were in the men's clothing industry. Buchalter helped organize truck owners and self-employed drivers into an employers' trade association which was perhaps the most significant act in the development of what should be called business racketeering. To make the point clearer, one of the first actions of the association was to raise the cartage costs for men's clothing followed by the sharing of the windfall profits by the members of the association (Hutchinson, 1970: 76). At about the same time Buchalter became what John Hutchinson modestly calls: "influential in the clothing drivers' local of the Amalgamated," thus completing what we will see is the classic equation of business racketeering. Finally, it was at this time that Buchalter and Shapiro bought into some clothing firms, thus moving into the arena of business crime.

Let us expand upon the methods by which racketeers became entrepreneurs. First consider the details of Buchalter's and Shapiro's relationship with businessman Joseph Miller as reported by the FBI:

Miller has been in the coat front manufacturing

business since 1907, and in 1933, the name of his firm was changed to the Pioneer Coat Front Company, Inc. In that year, Miller took Shapiro and Buchalter into his business as one-third partners, following their investment of $20,000 each. In 1934, Miller sold his New York plant to Samuel Weiner for $50,000 and moved to Philadelphia. At this time Weiner ascertained that Buchalter and Shapiro were stockholders in the New York Pioneer Company and they demanded to be placed on Weiner's payroll, stating even though Miller had moved to Philadelphia under an agreement not to open up in the coat front manufacturing business in New York City nor to sell to his old customers, nevertheless, he would not keep his agreement and Weiner would need the services of Buchalter and Shapiro for forcing Miller to keep his promise. At this time, Buchalter and Shapiro, without any capital investment whatsoever, were taken into the Perfection Coat Front Manufacturing Company, and received $300 each, weekly. They were not satisfied with the salaries paid them by Weiner and took additional money from the Perfection Company in the nature of loans, resulting in losses to this organization of $75,000 from April 12 to September 1, 1934. The company then could not obtain additional credit unless Joseph Miller returned to New York to take over management of the company. Buchalter and Shapiro, in an effort to force Miller to return to New York from Philadelphia, stopped him from selling coat fronts manufactured in Philadelphia to his New York customers (FBI, 1939: 9).

What seems clear from the FBI account, although not commented on by them, is that Buchalter, Shapiro and Miller had entered into a scheme to defraud Weiner. Obviously, Miller had not lived up to his part of the original agreement and was busy selling to his former New York customers. It is also apparent that both Buchalter and Shapiro knew well in advance that Miller would fail to fulfill his contract and that would provide their rationale for bilking Weiner which would cause Miller to be brought back into the business.

A further indication of the business machinations engaged in by Buchalter and Shapiro along with Miller concerns the formation in 1933 of Leo Greenberg & Company, Inc. This corporation was founded with Nathan Borish and Joseph Miller investing $10,000 and $5,000 each. Then in 1934, Jacob Shapiro also invested in the company in sufficient amount to obtain a half interest. The company's name was changed to Greenberg and Shapiro and Jacob Shapiro placed his brother Carl in as manager of the company. The following year the company was reorganized into the Raleigh Manufacturers Company with Nathan Borish, Carl Shapiro, Jacob Shapiro, Louis Buchalter and Louis Miller each having a 20 percent interest.

One final example of the methods by which Buchalter, Shapiro and other "union organizers" joined the ranks of the owners deals with the outcome of a work stoppage called by the Amalgamated to prevent garment work from being carted out of New York to non-union firms primarily located in Pennsylvania. One of the garment trucking firms balked at the stoppage, claiming that it had been "double-crossed by the Amalgamated once before" (Court of Appeals—Brooklyn, New York, 1942: 1333-47). Buchalter countered that argument by assuring the boss of the company, Louis Cooper, that he had nothing to worry about, that he (Buchalter) was now the Amalgamated. Cooper responded that he would only agree to stop his trucks if Buchalter would become his partner. Buchalter agreed and the trucks stopped (Court of Appeals—Brooklyn, New York, 1942).

In 1931, Buchalter attempted to take control of the cutters' union, Local 4, of the Amalgamated and thereby precipitated what Matthew Josephson, in his laudatory biography of Sidney Hillman, terms the "terrible emergency" (Josephson, 1952: 336-39). The strategic importance of the cutters' union is described by Joel Seidman:

> The jobber-contractor system is particularly vulnerable to gangster influence. Under the system of inside production, with workers of all degrees of skills under the same roof, the superior economic power of the highly skilled worker can be utilized to help unionize the entire plant; so long as the relatively small number of skilled workers refuse to work under nonunion conditions, the plant can scarcely operate, whether or not it enjoys the protection of gangsters. Under the contracting system, however, the cutters, comprising a large percentage of the skilled workers, may work in the jobber's shop under union conditions. If the cut goods can then be shipped to nonunion contracting shops, anywhere within a radius of a hundred miles or even more, the enterprise can under-sell its completely unionized competition. The function of the gangsters is then to protect the trucks that haul the cut goods to the contractor and bring the finished product back. Protection of trucking at or near the jobber's office is more important than safeguarding the contract shop against union organizers: the gangster may indeed perform both functions, though in many small towns, the police may stand ready to repel the union organizing drives, without extra cost to the garment manufacturer.

> The two points of control are therefore the cutting room and trucking. When the union is functioning properly, it checks the volume of goods cut with the volume received by inside and authorised contract shops, and learns from the truckers where the balance is being taken. If some of the cutters can be persuaded to send false figures to the union office, however, receiving part of the net savings as their share of the loot, and if in addition, the metropolitan politicians

or police are bought off so that the gangsters riding the trucks are not molested in the performance of their duties, then indeed the business that receives gangster protection will prosper, and the union tailors and the legitimate employers will suffer (Seidman, 1942: 190-91).

Seidman adds that this was exactly the situation in the metropolitan New York men's clothing industry.

Buchalter gained control of the cutters, according to Assistant District Attorney Burton Turkus, by convincing certain of their leaders that it would be advantageous if his mob replaced Terry Burns and Ab Slabow, who were then Local 4's enforcers. At the same time, Orlofsky who had been a business agent for the union became the manager of the cutters' local. In the battle between Hillman and Orlofsky, Turkus contends that Buchalter used Orlofsky as a pawn, trading him off for a deal with Hillman. This maneuver was followed by the designation of Bruno Belea, the general organizer of the Amalgamated, and of two Buchalter hoods, Paul Berger and Danny Fields, as the new intermediaries between Buchalter and the union. Later, another of Buchalter's men received $25,000 from Hillman himself for delivery to Buchalter. With his position concerning the Amalgamated suppoedly secured, Buchalter next turned to management. He extorted anywhere from $5,000 to $50,000 from both truckers and individual manufacturers. One of Buchalter's most important operatives, Max Rubin, stated that from 1934 to 1937 he took part in shakedowns of $400 to $700 per week—and he was only one of many collectors. Turkus also notes that it had been charged "that reputable garment trucking firms alone yielded Lepke a million dollars a year for ten years"(Turkus and Feder, 1951: 338-43). Not calculated, however, was the amount of money saved by employers engaged in price-fixing, restraint of trade and wage freezes.

By 1932, Buchalter became involved in the fur dressing trade. Buchalter was approached by members of the fur dressing industry and asked if he would help in overcoming resistance to an organization of manufacturers. The request, obviously criminal in intent, called for the formation of a syndicate under Buchalter's direction which would work in concert with an earlier criminal conspiracy formed by employers. As we have already seen with the formation of an employers' association among garment truckers, so-called labor racketeering "flourishes most effectively in conjunction with trade associations formed and maintained in demoralized industries" (Columbia Law Review, 1939: 994-95). These employer associations are, of course, a device to stabilize competition and to raise commodity prices. In some cases, however, "the temptation to attract business by price cutting may be so strong, that coercion becomes necessary to compel members to remain in the association or competitors to join it." In these kinds of situations, racketeers, usually through intimidation of local union leadership or as partners with corrupt trade unionists, are able to threaten labor problems against those recalcitrant firms attracted by the advantages of price cutting.

The fur industry was both demoralized and exceedingly competitive, according to Hutchinson. Because fur manufacturing was a skilled trade, resistant to mechanization and performed largely by hand, access into the industry was simple. The majority of firms were small: about 25 percent had only one or two employees; and over half employed four workers or less. In addition, Hutchinson writes that the fur trade was highly susceptible to fashion changes, quite unstable in prices, an arena replete with business and economic failures, and, finally, a kind of ethical wasteland. Also. the Depression struck the fur industry harder than any of the other needle trades with fur imports dropping by 1932 to one-quarter, and exports to one-third of the 1929 base. These grave difficulties increased the employers' normally competitive, secretive and suspicious behavior towards each other. They were notoriously uncooperative in facing common industry problems.

Prodded by desperate competition after three years of the Great Depression in what was probably the most cutthroat part of the fur industry, the fur dressers invented two organizations they hoped would promote both stability and profit. Formed early in 1932 were the Protective Fur Dressers Corporation (Protective) consisting of 17 of the largest rabbit skin dressing companies in the country and the Fur Dressers Factor Corporation (Factor), which included 46 of the largest dressers of furs other than rabbit skins. As outlined later by the Federal Bureau of Investigation, the purposes and functions of the two corporations were to eliminate from the industry all dressing firms which were not members, to persuade all dealers to work only with firms which belonged to the corporations and/or to prevent them from dealing with nonmembers (FBI, 1939: 9). The associations were to set prices and to implement a quota system insuring that the different members of the corporations received a fixed percentage of the entire business handled by the member firms. Also, the associations set up a system of credit which enforced frequent settlements and blacklisted dealers who did not pay on time.

Once the corporations were organized, all the dealers and manufacturers were notified that henceforth their business was to be given to a firm designated by the Association. They were also told that prices would be increased immediately and all accounts were to be settled every Friday in full. When the Protective was first organized, the individual members set the price for dressing the cheapest rabbit skins at five cents apiece; subsequently, prices were raised until the minimum was seven and the maximum ten cents. The FBI estimated that this association controlled about 80 to 90 percent of the trade in 1932 and around 50 percent the following year. Those dealers and manufacturers who refused to cooperate with the Protective and continued doing business with independent fur dressers were subject first to telephone warnings, and then to beatings and the destruction of their goods and plants by corrosive acids and stench bombs. In extreme cases some firms were told to permanently close down or be blown up (FBI, 1939: 10).

Buchalter and Shapiro were brought into the fur industry through the efforts of Abraham Beckerman,

New York garment workers

previously a high official in the Amalgamated and subsequently general manager of the Fur Dressers Factor Corporation and the Associated Employers of Fur Workers, Inc. Beckerman's initial problems as general manager of the Factor were organizational, and accordingly he solicited the help of Buchalter and Shapiro, both of whom he had known from the Amalgamated. Beckerman explained to Buchalter and Shapiro that there was a need for "organizational work," meaning violent coercion. Beckerman then said, according to the FBI, that before he became associated with the Factor, it had contracted with gangster Jerry Sullivan, a member of the Owney Madden gang, to handle the organizational problems (FBI, 1939: 11). Sullivan's work was unsatisfactory and Beckerman had been requested to get the association out of the deal. This he had now done by contracting with Buchalter and Shapiro.

The work performed was the obvious: informed by contact men within the industry which dealers, dressers, manufacturers and union officials were not cooperating, they directed their men to intimidate and coerce these individuals into joining the Association. The FBI concluded that all together, more than 50 telephone threats were made along with twelve assaults, ten bombings, three cases of acid throwing, two of arson, and one kidnapping (FBI, 1939: 12).

Buchalter and Shapiro had a relatively short career in the fur industry; they lasted from April of 1932 until the summer or fall of 1933. The decisive factor in the termination of their activities lay in the deteriorating relationship between the Protective and the Needle Trade Workers' Industrial Union, perhaps the most radical union in the garment industry (Hutchinson, 1970: 81). It is not clear in Hutchinson's account why this turn of events was, in fact, decisive unless it displayed Buchalter's inability to control labor in the industry and, therefore, turned the employers against him. Perhaps as important was a federal investigation which resulted in indictments of the two trade associations, Buchalter and Shapiro, and others in the fall of 1933. In any case, by the spring of 1933 something like open warfare existed between Buchalter and the Industrial Union. A telling incident that is descriptive of the fragmenting cooperation or unalterable opposition between the Protective and the union concerned Morris Langer, one of the union leaders. Langer, called by Foner a "Martyr of Labor" (Foner, 1950: 388-401), and by Hutchinson an organizer for the Protective (Hutchinson, 1970: 83), was told by the racketeers to organize strikes against three companies which had refused membership in the association. Langer balked because the firms were unionized. Langer also began to talk against the Protective. Before a month had passed, on March 23, 1933, Langer was blown up by a bomb placed under the hood of his car.

The event which finally ended Buchalter and Shapiro's involvement in the fur industry came in the form of a mini-war on April 24, 1933. During the morning, thugs hired by Buchalter and Shapiro staged an armed attack on the headquarters of the Industrial Union where a meeting was in progress. Contrary to expectations and even though armed with revolvers, lead pipes and knives, the gangsters were beaten back by the union men inside the building. As word of the attack spread, more workers streamed into the building and severely beat a number of the hoodlums who had been unable to escape. When it was all over, two men were dead and many injured; another man would die months later from injuries sustained in the battle (FBI, 1939: 15-16).

Buchalter and Shapiro had been hired by fur dressers in an effort to achieve the benefits of monopoly through forcing competitors into trade associations which dictated prices and allocated resources and markets. Garment manufacturers including fur dressers found it exceptionally difficult to escape competition and maintain profits through expansion because the industry was typically "confronted with a continually changing product" which hampered the development of large firms and dominant plants. This meant that garment businesses usually could not "afford to accept the rigidities involved in specialization and growth" (Hoover and Vernon, 1952: 61). Instead, manufacturers relied on subcontractors and others for operations and services which otherwise they might have considered providing from inside the firms. Also, the structure of the industry encouraged the entry of entrepreneurs with limited capital which further increased the competitiveness. In many cases, highly competitive, small sized, local product businesses such as the needle trades developed illegal associations staffed by gangsters. What all this means is that the logic of competitive capitalism in industries such as the clothing trades led inexorably to the formation of organized crime. Consumed by the desire for profit which, it seemed, could only be achieved by the creation of illegal monopolies and the elimination or more likely neutralization of trade unions, businessmen were instrumental in establishing some of the most vicious criminal syndicates in urban America. Paradoxically some employers were themselves the victims of terror campaigns waged by racketeers which sometimes rivaled those aimed at both progressive trade unionists and much of the rank and file. More often than not, however, the instigators of violence against employers were themselves employers.

It should be clear that even though extortion was practiced against some employers in the form of initiation fees and membership dues which ended up in the pockets of trade association racketeers, it was still monetarily advantageous for firms to belong. A graphic example of the benefits for employers in joining can be seen by looking momentarily at the restaurant racket operated by Arthur "Dutch Schultz" Flegenheimer. Flegenheimer worked along with a trade association "to extort initiation fees of $250 and membership dues of $260 annually, in addition to remunerative "shakedowns" of scores of restaurants in Manhattan. But because of Flegenheimer's dominance over restaurant locals, salaries were never raised despite what appeared to be vigorous union activity. It was estimated "on the basis of wage increases granted to the union in 1936 after the fall of the racket," that one employer saved about $136,000 from 1933-1936 even after paying $36,000 to the association. It is no wonder that it was strongly alleged that Flegenheimer "was brought in by the restaurant owners to stave off the activity of Locals 110 and 119" (*Columbia Law Review*, 1937: 998-99).

Finally, it must be added that the single most effective organization in combatting racketeers was the Needle Trade Workers' Union, surely the most radical trade union to confront organized crime in our sample. One might well want to argue, therefore, that the more progressive the union, the more militant the rank and file, the less likely it is to be penetrated and seduced by organized crime.

DAVE BECK OF THE TEAMSTERS

Toward the end of one of the hearings conducted by the McClellan Committee investigating corruption in the International Brotherhood of Teamsters, Senator Frank Church of Idaho delivered a most revealing opinion. Church stated: "I submit . . . that these men are capitalists and exploiters in the same tradition as the robber barons of old" (Hutchinson, 1970: 252). At that moment, Church was commenting on the character of certain Teamster leaders from Chicago, including Joseph Glimco, a notorious criminal and John T. O'Brien, secretary of Teamster Local 710 and a vice-president of the International Teamsters. The Committee had just finished listening to some of the most tawdry accounts of blatant stealing and corruption in the history of organized labor. What Church sensed and aptly noted was the triumph of capitalism as unregenerate greed at the very core of one of America's largest trade unions. The ideology sustaining the leaders of the International Teamsters was "gutter" capitalism, as far removed from the traditional ethos of trade unionism as Bonapartism was from Marxism in the 19th century. What is most unique about these modern robber barons, then, is the sordid but curious perversity of crooked capitalists running one of America's most significant national unions. In this case, it is organized labor as organized crime.

One of the most infamous of labor leaders and the man generally given credit for the unprecedented growth of the International Brotherhood of Teamsters (a union which began by organizing truckers but now includes a wide range of workers in many different types of industry) was Dave Beck. Beck's career as a Teamster began in Seattle, Washington, in 1920. At this time Beck was involved in relatively low-level union organizing activities and served as Business Agent for Teamsters Local 566. In 1924 Beck was elected secretary of the local and in 1925 the national organization hired him as a labor organizer.

The economic crash of 1929-1930 strengthened the unions' appeal to workers and the election of Franklin Delano Roosevelt in 1932 provided them with unprecedented political clout. In 1933 the National Recovery Act was signed and Section 7a of that Act provided that workers had the right ". . . to organize and bargain collec-

tively through representation of their own choosing . . ." The Seattle Teamsters chose Dave Beck to bargain for them.

Early attempts at union organization (in the late 1800's) in the United States met with an incredible amount of violence. Business and industry employed strikebreakers who did not hesitate to shoot or maim in order to break a strike. Fledgling unions in turn employed people who became virtually professional specialists in violence. Dave Beck was unusually effective in creating a coterie of union organizers who specialized in the selective enforcement of Beck's organizing activities.

Beck's more important innovations, however, were not along the lines of organized violence. They were in the area of union-management cooperation. Among other things, David Beck is generally given the dubious credit of having developed the "sweetheart contract," that is, a contract between the union and an owner which has the owner kicking back to union leaders a certain amount of money in exchange for a union contract that the owner finds favorable. More generally, Dave Beck's policies were from the beginning designed to create peace and harmony (he referred to it as "order") in the businesses with which he dealt. Beck said publicly in the early 1930's that "Some of the finest people I know are employers." Some years later, a Teamster worker remarked, "Dave used to say some of his best friends were bosses. Now I'll bet he tells the bosses some of his best friends drive trucks" (Morgan, 1951: 242).

In the early days of union organizing, as mentioned, the unions employed muscle-men to counterattack strikebreakers employed by owners. These muscle-men, however, in the case of the Seattle Teamsters were used for a variety of purposes including the intimidation of workers who did not readily accept Beck's leadership and his contracts.

"Professional bullyboys made it unhealthy to drive anything for pay if you didn't wear a Teamsters button. Trucks were sideswiped and overturned. Men who voted wrong at the Central Labor Council were beaten up. People heard the apocryphal Teamster slogan: 'vote no and go to the hospital' " (Morgan, 1951: 242).

These techniques of entering into secret pacts with owners and coercing workers to accept Beck's leadership were largely effective in maintaining stability for those who negotiated with the Teamsters. Occasionally businessmen who refused to cooperate were attacked and their businesses sometimes destroyed. Al Rosser, a Teamster organizer under Beck, was sent to prison for burning down a box factory when the owner had refused to allow the Teamsters to organize the workers.

Beck's most powerful weapon, however, and the one that eventually enabled him to become one of the nation's most influential labor leaders, was his willingness to cooperate with the owners. It was often said, as often by Beck as by business, that Seattle had the most peaceful labor relations in the country. These relations were built upon the complicity of union leaders with business interests. A complicity that not only meant wage agreements that were favorable to business but that involved labor leaders in a set of economic links with the owners.

Dave Beck was not the only West Coast union leader to gain national prominence in the thirties. Harry Bridges of the Longshoremen's Union, which was based in San Francisco, was also rapidly rising as a labor leader to be contended with. Bridges and Beck came head-to-head in Seattle where Beck's union was allied with the AFL and Bridges' with the recently formed CIO. In Seattle, Teamsters and Longshoremen literally carried on a war. Longshoremen and sailors armed themselves with grappling hooks and fists wrapped in steel tape; Teamsters relied on sawed-off baseball bats that fit under their coat sleeves. In the end, the Teamsters won this war because the local politicians, businessmen and police supported them. Longshoremen were arrested while Teamsters were allowed to go free from confrontations. Bridges was described by business as "the worst red peril to hit America since the Russian Revolution." Beck put the matter squarely when he addressed Seattle's businessmen and told them: "The town is going to be organized. Choose me or Bridges" (Morgan, 1951: 250). They chose Beck; a wise (and realistic) choice from their point of view. Beck promised and delivered labor stability:

Our aim has been to develop better understanding between industry and labor. This is our contribution toward good government and the community. We have inculcated the concept that there is a definite understanding between those employed and those who invest capital. We do our part to make the system work. We observe our contracts to the letter.

Small wonder the business and political community of Seattle backed Beck in his struggle for power against Bridges. It was Harry Bridges who had said in Seattle:

We take the stand that we as workers have nothing in common with the employers. We are in a class struggle, and we subscribe to the belief that if the employer is not in business, his products will still be necessary and we still will be providing them when there is no employing class. We frankly believe that day is coming (Morgan, 1951: 248).

Dave Beck, by contrast, was an anticommunist, believed that private property was sacred and should not be blemished by "sit down strikes." As a member of the Board of Trustees of the University of Washington, Dave Beck recommended that faculty members who refused to testify about their alleged Communist Party affiliations before congressional committees on the state and national level should be fired.

Beck bought stock in some of the companies and worked not only to assure labor stability but price stability as well. When some of the breweries of the Northwest lowered prices to gain a competitive edge, Beck approached the owners and threatened union action if they did not fall into line with the prices set by the majority of other brewery owners, including himself.

By 1947, the Teamsters were the largest labor union in the United States and Dave Beck was the national union's executive vice-president. In 1952, Beck took over as president of the national union. He continued to do favors for local businessmen and to organize the Teamsters around racketeering practices that served business interests. Beck was active in both stealing and corruption and he permitted or condoned it on the part of others in positions of leadership (Chambliss, 1978). No better example of the type of activities that were rampant in the Teamsters during Beck's leadership can be found than in some of the highlights of the career of Johnny "Dio" Dioguardi. In the early 1950's, Dioguardi was the regional director of the UAW-AFL in addition to being the business manager of one of the New York locals. Dioguardi concentrated his attention at this time on paper locals composed of the most abused segments of the working class population—blacks and Puerto Ricans. The vast majority of these locals were operated as money machines for Dioguardi and his associates.

The typical contract was never seen by the employees, provided a wage rate below or just slightly above the federal minimum wage, offered no other benefits, and was unenforced. There were no union elections, no general meetings of the members, and employers usually attended the shop meetings that were held. There was no grievance process, and in many cases the union officials involved were unknown to the members (Hutchinson, 1970: 234).

In investigating the activities of Dioguardi, a Senate Committee's only analogy to the conditions uncovered in Dioguardi's locals was the condition of the serfs of the Middle Ages. So blatantly rotten were these conditions, so obviously criminal, that Dioguardi was expelled from the UAW-AFL in 1954. But his career as a leader of organized labor was hardly over. The following year Dioguardi and several of his associates received charters for four local Teamster unions. Concerning these new Teamster locals, the McClellan Committee noted:

The officers and directors of these locals read like a rogue's gallery of the New York labor movement. They include such convicted extortionists as Joseph Cohen, Nathan Carmel, Aaron Kleinman, Milton Levine, Dominic Santa Maria, Harry Davidoff, Sam Goldstein, and Max Chester. So phony were these locals that, in the mad dash which occurred in the Teamsters to get them chartered, officials were chosen who had never been members of the union, false addresses were given for the offices, and the stationery of five of the locals was jointly printed and kept under wraps in the office of one of the locals (Hutchinson, 1970: 234-35).

As far as Beck himself is concerned, probably the least criminal or corrupt activity he engaged in was the transfer of large amounts of Teamster funds (the Central States Pension Fund alone by 1952 contained over 20 million dollars) out of Indianapolis banks (where the union was headquartered) to Seattle banks. Among the rest of his deals consummated while president of the Teamsters were highly unethical if not illegal ones involving the Fruehauf Trailor Company, a toy manufacturing company, the Occidental Life Insurance Company and the Seattle First National Bank.

Dave Beck's friendship and support of politicians was, however, eventually his undoing. He built his empire on cooperation with businessmen and with successful politicians. From 1932 to 1952, successful politics meant Democratic politics. With Eisenhower's election to President (and Richard Nixon his Vice-President) Beck's empire was in trouble. Federal investigators uncovered enough evidence of Beck's misuse of union funds to send him to prison in 1956. He was replaced by Jimmy Hoffa as president, who himself was sent to prison a decade later.

Beck's rise and fall in the Teamster Union is illustrative of the extent to which the "success" of union organizers in the United States in the 1930's, 40's, and 50's depended upon their being able to cooperate with business and politics sufficiently to receive their support. The workers were for the most part organized by coercion and violence. Business support was gained through offering labor stability and an alternative to radical labor representation (such as Harry Bridges), and politicians were bought through campaign contributions and votes. The racketeering that transpired was indeed rampant; the corruption ubiquitous; but it was a racketeering and corruption which did not emerge from the "needs of the system" or from the seamy character of union leaders but rather from the ability of business and politics to support their kind of union leader-

ship and squelch opposition. In the end, labor racketeering was in reality business racketeering, which was "functional" all right, for business interests and business profits, but "dysfunctional" for workers and for labor unions as a force in American politics and economics.[2]

THE BOSSES AND THE UMW

So far we have dealt with two classic examples of business racketeering erroneously labeled labor racketeering, a device to shift the onus of blame for aspects of organized crime onto the trade union movement and away from competitive and corporate capitalism. Our last example, however, is in large part such an obvious case of corporate gangsterism that only rarely and in special circumstances has the term labor racketeering been applied. What follows then is primarily an account of business racketeering in its most primitive form: the use of criminals (goons, thugs, enforcers) to prevent labor from organizing. The social environment in this case is so unsophisticated that we are confronted with pure criminal conspiracies engineered by corporate leaders who could almost at whim marshal criminal armies to bully, if not murder, nascent trade unionists. This is a world apart from the political economy of mid-century New York or Seattle where so many contentious, squabbling urban entrepreneurs were anxiously willing to deal with local power brokers like Buchalter, Dutch Schultz or Beck to insure profits. Equally removed from this world are the machinations of pseudo-trade unionists like Dioguardi, Jimmy Hoffa and Joseph Glimco whose romance with corporate capitalism was built on the backs of rank and file.

The coal mines of the Cumberland Plateau located in the hills of Kentucky, West Virginia and Tennessee suffered along with the rest of the nation in the economic crisis of the 1920's and 30's. The time was ripe for labor unions and the National Recovery Act of 1933 gave formal legal support for organizing. The U.S. Supreme Court, however, quickly declared the Act unconstitutional:

> The darkness of despair descended upon the region when the Supreme Court shattered the Recovery Program by declaring the Congressional Act unconstitutional. By the mandate of the court, the fair codes were dissolved and prices and wages plummeted to the old subterranean levels. In the gloom that followed the apparition of trade unionism was replaced by the appearance of the genuine article. Organizers for the United Mine Workers of America entered the field under the determined direction of a battle-hardened warrier, John L. Lewis" (Caudill: 123).

Few of the miners had had any real experience with the union movement. Any movement toward collective bargaining was often viewed as an infringement on the right of the individual to work for such employer, and at such wage, as the workman might choose. In the union membership drives of the early 1920's, most miners spurned the entreaties of the "field workers."

But in the intervening years their outlook changed radically. They were now willing to listen to anyone who offered a possible solution for their problems. No longer were the advocates of unionism disdained. To the contrary, when rumor spread the word that a representative of the union was in the vicinity, miners began to seek him out.

The organizing of local unions was bafflingly difficult. The operators knew each man in their respective camps. Any act or word indicating pro-union leanings came promptly to the attention of the new bosses. The sheriffs and judges were little less than hirelings of the coal corporations, and the men who successively occupied the governor's office were wholeheartedly sympathetic with the operators' point of view. Sheriffs could be counted upon to arrest any union representative who "loitered" or "breached the peace," and the judges were certain to reform him with swift jail sentences. In a pinch, the governor could be relied on to send national guard units "to preserve the peace" in the coal towns. The majesty and power of the law were on the side of the operators.

Under statutes then in effect, "industrial peace officers" were employed by the coal companies. It was their duty to protect company property and preserve the peace. The larger coal companies and associations of the smaller ones hired little armies of such industrial policemen. The sheriffs appointed many of them deputies so they could act both as private and public peace officers, as occasions might require. In addition, little swarms of private sleuths were engaged from Pinkerton's Detective Agency and other similar firms. These latter sometimes masqueraded as miners, finding underground employment and ferreting out evidence of union activities among their fellow workmen.

"Bloody" Harlan County acquired its famous prefix during these years because there the Harlan County Coal Operators Association, marshaled by the United States Coal and Coke Company, fought a violent, years-long campaign to prevent their employees from taking the "obligation" required of United Mine Workers.

The blacklists came back, and any man who was known to have joined the union or was suspected of being sympathetic to its objectives was summarily fired and his name added to the ban. Some companies publicly posted their blacklists by the payroll windows. Gangs of heavily armed "goons" were imported from Chicago and other crime-ridden cities to beat, murder and intimidate organizers and miners. In automobiles and on motorcycles, they patrolled the camps and highways of the county. They wore the uniforms of the iniquitous industrial police and were as arrogant as Nazi storm troopers. Their testimony was accepted by the courts in preference to that of any number of coal miners. The tactics of these desperados violated both state and federal constitutions and have rarely been outdone.

The company-directed law officers were unbelievably numerous, and were on constant outlook for union agents. If a stranger came into a coal camp he was accosted and his business and identity demanded. If he could offer no explanation for his presence that suited the company, he was told in no uncertain terms to "get off company property and out of town."

Despite these tactics and the goons employed by owners, the realization that organization and collective action was essential to their future led increasing numbers of workers to join the United Mine Workers (UMW). Under the tough and experienced leadership of John L. Lewis the workers struck back: "When his wife packed the miner's dinner bucket she frequently reserved space for his .38 caliber revolver. And the armed and sullen men began to strike back with violence as deadly as any of the companies meted out" (Caudill: 187).

In the end the mine owners were forced to sign contracts with the union. Then came the inevitable attempts to slander and discredit. The UMW was accused of being a communist front which took orders from Moscow. This chorus was sung not only by mine owners but by their lawyers, local law enforcement officers, the mass media and even the governor of the State of Kentucky. In the years to come, however, the complaints lessened. As was the case elsewhere, the owners quickly came to realize that the UMW might be the lesser of alternative evils. The Progressive Miners Union tried to organize a more militant brand of labor organization. They were crushed by a coalition of the UMW and the mine owners.

John L. Lewis was, from the outset, a staunch advocate of technological innovation in the mining industry. The rhetoric was impressive: more machines would reduce the arduousness of the job and increase the safety in the mines. It would also increase profits for the owners and, though this was not mentioned, swell the ranks of the unemployed. As the courts began to see the benefits of technology and strong union leadership, they increasingly supported the UMW.

The advance of technology to increase profits was rapid and effective. The electric drill replaced the manual breast auger, the cutting machine displaced the pick. Conveyor belts carried the coal out of the mines and the

The Collaborators

ultimate in coal mining equipment, "the coal mole," drilled mercilessly into the mountains of black earth and transformed the industry. The increased profits were shared by the owners, union leaders and to a lesser extent those miners who were not made redundant by mechanization: "production capacity climbed while payrolls shriveled. The same industry which had required 700,000 men in 1910 was able to provide all of the same fuel required by a vastly larger nation in 1958 with fewer than 200,000 men." (Caudill: 27). The union did nothing for the 500,000 men and their families who were displaced.

Meanwhile, the UMW with the aid and support of the mine owners institutionalized racketeering practices second only to the International Brotherhood of Teamsters. Sweetheart contracts, a blind eye to company policies, use of union funds for personal gain by union leadership, profit sharing with owners, and outright stock ownership by union leaders assured a relatively peaceful and predictable (albeit somewhat higher paid) labor force (NACLA, 1977: 9; Caudill, 1962). To secure the position of the union, members who complained were fired, threatened and if necessary, shot.

Most interesting, the profit potential of a violently conservative labor union was recognized by others besides the collaborationists in charge of the union and the corporate capitalists whose attitude had shifted from opposition to contented acceptance. The professional classes, for instance, also enriched themselves at the expense of the rank and file and thus became supporters of the union. Doctors and morticians dipped into union funds by operating on anyone who came near the examining room of the doctor, and billing the union pension fund for exorbitant burial fees for those who died:

> Despite the bellowing of the American Medical Association that the UMW medical fund was a venture in 'socialized' medicine, many camp doctors promptly recognized the Welfare Fund as a gravy train. They climbed aboard with alacrity and plundered it with great skill. The empty rooms in their little hospitals were filled with beds and new cubicles were opened. Chronic ailments for which the patient had already taken bags of pills and gallons of tonics now required bed rest and hospitalization. Surgery was undertaken for trivial complaints. Bushels of tonsils, adenoids and appendices were removed. The "head nurse" at one of these establishments described the situation in her hospital in inelegant terms: "It's all a woman's sex life is worth to even walk through this place. It's got so the doctors spay every woman who comes in the door!" (Caudill: 44).

Mine owners, union leaders, medical doctors, morticians, politicians, law enforcers—all were made richer by unionization. Complaints by miners of misuse of union funds were, if heeded at all, easily and quixotically dismissed as the inevitable result of labor racketeering. What, after all, could you expect from a bunch of lower class types whose success in union organizing was a function of their ability to corner the use of violence? No one asked why those tactics had been necessary; no one asked why the companies chose some unions rather than others with which to sign contracts. No one asked of the process by which these racketeering practices evolved. After all, the mines kept operating, the coal kept spewing out, and profits remained high. And when profits were finally exhausted, the owners sold out, the union withdrew, and the medical clinics and mortuaries closed.

CONCLUSION

Wherever one delves into the development of rackets or corruption in labor unions the same theme is repeated: business and industry are frightened by unionization, in the face of militant and demanding union leadership, compliant unions or union leaders (often with a background in strike-breaking) are sought out and encouraged, contracts drawn up which sometimes raise wages and improve conditions while simultaneously establishing a network of collaboration between union leadership and owners. Labor stability is thereby assured, profits increased and the threat of unionization turned into a mild annoyance. There are, of course, a host of even more vicious scenes in which the working class is simply brutalized as a prelude to the drive for monopolization.

Clearly, "labor racketeering" is a most inappropriate and misleading term for describing what takes place in the corruption of unions and in the arena of "labor-management relations." Business co-optation of the labor movement through corruption and violence to protect the short term interests of business and union leaders is a more apt description. But the tenacity of the term "labor racketeering" signals a deep-seated prejudice against organized labor. It also points out how deeply ingrained are the myths of private enterprise as the engine of public good. Labor unions are per se suspect; criminal capitalists are simply the bad bananas of an otherwise efficient, if not benevolent bunch. Consequently, social scientists and popular writers alike focus on the "racketeers" and on the "rackets" rather than on the symbiosis between business and corrupt labor practices.[3]

From the perspective of functional theory in sociology, racketeering is understood as emerging and persisting because it solves a problem of order and predictability for "the system." This functional perspective is more interesting for the things it fails to see than for those it reveals. It certainly highlights the extent to which economic realities shape the development of labor union activities. But, it is unable to adequately analyze the phenomenon because of its premature closure of the analysis by failing to see both sides of this functional argument: for while the development of racket-ridden unions may be "functional" for business and labor racketeers, it is "dysfunctional" for the workers and for the development of organized labor. The creation of racket-ridden unions makes possible the manipulation of union leadership by owners at the expense of an independent labor union that would represent the interests of the workers. Quite a different picture of union racketeering emerges if we look more systematically at the historical roots of union racketeering which suggest that the development of corruption and racketeering comes about through a coalition between the least desirable elements in the trade union movement and the owners of business and industry. More importantly, the impetus for criminal conspiracies comes from employers. The conspiracies, dominated by the needs of both large and small capitalists in a variety of industries, provide the groundwork for the more publicized kind of corruption – the domination of both locals and certain national unions by the likes of Jimmy Hoffa, Frank Fitzsimmons, Dave Beck and Tony Boyle who enrich themselves and their associates in the business world by looting union treasuries and who steal from the rank and file through institutionalized loan sharking and other criminal activities. This mutuality of interest beween employers and union leaders also serves the "function" of eliminating radical and miliant trade union efforts.

Robert K. Merton (1968) in his discussion of political machines and criminal rackets clearly recognized the "function" of racketeering for business:

> Business corporations, among which the public utilities . . . are simply the most conspicuous in this regard, seek special political dispensations which will enable them to stabilize their situation and to near their objective of maximizing profits.

The results of our study of the emergence and development of racketeering in labor unions make essentially the same point: racket-ridden labor unions are in the interests of business and for a few labor leaders. In other words, the struggle between social classes for control of the profits from production led to a situation in the early 1900's where business was faced with a serious challenge to its control of labor. The inherent contradiction between labor and capital created organizational efforts on the part of labor unions sufficient to threaten the owners with the very real possibility that they would lose control of the labor force. Among other serious threats perceived by capital was the introduction of communist and socialist ideology into the labor movement. The dilemma thus created for business was whether to join into an unholy alliance with some union leaders or risk the possibility of losing the entire game in the form of a labor force that would demand not just higher wages but control of the means of production. The dilemma was resolved in favor of supporting and joining those in the labor movement who employed illegal and violent means to circumvent the demands of workers.

FOOTNOTES

1. Information on Fein, Wexler and other organized criminals involved with the United Hebrew Trades can be found in the Judah L. Magnes Archives, the Central Archives for the History of the Jewish People, Jerusalem, Israel. Specifically check reports Number 1, 700, 719, and 871.

2. It is tempting to speculate, for example, that the failure of America to develop a Labor Party similar to those that emerged in Sweden, Norway and Denmark during the 1920's and 1930's was the result of the difference in the effective co-optation of unions in the United States as compared to other countries.

3. A recent *Washington Post* article suggests that the symbiosis may take many forms. For example, the practice of "lumping" in the trucking industry. "Lumpers" are non-union gangs who load large trucks for warehouses and who charge the truck drivers for this service. As a report in the *Washington Post* (Tuesday, March 21, 1978, p. C1) noted: "Receivers of perishable goods, such as larger supermarket warehouses, allow the 'lumpers' to avoid hiring additional laborers."

REFERENCES

Bell, Daniel
  1962 "Racket-Ridden Longshoremen: The Web of Economics and Politics." In The End of Ideology. Free Press.

Bernstein, Irving
  1966 The Lean Years: A History of the American Worker, 1920-1933. Penguin.

Block, Alan A.
  1978 East Side – West Side: Organizing Crime in New York, 1930-1950. (Forthcoming).

Boyer, Richard O., and Herbert M. Morais
  1955 A History of the American Labour Movement. J. Calder.

Court of Appeals, Brooklyn, New York
  1942 The People of the State of New York against Louis Buchalter, Emmanuel Weiss, Louis Capone. May-June; 7944, Vols. 1-5.

Caudill, Harry M.
  1962 Night Comes to the Cumberlands. Little Brown.

Chambliss, William J.
  1978 On The Take: From Petty Crooks to Presidents. Indiana University Press.

District Attorney of Kings County and the December 1949 Grand Jury
  1955 Presentment. February 1.

Dubofsky, Melvyn
  1969 We Shall Be All: A History of the Industrial Workers of the World. Quadrangle.

Foner, Philip S.
  1950 Fur and Leather Workers' Union: A Story of Dramatic Struggles and Achievements. Nordan Press.

Foner, Philip S.
  1965 The Industrial Workers of the World, 1905-1917. International Publishers.

Herberg, Will
  1952 "The Jewish Labor Movement in the United States." In American Jewish Yearbook. Vol. 53.

Hoover, Edgar M. and Raymond Vernon
  1962 Anatomy of a Metropolis: The Changing Distribution of People and Jobs Within the New York Metropolitan Region. Doubleday and Company, Inc.

Huberman, Leo
  1937 The Labor Spy Racket. Modern Age Books, Inc.

Hutchinson, John
    1970 The Imperfect Union: A History of Corruption in
          American Trade Unions. E. P. Dutton Co., Inc.

Jeffreys-Jones, G.R.
    1974 "Plug-Uglies in the Progressive Era." In Donald Fleming
          and Bernard Bailyn (eds.), Perspectives in American
          History. Charles Warren Center for Studies in American
          History.

Josephson, Matthew
    1952 Sidney Hillman: Statesman of American Labor. Doubleday
          and Company.

Columbia Law Review
    1937 "Legal Implications of Labor Racketeering." (Summer).

Lens, Sidney
    1973 The Labor Wars: From the Molly Maguires to the Sit-
          Downs. Doubleday.

Merton, Robert K.
    1968 Social Theory and Social Structure. The Free Press.

Morgan, Murray
    1951 Skid Road. Ballantine Books.

North American Congress on Latin America
    1977 "Channeling Labor's Early Struggles." In Latin America
          and Empire Report XI (5) (May-June).

Rischin, Moses
    1970 The Promised City: New York's Jews, 1870-1914. Harper
          and Row.

Seidman, Joel Isaac
    1942 The Needle Trades. Farrar and Rinehart.

Seligman, Ben B.
    1950 "The American Jew: Some Demographic Features." In
          American Jewish Yearbook, Vol. 53.

Turkus, Burton B. and Sid Feder
    1951 Murder, Inc.: The Story of the Syndicate. Farrar, Straus
          and Young.

U.S. Department of Justice, FBI "The Fur Dress Case" I.C. 60-1501.
    1939 November 7.

Yellen, Samuel
    1936 American Labor Struggles. Harcourt, Brace and Co.

6

I Cheat, Therefore I Exist?
The BCCI Scandal
in Context

Nikos Passas

The Bank of Credit and Commerce International (BCCI) was founded by Agha Hasan Abedi whose ambition was to make it the largest Third World bank and a bridge between the First and the Third Worlds. By presenting itself as the bank that would serve "little countries" and "little people" it appeared to be an unprecendented "social investment." Yet, BCCI is now known as the perpetrator of the biggest bank fraud in history (*Financial Times* [*FT*], November 9–10, 1991). The current director of the CIA had nicknamed it as the "bank of crooks and criminals international" in 1988, while the head of the Bank of England suggested that BCCI was dominated by a "criminal culture" (*FT*, July 24, 1991). Ironically, the primary victims of BCCI and its closure are the intended beneficiaries of the bank: Third World depositors and governments. Substantial dollar deposits by central banks of some of the poorest countries were lost. In Gabon, the social security fund was wiped out, leaving people who worked all their lives without pension ("Sunday Today", NBC, February 23, 1992). Significant business and UN project disruption, nonpayment of employees, corruption investigations, and riots are among the disturbing consequences (e.g., *FT*, August 6, 1991; *Los Angeles Times* [*LA Times*], August 10, 1991; *Wall Street Journal* [*WSJ*], August 6, 1991; U.S. Senate Committee on Foreign Relations [U.S. SFR] 1992a, 1992c).

BCCI's liabilities are about $10 billion to 800,000 depositors in 1.2 million accounts in over 70 countries (*FT*, December 3, 1991, February 22–23, 1992; U.S. SFR 1992a). The "culprits" and those implicated in the scandal include highly respected individuals, legitimate organizations (e.g., intelligence and other government bodies), illegitimate organizations (e.g., terrorist groups), and even "gangsters" who "enforced" certain decisions to ensure that people knowledgeable of BCCI's inner workings remained silent.

BCCI's illegal activities covered an impressive range: "Ponzi" schemes, deceitful accounting, frauds against depositors, money laundering, financing of illegal arms deals and nuclear programs, corruption of politicians and other influential individuals, illegal control of financial institutions, and assistance to intelligence agencies for illicit operations (Lacayo 1991; U.S. House Banking Committee [U.S. HBC] 1991, 1992a, 1992b, 1992c; Adams and Frantz 1992; U.S. Senate Committee on Banking, Housing, and Urban Affairs [U.S. SBC] 1992; US SFR 1992a, 1992b, 1992c).

The significance and complexity of the BCCI affair cannot be overstated, because unethical and criminal acts were perpetrated by top BCCI people. The objective here is to place the BCCI saga in context and to raise issues that ought to be pursued in further research. The chapter is based on press reports, indictments, plea bargain agreements, Congressional hearings, and short private conversations with investigators and officials. It is emphasized that investigations are still going on in many parts of the world and that the jigsaw puzzle is still incomplete. Indeed, given that national security issues have been raised and many documents have not been disclosed, the full picture may never be seen. For these reasons, caution is warranted in the analysis and interpretation of the facts.

IN SEARCH OF EXPLANATIONS

According to the Justice Department, BCCI "was set up deliberately to avoid centralized regulatory review. Its officers were sophisticated international bankers whose apparent objective was to commit fraud on a massive scale" (U.S. SFR 1992c, 788). The implication is that BCCI existed in order to cheat, that it was a criminal enterprise by design. It has been argued that BCCI was set up criminally (by deviously obtained and never repaid loans) and would not have been able to operate without the support of its systematic criminal activities ("MacNeil/Lehrer Newshour," September 30, 1991, interview with journalist Tariq Ali).

Another plausible scenario is that BCCI started out with good intentions and noble goals, ran into trouble, and resorted to illegal practices to remain afloat (i.e., it cheated in order to exist). Further, evidence suggests that BCCI was used by some of its managers, employees, and (especially) customers to serve their illegitimate purposes. Knowingly or not, BCCI has facilitated many people's crimes and satisfied illicit demands. In many respects, rather than the "source of global evil," BCCI has been a "mirror of global evil."

These are not necessarily competing interpretations; in a mind-boggling case like this, it would be unrealistic to seek a single theory to explain everything. It seems more likely that each of the above general statements account for different aspects of this world-wide debacle, each corresponds to parts of a perplexing reality. In our search for causes and facilitating factors, we must keep these lines of inquiry separate. It is imperative for theorists and practitioners alike to distinguish corporate (criminal) policy from individual managers' misconduct and shady operations of customers who took advantage of BCCI policies. Confusing all types of situations and motives can only send misleading signals to policymakers keen on avoiding such disasters in the future.

The focus in this limited space will not be on the "I exist in order to cheat" version, which is not to deny its tremendous significance and supporting evidence. Rather, the aim is to explore comparatively neglected aspects of the affair that may involve other disquieting sources of unethical conduct.

BCCI CULTURE

Much has been written about Abedi's background, character, philosophy and intentions (Adams and Frantz 1992; U.S. SFR 1992a, 1992b, 1992c). Abedi started his banking career at the Habib Bank of Pakistan. As he was rising through the ranks of the bank, he persuaded a prominent Pakistani businessman to finance the start of United Bank Ltd. Much like BCCI later, the new bank (under the management of Abedi) opened branches in poor regions, even at the risk of making no profits, in order to serve poor farmers. In 1972, Bhutto's government decided to nationalize many industries including the banking sector. He placed a number of their executives under house arrest; Abedi was one of them.

Following this experience, Abedi devoted his energy to his developing vision of a truly international bank that would serve the underprivileged while being beyond the control of any government. This would be the "immigrant's" bank; Third World people and countries would no longer have to do business with the less understanding and colonial banks of the West. The ambitious, cunning, and charismatic banker took his ideas to the ruler of Abu Dhabi and other increasingly wealthy sheiks, who agreed to finance BCCI and saw in Abedi a trusted financial adviser (Adams and Frantz 1992).

Many BCCI policies can be better understood in view of Islamic principles of banking. Abedi, and others in the Muslim world, believed that it is usury for banks to charge excessive interest. In addition to profit-making, banks have a social role and must be partners in the building of a better society (Adams and Frantz 1992). Depositors in much of the Arab world do not receive interest on their money—instead, they engage in productive investments (*FT*, November 12, 1991; *WSJ*, August 6, 1991). For their money and influence, the sheiks, devout Muslims themselves, were rewarded by BCCI through other services. When important customers visited London, for instance, BCCI would welcome them in limousines and take care of their accommodation, business and (occasionally extravagant) entertainment needs.

For his international bank, Abedi also needed associates in the United States.

After a few meetings and communications, a quarter of the start-up capital for BCCI came from the Bank of America, a California bank with a similar pro-social philosophy, which thus gained access to the generally closed Middle Eastern market.

BCCI was initially run like a family business, in which Abedi had the authority to decide on people, organization, and external relations. A master of personal relationships, Abedi routinely cultivated contacts and partnerships with key people in every place where the fast-expanding bank was opening offices.

By themselves, these tactics were legitimate. It is not uncommon for international organizations to try to recruit the best available people and associate with them. The "social investment" side of BCCI helped Abedi in the courting of individuals like Perez de Cuellar, Henry Kissinger, Jimmy Carter, James Callaghan, Clark Clifford, and Deng Xiaoping, among many others. Such associations lent BCCI a valuable veneer of respectability.

BCCI was promoting itself as the friendly, "can-do" bank. It was extremely fast at providing letters of credit or loans, it was more personal than other major banks, and had "no questions asked" policies. By cutting a lot of red tape, BCCI claimed a growing share of the international market—especially customers other banks turned down or ill-served. It operated in countries which major international institutions were fleeing due to declining and/or unstable economies; it came to the aid of Third World governments, businesses, and individuals having difficulty with their budgets or credit-worthiness (Adams and Frantz 1992; *WSJ*, August 5, 1991). Worthy contributions and charity work—though many argue that this was a mere facade (*LA Times*, August 9, 1991)—were publicized at BCCI conferences where success stories were exchanged among senior executives, and Abedi gave his mystical speeches about "cosmic energy," dynamics, and power (*FT*, November 11, 1991; U.S. SFR 1992a).

Thanks to its services, the promotion of Third World interests, the backing and participation of the Bank of America, the financial support of wealthy Arabs, and legitimate businesspeople who were repatriating a good deal of oil money in the West (US HBC 1992c; US SFR 1992c), BCCI did not look bad at the beginning. It seemed to be doing quite well for some time: it became the seventh largest private bank in the world, operating in 73 countries with 14,000 employees of 83 nationalities and $21 billion in assets.

ILLEGITIMATE OPPORTUNITIES OF A GLOBAL SCALE

With its local connections and global organization, BCCI claimed to be a "local bank internationally." Its structure made possible the transfer of immigrants' earnings back home, facilitated international aid projects and business transactions, minimized costs and taxes for the bank, and maximized certain benefits for depositors. Such goals are pursued routinely by major financial institutions, which use the international system, its loopholes, and the lax regulation in several countries to their advantage (Blum 1984; Lernoux 1984; Lohr

1992). In themselves, these are common methods of achieving mainstream objectives.

However, BCCI was "located everywhere, but regulated nowhere"—it was officially headquartered in Luxembourg and the Cayman Islands and had two auditing firms until 1985. In the mid-1980s, the Luxembourg Monetary Institute and BCCI requested that the Bank of England [BoE] become its central bank and regulator. Citing fears that the BoE may convey the impression of supervising the whole BCCI group, though the obscure Caymans side would be beyond its authority, BoE turned down the request (*FT*, August 10/11, 1991).

The absence of consolidated control of the BCCI giant enhanced secrecy and confidentiality enjoyed by ordinary customers, but also furnished massive opportunities for unlawful transactions. The combination of such opportunities with the protective shield of respectability, which further lowered the risk of detection and sanctions, invited fraud and abuse (U.S. HBC 1991). In addition to very highly placed individuals, for a variety of reasons, BCCI officials themselves could also take advantage of this situation.

Some could use the opportunities for personal gain. Local managers perhaps needed to hide and cover up mistakes or losses. Others may have sought their own advancement by exceeding their superiors' expectations. Still others, having accepted Abedi's rhetoric, were overzealous in the promotion of BCCI and its causes and only reported what he wanted to hear. In the relentless pursuit of growth, nonconventional avenues were followed (U.S. SFR 1992b).

BCCI IN TROUBLED WATERS

The lavish style of some BCCI customers, its unorthodox practices, its frenzied growth, the anonymity of its owners, and the absence of consolidated supervision made regulators cautious or even suspicious of BCCI. Although instrumental in avoidance of nationalization and to being local internationally, BCCI's structure was at once a business handicap. Despite legal attempts to enter the U.S. market, BCCI was not allowed to open branches. BCCI resorted to illegitimate means of gaining the, in their eyes unjustifiably, denied access by secretly acquiring First American Bankshares—the holding company of First American Bank—and other financial institutions (U.S. HBC 1992b, 1992c; U.S. SBC 1992). No improprieties have been detected in the management of First American. So, the illegal acquisition could be rationalized by BCCI people as a technicality of little adverse consequence for anyone concerned. Moreover, BCCI was an outsider in an environment governed by Western rules; many felt the way it was treated by authorities was discriminatory (U.S. SFR 1992b). Bending the rules could be "justified" as a necessary line of defense.

Strain and survival, rather than concern with expansion, were behind another series of illegalities; when BCCI was in desperate need of cash, some of its people did not hesitate to welcome suspicious depositors, in line with its customer-friendly policies. A number of factors brought about fiscal crises at BCCI.

The bank was victimized by crooks who took advantage of its red-tape cutting practices and reliance on "reputations." For instance, a dummy corporation opened an account at BCCI's Panama branch and deposited $3.7 million in U.S. Treasury checks. These checks were transferred to the Bank of New York, cleared and withdrawn through checks in the name of the dummy corporation. On the same day, BCCI's local manager was informed that the Treasury checks were forged, and the credit was reversed. BCCI sustained a loss of nearly $3.7 million. Adopting deviant means to fill such significant holes might have been considered as an option.

The bank was also damaged by customers who mismanaged or squandered loans from BCCI. The Gokal brothers, for example, owners of one of the largest shipping groups (Gulf Group), caused a near-disaster for the whole BCCI group. Although their credit limit was $300 million, the total loan exposure reached $700 million (U.S. SFR 1992a). Speculative and instinct-based trading led to dramatic losses; when the Gulf Group appeared to be near collapse, it was feared that it would drag BCCI down with it. BCCI had an interest in continuing its support; so, it kept pouring in money, while a "special duties department" was working full time to conceal reality.

Additional bad loans were inevitable, given BCCI's services to "friends," its determination to stay in troubled countries, and its general openness to risky investments in the Third World. In this, however, BCCI was in good company as major banks have had to struggle with Third World debt following the theory that "governments cannot be bankrupted" (Channon 1988).

Mismanagement and imprudent risks against internal BCCI rules created other critical cash flow problems in the 1980s. The bank experienced about $450 million in loss by taking often "non-sensical" positions in commodity and treasury markets and by betting hugely over its trading limit of $1 billion (the bank's total exposure went to $11 billion) (U.S. HBC 1991; U.S. SFR 1992a).

Another blow to BCCI was money laundering charges filed against the bank and its officials in Florida. The negative publicity that the case attracted, the businesses that were consequently lost, and the litigation costs (costing $45 million [U.S. SFR 1992b]) worsened its financial situation.

Following Abedi's plea for assistance, the ruler of Abu Dhabi injected $150 million (U.S. SFR 1992a), but it was insufficient. A whole department was allegedly set up to cover-up the fiscal crisis through Ponzi schemes, capital shifts from branch to branch, false accounts, and other frauds. Bribes were allegedly paid to central bank officials in Peru and elsewhere, in order to attract dollar deposits (U.S. SFR 1992a). Finally, serving the Colombian drug cartels was bringing in needed business (e.g., U.S. SFR 1992c, 692–3). Seen from this angle, the "I cheat, therefore I exist" scenario does not appear implausible. Nevertheless, it is stressed that the benefits from frauds were not spread widely, and only a tiny fraction of all BCCI employees were involved (U.S. SFR 1992a, 1992b).

THE WORLD NEEDS US

All kinds of rationalizations and neutralizations of moral/social controls commonly employed by private and public sector managers are encountered in the BCCI saga (Steinberg and Austern 1990; Passas 1991). "Everybody does it anyway" (U.S. SFR 1992b) was an important one, because it is not totally unfounded. Although the overall BCCI case is extraordinary, most of its unlawful practices and underlying motives are not so unusual if examined separately.

The head of the BoE argued BCCI could not be closed down earlier because evidence on "systematic fraud" had not been obtained and added: "If we closed down a bank every time we had a fraud, we would have rather fewer banks than we have" (*FT*, July 24, 1991). Many cases of concealed fund transfers, deceptive accounting, phony, insider, and nominee loans have been well documented; the same applies to cases where owed favors, concern about growth, and lack of legitimate sources of money have led to imprudent banking, conscious solicitation of funds from dubious sources, or wilful blindness. We also know of banks set up for illicit purposes from the outset (Kwitny 1988; Lernoux 1984; Naylor 1987; Calavita and Pontell 1990; Block 1991).

There are reliable reports on widespread violations of the Bank Secrecy Act and money laundering of billions of dollars annually that all too often go undetected (U.S. Senate Committee on Governmental Affairs [U.S. SGA] 1985; Levi 1991). Contrary to the Basle Convention banking principle that you have to know your customer, numerous institutions "make a practice of not knowing their customer and even hiding their customers" (U.S. SFR 1992c, 52).

All this raises concerns about regulatory weaknesses as does the question of how was it possible for BCCI to commit all of the above offenses for years with impunity (Schumer 1991; U.S. HBC 1991; Passas 1992; U.S. SFR 1992a). For the present purposes, however, the point is that financial institutions everywhere engage in similar activities as there is a huge demand for them. One of Abedi's mottos was "the world needs us," which happened to be true, both for the legitimate and illegitimate services that BCCI rendered.

A MIRROR OF GLOBAL EVIL

Press reports on how BCCI bribed high-level government officials in several countries, and headlines with the names of global villains that were dealing with BCCI might convey the impression that BCCI was the source of unethical conduct around the world. Yet, on many occasions, BCCI did not initiate, but facilitated illegal practices. Ties between the bank and customers like Manuel Noriega, Saddam Hussein, Anastasio Somoza, Contra leaders, Ferdinand Marcos, and Duvalier alone are not sufficient evidence that BCCI was a "rogue bank." It is often unmentioned that all of the above have been U.S. allies or served U.S. policies and interests in the past.

During the last few months, hearing after hearing in Congress reveal that
BCCI and associates were useful to a plethora of powerful individuals and
intelligence agencies and governments. For instance, BCCI was used for Iran-
Contra transactions; CIA payments to Noriega and to Afghani rebels were made
through BCCI; being one of Noriega's banks, BCCI later assisted in his prosecution (Scott and Marshall 1991; U.S. HBC 1992c; U.S. SFR, 1992a, 1992b,
1992c). According to a recent report, a BCCI shareholder and former head of
the Saudi intelligence was instrumental in bringing about the Camp David Accord
("Frontline," PBS, April 21, 1992). BCCI's network of influence, no-questions-
asked practice, secrecy, and omnipresence made it an ideal conduit for international covert operations, legitimate and illegitimate.

For the same reasons, BCCI was also used for the financing of illegal arms
deals, illegal transfer of nuclear and other technology, and terrorism. At the
same time it was graciously bailing out countries with external debt that were
turned down by institutions like the International Monetary Fund, BCCI facilitated capital flight and money laundering operations. Whenever one's objective
was to evade regulations, bans or sanctions (BCCI had close dealings with South
Africans), BCCI would be the bank of choice. In short, BCCI served approximately 3,000 criminal customers, each one of whom could make front-page
stories ("MacNeil/Lehrer Newshour," August 13, 1991, interview with former
Senate investigator Jack Blum).

The "full service bank" responded and catered to demands that clearly pre-
dated it; as an international bank, BCCI met international needs. To say that
BCCI assisted rather than initiated criminal operations is hardly to exonerate the
bank or its officials, but to point to deeper sources of unethical acts. Cultural,
political, and economic issues are at the core of the above transactions. Regional
conflicts, real and perceived inequities, mismanagement, exploitation and abuse,
foreign debt, political and economic instability, and conflicts between foreign
and domestic (open and covert) policy priorities are some of the global structural
problems reflected in the BCCI affair. In this sense, BCCI may be described as
the "mirror of global evil."

CONCLUSION

What is important is not only the BCCI scandal, but also the fact that many
scandals lead to BCCI. While BCCI's structure promoted certain legitimate
purposes, it simultaneously opened up global opportunities for illicit practices,
which were exploited by BCCI insiders and clients. Confronted with substantial
financial problems, BCCI also broke rules in order to survive; systematic and
sophisticated frauds were then initiated or intensified. Many of BCCI's unlawful
practices are not uncommon but reflected and satisfied illegitimate world-wide
demands.

A lesson to be drawn from this case is that, if we hope to prevent such
occurrences in the future, the regulatory gaps that the case has exposed must be

filled. Laws and regulations must certainly be amended and international co-operation strengthened. But such measures are no panacea. Breaking the "mirror of global evil" only eliminates its image, while much of the evil will remain intact. Attention and resources ought to be allocated to attend to the underlying structural problems and conflicts which cannot be legislated away.

Before moving to policy construction, however, a good deal of work has yet to be done. The BCCI patterns of misconduct lend support to theories of deviance not focusing solely on greed-profit motives, but also to the emphasis on goals such as survival, power, loyalty, and clientele service (features BCCI shares with other organizations, see Gross 1978; Passas 1990). Evidence points to the fact that there are multiple sources of misconduct. Policies designed to address medium- and longer-term concerns on both the national and international level must not be implemented without thorough investigation and analysis of (1) the various "criminogenic" factors; (2) the patterns of illegality that correspond to each factor; (3) the relative importance and impact of each pattern of illegality; and (4) the corrigibility of each problem and cost of reforms.

REFERENCES

Adams, J. R., and D. Frantz. 1992. *A Full Service Bank: How BCCI Stole Billions Around the World*. New York: Pocket Books.

Block, A. A. 1991. *Masters of Paradise: Organized Crime and the Internal Revenue Service in the Bahamas*. New Brunswick, NJ: Transaction Publishers.

Blum, R. H. 1984. *Offshore Haven Banks, Trusts and Companies*. New York: Praeger.

Calavita, K., and H. Pontell. 1990. " 'Heads I Win Tails You Lose': Deregulation, Crime and Crisis in the Savings and Loan Industry." *Crime and Delinquency* 36:309–41.

Channon, D. F. 1988. *Global Banking Strategy*. New York: John Wiley & Sons.

Gross, E. 1978. "Organizations as Criminal Actors." In *Two Faces of Deviance: Crimes of the Powerless and Powerful*, ed. P. Wilson and J. Braithwaite, 199–213. Brisbane: Queensland Univ. Press.

Kwitny, J. 1988. *The Crimes of Patriots: The True Tale of Dope, Dirty Money, and the CIA*. New York: W.W. Norton & Co.

Lacayo, R. 1991. "The Cover-Up Begins to Crack." In *Time*, July 22, 14–16.

Lernoux, P. 1984. *In Banks We Trust*. Garden City, N.Y.: Anchor Press/Doubleday.

Levi, M. 1991. "Regulating Money Laundering." *British Journal of Criminology* 31(2): 109–25.

Lohr, S. 1992. "Where The Money Washes Up." *New York Times Magazine*, March 29.

Naylor, R. T. 1987. *Hot Money and the Politics of Debt*. New York: Simon and Schuster.

Passas, N. 1990. "Anomie and Corporate Deviance." *Contemporary Crises* Vol. 14: 157–78.

Passas, N. 1991. *Frauds Affecting the Budget of the European Community*, Report to the Commission of the European Community, Brussels.

Passas, N. 1992. " 'Regulatory Anesthesia' or the Limits of Criminal Law? Going After

BCCI.'' Presented at the annual meeting of the Law and Society Association, Philadelphia.

Schumer, C. E. 1991. *Report Regarding Federal Law Enforcement's Handling of Allegations Involving the Bank of Credit and Commerce International*, House Judiciary Committee, staff report of the Subcommittee on Crime and Criminal Justice, September 5, 1991.

Scott, P. D., and J. Marshall. 1991. *Cocaine Politics: Drugs, Armies, and the CIA in Central America*. Berkeley and Los Angeles: Univ. of California Press.

Steinberg, Sheldon S., and David T. Austern. 1990. *Government, Ethics, and Managers: A Guide to Solving Ethical Dilemmas in the Public Sector*. New York: Quorum Books.

U.S. House Banking Committee (HBC). 1991. *BCCI and its Activities in the United States*, Minority Staff Report. Washington D.C.: U.S. Government Printing Office.

U.S. House Banking Committee (HBC). 1992a, b, c. [Parts 1, 2, 3] *Bank of Credit and Commerce International (BCCI) Investigation*, Hearing before the Committee on Banking, Finance and Urban Affairs, House of Representatives. Washington, D.C.: U.S. Government Printing Office.

U.S. Senate Committee on Banking, Housing, and Urban Affairs (SBC) 1992. *The Bank of Credit and Commerce International and S. 1019*, Hearing before the Subcommittee on Consumer and Regulatory Affairs. Washington, D.C.: U.S. Government Printing Office.

U.S. Senate Committee on Foreign Relations (SFR). 1992a, b, c. [Parts 1, 2, 3] *The BCCI Affair*, Hearings before the Subcommittee on Terrorism, Narcotics, and International Operations. Washington, D.C.: U.S. Government Printing Office.

U.S. Senate Committee on Governmental Affairs (SGA). 1985. *Domestic Money Laundering: The First National Bank of Boston*, Hearing before the Permanent Subcommittee on Investigations. Washington, D.C.: U.S. Government Printing Office.

[18]

SOCIAL PROBLEMS, Vol. 31, No. 1, October 1983

ARSON, URBAN ECONOMY, AND ORGANIZED CRIME: THE CASE OF BOSTON*

JAMES BRADY

Director, City of Boston Arson Strike Force;
University of Massachusetts, Boston

The deadly crime of arson is spreading at an alarming rate in the United States, leaving whole city neighborhoods devastated in its wake. Traditional methods of dealing with the problem are based on a view of arsonists as pyromaniacs or vandals. This paper shows a clear link between the policies of banks and insurance companies, on the one hand, and the arson-for-profit schemes of organized crime, professional arsonists, shady landlords, and corrupt public officials. I develop a sociology of arson, in the process analyzing several kinds of arson and describing specific bank investment practices and insurance industry underwriting policies which directly contribute to the problem. I conclude by assessing proposed new remedies for arson in the light of the conflicting interests of corporate institutions, on the one hand, and tenants and homeowners on the other.

We are accustomed to think of fires, like automobile crashes, as tragic accidents caused by carelessness or bad luck. While it is recognized that some blazes are deliberately set, the public has long been assured by fire officials, psychiatrists, and criminologists that such fires are the isolated acts of pathological "pyromaniacs" or juvenile "vandals" and pose no serious threat to cities guarded by modern fire-fighting companies. Unfortunately, the dramatic upsurge of arson fires in the United States since 1960 has made a shambles of these assurances. Arson now outstrips all other "index" crimes in terms of injuries, deaths, and property losses, forcing us to rethink both our current control measures and our notions about the causes of this menace.

INTRODUCTION: THEMES AND METHODS

This study breaks new ground in developing a sociology of arson, using demography and urban economics. It demonstrates that arson is essentially a consequence of economic decisions undertaken by the banking, real estate, and insurance industries, as well as the racketeering operations of organized crime syndicates. This is not to say that "pyromaniacs" and especially "vandals" do not set a substantial number of fires in addition to those set by more sophisticated professional "torches"—the preferred employees in arson-for-profit schemes. Nor do I mean to imply that bankers, realtors, and insurance agents are necessarily joined in conscious conspiracy with gangster syndicates, though this is clearly the case in some instances.[1]

I argue that routine profit-making practices of banks, realtors, and insurance companies lead to the processes of abandonment, gentrification, and neighborhood decline which destabilize urban communities and provide the context and motivation for several varieties of arson. Organized crime syndicates, professional firesetters, and corrupt officials all figure prominently in arson-for-profit schemes, but the urban economic context also lies behind the fires of vandals and small property owners desperate to escape losing investments by means of convenient fires.

---

* An earlier version of this paper was presented at the national meetings of the American Society of Criminology, Toronto, November, 1982. The author thanks his police and civilian colleagues of the Boston Arson Strike Force, particularly Michael N. Moore. Correspondence to: Department of Sociology, University of Massachusetts, Boston, MA 02125.

1. The symbiotic and sometimes consciously conspiratorial ties between legitimate corporations and gangster syndicates is hardly peculiar to arson. Scholars probing such criminal activities as narcotics trafficking, gambling, labor union corruption, loan sharking, and selling stolen goods have discovered the same kinds of links between racketeering, official corruption, and corporate profiteering. See Block and Chambliss (1981), Chambliss (1978), and Grutzner (1973).

2   BRADY

In advancing this social economy of arson I rely mainly on original materials drawn from my study of arson, neighborhood development, and organized crime in the city of Boston.[2]

The Boston data is drawn from several years of personal experience as a researcher and activist with anti-arson community organizations in the fire-ravaged Dorchester ghetto where I live and work. I am also director of the City of Boston Arson Strike Force, a special team of civilian experts and police detectives appointed by the mayor and charged with the investigation of local arson-for-profit syndicates. Our collected evidence was presented to the Suffolk County Grand Jury in April, 1983, preliminary to indictments and prosecution by the District Attorney. For obvious reasons, neither the targets of the Strike Force nor any of the confidential evidence collected in our work will be disclosed in this article.

The materials presented in this paper are derived entirely from publicly available sources, including the local press, television documentaries, and especially the scattered records of property transactions. These transactions include sales and resales of buildings and land, insurance policies and brokerage arrangements, mortgage lending, papers of incorporation for trusts and holding companies, taxes, housing and land court decisions, housing inspections, fire code inspections, and fire histories of individual buildings and landlords. These records are drawn especially from the Suffolk County Registry of Deeds, the Boston Rent Control Administration, the Boston Buildings Department, the Boston Housing Authority, the Boston Office of Community Development, the Metropolitan Area Planning Commission, the Boston and Lowell, Mass., Fire Departments, the Massachusetts State Commissions for Banking and Insurance, and the Massachusetts Secretary of State. I share with my police and civilian Strike Force colleagues the hope that we shall soon obtain criminal convictions of at least one major organized crime arson ring operating in Boston. Afterwards, it will perhaps be appropriate to divulge some of the investigative methods and findings of this effort, which combines police work and sociological research.

It might be helpful to define several terms here. *Arson* refers to the intentional destruction of property by fire. *Redlining* refers to the mortgage-lending practices of banks, and particularly to the illegal practice of denying mortgage loans for properties located in districts inhabited by poor and minority populations. *Gentrification* refers to the migration of more affluent professionals and middle-class families from the suburbs back to selected districts in the central city. Both of these phenomena are characteristic of Boston's contemporary social dynamic and central to an understanding of arson.

Jurisdiction over arson investigation has been traditionally the almost exclusive domain of local fire departments and their semi-specialized arson squads (though the latter often include a few local police detectives, since firefighters do not usually have the power to arrest). However, since 1972 the Federal Bureau of Alcohol, Tobacco, and Firearms (ATF) has been authorized to investigate fires in commercial buildings if an "explosive device" is suspected as the cause of the fire; since 1982 the ATF's jurisdiction has been broadened to include any commercial building destroyed "by explosion or by fire" (Murphy, 1983). The ATF has established teams of arson investigators in major cities across the United States who are supported by sophisticated, mobile, arson-detection laboratories; nevertheless, the organization still responds only to a small percentage of the total arson incidents in commercial buildings.

The United States Fire Administration (USFA) supports some limited research on fire scene investigation, insurance fraud techniques, and related arson topics, and provides standards for the modernization of local fire departments. The National Fire Protection Association (NFPA), largely supported by the insurance industry, also engages in periodic evaluations of the local fire departments, publishes some of the more important arson statistics and research findings, and

---

2. A parallel view of arson-for-profit racketeering in Tampa, Minneapolis, and Rochester, New York, is provided in U.S. Congress: Senate (1979).

is largely responsible for the drafting of fire codes used in building construction throughout the United States.

The discussion which follows is divided into four main sections. First, I survey the growth and impact of arson in the United States, the failure of law enforcement, and the contribution of deviance theory to our misunderstanding of the problem. Second, I develop a case study of arson patterns in Boston and link this to a discussion of urban speculation, bank mortgage lending policies, insurance industry underwriting practices, and demographic shifts as predictors and motivators for arson. Third, I discuss major varieties of arson for profit in Boston and present the property transactions of several arson-prone speculators and one local bank whose "problem properties" have a tendency to burn. Fourth, I describe contemporary arson control reforms and assess their prospects for success against the competing interests of the banking, real estate, and insurance industries. I also describe emerging movements of tenants and homeowners in threatened neighborhoods.

OVERVIEW: ARSON IN U.S. CITIES

From 1951 to 1977 the number of arson incidents reported by local fire departments across the United States to the National Fire Protection Association (NFPA) increased by over 3,100 percent, from 5,600 cases to over 177,000 cases (Carter, 1980:41). In 1964 arson was reported to have caused less than 3 percent of all fire losses (Carter, 1980:40); by 1981 it had risen to 30 percent (Karter, 1982:68). The federal Law Enforcement Assistance Administration (LEAA) estimated arson losses at closer to 40 percent of total fire damages in 1977 (Boudreau *et al.*, 1977:5; *Economist*, 1977:11); this higher estimate is corroborated by the Aerospace Corporation report to the Senate (U.S. Congress: Senate, 1979). In 1981 local fire departments estimated that "large loss" arson fires (those causing over a million dollars in damages each) resulted in over $1.5 billion in structural damage (LeBlanc and Redding, 1982:32). The National Insurance Service estimated that the industry paid approximately $5 billion in claims submitted in 1979–80 for arson-related fire losses (Karter, 1982; Lima, 1977b).

In 1981, 6,700 civilians died in burning buildings in the United States (Karter, 1982:68), three times more than the number killed by handguns (LeBlanc and Redding, 1982:50). Arson accounts for an increasing proportion of these fire deaths. During each year between 1977 and 1980, about one thousand civilians and another 120 firefighters were killed in deliberately set fires; an additional 30,000 civilians and 4,000 firefighters were injured (Carter, 1982; *Fire and Arson Investigator*, 1981:14).

These statistics understate the seriousness of the situation. Local fire departments count as "arson" only those fires whose origins are initially regarded as suspicious by firefighters on the scene and which are subsequently investigated by the local arson squad and judged to be "incendiary" or "suspicious." The standards of evidence required for these classifications are high, and a number of questionable fires are simply classified as "undetermined."[3] Still others are wrongly described as accidents. There is wide agreement among independent investigators that most of these fires are also arson.[4] Studies prepared by the LEAA count half of all "undetermined" fires as arson (Boudreau *et al.*, 1977:1). Such prominent pyrotechnic experts as former chief James Scollins of the Lynn Fire Department, Harvey Schmidt of First Security Investigators, Inc., Robert Carter of the National Fire Protection Association, and William Murphy of

---

3. Based on an interview (Nov. 17, 1982) with Robert Carter, former Chief Arson Investigator, Commonwealth of Virginia and presently Research Analyst at the National Fire Protection Association, Quincy, Massachusetts. His assessment is corroborated by my own professional experience in the field, and by that of every other investigator I have encountered.
4. My views on this are shared by John White, Fire Marshall and commander of the Boston Fire Department's arson squad. White is the liaison between the Strike Force and the fire department.

the ATF arson team all concur that an enormous number of deliberately set fires are wrongly classified as "electrical," "children playing with matches," or "careless disposal" (as in trash set afire). They also concur that damages are greatly under-reported even when arson is acknowledged as the cause, since fire departments only consider fire damage to structures and do not consider either smoke and water damages, or the destruction of building contents. Actual insurance payments (usually based on replacement costs for all damaged items) typically amount to between three and five times the loss estimates reported by fire departments, as attested to by the above experts and substantiated in my own investigative experience.[5]

The under-reporting of arson and fire damages is partly due to the shortages of staff and equipment which plague many arson squads and make it impossible to seriously investigate more than a fraction of the fires which are initially called to their attention (U.S. General Accounting Office, 1978). Fire chiefs are under pressure from mayors to show that fire protection has not declined despite cut-backs in city fire department budgets, as exemplified by department claims during the recent "proposition 2½" fiscal crisis in Boston (Harvey, 1981:6; Radin, 1981:3). The reputation of a city's fire protection services and the local department's evaluation by the NFPA affects both insurance premium rates and the bond ratings from municipal securities, which must be sold to balance mounting budget deficits (National Fire Prevention Administration, 1976).

Like other social problems, the cost of arson is not shared evenly. While national statistics are not available, the common impression of investigators and journalists alike is that most of those killed are poor people and minorities living in slum districts of urban centers (Lima, 1977b; Schall, 1977). The victims are often children or elderly people who are not quick enough to escape the flames. Typically, they die choking in their beds or trapped on staircases, the latter a favorite spot for arsonists to do their work because they provide an easy escape route and good updrafts for spreading the flames (ABC, 1978; Fraker, 1977).

Declining urban neighborhoods, particularly in the older cities of the Northeast and Midwest, are the most common arson sites (Karter, 1982). New York City recorded more than 40,000 arson fires resulting in over 180 civilian deaths from 1975 to 1978 (Catalina, 1979). The city's fires have been concentrated in the heavily black and Hispanic South Bronx district, which was gutted by more than 30,000 arson fires from 1970 to 1979 (Hanson, 1980). In New Jersey, arson caused 168 deaths and over $96 million in damages in 1978, mainly in the ghettoes of Hoboken and Patterson (U.S. Congress: Senate, 1979). Denver's central district was scarred by more than 3,000 arson fires in 1971–76, which destroyed 544 buildings and caused over a million dollars in structural damages (MacDonald, 1977).

The response of law enforcement agencies to the arson problem does not inspire confidence. Throughout the mounting arson wave of the 1970s, the Federal Bureau of Investigation (FBI) continued to list arson as a low priority offense, along with drunk driving and gambling; it finally added arson to the list of "index crimes" in 1981 on a provisional basis (Campbell, 1981). Local police departments reported in 1977 that less than 9 percent of all *reported* arson incidents resulted in an arrest, while less than 2 percent ended with a conviction (Boudreau, 1977:30). Federal budget allocations show that in 1977, only $1.7 million of the Law Enforcement Assistance Administration's budget of $2 billion was set aside for anti-arson programs, or less than 0.1 percent (ABC, 1978; U.S. Congress: Senate, 1979). This was increased to $17 million by 1980, but was cut back to $5 million by President Ronald Reagan's administration in 1982 (Gest, 1983).

---

5. Based on presentations made by Scollins, Murphy, and Schmidt at the Massachusetts Attorney General's Conference on Arson held at Worcester, Massachusetts, February 23, 1983. In addition I interviewed three of these experts during January and February, 1983, in the course of liaison responsibilities for the Boston Arson Strike Force. I interviewed Carter extensively at the National Fire Protection Association at Quincy, Massachusetts, on November 17, 1982.

MISUNDERSTANDING ARSON: THE LEGACY OF DEVIANCE THEORY

Solving arson, like any other crime, requires both sufficient resources and a logical theory which can link the available evidence and point to a particular suspect or a correct enforcement policy. It is not enough for investigators to uncover the right clues; they must also set aside the wrong ones. A "cold trail" can be particularly deceptive when it is well worn by long investigative tradition and well marked by orthodox criminological theory. Unfortunately, the trail followed in most analysis and investigation of arson is both "cold" and circular.

In the United States, arson has long been the almost exclusive concern of local fire departments; and arson squads in those departments have typically served as a sort of bureaucratic "pasture" for older firefighters and those no longer fit for active fire duty. Training for these squads has been limited and largely confined to forensics and pyrotechnics. In essence, arson squad investigators are taught to approach each fire as an individual technical problem whose solution lies in identifying the means and method of "ignition" found in the rubble the morning after. Once this evidence has been collected and any available eyewitnesses have been questioned, the arson squads consider their job done. If they suspect a particular person set the fire, squad members may later spend long hours in clandestine surveillance of that individual (Associated Press, 1981).

But there is a great deal of difference between locating the origin or even the "torch" for a particular fire and understanding the source of the arson problem. Fire department officials have little grasp of organized crime and even less appreciation of the complex socio-economic processes which lead to abandoned property, dramatic demographic changes, and ultimately arson. None of these larger issues seem relevant so long as arson is viewed as a crime without rational motive. Criminal investigation aims simply at linking physical evidence to particular arsonists whose impulsive, disturbed behavior makes them all the more elusive and unpredictable.

The dominant popular image of the arsonist is the classic "pyromaniac" who masturbates while watching the soaring flames from the shadows. While this portrayal has been slightly expanded to include the "juvenile vandal," arson is still widely regarded as a crime of rage, jealousy, mental disorder, and especially sexual perversity (Battle and Weston, 1975:91; Witkin, 1979). This image owes a great deal to the rather dubious contributions of Sigmund Freud. Though Freud actually examined few pyromaniacs, he wrote extensively on the subject, describing them as sexually immature or homosexually inclined psychotics or adolescents. His conclusions, based largely on speculation and a reading of mythology (Freud, 1932:405), formed the basis of most later psychiatric and criminological work on pyromania (Macht and Mack, 1968; Yarnell, 1940).

Contemporary clinical research, invariably based on examinations of only a few maladjusted adolescents or adult psychotics, continues to reinforce the Freudian image. Hurley (1969:4) claims "arson is often a manifestation of mental abnormality . . . the result of unconscious sexual conflict or as obsessive-compulsive or passive-aggressive behavior." Scott (1974) discusses arson as a crime of revenge or perversion committed by psychotics, alcoholics, homosexuals, and maladjusted children, though he concedes that "arson for profit" might be the motive for a few offenders. Inciardi (1970) concludes that most of the 138 imprisoned arsonists he studied were primarily motivated by sexual excitement or the desire for revenge, while only 7 percent burned buildings for profit. The latter he regards as an anachronism harking back to the 1930s "when arson was associated with organized crime" (1970:145). MacDonald (1977) also depicts arsonists as compulsive pyromaniacs, sexually excited by fire, but otherwise impotent, prone to bedwetting, transvestite behavior, and collecting obscene magazines.

The violent subculture theory is essentially an extension of the traditional explanations of arson as the product of individual deviance. However, the subculture theories regard whole communities—particularly urban ghetto dwellers—as prone to a variety of deviant behavior, includ-

6   BRADY

ing arson (Banfield, 1970; Miller, 1968; Moynihan, 1970). Both sorts of deviance theory regard arson as an irrational act, undertaken by pathological actors, for a variety of perverse individual or collective impulses. Both explanations find wide acceptance among officials responsible for combatting arson and are clearly reflected in unsuccessful anti-arson programs (Battle and Weston, 1975; Witkin, 1979).

There is a disturbing circularity in the deviance theories and the anti-arson programs which are based upon them. Researchers draw an image of the arsonist from the composite characteristics of those few who were captured and imprisoned. Enforcement agencies aim their investigations at the "sort of people" identified by researchers as arson prone (*Fire and Arson Investigator*, 1981). Orthodox assumptions about the motives and actors involved with arson remain largely unquestioned.

THE DEMOGRAPHY OF ARSON IN BOSTON

Boston burns almost nightly in deliberately set fires. From 1978 until the end of 1982 the city was scarred by more than 3,000 "incendiary" and "suspicious" fires. In 1981 and 1982 alone they caused more than $4.5 million in property losses and killed about 60 people (Gest, 1983; Scharfenberg, 1980; Slade, 1978; Vennochi, 1982). Local fire officials view these incidents as the work of "bored juveniles" and "firebugs" (Jahnke, 1982). They rely on expanded forensic laboratories, neighborhood arson watch programs, and rewards to control the mounting fire problem (Mahoney, 1982; Osgood, 1982). Not surprisingly, this approach has utterly failed. George Paul, the Boston Fire Commissioner, said, "There's no rhyme or reason to this, no pattern. We've plotted space, time patterns, nothing shows up" (McMillan, 1982:23).

There is, nevertheless, a pattern in Boston's fire history. Maps 1 and 2 show that arson is tightly concentrated within certain poor Boston neighborhoods, particularly Roxbury, North Dorchester, East Boston, and Jamaica Plain. These districts are largely populated by blacks, Hispanics, and poor Irish and Italians. If pyromaniacs or juvenile vandals set these blazes in random irrational acts, as local officials insist, why do the arsonists so carefully respect neighborhood boundaries? If "bored youths idled by school vacation" (Dillon, 1982:4) were responsible for the wave of 300 arson fires in the summer of 1982, then must we assume that juveniles are bored only in certain districts?

Arson is more common in buildings owned by absentee landlords than in owner-occupied tenements in the same neighborhoods (National Urban League, 1971). Arson is rare in public housing projects, which are located in the heart of Boston's fire-ravaged districts and which house the poorest, most disproportionately non-white, single-parent families. These are, presumably, the angriest, most potentially "socio-pathic" people in the city. Rates of street crime in the housing projects are the highest in the city, so serious indeed that the buildings were placed in receivership by the federal courts during 1982–83 while security arrangements for tenants were improved.[6] Yet the Boston Housing Authority does *not* have a significant arson problem, with only four arson fires reported for 1981 in buildings which housed over 13,000 people (Fox, 1983).

Finally, incendiary techniques employed by arsonists have become increasingly sophisticated (Horn, 1976). Pyrotechnic experts draw particular attention to the 1982–83 blazes set in Roxbury's Highland Park, along the South Boston waterfront, and those straddling the new Southwest Corridor mass transit construction zone.[7] Robert Carter[8] of the NFPA described these fires as follows:

---

6. Based on an interview with Jonathan Fox, Fire Safety Coordinator, Department of Public Safety, Boston Housing Authority, October 26, 1982. Fox also provided extensive notes on these matters.
7. Based on an interview with William Murphy, Federal Bureau of Alcohol, Tobacco and Firearms, November 11, 1982, and an interview with Robert Carter, November 17, 1982.
8. Based on an interview with Robert Carter, November 17, 1982.

MAP 1

Arson and Abandonment in Boston

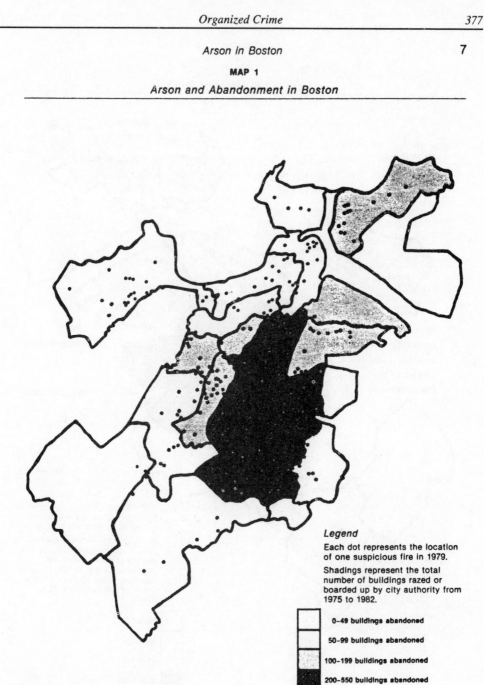

Legend

Each dot represents the location
of one suspicious fire in 1979.

Shadings represent the total
number of buildings razed or
boarded up by city authority from
1975 to 1982.

0–49 buildings abandoned

50–99 buildings abandoned

100–199 buildings abandoned

200–550 buildings abandoned

Sources

City divided according to ward boundaries used by the city's buildings department.

Arson fire locations plotted by Michael Moore, Boston Arson Strike Force.

Abandonment data from monthly and annual reports of the city's buildings and community development departments, available from Boston City Hall.

8   BRADY

MAP 2

Arson and Redlining in Boston

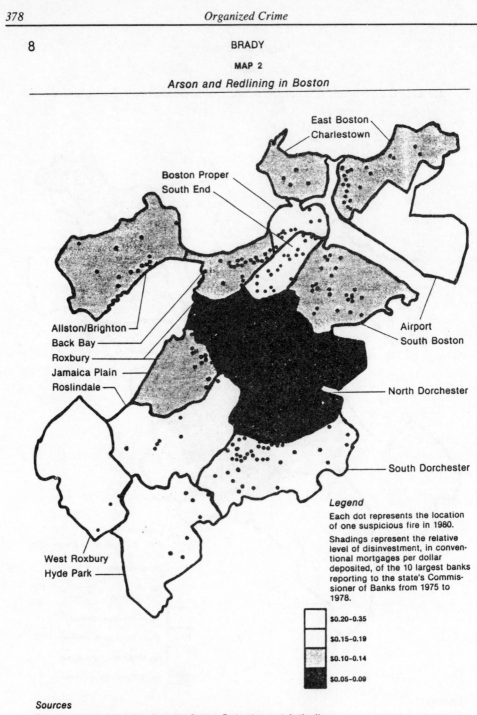

East Boston
Charlestown

Boston Proper
South End

Allston/Brighton
Back Bay
Roxbury
Jamaica Plain
Roslindale

Airport
South Boston

North Dorchester

South Dorchester

West Roxbury
Hyde Park

Legend

Each dot represents the location
of one suspicious fire in 1980.

Shadings represent the relative
level of disinvestment, in conventional mortgages per dollar
deposited, of the 10 largest banks
reporting to the state's Commissioner of Banks from 1975 to
1978.

$0.20–0.35
$0.15–0.19
$0.10–0.14
$0.05–0.09

Sources

City neighborhood divisions from the Boston Redevelopment Authority.

Arson fire locations plotted by Michael Moore, Boston Arson Strike Force.

Bank reinvestment patterns from Greenwald (1978).

These have been some of the most professional jobs we've seen in the city. Extensive quantities of hard-to-detect accelerants, such as paint thinner, have been used, typically placed in several waxed-paper containers positioned at key structural members of the buildings and linked together with trailers (streams) of accelerant, leading to a single ignition point, sometimes using photographic paper as a fuse device which leaves little residue.

Are we to believe that psychotic "pyromaniacs" or malicious juvenile vandals would employ such systematic and complex means of setting fires?

The answer, of course, is that arson is not primarily a result of deviant perversion, juvenile rage, or boredom. More complex economic motives are involved, which have to do with *where* buildings are situated and *who* owns them. I have discovered several discernable varieties of arson in Boston, all of these directly or indirectly linked to patterns of real estate speculation and to decisions aimed at profit-making in what are essentially business transactions.

THE ROLE OF BANKS: ARSON AND ABANDONMENT

Arson is both a barometer of changing values and a mechanism for accelerating changes in property values and in the social economy of the city. More than half of Boston's 3,000 arson fires from 1978 to 1982 occurred in abandoned buildings.[9] The relative frequency of abandonment in the city's neighborhoods can be ascertained by analyzing the monthly reports of city departments charged with boarding up or razing derelict buildings. The abandonment pattern corresponds closely to the arson distribution pattern as represented in Map 1. Across the city's 22 wards, an average of 41 buildings per ward were razed or boarded up from 1975 to 1982; in the depressed North Dorchester and Roxbury districts, there were between 220 and 540 buildings razed per ward.[10]

Abandoned buildings have long been recognized as a problem in urban neighborhoods, where the phenomenon is closely associated with declining local opportunities and mounting crime. An earlier generation of urban planners at the Federal Housing Administration (FHA) described abandonment as part of the "natural" process of "neighborhood evolution" wherein "high-rent neighborhoods move slowly but predictably across the urban landscape, creating a gravitational pull on the middle class, leaving behind the structure by which slums are made" (Hoyt, 1939:26). More recently, U.S. Housing and Urban Development analysts have attributed abandonment to the problem of "urban blight" brought on by the "influx of minority populations" (Real Estate Research Corp., 1975:22). Such prominent urban planners as Sternleib *et al.* (1974:33) also emphasize that "abandonment is a contagion problem" which is "most frequent in structures inhabited by blacks and Puerto Ricans."

These attempts to explain abandonment clearly echo the deviant subculture theory and, in their persistent use of language borrowed from physics or biology, give the impression that neighborhood decline is somehow natural or inevitable, or that poor and ethnic people are infected with the problem and are therefore responsible for it. The simple correlation of abandonment rates and minority census figures in fact proves nothing about *why* housing deteriorates; but such "explanations" again draw strength from implicit racist sentiments. Any further analysis of the problem is precluded by this orthodoxy, which is little more than a tautology.

There is a great deal more to be said about abandonment. National studies show that it is not minority landlords who most frequently abandon their buildings, but rather white landlords—in

9. Joseph O'Keefe, Massachusetts State Fire Marshall, on "People are Talking," WNEV–TV, Boston, November 11, 1982.
10. Statistics on razed and boarded-up properties drawn from tabulated monthly reports filed by Boston Buildings Department and Boston Office of Community Development at Boston City Hall. Note that these statistics are compiled by ward divisions, while the bank reinvestment statistics computed by Greenwald (1978) and presented in Map 2 are compiled with "neighborhood" districts drawn by the Boston Redevelopment Authority.

10　　　　　　　　　　　　　　　BRADY

particular absentee landlords with high incomes who own a number of buildings and who hold property titles indirectly through holding companies and real estate trusts (Sternleib *et al.*, 1974). Studies of abandonment in New York City, Cleveland, Chicago, Detroit, and Los Angeles consistently demonstrate that abandonment patterns follow closely the discriminatory mortgage-lending policies of banks which deny credit to certain districts of the inner city in order to invest in more profitable suburban real estate (Linton *et al.*, 1971; *Loyola Law Journal*, 1975; National Urban League, 1971). This disinvestment process is known as redlining. Devine (1973) documented the scale of this destructive redlining pattern in New York's South Bronx district, where the largest local banks systematically drained the district of capital by exporting local deposits and assets to investments in the suburbs. Berwyn (1974) showed that for every dollar deposited in major banks located in Chicago's predominantly black districts, less than eight cents was reinvested by those same banks in conventional mortgages loaned in those areas—though 31 cents was used by those banks to provide mortgage supports for the suburbs.

In Boston, the same pattern is evident. The State Commissioner of Banking, Carol Greenwald (1978:7), using statistics provided by the banks, found that for every dollar deposited in the city branches of the 10 largest banks from 1975 to 1978, the banks reinvested only 10 to 17 cents in conventional mortgages within the city. Some urban districts fared far worse than others: East Boston received between three and 11 cents, North Dorchester between five and 11 cents, Roxbury between four and 11 cents.

Redlining is a clear violation of both a bank's obligations, contained in state and federal charters, and the provisions of the Community Reinvestment Act adopted by the U.S. Congress in 1978 (Taggert, 1977). Yet no bank officers to my knowledge have ever been prosecuted for violation of the law or their local charters (Greenwald, 1980). Not all banks are equally involved with redlining. Greenwald (1978) found that the largest banks were the ones most systematically engaged in redlining. It should be noted that banks use redlining not so much to avoid losses as to maximize profits. In Boston the banks have consistently made profits from their investments in every section of the city, but suburban investments are more profitable (Metropolitan Area Planning Council, 1980).

Redlining is devastating to a neighborhood. Many small businesses are forced to close when they are unable to get bank loans (Bradford and Rubinowitz, 1975). As property values decline, landlords stop repairing their buildings and eventually abandon them when they become uninhabitable (Newfield and DuBrul, 1977; Stone, 1978). A severe housing shortage develops. In Boston, where housing for low- and moderate-income tenants is extremely scarce, the city authorities estimate that there were approximately 3,000 abandoned buildings in 1974 and nearly 5,000 in 1982 (Boston Redevelopment Authority, 1974; Flynn, 1982).

Arson has been concentrated in those Boston neighborhoods which have been most drained of capital and mortgage loans. The Boston Fire Department reports that there were an average of 12 arsons per ward across the city in 1980; but wards 14 and 15 in North Dorchester and Roxbury had a combined total of 82 arson fires, while ward 1 in East Boston had 21 arson fires.

Two sorts of arson fires can be seen as a direct result of redlining, and these might be described as escape fires and vandal fires. *Escape fires* are arranged by landlords and small business owners to collect insurance premiums on unprofitable properties and real estate investments. *Vandal fires* occur after owners abandon their properties and take a tax write-off on their losses. Their buildings become a hangout for juvenile gangs and, ultimately, a target for vandalism. Of course, redlining is not the only reason for neighborhood decline, which leads to vandal and escape fires; but redlining accelerates the downward spiral and makes recovery almost impossible (Duncan, 1975; Greenwald, 1980; Public Interest Research Group—District of Columbia, 1975).

While redlining has been found to be a common practice among the larger banks and an indirect contributor to arson, some individual banks and bank officers play a direct role in arson through their involvement with organized crime's arson-for-profit syndicates. Before discussing specific examples of collaboration between bankers and gangsters, I consider the general model that links criminal syndicates to redlining and abandonment.

BANKERS, GANGSTERS, AND PROBLEM PROPERTIES

Foreclosures on unpaid mortgages are one of the side effects of redlining. Many property owners in redlined areas cease making mortgage payments on losing investments. By the time foreclosure procedures have been completed and the bank seizes the buildings, the property has frequently been neglected and even abandoned for months or years. Such derelict buildings, hardly an attractive item on the real estate market, represent a potential loss for the banks.

Enter the organized crime racketeers. They offer to buy the "problem buildings," often at a price far greater than true market value, on condition that the bank write out a new mortgage for close to the full purchase price, and sometimes more, to cover the cost of "renovation." Thus, the racketeers acquire large numbers of properties with little investment of their own capital. In some cases they can further increase their "leverage" by arranging second, third, or fourth mortgages whose total value far exceeds the original inflated purchase price. Backed by mortgages from a major bank, it is fairly simple to arrange insurance coverage for the buildings at a level well above the total value of the mortgages.

The racketeers then hire professional "torches" to set fire to the over-mortgaged and over-insured buildings. Often a series of fires of escalating scale are set to net the owner several partial insurance payments before the building is totally destroyed in one final blaze. Racketeers' profits are further increased by hiring phony contractors to "repair" the fire damage. Corrupt building inspectors file false reports, concealing the fact that repairs were never made, then another fire is set to burn the "repaired" portion of the building.

The banks often profit more than the racketeers from this ruse, even without consciously joining in the conspiracy and without violating the law. Since state laws stipulate that the insurance company must pay the holder of the mortgage first in the event of a fire which destroys the building, arson represents the "final solution" to problem properties. Fire-prone speculators are the best possible risks for banks, since their mortgages are paid off in full and in short order. The potential losses represented by foreclosed properties are converted into a substantial profit for the bank because the new mortgage paid by the insurance company greatly exceeds the old bad debt assumed under foreclosure.

The relationship between bankers and racketeers can become quite cozy as the racketeers return again and again to the same bank and often the same loan officer. Unless bank officers engage in conscious conspiracy to burn for profit (and there *is* reason for them to do so), these transactions are perfectly legal—even if the buyer has recently been convicted for arson or has a long history of incendiary fires. Indeed, one might argue convincingly that a bank officer who failed to unload problem properties in such a profitable arrangement would be derelict in his obligation to protect the interests of the bank's shareholders.

The case of the South Boston Savings Bank, one of the largest financial institutions in Massachusetts, illustrates this point. From 1970 to 1977 the bank foreclosed on 76 properties, many of them in depressed neighborhoods. These parcels were covered by conventional mortgages written by the bank. In the same period 39 of these properties suffered a total of 79 fires, averaging about two fires per parcel. This may be compared with 69 parcels foreclosed by the same bank in the same period for mortgages written by the bank but guaranteed by the Veterans' Administration (VA) and the U.S. Department of Housing and Urban Development (HUD). These latter properties were in the same neighborhoods as the first group, and their original owners were actually poorer risks, since the VA and HUD required of them smaller initial down-payments than the bank demanded from holders of conventional mortgages. Still, the 69 government-guaranteed foreclosed properties suffered only 36 fires at 26 addresses, or approximately half the rate of loss at the foreclosed properties in which the bank's own money was at risk in a conventional mortgage (Zanger, 1978a,b).

The timing of these fires in the South Boston Savings Bank properties is also curious. One would expect more fires to occur in the year *before* foreclosure, when owners might turn to desperate means (such as an escape fire) to recoup their losses. This is precisely the pattern in the buildings foreclosed by the bank in which the mortgages were guaranteed by the U.S. government. However, the reverse is the case for properties foreclosed under conventional mortgages written by the bank. It was the *new* owners with properties acquired from the bank *after* foreclosure who had the "bad luck" with fires—most of which occurred in the first year after resale. Insurance payments for fires have brought millions of dollars in income to the South Boston Savings Bank, for properties which might otherwise have represented a serious loss (Zanger, 1978b).

In 1978 the South Boston Savings Bank's mortgage clients included many of Boston's most arson-prone property owners, of whom a mere dozen experienced more than a hundred suspicious fires from 1970 to 1977 (Zanger, 1978). The bank's clients during this period included: Caroll St. Germaine, convicted arsonist and murderer (over $500,000 to 1978); Russell Tardanico, convicted arsonist (over $730,000 in 16 mortgages to 1982); George Lincoln, confessed "torch" and arsonist who turned "state's witness" in exchange for immunity in a 1978–79 Boston arson conspiracy trial (over $150,000 in five mortgages to 1978); Nicholas Shaheen, convicted arsonist (over $100,000 in five mortgages to 1978). The bank's president, Alfred Archibald, has denied any knowledge that these and other fire-prone clients were "that sort of person" (WBZ, 1981), or that they had any "sort of fire problem" (Zanger, 1978a:1).

INSURANCE INDUSTRY POLICIES AND ARSON

Insurance companies in the United States paid an estimated $5 billion in arson-related losses in 1979–80 (Karter, 1982). Yet they have not been aggressive in pressing local, state, or federal governments to undertake vigorous anti-arson measures, such as the restriction of bank redlining; and their internal studies of arson are generally circulated quietly within the industry. With some important exceptions, which I discuss below, the insurance industry has not responded publicly to the arson problem.

There are three reasons for this attitude. First, the insurance companies themselves practice redlining (McDonough, 1980). In 1968, following ghetto riots in a number of U.S. cities, the insurance industry persuaded Congress to establish a network of FAIR Plan insurance consortiums to cover high-risk districts in urban centers (Massachusetts Property Insurance Underwriters Association, 1970; U.S. Housing and Urban Development, 1968). Under the FAIR Plans sponsored by 26 states with large urban centers, insurance losses in the high-risk areas are shared among all companies doing business in each state. A company's contribution to the state's FAIR Plan pool is based on that company's percentage of the total premium value of policies written in the state (U.S. Housing and Urban Development, 1968). The creation of the FAIR Plans accelerated the wholesale exodus of conventional insurance companies from the high-risk districts, and the FAIR Plans were obligated to provide insurance for virtually everyone and virtually all categories of real property. FAIR Plan losses to arson grew rapidly, amounting to an estimated $275 million for New York FAIR Plan and over $30 million for New Jersey FAIR Plan from 1968 to 1977 (*Economist*, 1977:11; Higgins, 1979:18). These are substantial losses for the FAIR Plans and their member insurance companies, but they can be simply passed along, in the form of higher premiums charged to all of those living in FAIR Plan districts where inhabitants cannot shop elsewhere for conventional coverage (U.S. Congress: Senate, 1979).

Second, insurance claims adjustors seldom recommend civil litigation against property owners making fire claims, even when arson for profit is suspected. The companies are reluctant to challenge claims, because they don't want to acquire a reputation for "being tough" and risk losing potential clients in the increasingly competitive scramble for policy underwriting. If a company challenges a claim, refuses prompt payment, and then loses the case in civil litigation, the judge will usually require the company to pay the claimant damages equal to three times the original claim (U.S. Congress: Senate, 1979). The poor record of the criminal justice system in investigating and prosecuting arson, and the inadequacy of often vague and sketchy arson squad reports, also leaves the insurance companies vulnerable to counter-suit when they are unsuccessful in challenging a client's claims. All of these considerations discourage serious arson control within the industry. George Clark, vice president for Cravens, Dargen Insurance Co., told a Congressional hearing on arson for profit:

> If we instruct our cause-of-loss investigators to send copies of their reports to District Attorneys, it looks as if the big insurance companies are trying to put the policy-holder in jail. If we voluntarily share the material and the District Attorney dismisses the case, we are wide open for a civil lawsuit. Punitive damages in some states will be the price we pay for sharing this valuable information with law enforcement authorities. There seems to be a lack of interest as far as law enforcement is concerned (U.S. Congress: Senate, 1979:22).

Third, the insurance industry is privileged: it is the only U.S. industry not restricted by federal anti-trust laws. Restrictions enacted by the individual state insurance commissions leave the companies tremendous flexibility in investing their premiums. Insurance companies are reluctant to admit the extent of the arson problem because they don't want closer regulation of the industry (Lima, 1980; Weese, 1971). The worst industry nightmare would be the repeal of the McCarran-Ferguson Act of 1945, which grants the industry exemption from federal regulation. This is precisely what has been demanded by some anti-arson activists and by some government-sponsored investigations of insurance fraud (U.S. Comptroller General, 1979; U.S. General Accounting Office, 1978; U.S. Congress: Senate, 1963).

The main impetus for insurance reform has come from community groups in fire-ravaged districts, such as Massachusetts Fair Share and the Symphony Tenants Organizing Project who made arson and insurance fraud a public issue in Massachusetts from 1977 to 1980 (Brady, 1981a, 1982a, b). They roundly criticized the local FAIR Plan for its inadequate attention to arson in the early 1970s, when Massachusetts FAIR Plan admitted that fully 60 percent of its total losses were due to arson-related claims (Golembeski, 1980, 1982). The state insurance commissioner, Michael Sabbagh, recognizing the mounting problem, granted enlightened FAIR Plan officials the authority to refuse certain coverage to clients with serious histories of suspicious fires. The Massachusetts FAIR Plan since 1979 has required all prospective clients to submit an "arson application" detailing all fires in every building in which they have held any financial interest (Golembeski, 1980). In 1976 the FAIR Plan also began to devote far greater resources to the investigation of suspicious fire claims, and has refused to write policies for a number of arson-prone landlords. The FAIR Plan's arson losses have declined from an estimated 60 percent of all fire claims in 1975 to less than 30 percent in 1981 (Golembeski, 1982).

Unfortunately, there is another form of insurance coverage still available to arson racketeers: the so-called *surplus line* insurance companies, which are based outside the state and often in another country. Though their premiums are often substantially higher than those of the conventional companies or the FAIR Plans, the surplus line companies insure almost anyone at levels of coverage not possible elsewhere (U.S. Congress: Senate, 1963). These companies operate without local licenses or regulation, except that their local brokers must be registered with state insurance commissions and must swear that their clients have been turned down by several conventional companies, making them eligible for "surplus" coverage (Bawcutt, 1978; Kwitney, 1973:158). These local brokers are largely unsupervised by their company's "home office," which

14   BRADY

is sometimes no more than a post office box in Bermuda, the Bahamas, or Delaware—a state notorious for its lack of corporate regulations. The brokers typically receive more than double the commissions allowed by conventional companies and often the same brokers are later responsible for claims adjustment (Lima, 1980; Weese, 1971).

The surplus line companies usually sell their premiums, and 98 to 99 percent of their policy liabilities, to foreign investors who are eager to break into the U.S. insurance market and are unaware of the scale of arson fraud in the United States. Thus, the broker and the surplus line company are not vulnerable to the losses sustained under the policies which they write, and policies of arson racketeers are buried within large investment bundles containing many more policies with legitimate insurance clients (Brenner, 1980; Daenzer, 1980). The surplus line market grew dramatically during the 1970s. From 1971 to 1977, the volume of surplus lines increased 533 percent, from $298 million to $1.6 billion dollars (National Association of Insurance Commissioners, 1980a). Since experts estimate that only about one-fourth of the actual premium volume is reported to the various states' insurance commissioners (Weese, 1971:81), the real premium volume was probably about $8 billion in 1980 (Chaput and Faxon, 1981; Daenzer, 1980; Lima, 1980:2).

The situation, in short, is ideal for arson racketeers driven out of their once lucrative FAIR Plan hunting grounds (U.S. Fire Administration, 1979). In 1978, the SASSE syndicate of surplus line brokers, operating in league with real estate speculators and gangsters in New York City, collected over $32 million in fraudulent insurance claims on grossly over-insured properties in the South Bronx (Brenner, 1980; Coppack, 1980). Some of these policies were backdated to cover previous fires, and "torches" were hired to set other buildings afire (Brenner, 1978; Lima, 1980). The SASSE syndicate consisted of New York City brokers representing a number of surplus line companies which were in turn investment conduits for Lloyds of London. The scale of this loss staggered even Lloyds and prompted New York State's insurance commissioner to implement the nation's most stringent underwriting procedures for surplus line companies (Chaput and Faxon, 1981).

In Massachusetts the implementation of effective anti-arson measures adopted by the FAIR Plan from 1976 to 1979 coincided with the dramatic expansion of the surplus line market. The total value of surplus line premiums reported to the state insurance commission increased by nearly 600 percent in 1976–77 alone, when it grew from $5.6 million to $32.8 million (Chaput and Faxon, 1981:4). The number of reported fire insurance policies written with surplus line companies doubled in 1981–82. Of course, there are many reasons for using surplus line coverage which are entirely legitimate, as are most brokers and surplus line clients. For example, an individual wishing to insure a vacant apartment building or an empty warehouse in a high-risk district would probably not be eligible (after 1978) for FAIR Plan or conventional insurance coverage (Golembeski, 1980). Nevertheless, the Boston Arson Strike Force discovered that 31 individuals and holding companies with serious arson histories on their properties contracted for new surplus line policies in 1980 and 1981. These policies totaled over $38 million in fire insurance coverage in these two years. Properties belonging to these 31 individuals and trust companies burned in 153 "incendiary," "suspicious," or "undetermined" fires from 1978 to 1982, with total structural damage estimated by the Boston Fire Department in excess of $2 million.[11] A handful of brokers represent nearly all of these suspicious property owners (Brady, 1982b; Moore, 1983).

---

11. Surplus line insurance affadavits are public records, on file at the Massachusetts Insurance Commission Office in Boston. Fire incidence and cause records are also public documents (though follow-up investigation reports of the Arson Squad are not). The public fire records may be obtained from the Central Headquarters, Boston Fire Department. Copies of insurance affadavits are available on request from the author.

"DOWNSCALE" ARSON AND THE TARDANICO SYNDICATE

The case of the Russell Tardanico/Robert Sherman syndicate in Dorchester illustrates one variety of arson racketeering in Boston. In 1970 Russell Tardanico was convicted of arson and "interfering with the duties of the Fire Department" while it was engaged in putting out another arson fire (Pappas, 1981). Tardanico and Sherman have, since the 1960s, owned whole blocks of commercial buildings and dozens of apartment units in Dorchester (Anner, 1982; Axelrod, 1982; Pappas, 1981). Following his arson conviction, Tardanico transferred title for most of his properties from his own name to those of his wife and children, and to Sherman, who are trustees of some dozen holding companies (Brady, 1982b). From 1973 to 1982, Tardanico/ Sherman properties have burned more than 35 times, with losses estimated at more than $600,000. The state FAIR Plan alone admits paying him more than $110,000 (Pappas, 1981).

Table 1 summarizes the Tardanico syndicate's transactions and a few of the more important fires to strike their properties, most of which were classified by the Boston Fire Department as "incendiary," "suspicious," "undetermined," or "burning trash." Most of these properties burned very shortly after they were purchased and insurance policies were arranged. Many of these properties were purchased from Arthur Pitnoff, a respected local entrepreneur with extensive holdings in Dorchester. Tardanico was until 1979 president of the Fields Corner (Dorchester) Merchants' Association (Zanger, 1978a).

The South Boston Savings Bank has consistently provided mortgages to the Tardanico syndicate, including six written while Tardanico was under a suspended prison sentence for arson, from 1971 to 1974. Between 1971 and 1979 the bank wrote 15 mortgages worth $730,000 for 13 different Tardanico properties.[12] Eleven of these buildings burned a total of 27 times, usually in "suspicious" or "incendiary" fires and usually a few months after purchase in suspicious fires. Backed by this powerful bank, Tardanico easily arranged large insurance policies for his properties. Along with the policies of several conventional companies, he arranged over $600,000 in coverage with the state's FAIR Plan from 1972 to 1979 (Brady, 1982b; Pappas, 1981).

Since 1979 the FAIR Plan has denied coverage to Tardanico (Pappas, 1981). He has become the object of considerable media attention (WBZ, 1981; WNEV, 1982) following four arson fires at Tardanico/syndicate-owned buildings at 318 Adams Street (August, 1981) and 1352 Dorchester Avenue (November, 1982) (Anner, 1982; Pappas, 1981). Despite his claims to the contrary (Pappas, 1981), Tardanico has not left the real estate business. Rather, Russell Tardanico has shifted property titles to a new set of trust companies now headed by his wife, Kathleen, and has drawn up a new series of comprehensive insurance policies (worth a total of over $1 million) with several surplus line insurance companies. The largest of these carries a value of $705,000 coverage for unspecified "buildings." The unnamed insurer, as a surplus line company, is not subject to state regulations, except that the broker was obligated to swear that Tardanico had been previously turned down by at least three conventional companies, making him eligible for surplus coverage.

"UPSCALE" ARSON AND THE CASE OF FREDERICK RUST

Another sort of arson has developed in Boston neighborhoods where property values are rising rapidly and landlords are trying to attract more affluent renters or buyers for condominiums created from former rental apartments (Jahnke, 1981b). Boston arson expert Michael Moore (1981) refers to this pattern as "upscale" arson in his seminal writings on the economics of arson. The "vacancy de-control" clause of Boston's rent control law and the eviction restrictions of the

---

12. South Boston Savings Bank mortgage contracts are public records, available from the Suffolk County Register of Deeds, Old County Courthouse, Government Center, Boston. Copies are available on request from the author.

TABLE 1

Real Estate Transactions and Fire History of the Tardanico Syndicate

Property	Date of Sale	Previous Owner	Buyer	Sale Price	Mortgage	Date of Fire	Fire Origin	Estimated Structural Damage
1350-8 Dorchester Avenue	11/17/76	South Boston Savings Bank	Russell Tardanico	$ 65,000	South Boston Savings Bank	11/16/82 11/20/82	suspicious suspicious	$ 10,000 $ 1,000
1374-78 Dorchester Avenue	5/13/75 1/2/80	City of Boston Russell Tardanico	Russell Tardanico Mass. Tex Corporation	$ 4,500 $ 70,000	Arthur Pitnoff	7/6/79	suspicious	$ 2,000
1377-79 Dorchester Avenue	2/24/74 7/23/76	Robert Pitnoff (Arthur's brother) Russell Tardanico	Russell Tardanico RKPSR Realty Trust (Russell Tardanico)	$ 45,000 $1	Meeting House Hill Bank South Boston Savings Bank	2/25/76 5/1/77	trash suspicious	$ 20,000 $ 2,500
1452-58 Dorchester Avenue	8/11/76	Mary Remy	RAB Realty Trust (Russell Tardanico)	$ 32,000	South Boston Savings Bank	10/9/76 1/20/79	trash Incendiary	$ 2,000 $ 1,500
1460-70 Dorchester Avenue	3/18/77	New England Mutual Life Insurance Co.	1460 Trust (Russell Tardanico)	$ 38,500	Mass. Cooperative Bank	4/27/77 2/16/78	suspicious Incendiary	$151,000 $ 1,000
1502-08 Dorchester Avenue	8/19/75	Simon Drasner	RAB Realty Trust (Russell Tardanico)	$ 45,000	South Boston Savings Bank	9/3/75 10/3/75	undetermined undetermined	$ 83,000 $ 25,000
1510-14 Dorchester Avenue	7/22/76	Arthur Pitnoff	RRR Realty Trust (Russell Tardanico)	$ 75,000	South Boston Savings Bank	11/6/76 1/2/77	undetermined undetermined	$ 6,500 $ 20,000
158 Adams Street	10/11/72 7/12/73 3/20/80	Arthur Pitnoff Russell Tardanico Arthur Pitnoff	Russell Tardanico Arthur Pitnoff Ronald Tardanico (Russell's brother)	$ 25,000 $ 12,000 $1	South Boston Savings Bank	11/30/72 4/11/73 3/15/77 6/18/78	undetermined suspicious undetermined undetermined	$ 2,500 $ 3,000 $ 40,000 $ 4,500
318-22 Adams Street	4/24/81	BayBank	RKPSR Realty Trust (Russell Tardanico)	$105,000	BayBank	4/26/81 3/25/81	suspicious suspicious	$ 1,000 $ 75,000
115 Hollingsworth Road	4/19/74	John Gornstein	Russell Tardanico	$ 48,000	South Boston Savings Bank	11/6/74 1/11/75	suspicious suspicious	$ 8,000 $ 37,400

Source:
Property sales and mortgages from documents at Suffolk County Registry of Deeds. Fire data and structural loss estimates from Boston Fire Department Arson Squad.

city's 1979 "condominium conversion" statute were specifically designed to protect long-term and elderly tenants from unwarranted rent increases or sudden displacement. Local tenants unions have won small but important victories in the courts and legislatures which restrict "free" speculation. As a consequence, arson has become increasingly popular among landlord-speculators as the final solution to "problem tenants," just as it has become popular among banks faced with "problem properties."

Boston's prime "condominium conversion" districts have been hard hit by arson. In 1980, arson rates increased by 400 percent in the Back Bay area, where property values have been soaring (Malaspina, 1981). This closely followed the 1979 passage of a city ordinance restricting the right of landlords to evict tenants for purposes of condominium conversion. Harvey Schmidt, an arson investigator for the Massachusetts FAIR Plan, noted:

> There are three basic upfront advantages that even a relatively unsophisticated owner might recognize in having a friendly fire on the premises: rendering the property uninhabitable, facilitating renovation by gutting the interior, and generating insurance money to finance conversion (McNamara and Kilbanoff, 1981:7).

City Councilman Ray Flynn, looking at the 1980 arson pattern in Brighton, a district undergoing extensive condominium conversion, stated:

> I am convinced that there is a correlation between building conversion and arson. There is nothing so effective as fire for circumventing eviction procedures. Just look at the money being made by conversions. It is second only to the lottery in the amount of money you can make in one shot (McNamara and Kilbanoff, 1981:7).

The upscale arson pattern is evident in the history of buildings owned by real estate magnate Frederick Rust. Since 1977, Rust has been engaged in a massive condominium conversion effort in the Brighton district (Jahnke, 1981b). His properties are extraordinarily "leveraged," in other words, with only small cash outlays he has obtained heavy second, third, and fourth mortgages whose total value often triples the original price within a few months of purchase. Rust is thus in a position to draw enormous fire insurance policies (Goodstine, 1982). For example, in 1977–78 Rust purchased four large Brighton buildings and, within four months, arranged second and third mortgages worth $1.7 million, more than double the purchase price. More than $1.3 million of the second mortgages for these four properties were provided by the Suffolk Franklin Savings Bank, where Rust was a member of the board of directors until 1981 (Goodstine, 1982; Jahnke, 1981b).

Rust's buildings are frequent targets for arson. Fires of "suspicious" or "undetermined" origin caused over $300,000 in estimated damages to his properties between 1978 and 1980. His building at 1673 Commonwealth Avenue burned in a "suspicious" fire in 1980; and one person burned to death in the August, 1980, "undetermined" fire at 1677 Commonwealth Avenue. Another "suspicious" fire occurred in 1980 at 232 Kelton Street, which Rust purchased for $96,000 in 1978 but which was mortgaged for a total of $950,000 in 1979. Rust purchased 248 Kelton Street (next door to 232) in 1980 from Joseph Mazzapica, who was convicted of arson and insurance fraud in the 1978 "Symphony Road" arson case (Zanger, 1980), and who, by virtue of his $100,000 second mortgage, remains an insurance beneficiary in the event of fire at 248 Kelton Street. Another of Rust's buildings, 362–6 Commonwealth Avenue, carried over $2 million in mortgages by 1980, three times its 1977 purchase price. Boston's largest financial institution, the First National Bank of Boston, provided third, fourth, and fifth mortgages worth $700,000 for that building (Goodstine, 1982) which burned in two arson fires during 1978 and 1980; total structural damages were estimated at $175,000 by the Boston Fire Department. The 1980 fire effectively evicted the tenants at 362–6 Commonwealth Avenue (Moore, 1980). When newspaper

18 BRADY

reports asked Rust about his plans to convert the building to condominiums after the fire, he replied:

> The building has a substantial amount of fire damage, and I had to make an economic decision. Not that you aren't sympathetic to the tenants involved, but it is an economic decision. . . . If you have a situation like that, it isn't absolutely strange for someone to decide to convert to condominiums under these circumstances (McNamara and Kilbanoff, 1981:7).

Rust's tenants have formed unions; they claimed Rust violated fire and building codes, clashed with his lawyers in housing courts, and pressed the Massachusetts Attorney General for a serious arson investigation (Jahnke, 1981a, b).

There are more than a dozen identifiable syndicates in Boston which have a history of suspicious fires and massive speculation. Elsewhere I have discussed the Sarah Cutler Trust operation in which John Kerrigan, a leading local politician and former member of the Boston City Council, was the silent beneficiary of this trust, which experienced dozens of arson fires from 1972 to 1980 (Brady, 1982a). Few residents of Boston are surprised by these kinds of revelations. Yet, local fire department officials and the state's fire marshall hold fast to their image of arsonists as vandals or pyromaniacs (Vennochi, 1982). In 1982 Boston Fire Commissioner George Paul said that the city did not have a serious arson problem and that the media was exaggerating the issue (WNEV, 1982). Such official denials, like the misunderstandings that spring from racism and social bias, not only preclude effective arson control, but can lead to the arrest of the innocent and the tolerance of those most culpable. The following two instances are cases in point.

THE SYMPHONY ROAD CONSPIRACY

In 1973–74 the Symphony Road district of Boston suffered more than 20 fires which left hundreds of people homeless and five dead (Blank, 1978; Brostoff, 1977; Lima, 1977a). The district was then inhabited by a mixture of the elderly, the poor, students, and newly arrived ethnic minorities. Local tenants groups repeatedly asked the state and local fire officials for an arson investigation, but Joseph Dolan, the Boston Fire Marshall, insisted, "I don't see any pattern of arson of any kind. Most of the fires in that area started in quarters where tenants were living. Most of them were caused by human error, human negligence" (Kenney and Richard, 1977:8).

Following the fifth arson death, a group of residents organized and began to systematically collect evidence of housing and fire code violations in local buildings and traced the pattern of sale, resale, and escalating insurance coverage on buildings which had burned (Schmidt, 1980). Presented with this information, State Police Lieutenant James De Furia, commanding the arson squad at the state fire marshall's office, continued to discourage the residents, saying, "Maybe an owner does hire a torch to do a job. But you can't prove it. It's a waste of time to try" (Blank, 1978:133). One of the leading neighborhood activists, David Scondras, recalled:

> Initially most people refused to believe that these were arson fires at all. They assumed that the kind of riff-raff that lives around here would naturally set fire to their buildings. There's some obscure notion in the minds of people that low-income people have a natural proclivity toward a variety of strange behavior, one of them being they burn down their homes (ABC, 1978).

The Symphony Road residents persisted in their research, and the publication of their findings prompted the state attorney general to investigate (Canavan, 1978). This year-long probe which followed was financially supported by the Massachusetts FAIR Plan, which provided funds for a staff of talented sleuths employed by the First Security Corporation (Schmidt, 1980). The case led ultimately to the indictment and conviction of 32 members of the largest arson ring in the United States: its profits surpassed $6 million from 1972 to 1977 (Harvey and Connolly, 1977; Zanger, 1977). Those convicted of charges varying from conspiracy and insurance fraud to arson and murder included six lawyers, four real estate agents, four insurance adjustors, six landlords, two finance company officers, two bookkeepers, two housing contractors, three small business-men, a city of Boston housing inspector, and two police officers (Cullen, 1977; Jones, 1978). The latter included the captain of the Boston arson squad and De Furia, the commander of the state fire marshall's arson squad, quoted above. None of the lawyers, insurance adjustors, finance executives, accountants, or the Boston arson squad captain served more than four months in jail; 10 of these 22 white-collar criminals received only probation or a suspended sen-tence, though all 22 were convicted of criminal conspiracy and many were also found guilty of insurance fraud (Zanger, 1980). The lenient sentences for fraud and conspiracy in this case are not unusual in the United States (*Fire and Arson Investigator*, 1980); in Massachusetts less than 4 percent of those convicted of arson from 1971 to 1979 were sent to prison (Roy *et al.*, 1980).

THE 1982 LOWELL FIRE: LAW ENFORCEMENT RESPONSE

It was a typical arson incident. A sudden 3 a.m. blaze roared through the decrepit wooden tenement at 32–36 Decatur Street in the Lowell, Massachusetts, Hispanic ghetto outside Boston. The eight bodies pulled from the rubble that March 1982 morning were typical victims: most were small children and none were white. The police response was also typical: they arrested a young man recently released from a mental hospital and two other young Hispanic men which the first named during interrogation. The motive ascribed to their crime was rage and drug-crazed irra-tionality (Thomases, 1982a).

When the three suspects were brought to trial, the ex-mental patient told the court that his confession had been obtained by torture and intimidation in the Lowell police station. The police department's own record showed, moreover, that all three defendants had remained at the scene of the fire throughout the night, trying with their neighbors to save those trapped in the flames (Lasalandra, 1982a). The judge dismissed the case against the two defendants implicated by the ex-patient, though, at the time of writing, the latter had spent nearly a year in jail still awaiting trial without bail (Thomases, 1982b). Meanwhile, leading figures in the Lowell community have mobilized the public to protest against this defendant's continued confinement and to demand a further investigation of the fire (Jordon, 1982b; Lasalandra, 1982b).

The police have apparently never questioned the owners of the building—the Spanos family. Fire department records show that there have been six previous "incendiary" fires at the same address since 1979, and that several of these started inside locked, vacant apartments. The title to this and other Spanos properties, which have been cited for numerous fire code violations, has been juggled among family members. Since legally a new owner is allowed an additional six months grace on fire code violations, continuous "resale" within the family precludes enforce-ment. The Spanos family owns over 20 tenements in Lowell's Hispanic ghetto (Lasalandra, 1982b; Thomases, 1982b).

Between 1974 and 1982 there were 86 "suspicious" fires at Spanos properties in Lowell (Jordon, 1982b). The insurance settlements for these fires remain confidential, protected from public scrutiny by state law. Massachusetts Insurance Commission records do show, however, that "William Spanos *et al*" contracted with a local broker for special package coverage by an unnamed, unlicensed surplus line company in 1981. That broker was the same one who arranged surplus line coverage for Russell Tardanico.

INNOVATIONS: LAW ENFORCEMENT

The public and policy makers alike have grown increasingly aware of the seriousness of the arson problem in Boston and the United States as a whole (Levey, 1982). Though some local fire officials continue to minimize this threat or cling to the traditional deviance explanations, there are signs of progress in the development of new arson control measures in Boston and elsewhere.

These fall into two main types: innovations in law enforcement aimed at strengthening prosecution or deterring arson-for-profit conspiracy, and regulatory reforms. A number of these deserve mention, but it is important to understand that powerful institutions with entrenched interests oppose any structural changes which might erode their autonomy or restrict their profitmaking.

The most promising criminal justice innovations established by local authorities include the police "strike force" approach and the computer-assisted arson prevention and prediction programs. The Boston Arson Strike Force, for example, combines the expertise of civilian criminologists and research analysts who are skilled in the analysis of urban demography, political economy, real estate mortgage, and insurance transactions, with police detectives skilled in discreet surveillance and the collection of testimony and physical evidence. The Boston Strike Force reports directly to the mayor and the district attorney. The fire department and its arson squad are excluded from the Strike Force, though fire department records are available for its use.

The identities of the syndicates which the Strike Force is watching are a closely guarded secret, as are the locations of buildings which are under surveillance as likely arson targets. Police experience with investigation of other types of racketeering is valuable, particularly in combination with civilian arson specialists; but the Strike Force is weak in the area of pyrotechnic expertise. The fire department's arson squad retains exclusive jurisdiction over investigations on the scene of fires, and the Strike Force is hampered by the vagueness and generally poor quality of arson squad reports. Other cities have also established similar strike forces (Fire and Arson Investigator, 1980).

Computers have been brought into action in programs designed to predict and prevent arson. Boston's Urban Educational Systems (UES) pioneered this approach (Rezendes, 1982). Unfortunately, that civilian-led program is a casualty of bitter infighting with the state's fire fighting establishment, particularly State Fire Marshall Joseph O'Keefe who, at the time of writing, was embroiled in a lawsuit with UES over the disbursement of funds appropriated for arson prevention by the legislature (Jordan, 1982a; Rezendes, 1982; Scharfenberg, 1980, 1981).

New Haven, Connecticut, has been more successful in institutionalizing its nationally renowned Arson Warning and Prevention System (AWAPS). Essentially, such computer-assisted programs try to predict buildings which are likely arson targets. The computers search through city records of fires, tax collections, and building inspections to locate properties whose individual histories fit a profile associated with arson (Miller, 1978). These characteristics include: previous structural fires, unpaid property taxes, building code violations, and outstanding liens for debt (Sauerteig and O'Connor, 1980). When the computer identifies a building with all of these characteristics, both the property owner and the insurance company are officially notified that the building is under the attention of law enforcement authorities (New Haven Fire Department, 1981).[13]

In 1980, a year after the AWAPS program was initiated, New Haven reported a 40 percent decline in total fire losses and arson losses, and a 20 percent decline in civilian death injuries and the total incidence of arson fires (*Security World*, 1981). These statistics have only limited meaning, however, since so many factors influence arson rates. The AWAPS program itself could have had only a tiny *direct* impact, since only 11 buildings were targeted as "arson prone" in 1980 (Sauerteig and O'Connor, 1980).

Deterrence is the central strategy for both the computer prediction/prevention programs and the strike force approach. These law enforcement innovations can make the arson problem more

---

13. It should be noted that the insurance industry, particularly Aetna Insurance Company and Factory Mutual Insurance Company, have contributed most substantially to the funding for the AWAPS program, along with the U.S. Fire Administration (*Security World*, 1981; Sauerteig and O'Connor, 1980).

visible and can raise the risks of what is still one of the safest and most lucrative crimes. Obviously, the very existence of such programs helps undermine the "deviant" image of the arsonist by concentrating on the arson-for-profit motive. Of course, neither the New Haven computer nor the Boston Arson Strike Force can hope to control arson, as long as its institutional sources remain intact.

STRUCTURAL REFORMS AND POLICY RECOMMENDATIONS

Efforts to address the structural economic causes of arson must begin with closer restriction of bank redlining. The federal Community Reinvestment Act of 1978 must be given greater investigatory powers and punitive sanctions. Federal anti-trust laws must be more energetically applied against bank mergers, because documented studies such as Greenwald (1978) show clearly that the larger banks are less sensitive to local community needs and are more systematically engaged in redlining than the smaller financial institutions.

The banks deny that they have ever engaged in redlining and bristle at the accusation from community groups, who have turned neighborhood disinvestment into a major urban political issue. In Massachusetts, the banks bitterly resented the regulatory activities of the former state bank commissioner, Carol Greenwald, who from 1974 to 1978 initiated the most aggressive anti-redlining enforcement in Massachusetts history. Indeed, the financial institutions were so angered that they refused, in 1976–77, to purchase state bonds unless the governor fired Greenwald. Governor Michael Dukakis refused to bow to this pressure, and was obliged to sell Massachusetts bonds to buyers in New York and the Midwest (Greenwald, 1980). Banking industry opposition was regarded by political analysts as one of the reasons for Dukakis' defeat in 1978; and since his re-election in 1982 he has pointedly assured the banking community that he will not appoint "another Greenwald" (Ball, 1983:23).

The Community Reinvestment Act requires banks to disclose their mortgage lending practices and aims especially at preventing and punishing redlining. Massachusetts regulatory statutes and the credit lending obligations imposed on banks by their state and federal charters, grant considerable powers to the banking commissioner (Greenwald, 1980). It remains to be seen whether the next commissioner will possess the will and the political mandate to press regulation on behalf of neighborhood preservation. Certainly the current pace of bank merger and agglomeration, together with the withdrawal of thrift institutions from the mortgage lending market, (Flad and Jones, 1982) will, if left unchecked, undermine hopes of recovery from arson and abandonment in urban neighborhoods (Stone, 1978).

Boston's city government, like that of most U.S. cities, has yet to formulate a coherent policy for dealing with the problem of abandoned buildings and unpaid property taxes. Long delays between notice of foreclosure and actual seizure and sale of properties for delinquent taxes are typical, and both vandal and escape fires occur most frequently in the interval. If a building survives this period of vulnerability, the city usually elects to sell it at a public auction to the highest bidder. This policy gives the illusion of securing maximum income for a city at a time of lean budgets; but the immediate gains on the auction block may be more than offset by later losses to arson fires, or speculators may choose to sit on newly acquired properties or convert them to uses which further destabilize property values in the neighborhood (Axelrod, 1982). A more rational approach would be to give or sell cheaply a substantial number of seized buildings for local homesteading families who would be obliged to rehabilitate and inhabit them (Flynn, 1982).

The insurance industry has failed abysmally to control arson fraud and it is therefore imperative that it be more tightly regulated. Local urban FAIR Plans should be given a longer grace period before payment of suspicious claims and they should be charged to devote more energies to investigation of prospective clients and especially fire losses. The growing surplus line sector of the insurance industry must be brought under immediate control, if not abolished outright.

22   BRADY

The National Association of Insurance Commissioners (NAIC, 1980a) study of the surplus line companies found extensive malpractice, swindling, and abuse. The NAIC formed a national information office in 1977 to keep track of these agencies (NAIC, 1979) and drafted a model law (NAIC, 1980b) to monitor the surplus line companies (Chaput and Faxon, 1981; Lima, 1980). Criminal penalties for fraud and malpractice by surplus line brokers carry maximum penalties of one year in prison and $500 fines. The NAIC model regulatory law should be adopted without delay as a minimum step, and criminal penalties for broker fraud should be substantially increased. Beyond this, the U.S. Comptroller General's (1979) report to Congress raised fundamental questions about the effectiveness of the present fragmented system in which 50 state insurance commissioners try to counter mounting fraud and corporate abuses of public trust. The privileged status of the insurance industry must be ended with the repeal of the McCarran-Ferguson Act and the imposition of stiff federal regulations on all aspects of the industry.

The insurance industry has fought with single-minded determination against all of these regulatory initiatives. The insurance lobbies have successfully blocked enactment of even the mild NAIC model law for surplus line insurance. The conventional companies do not regard the surplus line companies as mavericks, but rather as pathbreakers: if surplus line ventures are profitable in new sorts of risks, the conventional companies may later follow their lead (Chaput and Faxon, 1981; Lima, 1980). The conventional companies and their local FAIR Plans are not unduly disturbed about the surplus lines' vulnerability to arson racketeers. As John Golembeski,[14] general manager of the Massachusetts Property Insurance Underwriters Association, said:

> We realize that organized crime is moving to surplus line insurance; but our member [conventional] companies would resist any effort to abolish the surplus lines. We don't want to eat the losses if the arson rings are forced to come back to us.

The role of community activists in combatting arson and cutbacks in fire protection is crucial (Brady, 1981a; 1982a). Tenants' unions, taxpayers' and homeowners' associations, and firefighters' unions have played a leading role, particularly in Boston and New York where they have forced legislative reforms, prompted changes in insurance underwriting policies (Andrews, 1978; Stone and Zanger, 1979; Waterflow, 1977), and contributed decisively to the investigation of organized crime operations (Barry, 1979; Blank, 1978; Canavan, 1978; Johnson, 1981; Wyrough, 1981). At the same time, it is unfortunately true that the tensions of racial and social divisions and profound ideological differences among community groups have seriously undermined efforts to form broad coalitions able to challenge the banking and insurance industry or vigorously press for more effective law enforcement (Brady, 1982a). The community-based efforts are powerfully motivated and hold great potential, but have been fragmented thus far (Brady, 1981a, b).

CONCLUSION

Those critical of the existing order in the United States have long argued that crime is the product of socio-economic conditions engendered by capitalism; but they have been hard-pressed to show the operating linkage between the gross statistics of misery and the behavior patterns of the miserable—who may or may not commit street crimes. Radical critics have also argued that the corporations commit the most socially destructive crimes, but that their offenses are less visible and less personally threatening to the public. Arson, on the other hand, is the most visible and broadly threatening of crimes, and it cannot be explained without directly implicating the most central of capitalist institutions: the banking, insurance, and real estate industries. Moreover,

---

14. Based on interviews with Jack Golembeski, February 11, 1983.

Arson in Boston   23

the involvement of these institutions in the arson process cannot be ascribed to a few corrupt or irresponsible executives. The sociology of arson takes us right into the heart of the city, where corporate profiteering, gangster racketeering, and government corruption or ineptitude overlap with devastating impact on working-class communities. One needs no conspiratorial model or bogeyman visions here, for the processes that lead to neighborhood collapse, deteriorating housing, and arson are all logical consequences of good business practices.

REFERENCES

(ABC) American Broadcasting Corporation
   1978   "Fires for profit." Sixty Minutes Special, August 3.
Andrews, Tom
   1978   "Stop wins arson bill." Fenway News (Boston) 5(9):4.
Anner, John
   1982   "Fires plague Tardanico/Sherman buildings." Dorchester Community News (Boston), November 30:5.
Associated Press
   1981   "Arson detection: Part science, part art." Tulsa World, February 15:11.
Axelrod, Joan
   1982   "Auction program vulnerable." Boston Ledger, December 6:1, 3, 4.
Ball, Joanne
   1983   "Dukakis announces two more cabinet posts." Boston Globe, January 4:23.
Banfield, Edward
   1970   The Unheavenly City Revisited. Boston: Little, Brown.
Barry, Bill
   1979   "Fair Share carries its fight to City Hall." Worcester [Mass.] Telegraph, August 9:9, 16.
Battle, Brendan, and Paul Weston
   1975   Arson: A Handbook for Detection and Investigation. New York: Arco.
Bawcutt, Paul
   1978   "Offshore locations for captive insurance companies." Risk Management, October:32–48.
Berwyn, Robert
   1974   "Urban disinvestment in Chicago." In Redlining: Discrimination in Residential Mortgage Loans. Report to the Illinois General Assembly Legislature Investigation Commission. Chicago, General Assembly.
Blank, Joseph
   1978   "They're burning our neighborhood." Reader's Digest 110 (October):130–135.
Block, Alan, and William Chambliss
   1981   Organizing Crime. New York: Elsevier.
Boston Redevelopment Authority
   1974   "Abandonment: Executive summary." Unpublished report of the Boston Redevelopment Authority to the mayor, City of Boston, June. Boston Redevelopment Authority Library.
Boudreau, John, Quon Kwan, William Faragher, and Geneive Denault
   1977   Arson and Arson Investigation. Washington, D.C.: National Institute for Law Enforcement and Criminal Justice.
Bradford, Calvin, and Leonard Rubinowitz
   1975   "The urban–suburban investment-disinvestment process: Consequences for older neighborhoods." Annals of the American Academy of Political and Social Science 424 (November):77–86.
Brady, James
   1981a   "Towards a popular justice in the United States: Dialectus of community action." Contemporary Crisis 5(3):155–192.
   1981b   "Sorting out the exiles confusion: Dialogue on popular justice." Contemporary Crisis 5(1): 31–38.
   1982a   "Arson, fiscal crisis, and community action: Dialectics of urban crime and popular response." Crime and Delinquency 28(2):247–270.
   1982b   "Why is Boston burning?" Boston Observer, October 17:5–8.
Brenner, Lynn
   1978   "Lloyds syndicate cancelling U.S. commercial fire policies." Journal of Commerce (New York), May 15:8–11.
   1980   "Why reinsurers have the jitters." Institutional Investor 80(1):115–182.
Brostoff, Merna
   1977   "Arson in the Fenway." Fenway News (Boston) 4(8):1–2.
Campbell, Colin
   1981   "FBI begins collection of national arson statistics." Fire Chief 48 (October):10–13.

24   BRADY

Canavan, Jack
   1978   "Neighborhood foils arsonists." Parade, October 1:4–5.
Carter, Robert
   1980   "Arson and arson investigation in the United States." Fire Journal 74 (July):40–47.
Catalina, Frank
   1979   "From the legislatures: New York's attack on arson." Real Estate Law Journal 7(3):22–31.
Chambliss, William
   1978   On the Take: From Petty Crooks to Presidents. Bloomington: Indiana University Press.
Chaput, James, and Paul Faxon
   1981   "The potential for arson in the field of non-admitted insurance." Unpublished report to the
           National Fire Protection Association, Quincy, Massachusetts.
Coppack, Lee
   1980   "Sasse affair: Disciplinary action starts." Lloyd's List (London), July 14:13–14.
Cullen, John
   1977   "Over 100 probed in a 2 million dollar arson scheme." Boston Globe, September 22:1, 10.
Daenzer, Bernard
   1980   Surplus Line Manual. Santa Monica, CA: Merritt Company.
Devine, Richard
   1973   Where the Lender Looks First: A Case Study of Mortgage Disinvestment in Bronx County. New
           York: National Urban League.
Dillon, John
   1982   "Night into day for Boston's firefighters—ends with 9 alarm blaze." Boston Globe, June 3:4, 22.
Duncan, Marcia
   1975   "Redlining practices, racial resegregation, and urban decay." Urban Lawyer 7(3):510–539.
Economist
   1977   "The arsonists." Editorial. The Economist (London), May 27:11.
Epstein, Sidney
   1978   "LEAA and arson control." Fire Chief 45 (November):16–18.
Fire and Arson Investigator
   1980   "Dowsing arson rackets." Editorial. Fire and Arson Investigator 3(3):3–8.
   1981   "Analysis of arson and socio-economic backgrounds." Editorial. *Fire and Arson Investigator*
           31(3):3–16.
Flad, David, and DeWitt Jones
   1982   "Where credit is due." Boston Observer, October 29:12–14.
Flynn, Ray
   1982   "Residential Rehabilitation Act." Proposed City Ordinance drafted and submitted by Boston City
           Council member Ray Flynn, November 30, Boston City Council.
Fox, Johatham
   1983   "Fire and arson incidence in Boston Housing Authority buildings for 1981." Unpublished notes,
           Boston Housing Authority, Department of Public Safety.
Fraker, Francis
   1977   "Fastest growing crime." Newsweek, January 24:27.
Freud, Sigmund
   1932   "The acquisition of power over fire." International Journal of Psycho-Analysis 13(4):399–413.
Gest, Ted
   1983   "Are Boston's fires an omen for other cities?" U.S. News and World Report, February 7:55–56.
Golembeski, John
   1980   "The insurance mechanism and arson control." Unpublished paper presented to the Arson Control
           Conference of the Massachusetts Property Insurance Underwriters Association (MPIUA),
           Boston, May 10.
   1982   "Mass FAIR Plan and arson control." Boston Globe, September 4:12.
Goodstine, David
   1982   "History of speculation and rent increases in certain buildings in Brighton, Mass." Unpublished
           report to Comprehensive Arson Prevention and Enforcement Systems program, Boston. Avail-
           able from James Brady.
Greenwald, Carol
   1978   "Home mortgage lending patterns in metropolitan Boston." Publication no. 10252–45–300–2–
           78–CR, Banking Department, Commonwealth of Massachusetts, Boston.
   1980   Banks Are Dangerous To Your Wealth. New York: Prentice Hall.
Grutzner, Charles
   1973   "Organized crime and the businessman." Pp. 105–129 in Edwin Shur (ed.), The Crime Establish-
           ment. Englewood Cliffs, NJ: Prentice Hall.
Hanson, Frank
   1980   "Arson: Its effects and control." Fire Surveyor 9(3):32–36.

Harvey, Joseph
  1981   "Paul says Fire Department cuts have not affected response time." Boston Globe, April 14:6.
Harvey, Joseph, and Richard Connolly
  1977   "A huge conspiracy to burn Suffolk County for profit." Boston Globe, October 18:1, 3, 4.
Higgins, Richard
  1979   "Arson strike force." Boston Globe, October 18:18.
Horn, Jack
  1976   "The big business of arson: Building burners for hire." Psychology Today 9(9):52–57.
Hoyt, Homer
  1939   The structure and growth of residential neighborhoods in American cities. Washington, D.C.:
          Federal Housing Administration.
Hurley, Ward Monahan
  1969   "Arson: The criminal and the crime." British Journal of Criminology 9(1):4–13.
Inciardi, James
  1970   "The adult firesetter." Criminology 8(2):132–149.
Jahnke, Art
  1981a   "Upscale arson." Real Paper (Boston), January 1:4–6.
  1981b   "Rust never sleeps." Real Paper (Boston), March 26:11.
  1982   "Who's burning Boston?" Boston Magazine, December:144–149, 185–190.
Johnson, Eric
  1981   "Roger Smith gets 5 years in Concord." Community News (Boston), October–November:1.
Jones, Arthur
  1978   "Ex-officer pleads guilty in arson case." Boston Globe, March 8:2, 11.
Jordan, James
  1982a   "State's arson fighters await decision on renewed funding." Bay State Banner (Boston), February
          11:6.
  1982b   "Lowell Hispanics organize in wake of devastating blaze." Bay State Banner (Boston), June 3:4.
  1982c   "Old guard fights new in arson money tussel." Bay State Banner (Boston), June 17:7.
Karter, Michael
  1982   "Fire loss in the United States during 1981." Fire Journal 76 (September):68–86.
Kenny, Michael, and Ray Richard
  1977   "Symphony Road not like most declining areas." Boston Globe, March 21:8.
Kwitney, Jonathan
  1973   The Fountain-Pen Conspiracy. New York: Alfred Knopf.
Lasalandra, Michael
  1982a   "Garcias maintain innocence." The Sun (Lowell, Mass.) April 15:1, 10–12.
  1982b   "Area residents want probe to continue." The Sun (Lowell, Mass.) April 15:11–12.
LeBlanc, Paul, and Donald Redding
  1982   "Large loss fires in the United States: 1981." Fire Journal 74 (September):32–52.
Levey, Robert
  1982   "Boston as others see us." Boston Globe, September 23:28.
Lima, Alfred
  1977a   "Fire and death on Symphony Road." Unpublished report to the National Fire Prevention
          Administration. U.S. Fire Administration, Washington, D.C.
  1977b   "Fires in urban residential neighborhoods." Unpublished report to the National Fire Prevention
          Administration, September 28. Available from the U.S. Fire Administration, Washington, D.C.
  1980   "The influence of the non-admitted insurance market on arson for profit." Unpublished report
          to the U.S. Fire Administration, Washington, D.C. April 10.
Linton, Ron, John Mields, and William Coston
  1971   A Case Study of the Problems of Abandoned Housing and Recommendations for Action by the
          Federal Government. Report to the U.S. Department of Housing and Urban Development.
          Washington, D.C.: U.S. Department of Housing and Urban Development.
Loyola Law Journal
  1975   "Redlining: The fight against discrimination in mortgage funding." Editorial. Loyola Law Journal
          6(1):79–83.
Massachusetts Property Insurance Underwriting Association
  1970   "Plan of operation of Massachusetts FAIR Plan." Unpublished internal guidelines of the Massa-
          chusetts Property Insurance Underwriters Association, Boston.
Macht, Lee, and John Mack
  1968   "The firesetter syndrome." Psychiatry 31(3):277–278.
MacDonald, John
  1977   Bombers and Firesetters. Springfield, IL: Charles C. Thomas.
Mahoney, Frank
  1982   "Arson squad may get police powers." Boston Globe, November 19:1, 11.

26   BRADY

Malaspina, Ann
    1981   "Arson for profit on the increase." Allston/Brighton Citizen Item (Boston), May 14:19–20.
McDonough, John
    1980   "Redlining in Boston." The Phoenix (Boston), May 16:5–7, 18, 22–26.
McMillan, Gary
    1982   "A plague with no cure in sight." Boston Globe, October 14:11, 23.
McNamara, Eileen, and Hank Kilbanoff
    1981   "Condo evictions and fire." Boston Globe, May 31:7.
Metropolitan Area Planning Council
    1980   Mortgage Risk in Metropolitan Boston. Boston: Metropolitan Area Planning Council.
Miller, Walter
    1968   "Lower class culture as a generating milieu of gang delinquency." Journal of Social Issues 14(1):
            5–19.
Miller, Peter
    1978   "Preventing arson." Washington Post, September 14:A18, E33, E39.
Moore, Michael
    1980   "Deeds and fires of Frederick Rust III." Unpublished report to the comprehensive arson preven-
            tion and enforcement systems program, Boston. Available from James Brady.
    1981   "The Socio-economics of Arson in Boston." Unpublished report to the Comprehensive Arson
            Prevention and Enforcement Systems program, Boston. Available from James Brady.
    1983   "Notes on Surplus Line Clients with Significant Fire Histories." Memorandum to Arson Strike
            Force, Boston, February 12. Available from James Brady.
Moynihan, Daniel
    1969   On Understanding Poverty. New York: Basic Books.
Murphy, William
    1983   "Investigative strategies for arson control: The role of ATF." Unpublished remarks at the
            Attorney General's arson conference, Worcester, MA, February 22.
(NAIC) National Association of Insurance Commissioners
    1979   "Plan of operation for alien non-admitted insurances and reinsurers." NAIC Proceedings
            2:240–247.
    1980a   "A background study of the surplus line market." NAIC Proceedings 1:84–93.
    1980b   "Criteria which non-admitted insurers should meet to be eligible for placements by licensed surplus
            line brokers." NAIC Proceedings 1:120–128.
(NFPA) National Fire Prevention Administration
    1976   America's Malignant Crime. Washington, D.C: National Fire Prevention Administration.
National Urban League
    1971   The National Survey on Housing Abandonment. New York: Center for Community Changes.
Newfield, Jack, and Paul DuBrul
    1977   The Abuse of Power: The Permanent Government and the Fall of New York. New York: Prentice
            Hall.
New Haven Fire Department
    1981   "Arson warning and prevention strategy." Unpublished report to the mayor of New Haven,
            Conn. April.
Osgood, Viola
    1982   "Fire threat rouses section of Roxbury." Boston Globe, August 26:40.
Pappas, Kathy
    1981   "Fires in owner's Boston buildings probed." Boston Globe, December 3:1, 22–23.
Public Interest Research Group, District of Columbia
    1975   Redlining: Mortgage disinvestment in D.C. Washington, D.C.: Institute for Policy Studies.
Radin, Charles
    1981   "Study: 2 1/2 won't cripple protection." Boston Globe, April 29:3.
Real Estate Research Corporation
    1975   The Dynamics of Neighborhood Change. Washington, D.C.: U.S. Department of Housing and
            Urban Development.
Rezendes, Michael
    1982   "Playing with fire: Preventing arson prevention." Phoenix (Boston), June 8:1, 5, 16.
Roy, Marion, Linda Herbert, and Robert Copeland
    1980   "Arson in Massachusetts: Sentencing patterns." Unpublished report to Lt. Governor O'Neil's
            Arson Task Force by the Office of Probation, Commonwealth of Massachusetts, Boston.
Sauerteig, Ross, and Martin O'Connor
    1980   "New Haven's AWAPS program." Firehouse 5 (August):43–44, 48.
Schall, Dennis
    1977   "Neighborhoods burn across the country." The Guardian (New York), October 5:7.
Scharfenberg, Kirk
    1980   "Stopping the fires next time." Boston Globe, April 11:16.
    1981   "The best cure is. . . ." Boston Globe, November 2:13.

Schmidt, Harvey
  1980   "Boston's neighborhood arson fighters." International Fire Chief 46 (April):5–8.
Scott, Donald
  1974   Fire and Fire Raisers. Bristol, England: Duckworth.
Security World
  1981   "The New Haven arson program: One year later." Editorial. Security World (March):26–27.
Slade, Steven
  1978   "Arson: Business by other means–Boston." The Nation, March 18:23.
Sternlieb, George; Robert Burchell; James Hughes, and Franklin James
  1974   "Housing abandonment in the urban core." American Investment Planners Journal (September):
         321–332.
Stone, Michael
  1978   "Housing, mortgage lending, and the contradictions of capitalism." Pp. 178–208 in William Tabb
         and Larry Sawyer (eds.), Marxism and the Metropolis. New York: Oxford University Press.
Stone, Michael and Mark Zanger
  1979   The Research Manual for Arson. Urban Educational Systems, Boston.
Taggert, Tee
  1977   "Home mortgage lending patterns in metropolitan Boston." Report No. 11286 to the bank
         commissioner, Massachusetts Banking Department, Boston.
Thomases, Lawrence
  1982a "Hispanics, latest victims in the deadly game of arson." The American Gazette (Lowell, Mass.),
         August 19:3–5.
  1982b "Lowell's hispanics look back in anger," The American Gazette (Lowell, Mass.), August 26:7–9.
U.S. Comptroller General
  1979   Report to the Congress: Issues and Needed Improvements in State Regulations of the Insurance
         Business. Washington, D.C.: U.S. Government Printing Office.
U.S. Congress: Senate
  1963   Surplus Lines Insurance. Hearings pursuant to Senate Regulation 56 before Subcommittee on
         Anti-Trust and Monopolies of Senate Committee of Judiciary. 88th Congress, 1st session.
         Washington, D.C.: U.S. Government Printing Office.
  1979   Arson in America. Senate Committee on Government Affairs, Permanent Sub-Committee on
         Investigation. 96th Congress, 2nd session, Washington, D.C.: U.S. Government Printing Office.
U.S. Department of Housing and Urban Development
  1968   Urban Property Protection and Reinsurance Act of 1968. Washington, D.C.: U.S. Department
         of Housing and Urban Development.
U.S. Fire Administration
  1979   Report to Congress: Arson, The Federal Role in Arson Prevention and Control. Washington,
         D.C.: U.S. Government Printing Office.
U.S. General Accounting Office
  1978   Arson for Profit: More Could Be Done to Reduce It. Washington, D.C.: U.S. General Account-
         ing Office.
Vennochi, Joan
  1982   "Arson worst since 1977." Boston Globe, August 6:2–3.
WBZ–Television
  1981   "Eye team report: Arson for profit in Dorchester." Eye Team Investigative Report, Boston WBZ–
         Television, aired November 9–10.
WNEV–Television
  1982   "Arson in Boston." Chronicle investigative report, WNEV–Television, Boston, aired November
         16.
Waterflow, Anne
  1977   "Symphony STOP update." Fenway News (Boston), November:2.
Weese, Samuel
  1971   Non-Admitted Insurance in the U.S. Homewood, IL: Homewood.
Witkin, George
  1979   "All pyros are psychos." Fire and Arson Investigator 32(2):13–17.
Wyrough, Nancy
  1981   "Group's success story: Fewer fires." Dorchester Community News, (Boston), June 23:4.
Yarnell, Helen
  1940   "Firesetting in children." American Journal of Orthopsychiatry. 10(2):272–286.
Zanger, Mark
  1977   "Arson at the top." Fire Chief 44 (February):19–20.
  1978a "Playing with fire." Real Paper (Boston), April 22:1–7.
  1978b "The fire a month club." Real Paper (Boston), May 16:1–5.
  1980   "The fire last time." Real Paper (Boston), April 16:11.

[19]

CORPORATIONS, ORGANIZED CRIME, AND THE DISPOSAL OF HAZARDOUS WASTE: AN EXAMINATION OF THE MAKING OF A CRIMINOGENIC REGULATORY STRUCTURE*

ANDREW SZASZ

University of California, Santa Cruz

This paper explores the relationship between legitimate corporations that generate hazardous waste and elements of organized crime with whom they contract for the removal, treatment, or disposition of those wastes. The scope and importance of hazardous waste as a social problem is first described and the variety of organized crime participation in waste handling is summarized. The paper then explores the factors that enabled organized crime to become active in this sector of the economy. Lax implementation and enforcement, the most common explanations, are discussed. The formation of the Resource Conservation and Recovery Act of 1976 is analyzed to show that there was a prior and more fundamental factor: large corporate generators of hazardous waste fought for a regulatory structure that would prove to be highly vulnerable to organized crime intrusion. This fact is then used to discuss and critique two current explanations of the relationship of corporate generators to organized crime waste handlers: "ignorance" and "powerlessness." Finally, it is argued that although generators did not consciously intend to facilitate organized crime entry into hazardous waste hauling, they did subsequently enjoy tangible benefits from that entry.

The generation of hazardous waste is a necessary side effect of modern industrial production. Factories must cope daily with large accumulations of unrecyclable chemical byproducts generated by normal production techniques. The processing or disposal of these byproducts is a significant cost of production, a cost that, like all other costs of production, the prudent owner or manager minimizes.

Until recently, industrial hazardous waste was not legally distinguished from municipal garbage and other solid wastes. It was disposed of with ordinary garbage, at very low cost to the generator, mostly in coastal waters or in landfills unfit to adequately contain it. However, concern grew during the

---

* I wish to gratefully acknowledge that this paper has benefited from comments by Frank Henry, Judith Gerson, Wendy Strimling, Vern Baxter, John Campbell, Carroll Estes, members of the Pew Writing Seminar, and several anonymous reviewers.

2   SZASZ

1970s that improper disposal of hazardous waste was creating an environmental and public health burden of unknown but potentially massive scale. This concern finally moved some states and eventually the federal government to begin to legislate new regulations. The centerpiece of this regulatory effort was the federal Resource Conservation and Recovery Act (RCRA) of 1976. On paper, RCRA mandated comprehensive mechanisms to guarantee the safe disposal of hazardous waste. It established standards and procedures for classifying substances as hazardous. It authorized the states to register corporate generators of hazardous waste and license hauling and disposal firms. It mandated the creation of a manifest system that would document the movement of hazardous waste "from cradle to grave," from the generator, through the hands of the transporter, to the shipment's final destination at a licensed disposal site.

By legally distinguishing hazardous waste from other wastes and by directing that such wastes be treated differently than municipal solid waste, the new regulations dramatically increased, almost overnight, the demand for hazardous waste hauling and disposal services. Unhappily, recent state and federal investigations have documented both that illegal waste disposal is widespread (U.S. General Accounting Office, 1985; U.S. House of Representatives, 1980) and that organized crime elements traditionally active in garbage hauling and landfilling have entered this burgeoning and potentially profitable new market (Block and Scarpitti, 1985; U.S. House of Representatives, 1980, 1981a). Although the exact extent of organized crime involvement in hazardous waste hauling and disposal is uncertain,[1] the fact of that

---

1. The extent of involvement is unclear for two reasons:

First, investigation has focused on the New York, Connecticut, and New Jersey region. This is a strategic site for investigation because so much hazardous waste is produced in the Tri-State area (for example, New Jersey ranks number one in the nation in annual hazardous waste generation) and because mob involvement in garbage in this region has been thoroughly documented. But, for the same reasons, this region may not be typical of the rest of the nation. Recent investigatory reporting concerning environmental pollution and political corruption in Louisiana (Getschow and Petzinger, 1984; Petzinger and Getschow, 1984a, 1984b; Snyder, 1985a, 1985b, 1985c, 1985d, 1985e, 1985f) shows that waste disposal is a corrupt business there as well, but that corruption grows out of the specific history of oil industry domination of that state's economy and its politics and appears to be quite different from patterns of corruption in the Northeast. This suggests that the post-RCRA relationship between corporate generators and waste disposers may be heavily influenced by variations in regional history predating RCRA.

Second, on a more theoretical level, the boundary between organized crime and legitimate business is, at points, somewhat ambiguous. Take, for example, SCA, the nation's third largest hazardous waste company. SCA undertook a vigorous acquisition program in New Jersey and quickly bought up about 20 garbage hauling and landfill companies. Some of these were formerly owned by organized crime figures. SCA is a corporation whose stock is traded on the New York Stock Exchange and its corporate board boasts outside directors associated with IBM, Houghton-Mifflin Co., MIT, and the Boston Co. (U.S. House of Representatives, 1980, 1981a), but Congressional testimony indicates that when

ORGANIZED CRIME AND HAZARDOUS WASTE 3

involvement is beyond question. A situation exists, then, in which corporations, some at the heart of the American economy, discharge their regulatory obligations under RCRA by entering into direct contractual relationships with firms dominated by organized crime. The goal in this paper is to analyze in detail the complex nature of this relationship between corporate generators of hazardous waste and elements of organized crime that are active in industrial waste disposal. This goal will be approached by analyzing the formation and implementation of RCRA legislation.

The subject of this paper speaks to two distinct criminological literatures: works that examine the relationship between legitimate and illicit enterprise and works that examine crimogenic market structures. Recent scholarship has challenged the commonsense distinction between legitimate business and organized crime. Schelling (1967), Smith and Alba (1979), Smith (1980), and Albanese (1982) all argue that the most fundamental aspect of organized crime is that it is a form of entrepreneurial activity and that its ethnic or conspiratorial nature is of secondary importance. Recent scholarship also challenges the equally widely held belief that the relationship between the underworld and legitimate business consists solely of the former exploiting the latter through extortion, racketeering, and so on (Drucker, 1981). At minimum, it is argued that the relationship is one of mutually beneficial interdependence (Martens and Miller-Longfellow, 1982). This is clearly supported by excellent case studies of labor racketeering (Block and Chambliss, 1981), organized crime on the waterfront (Block, 1982), and arson (Brady, 1983). Chambliss (1978: 181-182) argues the even stronger view that organized crime can exist only because the structure of the legitimate economy and its accompanying political organization make its emergence possible and even inevitable. In a similar vein, Smith (1980) and Smith and Alba (1979) challenge the very distinction between business and organized crime and begin to dissolve that distinction in the common dynamic of a market economy. The study of organized crime participation in hazardous waste disposal presents an opportunity to once again examine this relationship between legitimate and illegitimate entrepreneurship.

The story of RCRA may also have links to the concept of crimogenic market processes. Farberman's (1975) and Leonard and Weber's (1977) studies of auto retailing and Denzin's (1977) study of the liquor industry showed that the normal operating logic of an industry may force some sectors of that industry into illegal activity in order to survive, much less thrive, in doing their part of the business. Needleman and Needleman (1979) subsequently expanded the concept by describing a second type of criminogenesis in which

---

SCA bought mob-owned firms, it hired the former owners as managers and appears to have allowed them free hand to run their businesses as they had before acquisition.

4   SZASZ

the criminal activity is not forced. It is, instead, an unwelcome drain on business, but it is unavoidable because the conditions that make it possible are necessary to the overall functioning of that industry and could not be altered without fundamentally affecting how business is conducted in that industry. Needleman and Needleman discussed securities fraud as an example of what they call a "crime-facilitative," as opposed to a "crime-coercive" market sector. The fact that RCRA not only cannot prevent illegal hazardous waste dumping but has also attracted organized crime participation in illegal hazardous waste activity suggests that the concept of criminogenesis may be fruitfully extended to regulatory processes as well.

In the first sections of this paper, some background is presented on hazardous waste as a social issue and the nature and extent of organized crime involvement in hazardous waste hauling and disposal is summarized. At the core of the paper, the conditions that made this involvement possible are analyzed. It is shown that the most common explanations—lax implementation and enforcement by state and local officials—are incomplete. Analysis of the formation of RCRA legislation shows that corporate generators of hazardous waste were instrumental in securing a regulatory structure that would prove highly attractive to and well suited for organized crime participation. In other words, generators are deeply implicated in the creation of conditions that made their relationship to organized crime possible. This finding is used to critique two explanations of this relationship suggested during Congressional hearings, generator "ignorance" and generator "powerlessness." It is then argued that the relationship has two other important aspects: generators did not consciously desire or intend this outcome, but they nonetheless benefitted from it once it occurred. The paper concludes with a discussion of the relevance of the findings to the two areas of criminological research mentioned above.

THE ISSUE BACKGROUND: HAZARDOUS WASTE FACTS

The Environmental Protection Agency (EPA) defines waste products as "hazardous" if they are flammable, explosive, corrosive, or toxic. Major industries central to the modern national economy, such as the petroleum, chemical, electronic, and pharmaceutical industries, generate copious amounts of hazardous waste. Although there is still great uncertainty about the exact effect of industrial hazardous waste on public health (Greenberg and Anderson, 1984: 84-105), improper management may result in explosions, fires, pollution of water resources, and other uncontrolled releases that put surrounding communities at risk and may result in physical harm ranging from skin irritation to increased incidence of cancer, lung disease, birth defects, and other serious illnesses.

ORGANIZED CRIME AND HAZARDOUS WASTE 5

How much hazardous waste has accumulated? How much is currently generated? Neither question can be answered confidently at this time. The generation and disposal of hazardous waste was completely unregulated until the late 1970s. In the absence of regulation, there was no systematic data-gathering effort. Consequently, there is great uncertainty about the magnitude and composition of hazardous waste accumulated up to the passage of the RCRA. Estimates have risen regularly as more sites are located and assessed. The EPA's most recent estimate is that there are 25,000 sites nationally that contain some hazardous waste. Of these, about 2,500 are priority sites judged by the EPA to be imminently hazardous to public health. More recent research by the General Accounting Office (GAO) and the Office of Technology Assessment (OTA) suggests that there may be 378,000 total sites nationally, perhaps 10,000 of them requiring priority attention (Shabecoff, 1985).

In theory, at least, the availability of data should have improved greatly following passage of the RCRA. Generators of hazardous waste were now required to create written documentation—the manifest—of the amount and content of every shipment of hazardous waste signed over to outside haulers and disposers. This documentation would be forwarded to state agencies following final disposition of each waste shipment. However, the actual quality of the data produced was compromised by several factors. First, there was little agreement over what substances should be defined as hazardous. Congressional and EPA testimony (U.S. Environmental Protection Agency, 1976, 1979; U.S. House of Representatives, 1975, 1976; U.S. Senate, 1974, 1979) shows that industrial spokesmen argued that too many substances had been unjustifiably included, while environmentalists argued that some materials had been improperly excluded. Second, firms generating less than one metric ton (2,200 lbs.) of hazardous waste per month are exempt from RCRA regulation (U.S. House of Representatives, 1983: 56, 60). There are over four million privately owned industrial sites in the nation. The "small generator" exemption leaves all but a few tens of thousands of these sites out of RCRA's registration and manifest system. Third, some firms that generate significant amounts of hazardous waste have either failed to cooperate with EPA requests for data (Williams and Matheny, 1984: 436-437) or have failed to identify themselves to the EPA as regulable generators (U.S. General Accounting Office, 1985: 14-20). Fourth, even those firms that appear to comply with reporting requirements may not be reporting accurately the types and quantities of hazardous waste they generate (U.S. GAO, 1985: 20-23). Consequently, knowledge of the amount and content of current hazardous waste generation is still imprecise. Estimates, like estimates of historical accumulation, have been rising. In 1974, the EPA was estimating hazardous waste generation at 10 million metric tons per year (U.S. Senate, 1974: 70). In 1980, the EPA estimate had risen to 40 million metric tons. In 1983, new

6   SZASZ

research led the EPA to nearly quadruple its estimate to 150 million metric
tons (Block and Scarpitti, 1985: 46), while the OTA was estimating 250 million metric tons per year (U.S. House of Representatives, 1983: 1).[2]

Where does hazardous waste end up? In response to EPA inquiries in
1981, 16% of generating firms reported treating their wastes completely on
site and another 22% reported treating part of their wastes on site. The
remaining 62% contracted with other parties to handle all of their wastes
(Block and Scarpitti, 1985: 48-49). Where do transported wastes actually end
up? The exemptions and noncooperation cited above leave an unknown fraction of total hazardous waste movement out of the paperwork of the manifest
system (U.S. GAO, 1985: 3-4, 14-24). The manifests that are filed are poorly
monitored and vulnerable to undetected falsification (Greenberg and Anderson, 1984: 242; U.S. GAO, 1985: 25-31; U.S. House of Representatives, 1980:
140, 1981b: 124). Consequently, this question also cannot be answered with
great certainty. On the basis of admittedly poor and incomplete data, the
OTA estimates that no more than 10% to 20% of all hazardous waste is
rendered harmless by incineration or by chemical or biological treatment.
There are few facilities that can treat wastes in these ways and the price of
treatment is much higher than the price of other means of disposal (U.S.
House of Representatives, 1983: 2, 5-6). The remaining 80% to 90% is either
landfilled or disposed of illegally. Only a small proportion of hazardous
waste goes into landfills that have the siting studies, proper containment practices, and continuous monitoring to be fully licensed by the EPA, since there
are only about 200 such landfills in the nation (Block and Scarpitti, 1985: 49;
U.S. House of Representatives, 1981b: 187). Even these top landfills are only
required by the EPA to keep wastes contained for 30 years (U.S. House of
Representatives, 1983: 2).[3] Most hazardous waste goes to landfills that have

---

2. Methods of estimation are discussed in depth by Greenberg and Anderson (1984).
3. It is generally admitted that even the best landfill is only temporary and inadequate: "No landfill can be made safe from all substances"—Albert Gore (U.S. House of
Representatives, 1983: 2). George J. Tyler, Assistant Commissioner of the New Jersey
Department of Environmental Protection, speaking about the Lone Pine landfill in Freehold, New Jersey (U.S. House of Representatives, 1981b: 188): "The landfill is leaking into
the water, but so does every landfill in the country." The landfill at Wilsonville, Illinois,
owned and operated by SCA (see Note 1), is, according to Dr. Raymond D. Harbison, a
toxicologist, EPA consultant, and professor of pharmacology at Vanderbuilt University,
"the most scientific landfill in this country" (U.S. House of Representatives, 1981a: 267).
Geological and soil permeability feasibility tests were conducted before construction was
begun. Trenches were carefully dug. Arriving waste is sampled and tested, then buried in
either nonleaking 55 gallon drums or double-walled paper bags. Monitoring wells sur-
round the site. Yet subsequent studies show that the soil is more porous than originally
thought and water is seeping in at rates greater than predicted. Furthermore, the landfill is
built over an abandoned coal mine and feasibility tests underestimated the likelihood of
"subsidence," land sinkage that may compromise the site's ability to keep substances safety
contained. If this is the best site in the nation, the Office of Technology Assessment is right

ORGANIZED CRIME AND HAZARDOUS WASTE 7

only interim license to operate, landfills that are of much poorer quality and are likely to pollute the surrounding land and water within a few years.

Illegal hazardous waste dumping is even more likely to have adverse short-term environmental and public health consequences. The full extent of illegal hazardous waste disposal is not known. State officials interviewed by the GAO agreed that illegal disposal was occurring, but had no firm information on the scope of this activity (U.S. GAO, 1985: 10). One study done for the EPA surveyed hazardous waste generators in 41 cities and estimated that one in seven generators had illegally disposed some of their wastes during the two years preceding the study (U.S. GAO, 1985: 10). A wide array of illegal disposal practices have been documented. Waste shipments may end up commingled with ordinary garbage. A 20 cubic yard "dumpster" full of dry garbage can be made to absorb up to sixty 55 gallon drums of liquid hazardous waste (U.S. House of Representatives, 1980: 63) and then be deposited in unlicensed municipal landfills never designed to contain hazardous waste. Liquid hazardous waste may be released along a roadway. An 8,000 gallon truck can be emptied in 8 minutes (U.S. House of Representatives, 1980: 101). Shipments may simply be stockpiled at sites awaiting alleged transfer that never happens or at disposal facilities that have no real disposal capability (U.S. House of Representatives, 1980: 10). Wastes may be drained into local city sewer systems, rivers, and oceans, or dumped in out-of-the-way rural spots (U.S. House of Representatives, 1980: 93). Flammable hazardous waste may be commingled with fuel oil and sold as pure heating oil (U.S. House of Representatives, 1980: 63-64) or sprayed on unsuspecting communities' roads for dust control (U.S. House of Representatives, 1980: 151).

ORGANIZED CRIME PARTICIPATION IN THE HAZARDOUS WASTE DISPOSAL INDUSTRY

Congressman Albert Gore: "At what point did companies picking up garbage begin to get into the toxic waste disposal business?"

Harold Kaufman: "To my knowledge, it's when the manifest system came out is when they found out the profit motive" (U.S. House of Representatives, 1980: 8).

New Jersey Attorney General John J. Degnan pointed out to a Congressional audience that organized crime activity accounts for only a fraction of the illegal dumping taking place in the United States (U.S. House of Representatives, 1980: 87). Nonetheless, organized crime was ideally suited to develop the methodology of illegal hazardous waste practices to the fullest.

---

to worry that current efforts to clean up the worst abandoned sites under the Superfund program only transfer the problem to other places and future times (Shabecoff, 1985: 31).

In those parts of the nation where garbage hauling and landfilling was historically controlled by organized crime, their movement into the newly created
hazardous waste market was an obvious extension of current activity. In
New Jersey, for example, organized crime had controlled the garbage industry through ownership of garbage hauling firms, through ownership of or
control of landfills, and through labor racketeering (U.S. House of Representatives, 1981: 1-45). The new regulations governing hazardous waste would
have had to have been carefully written and tenaciously enforced were organized crime to be kept from applying this highly developed infrastructure to
the new market. In fact, as will be shown below, the opposite happened and
organized crime easily entered both the hauling and the disposal phases of the
hazardous waste handling industry.

Hauling. Organized crime had dominated traditional garbage hauling in
states like New York and New Jersey for decades. Once associates of organized crime owned a number of hauling firms in any geographical area, they
established an organizational infrastructure that governed their relationships
and ensured high profits. Threats and violence persuaded other firms to join
that infrastructure and abide by its rules or to sell and get out. The keystone
of this infrastructure was the concept of "property rights" or "respect."
Municipal solid waste hauling contracts were illegally apportioned among
haulers. Having a property right meant that a hauler held rights to continue
picking up the contract at sites he currently serviced without competition
from others. Other firms would submit artificially high bids or would not bid
at all when a contract came up for renewal, thereby assuring that the contractor kept his traditional site. This system of *de facto* territorial monopolies
permitted noncompetitive pricing and made the lowly business of garbage
hauling a very lucrative activity. Property rights were recognized and
enforced by organized crime authorities. Conflicts were adjudicated in meetings of the Municipal Contractors Association. Decisions of the MCA were
enforced by threats and, if necessary, violence (U.S. House of Representatives, 1981a: 1-42).[4] As is shown below, when the RCRA mandated the
licensing of firms deemed fit to transport hazardous waste, mob-connected
garbage haulers found it easy to acquire state permits and declare themselves
to be hazardous waste haulers. Quite naturally, they brought their traditional
forms of social organization with them. Individual haulers holding established property rights assumed that they would transfer those property rights
to the new type of waste (U.S. House of Representatives, 1980: 22). They
also met as a group to set up a Trade Waste Association modeled after the
Municipal Contractors Association to apportion and enforce property rights

---

4. Of parenthetical interest here is the methodological similarity between organized
crime's property rights system in garbage and price-fixing by Westinghouse, General Electric, and other firms in the famous heavy electrical equipment price fixing scandal of 1961
(Geis, 1977).

ORGANIZED CRIME AND HAZARDOUS WASTE 9

in the new market (U.S. House of Representatives, 1980: 9-10, 1981a: 1-12, 212).

Disposal. The manifest system requires that someone be willing to sign off on the manifest and declare that a waste shipment has been properly disposed of. This means, as Congressman Florio (Democrat, New Jersey) pointed out (U.S. House of Representatives, 1980: 30), that mob control over hauling is not enough: organized crime figures had to have ownership of, or at least influence over, final disposal sites. This requirement did not prove to be a serious stumbling block, however. Many landfills were already owned wholly or in part by organized crime figures, a legacy of past mob involvement in the garbage business. These sites readily accepted dubious shipments of hazardous waste thinly disguised as ordinary municipal waste (U.S. House of Representatives 1981a: 228, 1981b). Landfill owners not directly associated with organized crime could be bribed to sign manifests for shipments never received or to accept hazardous waste that was manifested elsewhere (U.S. House of Representatives, 1980: 70, 90). In addition, known organized crime figures started or seized control of a network of phony disposal and "treatment" facilities such as Chemical Control Corporation, Elizabeth, New Jersey; Modern Transportation, Kearny, New Jersey; and Duane Marine, Perth Amboy, New Jersey.[5] Licensed by the state, these outfits could legally receive hazardous waste and sign off on the manifest. They would then either stockpile it on site (where it would stay until it exploded, burned, or otherwise came to the attention of authorities) or dump it along roadways, down municipal sewers, into the ocean, or elsewhere (Block and Scarpitti, 1985: 145, 158, 298; U.S. House of Representatives, 1980: 25). In the extreme, actual ownership of or access to disposal sites was unnecessary for those willing to file totally fanciful manifests. Congressman Gore cited one case in which several major corporations signed over their wastes to an out-of-state facility that subsequently was shown to simply not exist (U.S. House of Representatives, 1980: 70, 135).[6]

---

5. Modern Transportation, a firm that would ultimately receive half the manifested hazardous waste originating in northern New Jersey, was incorporated in 1972 by Richard Miele, co-owner with known organized crime figures of numerous garbage-related firms and landfills (Block and Scarpitti, 1985: 297). Chemical Control Corporation was taken over by Johnny Albert, one of the organizers of the New Jersey Trade Waste Association (Block and Scarpitti, 1985: 256-260; U.S. House of Representatives, 1980: 10). Duane Marine was so enmeshed in organized crime networks and activities that its former employee, Harold Kaufman, became the central federal informant on these activities.

6. Albert Gore in the case of Capital Recovery: "The subcommittee's investigation has uncovered evidence that since August, 1976, major industrial companies, such as Koppers, Inc., in one case Exxon, Union Chemical Company in the state of New Jersey certified that over 270,000 gallons of chemical waste were delivered to an out-of-state facility in Wilmington, Delaware, named Capital Recovery. From all the available evidence, Capital

10   SZASZ

ENABLING CAUSES: THE MAKING OF A
VULNERABLE REGULATORY STRUCTURE

In retrospect, it is hardly surprising that, given the opportunity, organized crime would enter the newly created market for hazardous waste handling. It was an extension of their current business activity. They had the equipment and organization. They had both the know-how and the will to corrupt the manifest system. It was an attractive prospect. Both the potential size of the market and the potential profits were enormous. Even if they charged only a fraction of the true price of legitimate disposal, that price would be much higher than the price they charged to move the same stuff when it was legally just garbage, but their operating expenses would stay the same (if they commingled hazardous waste with ordinary garbage) or decrease (if they simply dumped). Why organized crime would want to enter into relationship with corporate generators when the opportunity presented itself needs no subtle unraveling. The more complex task is to determine what political and social-structural conditions made it possible for them to "colonize" the hazardous waste disposal industry.

LAX IMPLEMENTATION, INCOMPETENT AND/OR
CORRUPT ENFORCEMENT

Explanations of organized crime presence in hazardous waste handling focused on lax implementation and improper enforcement. Congressional hearings produced dramatic evidence that, at least in New Jersey, the state where organized crime intrusion into hazardous waste is most thoroughly documented, the major provisions of the RCRA were poorly implemented and enforced. Interim hauling and disposal licenses were freely granted. The manifest system was not sufficiently monitored.

Interim Licensing. Congress had mandated an extended transition period during which both transporters and disposal firms would operate under temporary permits until an adequate national hazardous waste industry developed. Generators lobbied quite heavily on this point (U.S. EPA, 1976: 238, 1979: 153, 307; Gansberg, 1979) and Congress had to agree to this provision because the shortage of adequate hazardous waste facilities was so severe. American industry would have choked in its own accumulating wastes had it not been permitted to continue to use less-than-adequate means of disposal. A reasonable concession to economic realities, implementation of interim licensing was poorly managed. House of Representatives testimony shows that New Jersey issued hauling permits to any applicant who paid a nominal

---

Recovery is nothing more than a paper corporation. It has no offices or any site in Wilmington. There is no phone listing, no city or State real estate tax or business tax information no annual report has been filed . . ." (U.S. House of Representatives, 1980; 135-136).

ORGANIZED CRIME AND HAZARDOUS WASTE   11

$50 fee (U.S. House of Representatives, 1980: 14-15). Existing landfills and even totally bogus firms with no real disposal facilities found it equally easy to get interim disposal permits (U.S. House of Representatives, 1980: 10).

> Harold Kaufman (key FBI informant on mob involvement in hazardous waste disposal, testifying about his old firm, Duane Marine): "The State licensed us. We were the first ones licensed. . . ."
>
> Gore: "And this was a chemical waste disposal facility, is that right?"
>
> Kaufman: "Well, that is what it was called. It never disposed of anything, but you can call it that."

Manifest Oversight. Once a license was obtained, lax supervision of the manifest system made illegal and unsafe disposal of hazardous waste a relatively straightforward, low-risk activity (U.S. House of Representatives, 1980: 140).

> Gore: "What enforcement efforts are you making to prevent the abuse of the manifest system?"
>
> Edwin Stier (New Jersey Division of Criminal Justice): "The only way the manifest system is going to be properly, effectively enforced is through the proper analysis of the information that comes from the manifest. . . . Anyone who assumes that a manifest system which looks good on paper can control the flow and disposition of toxic waste without the kind of support both technical and manpower support that is necessary to make it effective, I think, is deluding himself. [However] . . . we aren't looking specifically for manifest case violations. We aren't pulling every manifest in that is filed with the department of environmental protection and looking for falsification of manifests specifically because we don't have the time, the resources, or the specific lead information to do that."

Congressional testimony revealed that until 1980 New Jersey did not have a single person assigned to monitor the manifests being filed in Trenton (U.S. House of Representatives, 1981b: 124). A recent study by the General Accounting Office (U.S. GAO, 1985: 25-31) found that the manifest system does not detect illegal disposal, in part because of inadequate monitoring.

Congressional hearings also produced evidence suggesting that the relevant New Jersey agencies—the Interagency Hazardous Waste Strike Force, the Division of Criminal Justice, and the Division of Environmental Protection—were incapable of producing effective enforcement even when tipped off to specific instances of hazardous waste dumping (U.S. House of Representatives, 1980: 144-146, 1981b: 110-124). Block and Scarpitti (1985) present many other examples that appear to show corruption or, at best, ineptitude on the part of state officials responsible for investigation and prosecution of illegal hazardous waste practices.

Lax implementation and enforcement undoubtedly played a big role in facilitating organized crime entry into the hazardous waste disposal industry.

12   SZASZ

There are, however, more fundamental conditioning factors that logically and
temporally preceded these causes. RCRA is a regulatory structure ripe with
potential for subversion. Why did Congress create a regulatory structure so
vulnerable to lax enforcement? A review of RCRA's legislative history shows
quite clearly that corporate generators moved decisively to shape the emerging federal intervention to their liking. They determinedly fought for and
achieved a regulatory form that would demand of them the least real change
and a form that would minimize their liability for potential violations of the
new regulations.

GENERATORS' STRATEGIC INTERVENTION IN THE
LEGISLATIVE DEBATE OVER THE FORM OF POLICY

Compared to the regulatory mechanism written into the final language of
the RCRA, some potential alternative forms that were proposed and then
rejected would have proved much less hospitable to noncompliance in general
and to the entry of organized crime in particular. The federal government
could have mandated specific treatment and disposal practices, or directed
generators to treat all of their wastes themselves, or legislated that generators
retain full responsibility for their wastes even if they assign them to other
parties for shipping and disposal. Generators, led by representatives of major
oil and chemical corporations, explicitly and vigorously opposed any such
language. They hammered away with striking unanimity at two fundamental
points: that the government should in no way interfere in firms' production
decisions, and that generators should not be held responsible for the ultimate
fate of their hazardous wastes.

Generators repeatedly warned Congress neither to appropriate to itself the
power to intervene in production processes nor to require generators to follow
specific waste treatment practices. They stressed, instead, that regulatory
controls are more properly imposed at the stage of final disposition. Here are
some representative statements:

> We believe that the disposal of wastes ought to be regulated instead of
> regulating the nature and use of the product or the type of manufactur-
> ing process used (E.I. DuPont de Nemours and Co., U.S. Senate, 1974:
> 454).
> Authority to control production, composition, and distribution of prod-
> ucts . . . would be devastating to free enterprise commerce (Dow Chemi-
> cal, U.S. Senate, 1974: 1,478).
> [Stauffer Chemical opposes generator permits which] would place con-
> trols on raw materials, manufacturing processes, products and distribu-
> tion (Stauffer, U.S. Senate, 1974: 1,745).
> . . . legislation should not impede the natural interaction of raw materi-
> als, market and other forces that ultimately control the nature, quality,

ORGANIZED CRIME AND HAZARDOUS WASTE 13

price, and success of products developed in our free enterprise system (Union Carbide, U.S. Senate, 1974: 1,748).

No specific requirements or prohibitions should be set governing the recovery, reuse or disposal of industrial wastes. . . . Generators should be free to increase or decrease waste production rates, terminate waste production, treat their own wastes, and negotiate treatment or disposal service contracts in a free and competitive market (American Petroleum Institute, U.S. EPA, 1976: 1,406, 1,410).

. . . the generator should be free to decide whether to treat or dispose of wastes (Manufacturing Chemists Association, U.S. EPA, 1976: 565).

. . . economic incentive alone should determine the degree of waste recycle and recovery. . . . We are opposed to regulations specifying the kind and amount of processing and recycle of wastes [by the generator]. [The] greatest emphasis should be placed on establishing standards which assure that the ultimate disposal method is satisfactory (DuPont, U.S. EPA, 1976: 72-73).[7]

Generator unanimity was equally impressive on the second issue of responsibility. They were willing to have limited responsibility, to label their wastes, and make sure they contracted only with firms approved by state authorities, but they vehemently opposed the idea that generators should bear legal responsibility for their wastes from cradle to grave. They argued that responsibility should pass to the party in physical possession of the hazardous waste. Under such a system, they further pointed out, only the hauler and disposer need to be licensed and the government should not license generators. Here are some representative statements:

We agree that the generator has some responsibility in the area, . . . [i.e.] make some determination that the disposer is competent and has the proper permits for disposal. . . . However, the waste hauler and disposer have responsibility to assure, respectively, that the wastes are delivered for disposal at the proper location and are properly disposed. Irresponsible action is invited if the person holding the waste has no responsibility for it (DuPont, U.S. EPA, 1976: 73-74).

[The generator should] confirm the competence and reliability of transporters, treaters and processors to whom the waste may be transferred. . . . Each transporter, treater and disposer should be responsible for his individual activities while the waste is in his possession (Monsanto, U.S. EPA, 1976: 410-411).

MCA recommends that the responsibility for the waste should be associated with physical possession of the waste, so that the generator should

---

7. Other companies and associations making the same argument during these hearings included Monsanto, Exxon, B.F. Goodrich, Alcoa, the Texas Chemical Council, and the Western Oil and Gas Association.

14   SZASZ

not be held liable for negligence of the transporter and the disposer of
the waste. (Manufacturing Chemists Association, U.S. EPA, 1976: 565).
We feel that permits should only be required of the disposal site operator
(B.F. Goodrich, U.S. Senate, 1974: 1,441).
. . . permits for both generation and disposal of hazardous waste is
doubly redundant. . . . A permit system for generators of wastes is
unneeded and would tend to stagnate technology at the level prevailing
at the time the permit was issued (Dow Chemical, U.S. Senate, 1974:
1,478-1,479).
. . . we consider permits for the generation of hazardous wastes to be
unneeded, and could result in unnecessary restriction of manufacturing
operations (Union Carbide, U.S. Senate, 1974: 464).[8]

The generators also lobbied for the other provisions to their liking—a narrow definition of what substances should be regulated as hazardous, flexible
time frames for implementation, and less stringent rules for on-site disposal[9]—but the two points above were the heart of their legislative intervention.
In the end, they didn't get everything they wanted. The government would
make generators register with the EPA. On-site, generator self-disposal
would be subject to the same rules that governed off-site disposal firms. However, the overall forms of RCRA passed by Congress embodied both of their
major demands.

THE LEGACY OF GENERATOR INATTENTION AND INACTION

The generators also contributed indirectly to the shaping of RCRA legislation through their historical lack of attention to proper hazardous waste disposal. The EPA estimated in 1974 that ocean dumping and improper
landfilling cost about 5% of the price of environmentally adequate disposal
and it reported that

Given this permissive legislative climate, generators of waste are under
little or no pressure to expend resources for adequate management of
their hazardous wastes. (U.S. Senate, 1974: 71)

Lack of generator demand for adequate disposal facilities discouraged the

---

8. The same point was also raised by Stauffer Chemicals, Marathon Oil, American
Cyanamid, Berylco, Shell, Alcoa, the Texas Chemical Council, the Western Oil and Gas
Association, the American Petroleum Institute, and the New Jersey Manufacturers
Association.

9. The issue of flexible time frames was raised by the National Association of Manu-
facturers (U.S. House of Representatives, 1976: 190) and Exxon (U.S. EPA, 1976: 940).
Arguing for a restricted definition of what is regulable hazardous waste were DuPont (U.S.
EPA, 1976: 69), the American Iron and Steel Institute (U.S. EPA, 1976: 100), American
Cyanamid (U.S. EPA, 1976: 1,550), B.F. Goodrich (U.S. Senate, 1974: 1,440), Stauffer
(U.S. Senate; 1974: 1,746). Monsanto (U.S. EPA, 1976: 406-407). and Dow (U.S. EPA.
1976: 956), argued for fewer restrictions for on-site disposal.

ORGANIZED CRIME AND HAZARDOUS WASTE 15

inflow of investment capital, and an adequate waste disposal industry had failed to develop by the time RCRA legislation was being debated. Had legislators ignored this situation and required an immediate shift to proper disposal, a production crisis could have been triggered as wastes accumulated and firms found few legal outlets for them. Industrial spokesmen predicted dire consequences. In a representative statement, a Union Carbide spokesman warned legislators:

> Those wastes which are non-incinerable and have no commercial value must be disposed of. To deny opportunity for disposal would effectively eliminate much of the chemical process industry. Disposal in or on the land or disposal in the oceans are the only viable alternatives available.
> (U.S. Senate, 1974: 461)

Neither individual officeholders nor whole governments stay in office long if they pass legislation which, even for the best and most popular of reasons, brings to a halt industrial sectors central to the national economy. Congressmen had to be realistic and mandate years of transition during which hazardous waste would be hauled and disposed by operators having only interim licenses. This reasonable concession to the reality of the situation, a legacy of generator inattention, created a loophole through which many less-than-qualified parties could legally participate as providers in the hazardous waste market.[10]

CORPORATE GENERATORS AND ORGANIZED CRIME: A COMPLEX RELATIONSHIP

The discussion of enabling causes leads from the surface explanation of lax implementation and enforcement back to the moment of creation of a regulatory structure ripe for subversion and subterfuge. Analysis of the formation of the RCRA shows that the actions of corporate generators were principally responsible for the passage of such a vulnerable structure. This is the most basic aspect of the generator-organized crime relationship. Answers to two

---

10. It should be noted that generators intervened not only in policy formation but also engaged in ongoing efforts to weaken regulatory impact during implementation. They appeared at EPA implementation hearings to emphasize that the criteria for declaring substances hazardous were still too broad, that proposed disposal requirements were too stringent, that interim standards were burdensome and inflexible, and that recordkeeping and reporting requirements were onerous. Especially active in this period were trade associations such as the Manufacturing Chemists Association, the Synthetic Organic Chemists Manufacturing Association, the American Petroleum Institute, and the National Paint and Coatings Association, as well as large individual corporations such as Dow and DuPont (U.S. EPA, 1979; U.S. Senate, 1979). EPA officials complained privately that "the millions of pages of testimony filed by representatives of industry on virtually each clause of every implementation proposal" created "a major obstacle" to timely implementation of RCRA (Shabecoff, 1979: 1).

16   SZASZ

questions may flesh out the analysis: did corporate generators intend this outcome? And what effect did it subsequently have upon them? One may also
ask how Congressional hearings did or did not deal with these issues. Discussion continues here with the latter line of exploration.

CONGRESS DISCUSSES THE ROLE OF CORPORATE GENERATORS

Having thoroughly documented organized crime presence in the hazardous
waste industry, Congressional scrutiny could have turned to the question of
how generators, legitimate economic actors, relate to that presence. However, the issue of corporate behavior or corporate responsibility was, for
whatever reason, never treated as a central topic of investigation during hearings.[11] There were only a few isolated attempts to broach the subject and
probe it even a little. Two explanations were tentatively suggested during
these brief interludes. These explanations are now critically examined in light
of the facts already at hand.

Ignorance and "Good Faith." Congressman Gore suggested to Harold
Kaufman, the former Duane Marine employee turned star witness, that per-
haps companies used Kaufman's phony "disposal" firm knowingly as a front.
In response, Kaufman articulated the theory of ignorance and good faith.

> Mr. Gore: "You offered a front to companies that wanted to pretend
> they were disposing of toxic waste."
> Mr. Kaufman: "No, that wasn't true. That wasn't true."
> Gore: "Well, explain it to me in your own words."
> Kaufman: "You're blaming the companies; 99 percent of these compa-
> nies in good faith thought that Duane Marine had the facility."
> Gore: "I see."
> Kaufman: "Because the State licensed us. We were the first ones
> licensed, Duane Marine. . . . these industrial people who in good faith
> wanted to follow the law, if they wanted to cheat, they wouldn't have
> brought the stuff to us, because we were charging a lot of money" (U.S.
> House, 1980: 10).
> Kaufman, later: "Forget about the generator. Let's not blame the peo-
> ple that are really trying to follow the manifest. . . . these companies

---

11. A concrete measure of inattention: in four Congressional hearings on organized
crime in hazardous waste, hearings totaling approximately 500 pages of transcript, a total
of five corporations are identified by name: Exxon, Union Chemical Co., 3M, Koppers,
Inc., and Monsanto. Discussion of corporate involvement was incidental to the main
themes of the hearings, which was the fact of mob involvement and criticism of law
enforcement efforts (U.S. House of Representatives, 1982). To their credit, Congressmen
appeared somewhat more willing to raise the question of corporate responsibility than
either federal regulatory officials or state legal authorities (see U.S. House of Representatives, 1980: 20,140, 1981a: 12, 1981b: 56,103,109-110, 153,158, 1983: 60).

ORGANIZED CRIME AND HAZARDOUS WASTE   17

operate in good faith—otherwise they wouldn't have called the people [i.e., Duane Marine], they would have thrown it in the nearest dump" (U.S. House, 1980: 16).

According to this scenario, managers and owners see the license, the State's seal of approval, and believe in good faith that the shipment of hazardous waste that they sign over will be properly disposed of by responsible operators. They do not know that their wastes end up stockpiled on an Atlantic Coast pier, poured down a municipal sewer, or burned, commingled with fuel oil, in a school furnace. They do not know they are dealing with organized crime. They are in fact being cheated because they pay large amounts for treatment and disposal that are not performed.

The issue of subjective awareness cannot be decisively resolved without in-depth interviewing of corporate managers in charge of waste disposal contracting, but the preponderance of circumstantial evidence makes claims of ignorance appear unconvincing. Organized crime control of garbage hauling and disposal had been considered a fact of life in New Jersey for decades. It had been the subject of numerous state hearings and investigations since 1958 (U.S. House of Representatives, 1981a: 15-16, 36, 39). Organized crime's rapid entry into hazardous waste was so readily apparent that New Jersey established an Inter-Agency Hazardous Waste Strike Force to investigate and attack the problem in 1978, shortly after the new system of licensing and manifesting was begun.   Management also knew—they themselves had stressed this fact when they had lobbied for extended transition periods in RCRA implementation—that there were few adequate hazardous waste facilities available, yet the feared shortage of disposal sites never materialized.

Rather than ignorance and good faith, these facts suggest that the rational industrial manager would have had ample reason to distrust the identity of their contractual partners. Had their suspicions been aroused, it would have been easy to hire investigators, as state and local officials had done, to follow some hazardous waste shipments and lay their doubts to rest:

> Congressman Rinaldo: "Is there any way these plants or companies could have discovered on their own that Duane Marine was a front, a fraud . . .?"
>
> Kaufman: "I guess they could have, sure. All they had to do was [go to Duane Marine and] see their stuff piled up and go to Chemical Control and see their stuff piled up" (U.S. House of Representatives, 1980: 20).[12]

---

12. Albert Gore speaks on Capital Recovery, the phony Delaware disposal firm: "The companies I mentioned, Koppers, Exxon, Union Chemical Co., probably were unaware, *maybe that is overly generous*, but from what I can ascertain from those documents, it is quite likely that the hauler was the person aware of the ultimate disposal site. *The company should have been aware, but they may very well not have been aware* of the fact that the Capital Recovery facility was nonexistent" (U.S. House of Representatives, 1980: 140, emphases added).

18   SZASZ

If managers and owners were indeed ignorant, that subjective state must either have been achieved through the hard work of vigilant inattention or have been the fruit of a profound lack of interest. Indeed, generators may have good material reasons to desire to stay ignorant. In its comments on the GAO's draft report on illegal waste disposal, the EPA states that the "key reason" why generators do not notify officials when they suspect that a waste shipment may have gone astray is "the unwillingness of the generator to "turn-in" its low-bid transporter. This is especially true for smaller volume generators who routinely have great difficulty finding transportation for their wastes" (U.S. GAO, 1985: 62). But, more to the point, the subjective state of awareness of owners and managers is irrelevant because their right to be ignorant is structured into the regulatory scheme of the RCRA. As has been shown, the generator bears no obligation to know its contractual partner beyond assuring itself that the firm has been licensed, declared fit to handle hazardous waste by one of the states. Rather than attempt to argue what corporate actors know, do not know, could know, or should have known, one must remember that generators explicitly fought for RCRA language that entitled them to a state of ignorance.

Powerlessness. Kaufman and New Jersey Deputy Attorney General Madonna suggested a second theory that also tends to absolve the generator of responsibility. Even if the corporate generator knows that it is dealing with organized crime, the "property rights" system forces it into a passive, powerless position:

> Madonna: ". . . numerous customers of garbage or solid waste collectors who have attempted to secure alternative collectors, for whatever reason, have found that it is virtually impossible to obtain a different garbage man to pick up their garbage" (U.S. House of Representatives, 1981a: 12).
> Congressman Marks: "If a disposer of chemical waste sought a different company to haul those waste, could that person voluntarily change without there being a problem?"
> Kaufman: "Not to my knowledge has it ever happened, because you see, most of the haulers of toxic wastes that are in the garbage business respect the same thing in toxics as solid, so he has no choice. He has a man there and nobody will go in" (U.S. House of Representatives, 1980: 22).

This claim of generator powerlessness is also undermined by the previous discussion of the generators' role in the shaping of RCRA legislation. Individual generators, especially smaller firms, may indeed find themselves unable to shop around among hazardous waste haulers once the property rights system had assigned their site to a specific hauler, but the discussion above suggests that one must look beyond individual firms to see how corporate power was exercised collectively. Industries that produce the bulk of hazardous

ORGANIZED CRIME AND HAZARDOUS WASTE 19

waste—oil, chemicals, pharmaceuticals, electronics—exert tremendous political power nationally and in states like New Jersey, where these four industries account for 36% of all industrial production (Governor's Commission, 1983: 18). These lobbying powerhouses used their collective political power during legislative debate over the form of RCRA to create a structure that, subsequently, permitted the emergence of a "property rights" system that can impose its will on some individual generators. Claims of generator powerlessness cannot be accepted without profound qualification.

The details of corporate intervention during the formation of the RCRA undermine any explanation that absolves them of all responsibility, but generator actions do not, by themselves, convey the full complexity of the resultant relationship. Two issues remain: why did the corporate generators do it? And what were the consequences for them?

THE QUESTION OF INTENT

The cohesiveness and unanimity of generator intervention to shape RCRA legislation certainly shows that they intended *something*. Nonetheless, no evidence was found in the research discussed here to support an argument that generators consciously intended to create a context for organized crime entry into the industrial waste disposal business, or even that they understood that such an outcome was possible. Rather, it appears much more likely that they acted out of a general tendency to resist full social responsibility for the "externalities," the environmental and public health consequences, of industrial production, and that they did not much care what, if any, unintended consequences would follow.

Why were generators so vehement that Congress not force them either to change production techniques or to assume full legal responsibility for proper waste disposal? These actions find their meaning within the larger context of industrial response to the whole spectrum of environmental, so-called "social" regulations. Industrial groups active during the passage of RCRA have consistently opposed Congressional passage of every piece of recent social regulation, intervened to weaken their form when passage seemed inevitable, and mobilized to limit their impact once they were implemented. They have done so with regard to the EPA, the Occupational Safety and Health Administration (OSHA), the Toxic Substances Control Act (TOSCA), the Superfund law (CERCLA), surface mining regulation, and right-to-know laws.[13]

---

13. For a discussion of similar industrial action to limit regulatory intervention in the area of worker safety and health, see Szasz (1982, 1984). Corporate vigilance concerning any government attempt to impose greater responsibility is both comprehensive and reveals exquisite attention to detail, especially by corporations and trade associations large enough to have the legal and lobbying staffing for ongoing analysis and intervention.

20   SZASZ

Policy committees composed of corporate leaders and elected officials often state that an intact environment and a healthy public are objectively in the long-run interest of the corporate sector. For example, the Governor's Commission on Science and Technology of the State of New Jersey (1983: 18) recently stated that "The safe disposal of hazardous and toxic substances is of enormous concern; if the problem is not solved, it will severely limit industrial growth." But this understanding is not reflected in the individual or the collective behavior of industrial firms. Regardless of objective or long-term interest, their behavior indicates that they do not wish to "internalize" the true cost of the undesirable side effects of modern industrial production.[14] Both generator failure to pay for proper waste disposal before RCRA and their talking points during RCRA legislative debate are manifestations of this posture. In some areas of regulation, such as worker safety and health, successful corporate intervention may delay passage of legislation, weaken its form, and lessen its impact through ongoing resistance to full implementation. But regulation of hazardous waste was a unique case because of the specific history of organized crime control of garbage. Because of this peculiar circumstance, corporate resistance to this regulation not only had the usual intended effect of avoiding the full internalization of responsibility and cost, it also had the effect—apparently unintended—of opening the door to mob colonization of the regulation-mandated market.

EVEN UNINTENDED OUTCOMES HAVE PAYOFFS

Generators mobilized when it became apparent that the political moment for regulation of hazardous waste had decisively arrived. There was sufficient public awareness, fear, and organized demand that the government would legislate something. They perceived, though, that the onerousness of impending federal intervention would be minimized if they could (1) ensure that regulation would not interfere with production decisions, and (2) they would not be fully liable for all possible costs associated with the ultimate fate of their wastes. A manifest-and-disposal-licensing structure was the generators' best-case damage control strategy. Undoubtedly, the greatest benefit would accure to the generators from their successful move to veto potentially more

---

14. There are always some owners and managers who advocate a more enlightened, long-range view of industrial interest in environmental matters. Producers of pollution control equipment of course support stronger regulation because it increases demand for their product. Nonetheless, historical and content analysis of past regulatory initiatives supports the view that the majority of industrial spokesmen vigorously oppose increases in government regulation of their health externalities. Crenson (1971), in the case of municipal regulation of air pollution, and Williams and Matheny (1984), in the case of state regulation of hazardous waste, have both shown statistically that the local presence of industry inhibits the imposition of regulation.

ORGANIZED CRIME AND HAZARDOUS WASTE 21

interventionist forms of regulation. The victory would hold the new regulation's impact to manageable proportions. However, the unintended effect of their legislative efforts then provided several important secondary benefits on top of the main payoff of defeating stronger forms of federal intervention.

Noninterruption of Vital Service. Industrial waste accumulates every day that a factory operates. It has to be dealt with. With passage of RCRA, firms faced new uncertainties in coping with their hazardous waste. They worried, quite realistically, that RCRA would uncover a fundamental shortage of legal off-site facilities at the same time that the new rules would require firms to upgrade their facilities if they wished to treat wastes themselves. Lax implementation of interim licensing allowed enough parties to enter the new market that potentially crisis-inducing bottlenecks of accumulating waste were avoided. This benefit accrued to industry as a whole and was of central importance in cushioning the potential adverse impact of the transition from an unregulated to regulated situation.

Cost. The transition to regulation also threatened an immense cost shock. As noted earlier, the EPA estimated in 1974 that firms were customarily paying no more than 5% of the price of adequate treatment (U.S. Senate, 1974: 71). If generators discharged their RCRA obligations by dealing with shady haulers and phony disposal firms, they would typically pay a higher price for disposal than they had before RCRA, but these charges could still be significantly less than the full price of adequate treatment. The Congressional hearings uncovered several instances of such cost savings by generators (U.S. House of Representatives, 1980: 189), but how often this benefit occurred was not fully explored.

Obfuscation of Origins. The final potential benefit follows from organized crime's facility at falsifying manifests. As hazardous waste travels through the maze of illegitimate haulers and disposers, it becomes equally impossible to trace its industrial origins or to locate its ultimate destination. Officials find that even if a waste shipment can be followed from the generator to a nondisposing "disposal" site like Duane Marine or Modern Transportation, its ultimate resting place still cannot be identified with any certainty.[15] Conversely, when improperly disposed wastes are found, it is nearly impossible to trace backward and identify their corporate origins (U.S. House of Representatives, 1981b: 153, 158).[16] The Superfund law, passed shortly after RCRA,

---

15. Modern Transportation, incorporated in 1972, quickly became the largest of New Jersey's 18 licensed disposal facilities. By 1980, it was receiving almost 50% of the hazardous waste manifested in northern New Jersey. The manifests allowed investigators to follow hazardous waste from generator to Modern Transportation, but they were unable to establish with any certainty where the waste actually went after arriving at this "disposal" firm that had no observable disposal facilities (Block and Scarpitti, 1985: 296-298; U.S. House of Representatives, 1981b: 115).

16. The effectiveness of "orphaning" one's hazardous waste, letting it be hauled and

provides that the original generators of abandoned wastes be identified and forced to pay for remedial cleanup. According to the Office of Technology Assessment, remedial cleanup can cost 10 to 100 times the cost of initial proper disposal (U.S. House of Representatives, 1983: 7). Therefore, a firm can expect to escape serious liabilities if manifest manipulation has successfully "orphaned" its wastes by obfuscating its origins.

DISCUSSION: CORPORATIONS, ORGANIZED CRIME, AND EXTERNALIZING CRIMINOGENESIS

As noted earlier, recent work has challenged the clear distinction between legitimate and illegitimate business, between corporate and organized crime. On the one hand, organized crime is described as entrepreneurial activity (Schelling, 1967; Smith, 1980; Smith and Alba, 1979; Albanese, 1982), and its most overtly deviant features—conspiracy, violence—are explained as organizational necessities for businesses that cannot turn to the legal structure to govern their internal relationships (Smith, 1980: 375). Chambliss (1978: 181) argues, furthermore, that it is "the logic of capitalism . . . [which makes] the emergence of crime networks inevitable." Others (Barnett, 1981) assert that the logic of capital constantly presses legitimate economic actors to violate socially defined limits of business conduct. Studies showing widespread illegal activity (including fraud, bribery, and pricefixing) by a majority of Fortune 500 corporations (Clinard, Yeager, Brissette, Petrashek, and Harries, 1979; Clinard and Yeager, 1980; Etzioni, 1985) support the view that the most powerful and legitimate enterprises routinely engage in highly rationalized criminal activity. The logical endpoint of this argument is the radical view that the process of capital accumulation is itself organized crime in some larger sense of that term.[17]

---

dumped without adequate records, is shown by the difficulties EPA has had in identifying the generators of wastes found in Superfund sites. One such site, the Lone Pine landfill in Freehold, New Jersey, where large amounts of improperly stored hazardous waste are leaching into the Manasquan River, was examined in detail in the U.S. House of Representatives (1981b). Both state and EPA officials stated that they could not identify the original generators of the material at the landfill. One New Jersey official stated, "It is very difficult to enforce against chemical waste surreptitiously going to a landfill" (1981b: 115). Richard Dewling, EPA Region II office, agreed that such information is often impossible to obtain because of insufficient data, stonewalling by guilty parties, and so on (1981b: 158). As a result, Dewling reported that "To the best of our knowledge, there is no reliable information presently available on generators whose wastes have been illegally disposed of at Lone Pine" (1981b: 153).

17. This perspective, most commonly associated with Marxist sociology, rests on the view that one must go beyond current social definitions of what is crime and strive to develop a definition of crime based on a more abstract and theoretical vision of what constitutes moral human conduct and social need. The most succinct statement of this perspective is still Proudhon's dictum that "Private property is theft." In line with the topic of this

ORGANIZED CRIME AND HAZARDOUS WASTE 23

Challenging the commonsense distinction between business and organized crime has the merit of drawing attention to the definitional processes whereby society labels some economic acts as legitimate and others as deviant. But even if one agrees that this distinction is a product of social construction and is on some level ideological, one can say that the central dynamic disclosed in this paper depends on continued social and legal acceptance of the reality of that definitional boundary. Widely accepted ideologies are more than pure illusion: they have important material consequences.

Exactly because there is a socially and legally recognized boundary between legitimate business and organized crime, ethically unacceptable activities that benefit legitimate businesses may happen without compromising their reputation because those acts are committed by and can be blamed on those whose social reputation is already sullied. Block and Chambliss's (1981) analysis of labor racketeering in trucking, restaurants, and the garment trades shows clearly that owners may gain great benefits, such as lower wages and labor peace, when labor unions are dominated by organized crime. Brady's (1983: 11) excellent analysis of arson in Boston shows that arson is an outcome of

> economic decisions undertaken by the banking, real estate, and insurance industries, as well as the racketeering organizations of organized crime syndicates. . . . [Although the actual arson is committed by organized crime,] banks often profit more than the racketeers . . . even without consciously joining in the conspiracy and without violating the law.

Societal acceptance of a definitional boundary between legitimate business and organized crime makes possible a type of criminogenic process different from the two types of criminogenesis defined by Needleman and Needleman (1979). Crimes that are functional for a particular industry are committed by actors that are not only not of that industry but are of a totally different economic world, the "underworld." One may think of this process as parallel to the process of externalizing the economic costs of production and call it "externalizing crimogenesis." What is externalized here is the legal liability and the social blame for those dirty little acts that quicken the wheels of commerce.

Analysis of the formation of hazardous waste disposal regulations captures such a criminogenic structure at the moment of its formation. In the mid-1970s, corporations faced the prospect of new legislation that would force them to bear the responsibility and cost of environmentally safe disposal of

---

paper, criticism of the environmental effects of capitalist industrial production often expresses the implicit view that such economic conduct is fundamentally "criminal." In this light, see Marx's remark (1967: 269) that "Capital . . . is in practice moved as much and as little by the sight of the coming degradation and final depopulation of the human race, as by the probable fall of the earth into the sun."

24   SZASZ

massive amounts of hazardous waste. They responded with a legislative campaign that effectively limited their liability. The regulatory structure they
advocated would prove to be highly vulnerable to the commission of disposal
crime, but these crimes would be committed by others, not by the generators
themselves. Even if generators did not intend this outcome, they were well
served by it because illegal disposal activity effectively slowed the pace of
change and cushioned the shock of transition from an unregulated to an
increasingly regulated context.

REFERENCES

Albanese, Jay S.
    1982   What Lockheed and La Cosa Nostra have in common: The effect of
            ideology on criminal justice policy. Crime and Delinquency 28: 211-232.

Barnett, Harold C.
    1981   Corporate capitalism, corporate crime. Crime and Delinquency 27: 4-23.

Block, Alan A.
    1982   "On the Waterfront" revisited: The criminology of waterfront organized
            crime. Contemporary Crisis 6: 373-396.

Block, Alan A. and William J. Chambliss
    1981   Organizing Crime. New York: Elsevier.

Block, Alan A. and Frank R. Scarpitti
    1985   Poisoning for Profit: The Mafia and Toxic Waste in America. New York:
            William Morrow.

Brady, James
    1983   Arson, urban economy and organized crime: The case of Boston. Social
            Problems 31: 1-27.

Chambliss, William J.
    1978   On the Take: From Petty Crooks to Presidents. Bloomington: Indiana
            University Press.

Clinard, Marshall B., Peter C. Yeager, Jeanne M. Brissette, David Petrashek, and
Elizabeth Harries
    1979   Illegal Corporate Behavior. Washington, D.C.: U.S. Government Printing
            Office.

Clinard, Marshall B. and Peter C. Yeager
    1980   Corporate Crime. New York: The Free Press.

Crenson, Matthew A.
    1971   The Un-Politics of Air Pollution: A Study of Non-Decisionmaking in the
            Cities. Baltimore: Johns Hopkins University Press.

Denzin, Norman K.
    1977   Notes on the crimogenic hypothesis: A case study of the American liquor
            industry. American Sociological Review 42: 905-920.

ORGANIZED CRIME AND HAZARDOUS WASTE   25

Drucker, Peter F.
1981   What is business ethics? The Public Interest 63: 18-36.

Etzioni, Amitai
1985   Shady corporate practices. New York Times. November 15.

Farberman, Harvey A.
1975   A crimogenic market structure: The automobile industry. Sociological
        Quarterly 16: 438-457.

Gansberg, Martin
1979   New Jersey Journal. New York Times. January 21.

Geis, Gilbert
1977   The heavy electrical equipment antitrust cases of 1961. In Gilbert Geis and
        Robert F. Meier (eds.), White-Collar Crime: Offenses in Business, Politics,
        and the Professions (rev. ed.). New York: Free Press.

Getschow, George and Thomas Petzinger, Jr.
1984   Oil's legacy: Louisiana marshlands, laced with oil canals, are rapidly
        vanishing. The Wall Street Journal. October 24.

Governor's Commission on Science and Technology for the State of New Jersey
1983   Report of the Governor's Commission on Science and Technology.

Greenberg, Michael R. and Richard F. Anderson
1984   Hazardous Waste Sites: The Credibility Gap. Piscataway, NJ: Center for
        Urban Policy Research.

Leonard, William N. and Marvin G. Weber
1977   Automakers and dealers: A study of crimogenic market forces. In Gilbert
        Geis and Robert F. Meier (eds.), White-Collar Crime: Offenses in Business,
        Politics, and the Professions (rev. ed.). New York: Free Press.

Martens, Frederick T. and Colleen Miller-Longfellow
1982   Shadows of substance: Organized crime reconsidered. Federal Probation 46:
        3-9.

Marx, Karl,
1967   Capital: A Critique of Political Economy, Vol. 1. New York: International
        Publishers.

Needleman, Martin L. and Carolyn Needleman
1979   Organizational crime: Two models of crimogenesis. Sociological Quarterly
        20: 517-528.

Petzinger, Thomas Jr. and George Getschow
1984a   Oil's legacy: In Louisiana, big oil is cozy with officials and benefit is mutual.
        The Wall Street Journal. October 22.
1984b   Oil's legacy: In Louisiana, pollution and cancer are rife in the petroleum
        area. The Wall Street Journal. October 23.

Shabecoff, Philip
1979   House unit attacks lags on toxic waste. New York Times. October 14.
1985   Toxic waste threat termed far greater than U.S. estimates. New York
        Times. March 10.

Schelling, Thomas C.
1967   Economics and criminal enterprise. The Public Interest 7: 61-78.

26   SZASZ

Smith, Dwight C., Jr.
   1980   Paragons, pariahs, and pirates: A spectrum-based theory of enterprise.
             Crime and Delinquency 26: 358-386.

Smith, Dwight C., Jr., and Richard D. Alba
   1979   Organized crime and American life. Society 3: 32-38.

Snyder, David
   1985a   Toxic scars crisscross Louisiana. The New Orleans Times-Picayune.
             September 8.
   1985b   Early action was met with disbelief. The New Orleans Times-Picayune.
             September 8.
   1985c   Wastes choke scenic bayous of St. Charles. The New Orleans Times-
             Picayune. September 10.
   1985d   Chemical specter fills Cajun paradise with sense of fear. The New Orleans
             Times-Picayune. September 11.
   1985e   He won't be stopped, landfill operator warns. The New Orleans Times-
             Picayune. September 11.
   1985f   10-year struggle to shut down waste site stymied by state. The New Orleans
             Times-Picayune. September 12.

Szasz, Andrew
   1982   The dynamics of social regulation: A study of the formation and evolution
             of the Occupational Safety and Health Administration. Unpublished
             doctoral dissertation. Madison: University of Wisconsin.
   1984   Industrial resistance to occupational safety and health legislation: 1971-
             1981. Social Problems 32: 103-116.

U.S. Environmental Protection Agency
   1976   Hazardous Waste Management: Public Meetings. December 2-11.
   1979   Public Hearings on the Proposed Regulations Implementing Sections 3001 to
             3004 of the Resource Conservation and Recovery Act. February 22-23.

U.S. General Accounting Office
   1985   Illegal Disposal of Hazardous Waste: Difficult to Detect or Deter.
             Comptroller General's Report to the Subcommittee on Investigations and
             Oversight, Committee on Public Works and Transportation, House of
             Representatives.

U.S. House of Representatives
   1975   Waste Control Act of 1975. Hearings held by the Subcommittee on
             Transportation and Commerce, Committee on Interstate and Foreign
             Commerce. April 8-11, 14-17.
   1976   Resource Conservation and Recovery Act of 1976. Hearings held by the
             Subcommittee on Transportation and Commerce, Committee on Interstate
             and Foreign Commerce. June 29-30.
   1980   Organized Crime and Hazardous Waste Disposal. Hearings held by
             Subcommittee on Oversight and Investigations, Committee on Interstate and
             Foreign Commerce. December 16.
   1981a   Organized Crime Links to the Waste Disposal Industry. Hearings held by
             Subcommittee on Oversight and Investigations, Committee on Energy and
             Commerce. May 28.
   1981b   Hazardous Waste Matters: A Case Study of Landfill Sites. Hearings held
             by Subcommittee on Oversight and Investigations, Committee on Energy
             and Commerce. June 9.

ORGANIZED CRIME AND HAZARDOUS WASTE   27

1982   Hazardous Waste Enforcement. Hearings held by Subcommittee on Oversight and Investigations, Committee on Energy and Commerce. December.
1983   Hazardous Waste Disposal. Hearings held by Subcommittee on Oversight and Investigations. Committee on Science and Technology. March 30 and May 4.

U.S. Senate
1974   The Need for a National Materials Policy. Hearings held by the Subcommittee on Environmental Pollution, Committee on Public Works. June 11-13, July 9-11, 15-18.
1979   Oversight of RCRA Implementation. Hearings held by the Subcommittee on Environmental Pollution and Resource Protection, Committee on Environmental and Public Works. March 28-29.

Williams, Bruce A. and Albert R. Matheny
984   Testing theories of social regulation: Hazardous waste regulation in the American states. Journal of Politics 46: 428-458.

Andrew Szasz pursues research on the political economy of environmental health hazards and on health care policy. He has been an Assistant Professor of Sociology at Rutgers University and a Pew Postdoctoral Fellow at the University of California at San Francisco. In 1986, Dr. Szasz joined the faculty of the University of California, Santa Cruz.

Part V
Regulation and Control of Organized Crime

SOCIAL PROBLEMS, Vol. 27, No. 4, April 1980

THREE MODELS OF ORGANIZATIONAL CORRUPTION
IN AGENCIES OF SOCIAL CONTROL*

LAWRENCE W. SHERMAN
State University of New York at Albany

In this paper I examine the processes by which agencies of social control become organizationally corrupt, as one instance of the more general social problem of organizations adopting deviant goals. I define organizational corruption, and present three models of how it may develop: (1) the co-optation by social control agencies of the subjects of control; (2) the capture of social control agencies by external exploiters of the "power to regulate" as a marketable commodity; and (3) the domination of the agency by internal exploiters of the marketability of regulatory authority. I explore and illustrate the conditions under which each model is found and suggest some tasks for future theoretical work.

One of Sutherland's greatest contributions to the sociological study of crime was his conception of organizations as deviant actors. Yet for almost forty years this contribution was all but ignored. Partly because Sutherland (1940, 1949) was inconsistent and contradictory in his use of the concept (Shapiro, 1976), and partly because sociologists of crime have been preoccupied with explaining the behavior of individuals, Sutherland's critics have been able to discredit the concept of deviant organizations as "economic anthropomorphism" (Geis, 1962). Bloch and Geis, for example, flatly pronounce that, "For the purposes of criminological analysis, . . . corporations cannot be considered persons" (1970:306). This narrow position not only ignores a major problem for inquiry into such central criminological concerns as violence and theft (Schrager and Short, 1978), it also ignores one of the most consequential shifts in the social structure of Western societies over the past several centuries: the emergence of organizations as the most powerful "persons" in society (Coleman, 1973, 1974).

In recent years, however, a growing number of sociologists have either employed or implied the concept of organizations as criminal or deviant actors, in both conceptual discussions (Reiss, 1966; Wheeler, 1976; Ermann and Lundman, 1978; Schrager and Short, 1978; Shover, 1978) and in research on such problems as consumer fraud in auto repairs (Leonard and Weber, 1970), police corruption (Sherman, 1978; Lundman, 1979) and occupational safety violations (Pearson, 1978). The concept of organizational deviance has become more widely accepted, but it has rarely been treated as a variable. Very little of the existing work on organizational deviance has attempted to explain why some organizations and not others engage in deviant conduct, or why some commit more deviant acts than others. The one theoretical framework that has been employed to answer this question, strain theory, was adapted from the individual level of explanation (Merton, 1968:Chapter VI), and it often fits the facts it is used to explain; but the strain theory explanations have been necessarily confined to organizational deviance involving the use of illegitimate means to achieve societally legitimate goals. *Organizational deviance involving the adoption of societally illegitimate organizational goals has yet to be explained.* The apparently growing social problem of corporations that lose money or go bankrupt through planned internal or external exploitation, religious organizations that deprive their members of liberty and life, and other organizations that *invert* (and not just displace) their manifest socially approved goals still await sociological examination as a general phenomenon.

One fertile area for developing theories of why organizations adopt deviant goals is the broad

* I wish to thank David Duffee, Michael Gottfredson, Clinton Terry and several anonymous reviewers for offering comments on an earlier draft of this paper, presented to the American Society of Criminology, Dallas, Texas, November, 1978.

category of agencies of official social control, defined as those organizations empowered by society to deprive people and organizations of their material wealth, their liberty or their lives.[1] The extensive literature on the corruption of social control agencies provides some basic descriptive material in which patterns of the adoption of deviant goals may be observed. After defining social control corruption and distinguishing its individual from its organizational forms, I present three models of the processes by which social control agencies adopt corrupt gain as an organizational goal and suggests some hypotheses about the conditions under which each model typically occurs. First, however, the unavoidable threshold issue that has stymied so much work on organizational deviance must be addressed: whether organizations are real actors.

ARE ORGANIZATIONS REAL, MORAL ACTORS?

The long dominant sociological view of organizations is that they have no reality apart from the existence of their members (Simon, 1964). More recent sociological discussions of organizations, however, speak of "the reality of organizations . . . as independent of their members" (Aldrich, 1979:2) derived from their ability to generate the actions of individuals (Hall, 1977:23–27), so that strictly organizational factors account for part of the behavior of individuals at all times in organizations. In this restated position in a very old debate (cf. Warriner, 1956), organizations can be said to act when individual agents (cf. Coleman, 1974) of the organization act under the influence of organizational factors. Since their actions are real, organizations can logically be labeled as conforming to or deviating from moral norms.

Whatever the philosophic objections might be to treating organizations as moral actors (e.g., Rawls, 1971:505), organizations are clearly defined as real in modern society. The legal system, for example, while struggling with several competing theories of how corporations are morally responsible for their acts, leaves no doubt that organizations are indeed to be held morally responsible; juries have even convicted corporations of crimes while acquitting individual corporate officers for the same offenses (Harvard Law Review, 1979b). Journalistic treatments and everyday language follow this conception. As Cohen (1966:21) points out, even philosophers and sociologists, when not engaged in disputing the reality of organizations, "do not doubt that the gas company" overcharged them or that "the university is not paying them what they are worth." The fact that much action in modern society is organizational action suggests that a conception of organizations as moral actors ought, at the least, to be admitted to the sociological floor for discussion; and the first question might well be why some organizations become corrupt.

DEFINING ORGANIZATIONAL CORRUPTION

The definitions of corruption in government vary widely among social scientists. Some definitions center on public office, while others use market situations or conceptions of the public interest, and other elements (Heidenheimer, 1970:4–6). The narrower category of corruption in agencies of social control may be most usefully defined in relation to the authority of public office (Goldstein, 1975:3–5; Sherman, 1978:30), but all of the definitions include the element of private gain (usually financial, although power, prestige and perquisites could be included) for individuals who exercise that authority. Those individuals include both the officials in whom the authority is formally vested and others who control those officials by participating in the agency's dominant administrative coalition.

As Thompson (1967:128) defines it, the dominant coalition is a process (not an entity) in which

---

1. While it is often observed that organizations cannot be put in jail, they can be deprived of life (Coleman, 1974).

certain individuals powerful enough to participate in any given decision determine the operative organizational goals:

> Almost inevitably this includes organizational members, but it may also incorporate significant outsiders. . . . In this view, organizational goals are established by individuals—but interdependent individuals who collectively have sufficient control of organizational resources to commit them in certain directions and withhold them from others (1967:128).

Corrupt acts by agents of social control may thus be defined as *the illegal misuse of public authority by social control agents resulting in private gain for the agents or others participating in the agency's dominant coalition*. This definition admittedly suffers from ambiguity about the key terms of "misuse" and its "resulting" in private gain. The term "misuse" opens the definition to a variety of conceptions of the public interest, and the term "result" belies the often complex causal connection between official decisions and private gain. A regulatory official, for example, who makes a decision favorable to a private corporation's interest and takes a highly paid position with that company five years later illustrates both problems. The example also illustrates the inadequacy of relying on official rules for a definition since the behavior in question is generally construed as perfectly legal and proper, but the broad legal definitions of bribery could conceivably be used to punish the behavior as illegal (see generally, Harvard Law Review, 1979a).

This definition explicitly rejects a definition of corruption as illicit attainment of organizational gain. The violation of laws in order to preserve or enhance the power or domain of an organization is an important social problem, and one which is often found in agencies of social control. But it is a distinct problem, with possibly distinct causes, from the problem of illicit attainment of individual gain.

The boundaries of a definition of corruption are no more or less clearly defined than the boundaries of definitions of all crime and deviance.[2] Yet the definition of corruption probably enjoys more consensus than the choice of criteria for distinguishing organizational deviance from individual deviance in organizations. Several definitions of organizational deviance have been suggested, but none of them has been widely adopted.

One definition of organizational deviance suggests that four characteristics would have to be present in order for social control corruption to be organizational rather than individual (Ermann and Lundman, 1978:7-9); the actions must be: (1) supported by the internal operating norms of an organization; (2) justified to new organizational members through a process of socialization inculcating those norms; (3) supported by fellow workers in the organization; and (4) supported by the dominant administrative coalition of the organization. This definition of organizational deviance repeats Sutherland's error of confusing elements of causation with the elements of the behavior itself (Shapiro, 1976). Operating norms (which can vary widely from one organizational unit to the next), organizational socialization into a deviant activity, and peer group support may all help to explain why organizational deviance occurs, but those characteristics are neither necessary nor useful for distinguishing organizational from individual deviance. All three characteristics apply to crimes committed *against* organizations by their employees, such as systematic employee theft (Mars, 1973), as well as to crimes committed by employees on *behalf of* their organizations, such as price-fixing (Geis, 1977). Only the fourth element of this definition (support by the dominant coalition) is essential for distinguishing deviance committed by individuals as representatives of the organization from deviance committed by individuals as personal actors.

Another definition relies solely on the support of the organization's dominant coalition to determine whether deviance is organizational or individual (Sherman, 1978:4-5), a position con-

---

2. For evidence that problems of definition are still very much alive, see the exchange between Black (1979) and Gottfredson and Hindelang (1979a,b) with regard to victimization data.

sistent with at least one legal theory (Harvard Law Review, 1979b:1250–1251). Whether a deviant act is committed against, within, or on behalf of an organization is thus defined by the operative or "real" goals of the organization, as distinct from the manifest or formal goals, and not by the nature of the act itself. Under this definition, employee theft from the organization, for example, would be individual deviance committed against the organization as long as the organization's operative goal set by the dominant coalition is to maximize profits (or for governmental and non-profit agencies, to keep down costs). But where employee theft is consistent with an operative organizational goal of maintaining internal harmony through "informal rewards" (Dalton, 1959:Chapter 7; Conklin, 1977:68) or of exploiting the organization's resources for the personal benefit of organizational employees (Raw *et al.*, 1972), then it would constitute organizational deviance. The objective behavior is the same, but the different operative goals set by the dominant coalition define the consequences of the behavior for the organization's interests differently at any given point in time.

When an individual acts "on behalf" of an organization, then, he or she is acting in accordance with the dominant coalition's operative goals. Thus it might seem appropriate to employ Shover's definition of organizational crime:

> ... criminal acts committed by individuals or groups of individuals ... during the normal course of their work as employees of organizations, which they intend to contribute to the achievement of goals or other objectives thought to be important for the organization as a whole, some subunit within the organization, or their own particular duties (1978:39).

It is difficult or impossible, however, to assess an individual's intent, even with direct observation of behavior, either sociologically (Shapiro, 1976) or in a criminal prosecution (Schrager and Short, 1978:409–410). It is possible to observe communications from the dominant coalition to organizational members, and to observe whether the member's behavior is consistent with those messages. A more practicable operational definition of organizational crime, then, is:

> Illegal acts of omission or commission committed by an individual or a group of individuals in a legitimate formal organization in accordance with the operative goals of the organization, which have a serious physical or economic impact on employees, consumers or the general public (Schrager and Short, 1978:411–412).

Rather than asking who benefits, the latter definition is more concerned with who is harmed and how much, something that is much easier to assess. The virtue of this definition, however, is also its failing. By including only clear cut cases of such serious harm as the Buffalo Creek Mining Disaster (Erikson, 1976), the definition excludes many deviant and criminal[3] acts which actually cause physical or economic harm to no one, either because they do not have the potential to do so or because they did not have that result. Many forms of corruption in social control agencies would be excluded by the Schrager and Short definition. Police bribe-taking to allow gambling is a clear example; a bribe taken by a Food and Drug Administration official to approve a new drug that had not been adequately tested but which did not turn out to have harmful effects would be another. But the criterion of serious harm is only relevant to the definition of deviant acts *per se*; it does not affect their distinction between individual and organizational action on the basis of operative organizational goals.

Three of the four definitions of organizational deviance (Ermann and Lundman, 1978;

---

3. By excluding illegal behavior that does not have a serious physical or economic impact, Schrager and Short solved the persistent problem of whether to call acts punishable by merely civil penalties "crime" (Sutherland, 1945; Tappan, 1947). In the process, however, they have allowed their own value judgment about impact to determine what will be labeled a crime, thereby violating the principle evident in their injunction not to "label some legal actions as criminal on moral grounds" (1978:412). Instead, they opted to use moral grounds to label some criminal actions as noncriminal.

Schrager and Short, 1978; Sherman, 1978), then, rely on the concept of operative organizational goals set by the dominant administrative coalition to distinguish individual and organizational action, and the fourth definition (Shover, 1978) implies a similar distinction. By combining this distinction with the admittedly provisional definition of social control corruption suggested above, organizational corruption in agencies of social control may be defined as *the illegal misuse of public authority in accordance with operative organizational goals for the private gain of social control agents or others participating in the agency's dominant administrative coalition.*

THEORIES OF ORGANIZATIONAL DEVIANCE

Given this definition of organizational corruption, the central problem is why some social control organizations and not others adopt operative goals consistent with corruption, or even adopt corruption itself as an operative goal. This is a very different problem from the one addressed by existing theories of specific types of organizational deviance, most of which are confined to strain theory explanations of the organizational use of societally illegitimate means in accordance with societally legitimate organizational goals. For business organizations, the usual problem for explanation is why some and not others break the law in order to achieve the societally legitimate goal of making a profit (Lane, 1953; Leonard and Weber, 1970; Farberman, 1975; Geis, 1977; Sonnenfeld and Lawrence, 1978).[4] For government organizations, the usual problem for explanation is why some and not others break the law in attempting to achieve such legitimate public interest goals as maintaining order (Marx, 1972).

None of these theories, however, can explain why a corporation would abandon the goal of profit making in order to milk corporate assets for the personal gain of organizational employees, or why a nursing home would abandon the goal of providing health care to the elderly in order to enrich its owners, or why a police department would abandon the goal of enforcing the law in favor of the goal of profiting from the sale of nonenforcement. Nor, for that matter, can the traditional theories of goal displacement, in which "an instrumental value becomes a terminal value" (Merton, 1968:253) or the imperatives of organizational survival "may lead to unanticipated consequences resulting in a deflection of original goals" (Selznick, 1949:259), explain the adoption of deviant goals. The displacement of one societally legitimate goal with another, such as the Tennessee Valley Authority's substitution of private land development for its original goal of conservation through public ownership, may enhance rather than threaten an organization's survival; but that is not necessarily the case for the adoption of a societally illegitimate goal. Even if the adoption of that goal enhances short-term prospects for survival and growth, in the long run it may make the organization vulnerable to punishment and even destruction.

The problem of organizational corruption in official agencies of social control is unlike any other problem for which theories have already been suggested, and is part of a larger gap in the sociology of organizational deviance. As a problem of organizational behavior, it may be better understood with three concepts taken from the sociology of formal organizations: co-optation, capture and shelter. Each of these concepts provide the basis for a model of how social control agencies become organizationally corrupt.

MODEL I: CO-OPTATION OF SUBJECTS OF CONTROL

One common pattern of social control corruption is co-optation: the participation of the subjects of social control in the policy-making process of the agency. Corruption in federal

---

4. The legitimacy of profit making, of course, is by no means universal, and a deviant label is now often applied to "excessive" profit levels, such as those of the oil companies (Parisi, 1979) during the energy crisis of 1973. But the idea of profit itself, it seems, is still far from being defined as deviant by a majority of the American public.

regulatory agencies is most often described in this manner, but local police departments sometimes fit this pattern as well. The colloquial usage of the concept implies that the subjects of control, threatened by the possibility that the control agencies will force them to cease their activity,
"co-opt" the control agency by making control agents identify with the interests of the subjects
of control. This imagery underlies the conventional interpretation of such behavior as Securities
and Exchange Commission employees accepting free trips and hotel rooms from securities industry groups (Conklin, 1977:123) or the "revolving door" through which employees of
regulated industries move into regulatory agency employment and back again, as did more than
half of the people appointed to nine of the federal regulatory agencies during 1970-75 (Burnham,
1975). Such "links" between the regulated and the regulators are said to reduce the effectiveness
of the control process (Conklin, 1977:123; Skolnick, 1978:159-167).

Both the concept of co-optation and this model of social control corruption are actually much
more subtle than the conventional imagery. As Selznick (1949:13) originally defined it, "co-
optation is the process of absorbing new elements into the leadership or policy-determining structure of an organization as a means of averting threats to its stability or existence," with the consequence that the organization's character, role and operative goals may be modified. It is not the
social control agencies which are co-opted; the regulators may pose a threat to the existence of the
regulated, but there is little evidence that, for example, the Mafia families or other businesses absorb social control agents into their leadership structures. Rather, in this model the reverse is true:
the regulated pose a threat to the regulators, and the regulators absorb the regulated into their
policy-making process of regulation.

To have the regulated threaten the regulators when the power of societally legitimated coercion
is on the side of the regulators may be counter-intuitive, but it makes sense from a sociological
view of organizations. The regulated's threat derives from the organizational imperatives of the
regulators. In order to accomplish (or appear to accomplish, through the production of enforcement statistics) their formal goal of regulation, the regulators may require expertise or information that is available only from the regulated (Wheeler, 1976). If the regulated withhold the information, expertise, or other resources that regulators require for accomplishing their formal goals,
they may threaten the stability or survival of the regulators (Leavitt *et al.*, 1978:271). In order to
be assured of the resources for accomplishing their formal goals, the regulators may absorb the
regulated into their policy-making structure. Once absorbed, however, the regulated may not
only displace the formal goals of the regulators, they may also invert them completely, inducing
the social control agency to adopt the deviant goal of selling its enforcement power.

Local police detectives, for example, have always depended on burglars for the information
necessary to arrest other burglars and to recover stolen property (Skolnick, 1966:126-137). In
order to accomplish these legitimate formal goals, detectives develop close personal relationships
with burglars—not unlike, in some respects, the relations of federal regulatory agents and those
they regulate. Through these relationships, (which Thompson, 1967:35, describes as "contracting," not "co-opting") the burglars help, in a sense, to make enforcement policy, through such
decisions as who will be arrested and who will not. The burglar-informants are often made to feel
that they are a part of the police department (Skolnick, 1966:130). The fact that the detectives
overlook their minor misdeeds (Westley, 1970:39) does not constitute misuse of public authority
for private gain, so the relationship itself cannot be termed corrupt. Sometimes such relationships
can go further, with detectives "licensing" burglars to operate in certain territories without fear
of arrest in exchange for cash payments (Steffens, 1931:222-223; Sutherland, 1937:117) or even
helping burglars to plan burglaries in order to split the reward for recovery of the stolen goods
(Laurie, 1970:214). Where such actions are in accordance with the operative goals of the social
control agency (our criterion for distinguishing organizational and individual behavior), they

constitute organizational corruption. The legitimate formal goal of arresting burglars may still be operative, but it takes second place to the illegitimate goal of profit through the sale of nonenforcement.

Similarly, when the Securities and Exchange Commission (SEC) was founded in 1934 to develop and enforce corporate financial reporting standards, its principal goal was to help stabilize the economy by preventing stock price manipulation and ruinous speculation, and by providing investors with reliable information. The financial community in general, and the accounting profession in particular, was so opposed to the SEC that it threatened to go on "strike" by halting capital investment and refusing to file audits (Chatov, 1975). In order to appear to be ensuring that investors receive reliable information, the SEC gave up its public mandate to develop corporate financial reporting standards to the private sector. Moreover, the SEC has also depended on the accounting and financial sector for expertise, a dependence reflected in the ancient principle that "it takes a thief to catch a thief." Just as the famous thief Eugene Francois Vidocq was hired in restoration France to establish the first centralized Criminal Investigation Division of the French Police and staff it with criminals (Stead, 1957:94), President Roosevelt and his successors have appointed corporate lawyers and accountants to both the staff and the Commissionerships of the SEC. Whether the "revolving door" of employment between the SEC and the private sector means that every SEC decision is made with a view to private gain is subject to debate, but there are those who would label such behavior as organizational corruption.

That it is often the regulated who threaten the regulators is further supported by the history of other federal independent regulatory agencies. The standard assumption that the regulatory agencies were all created to control deviance in a recalcitrant industry may only be true for some of the agencies, such as the Interstate Commerce Commission (Chatov, 1975:97; but see Stone, 1975:107; and Skolnick, 1978:166). Many others were created with the active support of the industries themselves in order to insure predictability and stable profits (Conklin, 1977:122). Both the Civil Aeronautics Board and the Federal Communications Commission, for example, have been described as having been "established by the regulated industries to operate a cartel in their behalf, and both have behaved according to the expectations of their creators, restricting entry and maintaining prices and industry profits" (Chatov, 1975:97).

Similarly, some gangsters have been able to use local police departments to guarantee themselves a monopoly on the local vice and gambling industries. Dependent on gangsters such as "Wincanton's" Irv Stern (Gardiner, 1970:23) for campaign contributions necessary to get elected, Mayors and City Council members sometimes allow the gangsters to set law enforcement policy and to choose top police officials. The high police officials then misuse their public authority for their own personal gain (in payoffs from the gangsters), but lower level officers may be compelled to misuse their public authority for the personal gain of the elective officials and their police superiors, not themselves (Gardiner, 1970:25; Sherman, 1978:36). The elective officials' dependence on campaign contributions leads them to co-opt the gangsters who then make corruption an operative organizational goal of the police department.

MODEL II: CAPTURE BY EXTERNAL EXPLOITERS OF CONTROL

A second pattern of social control corruption is capture: the exploitation of the agency's authority for the financial gain of outsiders who control significant resources of the agency. Unlike the co-optation of gambling organizations and airlines which use social control agencies as tools to restrict competition and to maintain price levels, politicians capture social control agencies to use them as marketable commodities. While some politicians may be so dependent on one source of campaign contributions (such as "Wincanton's" gangster boss, Irv Stern) that they are forced to co-opt that source, others may have a variety of sources of campaign funds interested in the policies and practices of the social control agencies under the control of elective officials.

Under those conditions, politicians need not co-opt anyone; they can sell control policy to the highest bidder, sometimes even on a case by case basis.

The exploitation of control power for the financial gain of politicians is only possible when the politicians have "captured" the control agency (Thompson, 1967:30, 37). That is, it is only when the politicians—either elective officials or party leaders (or any other environmental actors controlling organizational resources, for that matter)—have such complete power to constrain almost any action by the social control agency that the captors can market those actions. Not all social control agencies are captives of their environments. Some of them, including all of those described below under Model III, have a good deal of autonomy and insulation from environmental domination. Others may generally operate without interference, but they have the potential for capture whenever elective officials or others choose to interfere. Still others are directed on almost a day to day basis by elective and political party officials.

The basic tool of capture is control over jobs, both how many there will be and who will fill them. Enforcement personnel comprise the vital resource of social control agencies, and the loyalties of the personnel selected can do much to shape the character of those organizations. Where this resource is largely under the control of the agency itself, capture seems to be very rare. Where it is under the control of another autonomous agency, such as a civil service commission, capture also seems rare. But where elective and party officials obtain direct control over personnel, capture of the social control agency appears to be quite common.

The classic case of selling the law enforcement decisions of a captive social control agency is the politically-dominated corrupt police department. As described by Royko (1972), Fogelson (1977) and Sherman (1978), these police departments vary somewhat in the precise form of their political domination, but in all of them some aspects of the personnel process are controlled by outsiders and are used to influence enforcement decisions. In the nineteenth century police departments Fogelson (1977) describes, the political machines determined every aspect of every police officer's career, from hiring to assignment and promotion. In Sherman's (1978:35) study of the contemporary "Central City" Police Department, however, only promotions and assignments (and not hiring) were found to be under political control; and his study of the Oakland Police Department of the early 1950s found only assignment to be subject to political influence. Nevertheless, in each of these cases, patrol officers were ordered by their superiors to ignore law violations at certain vice establishments that paid the politicians controlling the police departments for the privilege to operate without police interference.[5]

While some police departments may be under the day to day direction of political figures for corrupt purposes, other social control agencies may only occasionally be captured for corrupt exploitation. In the U.S. Justice Department, for example, few antitrust prosecution decisions seem to be influenced by attempts of the President or his party leaders to sell the decisions to the organizations they threaten. Yet during the antitrust prosecution of International Telephone and Telegraph for its acquisition of the Hartford Fire Insurance Company, former President Nixon did just that: he directly ordered the (presidentially appointed) Attorney General not to prosecute the case, and negotiated a sizable campaign contribution from I.T.T. at about the same time (New York Times, 1974). Similar campaign contributions to the Nixon administration in return for aid in the federal prosecution of the contributor occurred with the S.E.C. (Sale, 1977:248)

---

5. A question beyond the scope of this paper is the nature of the process by which organizations are captured. In the case of urban police departments, however, the answer is very simple: they were created as captive organizations by the white Anglo-Saxon Protestant political machines which first established them to control the newer immigrants (Levett, 1975). The more interesting question, perhaps, is the nature of the process by which police departments were successfully liberated from external capture (see Fogelson, 1977; Sherman, 1978).

and other regulatory agencies, although the evidence of direct capture of the decision-making process by the President is less clear in those cases.

Even without blatant sale of particular decisions, of course, Presidents and their political aides can sell regulatory authority to regulated industries. When Nixon aide Herbert Kalmbach solicited corporate contributions for the 1972 campaign, he allegedly forced the corporations to give much more than they had planned by threatening to use the regulatory agencies against their interests (New York Times, 1973). Whether all such threats could have been implemented may be open to some question, given the civil service selection and tenure of regulatory agency employees (though not of the commissioners or board members); but judging by the Nixon administration's apparently successful capture of the National Transportation Safety Board—by installing what one career civil servant described as "the White House Mafia, the guys who were put in these agencies to get rid of people like me" (Berger, 1977:244)—the threats may well have been deliverable. If *any* of the enforcement decisions were influenced by the campaign contributions, then that behavior clearly constituted organizational corruption.

MODEL III: DOMINATION BY INTERNAL EXPLOITERS OF CONTROL

The political capture of social control agencies would not surprise the good-government reformers of the progressive era, whose solution to that problem was to insulate the agencies from political influence as much as possible. What would surprise them, however, is that even highly autonomous agencies of social control have adopted deviant goals and become organizationally corrupt. The dominant administrative coalitions of these "sheltered" (Thompson, 1967:152) organizations[6] have been taken over by organizational members who support the goal of personally profiting from the sale of law enforcement decisions. Where organizational members do not have to compete with outside captors, they may take advantage of the opportunity to exploit the power of official control for their own personal gain.

Certain police departments provide a classic example of this pattern. They also show how the autonomy necessary for this process of becoming corrupt need not be entirely formal or legal in nature. In New York City, for example, the historically corrupt police department has apparently been free from political capture for the sale of law enforcement decisions since Mayor O'Dwyer was almost indicted during a gambling payoff scandal in the early 1950s (Mockridge and Prall, 1954). The department went right on selling enforcement immunity for the gain of its own members, however, even after the political involvement ceased (Knapp, 1972). Even during the heyday of Tammany Hall, for that matter, the New York police were able to attain a fair amount of autonomy from political capture, apparently keeping the lion's share of the graft within the department (Steffens, 1931:248).

The Cincinnati Police Department would surprise the progressives even more. Restructured according to their ideal plan to provide almost complete isolation from politics, that department provided for civil service selection and promotion up to and including the rank of chief. Even the City Manager cannot remove the police chief except for cause, a structure that has been strongly endorsed by the International Association of Chiefs of Police (1976). For years, Cincinnati was widely reputed in police circles to have one of the most honest police departments in the country (Reppetto, 1970), a fact attributed to its great autonomy. In 1975, however, nine police officers alleged that a police chief had been selling arrest immunity to a number of vice establishments and directing enforcement policy accordingly (New York Times, 1975); the chief was later convicted on related criminal charges. The chief apparently imposed deviant operative goals on the

---

6. These organizations are, of course, still open to a variety of influences, but they are sheltered from direct external control of personnel promotions and assignments.

organization despite its apparent climate of integrity and (or perhaps because of) its great autonomy.

The federal-level law enforcement agencies, such as the Federal Bureau of Investigation and the Drug Enforcement Agency, have also experienced the same pattern of organizational corruption. Renowned for the high "quality" and college education of their agents as well as their general freedom from political interference, federal police agencies are often thought of as being above corruption. Yet that is far from true. The federal Drug Enforcement Agency has had a continuing problem of organizational corruption since the 1930s (Epstein, 1977:104–105). Similar problems have been found in the U.S. Immigration and Naturalization Service (New York Times, 1973). In one of the most extreme cases of organizational autonomy in federal law enforcement, the Federal Bureau of Investigation (which makes all its own personnel decisions internally) has recently lost its corruption-free image in a series of allegations from FBI agents (Crewdson, 1979; New York Times, 1979).

Internal domination by exploiters of control is not confined to police agencies. Civil service building inspectors in New York City, working without any political control, developed an almost universal practice of extorting bribes for issuing certificates of occupancy (Shipler, 1972), for which the majority of the building inspectors working in Manhattan between 1972 and 1974 were indicted (Ranzal, 1974). Grain inspectors officially licensed by the U.S. Department of Agriculture have developed a pattern of taking bribes to overlook violations (Robbins, 1975). Wherever organizations combine regulatory powers and a relatively sheltered system of organizational control from within, the potential for this pattern of corruption seems to be present.

PREDICTING THE MODELS

These three models demonstrate that there are a variety of conditions under which social control agencies adopt deviant operative goals and become organizationally corrupt. The brief illustrative material presented here probably identifies only a few of the possible conditions, and certainly fails to identify all of the necessary conditions of each model. As a first step towards explaining organizational corruption in social control agencies, however, three hypotheses can be induced from the models:

H_1: The more social control agencies depend upon their subjects to accomplish their formal goals, the more likely it is that organizational corruption will arise, if at all, through co-optation of the subjects of control.

H_2: The more vulnerable social control agencies' personnel decisions are to external manipulation, the more likely it is that organizational corruption will arise, if at all, through external capture of the agencies for the sale of enforcement decisions.

H_3: The more sheltered social control agencies are from dependence on outsiders, the more likely it is that organizational corruption will arise, if at all, through internal domination by sellers of enforcement decisions.

None of these hypotheses can predict *whether* a social control agency will become organizationally corrupt; they merely predict the model by which corruption would occur if it did arise. Indeed, hypotheses 2 and 3, if used to predict corruption, would lead to contradictory predictions: both an open system (H_2) and a closed system (H_3) will lead to organizational corruption. What is missing from both the hypotheses and the models is specification of the conditions under which threatened agencies do *not* corruptly co-opt their subjects of control, under which agencies with externally controlled personnel decisions are *not* captured by politicians, and under which highly autonomous agencies are *not* dominated by internal exploiters of regulatory authority. The concepts taken from the sociology of organizations help us understand why each of the

488   SHERMAN

models occur, but they do not explain why corruption does not occur when the conditions of each model are present.

The additional conditions needed to predict whether a social control agency will become corrupt might be drawn from a variety of types of explanation of crime borrowed from the individual level of analysis: differences in deterrence (Gibbs, 1975), opportunities to commit crime (Wilkins, 1965), or perhaps even the strength of organizational bonds to conventional social norms (Hirschi, 1969). Alternatively, explanations of organizational goal setting stressing the political economy of organizations (Zaid, 1970) and organizational conflict (Pfeffer, 1978) might be applied, although this explanatory perspective is even further away from being a theory than are explanations of individual criminality (Perrow, 1972).

Whatever direction theories of the organizational adoption of deviant operative goals may take, there would seem to be two priorities for theory construction. First, criminological concepts that apply only to the individuals must be separated from those appropriate for both levels of analysis. Sutherland once pointed out (in the unfair context of attempting to discredit psychoanalytic theory as an explanation of any crime) that it is unlikely that "the crimes of the Ford Motor Company are due to the Oedipus Complex, or those of the Aluminum Company of America to an Inferiority Complex" (1949:257). Yet there are many concepts used to explain individual crime, from commitment to stigma, which may well be applicable at the organizational level as well. The second task for theory construction is to identify those concepts which are only applicable at the organizational level of analysis. With more attention to such distinctively organizational issues as control of resources, conflicts over goals and the formation of dominant coalitions, as well as to the relevant explanations of individual crime, we may begin to understand the causes as well as the forms of organizational deviance.

REFERENCES

Aldrich, Howard E.
  1979   Organizations And Environments. Englewood Cliffs, N.J.: Prentice-Hall.
Berger, Dan
  1977   "Lethal smokescreen." Pp. 238–249 in J. D. Douglas and J. D. Grant (eds.), Official Deviance. Philadelphia: J. B. Lippincott.
Black, Donald
  1979   "Comment: Common sense in the sociology of law." American Sociological Review 44(1):18–27.
Bloch, Herbert A. and Gilbert Geis
  1970   Man, Crime and Society. New York: Random House.
Burnham, David
  1975   "Duality of appointments to U.S. agencies scored." The New York Times, November 7:14.
Chatov, Robert
  1975   Corporate Financial Reporting: Public or Private Control? New York: Free Press.
Cohen, Albert K.
  1966   Deviance and Control. Englewood Cliffs, N.J.: Prentice-Hall.
Coleman, James S.
  1973   "Loss of power." American Sociological Review 38:1–17.
  1974   Power and the Structure of Society. New York: W. W. Norton.
Conklin, John E.
  1977   'Illegal But Not Criminal': Business Crime In America. Englewood Cliffs, N.J.: Prentice-Hall.
Crewdson, John M.
  1979   "Former FBI agent tells investigators of widespread abuse and corruption." New York Times, January 20:8.
Dalton, Melville
  1959   Men Who Manage. New York: J. W. Wiley.
Epstein, Edward J.
  1977   Agency of Fear: Opiates and Political Power in America. New York: G. P. Putnam.
Erikson, Kai T.
  1976   Everything In Its Path: Destruction of Community in the Buffalo Creek Flood. New York: Simon and Schuster.

Ermann, M. David and Richard Lundman (eds.)
   1978   Corporate and Governmental Deviance: Problems of Organizational Behavior In Contemporary
           Society. New York: Oxford University Press.
Farberman, Harvey
   1975   "A criminogenic market structure: The automobile industry." Sociological Quarterly 16:438-57.
Fogelson, Robert
   1977   Big City Police. Cambridge: Harvard University Press.
Gardiner, John A.
   1970   The Politics of Corruption: Organized Crime in an American City. New York: Russell Sage Foun-
           dation.
Geis, Gilbert
   1962   "Toward a delineation of white collar offenses." Sociological Inquiry 32 (Spring):159-171.
   1977   "The heavy electrical equipment antitrust cases of 1961." Pp. 117-132 in G. Geis and R. F.
   [1967] Meier (eds.), White Collar Crime: Offenses in Business, Politics and the Professions. New York:
           Free Press.
Gibbs, Jack
   1975   Crime, Punishment, and Deterrence. New York: Elsevier.
Goldstein, Herman
   1975   Police Corruption: A Perspective On Its Nature And Control. Washington, D.C.: Police Founda-
           tion.
Gottfredson, Michael R. and Michael J. Hindelang
   1979a   "A study of the behavior of law." American Sociological Review 44(1):3-18.
   1979b   "Response: Theory and research in the sociology of law." American Sociological Review
           44(1):27-37.
Hall, Richard H.
   1977   Organizations: Structure and Process (2d. ed.). Englewood Cliffs, N.J.: Prentice-Hall.
Harvard Law Review
   1979a   "Campaign contributions and federal bribery law." Harvard Law Review 92(2):451-469.
   1979b   "Corporate crime: Regulating corporate behavior through criminal sanctions." Harvard Law
           Review 92(6):1227-1375.
Heidenheimer, Arnold J.
   1970   Political Corruption: Readings in Comparative Analysis. New York: Holt, Rinehart and Winston.
Hirschi, Travis
   1969   Causes of Delinquency. Berkeley: University of California Press.
International Association of Chiefs of Police
   1976   The Police Chief Executive Report. Washington, D.C.: U.S. Law Enforcement Assistance Ad-
           ministration.
Knapp, Whitman et al.
   1972   Report of the Commission to Investigate Allegations of Police Corruption and the City's Anti-
           Corruption Procedures. New York: Braziller.
Lane, Robert E.
   1977   "Why businessmen violate the law." Pp. 102-111 in G. Geis and R. Meier (eds.), White Collar
   [1953] Crime. New York: Free Press.
Laurie, Peter
   1970   Scotland Yard: A Personal Inquiry. London: The Bodley Head.
Leavitt, Harold J., William R. Dill and Henry B. Eyring
   1978   "Rulemakers and referees." Pp. 259-277 in M. D. Ermann and R. J. Lundman (eds.), Corporate
           and Governmental Deviance. New York: Oxford University Press.
Leonard, William N. and Marvin Glenn Weber
   1977   "Automakers and dealers: A study of criminogenic market forces." Pp. 133-148 in G. Geis and
   [1970] R. Meier (eds.), White Collar Crime. New York: Free Press.
Levett, Alan E.
   1975   "Centralization of city police in the nineteenth century United States." Doctoral dissertation,
           Department of Sociology, University of Michigan.
Lundman, Richard
   1979   "Police misconduct as organizational deviance." Law and Policy Quarterly l(1):81-100.
Mars, Geralds
   1973   "Hotel pilferage: A case study in occupational theft." Pp. 200-210 in Malcolm Warner (ed.),
           Sociology of the Workplace: An Interdisciplinary Approach. London: Allen and Unwin.
Marx, Gary T.
   1972   "Civil disorder and the agents of social control." Pp. 75-97 in Gary T. Marx (ed.), Muckraking
           Sociology. New Brunswick; N.J.: Transaction Books.
Merton, Robert K.
   1968   Social Theory and Social Structure. New York: Free Press.

Mockridge, Norton and Robert H. Prall
    1954   The Big Fix. New York: Henry Holt.
New York Times
    1979   "Ex-agent, alleging cover-up, sues FBI." Feb. 18:23.
    1975   "Jury indicts chief." Dec. 19:20.
    1974   "Kleindienst admits misdemeanor." May 17:1.
    1973   "Airline discloses illegal donation." July 7:1.
    1973   "Justice officials find corruption rife." May 21:1.
Parisi, Anthony J.
    1979   "Oil giants are worrying all the way to the bank." New York Times, March 11:3-1, 11.
Pearson, Jessica S.
    1978   "Organizational response to occupational injury and disease: The case of the uranium industry."
            Social Forces 57(1):23-41.
Perrow, Charles
    1972   Complex Organizations: A Critical Essay. Glenview, Ill.: Scott, Foresman.
Pfeffer, Jeffrey
    1978   "The micropolitics of organizations." Pp. 29-50 in Marshall W. Meyer and Associates, En-
            vironments and Organizations. San Francisco: Jossey-Bass.
Ranzal, Edwards
    1974   "City report finds building industry infested by graft." New York Times, November 8:1.
Raw, Charles, Godfrey Hodgson and Bruce Page
    1972   Do You Sincerely Want To Be Rich? Bernard Kornfeld and I.O.S.: An International Swindle.
            Newton Abbot: Readers Union.
Rawls, John
    1971   A Theory of Justice. Cambridge, Mass.: Harvard University Press.
Reiss, Albert J., Jr.
    1966   "The study of deviant behavior: Where the action is." The Ohio Valley Sociologist 32:1-12.
Reppetto, Thomas A.
    1970   "Changing the system: Models of municipal police organization." Doctoral dissertation, Harvard
            University.
Robbins, William
    1975   "Europe grain men press complaints." The New York Times, June 6:1, 36.
Royko, Mike
    1972   Boss: Richard J. Daley of Chicago. London: Paladin.
Sale, Kirkpatrick
    1977   "The world behind Watergate." Pp. 240-252 in G. Geis and R. Meier (eds.), White Collar Crime.
            New York: Free Press.
Schrager, Laura Shill and James F. Short, Jr.
    1978   "Toward a sociology of organizational crime." Social Problems 25(4):407-419.
Selznick, Philip
    1949   TVA and the Grass Roots: A Study in the Sociology of Formal Organization. Berkeley: University
            of California Press.
Shapiro, Susan
    1976   "A background paper on white collar crime." Unpublished manuscript, Yale University.
Sherman, Lawrence W.
    1978   Scandal and Reform: Controlling Police Corruption. Berkeley: University of California Press.
Shipler, David K.
    1972   "Study finds $25 million yearly in bribes is paid by city's construction industry." The New York
            Times, June 26: 1, 26.
Shover, Neal
    1978   "Defining organizational crime." Pp. 37-40 in M. D. Ermann and R. J. Lundman (eds.), Cor-
            porate and Governmental Deviance. New York: Oxford University Press.
Simon, Herbert A.
    1964   "On the concept of organizational goal." Administrative Science Quarterly 9(1):1-22.
Skolnick, Jerome H.
    1966   Justice Without Trial: Law Enforcement In Democratic Society. New York: Wiley.
    1978   House of Cards: The Legalization And Control Of Casino Gambling. Boston: Little, Brown.
Sonnenfeld, Jeffrey and Paul R. Lawrence
    1978   "Why do companies succumb to price-fixing?" Harvard Business Review 56(4):145-157.
Stead, Philip John
    1957   The Police of Paris. London: Staples.
Steffens, Lincoln
    1931   Autobiography. New York: Harcourt, Brace.
Stone, Christopher D.
    1975   Where the Law Ends: The Social Control of Corporate Behavior. New York: Harper and Row.

Sutherland, Edwin H.
  1937   The Professional Thief. Chicago: University of Chicago Press.
  1940   "White collar criminality." American Sociological Review 5:1-12.
  1945   "Is 'white collar crime' crime?" American Sociological Review 10 (April):132-139.
  1949   White Collar Crime. New York: Holt, Rinehart and Winston.
Tappan, Paul
  1947   "Who is the criminal?" American Sociological Review 12 (February):96-102.
Thompson, James D.
  1967   Organizations In Action. New York: McGraw-Hill.
Warriner, Charles K.
  1956   "Groups are real: A reaffirmation." American Sociological Review 21(5):549-554.
Westley, William A.
  1970   Violence and the Police. Cambridge, Mass.: Massachusetts Institute of Technology Press.
Wheeler, Stanton
  1976   "Trends and problems in the sociological study of crime." Social Problems 23(5):525-534.
Wilkins, Leslie T.
  1965   Social Deviance. London: Tavistock.
Zald, Mayer N.
  1970   Organizational Change: The Political Economy of the YMCA. Chicago: University of Chicago
          Press.

[21]

ANNALS, *AAPSS*, 474, July 1984

Police Regulation of Illegal Gambling: Frustrations of Symbolic Enforcement

By PETER REUTER

ABSTRACT: This article examines problems presented to the police by their gambling enforcement responsibilities during the four decades following Prohibition's repeal. In this period repeated gambling corruption scandals put the police in disrepute. These scandals accurately reflected the underlying corruption of an effort that was essentially symbolic and not supported by a significant element of the otherwise law-abiding population. The fundamental source of the corruption was the vulnerability of all illegal gambling organizations to police harassment. This corruption also contributed to organized crime's dominance in illegal gambling. The federal government mounted a major campaign against illegal gambling between 1962 and 1972. That effort failed to reduce the availability of gambling services but may have helped reduce the dominance of organized crime by depriving local police of their ability to franchise monopolies. Together with changing attitudes toward gambling, the entry of the state into many gambling markets, and changes in the nature of the games themselves, the federal enforcement effort helped end the era in which gambling enforcement was a major responsibility for the police.

Peter Reuter is a senior economist with the Rand Corporation in Washington, DC. His major research interests are the organization of illegal activities and the national income consequences of tax evasion. He is the author of Disorganized Crime: The Economics of the Visible Hand.

T HE moralistic legislatures of this nation have given American police a singularly heavy burden to regulate large-scale markets for illegal goods and services. From the prostitution that was so prominent a feature of American cities at the turn of the century to the markets for marijuana and cocaine that have become so pervasive since the 1970s, the police of this nation have always been required to devote a substantial effort to making it more difficult for large numbers of otherwise law-abiding citizens to buy certain goods and services.

Mass illegal markets present two generic problems to police. The first is that a significant portion of the population that otherwise cooperates with law enforcement disapproves of this police activity. The second is that there is rarely a complainant to initiate police action. Most police law enforcement is initiated by someone who is adversely affected by the crime and is in a position to bring an informative complaint, but illegal markets do not generate informative complaints. Rigorous enforcement is made unpopular by the first factor and difficult by the second.

Gambling was the most important illegal market for the police during the period from the repeal of Prohibition in 1933 to about 1970.[1] During that time, no responsibility posed a greater threat to the autonomy of police executives. Though gambling never consumed a large share of police resources, the constant threat of a gambling corruption scandal forced police managers to create

complex monitoring systems to assure that their departments could present a credible picture of aggressive and honest gambling enforcement. Given that the goals of enforcement were never articulated in a positive sense, the result was that the effort had a largely ritualistic quality to it, and the corruption problem was, if anything, exacerbated.

The era of intense gambling enforcement has passed. Not only have the numbers of gambling arrests declined,[2] but the prominence assigned to gambling in popular and political ratings of police departments has sharply diminished. It is now simply a minor duty of the police, accomplished with few resources and posing little threat of scandal.

This article reviews the problems that gambling enforcement posed to police departments during the period from 1933 to about 1970. It draws heavily on the experience of the New York Police Department, simply because more and better information is available for that department than for any other.[3] In describing the formalism and emptiness of local gambling enforcement, the article deals with familiar matters and reaches familiar conclusions.

More novel perhaps is the review here of federal intervention in gambling enforcement. Over a ten-year period, 1962-72, asserting the corruption of local efforts and the importance of gambling to organized crime, the Department of Justice made illegal gam-

---

1. Dating the end of the period is arbitrary. No single event ended it. There is justification for designating 1970 the date of the latest major New York gambling corruption scandal and the year in which non-heroin drug arrests began their great increase.

2. In 1960 the *Uniform Crime Reports* estimated 145,000 gambling arrests nationwide. By 1980 that figure had declined to 38,000. Estimates prior to 1960 are unreliable.

3. A major source on New York for the second half of the period is Alan Kornblum, *The Moral Hazards* (Lexington, MA: D. C. Heath, 1976).

bling the target of an expanded federal involvement in criminal law enforcement. The failure of this effort has its origins in some of the same factors that limited the effectiveness of local efforts: the ambivalence of many toward the impropriety of illegal gambling per se and the inability of agencies to show that enforcement had any significant effect on the targeted activity.

The failure of the federal effort also raised the issue of the true relationship between illegal gambling and organized crime. Some arguments are presented here to explain why that relationship may have changed over time, particularly as the result of alterations in the structure of politics and law enforcement.

THE GAMES AND THEIR STRUCTURE

Throughout the period we are considering, there was relatively little change in the major types of gambling offered illegally. Numbers, bookmaking, and casino games were all important, though illegal casinos declined after 1960.[4]

The common characteristics of all the games were that they required a fixed location and schedule. The bettor had to be able to come to a particular place at a particular time to place his or her bet. This made the gambling organization vulnerable to police intervention at precisely that point. The numbers collector could be easily identified by the flow of traffic at mid-morning. A large number of persons entering a retail store between 10:00 and 11:00 a.m. and emerging without any visible purchase would

immediately identify the store as a numbers outlet. The casino was, of course, even more obvious because it often required relatively elaborate facilities and generated a great deal of traffic at night. Bookmakers were vulnerable also at their own premises, which were often subject to elaborate protection for just that reason.[5]

GAMBLING CORRUPTION

Gambling operators, then, were strongly motivated to make payments to ensure that the police did not interrupt the routine operation of their businesses. The numbers banker, with collectors possibly dispersed throughout the city, needed protection from very large numbers of police, since the patrol cop in the neighborhood of any of his collectors posed a threat; the officer might seize not only the collector but also the pickup man that the banker dispatched to receive the day's betting slips. The individual casino did not need as wide a net of protection but certainly required the negation of all the officers in the precinct, since the rotation of officers assured that many of them would, at some time in their precinct assignment, become aware of its operation.

Thus the peculiar threat of illegal gambling to police integrity was its need for systematic and large-scale protection. A thief caught in the act may try to buy off the arresting officer. If the officer succumbs to the offer, that is the end of the matter; he does not need to involve any other police officer. That was not the case with respect to gambling. The corruption was effective only

4. A more detailed description of the operation and structure of numbers and bookmaking is contained in Peter Reuter, *Disorganized Crime: The Economics of the Visible Hand* (Cambridge, MA: MIT Press, 1983), chaps. 2 and 3.

5. The film *The Sting* provides a good depiction of the kinds of props that went into a bookmaker's parlor.

if all the officers in a position to enforce the law against the particular gambling business agreed to cooperate. A single zealous officer could put all his corrupt colleagues at risk. Thus there was a strong continued interest in testing the willingness of new officers to at least tolerate the ongoing corruption of the rest of the group.

We have a number of accounts of the working of this kind of systematic corruption. Whyte's classic study of organized crime in a Boston neighborhood, "Cornerville," offers perhaps the most detailed description of the organization of police protection of gambling operations.[6] The policeman who was unwilling to go along with the existing corruption might find himself transferred to patrol duty in the cemetery or given punitive overtime. Twenty-five years later the Knapp Commission,[7] investigating corruption in the New York Police Department, found similar protection of gambling throughout the city. In one instance, 24 out of 25 plainclothesmen— essentially specialized vice control officers—in an individual precinct were indicted for accepting payments from local gamblers.

Perhaps the account that best conveys the routinized character of gambling corruption is that of Rubinstein, dealing with the Philadelphia Police Department at the end of the 1960s. He described in detail the initiation process that a rookie went through before being included in the regular system of payoffs, a process that might take six months.

6. William F. Whyte, *Street Corner Society* (Chicago: University of Chicago Press, 1943).

7. Commission to Investigate Allegations of Police Corruption and the City's Anti-Corruption Program, *Report* (New York: George Braziller, 1973).

But he also underscored the petty nature of the payments.

One officer in a district which had a reputation for being one of the most "active" in the city estimated that he earned about ninety dollars a month in regular payoffs. . . . It can safely be assumed that his sergeant and lieutenant were earning at least double or triple his take.[8]

These were hardly significant sums.

The other disturbing feature of gambling corruption was that it reached beyond the police themselves. Gambling organizations were closely allied to political parties. Gamblers assured themselves of police protection by providing assistance to political figures; a zealous senior police officer might find himself called by a city council member, who had been supported financially in elections by the same gambling enterprise that the officer was currently harassing. This feature seems to have been much less prominent in the latter part of the period than in the earlier, for reasons we shall discuss in the following section.

The ability of gamblers to achieve political alliances, just like the general willingness of police to accept moneys from gamblers, was affected by the ambivalent moral status of gamblers and gambling during the period. Though there was little support for the legalization of gambling, apart from parimutuel betting at the racetrack, there was also a strong base of tolerance for gambling itself. This was particularly true among Irish immigrants, who were prominent in both police and urban politics during the first half of this century. Police and politicians who might resist allying themselves with the operators of brothels or heroin dealers had

8. Jonathan Rubinstein, *City Police* (New York: Farrar, Straus and Giroux, 1973), p. 390.

little hesitation in taking money from bookmakers or casino operators.

Moreover, the political alliance reflected the fact that some gambling operators had considerable organizational assets. The large numbers of retailers provided a very effective pool of labor for getting out the vote on election days.[9] It is also likely that the retailers had a certain status in the community, which made them effective advocates for the political organization supported by their banker. Block, in describing the evolution of the organization of illegal gambling in New York City, stresses the strength of the relationship between some of the major gambling organizations and the political machine of Tammany Hall.[10] A persuasive account of the ease with which New York detectives entered into corrupt relations with gamblers is provided by Reardon,[11] a central participant in the notorious Harry Gross scandal of 1950.

Senior police administrators were acutely conscious of the problems presented by gambling enforcement. No other responsibility was so likely to produce a major scandal. On the one hand, it was important to provide the appearance of rigorous enforcement; other-

wise, the department was assumed to be corrupt. On the other hand, the more intense the enforcement, the deeper the corruption it might engender.

The solution was highly ritualized enforcement practices. As usual, our best information concerns New York City. Kornblum describes in interesting detail the constant reorganization of the New York Police Department's gambling effort during the period 1950-70.[12] Though in theory every police officer had some gambling enforcement responsibility, patrol officers restricted their arrest activities to nuisance gambling, such as sidewalk card and dice games. The enforcement of laws against professional gambling organizations was given over to specialized units, the plainclothes squads. These were attached to all the various levels of command, from precinct to headquarters. They were notoriously corrupt units, and honest officers could only be recruited into them by the claim, which was correctly disbelieved, that this was a necessary step to becoming a detective and getting out of the uniformed branch.

One component of the solution to the control problem was to impose quotas on the plainclothesmen. They were required to make a certain number of gambling arrests every month. This assured at least a minimum amount of visible enforcement activity. Of course, it did nothing to prevent corruption. The plainclothesmen and gamblers worked out arrangements for the arrest of "stand-ins," persons of minor importance to the gambling business who agreed to be arrested—which imposed trivial risk of anything more serious than a modest fine—in return for some small amount of money.

---

9. Referring to an earlier period, 1880 to 1905, Haller says, "In many neighborhoods, it was not so much that gambling syndicates influenced local political organizations: rather gambling syndicates *were* the local political organizations." Mark Haller, "The Changing Structure of American Gambling in the Twentieth Century," *Journal of Social Issues,* 35(3):88 (1979).

10. Alan Block, *East Side-West Side* (Cardiff: University of Cardiff Press, 1980).

11. James Reardon, *The Sweet Life of Jimmy Riley* (New York: Wyndham Books, 1980). Though writing in the form of a novel, Reardon, who was convicted on corruption charges, uses actual names for most participants and clearly intends to provide his own account of what happened.

12. Kornblum, *Moral Hazards.*

Efforts to prevent this through centralized control were unsuccessful. The creation of an enormous central file system of known gamblers, or KGs, did not help. The KGs, of course, included all those persons who had previously been arrested for gambling, including the many stand-ins. The requirement that individual officers report on vice conditions in their area and check on all KGs on a regular basis did little to provide a method for monitoring the efficacy and integrity of gambling enforcement. There were in fact no objective indicators available to the central authority. The result was an enormous amount of worthless paperwork that simply reiterated the formal detail of corrupt gambling enforcement.

These corruption-control measures also made effective investigation more difficult. Given the lack of a plaintiff, the precautions adopted by gambling operators, and the lack of credible threats against arrested low-level employees, making it difficult to recruit them as informants, the gambling investigator faced substantial problems in trying to make a case against the bookmaker or numbers banker himself. The most plausible technique—undercover investigation—in which a police officer infiltrates the gambling milieu, was not an acceptable technique to senior management, whose prime concern was to avert scandal. Undercover officers required just the kind of unmonitored contact with gamblers that management attempted to prevent.

Even lower-level arrests presented serious difficulties for honest officers.

If the patrolman has no information regarding gambling, the only evidence he can look for is an exchange of money on the street or a person jotting something on a slip of paper. These acts could represent anything; nobody would argue that even in neighborhoods where gambling is common are they practiced exclusively by bookies or numbers writers.[13]

To make gambling arrests, the officer had to perjure himself. It may be argued that these management-induced illegalities were an important contribution to the process of corruption among police.

Prosecutors and judges

So far, only the problems that gambling presented to the police have been discussed. Other components of the criminal justice system—prosecutors and judges—did not face similar difficulties. While there is evidence of some corruption arising from their gambling responsibilities, it was in large part a police problem. The reasons are of some interest.

Judges have been unwilling for some decades to impose significant penalties on convicted gamblers. Dealing with the end of the 1933-70 period, Lasswell and McKenna found that not a single one of the 19,500 persons arrested on felony gambling charges in New York State between 1964 and 1969 received a state prison sentence.[14] Given the small threat posed by judicial sentencing practices, it was scarcely necessary to make payments to judges.

Prosecutors, similarly, were little interested in gambling cases. New York City provides a particularly interesting illustration of this. Despite the fact that the New York district attorney's office was the national leader in organized

13. Rubinstein, *City Police*, p. 379.
14. Harold Lasswell and Jeremiah McKenna, *Organized Crime in an Inner City Community* (Springfield, VA: National Technical Information Service, 1972).

42

crime investigations and routinely espoused the orthodox belief that illegal gambling was the most important activity of organized crime, little attention was in fact paid to gambling cases by the famous Rackets Bureau. Instead, most gambling cases during the 1950s and early 1960s were handled in a special gamblers' court. This was used as a training ground for new assistant district attorneys, who might handle 10 misdemeanor gambling cases in a day, watching police routinely perjure themselves in presenting formulaic evidence.

The distinction between the roles of police and prosecutors arose largely from the fact that the police could inflict significant harm on illegal gambling operations even without bringing a case to court. The arrest of persons holding gambling records was a serious inconvenience. For bookmakers it often involved payment of false claims to bettors who knew that a raid had occurred and that their claims could not be checked.[15] Numbers bankers did not usually pay claims on the day of a raid, but the raid did cause loss of money and consumer goodwill, as well as legal expenses for agents who were taken to court. The police had the ability to harass, without the assistance of the courts or prosecutors, and thus were the most important target for corrupt deals.

Were prosecutors unaware of gambling corruption among the police? Clearly, given the intimate involvement of local prosecutors in the workings of political machines, they must have been aware of the general phenomenon. However, they lacked either the tools or

15. Police, aware of this practice among bookmakers in New York, made efforts to ensure that bettors were aware of the raid, so as to maximize the bookmaker's loss from false claims.

the motivation for active prosecution of police corruption. In most cities the prosecutor's investigators were themselves members of the local police departments; enthusiasm for investigating their colleagues was limited. Moreover, corruption cases usually depended on the testimony of some gamblers willing to describe their ongoing relations with the police. There was little with which the prosecutor could threaten, and if they wished to later resume their gambling operations the protection of the police was essential.

Finally, prosecutors were themselves highly politicized figures. The selection of candidates for district attorney was a significant party activity, and party machines, strong through much of the period, were unlikely to choose candidates who would crusade against their gambling allies. The famous investigations of police corruption in New York, such as the Harry Gross scandal in 1950,[16] generally resulted from the actions of external groups—a newspaper in that particular case—rather than prosecutive initiative.

THE FEDERAL EPISODE

The federal government entered the gambling enforcement scene rather late in our period. Prior to 1950 federal authority was limited to very narrow matters, such as the operation of gambling ships, floating casinos that were located off the California coast, beyond state authority, in the 1930s and early 1940s. Then in 1951 a federal tax was placed on most forms of gambling. This was intended both to suppress illegal gambling and to raise significant revenues for the Korean conflict.

16. Kornblum, *Moral Hazards*, chap. 2.

These were clearly contradictory goals; the payment of the tax did not provide the payer with any protection from police enforcement actions. Indeed, until a Supreme Court decision in 1968,[17] it provided information that facilitated investigation. Consequently, it is not surprising that few illegal operators paid the tax. Revenues never came close to the original estimates. The maximum was $10 million in 1953 compared to congressional projections of $400 million per annum. The Internal Revenue Service, which was responsible for collection of the tax, made many criminal cases against gambling operators for failure to file. There is nothing to suggest that this significantly reduced the availability of illegal gambling opportunities to the public.

The passage of the tax was partially justified by the findings of the Kefauver Commission in 1951 that illegal gambling was the most important activity of organized crime. The apparent failure of the Internal Revenue Service to make much headway against organized crime, specifically the Mafia, encouraged Attorney General Robert Kennedy to sponsor a number of bills giving the Federal Bureau of Investigation jurisdiction over interstate gambling operations. A number of spectacular and highly publicized cases were made, and the efficacy of gambling laws as a tool against organized crime was apparently established.[18]

Thus in 1969 the Nixon administration, eager to expand the war against organized crime, as the effort was generally called, introduced a series of bills that even further extended federal jurisdiction over gambling offenses. Now federal prosecutors could bring cases against gambling operations involving more than 5 persons and involving either 30 continuous days of operation or $2000 per day in wagering.[19] This was justified by application of the commerce clause of the Constitution. Organized crime menaced the operation of interstate commerce, and gambling was central to organized crime. This represented only a mildly novel interpretation of a clause that had been much used recently to expand federal jurisdiction into areas long thought of as the sole province of the states.[20]

This extension of federal jurisdiction was also justified by claims of the corruption of local law enforcement. Numerous hearings of the McClellan Committee, following on the spectacular hearings of the Kefauver Committee in the early 1950s, had shown a great deal of local police corruption in the enforcement of gambling laws. This helped ease the passage of the Organized Crime Control Act of 1970.

With these expanded powers, the Federal Bureau of Investigation and the Department of Justice began to focus intense efforts on illegal gambling operations in many cities. The federal Organized Crime Strike Forces, interagency groups headed by career prosecutors, were set up in 17 major cities and initially put most of their resources into investigations of illegal gambling. It is impossible to find data on the allocation of strike force manpower across different offenses, but wiretap figures suggest

17. *Marchetti* v. *U.S.*, 390 U.S. 39, 88 Sup. Ct., 697, 19 L. Ed. 889 (1968).

18. This episode is discussed in Victor Navasky, *Kennedy Justice* (New York: Atheneum, 1971), chap. 10.

19. 18 U.S.C. 1955.

20. For example, the commerce clause is the basis for much of the federal civil rights legislation.

that gambling may have accounted for 60 percent or more of strike force time. Wiretaps, which had been authorized for the first time under the 1968 Safe Streets Act, were initially used almost entirely for gambling cases. In the first four years of the strike forces, which accounted for most of the federal wiretaps, some 72 percent of such surveillances were obtained for gambling offenses.

The federal effort came to an end very rapidly. The gambling cases produced numerous headlines but few prison sentences. Many of the early cases were dismissed as the result of technical problems with the wiretap applications or the operation of the surveillances themselves.[21] Judges were rarely willing to give long prison sentences to convicted gambling operators. Sentences averaged only 20 months, in contrast to, for example, 40 months for marijuana dealers.

By 1978 there were only 6 applications by federal authorities for gambling wiretaps, compared with over 200 annually during the early 1970s. The number of federal gambling indictments showed a similar decline. Despite the continued assertion that illegal gambling is the most significant source of revenue for "traditional organized crime," the current federal euphemism for the Mafia, little effort is made to investigate or prosecute illegal gamblers federally.

There are a number of possible interpretations of this episode in federal enforcement. One is that federal agencies

21. See, for example, the description of one major case provided in Jack Carlisle, "Gambling in Detroit: An Informal History" in *Gambling in America,* Commission on the Review of the National Policy toward Gambling (Washington, DC: Government Printing Office, 1976), app. 1.

simply lagged in their interpretation of the popular significance of illegal gambling. By the time they mounted their most serious effort, popular concern with the activity had diminished. The spread of state-operated lotteries around 1970, though it presented no threat to the revenues of illegal gambling operators, symbolized the end of a moral concern with gambling per se. Judges were unpersuaded by the claims of organized crime evils in sentencing operators whose primary sin they saw as failure to file taxes while competing with the state. The fact that few of those brought to court were either members of, or demonstrably close associates of, the Mafia also weakened the prosecutors' appeals to the judges at sentencing.

Another interpretation stresses the latter aspect. The federal effort explicitly assumed the importance of illegal gambling to the Mafia. Whether such importance ever did exist—and I am inclined to believe that it may have during the 1940s—it was not so clear by the time the federal government became most active. The credibility of the strategy is questionable in view of the continued failure of the federal agencies to show that this premise was correct.

What impact did the federal intervention have on the behavior of local police? A priori one can argue as plausibly that the federal agencies' efforts increased the intensity of local police enforcement as that it reduced the intensity. On the one hand, increased local enforcement might be a defensive response, an attempt to assure that the federal agencies did not show up the local police. Alternatively, the federal enforcement could be seen as cream-skimming; since the better-equipped federal agencies would take all the glamorous cases, local police might lose interest.

Unfortunately, it is not possible to test these hypotheses. For the nation as a whole, gambling arrests continued to decline, as they had done for the whole preceding decade. Analysis of differences between cities in which strike forces were present and those in which they were not has never been carried out. But the failure of the strike force campaign against gambling may be viewed as the final blow against intense gambling enforcement, by any level of government.

ILLEGAL GAMBLING AND ORGANIZED CRIME

From the time of the Kefauver Committee on, it has been held that illegal gambling was in fact the major activity of organized crime. It was argued that this gave a special importance to the suppression of the games, innocuous as they may seem. *The $2 Bet Means Murder,* the title of a book by J. Fred Cook in 1961,[22] presented the argument in its most direct form. Police constantly alleged that the income from gambling permitted participants in organized crime to finance their heroin operations, though no evidence was ever produced for this implausible statement.

The Kefauver Committee certainly made a case for the proposition that the major figures in gambling in a number of cities, such as Miami, Chicago, and Kansas City, were former bootleggers who also had considerable involvement in a number of other criminal activities in the postwar era. The committee asserted that the wire service, the telegraph system that provided bookmakers with the results of horse races throughout the nation, was the instrument for control of bookmaking in the individual cities. The committee's efforts to stitch together a national coordinated conspiracy, the Mafia, that ran this were less successful.

As reinterpreted by Schelling,[23] the committee's findings concerning the role of the wire service in the Mafia's control of bookmakers in particular cities came back to the role of police corruption. Organized crime was parasitic on bookmaking. The wire service provided a device for taxing all bookmakers uniformly. Corrupt police served as the prime instrument for collection of the tax. Arrest could be used as punishment of noncompliant bookmakers for their failure to pay. This also served to meet the police need for visible evidence of their gambling enforcement effort. The division of the spoils between the police and organized crime was a matter of bargaining and organizing initiative.

Slightly different arguments apply to casinos and numbers banks. There was no counterpart to the wire service to provide a connection between the operations of different cities. Probably the police were required to deal more directly with the gambling enterprises themselves. They could not merely collect from the organized crime operators of a wire service, as in bookmaking, but had to levy the tax directly. Indeed, the "bagmen" of the New York gambling squads seem to have been most heavily involved with numbers operations.

Nonetheless, the police allied themselves in many cities with organized crime in controlling the casino and numbers trades. For casinos, the explanation may be that the casino operation required more than just the skills of a gambling operator; the casino offered a

22. J. Fred Cook, *The $2 Bet Means Murder* (New York: Dial Press, 1961).

23. Thomas Schelling, "Economics and Criminal Enterprise," *Public Interest,* no. 7 (1967).

variety of illegal services, including prostitution, loansharking, and illegal liquor. Only broad-based criminal groups could be relied upon to provide all these services and assure that order would be maintained within the establishments, thus reducing the risk of public scandal.

The explanation for the organized crime involvement in numbers is, I believe, different. Haller has argued that, at least in New York, the major bootlegging gangs were able to take over numbers banks previously run by minority groups, in part because they offered more reliable service. Previous operators were undercapitalized.[24] In other instances, it may be that the political value of numbers enterprises with many members, already mentioned, gave political organizations an interest in assuring that they were under the control of gangs with whom they had already built stable alliances, namely the former bootleggers.

These explanations are highly speculative and, given the nature of the subject matter and the difficulty of obtaining documentation, are likely to remain so. However, they suggest that the relationship between organized crime and illegal gambling rested heavily on the necessity for gambling operators to protect themselves from police intervention. They suggest, too, the utility of organized crime in assuring that the relationships between the police and gambling operators were smooth.

They also help explain what appears to be a significant change in the relationship of illegal gambling and organized crime, beginning perhaps as early as the 1960s. A critical aspect of the arrange-

ments we have been describing is that the local police had sole responsibility for gambling enforcement. If the city police could be purchased, then the protection was total. No other agency had the legal and investigative resources to intervene.

This gradually changed over the period 1961-70. As already discussed, federal agencies became heavily involved in gambling enforcement. In a number of states, state police, previously essentially highway patrol agencies, became active criminal investigative agencies. It was no longer possible for local police to provide complete protection. Indeed, these higher-level investigative agencies were acutely interested, at least in some cities, in gambling corruption. That was, after all, one of the bases for Congress's giving the Department of Justice jurisdiction over intrastate gambling operations. Gamblers arrested by these other agencies might well find themselves offered the opportunity to get out of trouble by providing evidence of corruption by local police.

There were other changes that affected the organization of gambling and hence its relationship both to police corruption and organized crime. The growth of sports betting and the decline of horse betting had profound effects. Bookmakers no longer needed the wire service, and bettors had no interest in coming to the bookmaker's premises. Instead, the bookmaker became the operator of a telephone service only; police protection was far less important. Illegal casinos, because they almost all served customers from more than one state, had been badly affected by FBI raids during the early 1960s, under the interstate gambling statutes. The growth of Las Vegas probably also had a substantial negative effect. The breakdown of the

24. Haller, "Changing Structure of American Gambling," pp. 94-95.

old political machines in many cities led to ethnic groups' regaining control of their own numbers banks.

By the end of the 1960s it is likely that gambling had a very different relationship to broad-based criminal gangs such as the Mafia. The changes in the games and the structure of enforcement made it less feasible to use relations with political organizations to exert control over gambling through police corruption. Though many individual members of the gangs remained involved in the operation of particular gambling businesses, it is likely that gambling markets became substantially more competitive by the end of the era.[25]

CONCLUSION

Gambling enforcement was always a burden to the police departments of major American cities. The most that a department could hope for was an occasional arrest of a well-known racketeer and a lack of scandal. Not only could they not achieve their stated goal—suppression of organized gambling—but they could not produce any indicator that they were making any progress toward that goal.

25. The argument and evidence are given in detail in Reuter, *Disorganized Crime*, chap. 8.

The gradual decline in police responsibility for gambling enforcement has many roots. The entry of state governments into various forms of gambling certainly was important. So was the federal campaign against large-scale gambling organizations. I would also speculate that increased popular understanding of the inevitable failure of gambling enforcement and a concern that police devote their limited resources to other, more pressing activities may have been the most significant factors.

In any case, the end result is that gambling is no longer a major problem for local police. Few resources are devoted to it and, except for the occasional large-scale raid, it is given little attention. Narcotics enforcement has apparently taken its place as the responsibility that poses the greatest threat to police autonomy. Fortunately, it appears that changes in the structure of politics, in particular the demise of urban machines, and the different operating routines of drug traffic, in particular the lack of need for continued and systematic protection at the lowest operating level, make it likely that drug dealing will engender less organized corruption than did gambling in its heyday.

[22]
THE BRITISH JOURNAL
OF
CRIMINOLOGY

| Vol. 32 | Winter 1992 | No. 1 |

STREET PROSTITUTION CONTROL

Some Canadian Reflections on the Finsbury Park Experience

JOHN LOWMAN*

In Canada over the past ten years there has been extensive debate about street prostitution. Despite a variety of legal and other attempts to suppress it (including extensive enforcement of a new law making it an offence to 'communicate' in a public place for the purpose of buying or selling sexual services) the street trade persists. In several cities—this paper focuses on Vancouver—a mood of pessimism prevails. In stark contrast to this experience, Roger Matthews has claimed that, during the early 1980s, a 'multi-agency approach' successfully rid London's Finsbury Park of prostitution—and without displacing it to other areas. On the basis of this finding he concludes that prostitution is much more opportunistic than has often been supposed. But can this optimistic conclusion be drawn from the information that he presents to support it? And how should one interpret the very different experience in Vancouver, where there have been fourteen different prostitution strolls in the past ten years, and where the changing geography of street prostitution has been intimately related to law enforcement efforts? This paper sets out to answer such questions.

The content and overall objectives of sections of the Criminal Code relating to prostitution have been the subject of heated debate in Canada over the past ten years. Much of the initial concern was prompted by an apparent increase in street prostitution after a series of Supreme Court of Canada rulings were said to have rendered unenforceable the 'soliciting' law, which made it an offence to 'solicit any person in a public place for the purpose of prostitution'. In 1978, the first and most important of these decisions resolved a long-standing courtroom conflict concerning the meaning of the term 'solicit'. Police had interpreted the law as prohibiting the act of

* Professor, School of Criminology, Simon Fraser University, Canada.

JOHN LOWMAN

publicly offering sexual services for sale (Layton 1979; Winterton 1980).[1] Construed this way, it was a simple enough law to enforce. Undercover police officers posing as potential customers would approach street prostitutes; once the prostitute had offered to provide sexual services for a fee, he or she would be charged with 'soliciting'. But in 1978 the Supreme Court upheld a lower court ruling that 'soliciting' meant 'pressing and persistent' behaviour (*R.* v. *Hutt* [1978] 2 SCR 476). The implication of this decision was that a prostitute's conduct in the process of offering sexual services had to constitute a tangible 'nuisance' to be considered an offence. Since few prostitutes were 'pressing and persistent' in the course of offering their services, it became considerably more difficult to obtain convictions. The conventional wisdom suggests that because the police were no longer able to contain it, street prostitution spilled out of its traditional city environs. Whether this account makes sense is another matter. Below I suggest that, in the case of Vancouver, since the expansion of street prostitution occurred before 1978, a different sort of explanation of the problems besetting Canadian prostitution law is in order. But for the moment it is sufficient to note that the ensuing furore over street prostitution[2] led in 1983 to the convening of the Special Committee on Pornography and Prostitution (the Fraser Committee) to ponder the situation[3] and, in 1985, to the repeal of the soliciting law and enactment of a new Criminal Code section that makes it an offence to communicate in a public place for the purpose of buying or selling sexual services.

The same concern about the visibility of prostitution and its effect on inner-city neighbourhoods appears to have surfaced in England at about the same time as it did in Canada, and there would seem to be more parallels than there are differences between the experiences of the two countries. In Vancouver, the many different strategies described below that have been employed to suppress street prostitution—including enforcement of the 'communicating' law—have had little impact on levels of street prostitution (although they have often had a dramatic effect on its location). A feeling of pessimism prevails. Short of longer prison sentences for prostitutes (the solution now being mooted by many municipal councils, residents' groups and the Canadian Association of Chiefs of Police), nothing seems to work. When it comes to prostitution more generally, this pessimism is symptomatic of an even wider 'impossibilism' that suggests that, try as we might, prostitution is here to stay; the best we can hope for is its containment.

In marked contrast to these views, Roger Matthews' research on the experience of street prostitution control during the early 1980s in London's Finsbury Park suggests that a 'multi-agency approach' dealt with the problems of street prostitution 'extremely effectively [and] also provided what would appear to be a long term solution' (1986a: 4) to such problems. Given that the difficulties being experienced in several Canadian cities

[1] In practice, the soliciting law was almost always used against prostitutes but not their customers. In those rare instances when customers were charged, courts in different provinces made contradictory rulings as to whether s.195.1 was applicable to customers: the British Columbia Court of Appeal ruled that it was not (*R.* v. *Dudak* (1978), 41 CCC (2d) 31 BCCA) in opposition to the Ontario Court of Appeal, which upheld the conviction of a customer (*R* v. *DiPaola* (1978) 4 CR (3d) 121 (Ont.CA)).
[2] According to testimony at public hearings held across Canada in 1984, the cities most seriously affected by street prostitution were Vancouver, Toronto, Montreal, Calgary, Halifax and Niagara Falls (Fraser Committee 1985: 346).
[3] Another Committee (the Committee on Sexual Offences against Children and Youth, or the Badgley Committee) was also concerned with prostitution, interviewing 229 persons under the age of 20 in the course of its 'Youth Prostitution Survey'.

throughout the 1980s have been very similar to the situation in Finsbury Park as it stood in 1982, and that Canadian efforts to control street prostitution have nevertheless met with such little success, the two experiences would seem to invite comparison.

The Finsbury Park Initiative: Designing Out Prostitution

According to Matthews (1986a), while Finsbury Park has had a long-standing association with prostitution, it was in the late 1970s that a particularly dramatic increase in street prostitution occurred, with consequences that are only too familiar to Canadians:

The more visible presence of prostitutes, often congregating in groups, as well as the growing problem of kerb-crawling began by the early eighties to seriously effect [*sic*] the daily lives of all those living and working in the area—particularly of women. For some, even the simple business of walking along the street, waiting for a bus, or going shopping was a hazardous experience. Noise, harassment, frequent obscenities, the spectre of prostitutes and their clients or ponces haggling or arguing in the street—erupting occasionally into overt violence—became a common feature of everyday life. At night the frequent screaming and shouting was drowned by the irregular and piercing tones of car horns. (Matthews 1986a: 5)

As in Canada, complaints to the police about prostitutes and kerb-crawlers produced little action, the police maintaining that there was little they could do. Then various local residents' associations combined to form the 'Finsbury Park Action Group' that 'set about orchestrating a general campaign to improve the area and in particular to reduce the problems which are generally associated with prostitution' (Matthews 1986a: 7). Matthews maintains that in less than two years prostitution and kerb-crawling were virtually removed from the area by a two-pronged police and local council initiative involving the policing of prostitution-related offences and road closures, with the result that Finsbury Park 'was transformed from a noisy and hazardous red light district into a relatively tranquil and cohesive residential area' (Matthews 1986a: 7). And all this was achieved before the enactment in 1985 of the Street Offences Act, legislation specifically designed to deal with the problems created by street prostitution in communities across England and Wales.

In terms of the comparison being undertaken here, one of the most noteworthy aspects of the Finsbury Park initiative is that residents' associations in surrounding areas initially opposed the system of road closures for fear that the street trade would be displaced to surrounding areas. But when the barriers were eventually erected, Matthews claims that 'There was no sign of prostitution or kerb-crawling moving into neighbouring streets and since they had both noticeably been virtually removed from the Finsbury Park area it was widely assumed that prostitution had moved to other parts of London and to Amhurst Park in particular since it was the nearest well known red light district' (1986a: 15). A check on the names of persons arrested in Amhurst Park during the six months following the road closures revealed that only three or four of the women who had been arrested in Finsbury Park prior to the closures were re-arrested in Amhurst Park subsequent to them. Matthews notes that it has usually been thought that prostitution is not the kind of *opportunistic* activity that can be affected by 'situational crime prevention' strategies. However, from the experience of the effects of the Finsbury Park road barriers, Matthews concludes that while 'it is possible . . . that the prostitutes moved to other parts of London . . . the fact that they did not move into the neighbouring

3

JOHN LOWMAN

streets of Finsbury Park or over to Amhurst Park suggests that the problem might not be as intractable as is often assumed and that the displacement effect of "designing out" a red light district may, under controlled conditions, be minimal' (1986*a*: 15).

With these provocative comments in mind, let us now turn to the experience of street prostitution control in Canada. To provide some context for this discussion. it begins with a description of Canadian prostitution laws.

Prostitution Law in Canada

As the Canadian Criminal Code currently stands, a variety of activities related to prostitution are prohibited, although *prostitution itself is legal*. There are five clusters of statutes relating to prostitution. (1) 'Bawdy house' laws prohibit the keeping of 'places' as prostitution establishments or the frequenting of such places; in contrast to English law *a single prostitute in Canada is not exempt from the offence of keeping a bawdy house*. (2) A series of statutes prohibit living on the avails of prostitution and (3) the procuring of prostitutes for other persons. (4) One altogether new statute enacted on 1 January 1988 criminalizes the purchase of, or offer to purchase, sexual services from anyone under 18 years of age. (5) Finally, the 'communicating law' prohibits the public purchase or sale of sexual services or the offer to purchase or sell such services. In combination these five clusters of statutes make it almost impossible to practise prostitution on a continuing basis without committing an offence.

Street Prostitution in Vancouver, 1970–1989

My discussion concentrates on the history of prostitution law enforcement in Vancouver, first because it is the Canadian city for which the most detailed information is available, second because it is the city where the court decisions said to be responsible for the demise of the soliciting law originated, and third because a variety of different strategies (including a 'multi-agency' approach) have been employed there in attempts to suppress the street prostitution trade. Figure 1 depicts the prostitution 'strolls' that have existed at various times in Vancouver between 1970 and 1990 and gives an indication of the extensiveness of the areas affected. Some fourteen distinct strolls have existed at one time or other during this period. Generally, from three to five strolls were in use at any one time. Vancouver's downtown (a retail, hotel, and office district) is located on the peninsula between areas 1 and 4; the areas to the east and south are primarily residential.

In 1970 there were four strolls (all located in or adjacent to the downtown): a section of Davie Street (a retail store area with a few hotels and night clubs), the main thoroughfare of the West End high-rise residential district which is the most densely populated square mile in Canada (area 1a); the downtown section of Granville Street, an area of cheap hotels, bars, and an assortment of 'porn' and 'head' shops (area 2); the Columbia–Cordova intersection located one block away from Vancouver's 'skid row', an area of cheap hotels, bars, and rooming houses (area 3); and the Gore–Keefer–Union area (a mix of residential and commercial land uses) sandwiched between the Chinatown commercial district and Strathcona, the residential neighbourhood with the lowest average annual family income in Vancouver (area 4).

It is difficult to tell how levels of street prostitution in the early 1970s compared to

STREET PROSTITUTION CONTROL

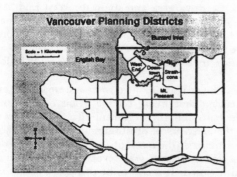

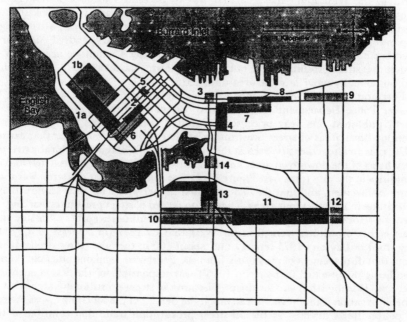

FIG. 1 Vancouver prostitution strolls, 1970–1990
1a West End; 1b West End, extended area; 2 Granville Street; 3 Columbia–Hastings–Cordova (skid row); 4 Gore–Keefer–Union (Strathcona); 5 West Georgia; 6 Richards–Seymour; 7 Strathcona Central; 8 Strathcona North; 9 Hastings–Commercial; 10 Mount Pleasant West; 11 Mount Pleasant East; 12 Grandview Woodlands; 13 Mount Pleasant North; 14 Main–Second Avenue

5

JOHN LOWMAN

levels after 1978 (the year of the *Hutt* decision). In a study prepared for the British Columbia Police Commission, Layton (1975: 103) cited figures from police files indicating that fifteen women worked in the Granville Street area, twenty-two in Chinatown, twelve in the Columbia–Cordova area and six in the West End. Apart from the small stroll in the West End, street prostitution was restricted to mainly commercial land-use areas. Layton's figures indicate that a larger number of prostitutes worked in certain cabaret clubs, particularly in the Penthouse (located only a few blocks from the West End) where some sixty to one hundred prostitutes could be found on any given night.

In December 1975, after a six-month investigation, the owners and employees of the Penthouse were charged with procuring and living on the avails of prostitution (Lowman 1986). The charges were based on the argument that the owners and employees knowingly profited from the activities of prostitutes in the club. Although the persons charged were eventually acquitted (the result of a successful appeal against their initial convictions) the club's liquor licence was revoked immediately after criminal charges had been laid, and it closed. It seems to be this police action more than anything else that lay behind the substantial increase of street prostitution after 1975 in the West End—the area that was to become Vancouver's most populous prostitution stroll in the early 1980s—although local politicians, police spokesmen, and 'residents' groups[4] reconstructed the history of 'what went wrong', attributing this expansion instead to the decisions of a permissive judiciary. Indeed, the founding member of a West End group testifying at the Fraser Committee hearings in 1984 stated that street prostitution did not occur in the area until after 1978 (even though he did not actually move into the area until 1979).

Foremost among several reasons for rejecting the conventional wisdom is a Vancouver Police Department report entitled 'Street Prostitution in Vancouver's West End', published one year prior to the *Hutt* decision (Forbes 1977).[5] This report identified five areas of street prostitution at that time: the four areas that existed in 1970, plus an altogether new area at the intersection of Georgia and Hornby streets, the very heart of the downtown area, amidst some of the most prestigious hotels and office buildings in the city (area 5 in Figure 1). It was estimated that this stroll was used by some 200 women, and that they commanded higher prices for their services than the prostitutes in the other four areas. There is no record of street prostitutes working in the Georgia–Hornby area prior to the closure of the Penthouse. Forbes estimated that at least eighty prostitutes worked in the West End by 1977 (in contrast to the handful described in Layton's 1975 report), and about 100 in the other three strolls. It would seem that displacement of prostitutes from the Penthouse (and one other club that was also being investigated by police in 1975[6]) was responsible for the development of the Georgia–Hornby stroll and for the proliferation of street prostitution in the West End. The implication is that it was not so much the demise of the soliciting law as the results of police efforts directed at the off-street prostitution trade that contributed to the expansion of street prostitution in the mid-1970s.

[4] The quote marks are in recognition of the fact that prostitutes often reside in the areas they work although their status as residents is often effectively denied by this common parlance.

[5] And, as we have already seen, Layton (1975) found mention of prostitutes working in the West End in police reports written in 1974. Indeed, a day-by-day search of Vancouver newspaper articles (part of a study of prostitution news from 1886 to the present) reveals that the first mention of West End street prostitution was on 10 October 1972.

[6] This club, the Zanzibar, was burned to the ground; the owner was charged with arson, but acquitted.

6

STREET PROSTITUTION CONTROL

The first wave of complaints about street prostitution in the aftermath of the Penthouse investigation emanated from Georgia Street hotel operators and West End retail store owners in 1977. It was during the police response to these complaints (in the form of a special street prostitution Task Force) that the Supreme Court ruled that a prostitute had to behave in a 'pressing and persistent' manner in order to be found guilty of 'soliciting'. At that point, Vancouver police gave up enforcing the soliciting law. In 1979 they adopted the Toronto Police Department tactic of charging prostitutes who approached several customers in turn, reasoning that such serial approaches constituted 'pressing and persistent' conduct. But this tactic was abandoned when the Supreme Court ruled that the soliciting law dealt with the circumstances of a single communication only *(R.* v. *Whitter*; *R.* v. *Galjot* [1981] 2 SCR 606).

Pressure to 'get tough' with street prostitutes continued to escalate, especially in the West End. In 1979, and again in 1981, a Prostitution Task Force was established to devise strategies to combat the street trade. Task Force activities included the use of general purpose public order laws (such as loitering and littering) to try to harass prostitutes out of certain areas, or off the street altogether. According to prostitutes (Lowman 1984), it was during this period that police urged prostitutes to move off Davie into the back streets so that they would be less visible to merchants and shoppers. Prostitutes must have become all the more visible to residents in surrounding areas as a result, a visibility that may well have fuelled the belief that street prostitution was spreading. By 1983 a district of some eighteen to twenty blocks (Figure 1, areas 1a and 1b) was cruised by prostitutes and their customers. Of course, it may well have been that street prostitution *was* spreading. Indeed, it would appear that prostitution generally was expanding in Vancouver during the early 1980s,[7] although this expansion may have had little to do with law enforcement patterns.

In 1981 the 'Concerned Residents of the West End' (CROWE)[8] began to organize around the single purpose of ridding the neighbourhood of prostitution. The group made a series of submissions to the city council and police department demanding that prostitution be removed from the area—regardless of where it might end up.

One of the first steps taken by Vancouver Council to respond to the remonstrations of CROWE was to install a series of traffic diverters throughout the West End, and another police Task Force was convened. Shortly thereafter, one of the local newspapers published a photograph of a women sitting astride one of the diverters waiting for a customer. Several other prostitutes were quoted as saying that the diverters were

[7] And to the extent that it was, we find further grounds to question the conventional explanation of 'what went wrong'. The conventional wisdom suggests that prostitution spilled on to the streets as the law, rendered unenforceable, was no longer able to contain it. While it is difficult to measure levels of off-street prostitution, one index is provided by the number of escort agencies advertising in newspapers and other publications. Recent Canadian research (e.g. Brannigan *et al.* 1989; Lowman 1989) leaves no doubt that escort agencies are fronts for prostitution. Advertising patterns indicate that escort services did not begin to proliferate until after 1978—i.e. at exactly the time prostitution was supposed to be spilling on to the streets. In 1978 only one escort agency advertised in the telephone Yellow Pages. In 1979 and 1980 there were three; then the number increased to six in 1982, fifteen in 1983, nineteen in 1984. and thirty-eight in 1985. It would not appear that changes in other styles of off-street prostitution explain this expansion (for example, there was no corresponding reduction in the number of body-rub parlours).

[8] Significantly, the founder of this group—a man who has since become a city alderman—did not move into the West End until 1979. At the public hearings held by the Fraser Committee in 1984 he presented a series of maps that unequivocally asserted that street prostitution did not exist in the West End prior to the *Hutt* decision in 1978. suggesting instead that it progressively spread outwards from a single intersection only after that date to engulf much of the West End.

JOHN LOWMAN

'good for business' because they slowed down traffic nicely (*Vancouver Sun*, 23 November 1981). Then in 1982, following the advice of the federal minister of justice and the lead of several other municipalities, Vancouver Council enacted a by-law in an attempt to control the activities of both street prostitutes and their customers. By Christmas over 500 charges had been laid, but local journalists concluded that there had been no visible reduction in the number of prostitutes working West End streets (*Vancouver Sun*, 10 December 1982). In 1983 the by-law fell into disuse when a similar municipal law in Calgary was struck down because it encroached on criminal legislation,[9] which in Canada falls under the exclusive jurisdiction of the federal government. Similarly, provincial governments could not introduce legislation to control street prostitution since it remained the subject of criminal law.

While municipal and provincial governments could not tamper with federal law they did become involved in the campaign to persuade the federal government to revise the Criminal Code. In 1984 the Fraser Committee held a series of public hearings in major cities across Canada in order to facilitate its review of prostitution policy, and the Department of Justice commissioned a series of studies to provide background information for the Committee.[10] Calling the Special Committee a stalling tactic, lobby groups continued to press for more immediate action. In 1984 a group of West End residents formed another organization, 'Shame the Johns',[11] that picketed prostitutes and recorded the licence plate numbers of cruising cars, threatening to picket the owners at their homes.

Systematic head counts of prostitutes[12] indicate that the tactics adopted by Shame the Johns, like the by-law and various police Task Forces before, did not have any noticeable impact on levels of street prostitution, although they did move prostitutes around (Lowman 1984). What the emergence of this vigilante movement did achieve was the impression that the Police Department had lost control of the city's streets. It was during these protestations that the provincial government devised an extraordinary legal strategy that ultimately did clear the West End of prostitutes; it issued a warning that some fifty prostitutes would be compelled to leave the West End by a civil nuisance injunction if they continued meeting customers in the area. The important point about this strategy is that it was *geographically limited*; the injunctions would have applied only to prostitutes working west of Burrard Street, the eastern boundary of the West End high-rise district. A group of prostitutes, aided by the 'Alliance for the Safety of Prostitutes' (a Vancouver-based prostitutes' rights organization), pooled resources

---

[9] *R* v. *Westendorp* (1983), 2CCC (3d) 330, (SCC).

[10] In terms of prostitution, the relevant studies are: Crook (1984); El Komos (1984); Fleischman (1984 : Gemme *et al.* (1984); Haug and Cini (1984); Jaywardene *et al.* (1984); Kiedrowski and van Dijk (1984); Lautt (1984); Lowman (1984); Peat, Marwick and Partners (1984); and Sansfacon (1984a, b, 1985).

[11] 'John' is a colloquial term for the prostitute's customer.

[12] The counts involve a tally of the number of prostitutes observable on a single traverse of all the streets and alleyways in each of the known strolls at various times through the day and week. A weekly count was (and still is) conducted every Thursday night from 10.00 to 11.00 p.m. Counts have also been made at that time each day of the week for various periods and throughout selected days. Comparison of counts by the Vancouver Police Department and an independent research team yielded strikingly similar results indicating that the counts provide a fairly accurate image of the geography of street prostitution and a useful impression of trends in the number of street prostitutes operating throughout the day, on different days of the week, seasonally and year by year. Figure 1 is based on these counts. Information about displacement of prostitutes provided by the head counts was confirmed by information from a series of interviews with prostitutes—forty-eight in 1984 (Lowman 1984) and forty-five in 1987–8 (Lowman 1989)—police officers, and social workers.

and sought legal advice. Because of escalating problems in the West End. and because by default the injunction strategy offered some indication as to where they could work, they decided to move. No legal challenge to the injunction was made, although it is quite likely that it too would have been found to infringe upon federal jurisdiction in the same way that the municipal by-law did (Cassels 1985). Indeed, the Supreme Court of Nova Scotia ruled that a similar injunction in Halifax infringed upon federal powers.

Patterns of Displacement

Observations of street activities and interviews with prostitutes (Lowman 1984) indicate that if the West End was successfully cleared of prostitutes, it was only at the expense of their displacement to other areas. Presumably the engineers of the injunctions hoped that prostitutes would relocate in the four other strolls in use at that time, all of which were mainly non-residential areas. But, unlike West End prostitutes, many of the women working in the traditional skid row areas were heroin users, and generally commanded much lower prices than their West End counterparts. And the women in area 5 (Georgia Street, at the heart of downtown Vancouver) differed to the extent that they were almost exclusively controlled by pimps, whereas many women in the West End worked independently. Also, male prostitutes had traditionally worked in the West End (the first area in Vancouver where males dressing as males worked as street prostitutes) and required a new location to meet customers.

Many West End prostitutes moved to Richards and Seymour streets (Figure 1, area 6), adjacent to the stroll that already existed on Granville Street. But for a variety of reasons, not the least of which related to competition in the new stroll, many prostitutes moved to an area in Mount Pleasant (Figure 1, area 11), a working-class residential area where prostitutes had occasionally worked since 1980. Apart from Strathcona—where a stroll has existed throughout the postwar period—Mount Pleasant has the lowest average family income in Vancouver. After the dislocation of street prostitution from the West End, Georgia Street prostitutes gradually moved into the Richards–Seymour area and the Georgia Street stroll disappeared. The greater competition occasioned by this merging of strolls presumably created a further incentive for some women to work in the Mount Pleasant stroll where fewer prostitutes operated.

Between 1985 and 1988, police and resident group activity displaced street prostitution within Mount Pleasant several times, sometimes unwittingly, sometimes deliberately. The first stroll was located in an area of single-family dwellings and small apartment buildings between Main and Clark on Broadway, the main thoroughfare of Mount Pleasant (Figure 1, area 11). It did not take long for area residents to complain to civic officials about the same sorts of problems that had been suggested as besetting the West End, and in the summer of 1985 a demonstration was held on Broadway (*Vancouver Sun*, 26 June 1985). Protestors wanted to know why the provincial Attorney-General would not use nuisance injunctions to oust prostitutes from Mount Pleasant, given that the tactic had been successful in the West End. They were told that since the Fraser Committee's Report had just been released and that changes to the Criminal Code were imminent, the assistance of the provincial government would not be necessary.

In the fall of 1985 the Police Department did, however, persuade prostitutes to move

JOHN LOWMAN

out of the residential area they initially occupied and relocate in what was considered to be a mainly industrial area on the north-western side of Mount Pleasant (Figure 1, area 10). In so doing they moved street prostitution to the front doorstep of a woman who was to become prominent in the 'Mount Pleasant Action Group', another one-issue lobby group organized to confront street prostitution. Infuriated at the lack of government response to their complaints, the Action Group staged a 'sleep-in' at City Hall, saying that since it was impossible to get any rest in their own neighbourhood they would sleep in the council chambers (*The Province*. 1 October 1985). In response to these protestations, the City Council established what local newspapers referred to as an informal red light district (*Vancouver Sun*, 10 October 1985) by erecting street barriers around the residential area of west Mount Pleasant. With police assistance prostitutes were displaced north into an almost exclusively industrial district (Figure 1, area 13). On 20 December 1985 the Conservative federal government attempted to turn back the clock by repealing the soliciting law, and enacting in its place a provision that made it an offence in a public place or any place open to public view to 'in any manner communicate or attempt to communicate with any person for the purpose of engaging in prostitution or of obtaining the services of a prostitute' (the communicating law).

The logic of the communicating law directly contradicted the recommendations of the Special Committee on Pornography and Prostitution, which had released its report in May 1985. The Committee proposed sweeping changes to the Criminal Code, noting that while prostitution was technically legal in Canada, almost every aspect of the trade was effectively criminalized. They suggested that levels of street prostitution would probably not abate until legislators told prostitutes where they *could* work, and recommended, among other things, that two prostitutes working from a single premise be exempt from bawdy house statutes and that the provinces be empowered to license small-scale prostitution establishments (Fraser Committee 1985: 530–53). The federal government rejected this logic on the grounds that it would be tantamount to condoning prostitution.

The Communicating Law in Action

For the first few months after the enactment of the communicating law the local newspapers kept a tally of the number of charges laid. Initially, the general opinion was that the street prostitution situation was once again under control, an impression that is confirmed by the trends in head counts of prostitutes depicted in Figure 2. But these counts, like subsequent newspaper reports, indicate that the reduction was short-lived. By the summer of 1986 Mount Pleasant activists were once again lobbying for more drastic measures to oust the street prostitution trade which by that time, they said, had returned to 1985 levels. At this time the Action Group began street patrols and sought open confrontation with prostitutes. They were successful to the extent that they drove prostitutes back into the eastern section of Mount Pleasant (Figure 1, area 11). Head counts indicate that by 1987 street prostitution levels were as high as or higher than they had been during the year prior to the enactment of the law. Interviews with prostitutes and police officers suggest that the gradual increase in numbers through 1986 was the result of a return of prostitutes to the street rather than an increase in the overall number of prostitutes (Lowman 1989). And, as judges imposed area restrictions

10

STREET PROSTITUTION CONTROL

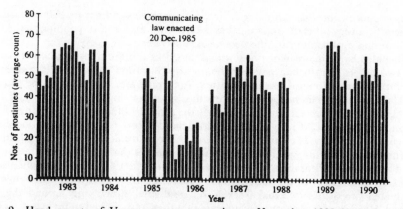

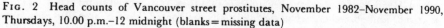

FIG. 2 Head counts of Vancouver street prostitutes, November 1982–November 1990, Thursdays, 10.00 p.m.–12 midnight (blanks = missing data)

on prostitutes as part of the conditions of their release pending trial, the prostitution stroll expanded as prostitutes occupied street corners just outside the boundaries of the restrictions (Figure 1, area 12).

In 1987 the federal government sponsored a series of studies (Brannigan *et al.* 1989; Gemme *et al.* 1989; Lowman 1989; Moyer and Carrington 1989) as part of its evaluation of the communicating law. These studies suggest that, in most cities, the new law has not had much impact on levels of street prostitution (Department of Justice Canada 1989: 69–75). In 1986 and 1987, just over 15,000 charges were laid in Canada, of which 2,180 were in Vancouver (1,648 involving prostitutes, 532 involving customers[13]); the fact that 15,000 charges could be laid at all indicates the durability of the street prostitution trade.

In the summer of 1987 the activities of the Action Group and a similar organization in east Mount Pleasant ('Mount Pleasant Watch') intensified and the general impression of lawlessness—in terms both of the relentlessness of the street prostitution trade and of the intensification of lobby group activity to combat it—was amplified. In response to lobby group pressure, the Police Department established the Mount Pleasant Prostitution Task Force to supplement enforcement of the communicating law. Task Force activities involved the use of various kinds of harassment techniques (checking prostitute identities; parking police cruisers by prostitutes; charging prostitutes for jaywalking or littering offences whenever possible; prosecution of kerb-crawlers for all manner of traffic violations) to drive the prostitution trade out of the neighbourhood. Interviews with prostitutes, police, and Action Group representatives indicate that the Task Force did indeed suppress prostitution in Mount Pleasant, but again only by displacing it to other areas, particularly to the stroll already existing in Strathcona (Lowman 1989). Residents of Strathcona must have wondered why a

---

[13] In the ten cities where studies of the communicating law were conducted, in all but one (London, where only sixty-five charges were laid) more prostitutes than customers were charged. Overall, 66.8 per cent of charges were laid against prostitutes, 33.2 per cent against customers. For more commentary on these enforcement patterns see Lowman (1990).

11

similar police effort was not made to deal with problems in their neighbourhood. But generally, a very different approach has been taken thus far in responding to the street prostitution problem in this, the poorest area of Vancouver.

Bounded by Chinatown on one side and the docks and the transcontinental railroad on two others, Strathcona has been home to prostitution throughout the twentieth century. From 1945 until recently prostitutes generally met customers on the commercial land-use streets immediately adjacent to Chinatown (Figure 1, areas 3[14] and 4). In 1986, a combination of factors, particularly the activities of several youth gangs, forced prostitutes from area 4 into the mainly residential streets east of the traditional stroll (Figure 1, area 7). The initial reaction of this community to street prostitution is particularly interesting given the confrontational tactics that were adopted in the West End and Mount Pleasant. After a series of meetings in 1987 involving police, social workers, and residents, a neighbourhood committee drew up a map and notice that requested prostitutes to avoid working on residential streets and around the local school. Head counts of prostitutes indicate that they have moved to the streets (Figure 1, area 8) immediately north of the informally designated 'No-Go' area. But escalating police activity (mainly in response to the complaints of a group of residents not satisfied with this solution) has resulted in some prostitutes moving further east along Hastings Street so that now a new stroll is developing in the Hastings Street–Commercial Drive area (Figure 1, area 9).

The Mount Pleasant Prostitution Task Force has been reconvened each summer, as prostitutes and their customers have filtered back into the area during the winter months when the Task Force was disbanded. According to head counts taken since 1982, levels of street prostitution in Strathcona reached their highest point in 1990. It has thus been more difficult to displace prostitutes out of Mount Pleasant because of the increased competition in Strathcona. As a result, the Task Force adopted a new tactic, asking prostitutes to relocate in the mainly commercial district along Main Street at the northern corner of Mount Pleasant (Figure 1, area 14). It may well turn out that the development of a stroll in this area will prevent prostitutes and their customers from returning to the residential area of Mount Pleasant. But now a new problem is emerging. The City Planning Office recently convened a meeting of police, social workers, and researchers to discuss the fate of the Richards–Seymour stroll. It turns out that although land use in this area is primarily commercial, over the next five years it is slated to become the highest density residential area in Vancouver. When it does, we will probably see a new round of demands to clean up the streets.

The main response of local politicians, the police administration (Vancouver Police Department 1987), and Mount Pleasant lobby groups to the failure of the communicating law has been to call for tougher sentences and to make 'communication' an indictable offence.[15] It is doubtful that the sentences being proposed (short jail terms) would, by themselves, have any noticeable effect on levels of street prostitution since they are not much different from the sentences already given in Vancouver during the first eighteen months of communicating law enforcement (Lowman 1989: 165–71). If

[14] Since 1982 head counts suggest that area 3 has been a minor stroll with only one or two prostitutes working on any given night—that is, when there were any at all.
[15] One is left wondering why the first version of s.195.1 is thought to have been effective in controlling street prostitution prior to the court decisions that rendered it unenforceable, since it too was a summary offence with similar penalties.

12

STREET PROSTITUTION CONTROL

sentences were to be made more severe than this (in the realm of months and years) the Canadian government might have to increase the holding capacity of women's prisons to perhaps five or six times its present size to accommodate the accelerated flow of prostitutes.

An alternative solution is to tackle the problem identified by the Special Committee on Pornography and Prostitution—i.e. the contradictory and often self-defeating nature of prostitution law. One of the most poignant examples of this muddled legal structure was the impact of the closure of the Penthouse Cabaret on levels of street prostitution in the mid-1970s. But a review of one hundred years of prostitution law enforcement in Vancouver (Lowman 1989: 178–94; Nilsen 1980) reveals many such examples. The result of this contradictory legal structure today is that in order to keep street prostitution under control, the Vancouver police have ignored the activities of escort agencies, despite the fact that when the owners and operators of such businesses have been charged with procuring and with living on the avails of prostitution—both indictable offences—they have been successfully prosecuted. Thus police effectively have to ignore what legislators have deemed to be more serious offences in order to concentrate on the summary offence of communicating.

Once again, Canadian legislators are faced with the task of amending prostitution policy as the review of the communicating law approaches completion. It is in this context that the experience of other jurisdictions, such as that described by Roger Matthews, would appear to be particularly relevant.

Implications of the Finsbury Park Study

Matthews suggests that street prostitution, at least in parts of England, may be much more opportunistic than has normally been thought. The history of street prostitution control in Vancouver would seem flatly to contradict this optimism. The question is, what might account for the differences that we see here?

One obvious possibility is that prostitution in London and in Vancouver is so different that comparison is imprudent. It is possible that differences in welfare systems and patterns of illicit drug consumption in different cultural settings influence the propensity to practise prostitution in distinct ways. Perhaps the factors surrounding a person's drift into prostitution are quite different. Alternatively, it is possible that prostitution in Finsbury Park is not actually as opportunistic as Matthews suggests.

Measuring displacement: problems with the Finsbury Park study

The implication of the Finsbury Park study is that prostitutes simply quit the game when their efforts to work in a certain area were frustrated. Given that this optimistic conclusion so flatly contradicts conventional wisdom, one might expect scrupulous attention to the methodology on which any such reasoning is based. But one problem with Matthews' study is that we do not actually know what happened to the prostitutes who were 'designed out' of Finsbury Park. One wonders if the desire to counter impossibilism compromises the realism of the conclusions reached.

Certainly Matthews did try to see if known Finsbury Park prostitutes had moved to the closest prostitution stroll by checking to see if their names appeared in police records of arrests in Amhurst Park, although whether this technique by itself is

13

sufficient to detect displacement is debatable. He recognizes that Finsbury Park women may have relocated further afield, but offers no way of testing this possibility. He also maintains that prostitutes did not move to indoor locations within Finsbury Park, but this still leaves the possibility that they had moved indoors in some other area (how would customers get past the barricades to travel to indoor locations within Finsbury Park anyway?). A more reliable analysis would have involved canvassing prostitutes about their adjustments in response to road barriers and police initiatives.

Another problem with Matthews' methodology is that he does not consider the possibility that his commentary was written before sufficient time had elapsed to account for every kind of displacement that may have occurred. The Finsbury Park barricades were erected in the spring of 1985; Matthews' report was published in October 1986. In some cases this is undoubtedly a long enough period to detect certain kinds of displacement. In Vancouver displacement of prostitutes to contiguous streets has often occurred the very night after law enforcement initiatives have been taken; but other displacements, such as the movement of prostitutes from the West End to Mount Pleasant, took longer to materialize (or be noticed). No matter how one looks at it, discussion about the 'long-term effects' of any criminal justice policy only a year after it was put into effect would seem to be premature. One wonders what the situation in Finsbury Park and other parts of London is like today.

Legal milieu

Because of the lack of any information about whether Finsbury Park women moved to off-street locations, it is difficult to ascertain the impact of differences in English and Canadian legal systems on street prostitution. As already noted, the most important difference between British and Canadian law is that in Canada a single prostitute cannot work alone out of a premise. Thus it may be that in the English legal environment *street* prostitution *is* more opportunistic than it is in Canada, because there are other legal opportunities for English prostitutes to turn to when the heat is turned up on the street trade.

In Vancouver there is a considerable amount of off-street prostitution, the most important component of which is provided by escort agencies. There are also several strip clubs where prostitutes congregate, and at least two massage parlours where men can purchase sexual services. Many prostitutes are not able to work for escort services because they cannot meet the standards of dress and physical appearance that most escort agency operators require. Escorts are more expensive than street prostitutes (usually in excess of $200 per encounter as compared to $40 to $120 on the street) and probably beyond the resources of many blue-collar men.[16] Thus while enforcement of the communicating law provides an incentive for prostitutes to leave the street, a variety of countervailing forces pull them back, not the least of which involve the habits of the consumers of their services. According to prostitute accounts, their rapid return to Vancouver's streets after the enactment of the communicating law reflected their inability to make enough money in other locations; there is simply more money to be earned on the street.

[16] Most of the customers convicted under the communicating law in Vancouver have been lower-class men (Lowman 1990).

STREET PROSTITUTION CONTROL

Conclusions

If prostitution itself is to remain legal in Canada, the interests of residents bothered by street prostitution would probably best be served by a legal system which identifies where prostitutes *can* work, rather than pursuing the current punitive strategy which, time and again, has produced unplanned displacement and often more intractable nuisance problems in the process. Prostitutes, too, would benefit from a legal system which protects them from the violence of the street (in Vancouver, twelve street prostitutes have been murdered during the past two years). From a purely instrumental perspective, the debate should focus on where prostitution ought to be located and how it should be organized, rather than entrenching a contradictory and often self-defeating system of criminal control. Of course, there is much more to the issue of designing prostitution policy than this. Canadian politicians have consistently opposed tackling the issue of where prostitution ought to be located on the grounds that to do so would be implicitly to condone prostitution. In similar fashion, Roger Matthews (1986*b*) has argued against decriminalization on the grounds that it would simply create a sexual free-for-all for men.[17] And yet neither Canadian legislators nor Matthews have recommended the criminalization of either the sale or purchase of sexual services, thereby still leaving a variety of questions about where prostitutes should meet their customers. It would seem that one simply cannot have it both ways.

References

BADGLEY COMMITTEE (1984), *Sexual Offences Against Children*. Report of the Committee on Sexual Offences against Children and Youth. Ottawa: Department of Supply and Services.

BRANNIGAN, K., KNAFLA, L., and LEVY, C. (1989), *Street Prostitution, Assessing the Impact of the Law: Calgary, Regina and Winnipeg*. Ottawa: Department of Justice Canada.

CASSELS, J. (1985), 'Prostitution and Public Nuisance: Desperate Measures and the Limits of Civil Adjudication', *Canadian Bar Review*, 63: 764–804.

CROOK, N. (1984), *A Report on Prostitution in the Atlantic Provinces*, Working Papers on Pornography and Prostitution, Report no. 12. Ottawa: Department of Justice Canada.

DEPARTMENT OF JUSTICE CANADA (1989), *Street Prostitution, Assessing the Impact of the Law: Synthesis Report*. Ottawa: Department of Justice Canada.

EL KOMOS, M. (1984), *Canadian Newspapers' Coverage of Pornography and Prostitution*, Working Papers on Pornography and Prostitution, Report no. 5. Ottawa: Department of Justice Canada.

FLEISCHMAN, J. (1984), *A Report on Prostitution in Ontario*, Working Papers on Pornography and Prostitution no. 10. Ottawa: Department of Justice Canada.

FORBES, G. A. (1977), 'Street Prostitution in Vancouver's West End', mimeo, report prepared for the Vancouver City Council and Police Board.

FRASER COMMITTEE (1985), *Pornography and Prostitution in Canada*. Report of the Special Committee on Pornography and Prostitution. Ottawa: Department of Supply and Services.

GEMME, R., MURPHY, A., BOURQUE, M., NEMEH, M. A., and PAYMENT, N. (1984). *A Report on Prostitution in Quebec*, Working Papers on Pornography and Prostitution, Report no. 11. Ottawa: Department of Justice Canada.

---

[17] For further commentary, see Lowman (1991).

JOHN LOWMAN

GEMME, R., PAYMENT, N., and MALENFANT, L. (1989), *Street Prostitution, Assessing the Impact of the Law: Montreal*. Ottawa: Department of Justice Canada.

GRAVES, F. (1989), *Street Prostitution, Assessing the Impact of the Law: Halifax*. Ottawa: Department of Justice Canada.

HAUG, M., and CINI, M. (1984), *The Ladies (and Gentlemen) of the Night and the Spread of Sexually Transmitted Diseases*, Working Papers on Pornography and Prostitution, Report no. 7. Ottawa: Department of Justice Canada.

JAYWARDENE, C. H. S., JULIANI, T. J., and TALBOT, C. K. (1984), *Pornography and Prostitution in Selected Countries*, Working Papers on Pornography and Prostitution, Report no. 4. Ottawa: Department of Justice Canada.

KIEDROWSKI, J., and VAN DIJK, J. M. (1984), *Pornography and Prostitution in Denmark, France, West Germany, the Netherlands, and Sweden*, Working Papers on Pornography and Prostitution, Report no. 1. Ottawa: Department of Justice Canada.

LAUTT, M. (1984), *A Report on Prostitution in the Prairie Provinces*, Working Papers on Pornography and Prostitution, Report no. 9. Ottawa: Department of Justice Canada.

LAYTON, M. (1975), 'Report on Prostitution in Vancouver: Official and Unofficial Reports', unpublished report to the British Columbia Police Commission.

—— (1979), 'The Ambiguities of the Law or the Street Walker's Dilemma', *Chitty's Law Journal*, 27/4: 109–20.

LOWMAN, J. (1984), *Vancouver Field Study of Prostitution*, Working Papers on Pornography and Prostitution, no. 8. Ottawa: Department of Justice Canada.

—— (1986), 'Street Prostitution in Vancouver: Some Notes on the Genesis of a Social Problem', *Canadian Journal of Criminology*, 28/1: 1–16.

—— (1989), *Street Prostitution. Assessing the Impact of the Law: Vancouver*. Ottawa: Department of Justice Canada.

—— (1990), 'Notions of Formal Equality Before the Law: The Experience of Street Prostitutes and Their Customers', *Journal of Human Justice*, 1/2: 55–73.

—— (1991), 'The "Left Regulation" of Prostitution', in J. Lowman and B. MacLean (eds.), *Realist Criminology: Crime Control and Policing in the 1990s*. Vancouver: The Collective Press.

MATTHEWS, R. (1986a), 'Policing Prostitution: A Multi-Agency Approach' Middlesex Polytechnic, Centre for Criminology, Paper no. 1.

—— (1986b), 'Beyond Wolfenden? Prostitution, Politics and the Law', in Matthews and Young, *Confronting Crime*: 188–210.

MATTHEWS, R., and YOUNG, J. (eds.), *Confronting Crime*. London: Sage.

MOYER, S., and CARRINGTON, P. (1989), *Street Prostitution, Assessing the Impact of the Law: Toronto*. Ottawa: Department of Justice Canada.

NILSEN, D. (1980), 'The "Social Evil": Prostitution in Vancouver, 1900–1920', in B. Latham and C. Kess (eds.), *In Her Own Right: Selected Essays on Women's History in B.C.*: 205–28. Victoria: Camosun College.

PEAT, MARWICK, and PARTNERS (1984), *A National Population Study of Pornography and Prostitution*, Working Papers on Pornography and Prostitution, Report no. 6. Ottawa: Department of Justice Canada.

SANSFACON, D. (1984a), *Pornography and Prostitution in the United States*, Working Papers on Pornography and Prostitution, Report no. 2. Ottawa: Department of Justice Canada.

—— (1984b), *Agreements and Conventions of the United Nations with Respect to Pornography and Prostitution*, Working Papers on Pornography and Prostitution, Report no. 3. Ottawa: Department of Justice Canada.

16

STREET PROSTITUTION CONTROL

—— (1985), *Prostitution in Canada: A Research Review Report*. Ottawa: Department of Justice Canada.

VANCOUVER POLICE DEPARTMENT (1987), 'Street Solicitation: A Review by the Vancouver Police Department', mimeo.

WILLIAMS, D. H. (1941), 'The Suppression of Commercialized Prostitution in the City of Vancouver', *Journal of Social Hygiene*, 27: 364–372.

WINTERTON, D. L. (1980), 'The Dilemma of our Prostitution Laws', *Canadian Police Chief*, April: 5–6.

YOUNG, J. (1987), 'The Tasks Facing a Realist Criminology', *Contemporary Crises*, 11 4: 337–56.

17

REGULATING STREET PROSTITUTION AND KERB-CRAWLING

A Reply to John Lowman

ROGER MATTHEWS*

There has been a renewed interest over the last few years in public order offences. This has occurred for a number of reasons. First, criminologists and others have become increasingly aware that problems of what is generally termed 'disorder' can have a devastating effect upon social life and community cohesion (Skogan 1990; Wilson and Kelling 1982). In some cases the effects of disorder or 'incivilities' may be even more destructive than those of crime. Secondly, problems of disorder tend to be not so much a series of discrete acts as a 'condition', and may become an integrated feature of social relations (Kelling 1987). Thirdly, problems of disorder tend to be localized, concentrated in certain inner-city areas. Many of these may also be high-crime areas, but this is not necessarily so (Hope and Hough 1988; Matthews 1991a). Fourthly, and consequentially, public order problems create particular problems of regulation (Ramsey 1989): they are rarely amenable to traditional methods of policing and call for more comprehensive and imaginative responses.

There have been significant changes both in the prevalence of disorder and in public attitudes towards these issues. Interestingly, much of the impetus to develop new approaches appears to come from 'below' rather than 'above' and signals a change in the levels of public tolerance and changing conceptions of public and private space. As concern increases around issues such as street drug-trading, public drunkenness and rowdiness, intimidation, and harassment on the street, growing interest has been expressed by researchers and policy-makers in historical and cross-cultural research to help to develop an adequate response. John Lowman's (1992) article on the control of street prostitution is a welcome contribution to this development.

The question Lowman raises in his article is whether the approach which was employed to reduce the levels of street prostitution and kerb-crawling in Finsbury Park, in north London, could be adapted to the situation in Vancouver. The significance of the Finsbury Park initiative was that it transformed a well established 'red light' area into a relatively tranquil residential area over a two-year period. One of a number of attempts throughout the country to grapple with this issue (Matthews 1986a), it was different from most of the other interventions in that it was substantially more successful, and in that it not only provided a temporary reprieve from the problems associated with a high concentration of street prostitution, but did so with an apparently low level of displacement.

It was the visible signs of this transformation in the social and personal life of the residents in this area—particularly women—which initially attracted my attention. The research which was carried out indicated that it was the departure from traditional styles of policing towards a more comprehensive multi-agency approach, in which the

* Centre for Criminology, Middlesex Polytechnic.

local authority and the residents' associations played a central role, that produced this outcome. This can be seen as a movement away from an approach based on attrition towards a more strategic and integrated approach which operated simultaneously on a number of different levels, and at a number of different points in the process.

As Lowman correctly points out, the police when operating a policy of attrition and working largely on their own may well exacerbate the problem. The police also tend to see these kind of public order problems as low status 'rubbish' work and to adopt a less than wholehearted attitude towards solving them. Even where the police are persuaded to take these issues seriously they are normally only able to keep the problems within manageable limits. The financial and social costs of achieving this limited and often temporary result are extremely high.

The type of multi-agency initiative adopted in Finsbury Park offers an approach which also goes beyond a 'community policing' model. It demonstrated that where a well supported and fully co-ordinated intervention is implemented, in which the residents are the driving force and where the police and local authority are responsive, the effects can be impressive. It is, therefore, not surprising that the type of approach has been followed to good effect in other parts of the country—most notably in Luton and in Streatham in south London—and that it has influenced policy developments in America and Australia (Levine 1990; Matthews 1991*b*).

Despite the success of the type of multi-agency approach adopted in Finsbury Park, there is no guarantee—as Lowman rightly points out— that such an approach will work elsewhere. His assessment, however, is overly pessimistic and as a result fails to explore fully some of the dimensions of the issue. He touches upon three key themes in his discussion which would benefit from further investigation: the issue of 'displacement'; the role of 'multi-agency' interventions; and the question of motivation.

Displacement

A frequent response from critics to the visible successes in Finsbury Park is that the problem *must* have been displaced elsewhere. The more cynical and impossibilist versions of this critique claim that it must have been displaced into more hidden and sinister forms. Other versions, like the one presented by Lowman, claim that the measures of displacement were inadequate and that, although the research design attempted to provide some gauge of the nature of geographical displacement, the results were not convincing. All the available evidence, however, both formal and informal, indicated that although a few of the women working as prostitutes in the Finsbury Park area moved to other parts of London, most of the women for whom there were records (approximately one-sixth of the total) were not working as prostitutes three years after the intervention was implemented.

But to see evidence of displacement in itself as a sign of failure involves a limited conception of the problem. In some cases, where a problem is simply pushed round the corner or down the street little may be achieved. But in relation to prostitution and kerb-crawling the location and organization of the trade can be extremely important in terms of its social impact. For this reason it is important to distinguish between benign and malign forms of displacement (Barr and Pease 1990). Because of the devastating effect that street prostitution and kerb-crawling can have on the social and personal life of people in affected neighbourhoods, displacement can be said to be benign where it

ROGER MATTHEWS

reduces the impact of disorder on vulnerable and deprived populations. As Barr and Pease (1990) argue there is no natural distribution of crime and disorder in society; the existing patterns are themselves a result of displacement. Displacement is, therefore, a continuous process. A central objective of intervention should be to influence existing patterns of distribution and promote more benign forms of displacement.

The issue of displacement is then not only a strategic but also a political question. This may well be why much contemporary 'administrative' criminology has studiously avoided dealing with the issue of displacement head-on (Rosenbaum 1986). The displacement or the deflection of crime and disorder from one area or form of organization to another is bound up with questions of strategy and in this case with the implementation of multi-agency initiatives.

Multi-Agency Initiatives

In many areas of policy formation multi-agency initiatives have become associated with positive and effective interventions. This belief is not without some foundation; but, as a number of commentators have pointed out, there is nothing intrinsically positive or beneficial about multi-agency approaches (Sampson *et al.* 1988). Such approaches, although overcoming some of the problems associated with single-agency initiatives, can generate other problems of co-ordination and accountability.

The evidence from a range of recent inititatives to reduce levels of street prostitution and kerb-crawling is that the police on their own or the implementation of environmental changes by themselves are likely to have a limited and possibly a negative effect. The complex and multi-dimensional nature of the problem indicates that some type of inter-agency approach will be needed. The Finsbury Park research indicated not only that the adoption of an inter-agency approach was required, but that it needed to involve certain components and that it needed to be implemented in a particular sequence. The level of organization and commitment of the residents proved crucial, as did the development of a close working relationship between the residents and the police.

The limitation of the Finsbury Park research was its inability to specify in detail the exact requirements for a successful intervention. Answering this question requires a closer examination of the application of this approach to various contexts. In each situation its potential significance will always be conditioned by the objective nature of the problem itself (i.e. by the size, organization and location of the trade) and by the motivation and commitment expressed by both the prostitutes and their clients.

Motivational Questions

The third issue Lowman raises is that of motivation and commitment. Clearly, the level of motivation which the prostitutes and the clients have to pursue their relative roles will have an impact on the effectiveness of any multi-agency initiative, and will also influence potential patterns of displacement. An interesting and important feature of the Finsbury Park situation was that many of the women involved expressed a relatively low level of commitment to prostitution as a career. For many of these women the decision to engage in prostitution was much more contingent and opportunistic than was expected. In other areas, such as Streatham and Merseyside, a

20

smaller, more committed group of women has been found and this has directly influenced the nature of intervention. In Merseyside, in particular, where almost four out of five female prostitutes were found to be intravenous drug users, the nature and organization of the trade were deeply involved with and conditioned by the demand and supply of illicit drugs (Matthews 1991*b*).

On the other side of the equation, research increasingly indicates that the commitment of the majority of clients is relatively low. The Finsbury Park research indicated that a low-level intervention is usually enough to deter clients. Subsequently, interventions in a number of areas have been increasingly directed towards this group.

Conclusion

Interestingly, at the end of his article, which seemed to be veering towards impossibilism, Lowman suggests that one way of squaring the circle of accepting the presence of street prostitution while trying to minimize its negative effects upon affected neighbourhoods is to adopt a zoning policy; he argues that certain streets should be designated for the use of prostitutes and their clients and that by implication prostitution should be decriminalized.

At first sight, the comments which I have made above on displacement might seem to suggest that I agree with Lowman's proposal of a zoning policy on the grounds that this would involve a form of benign displacement. Yet despite the apparent similarity our positions are in fact distinctly different. In contrast to Lowman, I would argue for *negative* zoning policy. By this I mean that rather than move prostitution to designated areas the aim should be to remove street prostitution and kerb-crawling *away* from those areas where they cause the most nuisance and have the most detrimental effects. This may appear merely to involve a difference of emphasis. But the difference is important. For it is a strategy which does not embrace the decriminalization of prostitution but rather incorporates the mobilization of legal sanctions in order to provide a more effective system of protection for vulnerable neighbourhoods.

Positive zoning has been tried extensively in America with little long-term success. The problem is that the decriminalization of prostitution encourages the continuous relocation of the trade in new areas potentially more lucrative than those designated. Moreover, the decriminalization of prostitution simultaneously encourages its further commercialization and an increase in the supply of sexual services.

The kind of regulationist policy I have argued for is designed to avoid these pitfalls (Matthews 1986*b*). It recognizes that, although the law in itself may be a blunt instrument for regulating activities of this type, the quasi-legal status of prostitution, and more recently kerb-crawling, provides an important framework for regulating the problems of nuisance associated with street prostitution and establishing some disincentive to those who may want to reap the vast potential profits which would be available if there were a free-for-all in commercialized sexual activity. Equally importantly, the quasi-legal status of prostitution may deter many who may be 'at risk' of adopting this option. Thus the value of the law relating to prostitution cannot be evaluated purely in terms of its immediate effects upon designated populations. Rather, it must also be considered in terms of the normative framework it constructs and its ability to limit the damaging effects of the trade on the more vulnerable sections of the population.

ROGER MATTHEWS

REFERENCES

BARR, R., and PEASE, K. (1990), 'Crime, Displacement and Placement', in M. Tonry and N. Morris (eds.) *Crime and Justice*, vol. 12. Chicago: University of Chicago Press.

HOPE, T., and HOUGH, M. (1988), 'Area, Crime and Incivility', in T. Hope and M. Shaw (eds.), *Communities and Crime Reduction*. London: HMSO.

KELLING, G. (1987), 'Acquiring a Taste For Order', *Crime and Delinquency*, 33 1: 90–103.

LEVINE, P. (1988), 'Prostitution in Florida, a report presented to the Gender Bias Study Commission of the Supreme Court of Florida.

MATTHEWS, R. (1986a), 'Policing Prostitution: A Multi-Agency Approach', Middlesex Polytechnic, Centre for Criminology, Paper no. 1.

—— (1986b), 'Beyond Wolfenden? Prostitution, Politics and the Law', in R. Matthews and J. Young (eds.), *Confronting Crime*: 188–210. London: Sage.

—— (1991a), 'Replacing Broken Windows: Crime, Incivilities and Urban Change', in R. Matthews and J. Young (eds.), *Issues in Realist Criminology*. London: Sage.

—— (1991b), 'Policing Prostitution: Disorder, Crime and Community Safety', report presented to the Home Office, March.

RAMSEY, M. (1989), *Downtown Drinkers: The Perceptions and Fears of the Public in a City Centre*. Crime Prevention Unit, Paper no. 19. London: Home Office.

ROSENBAUM, D. (1986), 'Community Crime Prevention: A Review and a Synthesis of the Literature', *Justice Quarterly*, 5/3: 323–93.

SAMPSON, A. *et al.* (1988) 'Crime, Localities and the Multi-Agency Approach', *British Journal of Criminology*, 28/4.

SKOGAN, W. (1990), *Disorder and Decline*. New York: Free Press; London: Macmillan.

WILSON, J.Q., and KELLING, G. (1982), 'Broken Windows: The Police and Neighbourhood Safety', *Atlantic Monthly*, March: 29–38.

LOWMAN, J. (1992), 'Street Prostitution Control: Some Canadian Reflections on the Finsbury Park Experience', *British Journal of Criminology*, 32/1: 1–17.

22

[24]

What Lockheed and La Cosa Nostra Have in Common

The Effect of Ideology on Criminal Justice Policy

Jay S. Albanese

A comparative analysis is presented of the testimony of A. Carl Kotchian, President of Lockheed Corporation, and that of Joseph Valachi, reputed member of La Cosa Nostra, before Senate investigative committees. In the Lockheed case, the corporation was found to be making illicit payments to foreign officials in order to secure sales abroad. The legislation enacted following the investigation was the Foreign Corrupt Practices Act of 1977, which established criminal penalties for any payment made by American corporations or employees in pursuit of sales contracts abroad.

Joseph Valachi, who had testified before the Senate about ten years before the Lockheed case, confirmed that there existed a nationwide criminal conspiracy, La Cosa Nostra. His testimony provided the major rationale for legislation permitting the federal government to use wiretapping evidence in court, Title III of the Omnibus Crime Control Act of 1968, and legislation allowing the government to force reluctant witnesses to testify before the grand jury, the Organized Crime Control Act of 1970.

There are several extraordinary similarities between these two cases. In both cases the legislation enacted as a result of the investigation ignored important aspects of the organizational behavior in question —seriously impairing the effectiveness of the legislation. In accounting for why important evidence was overlooked, the author suggests that the ideological position of the investigators predisposed them to pursue only the facts consistent with their beliefs about the causes of organizational crime.

A preliminary analysis is undertaken to illustrate the utility of general organization theory in explaining the misbehavior of the organizations in both the Lockheed and La Cosa Nostra cases. It is suggested that refinement of such a model can assist in the prediction of market conditions that are conducive to illicit organizational behavior.

In September 1963, Joseph Valachi appeared before the Senate Subcommittee on Investigations and testified to the existence of a na-

JAY S. ALBANESE: Assistant Professor, Department of Political Science and Criminal Justice, Niagara University, Niagara Falls, New York.

tionwide organization involved in widespread criminal activity. This testimony, together with more detailed information obtained by federal investigators during months of interviews with Valachi, represented the first time anyone ever admitted "belonging to or openly talk[ed] about a huge criminal conspiracy in this country, indeed an entire subculture of evil . . . the Cosa Nostra."[1] In addition to providing his view of the structure of organized crime in the United States, Valachi discussed the processes by which this organization engaged in crime in a systematic manner.

In February 1976, A. Carl Kotchian, president of Lockheed Corporation, testified before the Senate Subcommittee on Multinational Corporations about the extent to which Lockheed was making secret payments to foreign governments in order to sell airplanes overseas. Lockheed became one of the first corporations to admit that these payments were a common practice of United States multinational corporations. In a subsequent book, Kotchian described in detail the motives for, circumstances of, and manner in which these payments were made.

WHERE ORGANIZED AND
WHITE COLLAR CRIME MEET

The circumstances under which these two men testified are extraordinarily similar:

1. Both Valachi and Kotchian were the first "insiders" to detail how illicit activity, heretofore unknown to the federal government, was being carried out.

2. In each case, the activities described were characterized as true of the entire "industry."

3. The testimony of both men was heard as a result of circumstances unrelated to the operations themselves.

4. Finally, in both cases the stories were taken largely as fact by the Senate investigators and the public.

The implications of the testimony of these two men are far-reaching. In Valachi's case, the testimony was used as a rationale for legislation permitting more widespread use of wiretaps and special grand juries through Title III of the Omnibus Crime Control and Safe Streets Act of 1968 and the Organized Crime Control Act of 1970. For Lockheed, the result was the Foreign Corrupt Practices Act of 1977, prohibiting overseas payments made in pursuit of sales contracts. In both cases significant changes in

---

1. Peter Maas, *The Valachi Papers* (New York: Bantam, 1969), p. 1.

Lockheed and La Cosa Nostra **213**

public policy have occurred which have had important effects both for the targets of control and for the agencies charged with enforcing the provisions. Critics have argued that the legislation emanating from the Valachi hearings has resulted in abuses in the use of wiretaps as well as in the conduct of special federal grand jury proceedings.[2] A White House study group has recently reported that the Foreign Corrupt Practices Act could cost American corporations $1 billion a year in business lost to foreign manufacturers.[3] Those arguing in support of these legislative initiatives maintain that the possible abuse of the due process rights of a few is not too high a price to pay for more effective control of organized crime activity, and that some loss to American corporations is of little significance compared with the international repercussions that might result from corporate payments overseas.

The support one can gather in promoting any of these arguments is not impressive. In the literature surveyed for this paper it was found that, for every article in support of these laws, one could be found espousing the opposite view.[4] Although the supporters could provide no objective evidence that organized crime was being controlled more effectively today or that fewer corporate payments were being made to foreign officials, neither could the detractors make an impartial assessment showing any deleterious effects.[5]

The most fruitful approach in explaining this public policy outcome is to reconstruct the circumstances under which these problems became identified as such. Through an examination of the ideological assumptions underlying each investigation, I will show how the remedial legisla-

---

2. Sally Fly, "New Taps on Freedom," *Nation*, June 2, 1969, p. 697; "Judging the Grand Jury," *Time*, Feb. 7, 1972, p. 59.

3. *New York Times*, Jan. 12, 1979, p. 1.

4. Compare Hugh Scott, "Wiretapping and Organized Crime," *Howard Law Journal*, Winter 1968, p. 1, with "Senate Report No. 1097" (to accompany S. 917), Committee on the Judiciary, *U.S. Congressional and Administrative News*, Apr. 29, 1968, p. 2233; compare John McClellan, "The Organized Crime Control Act or Its Critics: Which Threatens Civil Liberties?" *Notre Dame Lawyer*, Fall 1970, p. 55, with "Organized Crime Control Act of 1970," *University of Michigan Journal of Law Reform*, Spring 1971, p. 546; compare "Senate Report No. 95-114" (to accompany S. 305), Committee on Banking, Housing, and Urban Affairs, *U.S. Congressional and Administrative News*, May 2, 1977, p. 4098, with "The Antibribery Bill Backfires," *Business Week*, Apr. 17, 1978, p. 143.

5. See, e.g., J. Estey and D. Marston, "Pitfalls (and Loopholes) in the Foreign Bribery Law," *Fortune*, Oct. 9, 1979, p. 182; Gerald T. McLaughlin, "The Criminalization of Questionable Foreign Payments by Corporations: A Comparative Legal Systems Analysis," *Fordham Law Review*, May 1978, p. 1071; "Law and Order," *New Republic*, June 29, 1968, p. 5; "Criminal Act," *New Republic*, Oct. 17, 1970, p. 4; "Ganging Up on the Mob," *Time*, May 2, 1969, p. 76; "Soft-Headed on Crime," *New Republic*, Oct. 24, 1970, p. 5.

214   **Jay S. Albanese**

tion may merely have been a reflection of ideological beliefs prevalent in each period. In a preliminary analysis I will then illustrate the comparability of these two forms of organized criminality using the perspective of organizational theory.

THE LOCKHEED CASE

S.E.C. *v.* Lockheed Aircraft Corporation

It was June 1972 when five men were arrested during a break-in of Democratic National Committee headquarters in the Watergate Office Building in Washington, D.C. In a search of their hotel rooms the following day, police discovered electronic bugging equipment, a notebook containing the name E. Howard Hunt, and $4,200 in new $100 bills with consecutive serial numbers.[6] In tracing the source of the $100 bills, the FBI found that one of the five, Bernard L. Barker, had withdrawn $89,000 from a Miami bank about a month earlier—money that was originally deposited in the form of Mexican checks contributed to President Nixon's re-election campaign.[7]

These disclosures spurred a General Accounting Office investigation into the financial records of the Committee to Re-elect the President (CREEP) to determine whether the Federal Election Campaign Act had been violated. On August 26, the Accounting Office released its report citing "apparent and possible violations" of the Federal Election Campaign Act by the Finance Committee to CREEP involving up to $350,000 in contributions to President Nixon's re-election campaign.[8] These findings were referred to the Department of Justice for further action, and subsequently became the responsibility of the Office of the Special Prosecutor.

In 1973, as a result of investigations by the special prosecutor, several corporations and corporate executives were charged with illegal use of corporate funds to contribute to domestic political campaigns. The Securities and Exchange Commission (SEC), recognizing the possible significance of these contributions to public investors and the possible violations of federal securities laws because of nondisclosure of these contributions, issued a policy statement on March 8, 1974, expressing concern about disclosing these matters in public filings.[9]

6. U.S., Congress, Senate, Select Committee on Presidential Campaign Activities, *Final Report*, 93rd cong., 2d sess. (no. 93-981) (Washington, D.C.: Govt. Printing Office, 1974).
7. Ibid., p. 37.
8. Milton S. Gwertzman, "GAO Report Asks Justice Inquiry into GOP Funds," *New York Times*, Aug. 27, 1972, p. 1.
9. Securities Act Release No. 5466, Mar. 8, 1974.

Lockheed and La Cosa Nostra   **215**

The SEC's subsequent investigation discovered that there had been such violations of securities laws:

> The staff discovered falsifications of corporate financial records, designed to disguise or conceal the source and application of corporate funds misused for illegal purposes, as well as the existence of secret "slush funds" disbursed outside the normal financial accountability system.[10]

The SEC found that these secret funds were sometimes used for "questionable or illegal" *foreign* payments as well. Within a year the SEC initiated injunctive actions against nine corporations. Lockheed was not among them.

After its later investigation of Lockheed in 1976, the SEC summarized the complaint against Lockheed to the Senate Committee on Banking, Housing, and Urban Affairs, as follows:

> *Lockheed Aircraft Corporation:* The Commission complaint named Lockheed, the Chairman of the Board of Directors from 1967 until February 1976, and the President of the company from 1967 until October, 1975. In particular, the Commission alleged that secret payments of at least $25 million (at times in cash) had been made to foreign government officials for the purpose of assisting Lockheed in procuring and maintaining contracts with foreign government customers, and in expediting permits to perform existing contracts. Among other things, it was alleged that the defendants disguised these secret payments on Lockheed's books and records by utilizing, or causing to be utilized, false accounting entries, cash or "bearer" drafts payable directly to foreign government officials, nominees and conduits for payments to government officials and other artifices and schemes. As a result of their activities, at least $750,000 was not expended for the purpose indicated on the books and records of Lockheed and its subsidiaries and was deposited instead in a secret Swiss bank account, and an additional $25 million was expended in secret payments to foreign officials. In addition, the Commission alleged that over $200 million was disbursed to consultants and commission agents without adequate records and controls to insure that the services were actually rendered. The practices were alleged to have resulted in the filing of inaccurate financial statements with the Commission with respect to the income, cost, and expenses of the company.[11]

It can be seen that the case against Lockheed alleges several things—not all of which are entirely clear.

10. U.S., Congress, Senate, Committee on Banking, Housing, and Urban Affairs, *Report of the Securities and Exchange Commission on Questionable and Illegal Corporate Payments and Practices*, 94th cong., 2d sess. (Washington, D.C.: Govt. Printing Office, 1976).
11. Ibid., Exhibit B-22.

216 Jay S. Albanese

Amount	Purpose
1. At least $25 million	Secret payments to foreign government officials to assist in procuring and maintaining foreign sales contracts.
2. At least $25 million	Disguised these payments on the books in various ways.
3. At least $750,000	Not expended for the purpose shown, but deposited in a Swiss bank account.
4. Over $200 million	Disbursed to consultants and sales agents without proper records and controls.

Broken down into these four particulars, an analysis shows that the first charge was not illegal at the time it occurred. Not until the Foreign Corrupt Practices Act was signed into law in December 1977 was it illegal to make any kind of payments in pursuit of foreign sales. Charges 2 and 3 are fairly obvious violations of federal securities laws relating to disclosure. Charge 4 is not an obvious violation, and may not be a violation at all, if it stems more from an accounting problem than from a deliberate attempt to disburse monies without proper accountability. With these final charges in mind, an assessment of the Lockheed testimony explaining the corporation's foreign sales activities can be better evaluated.

It should be pointed out that the testimony given by Kotchian to the Senate Subcommittee on Multinational Corporations was not a direct result of the SEC's findings. As noted previously, the SEC investigation was spurred by action of the special prosecutor, who moved against corporations making contributions to CREEP. Lockheed, however, made no contributions to CREEP. Therefore, it had to be through some other means that the SEC came to investigate Lockheed. Ironically, it was a result of testimony made by one of the company's competitors.

Having been found by the special prosecutor to have made illegal corporate contributions to CREEP, Northrop Corporation was fined $5,000 and its president fined an additional $1,000. Further investigation by the SEC uncovered political contributions that were made to foreign governments as well. This aroused the interest of the Senate Committee on Foreign Relations, which was concerned about the effects of these payments on United States foreign policy objectives, especially because Northrop's sales involved military aircraft. The result was a series of hearings conducted by the Subcommittee on Multinational Corporations during 1975–76 to determine the motives behind, and possible consequences of, such payments to foreign governments.

Officials from Northrop were the first to testify before the subcommittee in June 1975. During the questioning, subcommittee chairman Frank Church queried the Northrop president and its chairman, Thomas V.

Lockheed and La Cosa Nostra 217

Jones, about Northrop's method of paying foreign consultants (through a Swiss "dummy" corporation, Economic Development Corp., or EDC), set up exclusively for this purpose by Northrop to exert their influence in arranging overseas sales. Using supporting documentation obtained by the subcommittee from Northrop, Senator Church sought to uncover Northrop's inspiration in developing this complex financial arrangement.

> *Senator Church:* Was this whole arrangement patterned after the Lockheed arrangement? [referring to comments made in subpoenaed Northrop memos]
> *Mr. Jones:* Well, Mr. DeFrancis [the attorney who set up EDC] kept speaking of it as a Lockheed arrangement.
> *Senator Church:* Yes.
> *Mr. Jones:* I cannot vouch for really. . . .
> *Mr. Levinson* [counsel to the subcommittee]: You had a copy of the Lockheed contract?
> *Mr. Jones:* Yes, sir.
> *Mr. Levinson:* So you knew what the Lockheed arrangement was, and it was patterned after the Lockheed arrangement. It was not that Mr. DeFrancis said so, you had a contract to refer to.
> *Mr. Jones:* That's right. But how they had their reporting system, how they understood what they were doing, I cannot speak for. I am only speaking for Northrop. We have a contract.
> *Senator Church:* Your contract with EDC was patterned after the Lockheed contract?
> *Mr. Jones:* Yes.[12]

It was this exchange, more than anything else, that brought Lockheed into the investigation.[13] The exchange prompted the Lockheed Board of Directors to order a special investigation by the company's auditors to see whether there was any basis for the Northrop claims.[14] Three months later, Chairman Daniel J. Haughton was called to testify before the subcommittee. Senator Charles Percy confirms the connection with the Northrop investigation in his opening statement at the Haughton hearings:

> This morning's hearings are an outgrowth of this subcommittee's previous hearings on the sales practices of Northrop Corp. In the Northrop

12. U.S. Congress, Senate, Committee on Foreign Relations, Subcommittee on Multinational Corporations, *Multinational Corporations and U.S. Foreign Policy—Hearings Part 12*, 94th cong., 1st sess. (Washington, D.C.: Govt. Printing Office, 1976), pp. 159–60 (hereinafter cited as *Hearings—Part 12*).

13. In an interview with Kotchian, conducted in 1978, I questioned him about this exchange. He expressed doubt about whether Lockheed would ever have become involved in these hearings and investigations if this exchange had not taken place.

14. U.S., Congress, Senate, Committee on Foreign Relations, Subcommittee on Multinational Corporations, *Multinational Corporations and United States Foreign Policy—Hearings Part 14*, 94th cong., 2d sess. (Washington, D.C.: Govt. Printing Office, 1976), p. 303 (hereinafter cited as *Hearings—Part 14*).

documents there was repeated reference to the necessity of duplicating the sales structure of Lockheed.[15]

The Haughton testimony laid the groundwork for what was to be discussed during Kotchian's testimony in February 1976.[16] Because Kotchian was present during many of the overseas sales negotiations, he was able to confirm many of the specific allegations made by the subcommittee. Haughton, however, did make many of the assertions later repeated by Kotchian.

In his prepared statement, Haughton declared,

> Lockheed does not defend or condone the practice of payments to foreign officials. We only say that the practice exists, that in many countries it appeared, as a matter of business judgement, necessary in order to compete against both U.S. and foreign competitors.[17]

This was, perhaps, the most striking aspect of the Lockheed testimony. There was no question of whether payments had been made to foreign government officials. This was freely admitted during the course of the hearings. The questions that arose during the Senate hearings, as well as in the ensuing SEC investigation, were of five kinds:

1. How much money was spent in payments to foreign government officials, as opposed to normal and accepted payments for the services of foreign sales agents or consultants?

2. While the payments might not be against United States law, were any United States laws (i.e., tax or securities laws) broken in the *process* of Lockheed's making these payments?

3. How legitimate was the rationale offered by Lockheed in justifying these payments?

4. How serious are the consequences of foreign payments for multinational corporations and foreign relations?

5. What sort of remedial measures should be taken to correct this situation?

Unfortunately, the issues raised were never followed up sufficiently at any time during these investigations. The questions put to the Lockheed officials jumped from one topic to another, leaving the impression that more questions were raised during these hearings than were answered. Indeed, this is the case. Of the five questions above, the Senate hearings brought out what Lockheed's rationale was for making these payments,

---

15. *Hearings—Part 12*, pp. 342–43.

16. It should be noted that the testimony of both these men occurred before the *SEC* v. *Lockheed* settlement in April 1976. Therefore, there was little established as fact about these payments at the time of these hearings.

17. *Hearings—Part 12*, p. 346.

Lockheed and La Cosa Nostra **219**

but failed to establish its legitimacy, and also provided an indication of the subcommittee's position in instituting corrective measures.

Questions 1 and 2 were later answered largely through Lockheed's consent decree with the SEC in 1976, which was summarized earlier. These questions were pivotal, of course, in creating the new policy governing payments. The determination of the extent and nature of these payments was of primary concern and was established through SEC audits and interviews with corporate personnel and agents. The legitimacy of Lockheed's rationale for making these payments was also a crucial concern, as it would affect perceptions of responsibility for decisions made, an issue of fundamental importance in the possible recommendation of legislation affecting civil or criminal law.

How Much Money Was Paid to
Foreign Government Officials?

As set forth in the 1976 SEC complaint against Lockheed, the funds Lockheed was alleged to have misspent, or not to have accounted for properly, never became clearer than the figures cited earlier. That is, the most serious charge against Lockheed was that at least $750,000 was not expended for the purposes claimed, but was deposited in a Swiss bank account (and then, as was found by investigators, used to pay confidential agents with connections in influential government circles to assist in sales efforts). The second serious charge was that at least $25 million was disguised on Lockheed's books as something other than payments to foreign officials. It should be noted that the SEC complaint was settled with Lockheed in the form of a consent decree: There was no admission of guilt, but an agreement by the corporation to discontinue the practices alleged. Thus, either Lockheed may have made more payments to officials and placed more false entries in the books, but this was all the SEC could prove, or Lockheed agreed to this settlement rather than going to trial and risking greater exposure to events that were seen as having received too much attention already. In either case, the public disapprobation of Lockheed's sales activities overseas during this period was intense. Both editorial opinion and public reaction, as measured through opinion polls, overwhelmingly placed responsibility on the corporations for engaging in this questionable behavior.[18]

Public condemnation of these payments before their extent and rationale were made known suggests that there was already an ideological stance

18. See, e.g., Mark Green, "Crime Up in Big Business Too, SEC Discovers," *New York Times*, May 11, 1975, p. E17; W. Michael Blumenthal, "New Business Watchdog Needed," *New York Times*, May 25, 1975, p. 31; Andrew Hacker, "In Business, Ethics Is Not a Big Seller," *New York Times*, June 15, 1975, p. 31.

against corporations.[19] Several reasons can be offered for this critical attitude toward corporations. Most prominent is the fact that these disclosures of foreign payments immediately followed Watergate and the discovery of domestic political contributions by a number of corporations. Corporations were widely seen as "buying" influence in government affairs through their contributions. There may also have been disillusionment with institutions in general following Watergate and the illegal contributions to CREEP, leaving the public with a "them against us" attitude. In either case, there was a generally critical attitude toward corporations at the time these foreign payments were disclosed.

Were United States Laws Broken in the Process of the Corporate Payments?

Probably the most serious charge against the corporations involved was the violations of tax and securities laws in the failure to declare these payments to the Internal Revenue Service or to shareholders. It was not established, however, that these laws had been violated because consent decrees, which do not involve admissions of guilt, were reached with the SEC. In any event, most of the corporations involved did not reach settlements with the SEC until 1976, which was well after adverse public sentiment had been expressed.

Thus, it did not become clear during these corporate disclosures in 1975 that *any* laws had been broken. But this did not prevent public objections to unsavory corporate "morality," again suggesting that ideological position was an important factor in predisposing the public to adopt a critical view.

Was the Lockheed Rationale Legitimate?

As mentioned above, the legitimacy of Lockheed's rationale for making payments to foreign government officials is crucial in assessing culpability. The rationale offered by Kotchian consisted of the following:

> *Mr. Kotchian:* We had lost a sale of P-3 airplanes in The Netherlands which was a very important sale. We lost it to the French Atlantique. We immediately took the people who were working on that campaign to sell the Italians the P-3 airplanes.
>
> Here again, we lost to the French with the Atlantique. Our man, Mr. Wilder, who was mentioned earlier, was approached by an Italian Senator in

19. Ideology is used here in the same context as used by Walter Miller in "Ideology and Criminal Justice Policy," *Journal of Criminal Law and Criminology*, June 1973, p. 142. It refers "only to a set of general and abstract beliefs or assumptions about the correct or proper state of things, particularly with respect to the moral order and political arrangements, which serve to shape one's positions on specific issues."

the Italian Senate and told us we should obtain a consultant in Rome if we wished to sell planes.

Senator Percy: Could you go back through as to why you lost to the French? Did you lose to the French because of the technical superiority of the plane, or did you lose because they paid more in your judgment?

Mr. Kotchian: In my judgment it was the latter because our airplane was much superior.

Senator Percy: In other words, an inferior product was purchased because they were willing to pay more and those were the circumstances that you faced, then, in your campaign in Italy?

Mr. Kotchian: Yes, sir.

Kotchian described another, similar situation later in his testimony.

> *Mr. Kotchian:* While I was still in Italy, or it may have been when I went through there during this campaign, I remembered Mr. Lefevbre [Lockheed's sales agent in Italy] . . . said, "I'm embarrassed, and I'm just chagrined, but I'm going to have to recommend to you that you make some payments if you wish to sell airplanes in this country."
>
> *Senator Percy:* In other words, you just simply couldn't, no matter how superior a product was, you couldn't sell airplanes unless a bribe was paid.
>
> *Mr. Kotchian:* It was his opinion, and that was the case, sir.[20]

These passages exemplify the ambiguity that arises in assessing responsibility for these payments. In this Italian case it appears that Lockheed did not initiate these payments, but that the purchasing government demanded payments before it would consider purchasing aircraft.

Lockheed's experience in making sales in Japan during 1968–75 was the subject of a book written by Kotchian and published in Japan in 1976.[21] For these sales, the procedure was less ambiguous. Kotchian was told by Lockheed's trading company (a Japanese trading company representing Lockheed in sales efforts in Japan) representative, "If you wish to be successful in selling the aircraft, you would do well to pledge 500 million yen." This pledge of 500 million yen was to go to Japanese Prime Minister Tanaka.[22] Later in the sales mission, when it was still unclear which corporation would be awarded the contract, Kotchian was told by the representative that in order to complete the sale it will be necessary "to give $300,000 [90 million yen] to Mr. Wakasa [President of Japanese airline receiving planes] and also to make payments to six politicians."[23] These are two of a number of instances in which Kotchian was asked to make payments to government officials during the sales effort. According to Kotchian, payments in Japan totaled $12 million. Although ostensibly

20. *Hearings—Part 14,* p. 378–80.

21. *Rokkiedo Jiken* (Lockheed Incident), Book I: Lockheed Sales Mission (Tokyo, Japan: Asahi Shimbun, 1976).

22. Ibid., pp. 106ff.

23. Ibid., p. 196.

this is a huge sum, as he points out, it amounted to less than 3 percent of the expected $430 million for the total sale of twenty-one planes.[24] And these payments did not violate existing American laws.

Perhaps most important in Kotchian's defense of Lockheed's payments is the fact that they "were all requested by Mr. Okubo [Japanese representative] and were not brought up from my side."[25] This is of interest because it raises the question of whether Lockheed made these payments as bribes, or whether they were extorted from Lockheed. Kotchian maintains that the latter explanation is more accurate:

> When in August, 1972, I was requested by Mr. Okubo to make a pledge of 500 million yen to the office of Japan's Prime Minister, I at once expressed doubt by saying, "Couldn't Marubeni [the trading company] pay this out of its commission?" However, when I was told that I must make the pledge of 500 million yen, or we would not be successful, I was convinced that our competitors were doing the same thing; that is to say, I thought the pledge of money was like admission to a ballgame. And if you didn't pay the admission, you were not even qualified to participate in the game—your product would not even be considered.

He continues,

> Such was our conclusion; so the payment of money was not an offensive, but rather a defensive strategy to defend ourselves in the game of international trade.[26]

This explanation by Lockheed throws doubt on the prevailing feeling that corporations "bribed" foreign governments in order to obtain sales contracts. It appears that it would have been in order to check on the accuracy of Lockheed's claims.

*How Serious Have the Consequences
of These Payments Been?*

With the advantage of hindsight, it appears that the investigation of the payments, highlighted by the Senate public hearings, had more serious consequences than did the actual payments themselves. Several countries initiated investigations of government officials who were implicated by these disclosures in the United States, as, for example, the investigation of Prince Bernhard in The Netherlands, who was alleged by Lockheed to have received over $1 million.[27] The large-scale investigation in Japan of former Prime Minister Tanaka and a number of other Japanese government officials and businessmen mentioned in the Lockheed testimony and

24. Ibid., p. 230.
25. Ibid., p. 231.
26. Ibid., p. 236.
27. See David Boulton, *The Grease Machine* (New York: Harper & Row, 1978), ch. 5.

Lockheed and La Cosa Nostra

subpoenaed documents was the most notable. The conclusions drawn in 1977 by the Japanese prosecutors supported Kotchian's version of the events as he had recorded them in his book a year earlier,[28] lending even more credence to the view that these payments more closely resembled extortion than they did bribery.

It would seem that an analysis of the rationale for Lockheed's making these payments in other countries would have been conducted to see whether a similar distinction could be made between corporate bribery and foreign government extortion. Unfortunately, this did not take place. Senator Church mentioned during the hearings the possible effects of these payments on inflation,[29] and on gains made by the Communist party in Italy because of a widespread feeling that corruption at high levels of government was pervasive[30]; however, no investigation was carried out to determine whether or not the corporate payments really played a significant role in these developments. Although the subcommittee maintained that the primary concern in holding the hearings was the effect that foreign payments may have had on United States foreign policy objectives, no systematic analysis was ever conducted. Indeed, it appears the disclosures of these payments by the subcommittee had a more serious effect than did the payments themselves.

What Sort of Remedial Measures Were Correct?

From the first day of the hearings, legislation was seen as the means to a solution.[31] Both senators Church and Percy recognized, however, that international agreements would be the most effective way to eliminate undesirable payments.[32] Although this alternative was referred to the United Nations for consideration (the United Nations is still working on an international agreement), the subcommittee members, apparently feeling a need to propose some measure of their own, individually recommended changes in United States law.[33]

Haughton and Kotchian both emphasized the need for all corporations to be bound by the same rules, because they strongly suspected that their competitors (both United States and foreign) were also making payments.[34] The senators asked Haughton and Kotchian whether they felt

28. Transcript of Tanaka Trial, *Asahi Journal*, Feb. 11, 1977, pp. 4–84; Prosecutor's Opening Statement at Trial of Hashimoto et al., *Asahi Journal*, Feb. 18, 1977, pp. 87–118.
29. *Hearings—Part 12*, pp. 352–53, 388–90.
30. Ibid., p. 375; *Hearings—Part 14*, p. 1.
31. *Hearings—Part 12*, p. 2; *Hearings—Part 14*, pp. 1–2.
32. *Hearings—Part 12*, p. 356; *Hearings—Part 14*, p. 380.
33. No final committee report ever emerged from these hearings.
34. This was subsequently confirmed when Boeing, Grumman, McDonnell-Douglas, and Northrop were all charged by the SEC with making foreign payments abroad similar to Lockheed's.

public disclosure should be required of all commissions or agency payments made abroad. Neither regarded this as desirable in all cases, because the loss of secrecy would better enable other corporations to disparage the reputation of their competitors' consultants.[35]

The result of this ambiguity about the desirability of disclosure, international agreements, and the distinction between bribery and extortion was the Foreign Corrupt Practices Act of 1977.[36]

Foreign Corrupt Practices Act of 1977

The Foreign Corrupt Practices Act is divided into two titles covering the two main features of the bill: payments and disclosure. Title I, "Foreign Corrupt Practices," is summarized as follows:

> 1. Requires companies subject to the jurisdiction of the SEC to maintain strict accounting standards and management control over their assets;
> 2. Prohibits falsification of accounting records and the deceit of accountants auditing the books and records of such companies; and
> 3. Makes it a crime for U.S. companies to bribe a foreign government official for the specified corrupt purposes [influence in obtaining or maintaining sales]. Companies violating the criminal prohibitions face maximum fines of $500,000 (this was later changed in conference to $1 million). Individuals acting on behalf of such companies face a maximum fine of $10,000 and 5 years in jail.[37]

It is interesting to notice that even this official summary uses the word *bribe* to describe these payments made by corporations. It is useful at this point to refer back to Miller's explanation of ideological position; as this arguably bears on the government actions taken:

> Several aspects of ideology . . . should be noted. First, ideological assumptions are generally pre-conscious rather than explicit, and serve, under most circumstances, as unexamined presumptions underlying positions taken openly. Second, ideological assumptions bear a strong emotional charge. The charge is not always evident, but it can readily be activated by the appropriate stimuli, in particular by direct challenge.

Miller than describes the consequences of ideology:

> Ideology and its consequences exert a powerful influence on the policies and procedures of those who conduct the enterprise of criminal justice, and . . . the degree and kinds of influence go largely unrecognized. *Ideology is the permanent hidden agenda of criminal justice* (emphasis added).[38]

35. *Hearings—Part 12*, p. 383–84; *Hearings—Part 14*, p. 369.
36. Pub. Law 95-213.
37. "Senate Report No. 95-114," p. 4100.
38. Miller, "Ideology and Criminal Justice Policy," p. 142.

Lockheed and La Cosa Nostra 225

In spite of many statements made during the hearings about the extortionate aspects of these payments, and the fact that comparable payments were being made by foreign competitors, making some kind of international agreement necessary, the Foreign Corrupt Practices Act was signed into law restricting American multinational corporations from making payments abroad. Such a restriction placed responsibility on United States corporations for the character of the transactions and ignored the pressures of the international marketplace, which the testimony from Lockheed officials and others had pointed to as the reason for the payments.

Thus, the Senate investigators began their hearings referring to the payments as bribes, and legislation was passed despite evidence to the contrary. Ideological assumptions, "once established, . . . become relatively impervious to change, since they serve to receive or reject new evidence in terms of a self-contained and self-reinforcing system."[39] It appears that the ideological position of the Senate committee (and the SEC, which supported this act) had an important influence in this legislation.

THE VALACHI HEARINGS

As were the Lockheed officials, Valachi was testifying to the existence of activities not previously known by the United States government. As in the later hearings, Valachi's testimony came about because of circumstances extraneous to his involvement in these activities.

In the Valachi case, the witness's willingness to come forward stemmed from a prison murder. Believing himself marked to be killed in prison by his "boss," and to prevent that from happening, Valachi killed a fellow inmate who turned out to be an innocent bystander. To escape the death penalty for his crime, and feeling betrayed by his organization, Valachi agreed to cooperate with federal investigators.

Appearing before the Permanent Subcommittee on Investigations of the Senate Committee on Government Operations, Valachi described a number of activities and a structured criminal organization, providing information about the nature and extent of organized crime in the United States not heretofore known by the federal government. The two major subjects covered by Valachi were

1. A power struggle among Italian-American gangs during the early 1930s, called the Castellemmarese War.
2. The existence of a structured organization, called La Cosa Nostra, whose principal activities are criminal.

In addition, Valachi gave the details of a number of murders in New York

39. Ibid.

City which were confirmed as open cases by the New York City Police Department.

The veracity of Valachi's testimony became an important issue because of his unsavory past and also because he was facing a murder charge. The primary method used to establish the witness's reliability was the confirmation by police that the murders Valachi described had indeed occurred. Yet a number of questions about the evidence given remain unresolved.

For example, Valachi stated that, during the Castellemmarese War, up to sixty persons may have been killed. However, Valachi was only able to name a few of those killings.[40] Valachi also claimed that the Castellemmarese War was national in scope:

> *Mr. Alderman* [counsel to the committee]: Did Masseria declare or condemn anybody who came from that area [the Castellemmarese area of Sicily], no matter where they were in the United States, to death?
> *Mr. Valachi:* All Castellemmarese. That is the way I was told. I never found out the reason. I never asked for the reason. All I understand is that all the Castellemmarese were sentenced to death.
> *Senator McClellan:* That is when all-out war was declared by the other side?
> *Mr. Valachi:* That is, I would put it, national.
> *Senator McClellan:* It was made national.
> *Mr. Valachi:* It was made in all cities, wherever the members were—in Chicago, and Cleveland, and California.[41]

The question that arises here is, how does a gang fight become a national war when only a handful of sites are mentioned and actual events can only be described in one location (New York City)? This was not pursued further by the subcommittee. Neither was an alternate account of these same killings given a decade earlier.[42] Inexplicably, there was not even a check of whether sixty people were killed during this period in the manner Valachi described. Two separate subsequent historical works have confirmed only four or five deaths and no evidence of a national "gangland war."[43]

---

40. U.S. Congress, Senate, Committee on Government Operations, Permanent Subcommittee on Investigations, *Organized Crime and Illicit Traffic in Narcotics—Hearings Part I*, 88th cong., 1st sess. (Washington, D.C.: Govt. Printing Office, 1963) (hereinafter cited as *Hearings—Part I*).

41. Ibid., p. 180.

42. Burton B. Turkus and Sid Feder, *Murder, Inc.: The Story of "The Syndicate"* (New York: Bantam Books, 1951).

43. Alan A. Block, "History and the Study of Organized Crime," *Urban Life*, January 1978, pp. 455–74; Humbert S. Nelli, *The Business of Crime* (New York: Oxford University Press, 1976), pp. 179–218.

Lockheed and La Cosa Nostra   **227**

The Existence of La Cosa Nostra

Whereas the Lockheed hearings provided information that was ignored by investigators in subsequent legislation, Valachi's version of events was accepted by Senate investigators (and the Justice Department) in spite of incomplete evidence and available conflicting information. This is a serious concern, for Valachi's testimony to the existence and structure of the Cosa Nostra, and to the Castellemmarese War as its immediate precursor, has become the basis for many subsequent influential writings on organized crime and enforcement strategies.[44]

Valachi described the organizational structure as consisting of "the individual bosses of the individual families, and then we had an underboss, and then we had what we call a caporegima which is a lieutenant, and then we have what we call soldiers."[45] When it came to Valachi's specifying the role of the organization in the lives of its members, the Cosa Nostra appeared less organized.

> *Senator Javits:* Now, what he [Vito Genovese] got out of it then, your actions and those of other members of the family, was to kill off or otherwise deal with people who were bothering him; is that right?
>
> *Mr. Valachi:* Anybody bothering him, naturally he has the soldiers.
>
> *Senator Javits:* That is the function of the family?
>
> *Mr. Valachi:* Right.
>
> *Senator Javits:* That is mutual protection?
>
> *Mr. Valachi:* Right.
>
> *Senator Javits:* Through strong-arm methods by you and by other soldiers?
>
> *Mr. Valachi:* Right.
>
> *Senator Javits:* That is the total of it.
>
> *Mr. Valachi:* Right.
>
> *Senator Javits:* Otherwise, everybody operates by himself. They may take partners but that is their option.
>
> *Mr. Valachi:* Right.[46]

Given this scenario, it appears that if an organization existed at all, it was a very loose association.

Valachi also provided information about the members of the Cosa Nostra "families" in the New York area. Although all the law enforcement personnel who testified, including Attorney General Robert Ken-

---

44. See, e.g., President's Commission on Law Enforcement and Administration of Justice, *Task Force Report: Organized Crime* (Washington, D.C.: Govt. Printing Office, 1967); Donald Cressey, *Theft of the Nation: The Structure and Operations of Organized Crime in America* (New York: Harper and Row, 1969).

45. *Hearings—Part I,* p. 80.

46. Ibid., p. 116; see also p. 194.

nedy, claimed that a nationwide criminal organization did exist, no one could provide supporting information independent of Valachi's statements.[47]

> *Senator Muskie:* Would it have been possible for you to reconstruct these charts [of Cosa Nostra families] without his testimony?
> *Mr. Shanley:* [of the Intelligence Unit of the New York City Police Department]: No, sir.[48]

Other shortcomings of Valachi's story, such as why his testimony proved of little value in criminal prosecutions, have been fully assessed elsewhere.[49] Yet these shortcomings were ignored in the investigators' desire to accept the story being told. The subcommittee's willingness to accept Valachi's often uncorroborated testimony has been explained by Smith:

> The Subcommittee wanted to hear what Valachi told them, and once he had satisfied that desire there was little need to be skeptical or to press for additional, independent corroboration. It was a case of a story being true because it sounded like what ought to be heard.[50]

The unwillingness to make the distinction between "fact" and "value" makes it difficult, according to Miller, to estimate "the degree to which statements forwarded as established conclusions are based on ideological doctrine rather than empirically supportable evidence."[51] As a result, legislation coming from ideology, as opposed to fact, can be expected to address ideological questions rather than questions of fact. The subcommittee's ideological assumptions about the nature of organized crime guided the investigation and helped shape the subsequent legislation.

New Organized Crime Legislation

The reason why the Department of Justice had Valachi testify publicly was made clear by Attorney General Robert Kennedy at the beginning of the hearings:

> One major purpose in my appearing here is to seek the help of Congress in the form of additional legislation—the authority to provide immunity to witnesses in racketeering investigations; and reform and revision of the wiretapping law.[52]

47. Ibid., p. 262; see also pp. 6ff., 24, 52, 63.
48. Ibid., p. 262.
49. Dwight C. Smith, Jr., *The Mafia Mystique* (New York: Basic Books, 1975), ch. 8.
50. Ibid., p. 234.
51. Miller, "Ideology and Criminal Justice Policy," p. 154.
52. *Hearings—Part I*, p. 15.

Lockheed and La Cosa Nostra   229

Kennedy also pointed to the need for public support.

> We have yet to exploit properly our most powerful asset in the battle against the rackets: an aroused, informed, and insistent public.[53]

These and other similar statements make it obvious that Kennedy hoped to arouse the public, and, hence, Congressional indignation about organized crime (by telling them there was a nationwide criminal conspiracy). The result would be laws permitting wiretapping by federal law enforcement agencies and a provision enabling suspects to testify to incriminating activities through the use of immunity. These policy aims were not to be met until 1968, when civil liberties objections were overcome.[54]

The first law that was enacted as a result of the Valachi testimony (and its repetition in the 1967 President's Crime Commission Report) was the Omnibus Crime Control and Safe Streets Act of 1968.[55] Title III of this act provided law enforcement agencies with the power to wiretap in organized crime cases. Two years later, the Organized Crime Control Act of 1970 was passed establishing special grand juries and the power of immunity from prosecution to compel witnesses to testify.[56] As indicated earlier, both these acts had vehement defenders and critics, even though objective evidence was sparse.[57]

At this point it is interesting to look back at Attorney General Kennedy's testimony before the subcommittee in 1963.

> Senator, if those three bills were passed, the wiretapping, which is the most important, plus the immunity bills, then I would think that the need for this kind of hearing 5 years from now would not be necessary.
>
> I think you are still going to have organized crime, you are still going to have problems, but the major effect that it has, on people's lives and on communities would not exist 5 years from now.[58]

It was presumptive to have expected the wiretapping and immunity bills to make a difference in the effect of organized crime. If the existence of a nationwide criminal conspiracy could be established, if that organization demonstrably used the telephone to discuss criminal activity, and if its members would not testify because they could not get immunity, then these laws could be reasonably expected to have an effect. The Valachi

---

53. Ibid., p. 9.

54. For an interesting analysis of the debate and ultimate passage of the Omnibus Crime Control Act, see Richard Harris, *The Fear of Crime* (New York: Praeger, 1968).

55. Pub. Law 90-351; Statutes, vol. 82, p. 197.

56. Pub. Law 91-452; Statutes, vol. 84, p. 922.

57. See note 5.

58. *Hearings—Part I*, p. 19.

hearings provided no objective evidence that this was the case. Instead, the laws were built on the ideological assumptions of their authors.

This misdiagnosis could have been prevented if, rather than focusing on unsupported (and mostly secondhand) accounts of organized criminality, the Senate and Justice Department investigators had looked at the reasons behind organized criminal behavior.

AN ALTERNATE THEORY OF ENTERPRISE

Common to both the Lockheed and Valachi cases is the concept of "organization." In both cases, illicit activity was carried out through organizational processes. Furthermore, the behavior engaged in by Lockheed and La Cosa Nostra had an economic base. For Lockheed, the purpose of foreign payments was to obtain sales. For La Cosa Nostra, the purpose of the organization was, according to Valachi, protection from rival gangs in operating illegitimate business, consisting primarily of gambling. This similarity of purpose and organization has, until recently, been overlooked in explanations of organized criminal behavior. These factors, together with situational variables, can do much to clarify the genesis of organized illicit behavior.

While the nature of behavior prevalent in both corporate and organized crime has resembled conspiracy (i.e., corporations conspire to maximize profits without regard for law or morality, and organized crime conspires to sell illicit goods and services), recent writers have been giving more attention to the organizational aspects of this behavior. For example, although Cressey subscribes to the view of organized crime as a conspiracy, as indicated in his writings of the late 1960s,[59] in 1972 he published *Criminal Organization*, in which he examined organized crime from the point of view of structure.[60] Yet even in the later work Cressey places too much emphasis on the internal orderings of criminal organizations, with insufficient attention to the forces of the marketplace in which these organizations exist. Obviously, an organization cannot be criminal in a vacuum. It can only become criminal in performing an illegal act. Behavior is, therefore, the key criterion in determining criminality, and the interaction between the organization and what has been called its "task environment"[61] is critical in explaining organized criminal behavior. Overlooking this interaction, Cressey points to the single dimension of "rationality" as the motivational force behind organized criminal activity. This, however, does not help distinguish between legitimate and illegitimate behavior,

59. President's Commission on Law Enforcement and Administration of Justice, *Task Force Report*; Cressey, *Theft of the Nation*.

60. Donald Cressey, *Criminal Organization* (New York: Harper and Row, 1972).

61. Dwight C. Smith, Jr., "Organized Crime and Entrepreneurship," *International Journal of Criminology and Penology*, May 1978, p. 165.

nor does it provide a clue as to how illegitimate organizations or their activities come about.

A more useful approach was recently put forth by Smith,[62] who applies general organizational concepts drawn from organizational theory to what he calls a "spectrum-based theory of enterprise." As in traditional organizational theory, organizational functions are broken down into four main types:[63]

> *Long-linked Technology:* Usually entailing the manufacture of a product from raw material to marketable goods.
> *Intensive Technology:* When a number of goods and services are organized to service a particular consumer.
> *Mediating Technology:* When a good or service is provided that joins together a supplier and consumer.
> *Service Technology:* When a service is the product desired by the consumer.

Every organization has a particular technology that it employs to establish and maintain domain in its own industry, whether it be aircraft or a numbers bank. To examine both Lockheed and La Cosa Nostra in terms of Smith's enterprise theory, it is first necessary to look at the technologies of the two forms of organizational behavior.

While it can be said that Valachi's enterprise primarily involved a service technology and Kotchian's a long-linked technology, it is the mediating technology of each enterprise that was critical in prompting their testimony before the Senate subcommittees; that is, the mediating technology of power brokering was of primary concern in the Senate investigations. For Kotchian, payments to foreign officials were necessary to establish a "favorable climate" for selling aircraft overseas.[64] For Valachi, it was the bribery of public officials to gain protection for illegal goods and services.[65]

The problem of legitimacy was also a factor in both cases. In Lockheed, the distinction between legitimacy and illegitimacy was based on the answers to two questions: (1) Were the payments made legal as accepted consultant or commission fees? (2) Were securities and tax laws complied with in the reporting of these payments to stockholders and the SEC? The Lockheed hearings did not place in question the legitimacy of the enterprise itself (i.e., Lockheed as a corporation chartered to manufacture

---

62. Dwight C. Smith, Jr., "Paragons, Pariahs, and Pirates: A Spectrum-Based Theory of Enterprise," *Crime & Delinquency*, July 1980, pp. 358–86.

63. See James Thompson, *Organizations in Action* (New York: McGraw-Hill, 1967).

64. *Hearings—Part 14*, p. 349.

65. U.S., Congress, Senate, Committee on Government Operations, Permanent Subcommittee on Investigations, *Report on Organized Crime and Illicit Traffic in Narcotics*, 89th cong., 1st sess. (Washington, D.C.: Govt. Printing Office, 1965), p. 125.

aerospace equipment), but they did challenge the legitimacy of certain activities going on *within* that enterprise. The Valachi hearings differed from the Lockheed hearings in this respect.

The Valachi hearings were designed to prove the existence of an organized conspiracy to commit crime. The focus of the committee, as a consequence, was to propose ways to destroy this organized conspiracy rather than to deal with any particular form of illicit behavior going on within it. This, in all probability, doomed the committee to failure from the outset. Without looking at the dynamics causing the formation of organized criminal activity, attempts to destroy existing organizations will do nothing for others replacing them, especially if market forces caused the illicit activity in the first place.

It also appears that the problems encountered in the mediating technologies of both corporate and organized crime in these cases arose out of a failure to maintain or stabilize domain in the "industry." That is, the competitors in their respective fields (whether rival aerospace manufacturers or rival "families") were seen as the cause of the illicit activity in immediate question. In the Kotchian testimony, the understanding that competitors were making payments to obtain sales contracts was an important reason why Lockheed felt compelled to make payments of its own in order to maintain its domain.[66] In the Valachi testimony, the Castellemmarese War was explained as a rivalry over domain.[67]

This brief analysis suggests the potential of the enterprise perspective to explain organizational behaviors that have heretofore been explained by arguments infused with ideology. Comparable case studies could provide the knowledge enabling prediction of market conditions in which there is a high probability of illicit organized behavior. With further refinement of this model, and other emerging models,[68] the studies undertaken may be capable of ascertaining the facts behind organized criminal behavior and be more fruitful in their policy implications.

66. *Rokkiedo Jiken*, p. 196.
67. *Hearings—Part I*, p. 12.
68. See Lawrence W. Sherman, "Three Models of Organizational Corruption in Agencies of Social Control," *Social Problems*, April 1980, pp. 478–91.

[25]

Contemporary Crises **14**: 39–55, 1990.
© 1990 *Kluwer Academic Publishers. Printed in the Netherlands.*

A Trojan horse:[1] Anti-communism and the war on drugs

BRUCE BULLINGTON and ALAN A. BLOCK
Administration of Justice, 917 Oswald Tower, University Park, PA 16802, U.S.A

Abstract. This work argues the U.S. "War on Drugs" is a misnomer. We suggest, instead, that it is secondary to traditional anti-Communist foreign policy concerns. Thus, "the war on drugs" serves to mask the U.S. counter-intelligence and paramilitary presence abroad.

During the past decade a rhetorical "war on drugs" has taken the nation by storm. Hardly a politician can be found willing to consider any but the most severe punishments for drug dealers and users. "Zero tolerance" and calls for stiffer penalties are calculated to give the impression that the government will give drug merchants no quarter. It appears that a national panic has been manufactured; after months of television news proclaiming that drugs are the nation's number one problem, the story is confirmed by television polls asking television viewers what they think the nation's number one problem is. A less scientific more bogus effort is difficult to imagine. In this environment, suggesting that this Administration is using the drug issue to militarize American foreign policy in Latin America, is to invite ridicule. Yet there are now more than 30 U.S. government entities involved in the war on drugs in Latin America alone, including the DEA, U.S. Customs, the U.S. Information Agency, The Bureau of International Narcotic Matters, the FBI, the CIA, the Agency for International Development and a host of others.[2] In our view, their overall purpose is to implement traditional hemispheric American policies, using the pretext of drug trafficking to justify this remarkable paramilitary and intelligence presence.[3] Citing the cocaine menace, the U.S. has done overtly what it used to do only covertly – influence Latin governments, especially their military and police.

Recently, for instance, United States foreign aid allocations have been tied to cooperation with drug enforcement efforts, no matter how demanding and unrealistic these demands might be. Furthermore, the proportion of such aid that is earmarked for drug enforcement has increased dramatically. The amount of total aid to Colombia required to be spent on drug interdiction grew from 30 to 70 per cent between 1984 and 1987.[4] These requirements include close collaboration with U.S. drug and intelligence organizations in the destruction of cocaine production facilities. Recipient nations must also develop and arm special police and military units for joint drug interdiction efforts

40

under the control of U.S. authorities. Although these are generally described
as cooperative, bilateral agreements with American personnel acting in advisory capacities, they are actually unilateral demands to be carried out under
American supervision.

Historical antecedents: Drugs and anti-communism

In our view, the core of American drug policy lies within the traditional
concerns of U.S. foreign policy, and that has not changed in many decades. It
consists of standard fare anti-communism; this explains why the U.S. has
generously supported the Afghan rebels in their fight with the Soviet Union,
despite the fact that they are among western Asia's most notorious drug
smugglers. This situation is, of course, reminiscent of the American "presence" in Southeast Asia during the Vietnam War, when U.S. Special Forces
flew Golden Triangle opium and heroin to Bangkok and other centers for
distribution, and supported various hill tribes whose economy depended exclusively upon opium production. These groups received American assistance
as long as they remained stalwarts against Vietnamese communism.[5] Despite
the rhetoric about our nobility of purpose in Southeast Asia, the plain fact is
that we favored organized criminals in the drug trade as well as vice, currency,
precious metals, and extortion rackets.

Scholarship by Frances Fitzgerald, Alfred McCoy and William Corson
published two and three decades ago, demonstrated the subordination of drug
control to anti-Communism.[6] Corson, who was a Marine Intelligence officer in
Vietnam before he took up scholarship, understood the relationship perfectly.
That is why he blew up a U.S. forces clandestine narcotics factory in Laos, to
show his displeasure with the structure of foreign policy.[7]

Even before our formal involvement in the Vietnamese conflict. American
CIA officers were instrumental in promoting the region's narcotic trade.
Again, the "quid pro quo" was support against the Communist menace. In this
regard the actions and activities of banker, lawyer, and intelligence officer,
Paul Lionel Edward Helliwell, are instructive. During World War II, Helliwell
served in Army's G-2 Intelligence Group in the Middle East and then transferred to the Office of Strategic Services (OSS) as Chief of Intelligence in
China commanding 350 Army and Navy personnel.[8] It was Helliwell and
members of his OSS group who had contact with Ho Chi Minh during the latter
days of the war. Ho and Helliwell had three meetings between January and the
end of March 1945. At each encounter Ho requested arms and ammunition to
fight the Japanese; Helliwell refused unless Ho would give categorical assurances that the weapons would not be used against the despised French.[9] They
deadlocked over the issue. When the OSS disbanded at the end of the war,

Helliwell became Chief of the Far East Division of the Strategic Services Unit (SSU) of the War Department until the spring of 1946. The SSU was the interim intelligence unit bridging the gap between the dismantling of the OSS and the creation of the CIA in 1947.[10]

After Helliwell was mustered out of the military he joined a small Miami law firm specializing in real property, insurance, tax, trade regulation, and so forth.[11] He also worked for the CIA. Initially, his activities centered on Southeast Asian problems as he joined with the famous and controversial Major General Claire Chennault, known as an "acerbic warrior", at odds with his superiors for decades.[12]

Chennault was one of the first exponents of the Southeast Asian "domino theory" of Communist expansion. And he had a plan to stop this imagined catastrophe. In his vision, through the skillful use of air power supplying war material to more-or-less indigenous anti-Communist Chinese, coupled with the employment of American military advisers for training and planning, Chinese communism could be contained, thus saving all of Southeast Asia. The necessary logistical support for these operations would be furnished by certain civilian airlines, such as the Civil Air Transport (CAT), owned as it happened by Chennault and a partner.[13]

There were few takers in Washington for Chennault's plan even though he had the lobbying help of attorney Thomas G. "Tommy the Cork" Corcoran, an early FDR brain-truster, zealously committed to New Deal policies until he discovered how lucrative the other side was. Corcoran then became known for sleazy influence peddling, lobbying and backdoor deals.[14] Chennault was stymied until his friend Paul Helliwell intervened. It was Helliwell who broke the impasse by suggesting to Frank Wisner, an important CIA official, that he use CAT for Southeast Asian operations. The powerful and well-placed Wisner was at the time in charge of the Office of Policy Coordination, a covert action organization tied to both the CIA and Department of State in 1948–49, but soon entirely within the Agency. Wisner agreed, and requested that Helliwell figure out a clandestine way to subsidize the airline which was then in desperate financial trouble.[15]

In the autumn of 1949, a formal agreement was reached and signed by Corcoran for CAT and a CIA representative from the Office of Finance.[16] Helliwell helped construct the CIA's commercial cover organization for CAT and its Southeast Asian covert missions. This was the Sea Supply Corporation set up in Florida with its main office located in Bangkok, Thailand.[17] In 1952 Helliwell's law firm became General Counsel for Sea Supply. That same year Helliwell was made the General Counsel for the Royal Consulate of Thailand.[18]

Under the stewardship of Helliwell, Sea Supply did far more than cover the CAT operation. It channelled assistance to the Thai Chief of Police who was

42

deeply implicated in the region's extensive opium trade. With Sea Supply's help, the Chief built a police force of 42,833 men which rivalled, and most likely surpassed, the Thai army in organization, pay and efficiency.[19]

The Federal Bureau of Narcotics and the CIA

It is one thing to find CIA officers and operatives working hand in glove with foreign drug merchants, but quite another to find a long-standing arrangement between the Federal Bureau of Narcotics and U.S. Secret Services in which the concerns of the latter were always paramount. This had important institutional consequences, particularly within the Federal Bureau of Narcotics which provided excellent "cover" for CIA agents.

A case in point is the career of Henry L. Manfredi who had been in the Army's Criminal Investigation Division until October 1951. At that time, Manfredi was officially transferred to the Bureau of Narcotics.[20] But as a letter from CIA headquarters (signed by Richard Helms as Director of Secret Group One) to the Secretary of the Treasury in the autumn of 1967 disclosed, Manfredi's 1951 transfer was to the Agency, not the Narcotics Bureau.[21] Ironically enough, the found correspondence is a CIA recommendation to the FBN on Manfredi's behalf:

> I would like to bring to your personal attention the transfer of Mr. Henry L. Manfredi to a career position in Treasury's Bureau of Narcotics after more than fifteen years service in this agency. Mr. Manfredi's contribution to the attainment of the U.S. Government objectives abroad has been outstanding. I am confident that the Bureau is getting a superior officer and although he will be sorely missed by his colleagues here we are pleased that he is assuming an important position for which we feel he is uniquely qualified. I wish also to express my keen appreciation for the fine cooperation the Bureau of Narcotics, most recently under its present director Mr. Henry L. Giordano, has furnished us over the years. This is a particularly significant factor in the success of Mr. Manfredi's mission.

Manfredi was hardly an exception. He was part of a tradition of asymmetrical relations between the FBN and American clandestine organizations which began with the outbreak of World War II in Europe. Much of this hidden history can be glimpsed by looking very briefly at the careers of several significant FBN officers including the flamboyant George Hunter White and his FBN supervisor Garland Williams.[22] Williams and White both played key roles in the organization of American counter-espionage efforts and the training of special agents. As the head of the Corps of Intelligence Police, Williams took that raggle-taggle group and transformed it into the Army's Counter-Intelligence Corps. White followed Williams into the wartime clandestine world joining as soon as practicable the Office of Strategic Services (OSS).[23]

Williams designed a tough basic training program which specialized in teaching "special forces" the techniques of silent killing and demolitions. Advanced work called for agents to learn the ways of foreign undercover work including sabotage of enemy activities.[24] When White joined, he was initially assigned to a training facility in Oshawa, Canada, run by British Intelligence. White, in a famous remark, called the place the "Oshawa School of mayhem and murder."[25] He finished this first round of training and soon was chosen to head the New York X-2 training operation. X-2 was the designation given to the OSS counter-espionage group. White's headquarters for OSS X-2 training was the New York office of the FBN. Eventually he became the "director of all OSS counter-espionage training."[26]

To find key FBN officials hip-deep in counter-espionage activities during the war is interesting but hardly extraordinary. But it is remarkable and revealing to find them still diligently at work in the same activities years after. Their ongoing, *post-war*, clandestine work indicates the subordination of U.S. overseas narcotics operations to anti-Communist endeavors. The FBN hierarchy, from Commissioner Harry Anslinger through Williams, White and many of the men they recruited and trained as narcotics agents, functioned as a counterintelligence unit, attached to the CIA and, at times, the Army. Garland Williams, it appears, went into deep cover after the Korean War in order to help establish the counter-espionage capabilities of the Office of Public Safety located in the Agency for International Development (AID). Commissioner Anslinger, on the other hand, working with former OSS agents among others, set up a private intelligence organization (doubtless in close coordination with the CIA) which was especially concerned with Middle East projects.[27] George White's double life was perhaps the most bizarre as his "diaries" indicate. After his death in 1975, they were given by his widow to an electronics museum on the campus of Foothill College in Los Gatos, California.[28]

These little leather-bound volumes were White's appointment calendars – daily reminders of meetings, tasks, and expenses. The conjunction of his FBN work and Intelligence events is uncanny. In 1948, for instance, while the CIA was conducting one of its first operations, the subversion of Italian politics, White showed up in Rome for a meeting with his former OSS boss William Donovan.[29] More importantly, however, the diaries disclose that White, and his FBN protege, Charles Siragusa, were part of the "inner circle" of CIA officials who planned and carried out various lethal secret operations.

These activities, which in 1953 were known collectively as MK-ULTRA, began in 1950 with Project Bluebird directed by Sheffield Edwards.[30] Its

44

ostensible purpose was to determine if certain-drugs might improve interrogation methods. Within the year the direction of Bluebird passed to Allen Dulles who coordinated it with another drug experiment the Agency conducted for counterintelligence purposes named Project Artichoke. In ˏApril, 1953, Dulles, now the head of the CIA, instituted a program for "the covert use of biological and chemical materials" on Americans as part of the Agency's continuing efforts to control behavior. The decision to drug unwitting subjects spawned numerous efforts which were administered by Dr. Sidney Gottlieb who would become chief of the CIA's Technical Services Staff in the 1960s.[31] Gottlieb took control of these new ventures dubbed MK-ULTRA as well as the older Bluebird and Artichoke operations, and yet newer ones called Project Chatter and MK-Naomi.

There are several common threads linking these projects together: drug experimentation is one, political assassinations another. As John Ranelagh in his massive study of the Agency noted, the CIA found that "the doctors and biologists in the Technical Services Staff working on MK-ULTRA subprojects were ambitious to press the frontiers of their disciplines even further, to the point of 'executive action' capability – the agency's in-house euphemism for assasination."[32] It was not only the scientists who wished to move these projects to their logical end; members of the FBN hierarchy were also involved in these affairs, especially White and Siragusa.

There were several reasons for White's recruitment into MK-ULTRA, but the most important one was historical. Drug experimentation for counterintelligence purposes had been one of his important OSS missions.[33] Even before the Japanese attack on Pearl Harbor, General Donovan had approved a "truth drug program." Eventually, the plan was put under the supervision of Donovan's "chief scientist," Stanley Lovell and a committee which included the Director of FBI laboratories and FBN Commissioner Anslinger. White was the field officer responsible for testing various subjects, primarily with derivatives of cannabis. He also tested quite a lot of the "T" drug, as it was called, himself.

White's "diaries" show when and where he was contacted by the post-war architects of drug experiments and assassinations. In New York on March 20, 1950, he met with Allen Dulles and the following day had instructions for an FBN agent soon to be sent abroad who also doubled as a CIA operative. Indeed, on January 27, 1951, the FBN established its first overseas office sending Bureau agents Charles Siragusa, Joseph Amato and Martin Perna to Rome. Siragusa was in charge of the undertaking.

In November of 1951 White marked various meetings with the CIA in his calendar. A few months later he appears involved in "vetting" potential CIA operatives likely connected to Artichoke and Bluebird. These kinds of entries continue through April. However, in the middle of that month there are notes indicating his more complete induction into the projects. On April 15, 1952, he met in Boston with Stan Lovell and Colonel Harry Reynolds at what White described as the CIA's Algonquin Club. About three weeks later there was another CIA get together in Boston which was quickly followed by a talk between White and Gottlieb in Hartford, Connecticut. According to his notes, White called Anslinger the day after this meeting to inform him about the CIA drug ventures.

Through June and July, White had a series of meetings dealing with the projects. Late in August, the cast of characters directly involved in these experiments or knowledgeable about them broadened. White travelled to Washington, D.C. for a morning meeting with James Murphy, former head of OSS X-2. He and Murphy were later joined by James Jesus Angleton, dean of CIA counterintelligence. Angleton and White were old and apparently good friends, having met many times during the war and after. White's diaries reveal their friendliness, their many dinners in New York's Chinatown. The particular discussion in Washington that August between these veteran counter-intelligence officers concerned "a special teaching assignment" for White. Contacts between White, Murphy and Angleton continued. On Thanksgiving Day (November 27, 1952) White had dinner with Angleton on Long Island. The following day White's diary entry states that after nine in the evening he had taken LSD – "I had a delayed reaction" he wrote.

Meanwhile, it appears Gottlieb had an initial problem in securing White's formal assignment to what would be called the ULTRA projects. Apparently there were some within the CIA less enamored with White than Dulles, Angleton and Gottlieb. No matter. The difficulties were soon resolved and by the summer of 1953 ULTRA and White were moving comfortably forward. White had a new CIA codename, Morgan Hall, and an apartment on the fringe of Manhattan's Greenwich Village. He used this apartment for ULTRA experiments which seemed to consist largely of slipping LSD "mickeys" to unwitting subjects. White celebrated his 45th birthday on June 22, 1953. That day he phoned his old OSS boss, General William Donovan, from the ULTRA apartment to remind him of a meeting they were scheduled to have. The circle of those knowledgeable of the Agency's chemical experiments had obviously included Donovan, who seems never to have been in the dark about anything clandestine going on at CIA.

White left New York during the mid 1950s for San Francisco where he continued his Morgan Hall activities from two locations, one described as "a national-security whorehouse on Telegraph Hill."[34] The San Francisco CIA/drug venture was aptly called Operation Midnight Climax, according to commentator Warren Hinckle, and White who was never shy about his activities was characterized as "the best party-dog spy the CIA ever had." Hinckle noted that "White, who had the face of a friendly bulldog, was by day the head

46

of the Federal Narcotics Bureau here. By night, pop! Through the looking glass, he was a Kojak for the CIA, supervising wild drug experiments on unsuspecting johns procured by government-hired prostitutes who subjected their love objects to psychochemicals including LSD aerosols sprays, diarrhea-inducing drops and drug-coated swizzle sticks."[35] When White left New York, the CIA's east coast experiment did not miss a beat. The ULTRA apartment in the Village was taken over by Charles Siragusa who had been brought back from Rome to supervise the ongoing drug experiments in New York.

White's circle of CIA friends did indeed move forward into the arena of political assassination as Ranelagh states. No one was more eager to kill, it seems, than Gottlieb. He worked on "toxins to poison Fidel Castro and impregnated a handkerchief with poison to kill an Iraqi colonel."[36] Gottlieb also tried to assassinate Patrice Lumumba of the Congo using deadly bacteria. By this time, the CIA had developed several assassination programs. The one involved in the Lumumba plot was named Executive Action, later subsumed under the cryptonym ZR/RIFLE. The principal agent in charge of ZR/RIFLE field operations was known as QJ/WIN, supposedly a "foreign citizen with a criminal background recruited by the CIA for certain sensitive programs."[37] Although no one has yet satisfactorily identified QJ/WIN, one thing about this mystery seems certain. Charles Siragusa was either the mysterious QJ/WIN himself as some claim (including a former high official in the FBN and DEA) or at the least controlled him.[38] White's diaries, by the way, indicate that Gottlieb visited him in San Francisco just a short while before and then again right after his African mis-adventure to kill Lumumba. On the second visit Gottlieb was accompanied by Siragusa.

The FBN under the leadership of Anslinger, Williams, White, Siragusa, etc., was one of the lead organizations involved in foreign counterintelligence activities in pursuit of anti-communist objectives. So zealous was the Bureau in these matters that its highest officers committed numerous crimes ranging from drug distribution and drug use to planning foreign assassinations. To know that they committed these crimes while wearing their CIA hats in their Morgan Hall apartments is not comforting. The Narcotics Bureau had been subordinate to the CIA since the Agency's founding. But not everything was cover and counterintelligence. FBN pronouncements about overseas drug producers were often ludicrous propaganda statements about Communist intentions.

The China card

Drug villains shifted with the tides of foreign policy. That is why early in the

Cold War Communist China was alleged to be hard at work undermining American society by dumping drugs here at an alarming rate. This cuckoo theme, published by the Narcotics Bureau (doubtlessly under the CIA's spell), was first tried in the 1950s. For example, in 1954 Anslinger stated,

> The three-fold increase in some areas in the land devoted to the cultivation of the opium poppy in Communist China, the establishment of new heroin factories in Communist China, the continuation and expansion of a 20-year plan to finance political activities and spread addiction among free peoples through the sale of heroin and opium by the Communist regime in China, and the extension of the same pattern of narcotic activity to areas coming under the jurisdiction of Communist China has mushroomed the narcotic menace from Communist China into a multi-headed dragon threatening to mutilate and destroy whole segments of populations from whom the danger of addiction through ready availability of drugs had been removed during the past 40 years by the uncompromising work of the narcotic enforcement authorities in the free world.[39]

Thus while CAT was flying Thai opium in Southeast Asia, while George White and the Agency were doping the unsuspected with LSD, and while the remnant of Chiang Kai-Shek's Koumintang army which had been pushed into Southeast Asia positioned itself to control more and more of the region's opium traffic with American support, FBN press releases gobbled up by right-wing commentators and politicians called Red China the world's greatest narcotic menace.

But no matter how outlandish the charge, and how often it was shown false and intentionally misleading, the truth was not a deterrent. Always simmering, the tale of Communist perfidy in drugs returned with a rush in 1972 when a dangerous "crackpot" organization, the World Anti-Communist League, with support from the American clandestine community and its clone the Korean CIA, once again waved the "bloody Communist drug flag."[40] Using their Taiwan Chapter as the disseminator of narcotics information, it distributed bizarre pamphlets entitled "The Chinese Communist Plot to Drug the World," "Communist China and Drug Traffic," "True Facts of Chinese Communist Plot to Drug The World," and in 1976 "Chinese Communist Criminal Acts in Drugging the World."

The "True Facts" pamphlet contains the following pseudo-information under the heading THESE ARE THE ACCUSERS. In 1950, the U.S. reported to the U.N. that "Chinese Communists smuggle large amounts of opium into Burma and other countries." Four years later, Commissioner Anslinger stated the Red Chinese are "massively exporting opium in an attempt to drug

48

the world." Almost a decade after that, Harry Giordano (Anslinger's successor), identified in the pamphlet as the Chairman of the U.S. Commission on Narcotic Drugs, repeated Anslinger's comments. Giordano was quoted stating "the Chinese Communists are engaged in massive narcotics trafficking operations."

The litany of bunkum continued until the early 1970s when another problem appeared – President Nixon's rapproachment with China. The World Anti-Communist League was prepared, though, having American spokesmen ready to claim in one dumb remark or another that the Nixon doctrine was a "policy of disguise," pre-formulated to prevent government officials from revealing the Chinese Communist's true role in drug production and smuggling. Right-wing politicos, some on the Taiwan pad others supported by the South Korean CIA, angry with Nixon for dealing with China, issued these goofy statements to an increasingly incredulous world. Much to the despair of the Taiwanese and other Communist haters around the world, mainland China had finally proven acceptable to a broad spectrum of Americans. Improved relations with China stemmed the flow of drug accusations from all but the most cantankerous anti-Communists. In fact, David Musto recently claimed that the U.S. actually defended the Peoples Republic of China from allegations about drug running that had been published in a Soviet newspaper in the early 1970s.[41] If true, this certainly represented a major about-face on this touchy issue.

The contemporary scene – Latin America and the menace

That doesn't mean the broader theme – Communist imperialism equals drug smuggling to weaken the West's resolve – dried up, however. Throughout this decade the same tune has been played again and again, and a lot closer to home. Many Latin American countries have been targeted here for special attention in this regard. During 1988, for example, Panama, Mexico, The Bahamas, Jamaica, Paraguay, Bolivia, Peru and Colombia have all been identified as "problem" nations with regard to their contributions to the U.S. drug problem through "narcotrafficking." A key term that has been used repeatedly in press releases regarding these concerns is "narcoguerillas." Apparently the term was introduced in 1984 by Lewis Tambs, U.S. Ambassador to Colombia, who then announced the spectacular success of a raid on a jungle-based drug complex known as Tranquilandia. Tambs claimed that narcoguerillas – communist rebels – had been guarding the facility. The raid on the complex netted some 27,000 pounds of cocaine and was said to be largest coke bust ever.[42] The original Tambs' charge was never proven, yet the term stuck and became a stock phrase in the Reagan administration's rhetoric about the war on drugs being waged in Latin America.

In recent history Colombia has presented perhaps the most significant and lasting problem in terms of Latin-American based U.S. interdiction efforts. One writer has referred to Colombia as the "linchpin of America's narcopolitics." Colombia has been continually identified as a major contributor to our domestic drug problems by serving as a home and base of operations for many of the world's most notorious cocaine traffickers, presently dominated by the Medellin and Cali cartels. Recent newspaper accounts indicate that the two factions are now involved in a dispute over control of the New York market. In this dispute, gang members have been killing one another and providing enforcement officials with information regarding the other group's drug shipments.[43]

Colombia's reputation for complicity in drug running has been almost legendary in this decade. That nation's current Attorney General, whose predecessor was shot to death allegedly by drug traffickers, suggested earlier this year that perhaps the drug dealers would have to be appeased and that negotiations with them should include discussions of the possible legalization of cocaine. A U.S. State Department official responded, "It's an outrage, an absolute outrage. This man is charged with upholding the law of the land and he's saying that the job's too difficult."[44] Another Colombian government representative quickly denied that the Attorney General's remarks in any way reflected that government's policies or commitment to narcotics enforcement.[45] The current Vargas regime is especially concerned with bad relations with the U.S. and has actually gone so far as to hire a consulting firm in the U.S. to help improve that country's image here regarding their anti-drug efforts.[46]

Linking Colombia's drug lords with communism occurred initially during the bloodbath that took place at the Palace of Justice on November 6–7, 1985. During that confrontation more than 100 people were killed including the President of the Supreme Court, other magistrates and their assistants, canteen workers, government soldiers and guerilla members of the M-19 communist organization. At the time the M-19 soldiers were said to have been sponsored by drug traffickers who were distressed over a pending extradition treaty with the U.S.[47] That charge has been repeated ever since, despite the fact that two commissions of inquiry never found any evidence that M-19 had been working either with or for drug traffickers! With regard to these events, Dr. Rosa Del Olmo states,

It is worthwhile that what happened in Colombia is not unique in this respect. Attempts at protest, in Latin America, are all too often smeared –

50

by those with vested interests in suppressing criticism – with the labels of drugs and subversion, along the lines imputed and/or believed to be set by the U.S. government.[48]

The communism – drug theme surfaced again in the 1986 indictment of the notorious Colombian smuggler Carlos Lehder and the Medellin Cartel "which consisted of controlling members of major international cocaine manufacturing and distribution organizations."[49] Charged along with Lehder and other cartel members was Federico Vaughan an "assistant to Tomas Borge, Minister of the Interior of Nicaragua."

Vaughan supposedly helped the cartel establish cocaine conversion laboratories and distribution facilities in Nicaragua. The argument in the indictment claims that actions by the Colombian government moved the cartel to set up part of its shop in Nicaragua. Later in the indictment, however, the following statement about cocaine transshipment and importation into the U.S. is made:

> The Cartel maintained airstrips in South and Central American and made arrangements for transshipments of cocaine and refueling of aircraft and vessels in the Caribbean Islands and in Mexico. Pilots retained by the Cartel would and did fly cocaine from processing laboratories in South and Central America to trans-shipment points in Colombia, the Bahamas [sic], Turks and Caicos Islands, Jamaica and Mexico. At these locations, aircraft would be loaded and unloaded, serviced, and protected by Cartel employees and independent organizations, including service organizations headed by *officials of the aforementioned countries* (our emphasis).[50]

The Reagan administration worked hard to implicate Nicaragua in the Medellin cartel's activities. This was done partly to counter the growing evidence of Contra drug smuggling, and to convince the wary that the Sandinista government was capable of anything in its war with America. It now appears likely that much of the Vaughan evidence was fabricated. In addition, the only allegedly credible witness against him was Adler Berriman Seal who was murdered in Louisiana by cartel gunmen. But even if Vaughan was guilty, his participation pales next to that of the "officials of aforementioned countries." Where are the Jamaican, Mexican, and especially Bahamian officials? The answer is obvious. They are missing because the administration has politicized the Caribbean drug traffic issue, wildly overstating Communist interest and minimizing the clear responsibility of important regional friends. The administration's intent was announced in the 1984 Republican platform which identified the "international drug traffickers who seem to irritate the Reagan Administration the most" – Cuba, Bulgaria, the Soviet Union, and Nicaragua.[51]

It is well known that Florida prosecutors have been anxious to indict the Prime Minister of The Bahamas, Lynden Pindling, for quite some time. Pindling's partnerships with drug smugglers, in particular Carlos Lehder, have been alleged for years. The House Select Committee on Narcotics has debated the Pindling issue "in camera" and instead of holding the public hearing which would doubtlessly establish Pindling's participation and enrichment in one drug conspiracy after another, have chosen another path.[52] For reasons that are not clear, the Committee lent its most knowledgeable drug consultant, John Cusack, to the Bahamian government.

The Bahamian story reveals the limits of narcotic enforcement as it clashes with the most fundamental element in America's Caribbean policy – regional anti-communism. Pindling has likely been protected because of The Bahamas long-standing role in the U.S. struggle against Cuba. It is no secret that The Bahamas has provided a base for American sponsored infiltration and sabotage teams bound for Cuba.[53] The Bahamas strategic importance goes beyond this, however. The U.S. has long had a vital submarine listening post on Andros Island, as well as other intelligence installations in The Bahamas. These stations have given Pindling significant leverage with both the State and Defense Departments which has been used to urge restraint on the implementation of U.S. drug policy.

Colombia, The Bahamas, Nicaragua, and so on provide only some of the many contemporary examples of U.S. drug policy confusion. Bolivia is another. In that nation, which contains some of the most important growing regions for coca, similar events have unfolded. There former Air Force Major Clarence Merwin was hired in 1984 by the State Department's Bureau of International Narcotics Matters to organize, train and supervise an elite paramilitary force to conduct raids on the various growers and refiners of coca.[54] The Coca Reduction Directorate had been created in the Bolivian government as a result of four narcotic treaties signed with the U.S. on August 11, 1983. It called for a five-year program for reduction in coca production to a level that would only support domestic chewers of the leaves (it was estimated at the beginning of this process that local production was then more than twenty times that required for indigenous consumers).[55]

Major Merwin trained the Mobile Rural Patrol Unit, popularly known as the Leopards, to serve as a model in the creation of similar anti-drug units elsewhere. He found every attempt made to utilize this force effectively thwarted. Not only was there corruption within its ranks (many officers had accepted bribes from drug barons), but the Bolivian government repeatedly failed to live up to its end of the bargain in providing supplies and paying the troops. According to Merwin, the U.S. government representative, Ambassador Edwin Corr, spent his time trying to "maintain stable relations with

52

unstable Bolivian governments" and refused to force them to honor the original commitment.[56]

The raids conducted by Merwin's Leopards failed to net any significant drug pushers and concentrated instead on peasants and low level producer-seller-processors. Based on these experiences, Merwin stated "there are simply no sanctions being applied against any but the lowest level of traffickers."[57] He quit his position in 1986 as it had become clear to him that he was not accomplishing anything of significance in Bolivia and that the U.S. government representatives were not supporting his efforts. At the end of his service the estimated number of acres of coca under cultivation in Bolivia, far from being dramatically restricted, had actually increased by at least 10 per cent over the pre-Leopard period. Since Merwin's departure the Leopards were involved in Operation Blast Furnance, a much publicized series of raids that were said by the State Department to have "disrupted the local cocaine industry." Actually only empty labs were found and not one important trafficker was arrested during the 256 separate raids.[58]

The lesson in Bolivia, like The Bahamas, is that relations with apparently friendly anti-communist governments will never be sacrificied for drug control. Despite the obvious unwillingness of the present Bolivian government to rigorously pursue local traffickers, and at time, the direct involvement of top government officials in the cocaine trade (as occurred in the famous cocaine coups of 1981), U.S. officials have not pushed the issue. Clearly something more important is on their agendas; we believe that traditional anti-communism fits the bill, although carried out under a new guise.

The contemporary examples discussed here are instructive in putting together the puzzle of U.S. drug policy in the region. The Reagan White House has been effective in linking in the public mind drug trafficking and communism. The charges that communist guerillas or regimes such as in Nicaragua are either directly involved in the drug trade or at least protecting drug producers in exchange for sorely needed currency to support their cause or government are repeated often enough to have assumed a life of their own.

It is obvious why the administration wants to present this linkage of very long standing. Foreign drug enforcement carried out by U.S. paramilitary units, directing and training indigenous forces, is the cover for hemispheric counter-insurgency efforts. High technology weapons and advanced radar equipment, Delta force teams, the stationing of American naval, customs and coast guard ships ever closer to key South American ports, are in place to counter the Communist menace. The effectiveness of the administration in convincing others that communism and narcotics march together may determine the success of the entire operation.

53

Notes

1. This paper in slightly different form was originally presented at the meeting of the Drug Policy Foundation. Washington. D.C.. October 1988.
2. David Kline. "How to Lose the Coke War." *Atlantic Monthly*, May 1987. 23.
3. The theme we develop below has been explored to one degree or another by other writers as well. See. for example, Johnathan Marshall. "Drugs and United States Foreign Policy." in Ronald Hamowy (ed.). *Dealing With Drugs* (Lexington. Mass.: D.C. Heath and Co., 1987), 137–176.
4. Bruce Michael Bagley. "Reflections on the U.S. Latin American Drug Trade: Losing the War on Drugs." in *Miami Report II: New Perspectives on Debt, Trade, and Investment* by the North South Center Graduate School of International Studies, University of Miami, Coral Gables, Fla., May 1988, 115.
5. See Alfred W. McCoy with Cathleen B. Read and Leonard P. Adams II. *The Politics of Heroin in Southeast Asia* (New York: Harper & Row, 1972).
6. Alfred McCoy, op. cit., Frances Fitzgerald, *Fire in the Lake* (New York: Random House, 1972); William Corson, *The Betrayal* (New York: W.W. Norton, 1968).
7. Authors' interview with William Corson in Washington D.C.. 1982.
8. See the William Donovan Papers, Carlisle War College. Carlisle. Pa., Paul L.E. Helliwell to Bernard B. Fall, "Letter," October 14, 1954, in which it is recounted that Helliwell was awarded the Oak Leaf Cluster to the Legion of Merit, the Asiatic Campaign Medal with two bronze stars, and similar awards for outstanding intelligence work in Egypt.
9. Ibid.
10. See William R. Corson, *Armies of Ignorance: The Rise of the American Intelligence Empire* (New York: Dial Press, 1977), 221–290.
11. Martindale and Hubbell. *Law Directory* (Florida. 1949), 453.
12. William L. Leary, *Perilous Missions: Civil Air Transport and CIA Covert Operations in Asia* (Montgomery. Alabama: University of Alabama Press, 1984), 3.
13. Ibid., 67–68.
14. Bob Woodward and Scott Armstrong, *The Brethren: Inside the Supreme Court* (New York: Avon Books, 1981), 88.
15. Leary, op. cit., 72.
16. Ibid., 82.
17. Ibid., 129; and see Martindale and Hubbell, op. cit., 1952, 661.
18. Ibid.
19. Noam Chomsky and Edward S. Herman. *The Washington Connection and Third World Fascism* (Boston: South End Press, 1979), 220–222.
20. This transfer "in accordance with Department of Army message #28367," was signed by Marvin A. Ruckman, Assistant Civilian Personnel Officer.
21. The Helms correspondence dealing with Manfredi's CIA service and FBN cover was left, inadvertently no doubt, in a box of otherwise innocuous material located at DEA headquarters in Washington, D.C. The authors taped the correspondence and later transcribed it, Spring 1988.
22. On White see John McWilliams and Alan A. Block, "All the Commissioner's Men: The Bureau of Narcotics and the Dewey-Luciano Affair, 1947–1954," *Intelligence and National Security* (forthcoming 1989); and Alan A. Block and John McWilliams, "On the Origins of American Counterintelligence: Building a Clandestine Network," *Journal of Policy History* (forthcoming 1989).
23. Ibid.
24. Corson, op. cit., 81.

54

25. This famous remark found in the George White Diaries (1943) located in the Perham Electronics Museum, Los Gatos, California.

26. David Stafford, *Camp X: Oss, "Intrepid", and the Allies North American Training Camp for Secret Agents, 1941–1945* (New York: Dodd, Mead and Co., 1986), 82.

27. See Block and McWilliams, op. cit.; and on the Agency for International Development see A.J. Langguth, *Hidden Terrors* (New York: Pantheon Books, 1978).

28. The authors reviewed these volumes on two occasions in 1986 and 1987 and tape recorded summaries of all relevant material. Transcriptions of these recordings were then made and have been used in the following analysis.

29. The operation aimed to crush the power of the Italian Communist Party and elevate the Christian Democratic Party.

30. See John Ranelagh, *The Agency: The Rise and Decline of the CIA* (New York: Simon and Schuster, 1986), 204.

31. Ibid. 202–216; also see Martin A. Lee and Bruce Shlain, *Acid Dreams: The CIA, LSD and the Sixties Rebellion* (New York: Grove Press, 1985).

32. Ranelagh, op. cit. 207.

33. McWilliams and Block, op. cit.

34. Warren Hinckle, *San Francisco Examiner* (November 7, 1985).

35. Ibid.

36. Ranelagh, op cit., 211.

37. U.S. Senate Select Committee to Study Governmental Operations with Respect to Intelligence Activities, *Alleged Assassination Plots Involving Foreign Leaders: An Interim Report* (Washington, D.C.: Government Printing Office, 1975), 189.

38. Authors' interview with John T. Cusack former FBN and DEA officer currently on leave from the House Select Committee on Narcotics. Other material on QJ/WIN was pried out of the CIA by the Assassination Archives and Research Center, Washington, D.C. and generously made available.

39. The Anslinger quote can be found in Richard L-G. Deverall, *Red China's Dirty Drug War* (Tokyo, 1954).

40. For an informative history of the League see Scott Anderson and Jon Lee Anderson, *Inside the League* (New York: Dodd, Mead and Co., 1986).

41. David Musto, "The History of Legislative Control Over Opium, Cocaine, and Their Derivatives," in Hamowy, op. cit., 68.

42. Merrill Collett, "The Myth of the Narco-Guerillas," *The Nation* (August 13/20, 1988), 129.

43. Alan Riding, "Gangs in Colombia Feud Over Cocaine," *The New York Times* (August 23, 1988), A-1. For an interesting discussion of historical and contemporary violence in Colombia, see E.J. Hobsbawm, "Murderous Colombia," *The New York Review of Books* (November 20, 1986), 27–35.

44. Elaine Sciolino, "Colombian Official Talks of Legalizing Cocaine," *The New York Times* (February 25, 1988), A-11.

45. Ibid.

46. James Petras, "Colombia: Neglected Dimensions of Violence," *Contemporary Crises: Law, Crime and Social Policy* 12: 3 (1988).

47. Rosa Del Olmo, "The Attack on the Supreme Court of Colombia: A Case Study of Guerilla and Government Violence," *Violence, Aggression and Terrorism* 2: 1 (1988), 57–84.

48. Ibid.

49. U.S. District Court, Southern District of Florida, *United States of America V. Jorge Ochoa-Vasquez et al.*, Indictment No. 86-697-Cr-Scott.

50. Ibid., 32.

51. "The Communist Connection," *The New York Times* (September 13, 1984), A-17.

55

52. Authors' interview with staff members of the House Select Committee on Narcotics, 1988.
53. *Report of the Royal Commission Appointed on the Recommendation of the Bahamas Government to Review the Hawksbill Creek Agreement,* Volume I, paragraph 133, p. 44.
54. David Kline, op. cit., 22.
55. Ibid.
56. Ibid., 24.
57. Ibid., 27.
58. Ibid.

[26]

Peter Reuter and Mark A. R. Kleiman

Risks and Prices: An Economic Analysis of Drug Enforcement

ABSTRACT

Marijuana and cocaine, two mass-market drugs, have been the object of a major campaign by the federal government over the past five years. That campaign apparently has not led to a significant tightening in the availability of the two drugs, though the relatively high prices of these drugs historically are a consequence of enforcement. The reason for this lack of response to recent law enforcement pressures may lie in structural characteristics of these markets rather than in a failure of tactics or of coordination of law enforcement efforts. The federal effort aims at importation and high-level distribution, which account for a modest share of the retail prices of these drugs. Increasing the risks to importers or high-level distributors is thus likely to have modest effects on the retail price and is unlikely to have any other effect on the conditions of use. Street-level enforcement is hindered by the sheer scale of the two markets and because so few of the final purchases occur in public settings. Many of the risks associated with drug trafficking come from the actions of other participants in the trades themselves, and this also limits the ability of law enforcement agencies to act in ways that will cause prices to increase or alter market conditions. Law enforcement efforts directed at heroin have been much more effective at restricting drug use.

Marijuana and cocaine are used by large numbers of Americans on a regular basis. The most recent national estimates (Miller et al. 1982) put

Peter Reuter is a Senior Economist at the Rand Corporation in Washington, D.C. Mark A. R. Kleiman is Research Associate at the John F. Kennedy School of Government, Harvard University. A different version of this essay will appear in J. M. Polich, R. K. Ellickson, P. H. Reuter, and J. Kahn, *Controlling Drug Abuse* (in press).

289

the numbers using these drugs at least once per month at 20 million for marijuana and 5 million for cocaine. It is generally, though not universally, thought that this is a significant social problem. The primary response to the problem has been, particularly since 1981, greatly to increase efforts at reducing the supply of these two drugs.

Despite the increased enforcement effort, which has yielded substantial results in terms of drug and asset seizures, arrests, and lengthy prison sentences, it appears that both marijuana and cocaine are still readily available. Indeed, the street price of cocaine, the best single short-run indicator of the efficacy of enforcement, has declined since the enforcement effort intensified. Cocaine consumption may have increased. Marijuana prices have risen slightly in real dollars, and there is some evidence of decreased consumption; however, that decline is more plausibly accounted for by changes in adolescent attitudes toward the health consequences of marijuana use than to intensified enforcement.

This essay attempts to account for the apparent lack of response of cocaine and marijuana consumption to the increased federal enforcement effort. We make frequent comparisons between these trades and the heroin trade, in which enforcement has led to dramatically tighter market conditions. Heroin is an appropriate comparison drug because, like the others, it starts as an agricultural product overseas, a fact which is of considerable significance for enforcement strategies. The essay also considers, albeit more briefly, the consequences of possible increases in local law enforcement efforts against retail markets in marijuana and cocaine.

Our results are simply stated. Federal enforcement efforts have great difficulty in imposing significant costs on mass-market drugs. The sheer size of the markets forces a concentration on crops in the field, export-import transactions, and high-level domestic dealing. However, these components of the production-distribution process account for a modest share of the final retail price of the drugs; about one-quarter for marijuana and one-tenth for cocaine. Thus, even if the federal effort were to succeed in raising the kilogram-level price of cocaine or the ton-level price of marijuana (those being roughly the units in which the drugs are sold in their first domestic transaction), this would have limited effect on the retail price. Since the federal efforts can do little except change prices, that is, they cannot much alter the other social and cultural conditions that affect use, they can only modestly reduce total consumption.

Intensified enforcement by local police against retail markets for cocaine and marijuana is not likely to be much more effective than the federal enforcement effort. Again, it is the already massive scale of these markets, together with the middle-class character of so many of the users, that lowers the efficacy of such enforcement. For heroin, by contrast, with a much smaller and more exposed consumer base, there is evidence that increased stringency might be effective in still further reducing consumption.

Some caveats to this analysis should be mentioned. We focus on the consequences of enforcement for price because that is the only element of the markets that is much affected by most of the enforcement activities with which we are concerned. It may well be that there are other general effects, particularly in terms of the display of social disapprobation coming from arrests, seizures, trials, and so on, which operate to lower use or keep levels of use from increasing. We do not deal with these, simply because there is no empirical basis for doing so. That is not to say that they do not exist.

We do not claim to have a complete model of the marijuana and cocaine markets. Our explanations of historic changes in the price of cocaine are tentative and point to important gaps in the research on these markets. We try to ensure that these limits in our model are made clear to the reader.

Given the length of this essay, we venture two other introductory comments. First, we believe that the specific policy conclusions are less important than is the framework that is provided for considering the evaluation of enforcement against illegal markets generally. To that extent the essay can be viewed as an exercise in industrial organization, focusing on the impact of external changes imposed through the actions of agencies. We work with even more than the average number of assumptions used in economics because the available data on illicit drug markets are so meager.

Second, our pessimistic conclusions about the effect of cocaine and marijuana enforcement on street-level prices are not condemnations of drug enforcement generally. Indeed, one purpose of providing contrasts with heroin is to suggest the conditions under which enforcement can be highly effective. Even if we are correct in our estimate of the relative ineffectiveness of additional federal expenditures on cocaine and marijuana enforcement, that does not imply either that less should be spent for such enforcement or that legalization is appropriate. It simply points to the limits of what can be achieved with certain instruments aimed at these two markets.

Section I presents certain statistical data that are important to the analysis and is followed in Section II by discussions of how drug enforcement affects illegal markets and the appropriateness of using price as an indicator of the efficacy of supply reduction efforts. Sections III and IV then consider the four instruments of enforcement or supply reduction: source-country control, interdiction, law enforcement aimed at high-level dealers, and law enforcement aimed at low-level dealers. The final section presents some policy conclusions.

I. Markets: Organization and Scale

Heroin, cocaine, and marijuana are all imported, though approximately one-eighth of the marijuana market is supplied from domestic sources. The distribution chain is long and typically involves sales between independent buyers and sellers. Each importer sells to a small number of high-level domestic dealers, each of whom in turn sells to a slightly larger number of middle-level dealers. The length of the chain is a matter of conjecture. For heroin there may be as many as five dealers between the importer and the final user and for marijuana as few as two. The length of the chain is probably variable, even for any one drug. Some importers bring in large shipments; others bring in smaller shipments. It is the size of the initial importation relative to the size of the typical consumer purchase that determines the length of the chain.

The distribution system is affected by the physical characteristics of the drug involved. For example, marijuana is far bulkier per unit value than cocaine. This requires that it be imported in relatively large, dedicated vessels. These are more easily subject to interception than are the vessels used for smuggling the very compact cocaine. Heroin is so compact per unit value that it can be concealed on passengers or in freight. The enforcement environment also makes a difference; the higher penalties levied on convicted heroin dealers make them more discreet than their cocaine and marijuana counterparts and less willing to deal with a large number of intermediate dealers.

A. Prices and Scale

These differences are also reflected in the price structure of the three drugs in 1980, the most recent year for which source-country price data have been published. Table 1 presents official data on the prices for the drugs at different points in the distribution system. Three aspects of

Drug Enforcement 293

TABLE 1

Structure of Drug Prices, 1980* (per Pure Kilogram)

	Heroin	Cocaine	Marijuana[†]
Farmgate	$350–$1,000[‡]	$1,300–$10,000	$7–$18
Processed	$6,000–$10,000	$3,000–$10,000	$55
Export	$95,000	$7,000–$20,000	$90–$180
Import[§]	$220,000–$240,000	$50,000	$365–$720
Retail	$1.6–$2.2 million	$650,000[‖]	$1,250–$2,090

SOURCE.—Adapted from National Narcotics Intelligence Consumers Committee (1982).

* No more recent data are available for source-country prices. It is not likely that there have been significant changes in the relationship of prices at different points in the distribution system.

† Prices are for Colombian-origin marijuana, estimated to account for 75 percent of total U.S. consumption in 1980.

‡ The price of the 10 kg of opium required to manufacture 1 kg of heroin.

§ The import price refers to price at first transaction within the United States. Marijuana is purchased roughly in ton lots, cocaine in multikilo lots, and heroin in kilo lots.

‖ The original data source reported a retail price of $800,000. Other DEA data, such as those reported in U.S. General Accounting Office (1983), consistently indicate prices in the range $600–$650,000 in 1980.

the table deserve mention. First, most of the value added comes in the domestic distribution of the drug, not in its production or export. Second, the price rise within the United States is proportionately much greater for heroin than for marijuana. Third, only for marijuana does the export-import sector account for a significant share of final price.

The estimation of the scale of drug markets has attracted considerable attention. Few newspaper stories or political speeches on drug enforcement fail to mention the official 1980 estimate of $80 billion in gross sales generated by illicit drugs (National Narcotics Intelligence Consumers Committee 1982). Yet the data are so poor that estimates of revenue can vary threefold (*Miami Herald* [June 17, 1985]). Even fewer data are available for estimating the sizes of the dealer populations and the distribution of incomes among dealers.

Table 2 presents some rough estimates of total income and dealer numbers for 1982, the most recent year for which data are available from the National Household Survey (Miller et al. 1982). Details of these calculations are contained in Kleiman (1985) and Reuter (1984*b*). Here we state only the basic principles and sources underlying the calculations. Both income and dealer numbers are based on the user estimates.

TABLE 2

Drug Market Income and Dealer Estimates, 1982

	Marijuana	Cocaine	Heroin
Regular users	20,000,000	4,500,000	450,000
Users per dealer	40	25	10
Dealers	500,000	180,000	45,000
Total consumption (kg)	6,400,000	23,000	4,000
Expenditure ($ million)	4,800	7,800	8,000
Official expenditure estimates ($ million), 1980*	15,480–21,930	19,500–24,180	7,960–9,500

* No more recent data are available.

The number of drug dealers is estimated by dividing the number of users by a very rough estimate of the number of customers with whom a retailer will be willing to transact. Moore (1977) suggests that ten is the right number for heroin retailers, not including "jugglers" or addicts who sell to a small number of addict friends in order to support their own habit. We certainly expect the number to be higher for cocaine than for heroin, given the higher risk that each customer poses to the heroin dealer relative to the cocaine dealer. Simon and Witte (1982) suggest that the number for cocaine is twenty; no source is given for this. We use twenty-five. This produces a smaller number of dealers and thus will raise our estimates of the effect of a given level of enforcement.

Marijuana retailing is still less risky than cocaine or heroin selling. We assume that the average number of customers per seller is consequently even higher. Carlson et al. (1983) used a figure of fifteen. Arbitrarily, we select the number forty. While no data are available, the former number seems too low in light of the modest risks that additional customers pose to a marijuana dealer.

Retailers are not the only participants in the supply network. Others include importers, wholesalers, and their employees. However, given the sharp pyramiding in the distribution system for marijuana and cocaine, where first-level wholesalers might sell to ten or fifteen retailers, higher-level dealers constitute a small fraction of the total number of participants. High-level heroin dealers, precisely because they deal in small physical volumes, need few employees.

Our marijuana and cocaine income estimates are very imprecise.

They are lower than the published official estimates for two principal reasons. First, the official estimates assume all final sales occur at retail price. In fact, as the National Narcotics Intelligence Consumers Committee (1983*a*) now concedes, a significant fraction of total sales is in larger units (e.g., half ounces of cocaine) at prices far below the retail level. Second, the official consumption estimates reflect unrealistic assumptions about frequency of use by regular users and dosage units. The heroin addict estimate, developed without survey data, is probably considerably too high (Reuter 1984*a*) and also raises the consumption and expenditure estimates. No data are available for an alternative estimate, so we use the official figures. If they are upwardly biased, this will exaggerate the differences between heroin and the other two markets.

B. Enforcement and Its Consequences: Some Data

A short version of this essay was prepared in mid-1983 (and appeared as chap. 3 in Polich et al. [1984]) using 1982 data. It asserted that very substantial increases in enforcement activity would have little effect on consumption of cocaine and marijuana. Now that 1984 data are available on the levels of enforcement and on prices (though not on quantities), we can see that there has been at least rough confirmation of this conclusion. The following figures appear to show that a dramatic increase in the level of enforcement activities has not affected the availability of the drugs.

Table 3 provides data on drug arrests by state and local agencies for 1980–84. The majority of these arrests are for simple possession of marijuana. The total number has risen modestly over the period. How-

TABLE 3

Drug Arrests (in Thousands), 1980–84

	1980	1981	1982	1983	1984
Heroin and cocaine (totals)	68	72	113	149	181
Possession	46	49	78	109	133
Sale/distribution	22	23	35	40	48
Marijuana (totals)	406	400	456	407	419
Possession	342	344	388	337	345
Sale/distribution	64	56	68	70	74

SOURCE.—Federal Bureau of Investigation (1981–84).

ever, that modest rise masks very large changes in the composition of arrests, particularly, a substantial increase in the risks faced by dealers as opposed to users. Total heroin and cocaine arrests have risen by more than 150 percent, while arrests for sale or distribution have more than doubled. The number of persons arrested on charges of sale, distribution, or production of marijuana has also risen, though only by 16 percent. Unfortunately, we lack any national data on the disposition of these arrests, but some fragments from California and New York are presented below.

Table 4 gives some data on the federal drug enforcement effort. Federal expenditures on drug enforcement have risen dramatically over the period 1980–84. The rise is even more striking in the context of declining budgets for treatment and prevention of drug abuse (White House 1984). In current dollars, the total expenditure has risen by 70 percent. The measured output of this effort has also risen substantially. The number of persons committed to prison as a result of DEA actions increased substantially between 1980 and 1984. Drug seizures do not show the same consistent pattern year to year. However, for all three drugs, seizures are much higher in 1984 than in 1980.

Despite all this, retail prices for drugs have changed surprisingly little over the last five years, as reported in official data (table 5). The marijuana figures are hard to interpret because of the great variation in the quality of the drug, as measured by THC content. It appears that, as the share of marijuana produced domestically rises, so does the average quality, as measured by THC content. To that extent, the average price for marijuana of a given quality may have actually fallen.

In summary, we start with the following basic facts. The intensity of enforcement against the major drug markets has increased very substantially over the last five years. More people are being arrested on more serious charges and, at least at the federal level, are receiving more severe sanctions. Yet the retail price of the three drugs does not appear to have increased significantly over the same period.

II. Risks and Prices: The Theory

The major objective of drug law enforcement and source control programs is reduced drug consumption. Retail price can be used as a measure of effectiveness, for these programs can reduce use only by making drug dealing, including production and importation, so risky that dealers will require higher compensation for continued participation. Local enforcement against heroin retailers is the only significant

TABLE 4
Some Measures of Federal Drug Enforcement, 1980–84.

	1980	1981	1982	1983	1984
Federal seizures:*					
Heroin	268	231	305	495	385
Cocaine	4,797	3,205	9,763	18,027	12,390
Marijuana	1,773,098	3,078,696	3,022,351	1,968,771	2,466,373
Federal incarcerations[†]	2,547	2,865	3,516	4,150	4,721[‡]
	(54.5)	(55.5)	(61.4)	(63.8)	(56.0)
Federal enforcement expenditures[§]	537	707	854	1,076	1,210

SOURCES.—For federal seizures, see U.S. Department of Justice (1984, 1985). For federal incarcerations for 1980–82, see Brown et al. (1984, p. 497), and for 1984, see Drug Enforcement Administration (1985); for federal enforcement expenditures, see White House (1984).

* Pure kilograms.

[†] The period covered is the 12 months prior to September 30 of the previous year. Average sentence length in months in parentheses.

[‡] The 1984 figure includes some persons convicted in state courts after investigations involving federal agents.

[§] Figures are for fiscal years in millions of dollars.

TABLE 5

Retail Prices (per Pure Gram), 1980–84

	1980	1981	1982	1983	1984
Heroin	2,210	2,340	2,310	2,500	2,340
Cocaine	710	790	710	330–415	330–400
Marijuana	1.30	1.66	1.10–1.75	1.40–2.25	1.40–2.25

SOURCE.—U.S. Department of Justice (1984, 1985).

exception to this statement and is considered separately below. There will always be as much of a drug physically available at the export point as U.S. customers are willing to purchase at the risk-determined retail price.[1]

There are numerous qualifications associated with use of price as an indicator of the effectiveness of drug enforcement strategies. First, price is determined by both demand and supply. A decline in price may occur either because the demand curve falls or because the supply curve rises. For purposes of evaluating the historic success of drug enforcement efforts, it is impossible to separate out the two kinds of influence. It is clear that there have been shifts in both supply and demand and that we lack a well-specified model of the drug market. However, to consider the effect of hypothetical changes in drug enforcement efforts, the major tool of this analysis, we need only consider the impact these have on price through shifts of the supply curve; we assume the direct demand effects of law enforcement to be negligible, again with the exception of heroin retailing.

The ultimate objective of drug law enforcement is to reduce consumption. Price is merely a surrogate, chosen for its notional simplicity of measurement. In fact, the available price data are poor and scarcely more reliable than consumption estimates.[2] Nonetheless, price ought to be a cheaper and more rapidly ascertainable indicator than any other. Estimates of total consumption require the cooperation of users and involve numerous sampling problems.

However, to extrapolate from price changes to consumption changes requires, at a minimum, an estimate of the price elasticity of demand,

[1] The inefficacy of interdiction and source-control programs in restricting the physical supply is discussed below.

[2] The problem is that federal agencies are poorly placed to collect retail price data and local police agencies are poorly motivated. For a discussion of the weakness of drug price data, see Reuter (1984a).

that is, by what percentage a 1 percent increase in price reduces demand. No such elasticity has been empirically estimated for any of the three drugs. We are forced to rely instead on impressions, reflecting knowledge of the characteristics of users and current consumption patterns.

We assume that the demand for marijuana is relatively inelastic around its current price level. The dosage price is modest compared with dosage prices for other recreational drugs, such as alcohol. Currently, it appears that a "joint" costs only about seventy-five cents and probably yields one to two hours of moderate euphoria.[3] To obtain the same effect from alcohol costs perhaps twice as much and has noticeably more unpleasant aftereffects.

Estimates of the pattern of consumption suggest that, even for heavy users, total marijuana expenditures are no more than 10 percent of total expenditures, except for the significant fraction of heavy users who are still full-time students. With the important exception of this latter group, it seems plausible to assume that a 10 percent increase in the price of marijuana would have very modest long- and short-term effects on marijuana consumption.[4]

Cocaine, by contrast, is expensive relative to other recreational drugs and to most other recreations. A session with cocaine may cost $30–$100. For many regular users, indulging three times per week, total cocaine expenditure is likely to be a significant fraction of disposable income. Moreover, cocaine apparently creates psychological dependence in some regular users. This suggests that the short-run price elasticity might be low because it is difficult for current heavy users, who account for most of the total consumption, to reduce their consumption level substantially. But the high cost of regular use suggests that the flow of users into and out of the heavy user category may be very sensitive to the current price, implying at least a modest long-term price elasticity for cocaine.

For heroin we have rather more data, though none of it sufficient for a precise estimate. It has often been assumed that the regular users of heroin, precisely because they are addicted to the drug, have very

[3] There is considerable variation in the potency of marijuana; the THC content, a measure of its potency, ranges from 1 to 12 percent. While high-potency marijuana is more expensive, it is not known whether the price per unit of THC is constant. Hence we can only give a very approximate measure of the cost of an hour of pleasure. See Kleiman (1985, chap. 1).

[4] Kleiman (1985, chap. 1) provides estimates of the annual expenditures by different classes of users and argues (chap. 5) for an elasticity of demand of between 0 and −0.5.

inelastic demand, that is, even very large increases in price would do little to reduce their daily consumption. However, a growing body of research (summarized in Kaplan 1983, chap. 1) suggests that quite the contrary is the case. Heroin takes such a large share of the total budget of many regular users, and they have to be so active criminally to maintain their consumption, that price increases may lead to almost proportional reductions in their intake. The elasticity of demand for heroin may be about -1 for heavy users. In addition, heroin users often cease heroin consumption, with or without medical assistance. Moreover, it is likely that the flow of novice users into the pool of heavy users is quite sensitive to retail prices. As a result, we assume the aggregate demand for heroin may have quite a high elasticity.

It is simply not possible to go beyond such broad statements at this time. We lack adequate data on price or consumption levels. The analysis will assume that the elasticity of demand is moderately high for heroin, a little lower for cocaine, and quite low for marijuana.

Throughout this analysis we assume that drug markets are competitive. The basis for this assumption is the lack of evidence for the alternative, namely, that drug markets are characterized by restrictions on entry or pricing at any level, and moderately plausible theoretical arguments that such restrictions are difficult to maintain in illegal markets without a unitary, corrupt police department (see Reuter 1983, chaps. 5, 6).[5] This assumption is critical to the analysis since the response of markets to a tax is determined by their structure.[6] It is also contrary to the official view of drug markets, though that view is enunciated in vague terms that make it difficult to determine precisely what structure officials believe these markets to have.

In part, the official view may be explained historically. It appears that there was a monopoly, in the hands of the Mafia, on heroin importation in the 1950s (see President's Commission on Law Enforcement and Administration of Justice 1967). The explanation for that monopoly may be found in any or all of three factors. First, the Mafia had considerable influence over the New York Police Department; no other criminal group had access to the corruption of that department. Second, through control of the International Longshoreman's Association,

---

[5] A ready supply of violent labor in major American cities among dealers, a lack of martial skills among the leaders, and the need to compensate agents for not attempting coups are the essential elements of the argument.

[6] Moore (1977, chap. 1) provides a good discussion of this issue with respect to the heroin market.

the Mafia had command of the docks, so it was able to protect its own shipments of heroin and increase the hazards faced by all other importers. Third, the heroin refiners were located in southern France and Italy, and there were historic and ethnic ties between them and the American Mafia members.

The point of listing these factors is to suggest how specific the circumstances were under which the Mafia was able to attain market power with respect to heroin importation. None of those conditions are any longer relevant. The New York Police Department is no longer so centrally corrupt or powerful, the docks are no longer the locus of importation since air traffic has become so large, and the refining laboratories are now located in many parts of the world. If market power still exists in the heroin importation market, then it must have some other basis.

There is, in fact, little reliable information available on the structure of drug markets at various levels. Each drug is brought in from a multitude of nations, and international collaboration among traffickers to restrict the supply and thus boost profits seems quite implausible. The relatively small share of final price received by exporters is also consistent with the claim that there is no market power at the point of export, though it is certainly not conclusive evidence. At the retail level it is apparently easy to enter the business.

That leaves intermediate distribution levels as possible locations of market power. It might be the case that the wholesale cocaine market in, say, Denver is controlled by a small number of dealers. Their power might be based on the ability to exclude other wholesalers through threats of violence. Alternatively, other Denver market participants might be unable to locate sources of wholesale quantities.

It is impossible to obtain relevant evidence on this matter. There does seem to be some violence at the higher levels of the cocaine and marijuana markets. It is estimated that a large share of all homicides in the Miami area are the result of drug trafficking activities (U.S. Senate 1980). Whether that results from efforts to monopolize or whether it represents contractual disputes or robberies cannot be determined.

A. Two Kinds of Cost

The costs imposed by enforcement on the illicit drug industry are of two kinds: costs of avoidance and costs of losses actually suffered. The first can be as readily calculated in advance, by the dealer, as any other cost of doing business. If he buys a scanner to monitor police communications, he knows in advance what the scanner costs. Losses actually suffered, on the other hand, are not known in advance.[7] From the viewpoint of enforcement agencies (or researchers), ex post, the reverse is true; incurred (imposed) costs are measurable, while the costs of avoidance can only be guessed at.

Two Meanings of "Risk."   One measure of the enforcement threat a given transaction faces is the expected value of incurred enforcement losses, that is, the sum, for each possible kind of enforcement-induced loss, of its value times its probability. If a boatload of marijuana that costs a dealer $1 million faces one chance in ten of being seized by the Coast Guard, then the expected value of incurred enforcement losses in that transaction is $100,000. That one-in-ten chance is one meaning of "risk"; tougher enforcement makes the probability of loss higher and the transaction riskier.

But "risk" can also mean the special costs that go with uncertainty. If five $200,000 transactions were involved, each with a one-in-ten chance of going wrong, rather than one $1 million transaction, the expected value of incurred enforcement losses would be the same (assuming that the only loss is the loss of the marijuana): each of the five smaller transactions would have an expected value of incurred enforcement losses of $20,000 (one-tenth of $200,000) for a total of $100,000. But the transaction would be far less risky because the chances of a catastrophic loss would be much less.

Risk in this second sense—uncertainty—is also costly. A trafficker who is willing to treat a 35 percent probability of a one-year stretch in prison as a cost of doing business, one to be measured against current consumption and the nest egg waiting on release, may find a 5 percent probability of a seven-year stretch daunting (partly because of the potential lapse of years before that nest egg can be enjoyed). Thus entrepreneurs may require larger potential profits and employees higher wages to face the same expected-value time in prison if the time is more unequally distributed.[8]

[7] That is, losses are not known in advance unless a dealer's business consists of so many transactions, and the possible losses on any one transaction are so small, that the enterprise represents a statistical universe. This might be true of a pimp with a string of prostitutes; fines are a stochastic but predictable cost of doing business.

[8] This assertion runs contrary to the conclusion of deterrence studies that high-probability/low-severity regimes deter more than low-probability/high-severity regimes (Cook 1980). The explanation for the difference is that drug dealers, unlike most prisoners, are probably deferring the fruits of crime while in prison; each additional year of prison defers those fruits still further. For most property crimes, the fruits are enjoyed immediately; only the punishment is deferred.

Insurance is one of the many financial services whose unavailability helps distinguish illicit from licit trades. Drug dealers must, in general, bear the financial risks that enforcement imposes (though there is some evidence of quasi-insurance relationships between exporters and importers of marijuana that help spread the risks of marijuana smuggling).

In what follows, we attempt to quantify the costs imposed by enforcement on the illicit drug industry by comparing enforcement statistics—drug and asset seizures and years in prison—with estimated participant numbers and drug volumes. For example, we compute the days spent in prison per year in the marijuana business. It should be remembered, however, that these measures are all of expected-value losses and thus ignore the "risk premiums" due to the uncertain patterns of traffickers' enforcement-related losses. To compensate for this, we assign very high values to time in prison.

B. Costs in the Illicit Drug Trade

The price of any given drug at any given distribution level has five components: cost of drugs purchased, compensation of labor, cost of capital, operational expense, and proprietors' incomes.

Cost of Drugs. The cost of drugs at any level of the trade is influenced by enforcement pressures at higher levels. In addition, an entrepreneur at any given level risks having drugs seized after he has paid for them but before he has been paid for them. If, on average, a dealer loses a fraction p of the drugs he buys as a result of enforcement action, then he will need to buy $1/(1 - p)$ the quantity he sells, and his total cost of drugs purchased will be proportionately higher.

The cost a seizure adds to the drug traffic thus depends on the stage of the traffic at which it occurs as well as the physical volume of drugs involved. Seizing or destroying marijuana in a farmer's field adds to the traffic only the cost of growing more marijuana. This is what makes "street value" calculations so meaningless and lends a false importance to the huge quantities of drugs destroyed in source-country fields.

Compensation of Labor. Employees of drug-dealing organizations need to be compensated for their alternative occupational opportunities (licit or illicit) forgone; for the expected value of the danger of imprisonment (perhaps with a risk premium added); for the dangers from other illicit-market participants, including their employers, colleagues, customers, and competitors; and for forgone leisure time. Some of these elements represent fixed costs of being in the trade, and some are costs that vary with the number and volume of transactions engaged in.

Drug-market participants whose annual incomes, divided by the number of hours actively engaged in dealing drugs, suggest very high hourly wages may not in fact demand very much money to give up an additional hour of leisure because most of their current earnings are compensation simply for the risks of being dealers.[9]

Current employees of a firm are more valuable to the firm than otherwise equivalent new employees because the risks of employing them appear to be less; they are presumably less likely to be informants than are novices. Also, the disadvantages to them of persisting in the trade—in particular, the marginal imprisonment risk—are likely to be less than the costs faced by new entrants because the seasoned employees know that their associates are (relatively) trustworthy. This may allow most drug-market employees and entrepreneurs to reap inframarginal returns (i.e., to be better off than they would be at their best alternative employment), as long as the marginal transaction involves new participants, a likely condition in periods of rapid growth. This may explain why cocaine prices in 1978–82 seemed to be at levels far above those justified by the risks involved and why they subsequently fell, despite increased enforcement pressure; the high returns in the cocaine trade eventually attracted enough new entrants to force prices down.

Raising the level of enforcement pressure increases the risks faced by the employees of dealing firms. In turn this increases the compensation required to attract and keep employees since they now face higher risks from three sources—imprisonment, violence from their employing organization, and violence from other participants.

The increased imprisonment risk is straightforward. The increased risk from the organization is slightly more complicated to analyze. Organizations will vary from each other and over time in the willingness of their proprietors to use violence to silence potential or suspected employee informants and witnesses. Employees will have to be compensated for this risk as for any other. The optimal level of violence from the firm's viewpoint depends on the level of enforcement pressure. When pressure is low, the extra wages paid by high violence firms will put them at a competitive disadvantage. But as the pressure rises, less violent firms will feel it more severely since cases against them will be easier to make. This will force them either to leave the trade or to become more violent.

[9] Of course, there is an income effect: leisure is worth more to a wealthy individual than to a poor individual, even if the wage rate per hour is the same for the two.

Thus increased enforcement pressure will tend to increase the capacities for violence of drug-dealing firms. This increase in firms' violence capacities will in turn increase the risks to all employees from interfirm violence. Drug-market firms can use violence against each other to settle business disputes and enforce contracts in the absence of recourse to courts, to steal drugs or money, or to eliminate competition. The capacities that firms develop for internal violence in response to enforcement pressure will also be available for interfirm warfare and piracy.

Cost of Capital.   The cost of capital for drug dealers depends on the capital requirements of the business (determined by turnover rates, wholesale prices, and credit terms), the availability and cost of loan capital on the loan-shark market (or the equivalent), and the danger of capital loss. The higher the risk of loss, the higher the interest rate. Drug dealing may be largely internally financed once an enterprise is under way, but the cost of external capital, like the cost of new labor, may determine market prices if the market is expanding.[10]

As the price of drugs at higher levels rises, the capital cost of being a lower-level drug dealer rises as well, for the lower-level dealer must lay out more money per unit purchased. If, as we shall assume, it takes three months for marijuana to move from initial import to final sale, and if the annual cost of capital is 50 percent, then the added capital cost is 12.5 percent of the price increase. That is, a $1.00 increase in the imported price will lead to a $1.125 increase at the retail level.

Nondrug Supplies.   A drug dealer needs to buy, rent, or steal vehicles to transport drugs; buy or rent warehousing space; pay the costs of travel for himself and his employees; buy equipment (e.g., communications and communications-interception gear); and pay lawyers' fees, bribes to police, and other expenses of dealing with the criminal justice system.

There will be trade-offs between some of these expenditures and the dangers of enforcement losses. The higher the level of enforcement pressure, the more organizations will choose to invest in evasion rather than suffer enforcement action. Since these expenses, unlike the results of successful enforcement actions, will not in general be officially ob-

---

[10] There may be little direct connection between drug markets and conventional loan-sharking. Drug dealers may lack the attributes (personal reputation for violence or knowledge about credit risks) to be loan sharks. On the other hand, drug dealers, because they have relatively high risks of incarceration or death, may face difficulties in borrowing from loan sharks.

served, our estimates of enforcement-imposed costs will not include them and will thus tend to underestimate; seizures of nondrug assets (discussed below) suggest that these items constitute a very small share of total distribution costs.

Proprietors' Incomes.   Proprietors' incomes can be thought of as returns to their own labor and capital. They may be able to reap high rates of return in growing markets if there are significant barriers to entry. One effect of increasing enforcement pressure may be to make the markets differentially riskier for new players, thus creating entry barriers behind which existing entrepreneurs can pile up windfall profits.

Caveats.   There are three important caveats. (1) We observe two things about drug enforcement expenditure and outputs. Neither is exactly what we need to model effects on the market since we do not know enforcement pressure as a function of enforcement expenditure and since enforcement outputs do not measure avoidance costs or risks from other criminals. (2) Enforcement risks depend in part on the ratio of enforcement activity to trafficking activity. The more traffickers there are competing for the attention of any fixed number of agents, the safer the traffickers are. This may explain why Miami was so dominant for so long in marijuana and cocaine importing. It may also create positive-feedback effects from increased enforcement pressure. If enforcement succeeds in shrinking a market, the effective enforcement pressure corresponding with any given level of enforcement expenditure will rise as the number of targets falls. Static estimates of marginal enforcement risk underestimate the total effect of marginal enforcement on costs. (3) This model applies better to high-level than to street-level markets. Street-level costs involve large real transactions costs—search times on both sides—that no one captures as income.

With this conceptual apparatus established, we now turn to the four components of the supply reduction strategy.

III. Source Control[11]

Throughout the twentieth century, the government of the United States has maintained that the solution to the American drug abuse problem lies with the foreign nations that produce the most important illicit drugs. The official tone has become slightly less accusatory over

---

[11] This section is adapted, with permission, from Peter Reuter, "Eternal Hope: America's Quest for Narcotics Control," *Public Interest*, vol. 79 (Spring 1985).

the years, but there has been no change in the view that cutting exports from countries such as Burma, Colombia, and Pakistan is the best method for reducing U.S. consumption of heroin, cocaine, and marijuana. As the White House stated in 1982, "elimination of illegal drugs at or near their foreign source is the most effective means to reduce the domestic supply of these substances" (Drug Abuse Policy Office 1982, p. 31).

This notion became a genuine part of American foreign policy when President Nixon, under heavy congressional pressure, initiated a series of bilateral agreements with source countries to assist them in reducing their exports. These agreements have become a standard component of battles between the State Department and Congress, with Congress generally charging that the State Department gives too little high-level attention to the drug problem. But there is no political dispute about the centrality of these international programs to American drug policy. The only dispute concerns the appropriate levels of expenditure and the intensity of pressure to be exerted on other nations.

Unfortunately, there is ample evidence that U.S. foreign drug control efforts have been unsuccessful and that the failures of U.S. international programs are not simply the result of incompetence or inadequate resources but are inherent in the structure of the problem. The producer countries jointly lack either the motivation or the means to reduce total production. Even if such reduction were possible, it is unlikely that U.S. imports from each of these countries, apart from Mexico, would be much affected. Just as important, the set of source countries is readily expandable. The international programs may serve a useful function in curbing illicit drug use in some major source countries, but they will do little to reduce drug abuse in the United States.

A. U.S. Control Efforts

Efforts by the United States to suppress foreign production of illicit drugs go back at least to the Shanghai Treaty of 1909. Believing that the instability of China was very much bound up with the widespread use of opium, supplied through much of the nineteenth century from India by British merchants, the United States sought a treaty system that would require all nations to control the production of opium and its derivatives. Other nations were a great deal less enthusiastic, but in 1913 thirty-four nations signed a fairly comprehensive agreement that was later extended, again at the urging of the United States, to cocaine and marijuana. In that more innocent era there was enough faith in treaties per se that no program of assistance for enforcement was established.

The growth of heroin use in the late 1960s changed U.S. policy markedly. No longer content to work through the international treaty system, the United States for the first time began to seek bilateral agreements, involving the use of U.S. resources and personnel, to strike at production in nations deemed particularly important to the American heroin problem. These efforts have been expanded since 1979 to include cocaine and marijuana.

The United States has tried a number of approaches. Some efforts focus on production itself. Resources are provided to help local law enforcement agencies eradicate crops, either through the spraying of a herbicide (as was done in Mexico for opium poppies) or by manually uprooting plants (as is occasionally done with coca plants in Peru). A number of projects have been funded, either by the United States directly or through multilateral agencies (such as the UN Fund for Drug Abuse Control), that aim at providing alternative commercial crops for farmers growing coca (in Peru) or poppies (in Burma).

Since 1978, the State Department's Bureau of International Narcotics Matters (INM) has been responsible for foreign production control efforts through diplomatic efforts and targeted economic assistance programs. In fiscal year 1985, INM had a budget appropriation of $43 million. The DEA also assists foreign governments in law enforcement activities aimed at refining and distribution, particularly in source countries. It trains foreign police at U.S. facilities and has offices in major source and transshipment countries to help target traffickers particularly significant for the United States. Its international activities were budgeted at $38 million in fiscal year 1985.

The relatively small expenditures on the international programs have sometimes led Congress to charge that the executive branch is not taking the problem seriously enough. Indeed, in 1980 Congress forced the State Department to allocate $7 million to Colombia at a time when INM believed, correctly as it turned out, that the Colombian drug enforcement agencies would accomplish little with the money. Generally, officials in INM have been consistent in their view that the most important tools are diplomatic rather than financial, and they base their optimism on the apparent success of diplomatic efforts. They claim that there is increased interest on the part of senior U.S. officials in raising these issues with their foreign counterparts and that those counterparts are more willing to follow up on promises of action.

The recent success of the Pakistani government in greatly reducing the illicit cultivation of poppies in some areas of the country is cited as an instance of effective diplomatic pressure. Though a total national ban on opium production has not been implemented, new laws, increased police efforts, and low producer prices had reduced estimated Pakistani production levels to less than forty-five tons in 1984, compared to 800 tons in 1979.

In some countries that produce opium, local increases in heroin use may have increased the willingness of governments to implement crop reduction and traffic control programs. While estimates of the addict populations in countries such as Thailand and Pakistan are extremely unreliable, it is clear that these countries believe they have a substantial problem. While there were almost no heroin addicts in Pakistan ten years ago, INM now cites an estimate of 50,000. With a certain amount of skepticism, INM cites a figure of 400,000–600,000 Thai addicts, again an entirely new phenomenon. Domestic Colombian use of a dangerous combination of marijuana and cocaine residue is a cause of concern in that country.[12]

B. Down on the Farm

Despite the increasing concern with local drug use, there are many impediments to successful crop reduction efforts in producer countries. The first is that farmers usually do not have an easy alternative commercial crop; the high value to bulk of drugs compared to other farm products is crucial when the markets are distant and the roads bad. Currently, poppies may indeed be the only crop that can be produced in remote areas of Burma and Thailand to provide steady cash income. Everyone recognizes that increased law enforcement efforts against farmers will have little effect unless other productive opportunities are provided. This takes many years. Moreover, the coca and opium crops have important licit uses; for example, Peruvian coca leaves are used for pharmaceuticals and flavoring, and poppies provide peasant farmers in Turkey with an edible oil, fuel, and cattle feed.

The development of alternative cash crops requires, among other things, the creation of a new infrastructure (roads, in particular) to permit the efficient delivery of bulkier and more perishable crops to distant markets. Farmers must also learn how to produce crops entirely new to their regions, such as cacao in the Upper Huallaga valley of

[12] A discussion of foreign addiction problems is contained in U.S. Senate (1985).

Peru and kidney beans in the Chang Mai area of Thailand. Whether these efforts will turn out to be sufficient is a matter of speculation. Indeed, improving farmers' skills might have the perverse effect of increasing the productivity of their illicit farming. The programs in Thailand show promise but encompass a population of only a few thousand, and there are no instances in which crop substitution has actually been achieved on a large scale. Indeed, a piece of black humor from a Bolivian politician sums up the matter: "We have crop substitution; cocaine has been substituted for everything else" (State Department official, personal communication, 1983).

It should be noted that there is little talk of crop substitution for marijuana producers; enforcement alone is supposed to deal with the problem. Two arguments have been made for this policy. First, marijuana is grown solely for illicit commercial purposes, whereas poppies and coca have licit uses as well. Thus one can simply spray all marijuana fields without worrying whether one or another might in fact be legal. This would not work against coca producers in Peru, where there are some 9,000 licenses for coca production. Second, producers of marijuana are "mercenary"; they are not peasant farmers without a cash crop alternative. As one official suggested, it would scarcely be good policy to reward new marijuana source countries by granting them agricultural development assistance.

A second major obstacle to crop reduction is the generally weak control of governments in the producing areas. The Thai and Burmese governments have long been fighting insurgent movements in the hills that are home to the poppy growers. The Peruvian government has little effective control in some of the regions that produce coca leaves. Similar situations exist in Afghanistan, Pakistan, Bolivia, and Laos at least. Even where governments are in firm control, are strongly motivated, and have sensible plans, they are likely to have great difficulty implementing them. The ubiquitous corruption of source-country police adds yet another obstacle; in the case of Bolivia, at least one cabinet member was actively involved in the cocaine trade.

Third, some major source countries, notably Iran and Afghanistan, are hostile to the United States. Though they may adopt policies to reduce domestic consumption, they are unconcerned about U.S. imports. Fourth, U.S. relations with most of the other countries involved in drug production are very complex. The United States would like Pakistan to adopt certain policies with respect to Afghanistan. It seeks to retain bases in Thailand. It would like Colombia to take particular positions with respect to Central America. As a DEA official said, explaining the relatively light pressure being exerted on Jamaica, "Some analysts believe that if you came in with a severe narcotics program, you could affect the existence of the present government. . . . Drugs are a serious problem but communism is a greater problem" (Treaster 1984). Given all these considerations and the disinclination of diplomats and policymakers to concern themselves with such unseemly matters as the drug trade, it is difficult to put consistent pressure on source-country governments.

Finally, and perhaps most important, the set of producer countries is not fixed. New producers emerge all the time. Brazil is apparently witnessing a rapid growth in coca and marijuana production. Until five years ago, these crops were minor and were used only for peasant consumption; by 1983, the Brazilian authorities claimed to have destroyed or seized nearly 2,000 tons of marijuana (almost 30 percent of the best estimate of U.S. consumption). Belize, an enclave of 150,000 people in Central America, may have produced 700 tons of marijuana in 1983, all for export, where none was produced five years earlier (U.S. Department of State 1985). Pakistan produced little opium prior to 1948, the British being concerned to protect the markets of opium farmers in other parts of British India. Yet by the mid-1950s there was substantial licit and illicit opium production in the North West Frontier province. There is no reason to believe that other countries with large impoverished peasant populations and weak central governments will not become significant producers if the current producers cut back production greatly. A large or traditional local market turns out not to be essential. In the instance of marijuana, we must also note the rapid growth of production in the United States.

Lack of motivation is also a barrier to effective government action. The national governments in many of these countries believe that the political costs of reducing the cash income of farmers are very high. Indeed, in describing the recent Bolivian crackdown on coca producers in the Chapare region, which involved the moving in of troops, the *New York Times* reported: "On August 17, less than a week after the Chapare occupation, the government was forced to drop the peso's official value by more than half, from 2,000 to $1 to 5,000. And in Bolivia, the world's most politically unstable country, that is enough to start talk of a coup" (Brinkley 1984). Governments dealing with the enforced stringencies of the International Monetary Fund are likely to give pause to efforts that will add to their domestic economic worries. The extent to which foreign exchange earnings from drug exports matter is unclear: in most situations only a small share of these earnings enter the official accounts, but some amount certainly does.

C. The International Pipeline

Crop reduction is touted as a goal by the United States because it is assumed that the less each source country produces, the less will be exported to America. Clearly, if none is produced, then none can be exported. But it is also plausible that quite large reductions (or increases) in any particular country's production will have little impact on exports to the United States.

We start by observing that the price of opium in source countries is trivial relative to the price of heroin in the United States. As shown in table 1, the ten kilograms of opium in Thailand needed to make one kilogram of heroin cost at most $1,000. If that price fell to $100 or rose to $5,000, it would have little effect on the price of heroin delivered to the United States (roughly $200,000 per kilogram at the importation level). Yet the effect of crop reduction, short of elimination, is simply to raise local prices.

Moreover—and contrary to what we would expect in a smoothly working international market—it appears that quite large differences in source-country prices for particular drugs have little effect on the composition of U.S. imports from country to country. For example, in the oil market Nigeria has only to raise its price by 1 percent to lose a large share of its sales; its customers have little hesitation in shifting to other suppliers. Yet the bazaar price for opium in Burma can be half that in Pakistan without any rapid shift in the origins of American heroin imports.

One plausible explanation for this is that the U.S. price of a drug from a particular country is determined chiefly not by the source-country price but by the availability of efficient international distribution networks. This is certainly consistent with the fact that most of the export price of drugs represents payments to couriers and dealers for incurring risks. For example, Mexican-source heroin was relatively cheap not because of the price of opium in Mexico (which was very high relative to other producer countries) but because of the efficient Mexican networks for distribution. The reduction of the supply in Mexico that was achieved did cut the amount flowing through the pipeline. But if it were easy to smuggle heroin *into* Mexico, the loss of this local production would be of little consequence for the United States; the cheap distribution networks would remain. As it turns out, the Mexican government is reasonably effective at making it risky to bring heroin into that country, so the trafficking networks have been thwarted.

Similarly, the increased availability of Southwest Asian heroin in Western Europe and the United States shortly after 1979 may have had less to do with the price of opium in the local markets than with the growing density of traffic from Southwest Asia to Western Europe. Pakistan has substantial expatriate communities in Britain and West Germany. There are also large communities of Armenians and Lebanese in Europe, and Iranian immigration to the United States suddenly increased after 1977. These provide broad pipelines, so to speak, within which to hide the movement of drugs.

The international cocaine market provides some evidence consistent with this view. Most cocaine entering the United States comes from Colombia, though the raw material is produced mostly in Peru and Bolivia. The advantage of Colombia as an export source is partly that it is the largest South American source of migrants to the United States. On the other hand, most cocaine exported to Europe leaves from Brazil, which has the largest migrant population in Europe.

These broader pipelines have three important advantages for drug smuggling. First, they make it more likely that the courier will not be detected because surveillance decreases in intensity as the general traffic from a particular source country increases. If there is only one flight each day from Karachi to London, then it is possible to scrutinize every vaguely suspicious looking passenger; if there are ten per day, this becomes much more difficult and expensive. Second, the probability of finding a courier able and willing to carry the drugs increases with the size of the pipeline. When the only Pakistanis traveling to London are well-to-do tourists, it will probably be hard to find a courier. The lone peasant on a plane filled by the wealthy might well get caught. But when there is a steady flow of poor migrants, it will be easy to conceal a courier within the flow. Third, if there is a large population of immigrants from the source country in the consuming country, it is more likely that the exporter can find a local high-level distributor. The more Pakistanis resident in London, the higher the probability that a Pakistani exporter can find someone there who will know an English distributor.

If this is so, then we must ask why there are relatively sudden changes in the distribution patterns to source countries. After all, the immigrant flows and the heaviness of traffic from source to consuming countries change relatively slowly; the middle-class Iranian exodus of 1978–80 was unusual. There was not a sudden increase in the number of Pakistanis in Western Europe around 1980 to explain the great increase in the flow of heroin along that path.

The pipeline effect is likely to be nonlinear. There may be thresholds—in number and composition of travelers and in the size of the local community—that, once passed, lead to rapid changes in the efficiency of the distribution through a particular pipeline.

United States source control programs have occasionally had a noticeable impact in particular source countries. Three instances stand out: the elimination of illicit opium production in Turkey in 1972, the dramatic reduction of opium output in Mexico in the mid-1970s, and the slightly later reduction of the U.S. market for Mexican marijuana. The last instance is somewhat ambiguous. The major reason for the decline in American consumption of Mexican marijuana was not the reduction in Mexican production. Rather, it was U.S. consumers' fear that the drug might have been sprayed with paraquat, a potentially dangerous herbicide used to control Mexican production.

None of the three successes had lasting effect. Turkish-source opium was rapidly replaced by that from Mexico. Mexican marijuana was even more rapidly replaced by Colombian production. Only the decline in Mexican heroin production had more than a short-term effect; from 1975 to 1979 there appears to have been a decline in U.S. consumption that is related to availability. Changes in Southwest Asia led then to renewed growth in U.S. heroin consumption. Moreover, Mexico and Turkey represent somewhat special cases. In both countries the central government is quite strong. Equally important, illicit drugs were not very important to the national or major regional economies; the political cost of stringent enforcement was not high. This situation does not hold for many of the current and potential source countries.

The sad fact is that real long-term success stories have had nothing to do with international aid and law enforcement. Vastly more important is political and economic development. Macedonia was, prior to World War II, a significant producer of opium, mostly for domestic consumption. By the early 1970s, opium production had fallen to about 5 percent of its previous level. Some analysts plausibly attribute this to general economic progress in the producing area, which made the relatively labor-intensive crop less economically attractive (Bruun, Pan, and Rexed 1975).

On the political side, we have the success of China in its southwest provinces. Though some minority groups still produce for their own consumption, the major production areas have been eliminated since the establishment of the present regime. That is probably the result of the central government's repugnance for all symptoms of decadence in the old culture. It is hard to draw any but the most pessimistic lessons from these two examples, at least for the design of drug enforcement assistance programs.

IV. Interdiction

Interdiction aims at intercepting drug shipments just as, or just before, they enter the United States. It is expected to raise retail prices by imposing costs to replace seized shipments, by raising the risk of imprisonment for people who transport drugs, and by increasing the uncertainty of dealer supplies and income. Interdiction efforts account for about 33 percent of total federal expenditures to enforce drug laws, about $280 million out of $850 million spent in fiscal year 1982.[13] The amount and share have increased rapidly since 1977 (U.S. General Accounting Office 1983).

The Coast Guard and the Customs Service carry out most interdiction operations. The Coast Guard concentrates its interdiction efforts on sea patrols around Florida and the Caribbean, through which most of the Colombian and Jamaican marijuana passes. In the past few years, especially, it has seized enormous quantities of that marijuana, but little else. The Customs Service seizes drugs through both patrol and inspection at ports of entry. Its patrols account for the majority of all federal cocaine seizures, and its inspections at ports of entry garner significant quantities of marijuana. While nontrivial amounts of heroin are seized annually, this is largely the result of investigation rather than of random inspection; consequently, we ignore heroin in this section.

As shown in table 4, the combined efforts of Customs, the Coast Guard, and the DEA have resulted in substantial seizures of marijuana and cocaine, with a sharp upward trend for cocaine.[14] These amounts

[13] There is no breakdown of drug enforcement expenditures by function for the years after 1982. However, it should be noted that the drug enforcement budgets of the two major interdiction agencies increased from $387 million in fiscal year 1982 to $512 million in fiscal year 1984.

[14] Most DEA seizures took place as a result of investigations, not interdiction. We discuss the effectiveness of investigations later.

316   Peter Reuter and Mark Kleiman

TABLE 6
Estimated Interdiction Rates, 1984

	Cocaine (1,000 kg)		Marijuana (1,000 kg)	
Item Estimated	Lower Bound	Upper Bound	Lower Bound	Upper Bound
Seizures:				
Reported seizures*	12.4	12.4	2,466	2,466
Less overlap in reporting[†]	2.5	2.5	825	825
Estimated actual seizures	9.9	9.9	1,641	1,641
Shipments:				
Total estimated consumption	34.4	23.3	15,000	6,439
Less domestic production	.0	.0	1,650	704
Estimated amount imported	34.4	23.3	13,350	5,735
Total shipments to U.S. (actual seizures plus imported amount)	44.3	33.2	14,991	7,376
Seizures as percent of shipments	22.3	29.8	10.9	22.2

SOURCES.—For total reported seizures, see Organized Crime Drug Enforcement Task Force (1985, p. 68); for adjustment in reporting overlap, see U.S. General Accounting Office (1983).

* Total seizures reported by federal agencies.

[†] The adjustment represents rates of double reporting found by the U.S. General Accounting Office in reviewing 1982 data.

represent a significant proportion of total shipments of drugs destined for the United States—between 10 and 30 percent by our estimates (see table 6). To make these estimates, we first reduced reported seizures to correct for the overlap between the various agencies' reports, using data from the U.S. General Accounting Office (GAO) audit (1983). Then we calculated the seizure rate as a proportion of all imports (those shipments that were successfully imported plus those that were seized). Although the range of results indicates some uncertainties, it is clear that federal interdiction efforts currently impose significant costs on drug importers. Despite this, recent studies express continued skepticism about the ultimate effects of interdiction (General Accounting Office 1983; Mitchell and Bell 1980).

A. Drug Seizures

The reason for skepticism is rooted in the drug market's price structure, which is steeply graduated for all illicit drugs. As we noted in table 1, most of the retail price goes to domestic intermediaries, not to the grower, the exporter, or the importer, despite the fact that these latter parties bear the costs of production, processing, and international transportation. The universal practice of police agencies of valuing seizures at retail price vastly exaggerates the impact of seizures. The true impact is measured by the opportunity cost of those drugs at the point of seizure since that measures what it costs the distribution system to replace them.

Interdiction, treated purely as the seizure of drugs, raises price by requiring the distribution system to begin the shipment of more than one kilo of the drug for each kilo that reaches final customers. The price effect can be captured in a simple equation:

$$P_I = \frac{P_0}{1 - I},$$

where I is the interdiction rate, P_I is the price at that interdiction rate I, and P_0 is the price that would prevail at zero interdiction rate. We have observations of 1984 import selling prices and 1984 interdiction rates, from which we can deduce P_0.

For marijuana, the 1984 figures are an interdiction rate of about 0.22 and an import price of \$525 per kilo; this yields a P_0 of \$410. Consequently, doubling the interdiction rate to 44 percent will raise the importer selling price to \$732. Assuming the absolute price increase is 12.5 percent greater at final sale, retail price rises by \$237 per kilo or 13 percent. Table 7 traces out the consequences.

For cocaine, the import price increase from raising the interdiction to 60 percent from the current 30 percent (using the lower-bound con-

TABLE 7

Effects of Increased Interdiction Seizures on Marijuana Price

Item	Current Situation	Hypothetical Situation (Increased Interdiction)
Interdiction rate (%)	22	44
Amount exported to land 100 kg in U.S. (kg)	128	178
Amount seized (kg)	28	78
Amount landed in U.S. (kg)	100	100
Replacement cost of seizures (at \$410 per kg) (\$)	11,480	31,980
Total retail price (100 kg) (\$)	175,000	198,625
Increase in retail price (%)	. . .	13

sumption estimate) is $33,000. The final price increase of $37,000 is about 6 percent of the retail price. If we use the higher consumption figures, doubling interdiction volumes has correspondingly lower retail price effects.

The much greater impact for marijuana is a consequence of the much lower markup of prices as the drug moves from import to final sale. Our assumption that absolute price increases are marked up to the same extent in the two distribution systems may be incorrect precisely because cocaine distribution is a riskier business. Nonetheless, it seems reasonable that a 1 percent rise in import price will have a smaller retail price impact for cocaine than for marijuana.

B. Effects of Arresting Couriers

So far we have considered only how interdiction of goods affects the market. However, interdiction is also supposed to create increased risks for couriers: pilots of small aircraft carrying cocaine and crewmen on vessels carrying marijuana. These people are often captured along with the drugs during interdiction, and how they are treated, once caught, will affect their perceptions of risk. Raising their risk high enough might be expected, a priori, to affect the price of the drug.

It is very difficult to obtain data on the risks faced by couriers. Records of the disposition of interdiction arrests are incomplete, and the various agencies disagree on basic estimates, such as rates of indictment, conviction, and imprisonment (General Accounting Office 1983). Based on the very fragmentary available evidence, it seems that the probability that an arrested marijuana courier will go to prison is about 40 percent.[15] If the probability of a courier's arrest is the same as the seizure rate (22.2 percent), that would imply that a marijuana courier's risk of imprisonment per trip is approximately 9 percent. The time served by imprisoned crewmen probably averaged about one year.[16] No comparable data are available for cocaine couriers.

[15] Coast Guard information for 1981 (the most recent available) shows that, in the one district for which data are available, 68 percent of arrestees were indicted and 86 percent of indictments resulted in convictions (U.S. General Accounting Office 1983, app. X). The GAO examined records of 128 individuals who were arrested and convicted as a result of seizure operations; 67 percent of these received a prison sentence. These rates are likely to be upper bounds (since, e.g., the GAO sample was missing information for many other arrestees), but taken together they suggest a maximum rate of imprisonments per arrest equal to .39 (i.e., .68 × .86 × .67).

[16] The Coast Guard reports prison sentences in South Florida, the jurisdiction accounting for most interdiction arrests, of 1.9 years. Federal offenders serve approximately 50 percent of their sentences prior to first release.

What if the government were able to raise the marijuana courier's risk radically, say, from 9 to 18 percent? The result would probably differ between marijuana and cocaine because different types of couriers may be involved. Interdiction experience indicates that a large majority of marijuana arrives by sea, mostly in small vessels operated by unskilled Colombian or other foreign nationals (National Narcotics Intelligence Consumers Committee 1984, p. 10). A significant proportion of cocaine appears to be smuggled in dedicated airplanes by skilled pilots, though there have been a number of enormous seizures (500 kg or more) of cocaine in commercial planes (see National Narcotics Intelligence Consumers Committee 1984, p. 20). In the case of marijuana boats, few crewmen have alternative earning opportunities that pay as well as smuggling. For this reason, if the risks of the activity increase, it is likely that an increase in the compensation offered will ensure an adequate supply of Colombian crewmen.

To suggest the consequences of increasing risk we use a model based on expected value of imprisonment time. A study for the Coast Guard concerning seized marijuana boats shows that the average crew numbered about six and carried about ten metric tons (10,000 kg) of marijuana (Mitchell and Bell 1980). If interdiction and prosecution rates could be raised to make crewmen's risk of one year in prison 18 percent rather than 9 percent, and if the average crewman values his freedom at $50,000 a year, each crewman would have to get $4,500 more (.09 × $50,000) per trip to compensate him for the additional risk of prison time. For a crew of six, that would raise the cost of shipping 10,000 kg by $27,000. That change increases the cost of shipment per kilogram by only $2.70—which is 0.5 percent of the importer's selling price. This would raise retail price by only $3.00 per kilo or about 0.2 percent.

Interdiction of cocaine couriers may be another story. At least some pilots bringing in drugs receive severe sentences (U.S. Senate 1981). Pilots skilled enough to fly small planes into remote airstrips at night probably have substantial alternative earning opportunities. With a high enough interdiction rate and severe enough penalties, it might be possible to deter most or all of them. The number of skilled pilots willing to incur a high probability of a long prison sentence may be very limited indeed. Nevertheless, that constraint would last only as long as it took the cocaine trade to adapt. Planes and boats are completely interchangeable for bringing in cocaine. If flying becomes too risky, importers can always revert to shipment by sea.

C. The Possibilities for Adaptation

That consideration brings us to the last point concerning the effectiveness of interdiction, namely, the ease with which cocaine and marijuana smugglers can adapt to interdiction pressure. Even if we assume that the stringency of interdiction could be greatly intensified, we cannot assume that drug smugglers will go on using the same methods once these begin to expose them to very high risks. If the seizure rate begins to rise sharply, they might change their procedures.

At present, cocaine is brought into the United States in relatively large units, often in twenty-five-kilogram loads, on dedicated planes flown by skilled pilots who assume the risk of being apprehended as cocaine couriers. This contrasts sharply with the mode of importing heroin. That drug is brought in in small units (frequently less than 2.5 kg) on general cargo or transportation vessels (both ships and planes) and by unskilled couriers, typically crewmen or air stewards. The second mode of importation appears to be less efficient. At least it is true that the absolute price increase in the export-import transaction is higher for heroin than for cocaine.

Let us assume that interdiction efforts aimed at the specialized cocaine planes become effective enough that skilled pilots could not be found to fly in the drug. More cocaine importers could then adopt the heroin mode of importation currently used by some cocaine smugglers. To see the effect of that on the final price of the drug, we can compare the costs of the two modes. The comparison is complicated by the fact that distribution is itself expensive. By importing cocaine in much smaller units, the importers are able to eliminate one level of distribution and sell further down the chain at a higher per-unit price. Taking this into account, and assuming that the price rises by 85 percent at each transaction point,[17] we can show that the middle-level price of cocaine would rise by less than $100,000 and the final price by less than $150,000 or about 20 percent.

This is not additive with the drug seizure effect since the adaptation takes place precisely to lower that seizure rate. Our models are not sufficiently refined to permit determination of the interdiction rate at which it becomes optimal to switch importing modes; in any case, it will differ among organizations. It should also be noted that the heroin

[17] This is consistent with a three-level distribution chain between importer and retailer and a thirteenfold price rise. Different figures would apply for marijuana.

mode price effect estimate is an upper bound since heroin couriers are probably subject to more severe penalties than are cocaine couriers if caught; that is, heroin couriers demand more money for a given size shipment.

Marijuana importers would have more difficulty adapting to extreme enforcement pressure. The bulkiness of the drug per-unit value means that the value of much smaller units simply would not compensate for the risks of smuggling them. Moreover, marijuana has a distinctive odor that is hard to mask. The heroin importation mode is not feasible. Nonetheless, importers could shift to forms of cannabis that have less bulk for a particular quantity of THC—higher potency marijuana, hashish, or hashish oil. Under current conditions, the higher labor costs of hashish production make it unattractive to market, but that could change if the risks of transporting marijuana rose.

The optimal adaptation for modest increases in pressure may simply be scaling down the size of shipment brought in by specialized vessels. Instead of bringing up "mother" ships from Colombia with fifty tons of marijuana and then off-loading to smaller coastal vessels, much marijuana is now smuggled in small, very fast oceangoing boats, known as "cigarettes." This is reflected in the failure of quantities seized to rise along with Coast Guard expenditures.

Although this adaptation raises transportation costs, it is less feasible to stop many small, fast boats than a few large ones. Since a major portion of the cost in interdiction is a Coast Guard ship's "waiting time" between sighting and boarding a smuggling vessel and returning the smuggler's boat to port (Coast Guard, personal communication, 1983), a switch to smaller smuggling craft requires much greater resources to achieve a given interdiction ratio. Moreover, with this mode of transportation, the drug again passes through fewer distribution levels, thus avoiding the markups at those levels.

Higher interdiction could also result in higher domestic production. This is not strictly an adaptation by the import business, but it could frustrate the ultimate objective of interdiction. We have little systematic data on either current or potential domestic production, but the recent increase in apparent availability of sinsemilla, Hawaiian, and other high-THC specialty varieties of marijuana suggests a substantial expansion in domestic capacity. The most recent official estimate is that 11 percent (by weight) of U.S. marijuana consumption comes from domestic sources (National Narcotics Intelligence Consumers Committee 1984, p. 9). Since domestic marijuana is of higher potency and price than imported marijuana, the domestic share of total expenditures may be much higher.

Finally, note that the cost of achieving a doubling in the interdiction rates for cocaine and marijuana may be very high indeed. The Coast Guard more than doubled its expenditures on interdiction between fiscal years 1978 and 1982 (a real increase of about 50 percent) yet seized scarcely more marijuana (and trivial amounts of any other drug) in the latter year. The interdiction rate may actually have gone down since the market probably expanded somewhat over the same period. It appears that the interdiction rate for cocaine increased substantially in 1983; that may, however, reflect a decline in the export price induced by overplanting in producer countries. Lower export price would reduce the replacement cost of seized drugs and hence the incentives to invest in costly interdiction-avoiding expenditures.

To sum up, interdiction rates currently seem to intercept about 10–30 percent of the marijuana and cocaine shipped to this country. Our analysis suggests that, unless some unforeseen change creates a strong constraint on supply in the producing countries, even much higher interdiction rates would not raise retail prices very greatly and would be very costly to achieve. If interdiction efforts were to rise sharply, cocaine and marijuana traffickers could change transportation methods that make them vulnerable to present enforcement tactics and lower the effectiveness of these efforts.

V. Actions against High-Level Domestic Distributors

The federal government has for many years conducted investigations aimed at arresting and incarcerating high-level distributors. It has recently greatly intensified that effort, as indicated by increases in the number of arrestees (table 3) and in the numbers classified as high-level dealers (Drug Enforcement Administration 1985). The DEA now devotes most of its resources to making cases against such dealers. The Treasury Department, through the Customs Service and the Internal Revenue Service (IRS), also conducts its own investigations against major dealers. These actions take the form of undercover investigation—"sting" operations—tracing dealers' finances through Currency Transaction Reports (CTRs), asset seizures, and taxation of drug-related income (National Narcotics Intelligence Consumers Committee 1983a). They have produced very visible results in the form of large drug seizures, arrests (and long prison sentences) for tens of principals in big importing and distribution enterprises, and seizures of many millions of dollars of assets. The federal drug enforcement program now accounts for a significant share of all federal law enforcement effort. For example, drug offenses accounted for 19.7 percent of all defendants disposed of in federal court in 1982, compared with 13.8 percent in 1972.

A. *Types of Actions*

In many recent successful investigations, federal agencies have mounted sting operations that capitalize on the drug trade's need for certain services. Cocaine smugglers need to obtain planes and pilots. Marijuana importers need to off-load tons of the drug very rapidly once it comes ashore and to find safe warehouses where it can be stored until sold. And high-level dealers in both trades need financial services to protect their very large incomes from detection and to invest them profitably. In buying these services from independent entrepreneurs, dealers make themselves vulnerable to investigators. In a number of cases, DEA agents have set up transportation and financial "firms," building strong cases against dealers who sought their services. For example, a federal agent with the improbable name of Ted Weed set up what became the largest off-loading enterprise in the marijuana business, leading eventually to hundreds of arrests and the seizure of hundreds of tons of marijuana (Kleiman 1985, chap. 2). In addition, federal agencies continue their more traditional types of investigations using undercover drug purchases and informants.

It has been argued that the newer investigative approaches such as sting operations have the great virtue of producing large effects because they are targeted on organizations rather than on individuals. It takes time and money for traffickers to re-create large organizations because of the need to rebuild contacts, relationships of trust, and so forth. Thus removing fifty individuals from one organization may have a larger effect than removing fifty randomly selected individuals from many organizations.

However, despite the success of such techniques in building cases, we are skeptical that eliminating organizations has much additional effect simply because there are many successful dealers who operate on a much smaller scale. If large-scale organizations were made unprofitable because of excessive exposure to law enforcement, their place would be taken by smaller-scale ones; since many smaller-scale organizations now operate, they can apparently compete with the large ones at current prices.

Apart from undercover operations, federal agencies have also begun regularly using CTRs to make cases against high-level distributors. Federal regulations require financial institutions to file CTRs for transactions of $10,000 or more. Agents have analyzed CTRs to identify members of major dealer organizations and to locate their assets for later seizure and taxation. In addition, failure to file CTRs has served as the basis for prosecution, and bribery attempts to keep bank officials from filing have provided investigative leads.[18]

Federal agencies also have authority to seize the assets of drug dealers, including vessels, aircraft, vehicles, real estate, front businesses, cash, and bank accounts. The DEA can seize assets if they are used in the drug traffic or if they were purchased with drug-produced income. The Customs Service can confiscate vehicles, aircraft, and boats used in attempts to smuggle contraband and can also seize cash entering or leaving the country in violation of currency reporting laws (reports must be filed for all cash or bearer-negotiable instruments in excess of $5,000). In addition, the IRS has used procedures such as jeopardy assessments that also enable the government to take assets quickly to satisfy tax claims.

B. *Effects of Asset Seizures*

Let us consider the effects of asset seizures first because the analysis is quite straightforward. The various asset seizure programs have an obvious attraction as devices for attacking the drug trade. They are relatively speedy compared with the trials of well-defended traffickers. They immobilize assets during court proceedings, thus disrupting the cash flow of criminal organizations. They serve as a condign punishment since, given that dealers enter the drug trade because they seek large incomes, it seems appropriate that they lose the assets generated by that trade. Finally, they generate revenues that help offset the costs of enforcement.

Nonetheless, it appears that these seizure programs have little prospect of making a significant difference in the retail price of drugs. The amounts reported seized do not represent the actual financial penalty

---

[18] The strengths and weaknesses of this approach have been examined in a recent report by the President's Commission on Organized Crime (1984).

imposed on a trafficker. A two-stage procedure is involved: in the first phase (seizure), the agency freezes the assets to prevent the dealer from removing them beyond the government's reach; in the second phase (forfeiture), ownership finally passes to the government after legal proceedings. After litigation, the amount realized is likely to be much lower than the amount originally seized.[19] In fact, counting actions for all types of drugs, in 1981 the DEA actually obtained only $13 million in forfeitures from its asset removal program, though seizures totaled $161 million (National Narcotics Intelligence Consumers Committee 1983*b*). For more recent years, we have only seizure figures, which in 1984 totaled $134 million. Forfeitures probably were less than half that amount.

These amounts are not large in relation to the retail value of all drugs ($20 billion for marijuana, cocaine, and heroin together, according to our lower-bound estimates). Even if federal agencies managed to realize considerably more in the future, the effect on final retail price would be modest. For example, let us suppose that the agencies could triple the value of the dealers' assets that are forfeited or taxed and that 50 percent of that value came from marijuana dealers. Although those are improbably high figures, they would raise the retail price of marijuana by less than 1 percent, treating the seizures as a tax on marijuana imports.

C. The Possibilities for Increased Investigative Effort

The prospects for making progress through intensified enforcement are a little better. One constraint that presents a major problem for local enforcement is not present; prison space can be expanded if the federal government significantly increases the numbers of those convicted of drug offenses. Also in contrast to local drug enforcement efforts, the federal government has had little difficulty in obtaining convictions and prison sentences for those it charges with violations of drug laws.

In 1984, the DEA reported 10,939 persons convicted for drug violations resulting from federal investigations (Drug Enforcement Administration 1985). In federal court, the conviction rate has been about 80 percent in recent years. Of the 10,939 convictions in 1984, 72 percent

[19] For instance, if a seized house is mortgaged, the mortgage holder may successfully petition for return of the property. Claims of a wife or a family may be accepted. Valuation of real property may be overstated. Vehicles may deteriorate in storage during forfeiture proceedings. In tax proceedings, the IRS may seize large amounts of assets before closure, but the amount seized may bear no relation to the actual tax assessment. Finally, the agency may lose its claim in court.

resulted in prison sentences, and the average sentence was approximately fifty-six months.[20] Though the data series available to us are not perfectly comparable, it appears that the numbers of persons convicted and the average sentence length have risen very substantially, perhaps doubling over the period 1980–84. This increase roughly parallels the increase in resources devoted to high-level drug investigations; the principal investigative and prosecutive agencies (DEA, FBI, IRS, U.S. Attorneys, and Criminal Division of the Department of Justice) increased their expenditures on drug cases from $280 million in fiscal year 1982 to $512 million in fiscal year 1984.

The success of the increased investigative effort, in terms of persons arrested, convicted, and incarcerated, is impressive. We note, though, that there are adaptations that may reduce the long-run effectiveness of that effort. We suggest that they are likely to take some time to occur because they may come about only as a result of changes in the composition of the dealer population.

For example, the newer and more successful techniques, such as sting operations and analysis of CTRs, are defeated by relatively simple adaptations. Large smuggling or distributing organizations are vulnerable to undercover operations (e.g., selling financial or transportation services) precisely because of their scale. If these investigations present too much risk, organizations can simply scale down and handle smaller quantities of both goods and money. It is useful to note here that these investigations appear to have had little success with respect to heroin, where the relatively small import bundles are handled by much smaller organizations.

As for the analysis of CTRs, a dealer can avoid the CTR requirement by converting currency into other negotiable instruments without ever making a $10,000 transaction; it simply takes slightly smaller transactions with different financial institutions. Consequently, the effectiveness of CTR analysis may be self-limiting. Ease of entry into the marijuana and cocaine markets has meant that some people who have little education or familiarity with U.S. institutions and finances have amassed considerable wealth. Thus the CTR requirement may help to weed them out, leaving a more sophisticated dealer population. It is likely that there are enough potential dealers to keep the removal of the less competent from making a difference in the market.

---

[20] Note that drug violators, like other federal prisoners, are released after serving, on the average, less than half their sentence.

D. *Price Effects of Intensified Investigations*

Despite the difficulties just enumerated, it is conceivable that federal agencies could, through greatly increased efforts and resource expenditures, make many more cases against high-level dealers. Let us suppose that they achieved a very large increase, say, doubling the number of drug violators now sent to prison. What effect would that have on drug prices?

We again estimate the additional compensation that dealers would require to cover their increased risks of spending time in federal prison. From the sentencing data cited earlier, we estimate that about 29,800 years of prison time were imposed on drug dealers caught as a result of federal investigation of marijuana, cocaine, and heroin dealing. Given that dealers serve, on the average, only about 45 percent of their sentence, this implies about 13,371 actual years of imprisonment.[21] Now assume that this number were doubled, that is, that 13,371 more years were imposed on dealers. In response, dealers would require extra compensation for the added risk of imprisonment. Since these are high-level dealers, many of whom are earning very large incomes, it is reasonable to impute very high values. For highest-level dealers (class 1 violators as defined by the DEA), we use a figure of $250,000, for second-level (class 2) dealers $125,000, and for the remainder $75,000.[22] Assuming the distribution of classes of dealers remained the same under the new situation as it was in 1984, the added years of imprisonment would result in a total of $2 billion added to retail prices. Compared with the total retail value of drugs, this added cost would represent a price increase of only about 10 percent.[23]

Even this modest increase would probably not appear for a few years. There would probably be a substantial time lag between increasing expenditures and completing cases. It takes time to build a network of informants, to accumulate a pool of experienced agents, and to mount investigations. These considerations must be taken together with the possibilities of dealer adaptations and the probability of very high costs.

Of course, there are numerous uncertainties here; it may be that

[21] Details of these calculations are presented in Kleiman (1985, tables 2–4).

[22] In 1984, the DEA estimated that, of 10,839 total domestic drug dealers sentenced, 1,447 were class 1 dealers, 779 were class 2, and 8,613 were class 3 or 4 (Drug Enforcement Administration 1985).

[23] Most of these cases are made against persons involved in high-level domestic distribution. The markup to retail price is presumably significantly less than that which applies to rises in the import price.

dealers will not readily adapt, that the agencies could accommodate large budget increases quickly, or that further innovations in investigative techniques, such as targeting organizations, will pay off more than we expect. However, with currently available information it seems unlikely that even a dramatic expansion of investigative effort against high-level drug distributors would have a very large effect on the availability or price of drugs.

It is also important to note two possible adverse consequences from increasingly stringent enforcement. First, the price increase may raise high-level dealer incomes if the elasticity of demand is less than one, a highly plausible condition for marijuana and heroin. Second, more stringent enforcement may lead to more violent organizations, which are able to discipline agents more effectively, dominating the market.

VI. Local Law Enforcement

As shown in table 3, local police make numerous arrests for drug offenses. The figure has exceeded half a million annually since 1972, though most of these arrests are for simple possession of marijuana and result in little additional penalty beyond the confiscation of a small amount of the drug. However, local law enforcement does pose a major instrument against at least one of the markets, that for heroin.

This section is divided into two parts. The first deals with the peculiar virtues of street enforcement with respect to heroin. It also argues that street enforcement is not comparably effective for cocaine and marijuana. The second part then calculates the effect on cocaine and marijuana prices of a doubling of the efficacy of local enforcement.

A. The Virtues of Street-Level Enforcement

Enforcement activities directed at major distributors and wholesalers of drugs have most of their impact on money price. In effect, they raise the "raw materials" cost of the retail-level drug dealing business without changing other conditions. Thus if high-level enforcement succeeds in raising the wholesale price of a drug, users will have to pay more for their supplies of the drug, but their search time to find a connection will not tend to change. Whether the net result is more or fewer dollars spent on the drug depends on the price elasticity of demand.

By contrast, enforcement directed at retailers and first-level wholesalers can change the number of street dealers and the openness with which they flaunt their wares. As street-level enforcement increases, the typical user will not have to pay more for a given quantity of drugs but will have to search longer for a connection. This constitutes an increase in the nonmonetary costs of the drug.

The effects of this may be large or small, but they are unambiguously good (assuming only that drug consumption is on balance an evil). Both quantity consumed and dollars spent on drugs will decrease—and, consequently, so too will the earnings of drug merchants—as a result both of the drop in quantity (due to lower effective demand) and of the downward pressure that that drop puts on prices. In addition, insofar as heroin users commit property crimes to obtain money for drugs, an increase in search time will directly reduce their incentives to commit such crimes by making it harder to convert money into heroin.

But with street-level as with high-level enforcement, heroin is far more susceptible to the effects of increased pressure than is marijuana or cocaine. Again, a major reason is sheer size: measured by numbers of regular dealers, the heroin market is perhaps a fourth the size of the cocaine market. Imposing any given level of risk on the average cocaine dealer, therefore, requires four times as many arrests, prosecutions, convictions, and prison terms as are required to impose the same level of risk on the average heroin dealer.

Two other characteristics of retail heroin dealing make it particularly susceptible to enforcement pressure. First, heroin transactions take place largely outdoors because heroin dealers are reluctant to be alone inside with heroin consumers. Second, heroin users buy drugs daily because they find it difficult or impossible to hold onto personal inventories without consuming them all at once. By contrast, marijuana transactions are infrequent; while the conventional unit of marijuana consumption is the joint, the conventional unit of purchase is the ounce, roughly sixty joints. This suggests that marijuana consumers hold personal inventories. Consequently, it is difficult to impose substantial search-time costs on a regular marijuana user, but it is easy to impose them on a regular heroin user. Moreover, since the regular heroin user suffers some discomfort unless his consumption of the drug stays regular, a failure to connect has much more serious consequences for him than an equivalent failure for even a regular marijuana user whose personal inventory is exhausted. Increased search time for heroin users, combined with occasional failures to connect, may lead users to enter drug treatment or simply to quit unassisted as the attractiveness of the user life-style decreases.

As in any drug market, if enforcement succeeds in shrinking the number of participants, the same level of enforcement resources will impose a greater level of risk on the remaining participants. In addition, a second kind of positive feedback, one due to the behavior of search time as the number of participants shrinks, may be at work in the heroin retail market. The possibility that cruising around will lead to a successful meeting whether one is a buyer looking for a seller or a seller looking for a buyer depends on the number of buyers and sellers in the market in a given region. But the number of buyers and sellers itself depends in part on the probability of a successful meeting: the search time to "score" from the buyer's perspective, the waiting time between customers from the seller's.

Unlike a higher-level dealer, a heroin retailer facing increased risks and the need to operate more discreetly may have difficulty raising his prices. He, like his customer, spends considerable time waiting for an opportunity to do business. When a willing buyer meets a willing seller, both have substantial investments in being able to take care of business right then. The situation is one of temporary bilateral monopoly, which may account for conventional pricing in the retail heroin market; no one wants to take the risk of an unsuccessful negotiation. Increased search time due to tougher enforcement increases the sunk costs on both sides; if the dealer refuses to deal with new customers, his old customers are that much more valuable to him. Thus dealers are likely to make fewer transactions without being able to raise margins. This may cause some of them to leave the business.

If, then, increasing search time in the heroin market decreases the number of active users, the decrease in the number and aggressiveness of retail dealers may not create opportunities for new entry because the smaller number of active users tends to increase dealer search time and reduce the financial rewards of the business. This combination of positive feedbacks might, in some cases, cause a local market to drop below the minimum size at which it remains self-sustaining, establishing a new equilibrium with no active users and no sellers. This is, after all, the condition that obtains throughout most of the country and even in most neighborhoods in the cities where heroin is a problem.

There is now some empirical evidence that local enforcement initiatives against heroin dealing may be effective in reducing both drug consumption and some kinds of acquisitive crime. A recent study in Lynn, Massachusetts, found that burglaries fell 41 percent year to year after the introduction of a small heroin task force (six officers from a total force of 120 in a city of 80,000) that concentrated entirely on retail sales (Kleiman, Holland, and Hayes 1984).

That decrease in burglaries was more than four times the average declines nationally, statewide, and in other Massachusetts areas with heroin problems. During the same period, demand for heroin treatment in Lynn jumped 90 percent while remaining stable in the rest of Massachusetts. Similar results have been reported (anecdotally) on the Lower East Side of Manhattan and in Richmond, Virginia.

B. *Cocaine and Marijuana*

For cocaine and marijuana, the dominant effect of increased local enforcement is on dealer risk. We revert then to our earlier line of analysis and try to estimate the effect that this might have on retail prices.

Arrest is, of itself, a fairly minor sanction for most arrestees. To estimate the stringency of local law enforcement, it is also necessary to obtain data on the percentages of various kinds of drug arrests leading to jail or prison sentences. Unfortunately, we have only fragmentary data on these matters. We shall use the available data to estimate the current risks that dealers face from local police, namely, the probabilities of arrest, jail time, and at least one year in prison. As before, these calculations will require that we make many assumptions. In choosing those assumptions, we shall attempt to avoid downward bias in estimating the effectiveness of possible increases in the local police effort devoted to marijuana and cocaine. We will then consider the effect on cocaine and marijuana prices of doubling local police effort.

Table 8 presents estimates of the risk of arrest for marijuana, cocaine, and heroin dealers.[24] We assume that marijuana possession arrests do not include any dealers but that one-quarter of heroin and cocaine possession arrests are of dealers.[25]

Unfortunately, heroin and cocaine are lumped together in the FBI's annual *Uniform Crime Reports*. The sale and possession arrests for heroin and cocaine are assumed to be evenly divided between the two drugs; we would guess that the true figure is that three-quarters of the dealer arrests are of heroin dealers, but that is very impressionistic. Our assumption exaggerates the estimated efficacy of the cocaine enforcement increase.

Of the jail and prison rates resulting from arrests, we have only the following data elements. (1) On December 31, 1979, 15,500 out of

[24] Throughout this section we shall ignore risks posed by federal agencies, which eschew low-level investigations and arrests.

[25] Not including jugglers (Moore 1977), i.e., addicts supporting their habits through sales.

TABLE 8

Risks Faced by Drug Retailers, 1984

	Heroin	Cocaine	Marijuana
Dealers	45,000	180,000	500,000
Sale arrests	24,000	24,000	74,000
Dealer possession arrests	12,000	12,000	0
Total dealer arrests	36,000	36,000	74,000
Annual arrests per dealer	.8	.2	.15
Probability of jail, given arrest	.16	.16	.26
Probability of prison, given arrest	.07	.07	.02
Annual probability of jail	.32	.08	.04
Annual probability of prison	.14	.035	.001
Annual expected incarceration time (days)	131	33	4.3

175,000 inmates of state prisons were serving sentences for drug offenses (Brown et al. 1984, p. 577). For purposes of calculation we
assume that this is a steady-state number, that is, that 15,500 years of
prison time are allocated to drug dealers each year. (2) In California,
4,931 marijuana sales arrests in 1979 produced fifty-five prison sentences and 1,301 jail sentences. Felony arrests involving drugs other
than marijuana totaled 27,005 in 1979. These led to 807 prison sentences and 6,921 jail sentences.[26] (3) In New York City in 1980, there
were 11,600 nonmarijuana drug felony arrests. These produced 1,200
prison sentences and 850 jail sentences (Califano 1982).[27]

The second and third pieces of data are interesting in themselves.
California felony nonmarijuana drug arrestees face a 3 percent probability of a prison term, and those in New York City face over a 10
percent probability of the same outcome. But the probability of some
incarceration is higher in California (28.6 percent) than in New York
City (17.7 percent).

We have no data on the length of jail sentences; we know only that
they are less than one year. Califano (1982) reports that only 10 percent
of those jailed following conviction on misdemeanor drug arrests received more than thirty days. Let us assume, from now on, that a jail
sentence is ninety days. Again, this probably biases upward our estimate of efficacy.

[26] These figures come from unpublished Offender Based Transaction Statistics tables,
provided by the California Bureau of Justice Statistics.
[27] The 850 sentences were for misdemeanor convictions following felony arrest. A
very small portion may have received prison sentences of a little more than a year.

For marijuana, we shall double the frequency of California for the national imprisonment rate; 2 percent of sales arrests result in prison. Judicial attitudes in California toward marijuana dealers are probably more lenient than in most other states. The jail rate we shall leave at the California level. For heroin and cocaine, we average the California and New York prison and jail rates. The probability of state prison sentence following a felony sale or dealer arrest is 7 percent; the probability of jail is 16 percent. It should be noted that these are not much lower rates than for felony arrests generally.

Our final assumption concerns length of prison sentences. The probabilities calculated so far yield approximately 5,500 dealers going to prison each year. State prisons have 15,500 serving time for drug offenses. A significant share may be for drugs other than marijuana, cocaine, or heroin. In 1981, these other drugs accounted for 32,000 sale or manufacture arrests, nearly 30 percent of the total for sale or manufacture. If we allocate for these drugs the same percentage of drug prison time, then we have 11,000 years of prison time for our three drugs and an average sentence of two years actually served.

Use of this figure, together with our assumed ninety-day jail sentence, yields the last line of table 8. The average heroin dealer can expect to spend 35 percent of his dealing career incarcerated; marijuana dealers spend 1 percent of their time incarcerated. Let us assume now that local law enforcement agencies were able to double the present level of risk imposed on cocaine and marijuana dealers. This might well require more than doubling police expenditures on drug enforcement.

If arrest rates doubled and the probabilities of various outcomes following arrest remained unchanged, what might happen to the prices of marijuana and cocaine? We need to place a value on incarceration time and on arrest itself. Given that almost all these arrests are of retailers earning significant but not large incomes from being dealers, we place a modest value on the cost of time, $50,000 per year, or $137 per day. Since arrest is a penalty per se, we need to place a value on that. Surely $5,000 would seem a high enough value for a low-level dealer. Doubling arrest and incarceration rates then requires that cocaine dealers receive an additional $7,000 each; this raises total throughput cost for twenty-three tons of cocaine by $1.3 billion or about 16 percent. For marijuana, average dealer compensation must rise by about $1,340; this raises throughput costs by $620 million or about 14 percent.

These are extremely primitive calculations. They require the use of a very large number of quantitative assumptions. We have chosen in general to use assumptions that seem biased toward detecting large effects from the application of more resources to drug law enforcement. Even under those assumptions a dramatic increase in that enforcement seems to produce only quite modest price effects. An increase of 14 percent in the price of marijuana, from about seventy-five cents to eighty-six cents per joint, would appear to require very substantial reallocation of criminal justice system resources but would generate a decrease in consumption. At a time when there is a general concern about the system's ability to apprehend and punish offenders who commit property and violent crimes, it may be hard to justify such a diversion for such modest returns.

The apparent insensitivity of the system to increases in the stringency of local enforcement is somewhat puzzling; after all, that aims at the part of the distribution system that accounts for most of the final price. If doubling the risks of arrest and incarceration for retailers does not greatly increase the price of drugs, then we must ask why the retailers receive such large returns for their participation. We speculate that the answer lies in the discontinuities of dealer utility functions. A substantial part of their current return comes from entry into the trade and is not affected by marginal changes in the various risks associated with it. For example, the vulnerability that dealers may feel as a result of their inability to seek police protection when they are robbed is not something that changes with enforcement intensity.

Similarly, the indirect risks from other participants in the trades may not be much affected by increased enforcement intensity. For example, the measures a dealer adopts to ensure that he is fairly safe from customer robbery (such as giving his drugs to an associate while he collects the money) may be just as adequate when the price of heroin is $2.00 per milligram as when it is $2.50. Finally, we suggest that, for low-level dealers, an important part of their total compensation is the return to the investment of time. If our estimates of total marijuana income, dealer numbers, and markups are correct, then the average marijuana retailer earns only about $5,000 per year from the trade. A large part of that may simply be payment for making trips to suppliers and waiting around for customers. Enforcement will have little impact on that element of his costs.

VII. Some Policy Implications

This last section considers some implications of the foregoing four policy choices. We first present a brief summary of the major results. The second part then suggests what additional considerations should be taken into account in making decisions about the level of effort that should be devoted to supply reduction programs.

A. *Pessimistic Conclusions*

One obvious conclusion that might be drawn from this essay is that the enforcement-oriented strategy will not work. That is not correct, or at least not in such a simple form. We have looked only at what could be achieved by fairly large increases in the efforts, predominantly federal, aimed at the cocaine and marijuana markets. The analysis has not addressed the question of what has been accomplished by drug enforcement to date. We discuss that briefly before going to the implications of what we have done.

The most striking observation about illicit drugs in this country is their high prices. Even marijuana is vastly more expensive than it would be if legally available, mostly a consequence of illegality per se and of the enforcement of that illegality. Heroin surely represents the limits of enforcement effectiveness. A white powder, readily manufactured from poppy gum, which would cost only a few dollars if legal, instead costs about $2,000 per gram on the streets of American cities. Not only is it absurdly expensive and of extraordinarily low purity, but it can also be obtained only by incurring significant risks. One surely could ask no more of enforcement against an illegal market. Yet approximately half a million people are prepared to lead quite degraded lives in pursuit of the drug.

Enforcement against cocaine and marijuana has not accomplished as much as has heroin enforcement. It is not clear that it could, given the differences in characteristics of the drugs and, perhaps relatedly, their users. But cocaine and marijuana enforcement have certainly had significant consequences for the use of the two drugs in this nation.

The question that we have addressed is whether intensified enforcement, particularly by the federal government, can much further reduce consumption. We have concluded that this is not likely. The experience of the last five years, with its large increases in federal enforcement against these drugs and at least modest increases in the risks imposed by local agencies, does not contradict this. The cocaine market may have expanded, and price has certainly declined. Marijuana prices have increased modestly, but if there has been any significant decline in consumption, as indicated by the high school seniors survey, it is most probably explained by changed attitudes toward the health consequences of marijuana use.

Part of the problem is that so many of the enforcement resources are focused on a part of the drug distribution system that accounts for very little of the retail price of the drug. Limiting coca production in Peru, capturing Colombian crewmen on marijuana smuggling ships, or imprisoning importers of Iranian heroin produces impressive statistics but imposes relatively light costs on the drug distribution system. Even producing a lot more of these enforcement outputs will not much raise the costs of distributing drugs.

More stringent enforcement at the local level does not seem to offer better prospects, except for heroin. The scale of the markets, the significance of costs that are unrelated to enforcement, and the infrequency and privacy of individual transactions all mitigate against effective cocaine and marijuana enforcement. Only for heroin do we see much possibility for increased local enforcement to reduce the availability of the drug further.

It should be noted that our analysis makes use of very conservative estimates of the size of the cocaine and marijuana markets. That has the effect of biasing upward our estimate of the efficacy of increased enforcement. For example, if the marijuana market truly is 13,000 tons and generates revenues of $18 billion, as suggested in official publications, then the likely price effect of raising total marijuana seizures through interdiction to 4,000 tons is even smaller than we estimated.

It is useful to note again that our pessimism does not extend to drug enforcement generally. There are some markets in which increased enforcement has effectively reduced the availability of the drug. Methamphetamines and methaqualone are two recent instances. Whereas these drugs were readily available in the late 1970s, a combination of treaties with the small number of foreign producer countries, in which they were produced by pharmaceutical companies for legitimate medical purposes, and the targeting of abusive prescribers in the United States, greatly reduced their availability and use by 1984. The need for expensive centralized production facilities was probably critical in those cases.

B. *Evaluating Drug Enforcement Policies*

The analysis above lays the basis for evaluating drug enforcement policy choices, at least qualitatively. Those choices can be thought of as concerning (1) the overall budget; (2) its allocation between high-level (close to the source for the importer) and street-level (close to the final retail transaction) activities; and (3) its allocation among target drugs—

marijuana, cocaine, heroin, and the "dangerous drugs" (synthetics). The current federal strategy is to increase the resources available, direct attention toward high-level cases, and concentrate on marijuana and cocaine.

An evaluation ought to consider both the efficacy of a given set of enforcement activities (compared to their costs and the alternative uses of those resources) in reducing drug abuse and any unwanted side effects it may have.

The analysis above does not allow us to judge whether the increase in the overall federal drug enforcement budget is wise. The current budget of about $1.2 billion looks small in relation to either the $20–$35 billion Americans spend each year on illicit drugs or the recent $47 billion estimate of the total annual social costs of illicit drug abuse (Harwood et al. 1984). On the other hand, $1.2 billion is a healthy chunk of the total federal law enforcement budget—roughly $4 billion—and a multiple of the negligible sums spent on drug abuse prevention. One cannot say whether we should be spending more or less on drug enforcement overall without making assumptions about the alternative uses of those funds, unless it appears that some spending is either futile or likely to generate unwanted side effects of greater magnitude than its benefits.

Much of the current surge in federal drug enforcement spending may, however, be going into precisely such futile or counterproductive uses. High-level marijuana and cocaine enforcement is likely to be of very limited efficacy in reducing drug abuse both because of the limited ability of federal enforcement to increase prices and otherwise limit availability and because of the relatively inelastic demand for marijuana and cocaine. Inelastic demand—the tendency of marijuana and cocaine consumers to reduce consumption less than proportionately if prices increase—means that the total dollars paid for these drugs will tend to increase as enforcement increases prices. This creates two unwanted side effects, one on consumers' budgets and the other on illicit revenues; as consumers pay more, becoming poorer, drug market entrepreneurs earn more, becoming richer. If, in addition, toughened enforcement encourages the development of drug-dealing organizations that are more enforcement resistant because they are more violent and corrupt, the overall result of putting more pressure on the top levels of the marijuana and cocaine trades will be to give the most dangerous criminals a bigger share of a larger market.

Increasing enforcement directed against users and low-level dealers of marijuana and cocaine, though without the side effects of increasing high-level enforcement, is likely to be futile because of the sheer numbers involved. Local police already arrest 400,000 marijuana consumers per year; to make use significantly more risky would require a substantial rise in the share of scarce prison space allocated to users of the drug. Heroin, by contrast, trades in a much smaller market in which demand, we have argued, is likely to be relatively elastic to price. Both these factors boost the likely efficacy of increased enforcement pressure in reducing drug abuse, and elastic demand also means that dollars spent by addicts and earned by dealers will decrease rather than increase if enforcement tightens.

High-level heroin enforcement thus deserves a bigger share than it now receives of federal drug resources. In addition, since the size and structure of the retail heroin market make it a particularly attractive enforcement target, it might be desirable to find ways to funnel federal resources into street-level heroin enforcement. This could take the form of federal investigation and prosecution of retail-level cases—as exemplified by the DEA State-Local Task Forces (now largely moribund) or the prosecutions under Manhattan's Operation Pressure Point—or of federal funding of local agents and prosecutors.

Policy-making in a field as highly charged as drug abuse is not likely to be so rational—in the economic sense—as to make these relatively refined notions a central part of the debate. We hope, however, that the approach suggested here, and the numbers that the approach generates, will create a greater interest in determining just what will be accomplished by ever-increasing federal enforcement against the cocaine and marijuana trades.

REFERENCES

Brinkley, Joel. 1984. "Bolivia Drug Crackdown Brews Trouble." *New York Times* (September 12).

Brown, Edward, Timothy Flanagan, and Maureen McLeod. 1984. *Sourcebook of Criminal Justice Statistics, 1983*. Albany, N.Y.: Criminal Justice Research Center.

Bruun, Kettil, Lynn Pan, and Ingemar Rexed. 1975. *The Gentlemen's Club.* Chicago: University of Chicago Press.

Califano, Joseph. 1982. *The 1982 Report on Drug Abuse and Alcoholism: A Report to Hugh L. Carey, Governor, State of New York.* Albany, N.Y.

Carlson, Ken, Joan Peterson, Lindsey Stellwagen, Naomi Goldstein, and Herbert Weisberg. 1983. *Unreportable Taxable Income from Selected Illegal Activities*. Cambridge, Mass.: Abt.

Cook, Philip J. 1980. "Research in Criminal Deterrence: Laying the Groundwork for the Second Decade." In *Crime and Justice: An Annual Review of Research*, vol. 2, edited by Norval Morris and Michael Tonry. Chicago: University of Chicago Press.

Drug Abuse Policy Office. 1982. *Federal Strategy for Prevention of Drug Abuse and Drug Trafficking, 1982*. Washington, D.C.: White House.

Drug Enforcement Administration. 1985. *Statistical Report, Fiscal Year 1984*. Washington, D.C.: Drug Enforcement Administration.

Federal Bureau of Investigation. 1981–84. *Uniform Crime Reports*. Washington, D.C.: U.S. Government Printing Office.

Harwood, Henrick, Diane Napolitano, Patricia Kristiansen, and James Collins. 1984. *Economic Costs to Society of Alcohol and Drug Abuse and Mental Illness: 1980*. Research Triangle Park, N.C.: Research Triangle Institute.

Kaplan, John. 1983. *Heroin: The Hardest Drug*. Chicago: University of Chicago Press.

Kleiman, Mark. 1985. *Allocating Federal Drug Enforcement Resources: The Case of Marijuana*. Ph.D. dissertation, Harvard University.

Kleiman, Mark, William Holland, and Christopher Hayes. 1984. *Report to the District Attorney for Essex County: Evaluation of the Lynn Drug Task Force*. Cambridge, Mass.: Harvard University, John F. Kennedy School of Government, Program in Criminal Justice Policy and Management.

Miller, J. D., I. H. Cisin, H. Gardiner-Keaton, P. W. Wirtz, H. I. Abelson, and P. M. Fishburne. 1982. *National Survey on Drug Abuse: Main Findings, 1982*. Washington, D.C.: National Institute on Drug Abuse.

Mitchell, T., and R. Bell. 1980. *Drug Interdiction Operations by the Coast Guard*. Alexandria, Va.: Center for Naval Analysis.

Moore, Mark. 1977. *Buy and Bust*. Lexington, Mass.: Heath.

National Narcotics Intelligence Consumers Committee. 1982. *Narcotics Intelligence Estimate*. Washington, D.C.: Drug Enforcement Administration.

———. 1983a. *An Evaluation of the Methodologies for Producing Narcotics Intelligence Estimates*. Washington, D.C.: Drug Enforcement Administration.

———. 1983b. *Narcotics Intelligence Estimate*. Washington, D.C.: Drug Enforcement Administration.

———. 1984. *Narcotics Intelligence Estimate*. Washington, D.C.: Drug Enforcement Administration.

Polich, J. M., P. Ellickson, P. Reuter, and J. Kahan. 1984. *Strategies for Controlling Adolescent Drug Use*. Santa Monica, Calif.: Rand.

President's Commission on Law Enforcement and Administration of Justice. 1967. *Task Force Report: Organized Crime*. Washington, D.C.: President's Committee on Organized Crime, U.S. Government Printing Office.

President's Commission on Organized Crime. 1984. *The Cash Connection: Organized Crime, Financial Institutions, and Money Laundering*. Washington, D.C.: U.S. Government Printing Office.

340   Peter Reuter and Mark Kleiman

Reuter, Peter. 1983. *Disorganized Crime: The Economics of the Visible Hand*. Cambridge, Mass.: MIT Press.
————. 1984*a*. "The (Continuing) Vitality of Mythical Numbers." *Public Interest* 78 (Spring): 135–47.
————. 1984*b*. "The Economic Significance of Illegal Markets in the United States: Some Observations." In *L'Economie non-officielle*, edited by Edith Archambault and Xavier Greffe. Paris: Maspero.
Simon, Carl, and Ann Witte. 1982. *Beating the System*. Boston: Auburn.
Treaster, Joseph. 1984. "Jamaica, Close U.S. Ally, Does Little to Halt Drugs." *New York Times* (September 10).
U.S. Department of Justice. 1984. *Organized Crime Drug Enforcement Task Force Program: Annual Report*. Washington, D.C.: U.S. Department of Justice.
————. 1985. *Organized Crime Drug Enforcement Task Force Program: Annual Report*. Washington, D.C.: U.S. Department of Justice.
U.S. Department of State. Bureau of International Narcotics Matters. 1985. *Narcotics Profile Papers*. Washington, D.C.: U.S. Government Printing Office.
U.S. General Accounting Office. 1983. *Federal Drug Interdiction Efforts Need Strong Central Oversight*. Report GGD-83-52. Washington, D.C.: U.S. Government Printing Office.
U.S. Senate. 1980. *Organized Crime and the Use of Violence*. Hearings before the Permanent Subcommittee on Investigations of the Committee on Government Affairs. Washington, D.C.: U.S. Government Printing Office.
————. 1981. *International Narcotics Trafficking*. Hearings before the Permanent Subcommittee on Investigations of the Committee on Government Affairs. Washington, D.C.: U.S. Government Printing Office.
————. 1985. *International Narcotics Control*. Hearings before the Committee on Appropriations. Washington, D.C.
White House. 1984. *1984 National Strategy for Prevention of Drug Abuse and Drug Trafficking*. Washington, D.C.: U.S. Government Printing Office.

Name Index